Performance Modelling of Communication Networks and Computer Architectures

INTERNATIONAL COMPUTER SCIENCE SERIES

Consulting editor   **A D McGettrick**   University of Strathclyde

SELECTED TITLES IN THE SERIES

Functional Programming   *A J Field and P G Harrison*

Local Area Network Architectures   *D Hutchison*

Distributed Systems: Concepts and Design   *G Coulouris and J Dollimore*

Program Design with Modula-2   *S Eisenbach and C Sadler*

Parallel Processing: Principles and Practice   *E V Krishnamurthy*

Real Time Systems and their Programming Languages   *A Burns and A Wellings*

Prolog Programming for Artificial Intelligence (2nd Edn)   *I Bratko*

Introduction to Expert Systems (2nd Edn)   *P Jackson*

Logic for Computer Science   *S Reeves and M Clarke*

Computer Architecture   *M De Blasi*

The Programming Process: an Introduction using VDM and Pascal
  J T Latham, V J Bush and D Cottam

Analysis of Algorithms and Data Structures   *L Banachowski, A Kreczmar and
  W Rytter*

Handbook of Algorithms and Data Structures in Pascal and C (2nd Edn)
  G Gonnet and R Baeza-Yates

Algorithms and Data Structures   *J H Kingston*

Principles of Expert Systems   *P Lucas and L van der Gaag*

Discrete Mathematics for Computer Scientists   *J K Truss*

Programming in Ada plus Language Reference Manual (3rd Edn)
  J G P Barnes

Software Engineering (4th Edn)   *I Sommerville*

Distributed Database Systems   *D Bell and J Grimson*

Software Development with Z   *J B Wordsworth*

Program Verification   *N Francez*

Performance Modelling of Communication Networks and Computer Architectures

Peter G. Harrison

Imperial College of Science and Technology
University of London

Naresh M. Patel

Tandem Computers Inc.

ADDISON-WESLEY
PUBLISHING
COMPANY

Wokingham, England · Reading, Massachusetts · Menlo Park, California · New York
Don Mills, Ontario · Amsterdam · Bonn · Sydney · Singapore
Tokyo · Madrid · San Juan · Milan · Paris · Mexico City · Seoul · Taipei

Cover designed by Chris Eley and
printed by The Riverside Printing Co. (Reading) Ltd.
Typeset by Keytec Typesetting, Bridport, Dorset.
Printed in Great Britain by T. J. Press (Padstow) Ltd, Cornwall.

First printed 1992.

British Library Cataloguing in Publication Data
A catalogue record for this book is available from the British Library.

Library of Congress Cataloging in Publication Data
Harrison, Peter G.
    Performance modelling of communication networks and computer architectures / Peter G. Harrison, Naresh M. Patel.
        p.   cm. – (International computer science series)
    Includes bibliographical references and index.
    ISBN 0-201-54419-9
    1. Computer networks–Evaluation.   2. Computer architecture-
-Evaluation.   I. Patel, Naresh M.   II. Title.   III. Series.
TK5105.5.H37   1992
004.6–dc20   92-29632
                                                                                    CIP

Preface

Communication systems are becoming ever more complex as technological advances permit ever faster transmission over links of ever greater capacity. In telecommunications networks the information transmitted is generally in binary digital form, representing computer data, voice or video. Considerable resources and effort will be expended in coming years to allow interactive transcontinental and intercontinental collaboration through the sharing of information of these types. This will require the transmission of vast quantities of data in fractions of a second, particularly in the case of video where very many bits are needed to define each screen and many screens must be transmitted every second. Communication networks are organised hierarchically as Local Area Networks (LANs) for local communication, e.g. within a building, Metropolitan Area Networks (MANs), which contain geographically close nodes, e.g. within a city, and Wide Area Networks (WANs) for communication over longer distances up to thousands of miles. There may also be other levels in the hierarchy, for example using satellites. Communication between any two nodes in such a system may involve many intermediate nodes and meet contention from diverse traffic from many sources. The number of nodes in a network may run into thousands: they have diverse characteristics ranging from a local workstation to a gateway between sub-networks, and the links between nodes may also be of different types, e.g. Ethernet, radio, fibre-optic. The design of efficient communication systems, giving at least a minimum specified level of performance, is therefore of paramount importance.

Similarly, the world's insatiable appetite for high performance computing, supported by enormous advances in VLSI technology, has led to the development of a range of parallel computer architectures. These may involve a small or large number of processors cooperating to solve a problem in parallel, based on the partitioning of some algorithm. As with telecommunications systems, parallel computers can be extremely complex and again involve thousands of nodes which can be 'active' processors or 'passive' resources, such as memory modules or communication paths. Indeed, in a large parallel architecture, the central components are the interconnection networks (INs) between collections of nodes. These INs must be high speed and have high bandwidth, for example to facilitate fast memory accesses. Once again, the design of efficient parallel computer architectures is demanding but of the utmost importance.

Performance models of computer and communication systems have been studied for many years with a view to assisting optimization and guiding the design of new generations. To date, however, they have seen only limited use in practice: it has so far been reasonably effective to tune an optimization or new design using educated guesses and experimentation with existing similar systems – even though this process is often unreliable and requires expensive, exclusive use of the resources. Now, however, with the dramatic increase in complexity associated with the systems of the future, such intuitive understanding of system behaviour is much harder to acquire. Hence formal models of performance are necessary for efficient and reliable design and/or optimization. There are two main types of model available for this purpose: simulation and stochastic, the latter also often being referred to as analytic. Ideally, simulation should be used in combination with the analytical approach.

This book considers stochastic (queueing-based) models and is intended as a course text for computer science courses at the advanced undergraduate and Masters degree levels, as a reference for researchers in the field and as a handbook for professionals in the business of performance evaluation and design of communication networks, distributed systems and parallel computer architectures. It may also be relevant to courses in electrical engineering, operations research and applied probability, especially if these focus on telecommunications or computer applications. The emphasis is on modelling contention systems, which are mainly represented by queues or networks of queues. This provides a good abstract description of many physical systems, but there are other aspects of telecommunication networks which are not considered in any detail, for example network protocols and congestion control strategies. Nevertheless, the mathematical techniques described can be applied to such problems and there are a host of references in the literature that do just this.

The book has been written so as to be as self-contained as possible and the prerequisites for reading it are pre-university mathematics and some informal 'feel' for probability, for example as might be acquired in playing 'games of chance'. The material is presented in a rigorous way, appropriate to an academic course of lectures, but is structured so that the less mathematically sophisticated reader can often omit technical details yet still gain a thorough informal understanding. The intention is that the reader should rarely have to consult other texts to fill in the details of any model considered. For example, Chapter 4 covers the main properties of stochastic processes that form the foundations of most analytic models of computer/communication systems. At the same time, the book does not claim to be encyclopaedic and certain model types are not considered, for example those using Petri-nets.

The book is organized into 11 chapters, as outlined below, which interlink in various ways to provide a number of ways of reading (depending also on the degree of mathematical sophistication of the reader) and possible course structures. The first chapter gives an introduction to the conventional notion of probability and can be regarded in two ways: as a summary of the formal, axiomatic definition or at an intuitive level. Random variables are introduced in Chapter 2 and the main results on expectations – which can provide an alternative formalism for probability theory – are presented in Chapter 3. Chapter 4 is devoted to stochastic processes and may be used as a 'built-in' reference for basic properties used in later chapters. Markov processes and renewal processes are considered in some depth and the notion of reversibility, a powerful technique in queueing theory, is introduced. In fact, the mathematically experienced reader with a background in probability may skip all of the first four chapters on a first reading, using them only when referred to later if necessary. Chapter 5 considers single queues and their application to computer/communication systems; networks of queues are studied in Chapter 6. This analysis is extended to queueing networks with multiple classes of customers in Chapter 7 and the now well-known algorithms for solving such 'product form' networks are derived. Up to this point, the results obtained for queues and networks of queues are exact, but in real problems, networks are often too complex for their solutions to be numerically tractable and the assumptions required for an exact solution rarely hold. Chapter 8 therefore considers approximate, more efficient, methods of solution. In Chapter 9, distributions of time delays in networks are considered. This has become an important issue recently with the development of transaction processing systems for which benchmarks specifying quantiles for response times have been defined. Chapter 10 is devoted to blocking, which is another vital phenomenon which cannot be modelled by a product form network. Blocking occurs when the service of one queue is inhibited by another queue (of finite capacity) being full. This situation occurs in open queueing systems which contain finite capacity queues, for example in a communication network of nodes with finite buffers. Finally, the techniques described in the book are applied to model the performance of interconnection networks which arise in parallel computer systems and in telephone exchanges. Each chapter is supported by a set of exercises which serve to test the understanding of the reader, give practice for written examinations, elaborate on certain issues arising in the chapter and help a practitioner apply modelling techniques to real problems. Selected solutions are provided for about two thirds of the exercises at the end of the book. The exercises are given ratings, following Donald Knuth's notation, as follows:

00 = very easy (can be done immediately)
10 = simple exercise (up to two minutes)
20 = moderately difficult (up to 20 minutes)
30 = more difficult (up to an hour)
40 = very difficult (no time limit)

There are several courses that could be based upon this book, ranging from performance analysis in computer science or telecommunications to stochastic processes and their applications in these areas. Some possibilities are suggested in the following diagram.

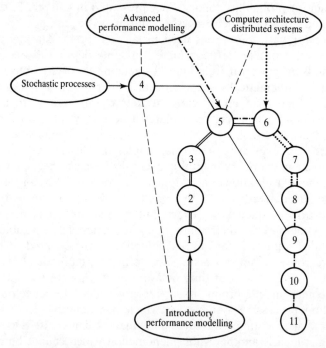

Two courses on performance modelling are proposed – one introductory, the other advanced – and the later chapters of the book could provide material to cover the performance aspects of courses on distributed systems and (parallel) computer architecture. The more theoretical material could be used as the main text for a course on stochastic processes, but would most likely be supported by other books unless this course were slanted towards communication and computing applications. Dashed lines indicate that a chapter would be used mainly for reference or support as a secondary text whereas other lines indicate a detailed study as part of the main course text.

Acknowledgements

This book is based partly on lectures given by Peter Harrison at Imperial College over several years, supported by Naresh Patel until he joined Tandem Computers Inc. in 1990. We therefore thank the students of these lectures for pointing out the deficiencies of earlier expositions, either directly or indirectly. Many of the authors' own results described in the later chapters were obtained in the course of a research project supported by the Science and Engineering Research Council of the United Kingdom under grant number GR/E/54986. More specifically, it is a pleasure to thank Tony Field for his enthusiasm and suggestions during our collaboration over several years and Edwige Pitel for her scrupulous comments on parts of the manuscript.

Peter Harrison
Naresh Patel
September 1992

Contents

Preface   v

Chapter 1   Essentials of Probability Theory   **1**

    1.1   Sample space, events and probability   3
    1.2   Conditional probability   9
    1.3   Independence   13
        Exercises   17

Chapter 2   Random Variables and Distributions   **19**

    2.1   Probability distribution functions   20
    2.2   Discrete random variables   23
    2.3   Continuous random variables   28
    2.4   Joint random variables   35
    2.5   Conditional distributions   39
    2.6   Independence and sums   44
        Exercises   48

Chapter 3   Expected Values and Moments   **51**

    3.1   Expectation   51
    3.2   Generating functions and transforms   63
    3.3   Asymptotic properties   72
        Exercises   79

Chapter 4   Stochastic Processes   **81**

    4.1   Random walks   83
    4.2   Markov chains   89
    4.3   Markov processes   112
    4.4   Reversibility   131
    4.5   Renewal theory   140
        Exercises   159

Chapter 5   Queues   **164**

    5.1   Simple Markovian queues   171
    5.2   The $M/G/1$ queue   188

5.3 The G/G/1 queue   207
Exercises   213

Chapter 6   Single Class Queueing Networks   **216**

6.1 Introduction   216
6.2 Open queueing networks   218
6.3 Closed queueing networks   231
6.4 Mean value analysis   238
6.5 Performance measures for the state-dependent case   245
6.6 The flow equivalent server method   249
Exercises   255

Chapter 7   Multi-class Queueing Networks   **258**

7.1 Service time distributions   259
7.2 Types of service centre   262
7.3 Multi-class traffic model   270
7.4 BCMP theorem   271
7.5 Properties and extensions of BCMP networks   275
7.6 Computational algorithms for BCMP networks   276
7.7 Priority disciplines   281
7.8 Quasi-reversibility   288
Exercises   295

Chapter 8   Approximate Methods   **298**
8.1 Decomposition   300
8.2 Fixed point methods   322
8.3 Diffusion approximation   328
8.4 Maximum entropy methods   337
Exercises   347

Chapter 9   Time Delays   **350**

9.1 Time delays in the single server queue   352
9.2 Time delays in networks of queues   360
9.3 Inversion of the Laplace transforms   372
9.4 Approximate methods   377
Exercises   379

Chapter 10   Blocking in Queueing Networks   **381**

10.1 Introduction   382
10.2 Types of blocking   383
10.3 Two finite queues in a closed network   388
10.4 Aggregating Markovian states   390
10.5 BAS blocking   392
10.6 BBS blocking   405
10.7 Repetitive service blocking   409
Exercises   414

Chapter 11   Switching Network Models   **416**

    11.1   Telephone networks   417
    11.2   Interconnection networks for parallel processing systems   420
    11.3   Models of the full crossbar switch   423
    11.4   Multi-stage interconnection networks   427
    11.5   Models of synchronous MINS   431
    11.6   Models of asynchronous MINS   433
    11.7   Interconnection networks in a queueing model   440
           Exercises   447

Appendix: Outline Solutions   **449**

References   **460**

Index   **465**

Chapter 1
Essentials of Probability Theory

1.1 Sample space, events
    and probability   3

1.2 Conditional probability   9
1.3 Independence   13

The complexity of contemporary computer and communication systems is such that no model, analytical or otherwise, could hope to capture every detail of their construction. Instead, the modeller must abstract the essential features which account for the cause and effect relationships that result in the observed behaviour of the system. This is exactly the situation that occurs in other fields of engineering, but even having been so abstracted, the essential features tend to be too many or impossible to quantify precisely, for example when human behaviour is involved. As a result, finely detailed features must be aggregated in some systematic way, leading to model components with manageable numbers of parameters. Moreover, prediction of observable quantities is rarely required at such a detailed level. Typically, an average of a collection of observations is preferred – a common form of aggregate. Aggregation is provided by probabilistic models which have been used successfully for this purpose in many applications, such as telephone systems, population processes and other biological models. In this book we will develop such models and show how they can be applied to make predictions about a variety of communication networks and parallel computer architectures.

Probability theory is often introduced by way of gambling applications in which a notion of 'chance' plays a prominent role. For example, the probability that a fair die will show a 'six' when thrown is intuitively $\frac{1}{6}$ in that one would expect, for a large number of throws, to see a 'six' one sixth of this number of times – or at least very nearly. Similarly, for two such dice thrown simultaneously, one would expect to get two 'sixes' one time in 36, provided the dice could not interact in any way. We have just used the concept of *independent events*: to say that the dice 'cannot interact' implies that their showing faces are independent, i.e. that knowledge of the number on one cannot affect the number on the other.

More generally, an observable event may have many facets which may be independent or dependent on each other. For example, consider the time taken by a person shopping in a supermarket. People have different shopping habits which will combine to produce a shopping time that will also depend on how many other people are shopping at the same time, since more people cause more queueing and so more delays. Both men and women shop; some shoppers will know the supermarket well and find what they want quickly; some will have a list and collect their goods systematically whereas others will wander about aimlessly wondering what they fancy for dinner; some people need many items, others just a few; and so on. How might we go about modelling such a process? Clearly we cannot account for every possible configuration of items in the supermarket, every characteristic of each shopper and every path taken by each shopper to model the contention delays. Even if we did, our predictions would be dependent on a large set of parameters representing the above scenarios. Instead, we assign probabilities to each characteristic and configuration using a **mass function** for a discrete set of possibilities and a **distribution function** for a continuous set. For example, a shopper is either male or female (to a good approximation) and a probability can be associated with each possibility, typically estimated as the respective proportions of male and female shoppers observed in a 'typical' day (or other period). This would define a two-point mass function. On the other hand, the time taken by a cashier to deal with one customer with a given set of purchases at the checkout will not come from a discrete set but from a continuum of real values. Thus, the probability measure required is that of the checkout time not exceeding a given value in this continuum – i.e. a distribution – and similarly for shopping time. Finally, the variables influencing shopping times will not, in general, be independent. For example, it may well be that men tend to have fewer purchases to make, do not know the supermarket well and buy more beer. These dependencies complicate the computation of the probability distribution of shopping time.

Thus, probability theory is important for simulation models. In this book, we will see how it is at least as important in analytical models. In fact, the analytical models we consider are essentially abstractions of the same physical systems as might be modelled by simulation: simulation provides an algorithmic abstraction, analytical models provide a mathematical abstraction. In the first three chapters we present the essential aspects of probability theory that will be used. The exposition is introductory in nature and is not intended to provide a full general introduction to the subject. There are several excellent texts that fulfil this role, for example Ross (1982) and Feller (1968).

1.1   Sample space, events and probability

Consider first an **experiment**, in some abstract sense, of which there is a set Ω of all possible **outcomes** or results. The bold terms are those conventionally used to introduce probability theory. The experiment need not be, and typically will not be, under the control of some experimenter but instead is intended to denote some physical system with measurable properties – its outcomes. For example, the 'experiment' might be a cricket match and the 'outcomes' the result of every ball bowled as written in the official scorebook (or similarly the result of every stroke in a golf match, or every point in a tennis match). In the context of computer performance modelling, the experiment might be the transmission of messages between two nodes in a communication network and the outcomes message transmission times, together with ∞, denoting a failed transmission. Notice that not all outcomes might be *observable*. In the first example, an observer might be reading the scorecard published in a newspaper which only records how many runs each batsman scored, the score at the fall of each wicket, summary bowling analyses etc. Each observable may be determined from the outcomes and indeed can be identified with a subset of the sample space; for example a batsman's score corresponds to the balls off which he scored runs. Similarly in the second case, timing information may not be available, the only information recorded being whether or not a message was transmitted successfully. In this case the observation 'successful transmission' corresponds to the complete set of possible transmission times, i.e. the whole sample space less ∞.

The notion of an observable is denoted by an **event** which is defined to be a subset of Ω – but not necessarily any subset. If the outcome of an experiment is a member of event E, we say that E has *occurred*. An event therefore has the interpretation of an observable in the above sense or of any *collection* of observables (denoted by a union of events). For example, the event $\{2, 3\}$ in the second of our examples represents the proposition that a message took either 2 or 3 seconds to transmit. We are now in a position to give the usual axiomatic definitions of the terms event space and probability. The formality should not be found obscure in the light of the preceding discussion, and the relationship between the axiomatic definition and a more intuitive notion of probability will be developed later. The most general, measure-theoretic definition of probability requires considerably more mathematical foundations and is outside the scope of this book. The interested reader is referred to Kingman and Taylor (1966).

We begin, as above, by defining a sample space Ω to be a set of outcomes of some experiment. We use the symbol \ to denote set difference and an overbar to denote set complementation. Thus $A \backslash B = \{x \in A | x \notin B\}$ and $\bar{A} = \Omega \backslash A$. An event space is now defined as follows:

Definition 1.1

An event space $\mathscr{E}$ over sample space Ω is a subset of 2^Ω, i.e. a collection of subsets of Ω, that satisfies the following properties:

(1) $\Omega \in \mathscr{E}$. This event will occur for every outcome of the experiment since it contains all outcomes.

(2)   If $E \in \mathscr{E}$ then $\bar{E} \in \mathscr{E}$. Thus if E denotes an observable, its complement denotes another, namely that 'E did not occur'.

(3)   If $E_i \in \mathscr{E}$ for $i = 1, 2, \ldots$ then $\bigcup_{i=1}^{\infty} E_i \in \mathscr{E}$. This means that if $E_1, E_2, \ldots$ denote observables then so does their union, i.e. '(the outcome is in) at least one of the E_i' or 'at least one of the E_i occurred' can be observed, which is clearly desirable.

In other words, an event space is a σ-field (also called a σ-algebra) but we will not make use of the more abstract properties of this definition.

By taking $E = \Omega$ in (2), which is valid by (1), we immediately find that $\varnothing \in \mathscr{E}$, i.e. that there is an event containing no outcomes. $\varnothing$ can never occur. From (3), a *finite* union, of n events say, is also an event, as may be seen by taking $E_i = \varnothing$ for $i > n$. Alternatively, we could take $E_i = E_n$ for $i > n$. In particular, if $E, F \in \mathscr{E}$ then $E \cup F \in \mathscr{E}$, and this property is sufficient for the event space to be closed under *finite* union. By De Morgan's laws, we also have that countable intersections of events are events since

$$\bigcap_{i=1}^{\infty} E_i = \overline{\left[\bigcup_{i=1}^{\infty} \bar{E}_i \right]}$$

Notice that the definition of $\mathscr{E}$ allows the trivial situation in which the only observable of an experiment is that the experiment occurred, i.e. 'something happened'. Another possibility is that every subset of Ω is in $\mathscr{E}$, corresponding to every outcome (and set thereof) being an observable.

Probability may now be defined as follows:

Definition 1.2

A probability measure P on an event space $\mathscr{E}$ with sample space Ω is a real-valued function satisfying the axioms:

(1) $\quad 0 \leq P(E) \leq 1 \qquad$ for all events $E \in \mathscr{E}$

(2) $\quad P(\Omega) = 1$

(3) $\quad P\left(\bigcup_{i=1}^{\infty} E_i\right) = \sum_{i=1}^{\infty} P(E_i)$

$$\text{for } E_1, E_2, \ldots \in \mathscr{E}, \; E_i \cap E_j = \varnothing \text{ for } i \neq j$$

Thus, axiom (1) states that all probabilities lie in the range $[0, 1]$ and axiom (2) states that the outcome of every experiment is in Ω with probability 1. Axiom (3) defines the probability of a countably infinite union of pairwise disjoint or **mutually exclusive** events, i.e. events E_1, $E_2, \ldots$ for which $E_i \cap E_j = \varnothing$ for $i \neq j$. The corresponding formula

$$P\left(\bigcup_{i=1}^{n} E_i\right) = \sum_{i=1}^{n} P(E_i)$$

holds for all finite n by taking $E_i = \varnothing$ for $i > n$ in axiom (3). This formula also follows from its instance with $n = 2$, i.e. from $P(E \cup F) = P(E) + P(F)$, and this is equivalent to axiom (3) for finite event spaces. However, the formula with finite n does not imply axiom (3) in the general case of an infinite event space.

We can deduce from axioms (2) and (3) that $P(\varnothing) = 0$ by taking $E_1 = \Omega$ and $E_i = \varnothing$ for $i > 1$ in (3); $\varnothing$ is mutually exclusive with any event. This gives $P(\Omega \cup \varnothing) = P(\Omega) + P(\varnothing)$, i.e. $1 = 1 + P(\varnothing)$ by axiom (2). Thus, the probability of the empty event is zero in *every* experiment, which is entirely reasonable since this event can never occur.

A set of events $\{E_1, E_2, \ldots\}$ is a **partition** of Ω if the E_i are mutually exclusive and $\bigcup_i E_i = \Omega$ so that $\sum_i P(E_i) = 1$. In other words, exactly one of the events E_i must occur. Suppose now that the sample space is *countable*, i.e. $\Omega = \{x_1, x_2, \ldots\}$. Then the sets $\{x_i\}$ for $i = 1, 2, \ldots$ form a partition of Ω (assuming they are valid events) and we can define $p_i = P(\{x_i\})$ so that $0 \leq p_i \leq 1$ by axiom (1) and $\sum_j p_j = 1$ by axioms (2) and (3). This is the elementary view of probability over a discrete sample space where the possible outcomes are assigned real numbers between 0 and 1 which sum to one.

Perhaps the most common intuitive notion of probability or chance is based upon expected values and long-term behaviour. If an experiment were repeated independently many times one might consider the probability of an event E to be the limiting value of the proportion of times that E was observed as the number of repetitions increased.

Thus one might take the *definition* of the probability of E to be

$$P(E) = \lim_{n \to \infty} \frac{N(E, n)}{n}$$

where $N(E, n)$ denotes the number of times that E occurred in the first n repetitions of the experiment. Whilst clearly intuitive, this is a very complicated definition in the mathematical sense since it is an asymptotic property. It also requires further assumptions. For example, it must be assumed that if another series of experiments were performed under the same conditions, the limiting value for $P(E)$ would turn out the same again. This complexity makes it harder to develop a theory of probability and the conventional approach uses the simple axioms given above and from them deduces asymptotic properties such as limit theorems and laws of large numbers, of which our alternative definition of $P(E)$ is an instance. We consider asymptotic properties in Section 3.3.

More generally, and more vaguely, probability can be considered as a 'measure of belief' in a very subjective sense. Here, a person attempts to quantify an opinion on some possibility by associating with it some chance value between 0 and 1, or a percentage. Some of the probability axioms are perfectly intuitive. For example, if a person thinks there is an 80% chance of rain, he or she will probably also believe that there is a 20% chance of no rain, consistent with axiom (3). However, if more than one event is being considered, intuition will not necessarily lead to consistency with the axioms. If there are many events with complex dependencies, it is hard, at the intuitive level, to keep track of all the probability. Although there are other theories of belief, such as Schafer (1976), inconsistency with the axioms of probability theory often implies a logical inconsistency in one's intuitive assignment of probabilities. It is easy to assign probabilities to the outcomes or disjoint subsets of the sample space – these just have to add up to one in a conventional theory – but it is harder to be consistent with mutually dependent and/or intersecting events. The probability axioms provide a good basis for consistency and more sophisticated theories of belief are often built on top of them, or some of them. There are various theories with applications in machine learning that violate the probability axioms, but we will not pursue this topic further.

There are some important fundamental results that follow directly from the axioms and we will use these extensively. We present them as the propositions below. We will frequently adopt the convention of omitting the $\cap$ symbol in finite intersections. In particular, we will usually write EF for $E \cap F$.

Proposition 1.1
$P(\bar{E}) = 1 - P(E)$ for event E.

Proof Since $E\bar{E} = \emptyset$, we have by (the finite form of) axiom (3) that $P(E \cup \bar{E}) = P(E) + P(\bar{E})$. But $E \cup \bar{E} = \Omega$ and so by axiom (2), $1 = P(E) + P(\bar{E})$. ∎

This result simply states the intuitive property that the probability that an event does not occur is obtained by subtracting from 1 the probability that it does occur. For example, if the probability that a tossed coin will come up 'heads' is 0.9, the probability that it will come up 'tails' is 0.1. Our previous result that $P(\emptyset) = 0$ is a direct consequence of this proposition.

Proposition 1.2

For events E, F, $P(E \cup F) = P(E) + P(F) - P(EF)$.

Proof Thinking of a Venn diagram, we first write $E \cup F = (E\backslash F) \cup (F\backslash E) \cup (E \cap F)$, noting that the components in the union on the right-hand side are mutually exclusive. Thus we have

$$P(E \cup F) = P(E\backslash F) + P(F\backslash E) + P(EF)$$

Now, $E = (E\backslash F) \cup (EF)$ so that $P(E) = P(E\backslash F) + P(EF)$ and $P(F) = P(F\backslash E) + P(EF)$ similarly. Eliminating $P(E\backslash F)$ and $P(F\backslash E)$ then gives

$$P(E \cup F) = P(E) - P(EF) + P(F) - P(EF) + P(EF)$$

∎

A more general result for the probability of finite unions of events can be proved by induction (see Exercise 1.2):

$$P(E_1 \cup \ldots \cup E_n) = \sum_{i=1}^{n} P(E_i) - \sum_{i_1 < i_2} P(E_{i_1} E_{i_2}) + \ldots$$

$$+ (-1)^{r+1} \sum_{i_1 < \ldots < i_r} P(E_{i_1} \ldots E_{i_r}) + \ldots$$

$$+ (-1)^{n+1} P(E_{i_1} \ldots E_{i_n})$$

(Notice that the domain of the rth sum on the right-hand side has $\binom{n}{r}$ elements corresponding to each of the (ordered) subsets of $\{1, 2, \ldots, n\}$ of size r.)

Proposition 1.3

If $E \subseteq F$, then $P(E) \leq P(F)$.

Proof We can write $F = E \cup \bar{E}F$. Since E and $\bar{E}F$ are mutually exclusive, $P(F) = P(E) + P(\bar{E}F)$ and since all probabilities are non-negative, the result follows. ∎

Corollary P is a continuous function on $\mathscr{E}$. In other words, if the events $\{E_1, E_2, \ldots\}$ are increasing according to the set-inclusion ordering, i.e. $E_1 \subseteq E_2 \subseteq \ldots$, then

$$P\left(\bigcup_{i=1}^{\infty} E_i\right) = \lim_{n \to \infty} P(E_n)$$

Similarly, if the events $\{E_1, E_2, \ldots\}$ are decreasing, i.e. $E_1 \supseteq E_2 \supseteq \ldots$, then

$$P\left(\bigcap_{i=1}^{\infty} E_i\right) = \lim_{n \to \infty} P(E_n)$$

(The limit of an increasing (respectively decreasing) sequence in $\mathscr{E}$ is its union (respectively intersection).)

Proof We define $F_1 = E_1$ and $F_i = E_i E_{i-1}$ for $i > 1$. Then the F_i are mutually exclusive and $\bigcup_{i=1}^{\infty} E_i = \bigcup_{i=1}^{\infty} F_i$. The result then follows via axiom (3) of Definition 1.2; similarly for decreasing sequences of events.

We conclude this section with two examples.

Example 1.1 ────────────────────────────────

If a fair die is tossed twice independently (see Section 1.3), the probability of each distinct ordered pair of numbers coming up is $\frac{1}{36}$. We require the probability that at least one of the numbers is a six, i.e. $P(E \cup F)$ where E and F are the events that the first and second throws respectively gave a six. Now, $P(E) = P\{(6, 1), (6, 2), \ldots, (6, 6)\} = \frac{6}{36} = \frac{1}{6} = P(F)$ similarly. (In fact these probabilities follow directly from the assumption of independence.) Thus,

$$P(E \cup F) = \tfrac{1}{6} + \tfrac{1}{6} - P\{(6, 6)\} = \tfrac{1}{3} - \tfrac{1}{36} = \tfrac{11}{36}$$

Alternatively, we could have worked out this result by observing that the required event is the complement of the event that neither throw gave a six. There are five possible values for each throw that achieve this and so 25 outcomes in our sample space. Thus the required probability is $1 - \frac{25}{36} = \frac{11}{36}$.

Example 1.2 ————————————————————————————————

In a hand of five-card poker, suppose we want the probability of being dealt (fairly) either a run (cards have successive values in any suits) or a flush (cards all of the same suit). Let these events be denoted by E and F respectively. There are 10 runs from $\{A, 2, 3, 4, 5\}$ to $\{10, J, Q, K, A\}$. Since the suits are not important, there are 4^5 hands which yield each run and so 10×4^5 hands which are runs of any type. The number of hands which are all (say) spades is just the number of ways of picking 5 indistinguishable items from 13, i.e. $\binom{13}{5}$. (From first principles, observe that there are 13 possibilities for the first card, 12 for the second and 11, 10, 9 for the third, fourth, fifth respectively, giving $13 \dots 9$ permutations in all. However, this distinguishes permutations within a given hand and so must be divided by 5!). The number of hands is, similarly, $\binom{52}{5}$ and so we have

$$P(E) = \frac{10 \times 4^5}{\binom{52}{5}} \approx 0.003\,94 \approx \frac{1}{254}$$

$$P(F) = \frac{4\binom{13}{5}}{\binom{52}{5}} \approx 0.001\,98 \approx \frac{1}{505}$$

Finally, $P(EF)$ is the probability of a running flush, i.e. a run in a single suit. There are only 10 of these in each suit and so 40 in all. Thus,

$$P(EF) = \frac{40}{\binom{52}{5}} \approx 0.000\,015 \approx \frac{1}{64\,974}$$

and so the required probability is (to six decimal places)

$$0.003\,940 + 0.001\,980 - 0.000\,015 = 0.005\,905$$

E and F are 'nearly disjoint', but the example shows some common combinatorial techniques.

1.2 Conditional probability

When determining the probability of an event we often have partial information about related events, i.e. about the outcomes of the same experiment. The probability we calculate is then **conditional** on this information. We also often use conditional probabilities as a means of calculating unconditional probabilities by first conditioning on some events whose probabilities we know.

The conditional probability that event E occurs given that F has occurred is written $P(E|F)$ and is computed in terms of $P(EF)$ according to the following reasoning. First, since we know that F has occurred, the sample space of our new 'conditional' experiment is reduced to F. Secondly, if E occurs as well as F, the outcome of the new experiment must be in EF. The probability of the conditional event $E|F$ is therefore the probability of EF *relative* to F. We therefore take the following:

Definition 1.3

If $P(F) > 0$, the conditional probability of E given F is

$$P(E|F) = \frac{P(EF)}{P(F)}$$

Notice that this is a definition rather than a proposition. We have introduced informally the concepts of a conditional probability, experiment and event. Definition 1.3 makes this intuition rigorous. However, in theories of knowledge with uncertainty, a more elaborate formulation is necessary to achieve greater expressive power. This may involve different 'worlds' with their own sets of probabilities for a given set of events; see for example Fagin and Halpern (1988a, b). Such problems will not concern us, however. The definition is illustrated by two simple examples. We then prove that $P(\cdot|F)$ does define a probability.

Example 1.3 ————————————————————————

A coin is tossed twice and each of the four outcomes in the sample space $\Omega = \{(h, h), (h, t), (t, h), (t, t)\}$ are equally likely. If it is known that at least one toss came up 'heads', we wish to find the probability that both did. Let F denote the event that at least one toss came up heads. Then the solution is

$$P(\{(h, h)\}|F) = \frac{P(\{(h, h)\}F)}{P(F)} = \frac{P(\{(h, h)\})}{P(\{(h, h), (h, t), (t, h)\})}$$

$$= \frac{\frac{1}{4}}{\frac{3}{4}} = \frac{1}{3}$$

Notice that the result is *not* $\frac{1}{2}$ which one might conclude by mistakenly reasoning that 'one toss was heads, so the other is also heads with probability a half'. The source of the error is that the knowledge that one toss was a head reduces the sample space to three outcomes of which two include a tail. Therefore the probability of the other toss being a tail is double that of its being a head. Equivalently one can note that of all the three outcomes with heads appearing in Ω, two also have tails and one does not.

Example 1.4 _____

In a communication network, there are two routes, A and B, between a particular pair of nodes which are chosen with equal probability. Message transmission time along route A is 1 second and along route B is 3 seconds. However, the probability of a transmission error is 0.2 on route A and 0.1 on route B. We wish to find the probability of a message being transmitted correctly in 1 second.

To solve this, let the event that a message is transmitted correctly be denoted by C. Then by hypothesis we have $P(C|A) = 0.8$, $P(C|B) = 0.9$ where the events A and B denote the choice of routes A and B respectively. The solution to the problem is $P(CA)$ which we now obtain as:

$$P(CA) = P(C|A) \times P(A) = 0.8 \times 0.5 = 0.4$$

Proposition 1.4

For event space $\mathscr{E}$, the function $P(\cdot|F)$, defined in Definition 1.3 for event $F \in \mathscr{E}$ with $P(F) > 0$, is a probability.

Proof Given $F \in \mathscr{E}$, we prove that the function of $E \in \mathscr{E}$, $P(EF)/P(F)$, satisfies each of the probability axioms of Definition 1.2 in turn.

(1) $EF \subseteq F \Rightarrow P(EF) \leqslant P(F) \Rightarrow \dfrac{P(EF)}{P(F)} \leqslant 1$

It is clear that $P(EF)/P(F) \geqslant 0$.

(2) $\dfrac{P(\Omega F)}{P(F)} = \dfrac{P(F)}{P(F)} = 1$

(3) $\dfrac{P\left(\left(\bigcup\limits_{i=1}^{\infty} E_i\right)F\right)}{P(F)} = \dfrac{P\left(\bigcup\limits_{i=1}^{\infty} E_iF\right)}{P(F)}$

since $\cap$ distributes with unions

$$= \sum_{i=1}^{\infty} \frac{P(E_iF)}{P(F)}$$

since the events E_iF are mutually exclusive if the E_i are. ∎

Because of Proposition 1.4, we can apply any result obtained for a normal probability to a conditional probability, including results about conditional probabilities. For example we could use conditional probabilities for the probabilities used in the next section.

1.2.1   Law of Total Probability and Bayes' Formula

Given any partition $\{G_1, G_2, \ldots\}$ of Ω, we can write *any* event E in the form

$$E = \bigcup_{i=1}^{\infty} EG_i$$

where the events EG_i are mutually exclusive. This is easy to prove using an argument based on Venn diagrams for the case of a partition of two events. We have given the result for an infinite partition. However, this includes the case of finite partitions also since a partition of n events is equivalent to an infinite one with the same first n events and $G_i = \varnothing$ for $i > n$; compare the discussion after Definition 1.1. In the sequel we will often omit the upper limit on unions and summations where the result is equally valid for both the finite and infinite cases. We now have the 'Law of Total Probability' or 'Complete Probability Formula':

$$P(E) = \sum_i P(EG_i) = \sum_i P(E|G_i)P(G_i)$$

Thus we can calculate $P(E)$ by first conditioning on each of the G_i, i.e. finding the probability of E given that G_i has occurred, and then computing the weighted average of the $P(E|G_i)$; the weights are the probabilities of the conditioning events G_i. The following proposition, a kind of inversion result for conditional probabilities, now follows immediately:

Proposition 1.5 (Bayes)

Given a partition $\{G_1, G_2, \ldots\}$ and event E,

$$P(G_i|E) = \frac{P(E|G_i)P(G_i)}{\sum_j P(E|G_j)P(G_j)}$$

This result is called **Bayes' Formula**.

Proof   The numerator on the right-hand side is $P(G_iE)$ by Definition 1.3 and the denominator is $P(E)$ by the Law of Total Probability.   ∎

Bayes' Formula is widely used in inference systems. Essentially it updates the probabilities assigned to the G_i, regarded as a collection of hypotheses or logical propositions about some scenario, in the light of the occurrence of the event E, regarded as new evidence. The updated probability is then $P(G_i|E)$. In fact we can weaken the requirement that the G_i form a partition in the Law of Total Probability and Bayes' Formula. The necessary and sufficient condition is that the events EG_i be mutually exclusive with union E.

As an example, we consider a simple well-known problem in probability theory with a solution that may not be obvious to all readers. Of three otherwise identical cards, one is red on both sides, one is yellow on both sides and one is red on one side and yellow on the other. A card is selected at random and is red on its upper side. What is the probability that the other side is yellow?

To solve this, let RR, YY, RY denote respectively the event that the card with two red sides, two yellow sides, a red and a yellow side was chosen. Let R_{up} denote the event that this card was red on its upper side. Then we have, since $\{RR, YY, RY\}$ is a partition,

$$
\begin{aligned}
P(RY|R_{up}) & \\
&= \frac{P(R_{up}|RY)P(RY)}{P(R_{up}|RR)P(RR) + P(R_{up}|YY)P(YY) + P(R_{up}|RY)P(RY)} \\
&= \frac{\frac{1}{2} \times \frac{1}{3}}{1 \times \frac{1}{3} + 0 \times \frac{1}{3} + \frac{1}{2} \times \frac{1}{3}} \\
&= \frac{1}{3}
\end{aligned}
$$

It is tempting to reason that, given the upper side of the selected card is red, only two of the three cards could have been selected, and these with equal probability. Exactly one of these would have a yellow side and so the answer is a half. This reasoning is wrong because it fails to take into account that there are two ways of having a red side face up if the two red sided card is chosen. To reason correctly in this way, we observe that there are three equally likely ways of having a red face up, because there are three red sides in all. Only one out of these three has a yellow bottom side.

1.3 Independence

Two events E and F are independent if the probability of E conditioned on F is equal to the unconditional probability of E, i.e. $P(E|F) = P(E)$. Since $P(E|F) = P(EF)/P(F)$, we have the following definition:

Definition 1.4

Two events E and F are **independent** if and only if $P(EF) = P(E)P(F)$. Otherwise, the two events are **dependent**.

Notice the symmetry in this definition between E and F: E is independent of F if and only if F is independent of E. This is consistent with the symmetrical intuitive notion of independence.

Example 1.5

Two fair dice are thrown simultaneously such that all 36 outcomes, i.e. pairs of values, are equally likely. Let E be the event that the first die shows a six and F be the event that the second die shows a one. Then EF is the event that the outcome of the experiment is $(6, 1)$, so that $P(EF) = \frac{1}{36}$. But $P(E) = P(\{(6, 1), (6, 2), (6, 3), (6, 4), (6, 5), (6, 6)\}) = \frac{6}{36} = \frac{1}{6}$. Similarly, $P(F) = \frac{1}{6}$ so that E and F are independent.

Example 1.6

Two fair dice are thrown simultaneously. Let E be the event that the first die shows a six and F be the event that the sum of the dice is nine. Then $EF = \{(6, 3)\}$ and so $P(EF) = \frac{1}{36}$. Now, $P(E) = \frac{1}{6}$ and $P(F) = \frac{4}{36}$ since $F = \{(3, 6), (4, 5), (5, 4), (6, 3)\}$. Thus $P(E)P(F) = \frac{1}{54}$ so that E and F are dependent.

Suppose instead that F is the event that the sum is seven, E remaining the same. Then $F = \{(1, 6), (2, 5), (3, 4), (4, 3), (5, 2), (6, 1)\}$ so that $P(F) = \frac{1}{6}$ and E and F are independent. The same would apply if E were the event that the first die showed any number between one and six.

This determination of independence has been purely mechanical, based on Definition 1.4. The intuitive argument is the following. If the sum of the two dice is to be seven, then given any value on the first, there is a unique value on the second that gives this sum. Moreover, this value will occur with probability $\frac{1}{6}$. Conversely, if the sum is to be anything other than seven, there will be at least one value on the first die that makes this sum impossible to achieve. For example, if the sum specified is nine, then a one or a two on the first die ensures that the sum will not be achieved. Thus, the probability of getting the specified sum depends on the value of the first die.

The following two propositions relate well with intuition.

Proposition 1.6

If E and F are independent events, then so are E and $\bar{F}$, $\bar{E}$ and F, $\bar{E}$ and $\bar{F}$.

Proof Since $E = EF \cup E\bar{F}$ and EF, $E\bar{F}$ are mutually exclusive, we may write

$$P(E) = P(EF) + P(E\bar{F}) = P(E)P(F) + P(E\bar{F})$$

by hypothesis

Thus, $P(E\bar{F}) = P(E)[1 - P(F)] = P(E)P(\bar{F})$. The second case follows by symmetry, interchanging E and F, and the third by applying the first case to the events $\bar{E}$, F which are independent by the second case.   ∎

Proposition 1.7

If E and F are independent, $P(E \cup F) = 1 - P(\bar{E})P(\bar{F})$.

Proof

$$P(E \cup F) = P(E) + P(F) - P(EF)$$

by Proposition 1.2

$$= P(E) + P(F) - P(E)P(F)$$

since E and F are independent by hypothesis

$$= 1 - [1 - P(E)][1 - P(F)]$$

Alternatively, we may write $E \cup F = (\overline{\bar{E}\bar{F}})$ so that $P(E \cup F) = 1 - P(\bar{E}\bar{F}) = 1 - P(\bar{E})P(\bar{F})$ by Proposition 1.6.   ∎

Example 1.7

A game is played with two biased dice, A and B. Die A gives a one with probability $\frac{1}{2}$ and all other numbers (between two and six) with probability $\frac{1}{10}$. Die B gives a one with probability $\frac{1}{16}$ and all other numbers with probability $\frac{3}{16}$. Die A is thrown first and if it shows an even number, it is thrown again; otherwise die B is used for the second throw. We require the probability that the sum of the two throws is five.

Let the events E_i be 'the first throw is i', the events F_i be 'the second throw is i' $(1 \leqslant i \leqslant 6)$ and the event S be 'the sum of the two throws is five'. Then

$$P(S) = P(E_1F_4 \cup E_4F_1 \cup E_2F_3 \cup E_3F_2)$$

$$= P(E_1F_4) + P(E_4F_1) + P(E_2F_3) + P(E_3F_2)$$

(since the unioned events are disjoint)

$$= P(F_4|E_1)P(E_1) + P(F_1|E_4)P(E_4) + P(F_3|E_2)P(E_2)$$

$$+ P(F_2|E_3)P(E_3)$$

$$= \tfrac{3}{16} \times \tfrac{1}{2} + \tfrac{1}{2} \times \tfrac{1}{10} + \tfrac{1}{10} \times \tfrac{1}{10} + \tfrac{3}{16} \times \tfrac{1}{10}$$

$$= \tfrac{69}{400}$$

Notice the use of the Law of Total Probability and the choice of conditioning. We conditioned on the E_i which influence the probabilities of the F_j in a known way. We could have conditioned the E_j on the F_i instead, but since we have no information on how the probabilities of the first throw's values depend on the values of the second throw, this would not have helped and we would have got stuck.

Finally in this section, we extend the definition of independence to more than two events. It is not sufficient to say that the events are pairwise independent since this does not imply that, in the case of three events, $P(E|FG) = P(E)$. Instead we have the following definition:

Definition 1.5

The events $E_1, \ldots, E_n$ ($n \geqslant 2$) are independent iff

$$P(E_{\pi(1)} \ldots E_{\pi(r)}) = P(E_{\pi(1)}) \ldots P(E_{\pi(r)})$$

for $2 \leqslant r \leqslant n$, where π is any permutation function on the numbers $\{1, \ldots, n\}$. This is equivalent to the inductive definition that the events are independent if and only if

$$P(E_1 \ldots E_n) = P(E_1) \ldots P(E_n)$$

and every proper subset with at least two events is independent. We extend this to infinite sets by defining an infinite set of events to be independent iff every finite subset with at least two events is independent.

Some experiments consist of a sequence of sub-experiments, such as repeatedly tossing a coin or throwing a die, as in Example 1.7. Often these sub-experiments are independent in that the outcome of one cannot influence the outcome of any of the others. More precisely, this means that if the event E_i and its probability is defined only by the ith sub-experiment ($i \geqslant 1$), then the sequence of events (E_i) must be independent. Experiments with the same probability function (and hence same sample space) are called **identical**, and identical sub-experiments are called **trials**. We will often have cause to consider sequences of independent trials; see in particular the discussion of the binomial distribution in Section 2.2.

SUMMARY

- Probability is important in modelling many systems in the real world, especially communications networks and computer architectures.

- Probability theory has a natural, intuitive interpretation and simple mathematical axioms.
- Dependent events are handled by conditional probability.
- The law of total probability allows problems to be decomposed and is a vital tool in stochastic modelling.
- The probability of the intersection of independent events is the product of the probabilities of each event.

EXERCISES

1.1 (00 Independence)
Consider an experiment consisting of tossing two true dice. Let X, Y and Z be the numbers shown on the first die, the second die and the total on both dice, respectively. Find $P(X \leqslant 1, Z \leqslant 2)$ and $P(X \leqslant 1)P(Z \leqslant 2)$ to show that X and Z are not independent.

1.2 (20 Union of events)
Show that for n events $E_1, E_2, \ldots, E_n$ in a sample space Ω:

$$P(E_1 \cup \ldots \cup E_n) = \sum_{i=1}^{n} P(E_i) - \sum_{i_1 < i_2} P(E_{i_1} E_{i_2}) + \ldots$$

$$+ (-1)^{r+1} \sum_{i_1 < \ldots < i_r} P(E_{i_1} \ldots E_{i_r})$$

$$+ \ldots + (-1)^{n+1} P(E_{i_1} \ldots E_{i_n})$$

1.3 (20 Ball in urn)
How many ways can N balls be arranged in M urns, assuming that each urn can accommodate all N balls?

1.4 (20 Conditional probability)
A proportion p of people in a particular group have a given disease. A test is developed with sensitivity v (i.e. the probability that a person who has the disease gets a positive test result) and specificity c (i.e. the probability that a person who does not have the disease gets a negative test result). Clearly both v and c should be close to one for a good test. Given that a person tests positive for the disease, what is the probability that he or she has the disease?

1.5 (30 Choice in game show)
In a game show, the grand prize is hidden behind one of three

closed doors and bogus prizes are behind the other doors. The final contestant chooses one of the doors by standing in front of it. The host (knowing where the grand prize is) then opens one of the other doors to reveal a bogus prize and asks the contestant if he or she wants to change the selection. In order to maximize the probability of winning the grand prize, should the contestant keep the first selection, change to the other closed door, or does it make no difference?

Chapter 2
Random Variables and Distributions

2.1 Probability distribution
functions   20
2.2 Discrete random
variables   23
2.3 Continuous random
variables   28
2.4 Joint random variables   35
2.5 Conditional distributions   39
2.6 Independence and sums   44

Rather than the outcomes or events of an experiment *per se*, we are often more interested in a numerical value that describes some property of the outcomes. Examples include:

- the total number of tasks using a communication system rather than the number at each node;

- the number of successful message transmissions in a given time rather than the status of every message;

- the number of heads in a sequence of coin-tossing trials rather than the sequence of outcomes of each trial.

Not all of these values will be integers. For example, we might be interested in the transmission time of a message or the average number shown by a die in a sequence of trials. These values will be real numbers and in the former case the sample space itself would be the positive reals. A function which maps the sample space of an experiment to the real numbers is called a **random variable**. We refer to the **value** of a random variable as the result it produces when applied to a given outcome. To each of the possible sets of values of a random variable, we can assign a probability equal to that of its inverse image in the sample space, provided that this is an event. Thus, the probability that a random variable R is in the subset X of the reals is defined by

$$P(R \in X) = P(A)$$

where $R(a) \in X$ iff $a \in A$ and A is an event. Notice in the left-hand side we use the abbreviation '$R \in X$' to mean '$R(w) \in X$ for some $w \in \Omega$'. We shall assume that all subsets of the real line have inverse images in the sample space which are events for all random variables. Consequently, the proposition that a random variable is in a given set of reals may be regarded as, and is equivalent to, an event in the space of the real line, i.e. a subset of $(-\infty, \infty)$. This event has probability equal to the probability of its inverse image in the original sample space. Moreover, since random variables are well defined functions, disjoint subsets of $(-\infty, \infty)$ have mutually exclusive inverse images and the inverse image of $(-\infty, \infty)$ is the whole event space Ω. Thus, the sum of the probabilities of disjoint (images of) random variables that cover the real line must be one.

Example 2.1 ────────────────────────────────

Two fair coins are tossed independently; i.e. the tosses comprise independent, identical sub-experiments. The random variable X is the number of heads, so that $X \in \{0, 1, 2\}$ and has the following probabilities:

$$P(X = 0) = P(\{(t, t)\}) = \tfrac{1}{4}$$
$$P(X = 1) = P(\{(h, t), (t, h)\}) = \tfrac{1}{2}$$
$$P(X = 2) = P(\{(h, h)\}) = \tfrac{1}{4}$$

Notice that the events corresponding to $X = 0, 1, 2$ are mutually exclusive and that the assigned probabilities sum to 1 as required.

2.1 Probability distribution functions

Any interval on the real line which is open on the left and closed on the right, $(a, b]$ say, can be expressed as a difference between intervals of the form $(-\infty, x]$ for some real x, here $(-\infty, b]\backslash(-\infty, a]$. The probability assigned to such an interval for some random variable is therefore the difference between the probabilities assigned to the corresponding intervals of the form $(-\infty, x]$. The probability of an arbitrary interval, open or closed at either end, can then be determined by continuity; see Proposition 1.3. The probabilistic characteristics of a random variable X

can therefore be defined entirely in terms of its **cumulative distribution function**, more commonly abbreviated to just **distribution function**, which is defined for real number x by

$$F(x) = P(X \leq x)$$

$F(x)$ is simply the probability that the value of the random variable X is less than or equal to x. Distribution functions satisfy four important properties.

Proposition 2.1

Given the distribution function F,

(1) If $x \leq y$, then $F(x) \leq F(y)$, i.e. F is non-decreasing

(2) $\lim\limits_{x \to \infty} F(x) = 1$

(3) $\lim\limits_{x \to -\infty} F(x) = 0$

(4) F is right continuous, i.e. if $x_1, x_2, \ldots$ is a decreasing sequence with limit x, then

$$\lim_{n \to \infty} F(x_n) = F(x)$$

Proof   First, (1) follows since $x \leq y \Rightarrow (-\infty, x] \subseteq (-\infty, y]$.

For (2), note that the events $X \leq x_n$ are increasing as n and x_n increase, and that their union is the event $X < \infty$ as $x_n \to \infty$. Thus $\lim_{x \to \infty} P(X \leq x) = \lim_{n \to \infty} P(X \leq x_n) = P(X < \infty) = 1$ by the continuity property for increasing sequences, Proposition 1.3. The proof of (3) is similar.

Finally, (4) is a consequence of the continuity property for decreasing sequences. Since the x_n decrease to x as n increases, the intersection of the (decreasing) events $X \leq x_n$ is $X \leq x$. Thus,

$$\lim_{n \to \infty} P(X \leq x_n) = P(X \leq x) \qquad \blacksquare$$

The probability that X is in the left-open, right-closed interval $(a, b]$ for $a < b$, i.e. $P(a < X \leq b)$, can now be obtained using

$$(-\infty, b] = (-\infty, a] \cup (a, b]$$

and that the events $(-\infty, a]$ and $(a, b]$ are disjoint. This gives

$$P(X \leq b) = P(X \leq a) + P(a < X \leq b)$$

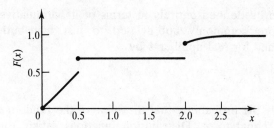

Figure 2.1   Graph of the distribution $F(x)$.

and so

$$P(a < X \leqslant b) = F(b) - F(a)$$

For other sorts of interval, we need the probability that $X < b$. This we can compute using continuity once more as follows.

$$P(X < b) = P\left(\bigcup_{n=1}^{\infty} \left\{X \leqslant b - \frac{1}{n}\right\}\right) = \lim_{n \to \infty} P\left(X \leqslant b - \frac{1}{n}\right)$$

$$= \lim_{n \to \infty} F\left(b - \frac{1}{n}\right) = F(b^-)$$

where b^- is the limit of $F(x)$ as $x \to b$ from the left. Notice that if F is continuous at the point x, then $P(X = x) = 0$; note that this means that the event $X = x$ cannot occur since in general we will have an infinite sample space. We compute the probability that a random variable is *equal* to a given value by writing

$$P(X = b) = P(X \leqslant b) - P(X < b) = F(b) - F(b^-)$$

These results are illustrated in the following example.

Example 2.2

Let the random variable X have distribution function F defined by

$$
\begin{aligned}
F(x) &= 0 & & x < 0 \\
&\ x & & 0 \leqslant x < \tfrac{1}{2} \\
&\ \tfrac{2}{3} & & \tfrac{1}{2} \leqslant x < 2 \\
&\ 1 - e^{-(\ln 2)x} & & 2 \leqslant x
\end{aligned}
$$

The graph of this distribution is shown in Figure 2.1. We can now read off various probabilities from the definition or graph. For instance:

$$P(0.25 < X \le 1) = F(1) - F(0.25) = \tfrac{2}{3} - \tfrac{1}{4} = \tfrac{5}{12}$$

$$P(X > 0.5) = 1 - F(0.5) = 1 - \tfrac{2}{3} = \tfrac{1}{3}$$

$$P(X = 2) = F(2) - F(2^-) = \tfrac{3}{4} - \tfrac{2}{3} = \tfrac{1}{12}$$

$$P(X < 2) = F(2^-) = \tfrac{2}{3}$$

2.2 Discrete random variables

If the image of a random variable, i.e. the complete set of values it can take, is finite or countably infinite, the random variable is called **discrete**. The **probability mass function** p of a discrete random variable X is defined by

$$p(x) = P(X = x)$$

for real x. Thus, if the image of X is $\{x_1, x_2, \ldots\}$, then $p(x_i) \ge 0$ ($i \ge 1$) and $p(x) = 0$ if $x \notin \{x_1, x_2, \ldots\}$. Since $P(X \in \{x_1, x_2, \ldots\}) = 1$,

$$\sum_{i=1}^{\infty} p(x_i) = 1$$

For example, if X is the number of heads when two fair coins are tossed independently,

$$p(0) = \tfrac{1}{4}, \qquad p(1) = \tfrac{1}{2}, \qquad p(2) = \tfrac{1}{4}, \qquad p(x) = 0 \text{ otherwise}$$

There is an analogy between this presentation of the probability function of a discrete random variable and the distribution of point masses along the real line; hence the term 'mass function'. A similar analogy will be found in the case of continuous random variables in the next section. The terms 'distribution' or 'distribution function' will sometimes be found in the literature instead of 'mass function', but we prefer to reserve the use of these terms for the cumulative distribution function. The cumulative distribution function F can, of course, be defined in terms of the mass function p by

$$F(x) = \sum_{y \le x} p(y)$$

In the rest of this section we consider a selection of important discrete random variables and their mass functions.

2.2.1 Bernoulli random variable

Suppose that a simple experiment has two outcomes: success and failure. Let the random variable $X = 1$ if the outcome of the experiment is 'success' and $X = 0$ if the outcome is 'failure'. Then X has probability mass function p defined by

$$p(0) = 1 - q \text{ and } p(1) = q$$

where q is the probability that the experiment's outcome is 'success' $(0 \leqslant q \leqslant 1)$. X defined thus is called a **Bernoulli random variable** with parameter q if $0 < q < 1$. For example, the experiment might be tossing a coin with 'heads' being regarded as success $(X = 1)$ and 'tails' as failure $(X = 0)$. The most common usage of Bernoulli random variables is in sequences of **Bernoulli trials**, i.e. identical experiments of the above type.

2.2.2 Geometric random variable

In a sequence of independent Bernoulli trials with parameter p, let X be the number of trials up to and including the first success. Then $X = i$ if the sequence of outcomes of the trials consists of $(i - 1)$ failures followed by a success. Now, each of the failures occurs with probability $1 - p$ and the success occurs with probability p. Thus, by independence,

$$p(i) = (1 - p)^{i-1} p$$

The sequence $p(i)$ is geometric and a random variable X with this form of mass function is called a **geometric** random variable. Clearly $\sum_{i=1}^{\infty} p(i) = 1$, as we can see by summing the simple geometric series. The notions of 'success' and 'failure' are somewhat arbitrary, and their interpretations are often interchanged. In other words, we may take p to be the probability of failure instead of success, so that p is replaced by $1 - p$ in the above and we obtain

$$p(i) = (1 - p) p^{i-1}$$

We will often use this alternative form of the mass function.

2.2.3 Binomial random variable

Consider now a sequence of n independent Bernoulli trials with parameter p. Let X be the number of successes that occur in the n trials. Then X is called a **binomial** random variable with parameters

(n, p) and mass function defined by

$$p(i) = \binom{n}{i} p^i (1 - p)^{n-i} \qquad (0 \leqslant i \leqslant n)$$

This follows since the probability of any given sequence of outcomes with i successes and $n - i$ failures in specified positions is $p^i (1 - p)^{n-i}$ by independence. However, the number of such sequences is equal to the number of different ways of selecting i objects (here, successes) out of n. Hence there are $\binom{n}{i}$ such sequences which are mutually exclusive. The probabilities $p(i)$ sum to one by the binomial theorem. Notice that a binomial random variable with parameters $(1, p)$ is a Bernoulli random variable with parameter p.

A variant of the binomial random variable is the **negative binomial**. Again, suppose we have n independent trials, each with probability p of success. The random variable X denoting the number of trials performed until r successes have occurred in total is called negative binomial with parameters (r, p). Then if $X = i$, there must have been $r - 1$ successes in the first $i - 1$ trials and the ith must have been a success. Thus by independence,

$$p(i) = \binom{i - 1}{r - 1} p^{r-1} (1 - p)^{i-r} p = \binom{i - 1}{r - 1} p^r (1 - p)^{i-r}$$

$$(r \leqslant i < \infty)$$

To verify that this is a mass function we compute

$$\sum_{i=r}^{\infty} \binom{i - 1}{r - 1} p^r (1 - p)^{i-r} = p^r \sum_{j=0}^{\infty} \binom{r + j - 1}{r - 1} (1 - p)^j$$

$$= p^r (1 - (1 - p))^{-r} = 1$$

Hence the name 'negative binomial'. Notice that a negative binomial random variable with parameters $(1, p)$ is a geometric random variable with parameter p.

2.2.4 Discrete uniform random variable

Another extremely simple, yet ubiquitous, random variable has a finite image $\{x_1, \ldots, x_n\}$ for $n \geqslant 1$, and mass function p defined by

$$p(x_i) = \frac{1}{n} \qquad \text{for every } i \ (1 \leqslant i \leqslant n)$$

Such a random variable is called **uniform**, since its mass function is spread uniformly over its image. For example, a Bernoulli random variable with $p(0) = p(1) = \frac{1}{2}$ is uniform as is the random variable denoting the number thrown on a fair die. Similarly, if a card is selected at random from an ordinary pack, the random variable denoting the number on the card is uniform over the set $\{1, \ldots, 13\}$, where 'ace', 'jack', 'queen', 'king' are regarded as 1, 11, 12, 13 respectively.

2.2.5 Poisson random variable

A **Poisson** random variable X with parameter λ has image $\{0, 1, \ldots\}$ and mass function defined by

$$p(i) = e^{-\lambda} \frac{\lambda^i}{i!} \qquad (i \geq 0)$$

This is well defined since $\sum_{i=0}^{\infty} p(i) = e^{-\lambda} \sum_{i=0}^{\infty} \lambda^i/i! = 1$ by definition of the exponential function.

The Poisson random variable arises frequently in communication systems modelling and has numerous other applications. It is typically used to denote the number of 'events' that occur in a given period of time; for example, the number of arrivals at a communication network node in one minute, the number of tasks completed by a computer in one hour or the number of radioactive particles from some source observed in one day. Analogously, the number of typographical errors in a page of a book is often approximated well by a Poisson random variable. One reason for its diverse applicability is that it is an approximation for a binomial random variable which it approaches in the appropriate limit, as we shall now see.

Suppose that X is a binomial random variable with parameters (n, p) and let $\lambda = np$. We consider the limit in which $n \to \infty$ and $p \to 0$ such that $np = \lambda$. In other words, we have $p = \lambda/n$ and $n \to \infty$. Then,

$$\begin{aligned}
P(X = i) &= \frac{n(n-1) \ldots (n-i+1)}{i!} \left(\frac{\lambda}{n}\right)^i \left(1 - \frac{\lambda}{n}\right)^{n-i} \\
&= \left(\frac{n}{n}\right)\left(\frac{n-1}{n}\right) \ldots \left(\frac{n-i+1}{n}\right) \frac{\lambda^i}{i!} \frac{\left(1 - \dfrac{\lambda}{n}\right)^n}{\left(1 - \dfrac{\lambda}{n}\right)^i} \\
&\to e^{-\lambda} \frac{\lambda^i}{i!}
\end{aligned}$$

as $n \to \infty$ for finite i since $\lim_{n \to \infty} [1 - (\lambda/n)]^n = e^{-\lambda}$.

In fact it can be shown (see Chapter 4) that if

- one event occurs with probability $\lambda h + o(h)$ in any interval of length h,
- two or more events occur with probability $o(h)$ in any interval of length h, and
- the numbers of events occurring in disjoint intervals are independent,

then the random variable denoting the number of events in any interval of length t is Poisson with parameter λt. (In the 'o-notation' we have used, $o(h)$ denotes an expression $f(h)$ such that $\lim_{h\to 0} f(h)/h = 0$.) These conditions can be taken as a *definition* of a Poisson random variable, and it is from their mildness that the diversity of this random variable arises. This will be discussed further in the context of Poisson processes in Chapter 4.

The Poisson random variable approximates well the number of successes in a sequence of independent trials, but it is also quite accurate when the trials are dependent in a 'weak' way. Consider the well-known 'birthday problem' in which there are n independent people in a room, each of which is equally likely to have their birthday on any day of the year, neglecting leap years. The problem is to find the least n such that two people have the same birthday with probability greater than a half. This is not difficult to solve exactly by a combinatorial argument, even if the solution is computationally expensive, giving the answer 23.

Instead, consider the sequence of $\binom{n}{2}$ trials which compare the birthdays of each pair of people. A trial is a success if the birthdays are the same. These trials are not independent: if it is known that both of the pairs (p_1, p_2) and (p_2, p_3) share a birthday then p_1 and p_3 have the same birthday with probability 1. However, the trials are *pairwise* independent and so it is plausible that their dependence can be considered weak. Thus the Poisson random variable might be expected to provide a good approximation to the number of successes in the sequence of trials. The corresponding binomial random variable would have parameters $(\binom{n}{2}, \frac{1}{365})$ and so the Poisson random variable has parameter $n(n-1)/730$. Hence,

$$P(\text{no successes}) \approx e^{-n(n-1)/730}$$

This is the probability that no two birthdays are the same, so we want the smallest n for which it is less than a half, i.e. for which

$$e^{n(n-1)/730} > 2 \text{ or } n(n-1) > 730 \ln 2 \approx 506$$

This gives $n = 23$ as required. Notice that if $n = 366$, then there are no successes with probability 0. The Poisson approximation yields a very close e^{-183}. If $n = 2$, there are no successes with probability $\frac{364}{365}$ which is approximated well by $e^{-1/365}$

2.3 Continuous random variables

Random variables whose range of possible values is uncountable are at least as important as those that are discrete. For example, the length of time between successive arriving messages at a communication network node or a message transmission time may take any real value. A random variable with an uncountably infinite image is said to be **continuous**. Most continuous random variables 'in everyday use' have a **probability density function**, f say, which is a non-negative valued function defined on the whole real line $(-\infty, \infty)$ such that for any subset $S \subseteq (-\infty, \infty)$,

$$P(X \in S) = \int_S f(x)\,dx \tag{2.1}$$

Thus, any density function f must satisfy the **normalizing condition** that

$$\int_{-\infty}^{\infty} f(x)\,dx = P(-\infty < X < \infty) = 1$$

The correspondence between density function and mass function is in direct analogy with the correspondence in applied statics between the distribution of a continuum of mass and the distribution of point masses in one dimension. Probability is interpreted as mass and the analogy persists in many of the integrals and summations we derive. All probabilistic characteristics of a random variable may be determined from its density function and, not surprisingly, there is a simple relationship between the density and distribution function; recall that the distribution function is also sufficient. If $S = (a, b]$ in Equation (2.1), we have

$$P(a < X \leq b) = \int_a^b f(x)\,dx$$

and if a is set to $-\infty$,

$$P(X \leq b) = F(b) = \int_{-\infty}^b f(x)\,dx$$

Thus, the density function f is the derivative of the distribution function F. This means that the necessary and sufficient condition for a random variable to have a density function is that its distribution function be everywhere differentiable. All the continuous random variables we will be considering in this book will have densities.[1] A further consequence of this (actually of a distribution function being everywhere continuous) is that

$$P(X = b) = \int_b^b f(x)\,dx = 0$$

so that

$$P(a < X < b) = P(a < X \leqslant b)$$
$$= P(a \leqslant X < b) = P(a \leqslant X \leqslant b)$$

Hence we need not worry about the precise nature of the end-points of the intervals over which we require probabilities for our continuous random variables. We will use $P(a < X \leqslant b)$ for consistency.

Recall that discrete random variables have discontinuities in their distributions (at the points where the mass function is defined) and so are not differentiable. However, we can define a density in terms of the mathematical device known as the *Dirac delta function*, which is defined on the reals and denoted by δ. Informally, $\delta(x)$ is an 'infinite spike' at the point $x = 0$ and zero everywhere else, with the property that its integral over the real line is equal to 1. It is defined rigorously as the limit of a sequence of functions and its application involves interchanging this limit with that of integration. In particular, a function F with a simple discontinuity at the point b can be considered as differentiable at b with derivative $F'(x) = [F(b^+) - F(b^-)]\delta(x - b)$ at $x = b$. Then, assuming F to be differentiable on the interval $[a, b)$, we have (non-rigorously)

$$\int_a^{b^+} F'(u)\,du = \int_a^{b^-} F'(u)\,du + \int_{b^-}^{b^+} F'(u)\,du$$
$$= F(b^-) - F(a) + F(b^+) - F(b^-)$$
$$= F(b^+) - F(a)$$

as required. With this definition of δ, a discrete random variable X with image I and mass function p is equivalent to a continuous random

---

[1] In some cases we will use mixed discrete–continuous random variables, for example the generalized exponential random variable considered in Chapters 5, 7 and 8. The discontinuities in the distribution are represented by Dirac delta functions in the density.

variable X' with density f defined by

$$f(x) = \sum_{x_i \in I} p(x_i)\delta(x - x_i)$$

since $p(x_i) = \int_{x_i^-}^{x_i^+} f(u)\,du$ for $x_i \in I$ and $p(x) = 0$ for $x \notin I$.

Thus, discrete random variables are subsumed by continuous random variables and, in this sense, the 'at least as' in the first sentence of this section could be replaced by 'more'. In fact, we will only derive some of our results for the continuous case, the discrete case being obtained by using the appropriate delta functions in the density.

We will often abuse notation slightly by writing $f(x)\,dx$ for $P(X = x)$. This is equal to zero for a continuous random variable X (excluding delta functions), which is acceptable since dx is zero in the limit of integration. What we mean rigorously when writing this is $f(x) = dP(X \leqslant x)/dx$, where $dP(X \leqslant x) = P(X \leqslant x + dx) - P(X \leqslant x) = P(X \in (x, x + dx]) = P(X = x)$ when $dx = 0$. There are numerous examples of continuous random variables and we introduce the main ones used in this book next. Each has a probability density function and so has a continuous (and differentiable) distribution function.

2.3.1 Continuous uniform random variable

A random variable X with density function f which is *constant* over an interval (a, b) and zero elsewhere is called **uniform**. We can determine the value of this constant, c say, from the normalizing condition:

$$1 = \int_{-\infty}^{\infty} f(x)\,dx = \int_{a}^{b} c\,dx = c(b - a)$$

Thus, f is defined by

$$f(x) = \begin{cases} \dfrac{1}{b-a} & a < x < b \\ 0 & \text{otherwise} \end{cases}$$

The distribution function F of X is then obtained as $F(x) = \int_{-\infty}^{x} f(u)\,du$ giving

$$F(x) = \begin{cases} 0 & x \leqslant a \\ \dfrac{x-a}{b-a} & a < x < b \\ 1 & x \geqslant b \end{cases}$$

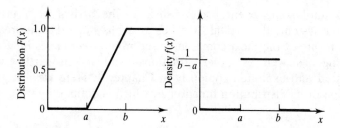

Figure 2.2 The uniform distribution and density.

Graphs of the distribution and density of the uniform random variable appear in Figure 2.2.

Example 2.3

Suppose a rotating disk in a computer system has 16 sectors and input/output requests specify the sector they wish to access. If, at the time a request arrives, the disk's head is within half a sector of the beginning of the sector required, the request cannot be serviced until the next revolution. Assuming that the rotational position of the disk at the time a request arrives is a uniform random variable, and neglecting inter-sector gaps, what is the probability that an extra rotation will be required?

The solution is the probability that, at the time of the arrival of the request, the disk's head is at a position strictly between the start of the required sector and half a sector before that. Let the random variable for this rotational position be denoted by X, measured in radians so that X is uniform over $(0, 2\pi)$. The required probability is

$$P\left(X < \frac{2\pi}{32}\right) = \frac{2\pi/32}{2\pi} = \frac{1}{32}$$

There are no surprises here, but the methodology should be clear.

2.3.2 Negative exponential random variable

A continuous random variable X with density function f defined by

$$f(x) = \begin{cases} \lambda e^{-\lambda x} & x \geq 0 \\ 0 & x < 0 \end{cases}$$

is called **negative exponential**, or sometimes just exponential, with parameter λ. This random variable is often used to denote the time elapsed until some event occurs, such as the arrival of a task at a computer system, the arrival of a bus at a bus-stop, the outbreak of a war. It is one of the most commonly used random variables in stochastic modelling, as well as other situations, and its properties will be introduced and exploited copiously in Chapter 4. Here we just give the definition of its distribution function F, which is defined by

$$F(x) = \int_0^x \lambda e^{-\lambda u}\, du \qquad x \geqslant 0$$

$$= [-e^{-\lambda u}]_0^x$$

$$= 1 - e^{-\lambda x}$$

As an illustration, suppose the lifetime X of an electric light bulb is a negative exponential random variable with mean $10\,000$ hours; it is shown in Chapter 3 that the expected value of an exponential random variable with parameter λ is $1/\lambda$. What is the probability that the bulb will last for more than $20\,000$ hours? The solution is clearly

$$P(X > 20\,000) = 1 - F(20\,000) = e^{-20\,000/10\,000} = e^{-2} \approx 0.135$$

2.3.3 Gamma random variable

A continuous random variable X with density function f defined by

$$f(x) = \begin{cases} \dfrac{\lambda(\lambda x)^{t-1} e^{-\lambda x}}{\Gamma(t)} & x \geqslant 0 \\[2mm] 0 & x < 0 \end{cases}$$

is called **gamma** with parameters (t, λ). The gamma function Γ is defined by

$$\Gamma(t) = \int_0^\infty e^{-u} u^{t-1}\, du$$

To verify that f really is a density, we check its normalizing condition as follows:

$$\int_0^\infty f(x)\, dx = \frac{\int_0^\infty (\lambda x)^{t-1} e^{-\lambda x} \lambda\, dx}{\Gamma(t)} = 1$$

by change of variable in the integrand $u = \lambda x$. Integrating the defining expression of $\Gamma(t)$ by parts, we obtain

$$\Gamma(t) = [-e^{-u}u^{t-1}]_0^\infty + \int_0^\infty e^{-u}(t-1)u^{t-2}\,du = (t-1)\Gamma(t-1)$$

Moreover, $\Gamma(1) = \int_0^\infty e^{-u}\,du = 1$ so that for integer $n \geqslant 1$, $\Gamma(n) = (n-1)!$

In the case that $\lambda = \frac{1}{2}$ and $t = n/2$ for integer $n > 0$, the gamma random variable becomes the chi-square with n degrees of freedom, much used in statistics, for example in the analysis of simulation output data. Although this case will not concern us, we will encounter the following one frequently. When $t = n$, a positive integer as above, the gamma random variable has density function f defined on the non-negative reals by

$$f(x) = \frac{\lambda(\lambda x)^{n-1}e^{-\lambda x}}{(n-1)!}$$

and zero elsewhere. This density (and random variable) is also called **Erlang-n** with parameter λ. Notice that the negative exponential random variable is Erlang-1. An important property of the Erlang-n random variable is the following.

Proposition 2.2

Suppose that the number of occurrences of some event in a time interval of length t is a Poisson random variable with parameter λt. Then the elapsed time between any event and the nth event after it is an Erlang-n random variable with parameter λ.

Proof Let T_n denote the amount of time taken for n events to occur and N_t denote the number of events in $[0, t]$. Then we have

$$P(T_n \leqslant t) = P(N_t \geqslant n) = \sum_{i=n}^\infty P(N_t = i) = \sum_{i=n}^\infty \frac{e^{-\lambda t}(\lambda t)^i}{i!}$$

Denoting by f the density function of the random variable T_n, $f(t)$ is the derivative of this expression with respect to t, i.e.

$$f(t) = \sum_{i=n}^\infty \frac{e^{-\lambda t}i\lambda(\lambda t)^{i-1}}{i!} - \sum_{i=n}^\infty \frac{\lambda e^{-\lambda t}(\lambda t)^i}{i!}$$

$$= \sum_{i=n}^\infty \frac{\lambda e^{-\lambda t}(\lambda t)^{i-1}}{(i-1)!} - \sum_{i=n}^\infty \frac{\lambda e^{-\lambda t}(\lambda t)^i}{i!}$$

$$= \frac{\lambda(\lambda t)^{n-1}e^{-\lambda t}}{(n-1)!} \qquad \blacksquare$$

An alternative proof of this result will be obtained in the next section by considering directly the sum of the times between the events.

2.3.4 Normal random variable

A continuous random variable X is **normal** or **normally distributed** with parameters (μ, σ^2) if its density function f is defined by

$$f(x) = \frac{1}{\sqrt{2\pi}\,\sigma}\, e^{-(x-\mu)^2/2\sigma^2} \qquad -\infty < x < \infty$$

It is often said that X is $N(\mu, \sigma^2)$. The graph of the normal density is the familiar bell shape, symmetrical about $x = \mu$ and with spread increasing with σ. In fact, μ is the mean and σ^2 is the variance of the normal random variable; see Chapter 3. To verify that f is a (normalized) density, we require that

$$\frac{1}{\sqrt{2\pi}\,\sigma} \int_{-\infty}^{\infty} e^{-(x-\mu)^2/2\sigma^2}\, dx = 1$$

Changing the variable of integration to $z = (x - \mu)/\sigma$, the condition becomes

$$\frac{1}{\sqrt{2\pi}} \int_{-\infty}^{\infty} e^{-z^2/2}\, dz = 1$$

which is a standard result.

The normal distribution is central to the theory of probability and we will make use of it when we consider diffusion processes in Chapter 8. We now give some of the basic properties. First, if X is a normal random variable with parameters (μ, σ^2), then for real values $\alpha > 0$ and β, $Y = \alpha X + \beta$ is also normal with parameters $(\alpha\mu + \beta, \alpha^2\sigma^2)$. This follows since the distribution function of Y, F_Y, is defined by

$$F_Y(y) = P(Y \leq y) = P\left(X \leq \frac{y - \beta}{\alpha}\right) = F_X\left(\frac{y - \beta}{\alpha}\right)$$

where F_X is the distribution of X. Integrating the density of X from $-\infty$ to $(y - \beta)/\alpha$ and changing the variable of integration from x to $y = \alpha x + \beta$ gives the required result.

Taking $\alpha = 1/\sigma$ and $\beta = -\mu/\sigma$ we deduce that the random variable $Z = (X - \mu)/\sigma$ is normal with parameters $(0, 1)$. Z is said to be **standard normal**, often written $N(0, 1)$. The cumulative distribution function of Z is conventionally denoted by $\Phi(z)$ for $z \geq 0$. For negative z, the result that

$$\Phi(z) = 1 - \Phi(-z)$$

is used; this result follows by symmetry and is easily derived. The standard normal distribution Φ is well tabulated and *any* normal distribution can be evaluated at any point using it. If X is $N(\mu, \sigma^2)$ with distribution function F_X, we can standardize X by defining $Z = (X - \mu)/\sigma$ so that Z is $N(0, 1)$. We then have

$$F_X(x) = P(X \leq x) = P\left(Z \leq \frac{x - \mu}{\sigma}\right) = \Phi\left(\frac{x - \mu}{\sigma}\right)$$

Finally, the normal distribution is an important limiting distribution in that the (standardized) sum of a sequence of independent identical random variables approaches $N(0, 1)$ asymptotically under some mild conditions. This is discussed in Section 3.3 of Chapter 3.

2.4 Joint random variables

A single random variable describes an event of some experiment, but we also may be interested in probabilities relating to more than one random variable, for example to describe the intersection of events. To this end, we define the **joint cumulative probability distribution function** (or **joint distribution function**) F of the random variables $X_1, \ldots, X_n$ by

$$F(x_1, \ldots, x_n) = P(X_1 \leq x_1, \ldots, X_n \leq x_n) = P\left(\bigcap_{i=1}^{n} (X_i \leq x_i)\right)$$

for real numbers $x_1, \ldots, x_n$. Notice that we write commas to separate the events $X_i \leq x_i$ instead of $\cap$. This notation corresponds to the list of n arguments of the distribution function F and distinguishes the arguments of the probability operator P as set-memberships of random variables. We will assume that $n = 2$ in the rest of this section and consider the random variables X and Y; the generalization to an arbitrary finite n is straightforward.

All probabilistic characteristics of the random variables X and Y can be expressed in terms of their joint distribution function. For example,

$$P(x_1 < X \leq x_2, y_1 < Y \leq y_2) = F(x_2, y_2) + F(x_1, y_1)$$
$$- F(x_1, y_2) - F(x_2, y_1)$$

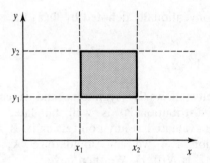

Figure 2.3   Joint random variables (X, Y).

since, referring to Figure 2.3, the shaded area represents

$$\{(X, Y)|x_1 < X \leq x_2, y_1 < Y \leq y_2\}$$
$$= \{(X, Y)|X \leq x_2, Y \leq y_2\}$$
$$\setminus\{(X, Y)|X \leq x_1, Y \leq y_2\}$$
$$\setminus\{(X, Y)|X \leq x_2, Y \leq y_1\}$$
$$\cup \{(X, Y)|X \leq x_1, Y \leq y_1\}$$

We can obtain the distribution function of X or Y from the joint distribution of X and Y. These are called the **marginal distributions** of X and Y, denoted by F_X and F_Y respectively. They are obtained as follows:

$$F_X(x) = P(X \leq x)$$
$$= P(X \leq x, Y < \infty)$$
$$= P\left(\lim_{y \to \infty} (X \leq x, Y \leq y)\right)$$
$$= \lim_{y \to \infty} F(x, y) \qquad \text{since } P \text{ is continuous}$$
$$= F(x, \infty)$$

Similarly, $F_Y(y) = F(\infty, y)$.

Let us now consider the density functions and mass functions of continuous and discrete random variables respectively. If the random variables X and Y are discrete, their **joint probability mass function** is defined by

$$p(x, y) = P(X = x, Y = y)$$

The **marginal probability mass function** p_X of X is then defined by

$$p_X(x) = P(X = x) = \sum_{y \in I_Y} p(x, y)$$

where I_Y is the image of Y (i.e. the complete set of real values Y can take) and similarly the marginal mass function of Y is defined by

$$p_Y(y) = \sum_{x \in I_X} p(x, y)$$

where I_X is the image of X.

The **joint probability density function**, or just joint density, of (jointly) continuous random variables X and Y, when it exists, is a non-negative valued function defined on the two-dimensional real plane, $(-\infty, \infty) \times (-\infty, \infty)$, such that for any set S of pairs of reals, i.e. any subset of the real plane,

$$P((X, Y) \in S) = \iint_{(u,v) \in S} f(u, v) \, du \, dv$$

The joint distribution function F of X and Y is obtained by taking $S = \{(u, v) | u \le x, v \le y\}$ for real values x, y, so that

$$F(x, y) = P(X \le x, Y \le y) = \int_{-\infty}^{x} \int_{-\infty}^{y} f(u, v) \, du \, dv$$

Thus, $f(x, y) = \partial^2 F(x, y)/\partial x \partial y$ provided the partial derivatives exist. Indeed, the existence of these derivatives everywhere is the necessary and sufficient condition for the existence of a joint density function; this will always exist for the joint random variables we consider in this book. As in the case of a single random variable, we will often write

$$f(x, y) \, dx \, dy \approx P(X = x, Y = y)$$

This is just an abbreviation for the definition of f as the double partial derivative of F, or equivalently

$$P(x < X \le x + dx, \, y < Y \le y + dy)$$
$$= \int_{x}^{x+dx} \int_{y}^{y+dy} f(u, v) \, du \, dv$$
$$\approx f(x, y) \, dx \, dy$$

at $dx, dy \approx 0$.

If X and Y have a joint density, we can obtain the **marginal densities** of X and Y as follows. For $S \subseteq (-\infty, \infty)$,

$$\int_S f_X(u)\,du = P(X \in S) = P(X \in S, -\infty < Y < \infty)$$

$$= \int_S \int_{-\infty}^{\infty} f(u, v)\,du\,dv$$

We therefore obtain $f_X(x) = \int_{-\infty}^{\infty} f(x, y)\,dy$ for the (marginal) density of X, and similarly $f_Y(y) = \int_{-\infty}^{\infty} f(x, y)\,dx$ for the marginal density of Y.

Example 2.4

Suppose a point is selected with a uniform distribution in a square with side of length 1. We require:

(1)   the probability that the horizontal distance of the point from the bottom-left corner of the square is less than h;

(2)   the probability that the distance of the point from this corner is less than d, assumed less than 1.

Let the pair of random variables (X, Y) denote the coordinates of the point chosen. Then X and Y have joint density function f defined by

$$f(x, y) = \begin{cases} c & \text{if } 0 \leqslant x < 1 \text{ and } 0 \leqslant y < 1 \\ 0 & \text{if } x > 1 \text{ or } y > 1 \end{cases}$$

The normalizing condition on f is

$$1 = \int_{-\infty}^{\infty}\int_{-\infty}^{\infty} f(x, y)\,dx\,dy = \int_0^1 \int_0^1 c\,dx\,dy$$

so that $c = 1$. The solution to (1) is therefore

$$P(X < h) = F_X(h) = F(h, \infty) = \int_0^h \int_0^1 dx\,dy = h$$

For (2) we require

$$P(X^2 + Y^2 < d^2) = \iint_{\substack{x^2+y^2<d^2 \\ 0 \leqslant x, y < 1}} dx\,dy$$

$$= \frac{\pi d^2}{4}$$

since $d < 1$ by hypothesis. For $1 < d < \sqrt{2}$ the same integral gives the required solution, but its evaluation is more complicated – or alternatively the geometrical problem involving the area cut off a square by a quadrant is harder.

As in the case of a single random variable, we can define a joint *mass function* in terms of a joint density by using the Dirac delta function. Here we need one for each dimension, however, and obtain

$$f(x, y) = \sum_{i \in I} \sum_{j \in J} p(i, j)\delta(x - i)\delta(y - j)$$

where I and J are the images of X and Y respectively.

2.5 Conditional distributions

Given random variables X and Y, the **conditional probability distribution function** of X on Y, $F_{X|Y}$, is defined by

$$F_{X|Y}(x|y) = P(X \leq x|Y = y)$$

for y such that $p_Y(y) > 0$ if Y is discrete or $f_Y(y) > 0$ if Y is continuous, where p_Y and f_Y are respectively the (marginal) mass function and density function of Y.

If X and Y are discrete with joint mass function p, the **conditional probability mass function** of X on Y, $p_{X|Y}$, is defined by

$$p_{X|Y}(x|y) = P(X = x|Y = y) = \frac{P(X = x, Y = y)}{P(Y = y)} = \frac{p(x, y)}{p_Y(y)}$$

for all y such that $p_Y(y) > 0$. Then,

$$F_{X|Y}(x|y) = \sum_{u \leq x} p_{X|Y}(u|y)$$

and

$$F(x, y) = \sum_{u \leq x} \sum_{v \leq y} p_{X|Y}(u|v)p_Y(v) = \sum_{v \leq y} F_{X|Y}(x|v)p_Y(v)$$

This is the **Law of Total Probability for Discrete Random Variables** (compare Section 1.2).

If X and Y are continuous and have a joint density function f, then the **conditional probability density function** of X on Y, $f_{X|Y}$, should satisfy the property that for any subset S of the reals,

$$P(X \in S | Y = y) = \int_{u \in S} f_{X|Y}(u|y) \, du$$

Taking $S = (-\infty, x]$ and differentiating with respect to x then gives

$$f_{X|Y}(x|y) = \frac{\partial}{\partial x} P(X \le x | Y = y)$$

$$= \lim_{\Delta x \to 0} \frac{P(X \le x + \Delta x, Y = y) - P(X \le x, Y = y)}{\Delta x P(Y = y)}$$

$$= \lim_{\substack{\Delta x \to 0 \\ \Delta y \to 0}} \frac{P(x < X \le x + \Delta x, y < Y \le y + \Delta y)}{\Delta x P(y < Y \le y + \Delta y)} \frac{\Delta y}{\Delta y}$$

$$= \frac{f(x, y)}{f_Y(y)}$$

Informally, we may write

$$f_{X|Y}(x|y) \, dx = \frac{f(x, y) \, dx \, dy}{f_Y(y) \, dy}$$

$$\approx P(x < X \le x + dx | y < Y \le y + dy)$$

which may be read as '$f_{X|Y}(x|y) \, dx$ is the conditional probability that X is in the infinitesimal interval $(x, x + dx]$ given that Y is in the infinitesimal interval $(y, y + dy]$, i.e. given that $Y = y$ at $dy = 0$'. In particular, when $S = (-\infty, x]$, we obtain the conditional distribution function

$$F_{X|Y}(x|y) = P(X \le x | Y = y) = \int_{-\infty}^{x} f_{X|Y}(u|y) \, du$$

so that

$$f_{X|Y}(x|y) = \frac{\partial}{\partial x} F_{X|Y}(x|y)$$

Finally, we extend the Law of Total Probability (Section 1.2) to random variables. There are various forms corresponding to the cases where the two random variables are discrete or continuous (i.e. four possibilities) and whether a cumulative distribution or a density is required. We have already obtained the result for the case of two discrete random variables. Suppose now that the random variables X and Y are continuous with joint density function f. Then we have

$$f_X(x) = \int_{-\infty}^{\infty} f(x, y)\,dy = \int_{-\infty}^{\infty} f_{X|Y}(x|y)f_Y(y)\,dy$$

and so

$$F_X(x) = \int_{-\infty}^{x} f_X(u)\,du = \int_{-\infty}^{x}\int_{-\infty}^{\infty} f_{X|Y}(u|y)f_Y(y)\,du\,dy$$

$$= \int_{-\infty}^{\infty} F_{X|Y}(x|y)f_Y(y)\,dy$$

There is a more general form of this result which does not require the existence of densities. A sketch of the derivation is the following:

$$d_y F(x, y) = P(X \leq x, y < Y \leq y + dy)$$
$$= P(X \leq x | y < Y \leq y + dy)P(y < Y \leq y + dy)$$
$$= F_{X|Y}(x|y)\,dF_Y(y)$$

Thus,

$$F_X(x) = \int_{-\infty}^{\infty} F_{X|Y}(x|y)\,dF_Y(y)$$

This expression is a **Stieltjes integral** which is a generalization of the Riemann integral and defined as follows.

Definition 2.1

(1)   For *finite* a, b and non-negative real valued function g, the Stieltjes integral is defined by:

$$\int_a^b g(x)\,dF(x) = \lim_{n \to \infty} \sum_{i=1}^{n} g(x_i)[F(x_i) - F(x_{i-1})]$$

where for each n, $a = x_0 < x_1 < \ldots < x_n = b$ defines a partition of the interval $[a, b]$.

(2)   In the case of infinite limits,

$$\int_{-\infty}^{b} g(x)\,dF(x) = \lim_{a \to -\infty} \int_a^b g(x)\,dF(x)$$

$$\int_a^{\infty} g(x)\,dF(x) = \lim_{b \to \infty} \int_a^b g(x)\,dF(x)$$

and

$$\int_{-\infty}^{\infty} g(x)\,dF(x) = \lim_{\substack{b\to\infty \\ a\to-\infty}} \int_a^b g(x)\,dF(x)$$

(3)   For an arbitrary function g defined on $(-\infty, \infty)$, let g^+ and g^- be defined by

$$g^+(x) = \begin{cases} g(x) & \text{if } g(x) \geq 0 \\ 0 & \text{if } g(x) < 0 \end{cases}$$

$$g^-(x) = \begin{cases} 0 & \text{if } g(x) \geq 0 \\ -g(x) & \text{if } g(x) < 0 \end{cases}$$

Then we may write $g(x) = g^+(x) - g^-(x)$ and the Stieltjes integral is defined by

$$\int_{-\infty}^{\infty} g(x)\,dF(x) = \int_{-\infty}^{\infty} g^+(x)\,dF(x) - \int_{-\infty}^{\infty} g^-(x)\,dF(x)$$

in terms of (2).

Part (3) of Definition 2.1 also holds for finite limits, i.e. with $-\infty$ replaced by a and/or ∞ replaced by b. This follows immediately by defining $g(x) = 0$ for $x < a$ or $x > b$.

The above expression for $F_X(x)$ can now be derived rigorously in terms of this definition. Of course, if F is differentiable with derivative f on $(-\infty, \infty)$, if follows that

$$\int_{-\infty}^{\infty} g(x)\,dF(x) = \int_{-\infty}^{\infty} g(x)f(x)\,dx$$

The Stieltjes integral then reduces to an ordinary Riemann integral and we return to our original formulation. Because of its greater generality, the Stieltjes integral is frequently used in more advanced texts and we shall meet it again briefly when we consider expectations in Chapter 3. However, we will not be forced to make use of it since we will always have a density function available.

Of course, it is not necessary for a random variable to be either purely discrete or purely continuous, as we saw in Example 2.2. However, the cases in which one of X and Y is discrete and the other continuous are simple extensions of the preceding theory and are left as an exercise.

Example 2.5

Each job's service time on a computer is exponentially distributed with mean $1/\mu$ and jobs have to queue for service in strict first come, first served, order. The number of jobs ahead of a newly arriving job has probability mass function $p(n) = (1 - p)p^n$ and we require the probability density function of the total time spent by a job at the computer, often called its **sojourn time** there.

The solution uses the memoryless property of the exponential random variable (see Chapter 4). This property allows us to assume that a job already in service at the instant of arrival of a new job has just started, i.e. that the random variable for its remaining time to be served is identical to that for a complete service time, namely exponential with parameter μ. Now, the probability that a new job's sojourn time is the time elapsed up to the $(n + 1)$st next service completion is $(1 - p)p^n$, $n \geq 0$, because there must have been n jobs ahead of the new job on arrival. By the result of Proposition 2.2, this elapsed time is an Erlang-$(n + 1)$ random variable with density $(\mu(\mu x)^n e^{-\mu x})/n!$. Let N denote the discrete random variable for the number of jobs in front of the new job on arrival and D denote the continuous random variable for the new job's sojourn time. Then D has density:

$$f(d) = \sum_{n=0}^{\infty} f_{D|N}(d|n)(1 - p)p^n = \sum_{n=0}^{\infty} \frac{\mu(\mu d)^n e^{-\mu d}}{n!} (1 - p)p^n$$

$$= (1 - p)\mu e^{-(1-p)\mu d}$$

Example 2.6

In the previous example, suppose that the number of jobs arriving in t units of time is a Poisson random variable with parameter λt. What is the probability mass function for the number of arrivals during a job's sojourn time at the computer?

Let A denote the number of jobs that arrive during a given job's visit. Then by hypothesis, the conditional mass function of A given that the sojourn time D of the given job is equal to d is Poisson with parameter λd. Thus A has probability mass function g defined by:

$$g(i) = \int_0^{\infty} g_{A|D}(i|v)f(v)\, dv$$

where f is the density of D obtained in the previous example. Thus

$$g(i) = \int_0^{\infty} e^{-\lambda v} \frac{(\lambda v)^i}{i!} (1 - p)\mu e^{-(1-p)\mu v}\, dv$$

$$= (1 - p)\mu \int_0^{\infty} \frac{(\lambda v)^i}{i!} e^{-(\lambda + (1-p)\mu)v}\, dv$$

2.6 Independence and sums

Two random variables X and Y are **independent** iff for all real numbers x and y

$$P(X \leqslant x, Y \leqslant y) = P(X \leqslant x)P(Y \leqslant y)$$

This condition is equivalent, by the probability axioms and continuity, to

$$P(X \in A, Y \in B) = P(X \in A)P(Y \in B)$$

$$\text{for all } A, B \subseteq (-\infty, \infty)$$

The independence condition is also equivalent to the following alternatives:

- If F is the joint distribution function of X and Y, for all reals x, y,

$$F(x, y) = F_X(x)F_Y(y)$$

   i.e.

$$F_{X|Y}(x|y) = F_X(x)$$

- If X and Y are discrete with joint mass function p, for all reals x, y,

$$p(x, y) = p_X(x)p_Y(y)$$

   i.e.

$$p_{X|Y}(x|y) = p_X(x)$$

- If X and Y are continuous with joint density function f, for all reals x, y,

$$f(x, y) = f_X(x)f_Y(y)$$

   i.e.

$$f_{X|Y}(x|y) = f_X(x)$$

As with events, a set of more than two random variables may be independent. We say n random variables $X_1, \ldots, X_n$ are independent if for all real numbers $x_1, \ldots, x_n$

$$P(X_1 \leqslant x_1, \ldots, X_n \leqslant x_n) = \prod_{i=1}^{n} P(X_i \leqslant x_i)$$

which is equivalent to, as above,

$$P(X_1 \in A_1, \ldots, X_n \in A_n) = \prod_{i=1}^{n} P(X_i \in A_i)$$

for all $A_i \subseteq (-\infty, \infty)$

Notice that this condition *implies* that all subsets of $\{X_1, \ldots, X_n\}$ are independent, unlike the case of events, because the X_i are disjoint and we can obtain the joint probability of $i < n$ of them by summing the other $n - i$ over $(-\infty, \infty)$. Finally, an infinite set of random variables is said to be independent if every finite subset is independent.

Example 2.7

Suppose we drop a matchstick 'randomly' on some floorboards of width equal to twice the length of the matchstick. What is the probability that the matchstick will lie across two boards? To solve this, we assume that the boards are 'perfectly laid' in that their edges form a set of equally spaced parallel lines. Without loss of generality, we assume that the distance between an adjacent pair of lines is 4 units and that the length of the matchstick is 2 units. By 'randomly' we mean that the distance D of the centre of the matchstick from the nearest line is uniformly distributed over $[0, 2]$, that the acute angle Θ the matchstick makes with the direction of the lines is uniformly distributed over $[0, \pi/2]$ and that D and Θ are independent.

The matchstick lies across two boards if it crosses one of the lines, i.e. if $D < \sin \theta$. The required probability is therefore:

$$
\begin{aligned}
P(D < \sin \theta) &= \iint_{x < \sin \theta} f_D(x) f_\Theta(\theta) \, dx \, d\theta \\
&= \frac{2}{\pi} \frac{1}{2} \int_0^{\pi/2} \int_0^2 \sin \theta \, d\theta \, dx \\
&= \frac{2}{\pi} \int_0^{\pi/2} \sin \theta \, d\theta \\
&= \frac{2}{\pi}
\end{aligned}
$$

In a more complicated version of this example, the matchstick is more likely to land at more acute angles θ, i.e. closer to parallel to the lines. Suppose Θ has a truncated exponential density with parameter λ, i.e.

$$
f_\Theta(\theta) = \begin{cases} \dfrac{\lambda}{1 - e^{-\lambda\pi/2}} e^{-\lambda\theta} & 0 \le \theta \le \pi/2 \\ 0 & \text{otherwise} \end{cases}
$$

Then we would have obtained

$$P(D < \sin \theta) = \frac{2\lambda}{\pi(1 - e^{-\lambda\pi/2})} \int_0^{\pi/2} e^{-\lambda\theta} \sin \theta \, d\theta$$

$$= \frac{2\lambda(1 - \lambda e^{-\lambda\pi/2})}{\pi(1 + \lambda^2)(1 - e^{-\lambda\pi/2})}$$

We will often be interested in a sum of random variables. First, let us consider the case of two continuous random variables X and Y with joint density f. If $X + Y$ has distribution function G (or F_{X+Y} in our notation above), we have

$$G(z) = P(X + Y \le z) = \iint_{x+y\le z} f(x, y) \, dx \, dy$$

$$= \iint_{x+y\le z} f_{X|Y}(x|y)f_Y(y) \, dy \, dx$$

$$= \int_{-\infty}^{\infty}\int_{-\infty}^{z-y} f_{X|Y}(x|y)f_Y(y) \, dy \, dx$$

$$= \int_{-\infty}^{\infty} F_{X|Y}(z - y|y)f_Y(y) \, dy$$

and by differentiating with respect to z, the density function of $X + Y$ is

$$g(z) = \int_{-\infty}^{\infty} f_{X|Y}(z - y|y)f_Y(y) \, dy$$

If X and Y are *independent*, we obtain

$$G(z) = \int_{-\infty}^{\infty} F_X(z - y)f_Y(y) \, dy$$

and

$$g(z) = \int_{-\infty}^{\infty} f_X(z - y)f_Y(y) \, dy$$

G (respectively g) is called the **convolution** of the distributions F_X and F_Y (respectively densities f_X and f_Y) which we denote by the (infix) symbol *, i.e. we write $G = F_X * F_Y$ and $g = f_X * f_Y$.

A sum of discrete random variables is analogous, using summations instead of integrals, and is left as an exercise. In fact if we had used Stieltjes integrals in the above, the discrete case would already be covered. In particular, the convolution of discrete, integer-valued random variables X, Y with probability mass functions p_X, p_Y respectively is given by

$$p_{X+Y}(i) = \sum_{j=-\infty}^{\infty} p_X(j)p_Y(i - j)$$

which is an immediate consequence of the law of total probability.

Example 2.8 ————————————————————————————————

What is the probability density function of a sum of two independent negative exponential random variables with the same parameter? The answer is, of course, the convolution of that negative exponential density with itself. Let the parameter be λ and the required density be g. Then we have, noting that the exponential density is zero at negative values,

$$g(z) = \int_0^z \lambda e^{-\lambda(z-y)} \lambda e^{-\lambda y}\, dy$$

$$= \lambda^2 e^{-\lambda z} \int_0^z dy$$

$$= \lambda(\lambda z)e^{-\lambda z}$$

Thus the required density is an Erlang-2 with parameter λ.

————————————————————————————————

In fact, the sum of $n \geq 1$ independent negative exponential random variables with the same parameter is Erlang-n, which is a special case of the following proposition. A consequence of this is that if the number of events in a time interval of length t is a Poisson random variable with parameter λt, the time elapsed between any event and the nth event after it is an Erlang-n random variable with parameter λ. This follows from properties of the Poisson random variable: the times between successive events are independent, negative exponential random variables with parameter λ (see Section 2.2 and Chapter 4). This proof is an alternative to that of Proposition 2.2.

Proposition 2.3

If $X_1, \ldots, X_n$ are independent gamma random variables with parameters $(t_1, \lambda), \ldots, (t_n, \lambda)$ respectively, then $\sum_{i=1}^{n} X_i$ is a gamma random variable with parameters $(\sum_{i=1}^{n} t_i, \lambda)$.

Proof We use induction on n and for $n = 1$, the result is trivial. Now, for $n \geqslant 1$, let $Y = \sum_{i=1}^{n} X_i$ and $t = \sum_{i=1}^{n} t_i$. By the inductive hypothesis, Y is gamma with parameters (t, λ) and we consider the random variable $Z = Y + X_{n+1}$ where X_{n+1} is gamma with parameters (t_{n+1}, λ). Let Z have density function f. Then

$$f(z) = \frac{1}{\Gamma(t)\Gamma(t_{n+1})} \int_0^z \lambda[\lambda(z - y)]^{t-1} e^{-\lambda(z-y)} \lambda(\lambda y)^{t_{n+1}-1} e^{-\lambda y} \, dy$$

$$= \frac{\lambda^{t+t_{n+1}} e^{-\lambda z}}{\Gamma(t)\Gamma(t_{n+1})} \int_0^z (z - y)^{t-1} y^{t_{n+1}-1} \, dy$$

$$= \frac{\lambda^{t+t_{n+1}} z^{t+t_{n+1}-1} e^{-\lambda z}}{\Gamma(t)\Gamma(t_{n+1})} \int_0^1 (1 - x)^{t-1} x^{t_{n+1}-1} \, dx$$

by change of variable to x where $y = xz$. The result that $f(z)$ is the gamma density with parameters $(t + t_{n+1}, \lambda)$ then follows either by showing that the integral evaluates to $\Gamma(t)\Gamma(t_{n+1})/\Gamma(t + t_{n+1})$ or else by noting that the density is proportional to $z^{t+t_{n+1}-1} e^{-\lambda z}$ and must be normalized. ∎

SUMMARY

- Random variables map outcomes to real numbers giving events a numerical interpretation.

- All probabilistic properties of a random variable are given by its distribution function.

- There are two types of random variable: discrete and continuous. The probability mass function and probability density function assign probabilities to values and infinitesimal intervals respectively for discrete and continuous random variables.

- The Poisson, negative exponential and Erlang random variables are important in modelling arrival processes.

- The normal random variable is fundamental in probability theory and statistics as a limiting distribution.

- Sets of random variables are considered jointly by a joint probability distribution function and dependent random variables are handled by a conditional distribution.

- The law of total probability extends to random variables.

- The distribution of a sum of independent random variables is the convolution of the individual distributions.

EXERCISES

2.1 (20 Birthday problem)
There are n people in a room, each of which is equally likely to

have their birthday on any day of the year, neglecting leap years. Find the probability that no two in the room have the same birthday. Hence find the least n such that two people have the same birthday with probability greater than a half.

2.2   (20 Exponential distribution – conditional)
A computer system completely crashes 10 times a year on average and the time to the next crash is memoryless. Given that there was exactly one crash in January, what is the probability that it occurred on 31 January?

2.3   (10/20 Exponential distribution – two transactions)
The times taken for transactions from sites A and B are exponentially distributed with means $1/\lambda$ and $1/\mu$ minutes respectively on a host computer system. If two transactions T_1 and T_2 arrive from A and B respectively and their service is started immediately in each case, what is the probability that T_2 finishes first?

2.4   (10/20 Exponential distribution – fork and join)
At a fork node a task forks into a pair of subtasks, which join independent servers with processing time that is exponentially distributed with parameter μ. After both tasks have been processed, they re-form the original task at a join node. What is the probability density function of the time interval between the fork and the join?

2.5   (20 Exponential distribution – direct proof)
Prove directly from the memoryless property for infinitesimal intervals that defines the Poisson process that inter-arrival times have negative exponential distribution with parameter the rate of the Poisson process.

2.6   (20 Distribution of the minimum of a set)
Find the distribution function of the minimum of a finite set of independent random variables $\{X_1, X_2, .., X_n\}$, where X_i has distribution function F_{X_i}. What is this distribution when X_i is exponential with a mean of $1/\mu_i$?

2.7   (20 Distribution of the maximum of a set)
Find the distribution function of the maximum of a finite set of independent random variables $\{X_1, X_2, \ldots, X_n\}$, where X_i has distribution function F_{X_i}. What is this distribution when X_i is exponential with a mean of $1/\mu_i$?

2.8   (20 Erlang-n distribution)
Let T_n be the instant of the nth arrival in a Poisson process with

rate λ. Show that the distribution function of T_n, $F_n(t)$, is given by

$$F_n(t) = 1 - \sum_{k=0}^{n-1} \frac{(\lambda t)^k}{k!} e^{-\lambda t}$$

2.9   (20 Erlang-n density, convolution)
Find an expression for $f_n(t)$, the n-fold convolution of the negative exponential density function with parameter λ, i.e. the Erlang-n density function.

2.10 (10/20 Next arrival)
Arrival processes 1 and 2 have inter-arrival times that are exponentially distributed with mean $1/\lambda$ and uniformly distributed over the interval $[0, 2/\lambda]$, respectively. Assuming that each process has an arrival at time 0, what is the probability that the next arrival from either process will be from process 1?

2.11 (20 Conditional probability)
Show that if X is continuous and Y is discrete

$$f_{X|Y}(x|y) = \frac{P(Y = y | X = x)}{P(Y = y)} f(x)$$

Hint: consider $P(x < X \leqslant x + dx | Y = y)/dx$

2.12 (40 Sum of dependent random variables)
Find the density function of the sum of two given *dependent* random variables, X and Y. For example, Y is exponential if $Y < X$ and Y is Erlang if $Y \geqslant X$.

Chapter 3
Expected Values and
Moments

3.1 Expectation   51   3.3 Asymptotic properties   72
3.2 Generating functions
    and transforms   63

The distribution function, or density function when it exists, provides a complete description of a random variable and hence is sufficient to define any property desired. However, it is neither necessary for the computation of any given property nor is it the only complete characterization of a random variable. The most important function of a random variable is its **expected value**, also called **expectation, mean value** or **mean**. This function gives the average value taken by a random variable in a rigorous sense, to be defined, which is also rich in intuition. Moreover, it is possible to define the distribution function of a random variable in terms of its expectation. Thus, expectation provides an alternative complete description of a random variable which has been used as a basis for the whole theory of probability; see for example Whittle (1970). For the pedantically minded, or functional programmer, observe that the expectation function is *higher-order* in the sense that it takes a function for its argument.

3.1 Expectation

The expectation of a discrete random variable X with mass function p is written $E[X]$ and defined by

$$E[X] = \sum_{x \in S} xp(x)$$

where $S = \{x \mid p(x) > 0\}$ is a subset of the image of X. If X is a continuous random variable with probability density function f, its expectation is

$$E[X] = \int_{-\infty}^{\infty} xf(x)\,dx$$

which has exactly the same interpretation as in the discrete case if we recall the infinitesimal property that

$$P(x < X \le x + dx) \approx f(x)\,dx$$

Both cases relate directly to the analogy with applied statics that we first observed in Section 2.3. The analogy here is between expectation and *centre of mass*. In the discrete case, if point masses $p(x_i)$ are placed at the points x_i on the real axis, the net moment about their expected value, defined as above, is zero – as for the centre of mass. This remark applies equally in the continuous case and the integral is the same as the one used in statics for the position of a centre of mass, where f is the (mass) density function.

In the following examples, expected values are derived for some of the random variables we introduced in the previous chapter. The others are derivable similarly and are well tabulated in other books on probability.

3.1.1 Bernoulli random variable

A Bernoulli random variable with parameter q has mass function defined by $p(0) = 1 - q$, $p(1) = q$. Thus its expectation is

$$E[X] = 0 \times (1 - q) + 1 \times q = q$$

Thus, the 'average value' of a success is the same as the probability of a success. Intuitively, we would expect the proportion of successes in a long sequence of independent Bernoulli trials to be q. (This intuition is borne out in Section 3.3.) We will show in Proposition 3.2 that the expectation of a sum of random variables is equal to the sum of their expectations. Hence the expected number of successes in n trials is nq and the proportion of successes is therefore q, as anticipated.

3.1.2 Binomial random variable

The argument just made about a sequence of Bernoulli trials proves that
the expectation of a binomial random variable X with parameters (n, q)
is nq since the number of successes in the sequence has the distribution
of X; see Section 2.2. The result can be derived directly as follows:

$$E[X] = \sum_{i=0}^{n} ip(i)$$

$$= \sum_{i=0}^{n} i\binom{n}{i} q^i (1 - q)^{n-i}$$

$$= \sum_{i=1}^{n} \frac{n!}{(n - i)!(i - 1)!} q^i (1 - q)^{n-i}$$

since $i = 0$ gives zero contribution

$$= \sum_{i=0}^{n-1} n \frac{(n - 1)!}{(n - 1 - i)!i!} qq^i (1 - q)^{n-1-i}$$

by change of variable $i \to i - 1$

$$= nq[q + (1 - q)]^{n-1}$$

$$= nq$$

3.1.3 Poisson random variable

We showed in Section 2.2 that a binomial random variable X_n with
parameters (n, q) approaches the Poisson random variable with parameter λ as $n \to \infty$ such that $nq = \lambda$. Since each binomial random
variable in the sequence (X_n) has mean λ, it follows, assuming the
appropriate convergence properties for sequences of random variables,
that a Poisson random variable with parameter λ also has expectation λ.
For a direct proof, let the random variable X be Poisson with parameter
λ. Then,

$$E[X] = \sum_{i=0}^{\infty} i e^{-\lambda} \frac{\lambda^i}{i!}$$

$$= \sum_{i=1}^{\infty} \lambda e^{-\lambda} \frac{\lambda^{i-1}}{(i - 1)!}$$

$$= \lambda e^{-\lambda} e^{\lambda}$$

$$= \lambda$$

3.1.4   Negative exponential random variable

Recall from Section 2.3 that an exponential random variable X with parameter λ has density function $f(x) = \lambda e^{-\lambda x}$ for $x \geq 0$ and zero otherwise. Thus,

$$E[X] = \int_0^\infty x \lambda e^{-\lambda x}\, dx$$

$$= [-x e^{-\lambda x}]_0^\infty + \int_0^\infty e^{-\lambda x}\, dx$$

$$= 0 + \left[-\frac{e^{-\lambda x}}{\lambda}\right]_0^\infty$$

$$= \frac{1}{\lambda}$$

3.1.5   Normal random variable

A normal random variable X with parameters (μ, σ^2) and density $[1/(2\pi\sigma)^{1/2}]e^{-(x-\mu)^2/2\sigma^2}$ has expected value

$$E[X] = \frac{1}{\sqrt{2\pi}\,\sigma} \int_{-\infty}^\infty x e^{-(x-\mu)^2/2\sigma^2}\, dx$$

Changing the integration variable to $z = (x - \mu)/\sigma$ then yields

$$E[X] = \frac{1}{\sqrt{2\pi}\,\sigma} \int_{-\infty}^\infty (\sigma z + \mu)e^{-z^2/2}\sigma\, dz$$

$$= \frac{1}{\sqrt{2\pi}\,\sigma} \left(\int_{-\infty}^\infty \sigma z e^{-z^2/2}\sigma\, dz + \int_{-\infty}^\infty \mu e^{-z^2/2}\sigma\, dz \right)$$

$$= \mu \left[\frac{1}{\sqrt{2\pi}} \int_{-\infty}^\infty e^{-z^2/2}\, dz \right]$$

since the first integral vanishes by symmetry

$$= \mu \Phi(\infty)$$

$$= \mu$$

3.1.6   Properties of expectation

The expectation of any discrete random variable or continuous random variable with a density function can be obtained as above. However, the most general definition of expectation does not require a random variable to have a density function, nor that it be purely discrete or purely continuous. See Example 2.2 for a random variable which is neither discrete nor continuous. Expectation can be defined solely in solely in terms of the *distribution function* of a random variable which *always* exists. The definition uses a Stieltjes integral of the type discussed in Section 2.5:

$$E[X] = \int_{-\infty}^{\infty} x \, dF(x)$$

which reduces to the forms we have defined when X is either discrete or continuous with a probability density function.

The expectation function has many important properties and from them a whole theory of probability can be developed (Whittle 1970). We have seen how expectation is defined in terms of the probability distribution function. To demonstrate the equivalence of the concepts of probability and expectation we must show how the probability of an arbitrary event can be expressed in terms of expected values. Given a sample space Ω, let the 'indicator' random variable I_E be defined on Ω by

$$I_E(w) = \begin{cases} 1 & \text{if } w \in E \\ 0 & \text{otherwise} \end{cases}$$

Then the expected value of I_E is

$$E[I_E] = 1 \times P(I_E = 1) + 0 \times P(I_E = 0) = P(w \in E)$$

just as we saw for a Bernoulli random variable. Thus we can define probability as an expectation and take axioms satisfied by an expectation function as the basis for an alternative theory. The *completeness* of a set of such expectation axioms would have to be proved to establish the equivalence of the theories; i.e. it must be proved that the probability axioms of Definition 1.2 can be derived. In fact, many of the properties of expectation we derive below in terms of probability are *assumed* as axioms in the alternative theory, but we will not pursue this.

The first property of expectation we consider, which is often taken for granted, concerns the expectation of a function of a random variable. It is given as Proposition 3.1 below. First, let us consider $E[\varphi(X)]$ for some real-valued function φ of the random variable X. Before we can compute the expectation, we require the distribution function, F_φ say, of the random variable $\varphi(X)$. This is defined by

$$F_\varphi(x) = P(\varphi(X) \leq x)$$

For a monotonically increasing function φ which is onto $(-\infty, \infty)$, we have

$$F_\varphi(x) = P(X \leq \varphi^{-1}(x)) = F_X(\varphi^{-1}(x))$$

where F_X is the distribution function of X. Thus, if we assume X to be continuous with density f_X,

$$f_\varphi(x) = \frac{f_X(\varphi^{-1}(x))}{\varphi'(\varphi^{-1}(x))}$$

and the required expectation is

$$E[\varphi(X)] = \int_{-\infty}^{\infty} x f_\varphi(x)\,dx$$

$$= \int_{-\infty}^{\infty} \varphi(y) f_X(y)\,dy$$

by change of variable to $y = \varphi^{-1}(x)$. This is the expected result, but we have had to work quite hard to get it and have restricted ourselves to functions φ which are monotonic increasing and onto $(-\infty, \infty)$. In fact, the result is true in general.

Proposition 3.1

If the random variable X has distribution function F and φ is any real-valued function defined on the reals, then

$$E[\varphi(X)] = \int_{-\infty}^{\infty} \varphi(x)\,dF_X(x)$$

If X is discrete with mass function p,

$$E[\varphi(X)] = \sum_{\substack{x \\ p(x)>0}} \varphi(x)p(x)$$

and if X is continuous with density function f,

$$E[\varphi(X)] = \int_{-\infty}^{\infty} \varphi(x)f(x)\,dx$$

Proof We just prove the discrete case. Let $D = \{y \mid y = \varphi(x)$ for some $x \in (-\infty, \infty)\}$. Then,

$$E[\varphi(X)] = \sum_{y \in D} yP(\varphi(X) = y) = \sum_{y \in D} yP(X \in \varphi^{-1}(y))$$

$$= \sum_{y \in D} \sum_{\substack{x \\ \varphi(x)=y}} yp(x)$$

$$= \sum_{x} \varphi(x)p(x)$$

The proof of the continuous case involves more complex handling of the integration domain and we omit it. The interested reader is referred to Ross (1988).   ■

The following corollaries state that the expectation of a constant is itself and that the expectation of a sum of functions of a random variable is the sum of the expectations of those functions.

Corollary 1 $E[a] = a$ for real constant a.

Proof The proof follows by taking $\varphi(x) = a$ for all x in the proposition. An alternative direct proof considers the random variable X which always takes the value a, with probability 1. Then $E[X] = P(X = a) \, a = a$.   ■

Corollary 2   If φ and ψ are any real-valued functions,

$$E[\varphi(X) + \psi(X)] = E[\varphi(X)] + E[\psi(X)]$$

Proof We assume that X is continuous with density f. The discrete case is analogous.

$$\begin{aligned}
E[\varphi(X) + \psi(X)] &= \int_{-\infty}^{\infty} [\varphi(x) + \psi(x)] f(x) \, dx \\
&= \int_{-\infty}^{\infty} \varphi(x) f(x) \, dx + \int_{-\infty}^{\infty} \psi(x) f(x) \, dx \\
&= E[\varphi(X)] + E[\psi(X)]
\end{aligned}$$ ■

Expectation of a random variable is also called the **first moment** out of an infinite set of moments which is defined as follows.

Definition 3.1

The **nth moment** $M_n(X)$ of a random variable X is defined by

$$M_n(X) = E[X^n]$$

for $n = 1, 2, \ldots$.

An expression for the nth moment of a random variable is given by Proposition 3.1 and stated as a third corollary:

Corollary 3 The nth moment $M_n(X)$ of a random variable X is given by:

$$M_n(X) = \begin{cases} \displaystyle\sum_{\substack{x \\ p(x)>0}} x^n p(x) & \text{if } X \text{ is discrete} \\[2em] \displaystyle\int_{-\infty}^{\infty} x^n f(x) \, dx & \text{if } X \text{ is continuous} \end{cases}$$

The case that X is neither discrete nor continuous is left as an exercise for the reader.   ∎

The second moment has particular importance since it defines the variance and standard deviation which are frequently used in statistics. The **variance** Var$[X]$ of a random variable X is defined by

$$\text{Var}[X] = E[(X - \mu^2)]$$

where $\mu = E[X]$ is the expected value of X. The variance is therefore a measure of the 'spread' of X about its mean. Its square root is called the **standard deviation** of X, written $\sigma[X]$, and has the same dimension as the mean, so providing a more realistic measure of the spread.

We can use the corollaries of Proposition 3.1 to express variance as

$$\text{Var}[X] = E[X^2 - 2\mu X + \mu^2] = E[X^2] - 2\mu E[X] + \mu^2$$
$$= M_2[X] - \mu^2$$

Using this formula, we can obtain the variance of all the random variables we have considered – and many more. This is left as an exercise, but we state the variance for two cases. First, the binomial random variable with parameters (n, p) has variance $np(1 - p)$, so what does this suggest for the variance of a Poisson distribution? (Hint: recall the argument used for the mean.) Secondly, the variance of the normal $N(\mu, \sigma^2)$ random variable is σ^2. Thus its parameters are its (mean, standard deviation) pair.

Proposition 3.1 generalizes to more than one dimension by considering joint random variables. The result is the following, which we state without proof.

Proposition 3.2

Given random variables $X_1, \ldots, X_n$ and any real-valued function φ of n real arguments, then:

(1)   If $X_1, \ldots, X_n$ are discrete with joint mass function p,

$$E[\varphi(X_1, \ldots, X_n)]$$

$$= \sum_{\substack{x_i | 1 \leqslant i \leqslant n \\ p(x_1, \ldots, x_n) > 0}} \varphi(x_1, \ldots, x_n) p(x_1, \ldots, x_n)$$

(2)   If $X_1, \ldots, X_n$ are continuous with joint density function f,

$$E[\varphi(X_1, \ldots, X_n)] =$$

$$\int_{-\infty}^{\infty} \cdots \int_{-\infty}^{\infty} \varphi(x_1, \ldots, x_n) f(x_1, \ldots, x_n) \, dx_1 \ldots dx_n$$

∎

An immediate consequence of this proposition is that the expectation operator is a *linear operator*. This is stated in the following corollary, the proof of which is straightforward and omitted.

Corollary For random variables $X_1, \ldots, X_n$ and real constants $a_1, \ldots, a_n$

$$E\left[\sum_{i=1}^{n} a_i X_i\right] = \sum_{i=1}^{n} a_i E[X_i]$$

where $E[X_i]$ is the marginal expectation of X_i, i.e. $E[X_i] = \int_{-\infty}^{\infty} x \, dF_{X_i}(x)$ which is equal to $\int_{-\infty}^{\infty} x f_{X_i}(x) \, dx$ if X_i has a density function, or a corresponding sum if X_i is discrete.   ∎

In particular, the expectation of a sum of random variables is equal to the sum of their expectations. This is precisely what the corollary states when $a_1 = \ldots = a_n = 1$. Notice that this holds whether or not the random variables X_i are independent. Using this result, we obtain np for the mean of a binomial random variable X with parameters (n, p) since X is a sum of n (actually independent) Bernoulli random variables with parameter p. Similarly, we saw in Section 2.6 that an Erlang-n random variable with parameter λ (i.e. gamma with parameters (n, λ)) is a sum of n (independent) negative exponential random variables each with parameter λ. Thus the Erlang-n distribution with parameter λ has expected value n/λ.

3.1.7 Conditional expectation

Finally, we consider the notion of conditional expectation, from which our results on conditional probability in Section 2.5 follow very neatly.

Definition 3.2

For random variables X and Y, the **conditional expectation** of X given that $Y = y$ is

$$E[X|Y = y] = \int_{-\infty}^{\infty} x \, dF_{X|Y}(x|y)$$

The Stieltjes integral covers all permutations of X and Y being discrete or continuous. In particular, the formula simplifies to:

(1) $E[X|Y = y] = \sum_x x p_{X|Y}(x|y)$

if X and Y are discrete and $p_Y(y) > 0$, where x is summed over $\{x | p_{X|Y}(x|y) > 0\}$

(2) $E[X|Y = y] = \int_{-\infty}^{\infty} x f_{X|Y}(x|y)\, dx$

if X and Y are continuous and $f_Y(y) > 0$

An important formula satisfied by the conditional expectation operator concerns the *random variable* $E[X|Y]$ which takes the value $E[X|Y = y]$ at $Y = y$. More generally, for the joint random variable $E[X|Y_1, \ldots, Y_n]$ (which takes the value $E[X|Y_1 = y_1, \ldots, Y_n = y_n]$ at $Y_1 = y_1, \ldots, Y_n = y_n$) we have:

Proposition 3.3

Given random variables $X, Y_1, \ldots, Y_n$,

$$E[X] = E[E[X|Y_1, \ldots, Y_n]]   (n \geq 1)$$

The proof is straightforward and follows directly from the results we obtained in Section 2.5 on conditional probability. However, the beauty of this expression is its generality and simplicity, being as general as the Stieltjes integral formulation but more concise. If Y is discrete with mass function p_Y, Proposition 3.3 yields:

$$E[X] = \sum_{y \in S} E[X|Y = y] p_Y(y)$$

where S is the image of Y. If Y is continuous with density function f_Y, it yields:

$$E[X] = \int_{-\infty}^{\infty} E[X|Y = y] f_Y(y)\, dy$$

In fact, we can recover our results on conditional probability by taking X to be the indicator random variable I_E for event E, as defined at the beginning of this section. Then $E[X] = P(E)$ and $E[X|Y = y] = P(E|Y = y)$ for random variable Y. Proposition 3.3 then gives:

$$P(E) = \int_{-\infty}^{\infty} P(E|Y = y) f_Y(y)\, dy$$

when Y is continuous, with a corresponding result when Y is discrete. Indeed, writing G_i to denote the event $Y = y_i$ in the discrete case (or $Y \in y_i \subseteq (-\infty, \infty)$ for a partition $\{y_i\}$), we recover our original version of the Law of Total Probability in Section 1.2.1.

The following useful corollary of Proposition 3.3 gives the expectation of a product of random variables in terms of conditional expectation.

Corollary   Given random variables X and Y,

$$E[XY] = E[YE[X|Y]]$$

Proof   The result follows directly from the proposition since $E[XY|Y = y] = yE[X|Y]$ ∎

Notice that if X and Y are independent, we have $E[XY] = E[YE[X]] = E[X]E[Y]$ by Proposition 3.1; see also Proposition 3.4 below.

Proposition 3.3 generalizes to provide the conditional expectation of X given $Y_1, \ldots, Y_n$ when we know the conditional expectation of X given $Y_1, \ldots, Y_n$ and further information $Y_{n+1}, \ldots, Y_{n+m}$. We state the result without proof; the reader is recommended to check at least the discrete case with small n and m.

Proposition 3.3'

Given random variables $X, Y_1, \ldots, Y_{n+m}$, $E[X|Y_1, \ldots, Y_n] = E[E[X|Y_1, \ldots, Y_{n+m}]|Y_1, \ldots, Y_n]$

We can also define the conditional variance of a random variable.

Definition 3.3

For random variables X and Y, the **conditional variance** of X given that $Y = y$ is

$$\text{Var}[X|Y] = E[(X - E[X|Y])^2|Y]$$

The corresponding formula satisfied by conditional variance is then

$$\text{Var}[X] = E[\text{Var}[X|Y]] + \text{Var}[E[X|Y]]$$

This is an appealing formula in view of its symmetry, but we will have no cause to use it!

Of course, if the random variables X and Y are independent $E[X|Y = y] = E[X]$. We also have the following important result:

Proposition 3.4

If X and Y are independent random variables, then for any real-valued functions φ and ψ,

$$E[\varphi(X)\psi(Y)] = E[\varphi(X)]E[\psi(Y)]$$

Proof We just consider the case where X and Y are continuous with joint density f; the discrete case is similar. Thus we have

$$E[\varphi(X)\psi(Y)] = \int_{-\infty}^{\infty} \int_{-\infty}^{\infty} \varphi(x)\psi(y)f(x, y)\,dx\,dy$$

by Proposition 3.2

$$= \int_{-\infty}^{\infty} \int_{-\infty}^{\infty} \varphi(x)\psi(y)f_X(x)f_Y(y)\,dx\,dy$$

by independence

$$= \int_{-\infty}^{\infty} \varphi(x)f_X(x)\,dx \int_{-\infty}^{\infty} \psi(y)f_Y(y)\,dy$$

$$= E[\varphi(X)]E[\psi(Y)]   \text{by Proposition 3.1} \blacksquare$$

If X and Y are not independent, we can easily prove the following generalization of the corollary to Proposition 3.3 (with obvious notation in the subscripts to E):

Corollary (generalization of the corollary to Proposition 3.3)

$$E[\varphi(X)\psi(Y)] = E_Y[\psi(Y)E_{X|Y}[\varphi(X)|Y]] \qquad\qquad \blacksquare$$

When considering the variance of sums of random variables, we need more than just the individual variances; contrast the case of expectations. Consider the sum of random variables X and Y. Then, using Propositions 3.1 and 3.2, we obtain

$$\begin{aligned}
\text{Var}[X + Y] &= E[(X + Y - E[X] - E[Y])^2] \\
&= E[(X - E[X])^2] + 2E[(X - E[X])(Y - E[Y])] \\
&\quad + E[(Y - E[Y])^2] \\
&= \text{Var}[X] + 2\,\text{Cov}[X, Y] + \text{Var}[Y]
\end{aligned}$$

where the **covariance** $\text{Cov}[X, Y]$ of two random variables X, Y is defined by

$$\text{Cov}[X, Y] = E[(X - E[X])(Y - E[Y])]$$

Expanding this definition and simplifying yields

$$\text{Cov}[X, Y] = E[XY] - E[X]E[Y]$$

Thus if X and Y are independent, $\mathrm{Cov}[X, Y] = 0$ by Proposition 3.4. However, the converse does not hold.

For a sum of n random variables $X_1, \ldots, X_n$ we can obtain similarly

$$\mathrm{Var}\left[\sum_{i=1}^{n} X_i\right] = \sum_{i=1}^{n} \mathrm{Var}[X_i] + 2 \sum_{1 \leq i < j \leq n} \mathrm{Cov}[X_i, X_j]$$

so that if the random variables are (pairwise) independent,

$$\mathrm{Var}\left[\sum_{i=1}^{n} X_i\right] = \sum_{i=1}^{n} \mathrm{Var}[X_i]$$

which now is consistent with the expectation operator. Notice that independence is a sufficient but not necessary condition for this result. However, variance is *not* a linear operator since, for constant c,

$$\mathrm{Var}[cX] = E[(cX - E[cX])^2] = E[c^2(X - E[X])^2]$$
$$= c^2 E[(X - E[X])^2] = c^2 \mathrm{Var}[X]$$

Standard deviation does vary linearly with c, i.e. $\sigma[cX] = c\sigma[X]$, but also is not a linear operator since $\sigma[X + Y] \neq \sigma[X] + \sigma[Y]$ even when X and Y are independent.

3.2 Generating functions and transforms

A generating function of a random variable is a parametrized expectation defined over that random variable's probability distribution, density or mass function. Their importance stems from the facts that:

- They may have a simple closed form, i.e. not involve an integral or summation;
- The moments of the distribution are readily obtained from them;
- The probability distribution can always be recovered from them in theory and often in practice;
- Certain operations on probability distributions are equivalent to much simpler operations on their generating functions;
- They often simplify the solution of recurrence relations.

We first define the generic *moment* generating function of a random variable in terms of which all the others follow. We then illustrate the usage of particular generating functions and transforms.

Definition 3.4

The moment generating function ϕ of a random variable X is defined for all complex values of t by

$$\phi(t) = E[e^{tX}] = \begin{cases} \displaystyle\sum_{\substack{x \\ p(x)>0}} e^{tx} p(x) \\ \qquad\qquad \text{if } X \text{ is discrete with mass function } p \\ \displaystyle\int_{-\infty}^{\infty} e^{tx} f(x)\,dx \\ \qquad\qquad \text{if } X \text{ is continuous with density function } f \end{cases}$$

As with any expectation, the definition in terms of the distribution function using a Stieltjes integral incorporates both of these possibilities.

It can be shown that the moment generating function uniquely characterizes a random variable. This result allows us to derive distributions in terms of their generating functions or transforms which are simpler. Then, for example, when the transform of a particular distribution is recognized, it can be inverted uniquely to give that distribution. Alternatively, there are also formulae for analytic and numerical inversion; see Chapter 9. The moments of a random variable can be obtained from its generating function by taking derivatives and setting the parameter t to zero. For the first moment, denoting differentiation with respect to t by a prime, we have

$$\phi'(t) = E\left[\frac{d}{dt} e^{tX}\right] = E[Xe^{tX}]$$

We are assuming we can interchange the operations of expectation and differentiation with respect to t, i.e. that the operations of integration (respectively summation) and differentiation can be interchanged in the continuous (respectively discrete) case. It is unusual for this assumption not to hold, and it certainly does hold for all the random variables used in this book. Assuming another interchange of limits operation to be valid, we can now let t approach zero to obtain

$$\phi'(0) = E[X] = M_1(X)$$

Similarly,

$$\phi''(t) = E\left[\frac{d^2}{dt^2} e^{tX}\right] = E[X^2 e^{tX}]$$

so that $\phi''(0) = M_2(X)$. In general, denoting the nth derivative of ϕ by $\phi^{(n)}$, we have $\phi^{(n)}(t) = E[X^n e^{tX}]$ so that $\phi^{(n)}(0) = M_n(X)$ for $n \geq 0$. Notice that the zeroth moment of any random variable is one by the normalization condition which is equivalent to $\phi(0) = 1$. Another important result gives the moment generating function of a convolution:

Proposition 3.5

If X and Y are independent random variables with moment generating functions ϕ_X and ϕ_Y respectively, then $X + Y$ has moment generating function ϕ_{X+Y} defined by

$$\phi_{X+Y}(t) = \phi_X(t)\phi_Y(t)$$

Proof By definition, $\phi_{X+Y}(t) = E[e^{t(X+Y)}] = E[e^{tX}e^{tY}] = E[e^{tX}]E[e^{tY}] = \phi_X(t)\phi_Y(t)$ by Proposition 3.4, since X and Y are independent. ∎

The result generalizes immediately to any finite sum of n independent random variables:

$$\phi_{X_1 + \ldots + X_n}(t) = \prod_{i=1}^{n} \phi_{X_i}(t)$$

In other words, the moment generating function of a convolution is the product of the moment generating functions of the components of that convolution.

In this book, we will be more concerned with two special cases of the moment generating function: the probability generating function for discrete random variables and the Laplace transform for continuous random variables. However, we now derive the moment generating function for the negative exponential distribution.

Example 3.1

The moment generating function of the negative exponential distribution with parameter λ is

$$\phi(t) = \int_0^\infty e^{tx} \lambda e^{-\lambda x}\, dx = \lambda \int_0^\infty e^{-(\lambda - t)x}\, dx = \frac{\lambda}{\lambda - t} \qquad \text{if } t < \lambda$$

If $t \geq \lambda$, the integral does not converge and $\phi(t)$ is undefined. Differentiating with respect to t gives

$$\phi^{(n)}(t) = \frac{n!\lambda}{(\lambda - t)^{n+1}}$$

so that the nth moment is $n!/\lambda^n$. In particular, the mean is $1/\lambda$ and the variance is $(2/\lambda^2) - (1/\lambda^2) = 1/\lambda^2$.

3.2.1 The probability generating function

Suppose that the discrete random variable X has image $\{x_i | i = 1, 2, \ldots\}$ and mass function p_X. Since the image of a discrete random variable is countable it can always be written in this form. Now let the random variable Y be defined by $Y = i$ iff $X = x_{i+1}$ for $i \geqslant 0$. Then the mass function p_Y of Y is defined by

$$p_Y(i) = p_X(x_{i+1})$$

for $i = 0, 1, \ldots$ and Y is equivalent to X. Thus without loss of generality we may assume that any discrete random variable has image $\{0, 1, 2, \ldots\}$. The probability generating function is defined for such random variables.

Definition 3.5

The **probability generating function** π of a random variable X whose values are the non-negative integers is defined by

$$\pi(z) = E[z^X] = \sum_{i=0}^{\infty} p_i z^i$$

where p is the mass function of X and $p_i = p_X(i)$ if $p_X(i) > 0$, $p_i = 0$ otherwise. (This allows for the possibility that the image of X is finite.)

Clearly the probability generating function becomes the moment generating function when $z = e^t$. The analogy of Proposition 3.5 therefore holds, with similar proof:

$$\pi_{X+Y}(z) = E[z^{X+Y}] = E[z^X z^Y] = E[z^X]E[z^Y] = \pi_X(z)\pi_Y(z)$$

for independent random variables X, Y with probability generating functions π_X, π_Y respectively. This extends in the obvious way to any finite sum.

However, the corresponding differentiations with respect to z and t are not quite the same. The probabilities p_i $(i \geqslant 0)$ and moments $M_n(X)$ $(n \geqslant 0)$ can be computed from the generating function using the following proposition.

Proposition 3.6

Let X be a non-negative integer-valued random variable with probability generating function π. Then

(1)   The mass function p of X is defined by

$$p(i) = \frac{\pi^{(i)}(0)}{i!} \quad \text{if } \pi^{(i)}(0) > 0$$

for $i = 0, 1, \ldots$ where $\pi^{(i)}(z)$ is the ith derivative of π at the point z

(2) $E[X(X-1) \ldots (X-i+1)] = \pi^{(i)}(1)$. This quantity is called the ***i*th factorial moment** of X.

Proof

(1)   For $i = 0$, $p(0) = \pi(0)$ since only the first term in the series for $\pi(z)$ has no factor z. For $i \geq 1$,

$$\pi^{(i)}(z) = \sum_{j=i}^{\infty} p_j j(j-1) \ldots (j-i+1) z^{j-i}$$

so that $\pi^{(i)}(0) = p_i i!$ for the same reason. The result then follows since $p(i) = p_i$ wherever $p_i > 0$.

(2)   From the proof of (1), $\pi^{(i)}(1) = \sum_{j=i}^{\infty} p_j j(j-1) \ldots (j-i+1) = E[X(X-1) \ldots (X-i+1)]$ as required.

■

The nth moment of X can be obtained from part (2) of the proposition by first successively computing the first, second, $\ldots$, $(n-1)$th moments and then the nth factorial moment. For example, $E[X] = M_1(X) = \pi^{(1)}(1)$ and $E[X(X-1)] = E[X^2] - E[X] = M_2(X) - M_1(X) = \pi^{(2)}(1)$. Hence,

$$M_2(X) = \pi^{(2)}(1) + \pi^{(1)}(1)$$

The probability generating function can be obtained in simple form for all the random variables we have considered and many more besides. We now consider two of them, from which others follow.

Geometric distribution

Recall that the geometric random variable with parameter p has mass function

$$p(i) = pq^{i-1}$$

for positive integer i, where $q = 1 - p$. Thus

$$p_i = pq^{i-1}$$

for $i > 0$ and $p_0 = 0$. The generating function is therefore

$$\pi(z) = \sum_{i=1}^{\infty} pq^{i-1}z^i = pz \sum_{i=1}^{\infty} (qz)^{i-1}$$

$$= \frac{pz}{1 - qz} = \frac{p}{q}\left(\frac{1}{1 - qz} - 1\right)$$

Thus, for $n \geqslant 1$,

$$\pi^{(n)}(z) = \frac{n!pq^{n-1}}{(1 - qz)^{n+1}}$$

Hence we can calculate the mean of the geometric distribution as

$$\pi'(1) = \frac{p}{(1 - q)^2} = \frac{1}{p}$$

and its second moment as

$$\pi'(1) + \pi''(1) = \frac{1}{p} + \frac{2q}{p^2} = \frac{1 + q}{p^2}$$

so that its variance is

$$\frac{q}{p^2}$$

From these results we can immediately deduce the mean and variance of the negative binomial random variable with parameters (n, p). Recalling its definition from Section 2.2, this is a sum of n independent geometric random variables with parameter p. Its mean is therefore np and, because of the independence, its variance is nq/p^2.

Binomial distribution

In the same way, we can obtain the generating function of the binomial distribution with parameters (n, p) as

$$\pi(z) = \sum_{i=0}^{n} \binom{n}{i} p^i(1 - p)^{n-i}z^i$$

$$= [pz + (1 - p)]^n$$

Alternatively, the generating function of a Bernoulli random variable X with parameter p is

$$\phi(z) = P(X = 0)z^0 + P(X = 1)z^1 = (1 - p) + pz$$

But since a binomial random variable with parameters (n, p) is a sum of n independent Bernoulli random variables with parameter p, we have $\pi(z) = [\phi(z)]^n$.

Now, given that $np = \lambda$, we can write

$$\pi(z) = \left(1 - \frac{(1 - z)\lambda}{n}\right)^n$$

so that as $n \to \infty$, $\pi(z) \to e^{-\lambda(1-z)}$. This is the probability generating function of the Poisson distribution, as may be verified directly.

3.2.2 The Laplace transform

An important instance of the moment generating function is obtained by restricting the parameter t to non-positive values and considering only non-negative valued random variables. This leads to the following definition of the Laplace transform.

Definition 3.6

For a function f defined on the non-negative reals, we define the **Laplace transform**, $f^*(s)$, by

$$f^*(s) = \int_0^\infty e^{-st} f(t) \, dt$$

for real values $s \geqslant 0$.

Of course, we will be interested in functions f which are the densities of non-negative random variables. For random variables that do not have a density, there is a more general definition, the **Laplace–Stieltjes transform**

$$f^*(s) = \int_0^\infty e^{-st} \, dF(t)$$

but we will not need this.

Of course, the Laplace transform is an expectation:

$$f^*(s) = E[e^{-sX}]$$

for non-negative random variable X with density f. Thus an instance of Proposition 3.5 holds in the form

$$f^*_{X+Y} = f^*_X f^*_Y$$

for independent non-negative random variables X and Y, with the obvious extension to an arbitrary finite sum. We will make extensive use of the Laplace transform in this book when we consider various time delays in queueing systems. These are composed of independent sums of sojourn times which are non-negative valued random variables.

Example 3.2 (Erlang-n density)

We have already obtained in Example 3.1 the moment generating function for the negative exponential (Erlang-1) distribution with parameter λ. The Laplace transform is obtained by taking $t = -s$ in Example 3.1 to give:

$$f^*(s) = \frac{\lambda}{s + \lambda}$$

Now, we saw in Proposition 3.1 that the Erlang-n density is the n-fold convolution of negative exponential densities, i.e. an Erlang-n random variable is a sum of n independent negative exponential random variables with the same parameter. The Laplace transform of the Erlang-n density g with parameter λ is therefore

$$g^*(s) = [f^*(s)]^n = \left(\frac{\lambda}{s + \lambda}\right)^n$$

The Laplace transform integrand is not in general suitable for random variables which may be negative, since the integral over the whole of the real line may not converge. Indeed, the same applies to the moment generating function with real parameter t where the positive region may be suspect. However, if we take t to be *imaginary* in the moment generating function, we obtain the **characteristic function** φ of a random variable X defined by

$$\varphi(s) = E[e^{isX}]$$

for real s, $-\infty < s < \infty$. Because $\varphi(s)$ always exists, it provides a more general and powerful tool for the analysis of probability distributions. It has all the features of the other variants of the moment generating function, for example the convolution result of Proposition 3.5 and a formula for the moments of its random variable. The principles are the same but the notation is a little more cumbersome in view of the use of complex numbers. We will not have cause to use it.

3.2.3 Solution of recurrence relations

An important use of generating functions, not necessarily probability generating functions, is to solve **recurrence relations** (also called recurrence formulae or just recurrences). These can often be transformed into a simple equation or a differential equation, with appropriate boundary conditions, having the generating function for its solution. This solution may or may not be determinable. Some problems, for example, can be transformed into a boundary value problem in the complex plane which also has the generating function for its solution. However, this technique is outside the scope of this book. From the generating function it is possible to obtain the solution of the recurrence relations, for example a set of discrete probabilities. Often, however, some aggregate quantity will be of greater interest and follow directly from the generating function, for example the mean and higher moments of a probability distribution.

We will make use of the former approach in various places in this book. In order to illustrate it, consider the recurrence

$$\sum_{i=0}^{n} a(i, d) p_{k+i} = 0 \qquad \text{for } k = 0, 1, \ldots$$

where it is required to determine p_n, p_{n+1}, $\ldots$ given appropriate boundary conditions for p_0, $\ldots$, p_{n-1}. Suppose that the coefficients $a(i, d)$ are polynomials in k of degree d. Then we can express $a(i, d)$ in the form

$$a(i, d) = \sum_{j=0}^{d} a_{ij}(k + i)(k + i - 1) \ldots (k + i + 1 - j)$$

Now, let $G(z) = \sum_{k=0}^{\infty} p_k z^k$. Then multiplying the recurrence formula by z^{k+n} and summing over k gives:

$$\sum_{k=0}^{\infty} \sum_{i=0}^{n} \sum_{j=0}^{d} a_{ij}(k + i)(k + i - 1) \ldots$$

$$(k + i + 1 - j)z^{j+n-i}p_{k+i}z^{k+i-j} = 0$$

i.e.

$$\sum_{i=0}^{n} \sum_{j=0}^{d} a_{ij} z^{j+n-i} \frac{\mathrm{d}^j}{\mathrm{d}z^j} \left(G(z) - \sum_{k=0}^{i-1} p_k z^k \right) = 0$$

The solution of this differential equation is the generating function $G(z)$. This technique extends to more than one dimension when we define a multidimensional generating function such as

$$G(z_1, z_2) = \sum_{j=0}^{\infty} \sum_{k=0}^{\infty} p_{jk} z_1^j z_2^k$$

and obtain a partial differential equation. Alternatively, we can define simple (one-dimensional) generating functions successively for each dimension of p. We will see several examples in this book. Here we consider a simple one.

Example 3.3

A processor has service times which are negative exponentially distributed with parameter μ and arrivals join the queue at the processor such that the time between successive arrivals is negative exponentially distributed with parameter λ. If the queue capacity is unbounded, we show in Chapter 4 that if p_k denotes the probability that there are k tasks at the processor at any time after the system has stabilized, then

$$\lambda p_0 = \mu p_1$$

$$(\lambda + \mu)p_n = \lambda p_{n-1} + \mu p_{n+1} \qquad (n \geq 1)$$

Multiplying throughout by z^{n+1} and summing yields

$$(\lambda + \mu)z[G(z) - p_0] = \lambda z^2 G(z) + \mu[G(z) - p_1 z - p_0]$$

where $G(z) = \sum_{k=0}^{\infty} p_k z^k$. Simplifying this equation then gives

$$G(z) = \frac{[\mu p_1 - (\lambda + \mu)p_0]z + \mu p_0}{\lambda z^2 - (\lambda + \mu)z + \mu}$$

$$= \frac{\mu p_0}{\mu - \lambda z}$$

by the boundary condition $\lambda p_0 = \mu p_1$. Thus, since we must have $G(1) = 1$, $p_0 = 1 - (\lambda/\mu)$ and $p_1 = G'(0) = p_0(\lambda/\mu)$. The mean number of tasks at the processor is $G'(1) = \lambda \mu p_0/(\mu - \lambda)^2 = \lambda/(\mu - \lambda)$.

3.3 Asymptotic properties

The asymptotic properties of a probability distribution, that is the limiting distribution of a sequence of random variables, demonstrate that the theory of probability we have defined in terms of a set of axioms is consistent with intuitive notions of chance. Moreover, they allow many complex situations to be analysed without representing every detail explicitly. For example, a sum of many independent random variables approaches a normal distribution: the Central Limit Theorem. This simplifies computation, since convolutions need not be calculated explicitly, and also explains why such sums exhibit bell-shaped histograms – the shape of the normal density. Another important class of results comprises the laws of large numbers. Roughly speaking, these show that the sum of a sequence of independent random variables divided by its length (i.e. its average) approaches a random variable which is equal to the expectation of the average with probability 1.

In this section, we consider the most basic results: the Central Limit Theorem and the weak and strong laws of large numbers. Many other asymptotic properties have been obtained in various areas of applied probability, for example simulation where efficient, unbiased estimators are sought. The reader is referred to Billingsley (1968) for a rigorous, general account and Heidelberger (1988) for simulation applications.

3.3.1   The Central Limit Theorem

The Central Limit Theorem has been proved in ever more general form since the 18th century. Initially it was restricted to a sum of independent and identical Bernoulli random variables. We do not require the random variables to be Bernoulli, but our conditions can be relaxed substantially further.

Proposition 3.7 (Central Limit Theorem)

If X_1, X_2, ... is a sequence of independent and identically distributed random variables with mean μ and variance σ^2, then

$$P\left(\frac{\sum_{i=1}^{n} X_i - n\mu}{\sqrt{n}\,\sigma} \le a\right) \to \Phi(a) \qquad \text{as } n \to \infty$$

Proof We may assume that $\mu = 0$ and $\sigma = 1$ since otherwise we just standardize each X_i to give $X_i' = (X_i - \mu)/\sigma$. Applying the result to the sequence (X_i') then yields the result required for (X_i).

Let each random variable X_i have moment generating function $\phi(t)$ so that $X_i/\sqrt{n}$ has moment generating function $\phi(t/\sqrt{n})$ and $\sum_{i=1}^{n} X_i/\sqrt{n}$ has moment generating function $[\phi(t/\sqrt{n})]^n$. Now we *assume* that, under appropriate continuity conditions, if the limit of a sequence of moment generating functions of random variables Y_1, Y_2, ... is equal to the moment generating function of a random variable Y, then the distribution of Y_n tends to the distribution of Y as $n \to \infty$. This is a consequence of the uniqueness of the moment generating function of a distribution together with continuity properties. It is left as an exercise to show that the moment generating function of the standard normal distribution is $e^{t^2/2}$.

To prove the proposition, it therefore remains to show that $[\phi(t/\sqrt{n})]^n \to e^{t^2/2}$ as $n \to \infty$, or equivalently that $n \ln \phi(t/\sqrt{n}) \to t^2/2$ or $[\ln \phi(t\sqrt{x})]/x \to t^2/2$ as $x \to 0$. This follows since

$$\lim_{x \to 0} \frac{\ln \phi(t\sqrt{x})}{x} = \frac{t\phi'(t\sqrt{x})}{2\sqrt{x}\phi(t\sqrt{x})} \qquad \text{by L'Hôpital's rule}$$

$$= \frac{t^2\phi''(t\sqrt{x})}{2\phi(t\sqrt{x}) + 2t\sqrt{x}\phi'(t\sqrt{x})}$$

by L'Hôpital's rule, since $E[X_i] = 0$ for each i

$$= \frac{t^2}{2} \qquad \text{since } \phi(0) = 1 \text{ and } \phi''(0) = 1 \qquad \blacksquare$$

A simple consequence of the Central Limit Theorem is that any random variable which is a sum of n independent identical random variables approximates a normal random variable as n becomes large, for example, a binomial random variable with parameters (n, p) or an Erlang-n random variable as $n \to \infty$. (Actually, independence is one of the assumptions we can drop.)

Example 3.4 _____

Suppose that on average one job is submitted to a computer system each minute with standard deviation 0.5, and that the numbers submitted in any sequence of minutes are independent. We require the probability that more than 68 jobs are submitted in one hour and four minutes.

The number X submitted in one hour and four minutes is the sum of 64 independent identical random variables with mean 1 and standard deviation 0.5. Thus, by the Central Limit Theorem,

$$P(X > 68) = 1 - P(X \le 68) = 1 - P\left(\frac{X - 64}{4} \le 1\right)$$

$$\approx 1 - \Phi(1) \approx 0.16$$

The Central Limit Theorem shows that the random variable $(\sum_{i=1}^{n} X_i - n\mu)/\sqrt{n}\sigma$ will very rarely exceed a given large value K as n becomes large – with negligible probability in most practical situations. However, it does not preclude the possibility that this happens for infinitely many n, even though these values of n will be very widely separated. A much more complex limit theorem is the **Law of the Iterated Logarithm** which states that the inequality

$$\frac{\sum_{i=1}^{n} X_i - n\mu}{\sqrt{n}\sigma} \geq c\{2\ln[\ln(n)]\}^{1/2}$$

is satisfied almost surely (i.e. with probability 1) for only finitely many n if $c > 1$ and for infinitely many n if $c < 1$. Notice that although it increases very slowly indeed with n, the right-hand side is unbounded. The full proof is very complex (Hartman and Wintner 1941), and the reader is referred to Kingman and Taylor (1966).

3.3.2 Laws of large numbers

There are two laws of large numbers which state properties about the average of a sequence of independent random variables as its length approaches infinity. We prove the weaker of the two – the weak law of large numbers – and just state the strong law. We will need another famous result, Chebyshev's inequality, which in turn uses the following proposition.

Proposition 3.8 (Markov's inequality)

For non-negative random variable X,

$$P(X \geq x) \leq \frac{E[X]}{x}$$

for all $x > 0$.

Proof   Here the use of Stieltjes integrals is very simple, enabling us to prove the result for any type of random variable X.

$$E[X] = \int_0^{\infty} u \, dF(u) = \int_0^{x} u \, dF(u) + \int_x^{\infty} u \, dF(u)$$

$$\geq \int_x^{\infty} u \, dF(u)$$

$$\geq x \int_x^{\infty} dF(u) = xP(X \geq x) \qquad \blacksquare$$

Chebyshev's inequality is actually just an application of Markov's inequality.

Proposition 3.9 (Chebyshev's inequality)

For random variable X with finite expectation μ and variance σ^2,

$$P(|X - \mu| \geq k) \leq \frac{\sigma^2}{k^2}$$

for all $k > 0$.

Proof By Markov's inequality applied to the non-negative random variable $(X - \mu)^2$, we have

$$P(|X - \mu| \geq k) = P((X - \mu)^2 \geq k^2) \leq \frac{E[(X - \mu)^2]}{k^2}$$

$$= \frac{\sigma^2}{k^2}$$

taking $x = k^2 > 0$.   ∎

These inequalities provide bounds on the probabilities that a random variable exceeds given values. They are very generally applicable since only the mean and variance of a probability distribution are required. However, a consequence of this generality is that the bounds tend to be very coarse. An important application, however, is the following:

Example 3.5 ────────────────────────────────

Show that if a random variable X has zero variance, then it is equal to a constant value with probability 1. It is sufficient to prove that

$$P(X = E[X]) = 1$$

if $\mathrm{Var}[X] = 0$, since the said constant value must be equal to the expectation of X. Now, by Chebyshev's inequality, if $\mu = E[X]$,

$$P(|X - \mu| > n^{-1}) = 0$$

for all $n > 0$, so that, by continuity (corollary to Proposition 1.3),

$$0 = \lim_{n \to \infty} P(|X - \mu| > n^{-1}) = P\left(\lim_{n \to \infty} (|X - \mu| > n^{-1})\right)$$

$$= P(X \neq \mu)$$

Proposition 3.10 (The weak law of large numbers)

Let X_1, X_2, ... be a sequence of independent and identically distributed random variables with $E[X_i] = \mu < \infty$ for each $i \geq 1$. Then for all $\varepsilon > 0$,

$$P\left(\left|\frac{\sum_{i=1}^{n} X_i}{n} - \mu\right| > \varepsilon\right) \rightarrow 0 \qquad \text{as } n \rightarrow \infty$$

Proof Assuming that $\text{Var}[X_i] = \sigma^2 < \infty$ for each i, the result follows immediately from Chebyshev's inequality by taking $X = \sum_{i=1}^{n} X_i/n$ so that, since the X_i are independent, $\text{Var}[X] = n\,\text{Var}[X_1/n] = \sigma^2/n$. We therefore have

$$P\left(\left|\frac{\sum_{i=1}^{n} X_i}{n} - \mu\right| > \varepsilon\right) \leq \frac{\sigma^2}{n\varepsilon^2} \rightarrow 0 \qquad \text{as } n \rightarrow \infty \qquad (3.1)$$

If the variance of X_i is not finite, we use the *method of truncation* to split the X_i into two, defining $X_i = U_i + V_i$ where $U_i = X_i$ and $V_i = 0$ if $|X_i| \leq \varepsilon n$ and $U_i = 0$ and $V_i = X_i$ if $|X_i| > \varepsilon n$. The result we have just proved then holds for the U_i and the contribution made by the V_i can be shown to be negligible. The reader is referred to Feller (1968) for the details. ∎

This law states that, for every n greater than some given large value N, the probability that $\sum_{i=1}^{n} X_i/n$ will not be within ε of μ is small, specifically of order n^{-1}. It says nothing about how often $|(\sum_{i=1}^{n} X_i/n) - \mu|$ can exceed ε except that this will be rare. In particular, it does not exclude the possibility that this might happen infinitely often. The strong law states that this possibility will occur only a finite number of times (almost surely).

Proposition 3.11 (The strong law of large numbers)

Let X_1, X_2, ... be a sequence of independent random variables with $E[X_i] = \mu_i < \infty$ and $\text{Var}[X_i] = \sigma_i^2 < \infty$ $(i \geq 1)$. Suppose further that $\sum_{i=1}^{\infty} \sigma_i^2/i^2 < \infty$. Then for all ε, $\delta > 0$, there exists an integer N such that for all $n \geq N$,

$$P\left(\left|\frac{\sum_{i=1}^{n} X_i - \sum_{i=1}^{n} \mu_i}{n}\right| < \varepsilon\right) \geq 1 - \delta$$

In other words, with probability 1,

$$\left| \frac{\sum_{i=1}^{n} X_i - \sum_{i=1}^{n} \mu_i}{n} \right| \to 0 \qquad \text{as } n \to \infty \qquad\qquad ■$$

An important instance of this law occurs when the random variables X_i are independent and identically distributed with finite mean μ and variance σ^2. In this case $\sum_{i=1}^{\infty} \sigma_i^2/i^2 = \sigma^2 \sum_{i=1}^{\infty} 1/i^2 < \infty$ and so, with probability 1,

$$\frac{\sum_{i=1}^{n} X_i}{n} \to \mu \qquad \text{as } n \to \infty$$

The difference between the weak and strong laws of large numbers lies in the bounds on the right-hand sides of Equation (3.1) and Proposition 3.11 respectively. For the weak law we had $\sigma^2/n\varepsilon^2$ which depends on ε, whereas for the strong law we had δ which was independent of ε. Thus, only the strong law asserts convergence *almost everywhere*, i.e. at all but a finite number of values of n.

SUMMARY

- Expectations or mean values or averages provide many of the most important predictions required of stochastic models.

- Many of the important distributions in stochastic modelling have simple expressions for their means.

- The concepts of probability and expectation are equivalent and the theory of probability can be based on the notion of expectation as primitive.

- Expectation is a linear operator.

- Variance is not a linear operator, but distributes over sums of independent random variables.

- The law of total probability has a particularly concise, general and powerful form in terms of expectations.

- Generating functions simplify the derivation of many properties of distributions, for example moments and convolutions. They can also be used to solve recurrence relations.

- The Laplace transform is an important generating function for non-negative, continuous random variables.

- Asymptotic properties are central to probability theory since they describe long-term behaviour and formalize intuition. The Laws of Large Numbers and the Central Limit Theorem are the most important and most general.

- The sum of many independent, identical random variables tends to a normal distribution.

EXERCISES

3.1 (00 Gambler gain or loss)
A gambler pays £3 for the privilege of throwing a single die. If the number that comes up is greater than 3, he will win that number of pounds; otherwise he will get nothing. Find the expected gain or loss.

3.2 (00 Expectation)
The probability density function of the rainfall random variable X is given by:

$$f(x) = \begin{cases} 0.02x & \text{if } 0 \leqslant x \leqslant 10 \\ 0 & \text{otherwise} \end{cases}$$

Find the average amount of rainfall.

3.3 (20 Expectation)
A random variable, X, takes value i with probability $1/2^i$ ($i = 1, 2, \ldots$). Calculate the expected value of X.

3.4 (20 Infinite first moment)
A random variable, X, takes value 2^i with probability $1/2^i$ ($i = 1, 2, \ldots$). Show that the probabilities sum to one, but the first moment is not finite.

3.5 (20 Bernoulli trials)
The outcome of a Bernoulli trial can be described by a random variable $X \in \{0, 1\}$ with probability of success $P(X = 1) = p$. Let the random variable $S_n \in \{0, \ldots, n\}$ represent the number of successes in n independent trials. For a Poisson process with rate λ, let the random variable K_t be the number of arrivals in an interval of length t.

(a)   Show that $E[S_n] = np$ and $\text{Var}[S_n] = np(1 - p)$
(b)   Using (a) show that $E[K_t] = \lambda t$ and $\text{Var}[K_t] = \lambda t$

3.6 (20 Moment generating function)
Show that the moment generating function of the standard normal distribution is $e^{t^2/2}$.

3.7 (10 Failure rate)
The probability that a component fails in unit time is p. What is the mean time before the component fails? Suppose n components are used to construct a part. Assuming that only components

fail, what is the probability that any one of the components on a given part fails? State any assumptions you make.

3.8   (20 Mirrored disk)

Suppose a disk volume is duplexed (i.e. 2 disks contain identical data) so that single failures can be tolerated provided that another failure does not occur during the repair time. If the mean time to failure for each disk is m cycles and the repair time for one disk is 1 cycle, show that the mean time to failure of the duplexed disk volume is m^2 cycles.

Chapter 4
Stochastic Processes

4.1 Random walks	83	4.4 Reversibility	131
4.2 Markov chains	89	4.5 Renewal theory	140
4.3 Markov processes	112		

Many physical systems, including computer and communication networks, *evolve* in time and often *dynamic* characteristics are important. For example, we may be interested in:

(1)   the length of a queue;
(2)   how long it takes for messages to be transmitted through a network;
(3)   the population of successive generations in animal breeding;
(4)   how much rain falls in successive years;
(5)   the proportion of students that pass their exams in performance modelling each year.

Stochastic processes provide models for such evolving systems by describing the sequences of states they enter. Technically, stochastic is a synonym for random, and just about any aspect of probability theory could therefore be considered as 'stochastic'. However, the term **stochastic process** is defined to be a *family of random variables* $\{X_t | t \in T\}$ say. T denotes the *parameter space* which indexes this set and the random variables X_t represent measurements of some physical characteristic of interest. Each X_t takes its values from some set S called the *state space* of the process. Any set of instances of $\{X_t | t \in T\}$ can be regarded as the path of a particle moving randomly in the state space S, its position at 'time' t being X_t. These paths are variously called **sample paths**, **trajectories** or **realizations** of the stochastic process, and values in the set T are often referred to as **times**.

Stochastic processes may be classified according to whether T and S are discrete (countable) or continuous (uncountable). For example, T is discrete in cases (3) to (5) above, while S is discrete in cases (1) and (3) and continuous in cases (4) and (5). In case (1), if queue lengths were measured every minute, T would again be discrete. On the other hand, if we specified that queue lengths were measured after every arrival from a Poisson process, T would be continuous. In case (2), if transmission time is a continuous random variable, measured at the end of a transmission, both S and T will be continuous. Typical objectives of a stochastic model, i.e. one based on the theory of stochastic processes, are to establish

- the probability that X_t takes a value in a particular subset of S at some given t – particularly in the *long term*, i.e. as $t \to \infty$, if the limit exists;

- the relationships between the random variables X_s and X_t for different indices s and t in T. This, of course, involves joint probability distributions;

- *hitting probabilities*, i.e. the probability that a given state in S will ever be entered (e.g that a particle ever hits a given point in S);

- distribution of *first passage times*. A first passage time between states A and $B \in S$ has the form $T_{B>A} - T_A$ where the random variable T_A is an instant at which the process enters A and $T_{B>A}$ is the least instant greater than T_A at which the process enters B. First passage times are important in the calculation of time delay distributions in networks, as we will see in Chapter 9.

The following terminology applies to any stochastic process with parameter space $T \subseteq \mathfrak{R}$.

- $\{X_t\}$ is **stationary** if for any $t_1, \ldots, t_n \in T$, $t_1 + \tau, \ldots, t_n + \tau \in T$ and integer $n \geqslant 1$,

$$F_{X_{t_1+\tau} \ldots X_{t_n+\tau}} = F_{X_{t_1} \ldots X_{t_n}}$$

That is, all the process's finite dimensional joint distributions are unchanged by a shift in the time axis.

- $\{X_t\}$ has **independent increments** if for any $t_1 < \ldots < t_n \in T$ and integer $n \geqslant 1$,

$$X_{t_2} - X_{t_1}, \ldots, X_{t_n} - X_{t_{n-1}}$$

are independent.

- $\{X_t\}$ has the **Markov property** and hence is a **Markov process**, if for any $\tau_0 < \ldots < \tau_m < t_1 < \ldots < t_n \in T$ and integers $m \geqslant 0$, $n \geqslant 1$,

$$F_{X_{t_1} \ldots X_{t_n} | X_{\tau_0} \ldots X_{\tau_m}}(x_1, \ldots, x_n | y_0, \ldots, y_m)$$
$$= F_{X_{t_1} \ldots X_{t_n} | X_{\tau_m}}(x_1, \ldots, x_n | y_m)$$

The Markov property is the weakest form of dependence in that given the value of X_t at some $t \in T$, the future path X_s for $s > t$ does not depend on knowledge of the past history X_u for $u < t$. Any process with independent increments has the Markov property; the proof of this is left to the reader. The theory of Markov processes is extensive and we introduce the basic results in Sections 4.2 and 4.3.

In this chapter, we introduce some of the most important results in the theory of stochastic processes which are required for modelling studies such as those described in the remainder of this book. We first consider the archetypal process, the random walk, in Section 4.1 and then go on to develop the theory of Markov chains. The Poisson process is considered in detail in Section 4.3, together with Markov processes. These are applied in birth–death models such as the simplest case of the single server queue. In Section 4.4 we introduce the concept of reversibility and demonstrate its potential in the solution of stationary Markov process models. Finally, we consider the more general renewal processes in Section 4.5.

4.1 Random walks

There is a whole theory of random walks in which a 'particle' moves in a number of dimensions in steps of one unit in the direction of each axis. Moves take place in discrete time, normally at intervals of one unit. There may be unbounded space, or there may exist reflecting barriers which force the particle to change direction, or there may be absorbing barriers which 'trap' the particle so that it remains at the same point forever after hitting the barrier. We will consider only random walks in one dimension, i.e. on a single discretely calibrated axis. This will introduce the use of sample paths and enable us to obtain some simple asymptotic results using the limit theorems of Chapter 3. We also consider the classic example of the 'gambler's ruin' as an application. The one-dimensional random walk is one of the simplest of stochastic processes and can be used to model many gambling games where fortunes can be accumulated and lost. There are also applications in communication systems modelling, for example in window flow control systems, but we prefer to move straight on to Markov chains after we have introduced this first simple usage of a stochastic model.

4.1.1 The unrestricted random walk in one dimension

Let $\{X_n | n \in \mathcal{N}_0\}$ be the stochastic process representing the movement of a particle along a single axis with discrete time points $\{\ldots, -1, 0, 1, \ldots\}$, where X_n is the position of the particle at (non-negative integer) time n. At each time n, the particle moves to the right with probability p and to the left with probability $q = 1 - p$ where p is constant. The process has the following properties:

- independent increments and hence the Markov property
- spatial homogeneity, i.e. $P(X_n = i + j | X_0 = j) = P(X_n = i | X_0 = 0)$
- time homogeneity, i.e. $P(X_{m+n} = i | X_m = 0) = P(X_n = i | X_0 = 0)$

Let each step $S_n \in \{-1, 1\}$ taken at time n (independent of every other step) have probability mass function defined by

$$P(S_n = 1) = p, \qquad P(S_n = -1) = q \qquad (n \geqslant 1)$$

We assume that the initial state of the random walk is $X_0 = 0$, i.e. the particle begins at the origin. Now, for $n \geqslant 1$,

$$X_n = S_1 + \ldots + S_n$$

where the S_i are independent.

We almost have a Bernoulli trial, except that the random variables S_i do not have values in $\{0, 1\}$. We therefore make a small transformation and define $Y_i = (S_i + 1)/2$ so that $Y_i \in \{0, 1\}$ and $P(Y_i = 1) = P[(S_i + 1)/2 = 1] = P(S_i = 1) = p$ and $P(Y_i = 0) = q$. Thus the random variable Z_n defined by

$$Z_n = \sum_{i=1}^{n} Y_i = \frac{X_n + n}{2}$$

for $n \geqslant 1$ is binomial with parameters (n, p). The position of the particle at time n, given that it was at the origin initially, is therefore described by

$$P(X_n = k | X_0 = 0) = P\left(Z_n = \frac{k+n}{2} \middle| X_0 = 0\right)$$

$$= P\left(Z_n = \frac{k+n}{2}\right)$$

$$= \begin{cases} \binom{n}{\frac{1}{2}(k+n)} p^{(k+n)/2} p^{(n-k)/2} \\ \qquad\qquad\qquad -n \leqslant k \leqslant n, \; k+n \text{ even} \\ 0 \qquad\qquad\qquad\qquad \text{otherwise} \end{cases}$$

Notice that $X_n + n$ is even with probability 1 since Z_n is an integer for all n (almost surely). This solves the problem for all finite times n, but it is more interesting to study the long-term behaviour. For example, by the strong law of large numbers (Proposition 3.3), we have, since the S_i are independent with mean $p - q$ (it is easy to show),

$$\frac{X_n - n(p - q)}{n} \to 0 \quad \text{with probability 1 as } n \to \infty$$

i.e.

$$\frac{X_n}{n} \xrightarrow{\text{as}} p - q \text{ as } n \to \infty$$

where $\xrightarrow{\text{as}}$ is read as 'converges almost surely'. Moreover, by the Central Limit Theorem, we have, since $\text{Var}[S_i] = (p + q)^2 - (p - q)^2 = 4pq$,

$$\frac{X_n - n(p - q)}{2(npq)^{1/2}} \xrightarrow{\mathcal{D}} N(0, 1) \qquad \text{as } n \to \infty$$

where $\xrightarrow{\mathcal{D}}$ denotes 'convergence in distribution'. In fact we can be even more precise by saying that the particle stays almost surely within the bounds given by

$$-2\{2npq \ln [\ln (n)]\}^{1/2} < X_n - n(p - q) < 2\{2npq \ln [\ln (n)]\}^{1/2}$$

except at a finite number of time points. This property follows from the Law of the Iterated Logarithm; see Section 3.3.

4.1.2 Random walks with barriers: the gambler's ruin

Consider now the random walk defined in the previous section, with initial state $X_0 = 0$ but with *absorbing barriers* at points $a < 0$ and $b > 0$; equivalently, a and b are *absorbing states*. The random walk

$\{X_n | n = 0, 1, \ldots\}$ is then such that $X_n = X_{n+1} = X_{n+2} = \ldots$ if $X_n = a$ or b, i.e. the walk remains in state X_n $(n > 0)$. If we take $a = -\alpha$, $b = \beta$ $(\alpha, \beta > 0)$, this process models a game played by two gamblers A and B in which the stake is £1 in each hand and A, B start with £α, £β respectively. X_n denotes A's net winnings after n hands. The end of the game is represented by entry into either state $-\alpha$ (B wins) or state β (A wins), and we might be interested in the probability that player A loses, for example.

Let the random variable Y be 1 if A eventually loses and 0 otherwise. Now, the walk still has the Markov property and we can write down a recurrence relation for the probabilities $p_i = P(Y = 1 | X_0 = i)$, $a \leq i \leq b$. The required probability is then p_0. This type of steady state analysis will be pursued in some detail in the next section when we consider ergodic Markov chains. However, in this simple case we proceed directly as follows. First, we observe that $p_i = P(Y = 1 | X_n = i)$ for all $n \geq 0$. Thus we have, for $a < i < b$,

$$
\begin{aligned}
p_i &= P(Y = 1 | X_0 = i) \\
&= P(Y = 1 \wedge X_1 = i - 1 | X_0 = i) \\
&\quad + P(Y = 1 \wedge X_1 = i + 1 | X_0 = i) \\
&= P(Y = 1 | X_1 = i - 1, X_0 = i) P(X_1 = i - 1 | X_0 = i) \\
&\quad + P(Y = 1 | X_1 = i + 1, X_0 = i) P(X_1 = i + 1 | X_0 = i) \\
&= q p_{i-1} + p p_{i+1}
\end{aligned}
$$

and boundary conditions $p_a = 1$, $p_b = 0$. This linear recurrence is easily solved, for example by noting that $p(p_{i+1} - p_i) = q(p_i - p_{i-1})$, to give

$$
p_0 = \begin{cases}
\dfrac{\rho^b - 1}{\rho^b - \rho^a} & \text{if } p \neq q \\[3mm]
\dfrac{b}{b - a} & \text{if } p = q = \tfrac{1}{2}
\end{cases}
$$

where $\rho = q/p$.

A more interesting problem is the *time to absorption*, T say, i.e. the length of the gambling game. Let this discrete random variable have conditional mass function m defined by

$$
m_{ij} = P(T = j | X_0 = i)
$$

Then, for $j > 0$ and $a < i < b$, we obtain the similar recurrence relation

$$
m_{ij} = q m_{i-1, j-1} + p m_{i+1, j-1}
$$

with boundary conditions

$$m_{aj} = m_{bj} = \delta_{j0}$$

where the function δ is the Kronecker delta, defined, for integers i, j, by $\delta_{ij} = 1$ if $i = j$, 0 if $i \neq j$. This two-dimensional difference equation can be solved using generating functions as described in Section 3.2. For example, we could first define

$$G_i(z) = \sum_{j=0}^{\infty} m_{ij} z^j$$

to obtain $G_i(z) = qzG_{i-1}(z) + pzG_{i+1}(z)$ for $a < i < b$, with $G_a(z) = G_b(z) = 1$. The new recurrence is simple to solve and left as an exercise.

We conclude this section by looking at the time to absorption in a more general random walk in which the step sizes are independent, identically distributed (i.i.d.) random variables. We first show that this time is finite with probability 1. This result is crucial since if it were not the case in our gambling example, a draw would be possible in the sense of a non-terminating game. We then derive a famous result relating the expectations of the time to absorption and state of the walk at that time – Wald's identity. The remainder of this section is a little more technical in nature and will not be required elsewhere in the book. It can therefore be omitted on first reading.

Let the random walk $\{X_n | n = 0, 1, \ldots\}$, with absorbing barriers at $a < 0$, $b > 0$, be defined by $X_0 = 0$, $X_n = S_1 + \ldots + S_n$ for $n \geq 1$ where the steps S_i are i.i.d. as the random variable S. Let $E[S] = \mu$, $\text{Var}[S] = \sigma^2$ and $P(S \neq 0) = 1$. The time to absorption is the random variable $T = \min_{X_n \notin (a,b)} (n)$.

Proposition 4.1

T is finite with probability 1.

Proof Assume the proposition is false. Then $P(X_n \in (a, b)$ for all $n) = 1$ and so, by the Central Limit Theorem, X_n approaches a normal distribution. However, the normal distribution is positive over the whole of the real line and so $P(X_n > b) > 0$ for sufficiently large n.   ∎

Proposition 4.2 (Wald's identity)

Let the moment generating function of S be $\phi(t) = E[e^{tS}]$. Then $E[\phi(t)^{-T} e^{tX_T}] = 1$ when $\phi(t) \geq 1$.

Proof Let $\Pi_n(t) = E[e^{tX_n} I_{T>n}]$ where I denotes the indicator function defined in Section 3.1. Then, by the corollary to Proposition 3.3, we have

$$\Pi_n(t) = E[I_{T>n}E[e^{tX_n}|I_{T>n}]]$$
$$= P(T > n)E[e^{tX_n}|I_{T>n} = 1]$$
$$= P(T > n)E[e^{tX_n}|T > n]$$

and

$$\Pi_0(t) = E[e^{tX_0}I_{T>0}] = 1$$

However, we may write $\phi(t) = E[e^{tS_{n+1}}|T > n]$ since S_{n+1} is independent of X_n and we have $I_{T>n} = I_{T=n+1} + I_{T>n+1}$. Thus we have, by independence,

$$\phi(t)\Pi_n(t) = P(T > n)E[e^{tX_n}e^{tS_{n+1}}|T > n]$$
$$= P(T > n)E[e^{tX_{n+1}}|T > n]$$
$$= E[e^{tX_{n+1}}I_{T>n}]$$
$$= E[e^{tX_{n+1}}I_{T=n+1}] + \Pi_{n+1}(t)$$

Multiplying by s^{n+1} and summing over $n \in [0, \infty)$ then yields, noting that $I_{T=n} \neq 0$ only for $n = T$,

$$s\phi(t)\Pi(t, s) = E[s^T e^{tX_T}] + \Pi(t, s) - \Pi_0(t)$$

where $\Pi(t, s) = \sum_{n=0}^{\infty} s^n \Pi_n(t)$. Thus we have, since $\Pi_0(t) = 1$,

$$E[s^T e^{tX_T}] = 1 - [1 - s\phi(t)]\Pi(t, s)$$

The result now follows by choosing t real such that $\phi(t) \geq 1$ and setting $s = [\phi(t)]^{-1} \leq 1$. ∎

One application of Wald's identity is obtained by differentiating it as follows; others are given in the exercises. Differentiation with respect to t yields

$$E[-T\phi(t)^{-T-1}\phi'(t)e^{tX_T} + X_T\phi(t)^{-T}e^{tX_T}] = 0$$

so that $E[-T\mu + X_T] = 0$, i.e. $E[X_T] = \mu E[T]$. This is entirely as expected!

There are numerous variations on the random walk problem. For example, instead of absorbing barriers we may have *reflecting barriers*; when the particle hits a reflecting barrier, it returns to its previous position, i.e. is 'reflected'. More generally, an *elastic barrier*, at the origin say, is defined as follows. Suppose the particle is at point 1 at time n. Then at time $n + 1$ it will

- go to point 2 with probability p;
- stay at point 1 with probability δq (i.e. be reflected);
- go to point 0 and be absorbed with probability $(1 - \delta)q$.

The constant δ may be regarded as a coefficient of elasticity: when $\delta = 0$ we have an absorbing barrier and when $\delta = 1$ we have a reflecting barrier. The method of solution is exactly the same – only the boundary conditions change. However, this results in solutions with widely differing properties.

Random walks in two and more dimensions involve correspondingly multidimensional state spaces and the complexity of the problem increases rapidly. The reader is referred to Cohen and Boxma (1983) for a thorough analysis. An important application of random walks is the modelling of *diffusion processes* and *Brownian motion*. This application is introduced in Feller (1968) and the models are the subject of Harrison (1985).

4.2 Markov chains

A **Markov chain** is a discrete time stochastic process

$$\{X_n \in S \mid n = 0, 1, 2, \ldots\}$$

with countable sample space S that has the Markov property. In other words, it is a Markov process for which both the parameter and sample spaces are countable. Often, the sample space will be *finite*. The **n-step transition probabilities** of a time homogeneous Markov chain with state space S are defined by

$$P_{ij}^{(n)} = P(X_{m+n} = j \mid X_m = i) \qquad (i, j \in S)$$

which is independent of m by definition of time homogeneity. We consider only time homogeneous Markov chains. The one-step transition probabilities are normally written p_{ij}, i.e.

$$p_{ij} \equiv p_{ij}^{(1)}$$

For example, consider the random walk with absorbing barriers at points a and b, which we observed was a Markov process in the previous section. This has one-step transition probabilities

$$p_{i,i+1} = p, \qquad p_{i,i-1} = q \qquad (a < i < b)$$

$$p_{aa} = p_{bb} = 1$$

$$p_{ij} = 0 \qquad \text{in all other cases}$$

A Markov chain is characterized entirely by its one-step transition probabilities as we will see in the following series of propositions. First, the joint distribution of the states of the chain at successive times is given by the following.

Proposition 4.3

For $i_0, i_1, \ldots, i_n \in S$, $P(X_0 = i_0, X_1 = i_1, \ldots, X_n = i_n)$
$= P(X_0 = i_0)p_{i_0 i_1} \cdots p_{i_{n-1} i_n}$.

Proof   By successively applying the result that

$$P(X_0 = i_0, \ldots, X_m = i_m)$$
$$= P(X_0 = i_0, \ldots, X_{m-1} = i_{m-1})$$
$$\times P(X_m = i_m | X_{m-1} = i_{m-1}, \ldots, X_0 = i_0)$$

for $m = 1, \ldots, n$, we obtain

$$P(X_0 = i_0, X_1 = i_1, \ldots, X_n = i_n)$$
$$= P(X_0 = i_0)P(X_1 = i_1 | X_0 = i_0) \cdots$$
$$\times P(X_n = i_n | X_{n-1} = i_{n-1}, \ldots, X_0 = i_0)$$

Thus by the Markov property,

$$P(X_0 = i_0, X_1 = i_1, \ldots, X_n = i_n)$$
$$= P(X_0 = i_0)P(X_1 = i_1 | X_0 = i_0)$$
$$\cdots P(X_n = i_n | X_{n-1} = i_{n-1})$$

and the result follows by time homogeneity.   ∎

A consequence of this proposition is that time homogeneity implies stationarity.

Equations are often simplified if we write transition probabilities in matrix form. Hence we define the **transition matrix** of the Markov chain by $P = [p_{ij} | i, j \in S]$, and the **$n$-step transition matrix** by $P^{(n)} = [p_{ij}^{(n)} | i, j \in S]$ ($n \geq 1$). For $n = 0$, we define $P^{(0)} = I$, the identity matrix. Since, for given $i \in S$ and $n \geq 1$, $\{p_{ij}^{(n)} | j \in S\}$ is a complete set of probabilities, $p_{ij}^{(n)} \geq 0$ for each $j \in S$ and $\sum_{j \in S} p_{ij}^{(n)} = 1$. (The same applies for $n = 0$ trivially.) A square matrix of non-negative real values in which every row sums to one is called a **stochastic matrix**. Thus each $P^{(n)}$ is a stochastic matrix. Stochastic matrices have the following property:

Proposition 4.4

If $P_1, \ldots, P_n$ are stochastic matrices of the same size ($n \geq 1$), so is their product $P_1 \ldots P_n$.

Proof The proof is by induction and since it is trivial for $n = 1$, we need only prove that AB is stochastic if $A = [a_{ij}]$ and $B = [b_{ij}]$ are both stochastic matrices. Now, $AB = [\sum_{k \in S} a_{ik} b_{kj}]$ and for all $i, j \in S$ we have

$$\sum_{k \in S} a_{ik} b_{kj} \geq 0 \qquad \text{since every summand is non-negative}$$

and

$$\sum_{j \in S} \sum_{k \in S} a_{ik} b_{kj} = \sum_{k \in S} a_{ik} \left\{ \sum_{j \in S} b_{kj} \right\}$$

$$= \sum_{k \in S} a_{ik} \qquad \text{since } B \text{ is stochastic}$$

$$= 1 \qquad \text{since } A \text{ is stochastic} \qquad \blacksquare$$

It therefore follows that every n-step transition matrix of a Markov chain is stochastic.

The next result shows how a multi-step transition matrix can be constructed and is fundamental to the theory of Markov and semi-Markov processes.

Proposition 4.5 (The Chapman–Kolmogorov equation)
For $m, n \geq 0$, $P^{(m+n)} = P^{(m)} P^{(n)}$, i.e. $p_{ij}^{(m+n)} = \sum_{k \in S} p_{ik}^{(m)} p_{kj}^{(n)}$ for all $i, j \in S$.

Proof The result is trivial when either $m = 0$ or $n = 0$. Otherwise, for $m, n > 0$,

$$p_{ij}^{(m+n)} = \sum_{k \in S} P(X_{m+n} = j, X_m = k | X_0 = i)$$

$$= \sum_{k \in S} P(X_{m+n} = j | X_m = k, X_0 = i) P(X_m = k | X_0 = i)$$

$$= \sum_{k \in S} P(X_{m+n} = j | X_m = k) P(X_m = k | X_0 = i) \qquad \text{by the Markov property}$$

$$= \sum_{k \in S} p_{kj}^{(n)} p_{ik}^{(m)} \qquad \text{by time homogeneity}$$

4.2.1 Direct solution for the state probabilities

An immediate consequence of Proposition 4.5 is that $P^{(n)} = P^n$ for all $n \geq 0$. At first sight, the Chapman–Kolmogorov equation gives us all we need to 'solve' a Markov chain, since it allows the probability distribution of the state to be determined at any time, conditional on that existing initially. We will see a simple example of this type of analysis next, but note that the computational complexity of determining the state space probabilities at times far in the future is likely to be prohibitive. This is because we must calculate P^n for large n and possibly a large matrix P. We will therefore turn to an asymptotic analysis later in this section, i.e. we will investigate properties of P^n as $n \to \infty$.

Example 4.1

The evolution of a binary system in discrete time can often be modelled by a two-state Markov chain. Consider, for example, a simple semaphore S in a concurrent computer control system. If it is free, the semaphore may be 'acquired' by a process on a clock pulse by means of a P-operation, whereupon it becomes held by the acquiring process. The semaphore may be released by a process holding it by means of a V-operation. Suppose that

(a)   If the semaphore is free on one clock pulse, it will be requested by a process before the next pulse with probability α and allocated to that process. Otherwise it will remain free. If more than one process requests it, all but one of them fail and abort.

(b)   If on one clock pulse the semaphore is held, it will be released at the next pulse with probability β and become free. Otherwise it will remain held. Any requests arriving between the pulses are lost. (Of course it would be more efficient to keep one request until the next pulse so that the semaphore can be allocated then in the event that the holding process releases it. This variation is easy to incorporate: the probability that the semaphore becomes free at the next pulse becomes $\beta(1 - \alpha)$.)

Clearly this defines a Markov chain. Let the state space $S = \{0, 1\}$ where 0 denotes that the semaphore is free and 1 denotes that it is held. The one-step state transition probability matrix P is then

$$P = \begin{bmatrix} 1 - \alpha & \alpha \\ \beta & 1 - \beta \end{bmatrix}$$

The same Markov chain can be used to model many other situations. For example, suppose that the weather tomorrow depends only on the weather today. In particular, suppose that it will rain tomorrow with probability α if it is not raining today and with probability $1 - \beta$ if it is. If the state 0 denotes 'not raining' and 1 denotes 'raining', the transition matrix is again P.

Let us now compute the matrix P^n for arbitrary integer n. To do this, we diagonalize the matrix P by finding a matrix M such that $P = M\Lambda M^{-1}$ where the matrix Λ has the eigenvalues of P on its diagonal and zeroes everywhere else. Standard techniques of linear algebra allow this to be done systematically, but here we just note that, except in the case $\alpha = \beta = 0$ (which we consider separately):

$$M = \begin{bmatrix} 1 & -\alpha \\ 1 & \beta \end{bmatrix}, \quad M^{-1} = \frac{1}{\alpha + \beta}\begin{bmatrix} \beta & \alpha \\ -1 & 1 \end{bmatrix} \quad \text{and} \quad \Lambda = \begin{bmatrix} 1 & 0 \\ 0 & \omega \end{bmatrix}$$

$$\text{where } \omega = 1 - \alpha - \beta$$

Thus,

$$P^n = M\Lambda^n M^{-1} = M\begin{bmatrix} 1 & 0 \\ 0 & \omega^n \end{bmatrix}M^{-1}$$

$$= \frac{1}{\alpha + \beta}\begin{bmatrix} \beta + \alpha\omega^n & \alpha(1 - \omega^n) \\ \beta(1 - \omega^n) & \alpha + \beta\omega^n \end{bmatrix}$$

$$= \frac{1}{\alpha + \beta}\begin{bmatrix} \beta & \alpha \\ \beta & \alpha \end{bmatrix} + \frac{\omega^n}{\alpha + \beta}\begin{bmatrix} \alpha & -\alpha \\ -\beta & \beta \end{bmatrix}$$

This is a sum of a constant matrix and one which decays to the null matrix exponentially fast, except in the case $\alpha = \beta = 1$ (i.e. $\omega = -1$ which is considered in the next paragraph). Thus,

$$\pi_0 \triangleq \lim_{n\to\infty} P(X_n = 0|X_0 = 0) = \lim_{n\to\infty} P(X_n = 0|X_0 = 1) = \frac{\beta}{\alpha + \beta}$$

$$\pi_1 \triangleq \lim_{n\to\infty} P(X_n = 1|X_0 = 0) = \lim_{n\to\infty} P(X_n = 1|X_0 = 1) = \frac{\alpha}{\alpha + \beta}$$

are the limiting probabilities that the Markov chain is in states 0, 1 respectively. Notice that these probabilities are *independent* of the initial state.

When $\alpha = \beta = 0$, the matrix M has no inverse and the method does not work. However, the transition matrix is the identity and so the process just remains in state X_0 forever: there is no steady state independent of the initial state. Finally, if $\alpha = \beta = 1$, the second contribution to P^n does not converge. In fact, the chain is *periodic*. $X_{2n} = X_0$ and $X_{2n+1} = 1 - X_0$ for $n = 0, 1, \ldots$; we will be considering periodicity very shortly.

The methodology of Example 4.1 can be applied to an arbitrary Markov chain with finite state space to find the asymptotic state probabilities. Moreover, it motivates the classification of states that we give in the next section. It consists of the following steps (for a sample space of size $s + 1$):

(1)   Find the eigenvalues $1, \lambda_1, \ldots, \lambda_s$ of the one-step transition matrix P. It is easy to check that 1 is always an eigenvalue of P and that

$|\lambda_i| \leqslant 1$ for $1 \leqslant i \leqslant s$; see Exercise 4.8. Now define the diagonal matrix $\Lambda = \mathrm{diag}(1, \lambda_1, \ldots, \lambda_s)$, i.e. the matrix $[\Lambda_{ij}]$ with $\Lambda_{00} = 1$, $\Lambda_{ii} = \lambda_i$ $(1 \leqslant i \leqslant s)$, $\Lambda_{ij} = 0$ $(i \neq j)$.

(2)   If $|\lambda_i| < 1$ for $1 \leqslant i \leqslant s$, $\Lambda^n \to \mathrm{diag}(1, 0, \ldots, 0)$ as $n \to \infty$. Thus,

$$P^n \to R \, \mathrm{diag}(1, 0, \ldots, 0) R^{-1} = [p_{ij}^\infty]$$

say, where R is the matrix $[r_{ij} | 0 \leqslant i, j \leqslant s]$ such that $P = R\Lambda R^{-1}$ which we know how to find by standard linear algebra. Its jth column is the jth eigenvector of P, i.e. the eigenvector of the eigenvalue equal to $\Lambda_{jj}(0 \leqslant j \leqslant s)$. Its first column is therefore $(1, \ldots, 1)$, and we have

$$P^n \to \begin{bmatrix} 1 \\ \vdots \\ 1 \end{bmatrix} \pi$$

where the row vector π is the first row of R^{-1}. We do not need actually to compute R since π is the *left eigenvector* of the eigenvalue 1. This follows from the fact that $P^{n+1} = P^n P$ for all $n \geqslant 0$ and taking the limit $n \to \infty$. This gives

$$\begin{bmatrix} 1 \\ \vdots \\ 1 \end{bmatrix} \pi = \begin{bmatrix} 1 \\ \vdots \\ 1 \end{bmatrix} \pi P$$

i.e.

$$\pi = \pi P$$

(3)   If some eigenvalues have modulus 1 but are not equal to 1, i.e. $\lambda_j = e^{i\theta}$ for some j $(1 \leqslant j \leqslant s)$ and $0 < \theta < 2\pi$, P^n will not converge and the Markov chain has no 'steady state'. In fact θ must be rational and so the chain is *periodic*, returning to the same state at regular intervals e.g. at alternate times as in the above example.

(4)   If P is a block matrix, it will be impossible for some states to be entered after some others. The simplest case is $P = I$, as in the above example, where the chain remains in the same state forever. In every case, there is no asymptotic solution independent of the initial state.

4.2.2 Classification of states of a Markov chain

The states of a Markov chain are first classified according to whether one state can be entered at some time in the future after the chain is in another state; i.e. in terms of the *accessibility* of one state from another.

We say that state i **leads to** state j, written $i \rightarrow j$, if for some integer $n \geq 0$, $p_{ij}^{(n)} > 0$; a state always leads to itself, taking $n = 0$. States i and j **communicate**, written $i \leftrightarrow j$, if $i \rightarrow j$ and $j \rightarrow i$, i.e. there exist integers m, $n \geq 0$ such that $p_{ij}^{(m)} > 0$ and $p_{ji}^{(n)} > 0$. It is easy to show that $\leftrightarrow$ is an *equivalence relation*. First it is reflexive since $p_{ii}^{(0)} = 1$. Secondly, $i \leftrightarrow j \Leftrightarrow j \leftrightarrow i$ by definition and so $\leftrightarrow$ is symmetric. Thirdly, suppose that $p_{ij}^{(m)} > 0$ and $p_{jk}^{(n)} > 0$ for some non-negative integers m, n. Then $p_{ik}^{(m+n)} = \sum_{h \in S} p_{ih}^{(m)} p_{hk}^{(n)} \geq p_{ij}^{(m)} p_{jk}^{(n)} > 0$ by hypothesis. Thus $i \rightarrow k$. Similarly, if $j \rightarrow i$ and $k \rightarrow j$ then $k \rightarrow i$. Thus $\leftrightarrow$ is transitive. The equivalence classes of $\leftrightarrow$ over the state space S are called the **irreducible classes** of states of the Markov chain. We denote the equivalence class of state $s \in S$ by $[s]$. Given an irreducible class C,

- if $i \in C$ and $i \leftrightarrow j$ then $j \in C$
- if $i \in C$ and it is *not* the case that $i \leftrightarrow j$, then $j \notin C$

In other words, if a state is removed from an irreducible class, the class is no longer irreducible, i.e. the irreducible classes are minimal. Whilst it may be possible for the chain to leave one irreducible class C_1 to enter a state in another C_2, no return to C_1 is possible: otherwise the state entered in C_2 (and hence all states in C_2) would communicate with every state in C_1.

Definition 4.1
A Markov chain with a state space which is an irreducible class (the only one) is called **irreducible**.

Example 4.2

The unrestricted random walk is an irreducible Markov chain since every state leads to every state. However, the random walk with absorbing barriers is not irreducible. If the barriers are at points a and b, $\{a + 1, a + 2, \ldots, b - 1\}$, $\{a\}$, $\{b\}$ are the irreducible classes.

The two-state Markov chain considered in Example 4.1 is irreducible unless $\alpha = \beta = 0$ whereupon the irreducible classes are $\{0\}$ and $\{1\}$. As we observed, in this case the chain remains in its initial irreducible class (i.e. a single state) forever and there was no asymptotic behaviour. However, suppose now that $\alpha = 0$, $\beta > 0$. Again we have the two irreducible classes $\{0\}$ and $\{1\}$ but transitions are possible from the second to the first, but not vice versa. The class $\{1\}$ is *transient*, as we define formally below.

We say that a property P defined on states is a **class property** if $P(i) \Rightarrow P(j)$ for all $j \in [i]$ ($i \in S$). In other words, either every state in a class satisfies P or none of them do. A state i is said to be **essential** if $i \to j \Rightarrow i \leftrightarrow j$, i.e. if it communicates with every state it leads to. A state which is not essential is called **inessential**.

Proposition 4.6

Essentiality is a class property, i.e. an essential state cannot lead to an inessential one.

Proof Let i be essential, $i \to j$ and $j \to k$. Then $i \to k$, by transitivity of $\to$, so that $k \to i$ since i is essential. Thus $k \to j$ by transitivity and hence $j \leftrightarrow k$. ∎

The **period** d_i of state i is the highest common factor of all positive integers n such that $p_{ii}^{(n)} > 0$. A state i is **periodic** with period d_i if

(1) $p_{ii}^{(n)} = 0$ if $n \neq md_i$ for any positive integer m;

(2) $p_{ii}^{(md_i)} \geq 0$ for $m = 1, 2, \ldots$ and $p_{ii}^{(md_i)} = 0$ for only finitely many m (i.e. $p_{ii}^{(md_i)} > 0$ for all sufficiently large m).

If $d_i = 1$, we say that i is **aperiodic**, which is the same as periodic with period 1.

Example 4.3 ───────────────────────────────

The period of every state of the unrestricted random walk is 2 since the particle can only return to any state in an even number of steps. The same applies to the non-absorbing states in the random walk with two absorbing barriers. However, in the random walk with *reflecting* barriers, all states are aperiodic. Why? What about the case of *elastic* barriers?

The **first return time** random variable T_{ii} is the time at which the Markov chain first returns to state i if $X_0 = i$. (By time homogeneity T_{ii} is also the elapsed time between any two successive entries into state i. We take the first at time 0 without loss of generality.) If $X_1 = i$, i.e. the chain remains in state i for unit time, $T_{ii} = 1$.

We can now further classify the states of a Markov chain.

Definition 4.2

A state i is **transient** if $P(T_{ii} < \infty) < 1$. A state i is **recurrent** (or **persistent**) if $P(T_{ii} < \infty) = 1$. A recurrent state i is **null-recurrent** if $E[T_{ii}] = \infty$ and **positive-recurrent** (or **non-null-recurrent**) if $E[T_{ii}] < \infty$.

Thus a state is transient if there is non-zero probability that there is *never* a return to it. A state is null-recurrent if it is not transient but the expected return time is infinite. A positive-recurrent state recurs infinitely often with finite expected recurrence times. These are class properties, as we show in Proposition 4.8 below. First, however, we need some preliminary results which are of interest in their own right.

Let the random variable T_{ij} denote the time for the chain to first enter state j when $X_0 = i$. T_{ij} is called the **first passage time** from i to j. By time homogeneity, it is also the random variable for the time elapsed between the chain entering state i at any time to the time it next enters j. Notice that if $i = j$, we get the return time T_{ii}. We define the generating functions F_{ij} and G_{ij} by

$$F_{ij}(z) = \sum_{n=1}^{\infty} f_{ij}^{(n)} z^n$$

where $f_{ij}^{(n)} = P(T_{ij} = n)$, and

$$G_{ij}(z) = \sum_{n=0}^{\infty} p_{ij}^{(n)} z^n$$

We then obtain the *renewal equation* (cf. Section 4.5) given in the following proposition.

Proposition 4.7

$$G_{ij}(z) - \delta_{ij} = F_{ij}(z) G_{jj}(z)$$

where δ is the Kronecker delta defined by $\delta_{ii} = 1$ and $\delta_{ij} = 0$ if $i \neq j$.

Proof By the law of total probability, for $n \geq 1$

$$p_{ij}^{(n)} = \sum_{k=1}^{n} P(X_n = j \mid X_0 = i, X_k = j \text{ for the 1st time})$$

$$\times P(X_k = j \text{ for the 1st time} \mid X_0 = i)$$

$$= \sum_{k=1}^{n} P(X_n = j \mid X_k = j) P(X_k = j \text{ for the 1st time} \mid X_0 = i)$$

by the Markov property

$$= \sum_{k=1}^{n} f_{ij}^{(k)} p_{jj}^{(n-k)}$$

Since $p_{ij}^{(0)} = \delta_{ij}$, we have

$$G_{ij}(z) = \delta_{ij} + \sum_{n=1}^{\infty} \sum_{k=1}^{n} f_{ij}^{(k)} p_{jj}^{(n-k)} z^k z^{n-k}$$

The summation domain is $\{(n, k)|1 \leqslant k \leqslant n\}$. Thus the limits of summation can be rewritten to yield

$$G_{ij}(z) = \delta_{ij} + \sum_{k=1}^{\infty} f_{ij}^{(k)} z^k \sum_{n=k}^{\infty} p_{jj}^{(n-k)} z^{n-k}$$

$$G_{ij}(z) = \delta_{ij} + F_{ij}(z) G_{jj}(z) \qquad \blacksquare$$

The following important corollaries provide tests for transience and recurrence.

Corollary 1   A state i is transient iff $G_{ii}(1) = \sum_{n=0}^{\infty} p_{ii}^{(n)} < \infty$ and recurrent iff $\sum_{n=0}^{\infty} p_{ii}^{(n)} = \infty$. For a transient state i, $p_{ii}^{(n)} \to 0$ as $n \to \infty$.

Proof   A state i is transient iff $F_{ii}(1) = P(T_{ii} < \infty) < 1$. But, setting $i = j$ in the proposition,

$$F_{ii}(z) = 1 - \frac{1}{G_{ii}(z)}$$

and the result follows. The proof for recurrence is similar. Since $G_{ii}(1)$ is finite for transient state i, we must have $p_{ii}^{(n)} \to 0$ as $n \to \infty$ $\qquad \blacksquare$

Corollary 2   If $p_{jj}^{(n)} \to 0$ as $n \to \infty$ for state j, then $p_{ij}^{(n)} \to 0$ as $n \to \infty$ for all states $i \in S$.

Proof   As in the proof of the proposition,

$$p_{ij}^{(n)} = \sum_{k=1}^{n} f_{ij}^{(k)} p_{jj}^{(n-k)}$$

Now, for all $\varepsilon > 0$, we can choose an integer u such that $\sum_{k=u}^{n} f_{ij}^{(k)} < \varepsilon/2$ for all $n > u$ since $F_{ij}(1) < \infty$. Moreover, $\{p_{jj}^{(m)} | m \geqslant 0\}$ is bounded above by 1. Thus,

$$\sum_{k=u}^{n} f_{ij}^{(k)} p_{jj}^{(n-k)} < \varepsilon/2$$

Similarly, since $\{f_{ij}^{(k)} | k \geqslant 0\}$ is bounded above by 1 and $p_{jj}^{(n)} \to 0$ as $n \to \infty$, $\sum_{k=1}^{u-1} f_{ij}^{(k)} p_{jj}^{(n-k)} < \varepsilon/2$ for sufficiently large n, because the sum is finite. Therefore,

$$\sum_{k=1}^{n} f_{ij}^{(k)} p_{jj}^{(n-k)} < \varepsilon$$

for sufficiently large n.   ∎

An immediate consequence of Corollary 2 is that for a transient state i, $p_{ji}^{(n)} \to 0$ as $n \to \infty$ for all states $j \in S$.

We can now show that our classification of states is a class property.

Proposition 4.8

Periodicity, transience, null-recurrence and positive-recurrence are class properties.

Proof For each property, we show that if $i \leftrightarrow j$, then i has the property if and only if j has it. The proofs are trivial when $i = j$ and so we assume that $i \neq j$. By definition of $\to$, there exist positive integers m, n such that $p_{ji}^{(m)} > 0$ and $p_{ij}^{(n)} > 0$. We now consider each property separately.

(a) *Periodicity*

We must show that $d_i = d_j$ for $i \neq j$. Now, by definition of period, we can choose a positive integer k such that $p_{ii}^{(k'd_i)} > 0$ for all $k' \geq k$. Thus, by Proposition 4.5 and our choices of m and n,

$$p_{jj}^{(m+kd_i+n)} \geq p_{ji}^{(m)} p_{ii}^{(kd_i)} p_{ij}^{(n)} > 0$$

Similarly, since $p_{ii}^{((k+1)d_i)} > 0$, $p_{jj}^{(m+(k+1)d_i+n)} > 0$. Therefore, d_j divides both $m + kd_i + n$ and $m + (k + 1)d_i + n$, and hence their difference, d_i. Interchanging i and j in the argument, we obtain similarly that d_i divides d_j. Hence $d_i = d_j$ as required.

(b) *Transience*

For all non-negative integers k,

$$p_{jj}^{(m+k+n)} \geq p_{ji}^{(m)} p_{ii}^{(k)} p_{ij}^{(n)}$$

Thus,

$$\sum_{k=0}^{\infty} p_{jj}^{(k)} \geq p_{ji}^{(m)} p_{ij}^{(n)} \sum_{k=0}^{\infty} p_{ii}^{(k)}$$

Hence,

$$\sum_{k=0}^{\infty} p_{jj}^{(k)} < \infty \Rightarrow \sum_{k=0}^{\infty} p_{ii}^{(k)} < \infty$$

Interchanging i and j in the proof (since $\leftrightarrow$ is symmetric) gives the reverse implication.

(c)   Recurrence

From the inequality obtained in (b), we deduce that

$$\sum_{k=0}^{\infty} p_{ii}^{(k)} = \infty \Rightarrow \sum_{k=0}^{\infty} p_{jj}^{(k)} = \infty$$

The reverse implication is obtained by interchanging i and j as before, and so recurrence is a class property. Now, we will see later in Proposition 4.10 that a necessary and sufficient condition for a recurrent state i to be null-recurrent is that $p_{ii}^{(k)} \rightarrow 0$ as $k \rightarrow \infty$. But we know that $p_{jj}^{(m+k+n)} \geqslant p_{ji}^{(m)} p_{ii}^{(k)} p_{ij}^{(n)}$ for all non-negative integers $k > 0$. Thus as $k \rightarrow \infty$, $p_{jj}^{(k)} \rightarrow 0 \Rightarrow p_{ii}^{(k)} \rightarrow 0$, and conversely by interchange of i and j. Thus j is null-recurrent if and only if i is null-recurrent, and similarly for positive recurrence. ∎

The following corollary is immediate.

Corollary In any Markov chain, the recurrent states can be divided uniquely into closed sets (the irreducible classes) such that any state in any one of them leads to all states in the same set and to no others. ∎

The closure of a recurrent state, together with its sub-matrix of transition probabilities, therefore defines an independent Markov chain. Analyses of recurrent states in a Markov chain can therefore assume, without loss of generality, that the chain is irreducible.

The preceding results are extremely important for determining not only the recurrence properties of a state but also when there exist asymptotic probabilities for the states in an irreducible class. These issues will be developed further in the next section. In practical applications of Markov chains to modelling systems, a major part of the effort may be devoted to identifying the irreducible classes and their properties. Proposition 4.8 is important since the properties need only be established for any *one* state in each class, whereupon it will hold for the whole class. For Markov chains with *finite state space* the problem is much simpler since we have:

Proposition 4.9

In a Markov chain with finite state space, at least one state is positive-recurrent and all recurrent states are positive-recurrent.

Proof Suppose all states are transient. Then, for all $i, j \in S$, $p_{ij}^{(n)} \rightarrow 0$ as $n \rightarrow \infty$ since $G_{jj}(1) < \infty$. Thus, since S is finite,

$$\sum_{j \in S} p_{ij}^{(n)} \to 0 \qquad \text{as } n \to \infty$$

which is a contradiction since the sum must be 1 for all n. There must therefore be at least one recurrent state. The same argument shows that not all states can be null-recurrent by Corollary 2 to Proposition 4.7. Therefore at least one state must be positive-recurrent. By the corollary to Proposition 4.8, we may assume without loss of generality that the chain is irreducible and hence that all states must be positive-recurrent.   ∎

Example 4.4

Consider again the unrestricted random walk in one dimension. All the cases with barriers are less interesting here since they have finite state spaces with all states positive-recurrent. In the symmetric case $(p = q = \frac{1}{2})$, we have $G_{ii}(z) = \sum_{n=0}^{\infty} p_{ii}^{(n)} z^n = \sum_{n=0}^{\infty} p_{ii}^{(2n)} z^{2n}$ since all states have period 2. Since, for all states i, $p_{ii}^{(2n)} = \binom{2n}{n} p^n q^n = \binom{2n}{n}(1/2^{2n})$, we see, by inspecting the binomial expansion of $(1 - z^2)^{-1/2}$, that

$$G_{ii}(z) = \frac{1}{(1 - z^2)^{1/2}}$$

Thus, since $G_{ii}(1) = \infty$, the Markov chain is recurrent. Furthermore,

$$F_{ii}(z) = 1 - (1 - z^2)^{1/2}$$

so that

$$F_{ii}'(1) = \lim_{z \to 1} \frac{z}{(1 - z^2)^{1/2}} = \infty$$

Hence the chain is null-recurrent. This conclusion also comes from the fact that $p_{ii}^{(n)} \to 0$ as $n \to \infty$; Stirling's formula yields $p_{ii}^{(2n)} \sim 1/(\pi n)^{1/2}$ at large n.

Example 4.5

Now let us see what happens with random walks in more than one dimension. Suppose first that we have two independent, symmetric random walks: one to give the x-coordinate and one for the y-coordinate. Considering point $(0, 0)$ – there is no need to consider any others since this chain is also irreducible – we have

$$p_{(0,0)(0,0)}^{(2n)} = \left[\binom{2n}{n} \frac{1}{2^{2n}} \right]^2$$

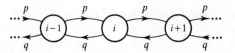

Figure 4.1   One-dimensional random walk.

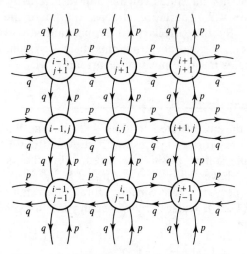

Figure 4.2   Two-dimensional random walk.

since each walk must return to state 0 at the same time, $2n$, and because they are independent. Thus,

$$p_{(0,0)(0,0)}^{(2n)} \sim \frac{1}{\pi n}$$

so that $G_{(0,0)(0,0)}(1) = \infty$ and $p_{(0,0)(0,0)}^{(2n)} \to 0$ as $n \to \infty$. The chain is therefore null-recurrent.

In three dimensions, proceeding in the same way yields

$$p_{(0,0,0)(0,0,0)}^{(2n)} \sim \left(\frac{1}{\pi n} \right)^{3/2}$$

Thus, $G_{(0,0,0)(0,0,0)}(1) < \infty$ and the chain is transient.

It is often helpful to visualize a Markov chain as a **state transition graph** (or diagram). The nodes represent states and the directed arcs between nodes represent the one-step transitions between states. Each node is labelled with the state it represents and an arc from node i to node j is labelled with p_{ij}. Thus, for the unrestricted random walk in one dimension, we would draw Figure 4.1, while for the two-dimensional case, this would be drawn as in Figure 4.2. Such diagrams are generally easy to draw since they provide a good abstraction of a physical system under investigation. Moreover, it is easy to read off the one-step transition probabilities to form the matrix P. We will also see that the equations for the limiting state probabilities are also easy to write down. This all applies equally to continuous time Markov processes for which the arcs are labelled slightly differently with instantaneous transition rates, as we will see in the next section. Perhaps most important of all, we can discover useful properties of a Markov process from its state transition graph; for example *reversibility*, discussed in Section 4.4.

Example 4.6

Consider the following model of a neuron. Discrete electrical signals arrive at the neuron and are accumulated in it as a 'charge'. At any level of charge, the neuron may 'fire', whereupon a signal is emitted and the accumulated charge is reduced to zero. We assume that charges are of constant size, so that the state space of the neuron is $\{0, 1, \ldots\}$ where state i represents i units of charge accumulated. At discrete times $t \in \{0, 1, \ldots\}$, in state i, either a new charge arrives with constant probability p_i or the neuron fires with probability $q_i = 1 - p_i$. Clearly this defines an irreducible Markov chain with infinite state space; any state can be reached from state 0, and state 0 can be reached from any state. The question is, under what conditions is the chain positive-recurrent?

This is a generic model which is relevant in several other practical situations, for example:

- In horse racing, the accumulated charge might be the accumulator.

- In games where a 'fault' causes a competitor to restart, the accumulator represents the current 'gain'.

- In tree-searching, the accumulator represents the current state and a return to state 0 represents a failed branch. In practice, we would probably not always want to go all the way back to the root of the tree but to a 'more recent' choice-node. This type of Markov chain can be used to model 'backtracking'.

The state transition diagram is shown in Figure 4.3. This gives rise to an infinite state transition matrix

$$
P = \begin{bmatrix}
q_0 & p_0 & 0 & 0 & 0 & \cdots \\
q_1 & 0 & p_1 & 0 & 0 & \cdots \\
q_2 & 0 & 0 & p_2 & 0 & \cdots \\
\vdots & \vdots & \vdots & \vdots & \vdots & \ddots
\end{bmatrix}
$$

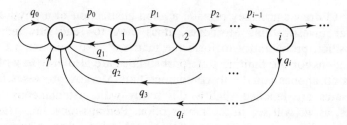

Figure 4.3

The chain is irreducible since for all states i, j, $p_{ij}^{(j+1)} = q_i p_0 \cdots p_{j-1} > 0$. Thus i can lead to j by first entering state 0 at the first step. For periodicity, we need only consider one state since period is a class property. Choosing state 0, $p_{00}^{(1)} = q_0 > 0$. Thus state 0, and hence the whole chain, is aperiodic. For recurrence,

$$P(T_{00} > n) = P(\text{first } n \text{ transitions are all to the right}) = \prod_{i=0}^{n-1} p_i$$

Thus state 0, and hence the chain, is recurrent iff $1 - \prod_{i=0}^{n-1} p_i \to 1$, i.e. $\prod_{i=0}^{n-1} p_i \to 0$ as $n \to \infty$. The chain is positive-recurrent iff $E[T_{00}] < \infty$. But,

$$E[T_{00}] = \sum_{n=1}^{\infty} n[P(T_{00} > n - 1) - P(T_{00} > n)]$$

Thus, assuming that $nP(T_{00} > n) \to 0$ as $n \to \infty$, which must be true if T_{00} has finite expectation,[1]

$$E[T_{00}] = \sum_{n=0}^{\infty} P(T_{00} > n) = \sum_{n=0}^{\infty} \prod_{i=0}^{n-1} p_i$$

Thus, defining $x_n = \prod_{i=0}^{n-1} p_i$, the chain is positive-recurrent iff $\sum_{n=0}^{\infty} x_n$ is convergent; this implies that $x_n \to 0$ as $n \to \infty$, which was required for recurrence. This result has an interesting interpretation. For the chain to be transient, the probability of returning to state 0 must eventually vanish at higher states, i.e. $q_n \to 0$ as $n \to \infty$. However, this condition is not sufficient. A stronger condition is that there must be a positive probability of passing to successively higher states forever, i.e. $\lim_{n \to \infty}(x_n) > 0$ as $n \to \infty$. This condition *is* sufficient and implies that $p_n \to 1$ and hence $q_n \to 0$ as $n \to \infty$. If we keep decreasing the p_n, x_n eventually has limit 0 and the chain becomes recurrent. However, we need to decrease the p_n a bit more to reach *positive* recurrence. The above result shows that null-recurrence turns into positive-recurrence when the p_n become small enough for $\sum_{n=0}^{\infty} x_n$ to converge.

---

[1] Consider $\sum_{i=n}^{\infty} iP(T_{00} = i)$ for arbitrarily large n.

The above neuron model is, of course, naïve. The signals may arrive in batches, i.e. the charge size may not be fixed; signals may be positive or negative 'inhibitors' which cancel some of the positive charges accumulated; and at some times, no event may occur. Any of these extensions could be incorporated into our model, although a simple solution might then be impossible. Also, events would more likely occur asynchronously; this can be handled by a continuous time model – see Section 4.3. Neuron models have been used in 'brain models' where a large network of neurons is interconnected according to some given topology. The signals produced on firing are transmitted to other neurons, and there are other sources of signals. The neuron models define nodes in stochastic networks which have been used with some success to describe neural networks; compare the extension of single server queues to queueing networks later in this book.

4.2.3 Steady state solutions: ergodic theorems

We now investigate the long-term behaviour of a Markov chain, i.e. the asymptotic behaviour of $p_{ij}^{(n)}$ as $n \to \infty$. If, for each j, $p_{ij}^{(n)}$ has a limit which is independent of i and defines a probability mass function on j, the chain is said to have a **steady state** or a state of **equilibrium**. The probabilities $p_{ij}^{(\infty)} = P(X_\infty = j)$ are called the **stationary** probabilities of the Markov chain (in equilibrium). Some steady state properties have already been obtained in the previous section, for example for transient chains. These are now extended to all classes in one of the most important results in the theory of Markov chains: Kolmogorov's theorem. For state $i \in S$, we will use μ_i to denote $E[T_{ii}]$. Thus we have

$$
\mu_i = \begin{cases}
\infty & \text{if } i \text{ is transient} \\
\infty & \text{if } i \text{ is null-recurrent} \\
\displaystyle\sum_{n=1}^{\infty} n f_{ii}^{(n)} & \text{if } i \text{ is positive-recurrent}
\end{cases}
$$

Proposition 4.10 (Kolmogorov's theorem)

In an irreducible, aperiodic Markov chain with state space S, for all states $i, j \in S$,

(a) $p_{ij}^{(n)} \to \mu_j^{-1} \geq 0$ as $n \to \infty$

(b)   The chain is positive-recurrent, i.e. $\mu_j < \infty$ for all $j \in S$, if and only if there exists a *unique* stationary distribution π such that $\pi = \pi P$ with $\pi_j = \mu_j^{-1}$.

A Markov chain which is irreducible, aperiodic and positive-recurrent is called **ergodic**. For ergodic chains, the matrix equation $\pi = \pi P$ is sometimes called the **steady state equation** (or steady state equations). The condition that the chain be irreducible is necessary since if it did not hold, the initial state would determine to which irreducible classes the chain could pass. Of course, once a recurrent class was entered, it could be treated as an independent chain; cf. the corollary to Proposition 4.8. The restriction is therefore not too severe. A similar remark applies to periodic chains, to which a corresponding theorem applies.

Proof First, suppose the Markov chain is transient. Then, by Corollary 1 to Proposition 4.7, $p_{jj}^{(n)} \to 0$ as $n \to \infty$. Now, for $i \neq j$, $G_{ij}(1) = F_{ij}(1) G_{jj}(1) \leq G_{jj}(1) < \infty$ by Proposition 4.7, and since j is transient. (The same result was obtained with more generality in Corollary 2 of the same proposition.) Thus, $p_{ij}^{(n)} \to \mu_j^{-1}$ for all i, $j \in S$.

Now suppose the chain is recurrent, and define $A_n = \sum_{m=n+1}^{\infty} f_{jj}^{(m)}$. Then we have

$$\sum_{n=0}^{\infty} A_n = \sum_{n=0}^{\infty} \sum_{m=n+1}^{\infty} f_{jj}^{(m)} = \sum_{0 \leq n < m < \infty} f_{jj}^{(m)}$$

$$= \sum_{m=1}^{\infty} \sum_{n=0}^{m-1} f_{jj}^{(m)} = \sum_{m=1}^{\infty} m f_{jj}^{(m)} = \mu_j$$

which may be finite or infinite. Furthermore, $A_0 = 1$ and $A_{m-1} - A_m = f_{jj}^{(m)}$ for $m > 0$. Thus, by Proposition 4.7, and omitting the subscript jj for brevity, for $n > 0$,

$$A_0 p^{(n)} = p^{(n)} = \sum_{m=1}^{n} f^{(m)} p^{(n-m)}$$

$$= \sum_{m=1}^{n} A_{m-1} p^{(n-m)} - \sum_{m=1}^{n} A_m p^{(n-m)}$$

Rearranging this equation yields

$$\sum_{m=0}^{n} A_m p^{(n-m)} = \sum_{m=1}^{n} A_{m-1} p^{(n-m)} = \sum_{m=0}^{n-1} A_m p^{(n-1-m)}$$

(changing the domain of summation). Thus, $\sum_{m=0}^{n} A_m p^{(n-m)}$ is independent of n and so, since $A_0 p^{(0)} = 1$, we have

$$1 = \sum_{m=0}^{\infty} A_m p^{(n-m)}$$

for all n, where we define $p^{(k)} = 0$ for $k < 0$. Now, since the chain is aperiodic, $p_{jj}^{(n)}$ converges as $n \to \infty$; this is shown in Lemma 4.1 below. The above series is absolutely convergent, being a sum of positive terms, and so it is valid to take the limit, $n \to \infty$, term by term. This gives

$$1 = \mu_j p_{jj}^{(\infty)}$$

as required. Now,

$$p_{ij}^{(n)} - \mu_j^{-1} \sum_{m=1}^{\infty} f_{ij}^{(m)} = \sum_{m=1}^{\infty} (p_{jj}^{(n-m)} - \mu_j^{-1}) f_{ij}^{(m)}$$

But

$$\sum_{m=1}^{\infty} |(p_{jj}^{(n-m)} - \mu_j^{-1}) f_{ij}^{(m)}| \le |1 + \mu_j^{-1}| \sum_{m=1}^{\infty} f_{ij}^{(m)} \le 1 + \mu_j^{-1} < \infty$$

since $F_{ij}(1) = 1$ in a recurrent chain and so the series is absolutely convergent. Letting $n \to \infty$ term by term then yields

$$p_{ij}^{(n)} \to \mu_j^{-1} \sum_{m=1}^{\infty} f_{ij}^{(m)} = \mu_j^{-1}$$

This completes the proof of (a).

Now, setting $n = 1$ in the Chapman–Kolmogorov equation gives

$$p_{ij}^{(m+1)} \ge \sum_{k \in S'} p_{ik}^{(m)} p_{kj}$$

where S' is an arbitrary finite subset of S. Letting $m \to \infty$, and writing π_j for $p_{jj}^{(\infty)}$ $(= \mu_j^{-1})$, we obtain

$$\pi_j \ge \sum_{k \in S} \pi_k p_{kj}$$

Summing both sides over $j \in S$ gives $\sum_{j \in S} \pi_j$ on both sides. Hence strict inequality is impossible and so

$$\pi_j = \sum_{k \in S} \pi_k p_{kj}$$

i.e. π is a stationary solution such that $\pi = \pi P$ as required. To prove uniqueness, suppose that ϕ is another stationary solution.

Then, multiplying by $p_{ji}^{(n)}$ and summing over $j \in S$ gives, since $\phi = \phi P^n$ for all $n \geq 0$,

$$\phi_i = \sum_{k \in S} \phi_k \sum_{j \in S} p_{kj} p_{ji}^{(n)} = \sum_{k \in S} \phi_k p_{ki}^{(n+1)}$$

Again we have an absolutely convergent series and letting $n \to \infty$ yields, for all $i \in S$,

$$\phi_i = \sum_{k \in S} \phi_k \pi_i = \pi_i$$

since ϕ is a probability distribution by hypothesis.   ∎

The missing part of the proof is included in the following lemma for completeness. The proof is given only in outline and can be omitted on a first reading.

Lemma 4.1

In an irreducible, aperiodic Markov chain, using the notation of Proposition 4.10, $p_{jj}^{(n)}$ converges as $n \to \infty$ for all $j \in S$.

Proof The transient case was handled in the proposition and we give a sketch of the proof for the recurrent case based on Feller (1968). To simplify the notation, given state $j \in S$, let $u_n = p_{jj}^{(n)}$ and $v_n = f_{jj}^{(n)}$ ($n \geq 0$). Then we have

$$u_n = \sum_{m=1}^{n} v_m u_{n-m} \quad \text{and} \quad \sum_{m=0}^{n} A_m u_{n-m} = 1$$

where $A_n = \sum_{m=n+1}^{\infty} v_m$. Let $\lambda = \limsup u_n$ which is finite since $u_n \leq 1$. Then for all $\varepsilon > 0$ and sufficiently large n, $u_n < \lambda + \varepsilon$. Moreover, there exists some sequence of integers $n_1, n_2, \ldots$ such that $u_{n_i} \to \lambda$. Since $F_{jj}(1) = 1$, we can choose a k such that $v_k > 0$ and claim that $u_{n_i-k} \to \lambda$. To prove this, suppose the contrary. Then there exists an integer N such that for infinitely many $n > N$,

$$u_n > \lambda - \varepsilon, \quad u_{n-k} < \lambda' < \lambda \quad \text{and} \quad A_N < \varepsilon$$

Thus, since every $u_i \leq 1$,

$$u_n \leq \sum_{m=1}^{N} v_m u_{n-m} + \varepsilon$$

For large enough n, $u_i < \lambda + \varepsilon$ ($n - N \leq i \leq n - 1$) and $u_{n-k} < \lambda'$. Therefore,

$$u_n < (\lambda + \varepsilon) \sum_{m \neq k} v_m + v_k \lambda' + \varepsilon$$

$$\leq (\lambda + \varepsilon)(1 - v_k) + v_k \lambda' + \varepsilon$$

$$< \lambda + 2\varepsilon - v_k(\lambda - \lambda')$$

We can now choose ε so small that $v_k(\lambda - \lambda') > 3\varepsilon$ and so $u_n < \lambda - \varepsilon$, giving a contradiction. Thus, $u_{n_i - k} \to \lambda$ and repeating the argument shows that $u_{n_i - rk} \to \lambda$ for $r = 0, 1, 2, \ldots$. If $k = 1$, we therefore have $u_{n_i - u} \to \lambda$ for every non-negative integer u. But since the chain is aperiodic, there must be a finite set of *coprime* integers $k_1, \ldots, k_a$ so that any integer $u = \sum_{i=1}^{a} c_i k_i$ for integer coefficients c_i. Thus, we do have the property that $u_{n_i - u} \to \lambda$ for every u.

Now, for $n_i > N$,

$$\sum_{m=0}^{N} A_m u_{n_i - m} \leq 1$$

and since every $u_{n_i - m} \to \lambda$, we conclude that $\lambda \sum_{m=0}^{N} A_m \leq 1$ for N sufficiently large. Thus as $N \to \infty$, $\lambda \mu_j \leq 1$. A similar argument using $\gamma = \liminf u_n$ instead of $\limsup u_n$ shows that $\gamma \mu_j \geq 1$. But since $\gamma \leq \lambda$, we must have $\gamma = \lambda = \mu_j^{-1}$. ∎

Example 4.7

Consider again the neuron model of Example 4.6. We noted that it was irreducible and aperiodic and so we can now apply Kolmogorov's theorem. We attempt to find a solution to the equation

$$\pi = \pi \begin{bmatrix} q_0 & p_0 & 0 & 0 & 0 & \cdots \\ q_1 & 0 & p_1 & 0 & 0 & \cdots \\ q_2 & 0 & 0 & p_2 & 0 & \cdots \\ \vdots & \vdots & \vdots & \vdots & \vdots & \ddots \end{bmatrix}$$

where $q_i = 1 - p_i$. This gives the system of equations

$$\pi_0 = \pi_0 q_0 + \pi_1 q_1 + \ldots$$

and

$$\pi_i = \pi_{i-1} p_{i-1} \qquad \text{for } i \geq 1$$

A stationary solution to all but the first of these equations is $\pi_i = \alpha \prod_{k=0}^{i-1} p_k$ where $\alpha \ (= \pi_0)$ is defined by normalizing π. The first equation imposes the condition that

$$1 = \sum_{i=0}^{\infty}(1 - p_i)\prod_{k=0}^{i-1} p_k = 1 - \lim_{i \to \infty}\prod_{k=0}^{i} p_k$$

i.e. that $\prod_{k=0}^{i} p_k \to 0$ as $i \to \infty$. This is exactly the condition obtained for recurrence in Example 4.6. The normalizing condition is

$$\alpha = \left(\sum_{i=0}^{\infty}\prod_{k=0}^{i-1} p_k\right)^{-1}$$

If the denominator converges, we have a solution for π which is a probability distribution. By Kolmogorov's theorem, this is the *only* solution and the chain is positive-recurrent. If the denominator diverges, there is no non-zero solution for π. Observe that the condition we obtained for positive-recurrence is the same as that obtained directly in Example 4.6.

Example 4.8

A variation on the previous example has a less sparse one-step transition matrix:

$$P = \begin{bmatrix} q_0 & p_0 & 0 & 0 & 0 & \cdots \\ q_1 & p_1 & p_0 & 0 & 0 & \cdots \\ q_2 & p_2 & p_1 & p_0 & 0 & \cdots \\ \vdots & \vdots & \vdots & \vdots & \vdots & \ddots \end{bmatrix}$$

This Markov chain is of interest in branching processes, for example in a tree searching algorithm with backtracking to nodes at levels other than the root of the tree. The steady state equations are now

$$\pi_0 = \pi_0 q_0 + \pi_1 q_1 + \ldots$$

and

$$\pi_{i+1} = \sum_{j=0}^{\infty}\pi_{i+j} p_j \qquad \text{for } i \geq 0$$

As a possible solution, we guess that $\pi_i = (1 - \rho)\rho^i$, i.e. the stationary distribution is geometric. This is already normalized and gives, for $i \geq 0$,

$$(1 - \rho)\rho^{i+1} = \sum_{j=0}^{\infty}(1 - \rho)\rho^{i+j} p_j$$

i.e. $\rho = \sum_{j=0}^{\infty}\rho^j p_j = G(\rho)$, where G is the generating function for $\{p_j | j \geq 0\}$. The condition imposed by the first equation is

$$1 - \rho = \sum_{i=0}^{\infty}q_i(1 - \rho)\rho^i$$

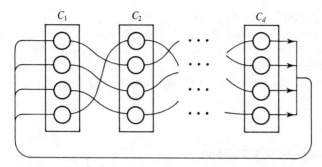

Figure 4.4

i.e. $Q(\rho) = 1$ where Q is the generating function of $\{q_j | j \geq 0\}$. Of course, this is not an independent condition since $q_i = 1 - \sum_{j=0}^{i} p_j$. Assuming this condition is satisfied, we can investigate solutions of the equation $\rho = G(\rho)$ by considering the intersection of the lines $y = G(x)$ and $y = x$. Assuming that G is a probability generating function, there is a solution at $(1, 1)$ giving $\rho = 1$, but this does not make π a probability distribution and so is no good. The only valid solutions lie between $(0, 0)$ and $(1, 1)$, corresponding to $0 < \rho < 1$ and, if $p_0 > 0$, a unique solution can exist only if $G'(1) \leq 1$. (If $p_0 = 0$, the chain is transient. Why?) Finally, observe that if $p_1 = p_2 = \ldots = 0$, this example is a special case of the previous one. It is left as an exercise to show that the chain in this case is positive-recurrent.

We have excluded the periodic case since we will have no cause to use it and it is rather involved notationally. However we state the following results. In an irreducible Markov chain with period d, the state space divides into d subclasses, $C_1, \ldots, C_d$ such that a one-step transition from any state in C_i always leads to a state in C_{i+1} $(1 \leq i \leq d$ where we identify C_{d+1} with C_1). If we consider the chain only at times nt $(n \geq 0)$, we get a new chain with one-step transition matrix P^d and in which each C_i is irreducible. The Markov chain defined on each C_i is aperiodic. Finally, the mean recurrence time of a state in this chain is clearly d^{-1} times that in the original chain. Hence, in the original chain, given states i and j, the sequence $p_{ij}^{(n)}$ comprises blocks of $d - 1$ zeros followed by a positive element with converges to $d\mu_j^{-1}$. A periodic chain can be visualized as any transition diagram organized as a cycle of 'banks' of states, such as that shown in Figure 4.4.

Most models of communication networks involve asynchronous systems and so require models in continuous time. However, some systems are synchronous in nature, such as control systems that update their state on successive pulses of a clock. One class of such systems comprises the synchronous interconnection networks; see Chapter 11. In addition, a Markov chain is often used to represent a continuous time system at times forming a discrete subset of the parameter space – *Markov times*. This 'embedded' chain is then used as the basis of a continuous time model. We will see a very important example of this usage when we analyse the $M/G/1$ queue in Chapter 5. Finally, discrete models have often been used successfully to approximate the behaviour of a continuous system.

4.3 Markov processes

We now consider stochastic processes which have the Markov property and a *continuous* parameter space. It is conventional in the literature for the term 'Markov process' to *imply* continuous time, but more correctly, such processes are called **Markov chains with continuous time parameters**. However, we will follow the convention for the sake of brevity and consistency. As we noted at the end of the previous section, Markov processes provide a more natural means for modelling physical systems where the state changes at arbitrary instants in time. We define a Markov process to be a stochastic process $\{X_t | t \in [0, \infty)\}$ with discrete state space S such that

$$P(X_{s+t} = j | X_u = x_u; u \leq s) = P(X_{s+t} = j | X_s = x_s)$$

We call this condition the **Markov property**. In words, it means that the sample path followed by the process after any time t depends only on the state X_t existing at that time. It can be shown that the Markov property, as stated at the beginning of this chapter, follows from this condition. Before introducing the general theory of Markov processes, we first consider the most important special case.

4.3.1 The Poisson process

The Poisson process not only provides the simplest, mathematically well-behaved example of a Markov process, it also possesses uniqueness properties that make it central to the general theory (although not for the more general Markov renewal processes which subsume both Markov processes and renewal processes, but are outside the scope of this book). The Poisson process is a *counting process* for the number of randomly occurring point-events observed in a given interval of time. Often we refer to these events as **arrivals**, for example messages or tasks arriving in the input buffer of a processor, customers arriving at a supermarket checkout, people joining a bus queue etc.

There are two definitions of the Poisson process which we prove to be equivalent in Proposition 4.11 below. Let the random variable $N_{t\tau}$ be the number of arrivals in the interval $(t, \tau]$.

Definition 4.3

The stochastic process $\{N_{0t}|t \geq 0\}$ is a Poisson process if, for t, $\tau \geq 0$,

(i)   it is *time-homogeneous*; i.e. for non-negative integer k, $P(N_{\tau,\tau+t} = k)$ is independent of τ, or equivalently, $N_{\tau,\tau+t}$ is equal in distribution to N_{0t};

(ii) it has *independent increments*, i.e. $N_{0\tau}$ and $N_{\tau,\tau+t}$ are independent;

(iii) it is *orderly*, i.e. $P(N_{\tau,\tau+t} \geq 2)/t \to 0$ as $t \to 0$.

An alternative definition is:

Definition 4.3′

The stochastic process $\{N_{0t}|t \geq 0\}$ is a Poisson process if there exists a positive number λ such that, for $t \geq 0$,

(a) $P(N_{t,t+h} = 0) = 1 - \lambda h + o(h)$;

(b) $P(N_{t,t+h} = 1) = \lambda h + o(h)$;

(c) $P(N_{t,t+h} \geq 2) = o(h)$;

(d) N_{0t} and $N_{t,t+h}$ are independent for all t, $h > 0$.

We call λ the *parameter* or *rate* of the Poisson process.

Proposition 4.11

Definitions 4.3 and 4.3′ are equivalent.

Proof   First (ii) is the same as (d) and (iii) is the same as (c). Furthermore, (b) is implied by (a) and (c) since $P(N_{t,t+h} \geq 0) = 1$. Now, since t does not occur on the right-hand sides of (a), (b) and (c), (i) must follow. (This will be made explicit in the proof below and in later propositions.)

It therefore remains to prove that (a) follows from Definition 4.3. Let $p_k(t) = P(N_{0t} = k) = P(N_{\tau,\tau+t} = k)$ for all $\tau \geq 0$ by (i). Then we have, for s, $t \geq 0$,

$$
\begin{aligned}
p_0(s + t) &= P(N_{0,s+t} = 0) \\
&= P((N_{0s} = 0) \cap (N_{s,s+t} = 0)) \\
&= P(N_{0s} = 0)P(N_{s,s+t} = 0) \qquad \text{by (ii)} \\
&= P(N_{0s} = 0)P(N_{0t} = 0) \qquad \text{by (i)} \\
&= p_0(s)p_0(t)
\end{aligned}
$$

Similarly, for any integer $n \geq 1$, $p_0(t_1 + \ldots + t_n) = p_0(t_1) \ldots$
$p_0(t_n)$, which follows from a simple induction Thus, since
$1 = \sum_{i=1}^{n} (1/n)$,

$$p_0(1) = \left[p_0\left(\frac{1}{n} \right) \right]^n .$$

Now, we may write $e^{-\lambda}$ for $p_0(1)$ where $0 < \lambda < \infty$ since the cases
$p_0(1) = 1$ and 0 are trivial. Thus,

$$p_0\left(\frac{1}{n} \right) = e^{-\lambda/n}$$

and by the same argument, $p_0(k/n) = e^{-k\lambda/n}$. Furthermore,
$p_0(s + t) \leq p_0(t)$, again because $p_0(s + t) = p_0(s)p_0(t)$, and so
$p_0(t)$ decreases as t increases. Now, for any $t \geq 0$, there is an
integer $k > 0$ such that $(k - 1)/n \leq t < k/n$. Thus we have

$$e^{-(k-1)\lambda/n} = p_0\left(\frac{k - 1}{n} \right) \geq p_0(t) > p_0\left(\frac{k}{n} \right) = e^{-k\lambda/n}$$

Therefore as $t \to \infty$, $p_0(t) \to e^{-\lambda t} = 1 - \lambda t + o(t)$ which proves
(a). ∎

We can now appeal to the conditions of both definitions arbitrarily when
dealing with Poisson processes, and will find this flexibility very convenient. Of course there is a connection between the Poisson process and
the Poisson distribution considered in Chapter 2. This is stated in the
following.

Proposition 4.12

N_{0t} is a Poisson random variable.

Proof The most concise proof uses probability generating functions as follows. First, consider N_{0h} for small h. Then, by (a), (b)
and (c) of Definition 4.3′,

$$E[z^{N_{0h}}] = (1 - \lambda h)z^0 + \lambda h z^1 + o(h)z^2$$
$$= 1 - \lambda(1 - z)h + o(h)$$
$$= e^{-\lambda(1-z)h + o(h)}$$

Now let $h = t/n$ for some positive integer n. Then,

$$E[z^{N_{0t}}] = E[z^{N_{0h}+N_{h,2h}+\ldots+N_{t-h,t}}]$$

$$= E[z^{N_{0h}}]^{t/h} \quad \text{by (i) and (ii) of Definition 4.3}$$

$$= [e^{-\lambda(1-z)h+o(h)}]^{t/h}$$

$$= [e^{-\lambda(1-z)t+o(1)}]$$

$$\rightarrow e^{-\lambda(1-z)t} \quad \text{as } h \rightarrow 0 \qquad \blacksquare$$

An alternative, direct proof is by induction and is also instructive. Let $p_n(t)$ denote $P(N_{0t} = n)$ as before and first consider $p_0(t)$. By Definition 4.3',

$$p_0(t + h) = p_0(t)(1 - \lambda h) + o(h)$$

and so

$$\frac{p_0(t + h) - p_0(t)}{h} = -\lambda p_0(t) + o(1)$$

Taking the limit $h \rightarrow 0$ then gives

$$\frac{dp_0(t)}{dt} = -\lambda p_0(t)$$

so that $p_0(t) = Ce^{-\lambda t}$ for some constant C. Since $p_0(0) = 1$ by (a), we have $C = 1$ and so $p_0(t) = e^{-\lambda t}$. (In fact we already knew this from the proof of Proposition 4.11.)

Now suppose inductively that

$$p_{n-1}(t) = [(\lambda t)^{n-1}/(n - 1)!]e^{-\lambda t}$$

for $n \geq 1$ and consider $p_n(t)$. By Definition 4.3' (all parts),

$$p_n(t + h) = p_n(t)(1 - \lambda h) + p_{n-1}(t)\lambda h + o(h)$$

i.e.

$$\frac{p_n(t + h) - p_n(t)}{h} = -\lambda p_n(t) + \lambda p_{n-1}(t) + o(1)$$

Thus, in the limit $h \rightarrow 0$,

$$\frac{dp_n(t)}{dt} = -\lambda p_n(t) + \lambda p_{n-1}(t)$$

i.e.

$$\frac{d}{dt} e^{\lambda t}p_n(t) = \lambda e^{\lambda t}p_{n-1}(t)$$

Hence, by the inductive hypothesis,

$$\frac{d}{dt} e^{\lambda t}p_n(t) = \lambda \frac{(\lambda t)^{n-1}}{(n - 1)!}$$

so that

$$p_n(t) = \left(\frac{(\lambda t)^n}{n!} + D\right) e^{-\lambda t}$$

for constant D. Since $p_n(0) = 0$ for $n > 0$, $D = 0$ and the proof is complete.   ■

A consequence of Proposition 4.12 is that the Poisson random variable is the only one satisfying the conditions of Definitions 4.3 and 4.3′.

Now, let us consider the time intervals between successive Poisson arrivals. Since we know that N_{0t} is a Poisson random variable, we know that the time interval between a given arrival and the nth arrival after it is an Erlang-n random variable by Proposition 2.2. For $n = 1$, we therefore have an exponential inter-arrival time. We now present this result based on the definition of the Poisson *process* given in this section.

Proposition 4.13

For a Poisson process with parameter λ, the time to the first arrival and the time interval between successive arrivals are both exponential random variables with parameter λ.

Proof   Let the time to the first arrival be denoted by A. Then,

$$P(A > t) = P(N_{0t} = 0) = e^{-\lambda t}$$

as we saw in the proof of Proposition 4.11. Thus, $P(A \leq t) = 1 - e^{-\lambda t}$. Let the inter-arrival time be denoted by T. To compute $P(T > t)$, we would like to argue that, given an arrival at time τ, the number of arrivals in $(\tau, \tau + t]$ is zero. However, the random variable N_{st} denotes the number of arrivals in the *interval* $(s, t]$. We therefore assume that there is an arrival at time τ and write

$$P(T > t) = \lim_{h \to 0} P(N_{\tau+h,\tau+h+t} = 0 | N_{\tau,\tau+h} = 1)$$

$$= \lim_{h \to 0} P(N_{\tau+h,\tau+h+t} = 0) \text{ by (ii) of Definition 4.3}$$

$$= P(N_{0t} = 0) \quad \text{by time-homogeneity}$$

$$= e^{-\lambda t} \quad \text{by the first part of the proposition} \quad ■$$

The negative exponential distribution is dual to the Poisson distribution in a Poisson process in the following sense. Exponential inter-arrival times in a point process imply that the number of arrivals occurring in a given interval is a Poisson random variable and that the process is Poisson. Conversely, given that the number of arrivals in any interval is a Poisson random variable, the inter-arrival times are exponential and the arrival process is Poisson. Exponentially distributed random variables are ubiquitous in stochastic modelling. This is partly because the smoothness of the exponential function often facilitates tractable analytic solutions. However, the main reason is that the exponential distribution is *memoryless*. We say that a random variable T is **memoryless**, or that the probability distribution of T is memoryless, if $P(T > t + \tau | T > \tau) = P(T > t)$. Essentially, this means that the probability of the time to the next arrival is independent of the time elapsed since the previous arrival. Moreover, the exponential distribution is the only continuous distribution with the memoryless property. We prove this in the following proposition.

Proposition 4.14

A continuous random variable is memoryless if and only if it is negative exponential.

Proof   For the 'if' implication, for an exponential random variable T with parameter λ, $P(T \leqslant t) = 1 - e^{-\lambda t}$. Hence,

$$P(T > t + \tau | T > \tau) = \frac{P(T > t + \tau)}{P(T > \tau)}$$

$$= \frac{e^{-\lambda(t+\tau)}}{e^{-\lambda \tau}} = e^{-\lambda t} = P(T > t)$$

Conversely, suppose that T has distribution function F and that $P(T > t) = P(T > t + \tau | T > \tau)$. Defining the function H by $H(t) = 1 - F(t)$, we have

$$H(t) = \frac{P(T > t + \tau)}{P(T > \tau)} = \frac{H(t + \tau)}{H(\tau)}$$

so that $H(t + \tau) = H(t)H(\tau)$. Since $0 \leqslant H(t) \leqslant 1$, we can apply the method used to prove Proposition 4.11 to show that $H(t) = e^{-\lambda t}$ for some λ. Thus, $F(t) = 1 - e^{-\lambda t}$ as required.   ■

For discrete random variables, there is a corresponding result which states that the geometric distribution is the only one with the memoryless property. The proof is analogous and left to the reader.

Returning now to the Poisson process, we have shown that inter-arrival times are exponential and that these times have the memoryless property. A further property of the Poisson process is the **random observer property**. Suppose a stochastic process $\{X_t\}$ includes

Poisson arrivals so that if there is an arrival at time τ, the state changes from X_{τ^-} to X_{τ^+}. For example, in a queue, X_t might denote the queue length and we would have $X_{\tau^+} = X_{\tau^-} + 1$. The random observer property states that the distribution of X_{τ^-} is independent of the event that there is an arrival at time τ. In other words, the state 'seen' by the arrival has the same distribution as the state seen by an external, 'random' observer.

A proof of this is as follows. First, the event 'there is an arrival in the interval $(\tau - h, \tau]$' is equivalent to $N_{\tau-h,\tau} \geqslant 1$ $(0 < h < \tau)$. But, the event $N_{\tau-h,\tau} \geqslant 1$ is independent of the history up to time $\tau - h$ by the memoryless property (and independent of the time $\tau - h$ itself for that matter). In particular, the events $X_{\tau-h} = x$ and $N_{\tau-h,\tau} \geqslant 1$ are independent. Thus,

$$P(X_{\tau-h} = x | N_{\tau-h,\tau} \geqslant 1) = P(X_{\tau-h} = x)$$

Letting $h \to 0$, the left-hand side approaches the probability that a new arrival at time τ 'sees' the state $X_{\tau^-} = x$ and so we have

$$P(X_{\tau^-} = x | \text{arrival at time } \tau) = P(X_{\tau^-} = x)$$

as required. Intuitively, the result uses applications of the memoryless property both forwards and backwards in time. That is, we also have $P(T > t + \tau | T > t) = P(T > \tau)$, which is proved in the same way as in Proposition 4.14, interchanging t and τ. Thus, the time interval between τ and the previous arrival is independent of the event 'there is an arrival at time τ'. We therefore conclude that the arrival at τ has exactly the same information about previous arrivals as an external observer.

Another important property is that the time to the next arrival from a *random* 'observation time point' – the **forward recurrence time** – has the same exponential distribution as the inter-arrival time. Moreover, it is independent of past history. Let the forward recurrence time at time t be denoted by V_t. The property is then proved as follows:

$$P(V_t \leqslant u | N_{0s} = n_s, s \leqslant t)$$
$$= P(N_{t,t+u} > 0 | N_{0s} = n_s, s \leqslant t)$$
$$= P(N_{t,t+u} > 0) \qquad \text{by independent increments}$$
$$= P(N_{0u} > 0) \qquad \text{by time homogeneity}$$
$$= 1 - P(N_{0u} = 0) = 1 - e^{-\lambda u}$$

We will show that this property is *unique* to the Poisson process in Section 4.5.

We conclude our discussion of the Poisson process with two further properties that we will use frequently in this book: the **superposi-

tion and **decomposition** properties. The superposition of m processes $\{N_{0t}^{(1)}|t \geq 0\}, \ldots, \{N_{0t}^{(m)}|t \geq 0\}$ is $\{N_{0t}^{(1)} + \ldots + N_{0t}^{(m)}|t \geq 0\}$, i.e. the arrivals in the superposed process are comprised of the union of the arrivals in the constituent processes. The m-way decomposition of a process A is a set of process–probability pairs $\{(D_1, q_1), \ldots, (D_m, q_m)\}$ for some integer $m \geq 2$, where $q_1 + \ldots + q_m = 1$. An arrival in process A is also an arrival in (exactly one) process D_i with probability q_i $(1 \leq i \leq m)$ and the sequence of assignments of arrivals in A to $\{D_i\}$ is i.i.d.

Proposition 4.15

(a)   Let $A_1, \ldots, A_n$ be independent Poisson processes with parameters $\lambda_1, \ldots, \lambda_n$ respectively. Then their superposition is also a Poisson process with parameter $\lambda_1 + \ldots + \lambda_n$;

(b)   Let A be a Poisson process with parameter λ. Then, in its m-way decomposition $\{(D_1, q_1), \ldots, (D_m, q_m)\}$, each process D_i is independent Poisson with parameter $q_i\lambda$.

Proof

(a)   Let $N_{\tau t}$ denote the number of arrivals in $(\tau, t]$ in the superposition of two Poisson processes $\{A_{0t}\}$ and $\{B_{0t}\}$ with parameters λ_1 and λ_2 respectively. Then, for $s, t \geq 0$,

$$P(N_{s,s+t} = n) = \sum_{i=0}^{n} P(A_{s,s+t} = i \cap B_{s,s+t} = n - i)$$

$$= \sum_{i=0}^{n} P(A_{s,s+t} = i) P(B_{s,s+t} = n - i)$$

$$\text{by independence}$$

$$= \sum_{i=0}^{n} \frac{(\lambda_1 t)^i}{i!} \frac{(\lambda_2 t)^{n-i}}{(n - i)!} e^{-\lambda_1 t} e^{-\lambda_2 t}$$

$$= \frac{e^{-\lambda_1 t} e^{-\lambda_2 t}}{n!} \sum_{i=0}^{n} \binom{n}{i} (\lambda_1 t)^i (\lambda_2 t)^{n-i}$$

$$= \frac{e^{-(\lambda_1 + \lambda_2)t}}{n!} [(\lambda_1 + \lambda_2)t]^n$$

This proves the result for two Poisson processes. Since the superposition is also Poisson, the result for $n \geq 3$ processes follows by an easy induction. Notice that an alternative proof is based on inter-arrival times. If the inter-arrival times of the n component processes are $T_1, \ldots, T_n$, the inter-arrival time of the superposition is $\min_{1 \leq i \leq n} T_i$. But since each T_i is exponential with parameter λ_i, the minimum is also exponential with parameter $\lambda_1 + \ldots + \lambda_n$; see Exercise 2.6.

(b)   Let $N_{\tau t}$, $N_{\tau t}^{(i)}$ denote the number of arrivals in $(\tau, t]$ in the Poisson process A and process D_i respectively $(1 \leq i \leq m)$. Then we have, for $s, t \geq 0$,

$$P(N_{s,s+t}^{(1)} = n_1, \ldots, N_{s,s+t}^{(m)} = n_m)$$

$$= P(N_{s,s+t}^{(1)} = n_1, \ldots, N_{s,s+t}^{(m)} = n_m | N_{s,s+t} = n_1 + \ldots + n_m)$$

$$\times P(N_{s,s+t} = n_1 + \ldots + n_m)$$

$$= \frac{(n_1 + \ldots + n_m)!}{n_1! \ldots n_m!} q_1^{n_1} \ldots q_m^{n_m} \frac{(\lambda t)^{n_1 + \ldots + n_m}}{(n_1 + \ldots + n_m)!} e^{-\lambda t}$$

since the assignments of arrivals to $\{D_i\}$ are i.i.d.

$$= \frac{(q_1 \lambda t)^{n_1}}{n_1!} e^{-q_1 \lambda t} \ldots \frac{(q_m \lambda t)^{n_m}}{n_m!} e^{-q_m \lambda t}$$

since $q_1 + \ldots + q_m = 1$. Thus the random variables $N_{s,s+t}^{(i)}$ are independent Poisson. ∎

4.3.2   Markov chains with continuous time parameters

A Markov process with discrete state space S is **time-homogeneous** if its transition probabilities,

$$p_{ij}(t) = P(X_{s+t} = j | X_s = i) \qquad (s, t \in [0, \infty), \ i, j \in S)$$

are independent of s, i.e. are time-homogeneous. We consider time-homogeneous Markov processes and assume that the transition matrix $P(t) = [p_{ij}(t) | i, j \in S]$ satisfies the following conditions (where, $i, j \in S$):

(a)   for all $t \in [0, \infty)$, $P(t)$ is a stochastic matrix, i.e. $p_{ij}(t) > 0$ and $\sum_{j \in S} p_{ij}(t) = 1$

(b) $P(t)$ is right-continuous at $t = 0$: $P(t) \to I$ as $t \to 0$, i.e. $p_{ij}(t) \to \delta_{ij}$ as $t \to 0$

(c)   the Chapman–Kolmogorov equation holds: $P(s + t) = P(s)P(t)$

In fact, (c) is a consequence of the Markov property, but it is often taken as an alternative axiom. This leads to two different formulations of the theory, as we will see. The derivation of the Chapman–Kolmogorov equation is analogous to the case of Markov chains. For $i, j \in S$, and $s, t \geq 0$,

$$p_{ij}(s + t) = P(X_{s+t} = j|X_0 = i)$$

$$= \sum_{k \in S} P(X_s = k|X_0 = i)P(X_{s+t} = j|X_s = k, X_0 = i)$$

$$= \sum_{k \in S} P(X_s = k|X_0 = i)P(X_{s+t} = j|X_s = k)$$

by the Markov property

$$= \sum_{k \in S} p_{ik}(s)p_{kj}(t) \qquad \text{by time-homogeneity}$$

From the above assumptions, we can prove two basic properties about $P(t)$ in the following.

Proposition 4.16

For all $t \geqslant 0$, $p_{ii}(t) > 0$ ($i \in S$).

Proof We use the argument used to prove Proposition 4.3.

$$p_{ii}(t) \geqslant P\left(\bigcap_{k=1}^{n} X_{kt/n} = i|X_0 = i\right)$$

$$= \left[p_{ii}\left(\frac{t}{n}\right)\right]^n$$

by the Markov property and time-homogeneity. But for sufficiently large, finite n, $p_{ii}(t/n) > 0$ since it approaches 1 as $n \rightarrow \infty$ by continuity. ∎

Proposition 4.17

For $i, j \in S$, $p_{ij}(t)$ is uniformly continuous in t on $[0, \infty)$ and uniform in j.

Proof For $s, t \geqslant 0$, by the Chapman–Kolmogorov equation,

$$p_{ij}(s + t) - p_{ij}(t) = (p_{ii}(s) - 1)p_{ij}(t) + \sum_{k \neq i} p_{ik}(s)p_{kj}(t)$$

$$\leqslant \sum_{k \neq i} p_{ik}(s)$$

$$= 1 - p_{ii}(s)$$

Similarly,

$$p_{ij}(s + t) - p_{ij}(t) \geqslant -p_{ij}(t)[1 - p_{ii}(s)]$$

$$\geqslant p_{ii}(s) - 1$$

Thus, $|p_{ij}(s + t) - p_{ij}(t)| \leq 1 - p_{ii}(s) \to 0$ as $s \to 0$ for all t and all j.   ∎

If a state $i \in S$ is entered at time t and the next state transition takes place at time $t + T$, we call T the **state holding time** of i. Now, by the Markov property, at any time point τ, the distribution of the time to the next change of state is independent of the time of the previous change of state. In other words, state holding times are memoryless and so have exponential distributions. Hence, at time τ, the probability that there is a state transition in the interval $(\tau, \tau + h]$ is $q_i h + o(h)$ where q_i is the parameter of the exponential distribution of holding time in state i which exists at time τ. Next, suppose that when a transition out of state i occurs, the new state is j with probability r_{ij}, which depends only on i and j by the Markov property. Thus we have, for $i \neq j \in S$,

$$P(X_{t+h} = j | X_t = i) = q_{ij} h + o(h)$$

where $q_{ij} = q_i r_{ij}$. The quantities q_{ij} are called the **instantaneous transition rates** or the **generators** of the Markov process which they characterize completely. In particular examples, these transition rates can often be written down immediately. For example, in the case of a Poisson process with rate λ, we have seen that

$$P(N_{0,t+h} = i + 1 | N_{0t} = i) = P(N_{t,t+h} = 1 | N_{0t} = i)$$
$$= P(N_{0h} = 1) = \lambda h + o(h)$$

Thus, $q_{i,i+1} = \lambda$. Generalizing this, we may have superposed Poisson processes leading to states $j_1, \ldots, j_m$ from state i with rates $\lambda_1, \ldots, \lambda_m$ respectively. Then $q_{ij_k} = \lambda_k$ $(1 \leq k \leq m)$. Similarly, the state may change according to a single Poisson process with rate λ, resulting in new states j_k being chosen with probability r_{ij_k}. By Proposition 4.15, this is equivalent to the superposition of m Poisson processes with rates λr_{ij_k} from state i to state j_k $(1 \leq k \leq m)$. This notion of rates is entirely intuitive, being analogous to 'fluid flows'. We will see this analogy strengthen later when we consider the steady state of a Markov process.

The above derivation of the generators of a Markov process is *probabilistic* in nature – i.e. it uses properties of probability distributions. An alternative, more mathematical derivation begins with the Chapman–Kolmogorov matrix equation, $P(s + t) = P(s)P(t)$, as follows. It can be shown that this equation has a unique solution: for $t \geq 0$,

$$P(t) = e^{tQ} \triangleq \sum_{n=0}^{\infty} \frac{(tQ)^n}{n!}$$

for some constant square matrix Q. This is analogous to the scalar case,

$f(s + t) = f(s)f(t)$ with solution $f(t) = e^{\lambda t}$, which we considered in the proof of Proposition 4.11. Thus, $P(0) = I$ and

$$P(h) = I + Qh + o(h)$$

in matrix notation. This is equivalent to $p_{ij}(0) = \delta_{ij}$ and $p_{ij}(h) = \delta_{ij} + q_{ij}h + o(h)$ at the element level. Consequently,

$$Q = \lim_{h \to 0} \frac{P(h) - I}{h} = \lim_{h \to 0} \frac{P(h) - P(0)}{h} = P'(0)$$

We therefore have $q_{ij} = p'_{ij}(0)$, and since $q_{ij}h = p_{ij}(h) + o(1)$ for $i \neq j$, $q_{ij}h$ is the probability that the state changes from i to j in a short time h – i.e. q_{ij} is the instantaneous transition rate from i to j. This is just as we had in the probabilistic derivation. However, now we also have $q_{ii} = p'_{ii}(0)$ which was previously undefined. Since $P(t)$ is stochastic, it follows immediately that the rows of $Q(t)$ sum to 0:

$$\sum_{j \in S} q_{ij} = \lim_{t \to 0} \left(\frac{d}{dt} \sum_{j \in S} p_{ij}(t) \right) = \lim_{t \to 0} \left(\frac{d}{dt} 1 \right) = 0$$

(We can interchange the limiting operations since the sum is absolutely convergent.) Thus, the q_i we defined above is equal to $-q_{ii} = \sum_{i \neq j} q_{ij}$. The equivalence between the two approaches is completed by the following.

Proposition 4.18

The holding time T in state $i \in S$ is exponential with parameter q_i.

Proof Let $u_n = [p_{ii}(t/n)]^n$, so that $u_n \to P(T > t)$ as $n \to \infty$. But, $p_{ii}(t/n) = 1 - q_i(t/n) + o(t/n)$ and so

$$\ln(u_n) = n \left\{ \ln \left[1 - q_i \frac{t}{n} + o\left(\frac{t}{n} \right) \right] \right\}$$

$$= n \left[-q_i \frac{t}{n} + o\left(\frac{t}{n} \right) \right] = -q_i t + t o(1) \to -q_i t$$

as $n \to \infty$. Thus, as $n \to \infty$, $u_n \to e^{-q_i t} = P(T > t)$. ∎

A state $i \in S$ is said to be **stable** if $0 \leq q_i < \infty$, **instantaneous** if $q_i = \infty$ and **absorbing** if $q_i = 0$.

The evolution of a Markov process is determined entirely by its generators through the **Kolmogorov equations**, which we present in the following proposition.

Proposition 4.19

For the Markov process described in this section,

(a)   The **forward Kolmogorov equation**,

$$P'(t) = P(t)Q$$

holds if there exists a real number M such that $q_i < M < \infty$ for all $i \in S$, i.e. if the q_i are bounded.

(b)   The **backward Kolmogorov equation**,

$$P'(t) = QP(t)$$

holds if $q_i < \infty$ for all $i \in S$, i.e. if the q_i are finite (whereupon we say Q is **conservative**).

Proof   By the Chapman–Kolmogorov equations,

$$P(t + h) = P(t)P(h) = P(h)P(t)$$

and so

$$\frac{P(t + h) - P(t)}{h} = P(t)\frac{P(h) - I}{h} = \frac{P(h) - I}{h}P(t)$$

Taking the limit $h \to 0$, assuming that the summations (in the matrix products) and the limit can be interchanged, proves both (a) and (b).[1]   ∎

4.3.3 The embedded Markov chain and stationarity

In a Markov process with initial state i, suppose that the state changes at times $\tau_1, \tau_2, \ldots$ and define the discrete time stochastic process $\{Z_n | n = 0, 1, \ldots\}$ where

---

[1]The interchange of summation and limit can only pose a problem if the state space is infinite, of course. If this is the case, we have, for the forward equations,

$$\frac{p_{ik}(t + h) - p_{ik}(t)}{h} = \sum_{j \neq k} p_{ij}(t)\frac{p_{jk}(h)}{h} + p_{ik}(t)\frac{p_{kk}(h) - 1}{h}$$

Now, it can be shown that if the q_j are bounded, for $j \neq k$, $p_{jk}(h)/h \to q_{jk}$ as $h \to 0$ uniformly in j. Since $\sum_{j \neq k} p_{ij}(t)$ is convergent, we can therefore take the limit inside the sum on the right-hand side to obtain

$$p'_{ik}(t) = \sum_{j \neq k} p_{ij}(t)q_{jk} + p_{ik}(t)q_{kk} = \sum_{j \in S} p_{ij}(t)q_{jk}$$

using the continuity assumption that $p_{kk}(0) = 1$. The proof of the backward equation is simpler since no extra uniformity assumption is required.

$$Z_0 = X_0$$

$$Z_n = X_{\tau_n^+} \qquad n \geqslant 1$$

In other words, X_n is the state entered immediately after the nth state transition $(n > 0)$. Since $\{X_t\}$ has the Markov property, it is clear that $\{Z_n\}$ is a Markov chain. Let $R = [r_{ij} | i, j \in S]$ be the one-step transition matrix of $\{Z_n\}$. Then, for $i \neq j$, by time homogeneity,

$$r_{ij} = \lim_{h \to 0} P(X_h = j | X_h \neq i, X_0 = i)$$

$$= \lim_{h \to 0} \frac{P(X_h = j \cap X_h \neq i | X_0 = i)}{P(X_h \neq i | X_0 = i)} = \lim_{h \to 0} \frac{p_{ij}(h)}{1 - p_{ii}(h)}$$

$$= \frac{q_{ij}}{q_i} \qquad \text{by application of L'Hôpital's rule}$$

$$r_{ii} = 0$$

Of course, this result is immediate from the probabilistic approach to deriving the generators of a Markov process; indeed, the matrix R was an integral part of that approach. We call the chain $\{Z_n\}$ the **embedded Markov chain** (EMC) of the Markov process $\{X_t\}$. Since it is unique, we can extend much of the terminology of Markov chains to Markov processes by allowing the latter to assume the properties of their EMCs. Thus, a Markov process is defined to be irreducible, transient, null-recurrent or positive-recurrent if its embedded Markov chain has the corresponding property. A Markov process with continuous parameter space cannot be periodic.

Let us now consider the asymptotic properties, when they exist, of a continuous time Markov process. Analogously to Markov chains, we seek, for $j \in S$,

$$\pi_j = \lim_{t \to \infty} p_{ij}(t)$$

which should be independent of the initial state i. The steady state result for Markov processes is the following.

Proposition 4.20

In an irreducible Markov process with state space S and generator matrix Q,

(a) $\pi_j = 0$ for all $j \in S$ if the process is transient or null-recurrent: there is no steady state

(b)   the process is positive-recurrent if and only if there exists a *unique* stationary distribution π such that $0 = \pi Q$

Proof (Sketch only)   If the EMC is transient or null-recurrent, $\lim_{n\to\infty} p_{ij}(\tau_n) = 0$ and (a) follows. Otherwise, the Markov process is positive-recurrent iff $v = vR$ has a solution with v a probability distribution; v is the stationary solution for the EMC. Now, the expected duration of a cycle in the EMC between successive visits to a state $i \in S$ is

$$q_i^{-1} + \sum_{j\neq i} q_j^{-1} \frac{v_j}{v_i} = \frac{1}{v_i} \sum_{j\in S} v_j q_j^{-1}$$

since the expected number of visits to state $j \neq i$ in the cycle is v_j/v_i. Thus, the expected proportion of time spent in state i in the cycle is

$$\pi_i = \frac{v_i q_i^{-1}}{\sum_{j\in S} v_j q_j^{-1}}$$

(This follows rigorously from a limit theorem of Markov renewal theory; see Section 4.5.3.) Thus, the vector $[q_i\pi_i | i \in S]$ satisfies $v = vR$, i.e.

$$q_i\pi_i = \sum_{j\neq i} \frac{q_j\pi_j q_{ji}}{q_j} = \sum_{j\neq i} \pi_j q_{ji}$$

i.e.

$$\sum_{j\in S} \pi_j q_{ji} = 0$$

as required.   ∎

Notice that if a Markov process has a steady state and satisfies the conditions of Proposition 4.19, then $PQ = 0$ and so $\pi Q = 0$ since each row of P is equal to π. ($QP = 0$ too, but this is merely a consequence of the fact that the rows of Q all sum to 0.) Notice too that an irreducible Markov process with finite state space is always positive-recurrent (because this is true of its EMC by Kolmogorov's theorem) and so a solution of the equations $\pi Q = 0$ always exists. This can often be found numerically, but perhaps more often direct solution is intractable because of the size of the state space.

Throughout this book, we will be concerned with Markov processes in a steady state, though some interesting time-dependent solutions can be obtained directly from the Kolmogorov equations. There is considerable intuition to be found in the steady state theorem for Markov processes which will facilitate simple solutions to quite complex problems and lead to the powerful technique of reversibility in the next section. We can rewrite the equation $\pi Q = 0$ in the form:

$$-\pi_i q_{ii} = \sum_{j \neq i} \pi_j q_{ji}$$

or

$$\sum_{j \neq i} \pi_i q_{ij} = \sum_{j \neq i} \pi_j q_{ji}$$

These equations are called the **balance equations** (or **balance conditions**) of the Markov process in equilibrium. They define a balance in the following sense. In equilibrium, π_i is the proportion of time that the process spends in state i and q_{ij} is the rate at which it leaves state i to go to state j. Thus, in unit time, the expected number of transitions from state i to state j is $\pi_i q_{ij}$; we call this quantity the **probability flux** from state i to state j. Now, the left-hand side of the above balance equation for state i is equal to the total flux out of state i – to *any* other state. Similarly, the right-hand side is the total flux into state i – *from* any other state. The balance equations state that these fluxes are equal, i.e. they 'balance'. If we can prove, or reasonably assume, that any Markovian system is in equilibrium, then we can apply the above intuition and write down the balance equations for every state. Notice that in the special case that $\pi_i q_{ij} = \pi_j q_{ji}$ for every pair (i, j), the balance equations are always satisfied. The process is then called *reversible*; we will consider this further in the next section.

In fact, we can do even better than analyse the balance equation for each state. Given an *arbitrary* subset of states, the sum of the left-hand sides of the corresponding balance equations is equal to the sum of the right-hand sides. Any line of probability flux between two states in this subset will appear on both sides of the resulting equation and so cancel out. The result is that the total flux going out of the whole subset is equal to the total flux going into the subset. In symbols, given any non-empty subset $A \subseteq S$,

$$\sum_{i \in A} \sum_{j \neq i} \pi_i q_{ij} = \sum_{i \in A} \sum_{j \neq i} \pi_j q_{ji}$$

Subtracting the identity

$$\sum_{\substack{i \in A \\ j \neq i}} \sum_{j \in A} \pi_i q_{ij} = \sum_{\substack{i \in A \\ j \neq i}} \sum_{j \in A} \pi_j q_{ji}$$

then gives the **aggregated balance equations**

$$\sum_{i \in A} \sum_{j \notin A} \pi_i q_{ij} = \sum_{i \in A} \sum_{j \notin A} \pi_j q_{ji}$$

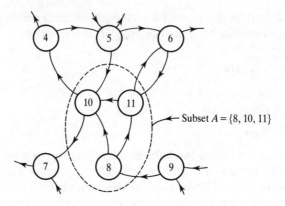

Figure 4.5

This is illustrated in Figure 4.5. The sum of the fluxes $f_{ij} = \pi_i q_{ij}$ on the outward arrows crossing the boundary drawn round the states in the chosen subset A is equal to the sum of the fluxes on the inward arrows crossing that boundary. All other arrows can be ignored. Thus we have

$$f_{10,4} + f_{11,6} + f_{10,7} = f_{5,10} + f_{6,11} + f_{9,8}$$

Three internal arrows have been omitted, leading to simpler balance equations.

Many Markov processes are analysed in this book. We now give a classic example, a simple birth and death process which demonstrates the effectiveness of the state-aggregation technique just described. Moreover, it will also be used to illustrate reversibility in the next section and provide the solution for the Markovian single server queue in the next chapter.

Example 4.9 (Birth and death process with immigration) _____

The origin of this Markov process (and its more general non-Markovian version considered in Section 4.5) is in population processes where the population of a colony of bacteria, pigs, humans etc. at time t was to be predicted given an initial population under certain assumptions. However, the process is important for many more applications, especially in computer and communication system modelling. In particular, *queues* are birth and death processes. A **birth and death process** is a stochastic process with state space $\{0, 1, \ldots\}$ in which a one-step transition can only change the current state by one unit, i.e. if $i \rightarrow j$, then $|i - j| = 1$. In general, we simplify the problem by allowing **immigration** which causes a state i to change to $i + 1$ $(i \geqslant 0)$. This ensures that the population need not become extinct when state 0 is reached and is exactly what we want when we consider queues, where arrivals certainly can join an empty queue, represented by state 0.

Alternatively, we can make states 0 and 1 absorbing and predict the probability of eventual extinction – indeed, this was one of the original motivations of the theory.

Consider the Markov process $\{X_t | t \geq 0\}$ where X_t is the population (or queue length) at time t and $X_0 = i$. In state j, the combination of births and immigration defines a Poisson process with rate λ_j and the combination of deaths and emigration defines a Poisson process with rate μ_j. Thus, if $X_t = j \geq 1$, considering the short interval $(t, t + h)$ yields

$$X_{t+h} = \begin{cases} j + 1 & \text{with probability } \lambda_j h + \text{o}(h) \\ & \text{(birth or arrival of an immi-} \\ & \text{grant)} \\ j - 1 & \text{with probability } \mu_j h + \text{o}(h) \\ & \text{(death or departure of an emi-} \\ & \text{grant)} \\ j & \text{with probability } 1 - (\lambda_j + \mu_j)h \\ & + \text{o}(h) \text{ (no change)} \\ k \neq j - 1, j, j + 1 & \text{with probability o}(h) \end{cases}$$

If $X_t = 0$, there are no departures or deaths and so we have instead

$$X_{t+h} = \begin{cases} 1 & \text{with probability } \lambda_0 h + \text{o}(h) \text{ (birth or arrival} \\ & \text{of an immigrant)} \\ 0 & \text{with probability } 1 - \lambda_0 h + \text{o}(h) \\ & \text{(no change)} \\ k > 1 & \text{with probability o}(h) \end{cases}$$

The instantaneous transition rate matrix, Q, is therefore

$$Q = \begin{bmatrix} -\lambda_0 & \lambda_0 & 0 & 0 & 0 & 0 & \cdots \\ \mu_1 & -(\lambda_1 + \mu_1) & \lambda_1 & 0 & 0 & 0 & \cdots \\ 0 & \mu_2 & -(\lambda_2 + \mu_2) & \lambda_2 & 0 & 0 & \cdots \\ 0 & 0 & \mu_3 & -(\lambda_3 + \mu_3) & \lambda_3 & 0 & \cdots \\ \vdots & \vdots & \vdots & \vdots & \vdots & \vdots & \ddots \end{bmatrix}$$

If we are only interested in the steady state (assuming this exists), we can write down the balance equations for the probability flux passing into and out of the states enclosed in the contour shown in Figure 4.6; we did not even have to define Q. In general, we should determine the conditions under which the equation $\pi Q = 0$ has a solution, although we can often verify that the solution of aggregated balance equations satisfies it. This kind of 'guessing' of solutions and appealing to uniqueness will be exploited further in the next section. There is only one arc leaving the contour and one incoming arc. The balance

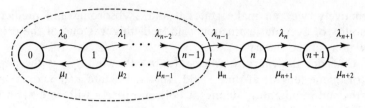

Figure 4.6

equations are therefore, for $j \geq 1$,

$$\lambda_{j-1}\pi_{j-1} = \mu_j\pi_j$$

with normalizing condition $\sum_{j=0}^{\infty}\pi_j = 1$. Notice how much simpler are these balance equations than $\pi Q = 0$ which yields $\lambda_0\pi_0 = \mu_1\pi_1$ and, for $j > 0$,

$$\lambda_{j-1}\pi_{j-1} - (\mu_j + \lambda_j)\pi_j + \mu_{j+1}\pi_{j+1} = 0$$

from which the balance equations follow. In more complex examples, the effort saved by a judicious choice of the subset of states can be considerably more than here.

The solution for π_j is now easily obtained as

$$\pi_j = \frac{\rho_j}{\sum_{k=0}^{\infty}\rho_k} \qquad (j \geq 0)$$

where $\rho_0 = 1$ and $\rho_j = \prod_{k=1}^{j}\lambda_{k-1}/\mu_k$ for $j > 0$. (For $j = 0$, we adopt the convention that an empty product is equal to one, i.e. $\rho_0 = 1$.) π will be a probability distribution if and only if $\sum_{k=0}^{\infty}\rho_k < \infty$, in which case it will be the unique stationary distribution of the Markov process which will be positive-recurrent.

We will see this Markov process again when we consider the M/M/1 queue in Chapter 5. However, there are still some interesting observations to be made about its time-dependent behaviour. First, let us consider the conditions of the Kolmogorov equations. For state j, the quantity $q_j = \lambda_j + \mu_j$. Now, in a general population process, we assume that individuals behave as independent Poisson processes, producing offspring at rate λ and dying at rate μ. Suppose that there is no emigration and that immigration is an independent Poisson process with rate ν. The net birth (including immigration) and death processes in state j are then both Poisson with respective rates $j\lambda + \nu$ and $j\mu$. Consequently, $q_j = j(\lambda + \mu) + \nu$. This is finite for any j, but the q_j are not bounded. Thus we can apply the Kolmogorov backward equation, but not necessarily the forward equation. However, that the q_j be bounded was not a necessary condition; we only needed a uniform convergence property. This can be established independently in this case – see Exercise 4.12 for an outline. Multiplying the forward equation for $p'_{ij}(t)$ by z^j and summing over $j \geq 0$ then yields the following partial differential equation for the generating function $G_i(z, t) = \sum_{j=0}^{\infty} p_{ij}(t)z^j$:

$$\frac{\partial G_i}{\partial t} + (\lambda z - \mu)(1 - z)\frac{\partial G_i}{\partial z} + \nu(1 - z)G_i = 0$$

This is a first-order equation which can be solved by Lagrange's method to give

$$G_i(z, t) = \left(\frac{z + \lambda t(1 - z)}{1 + \lambda t(1 - z)}\right)^i [1 + \lambda t(1 - z)]^{-\nu/\lambda}$$

The details are left to the enthusiastic reader. Notice that the first factor does not involve ν, i.e. the effects of immigration. From this result, it is straightforward to obtain the moments of $p_{ij}(t)$ by finding the partial derivatives of G_i with respect to z at $z = 1$. Differentiating the forward equation p times with respect to z and then setting $z = 1$ gives a first-order ordinary differential equation in t for the pth moment. The moments can then be computed iteratively. The reader is recommended to carry this out.

4.4   Reversibility

The analysis of stationary Markov processes, i.e. those in a steady state, can often be greatly simplified by considering a dual process which has the same state space but in which the direction of time is reversed, cf. viewing a video film backwards. This dual process is known as the *reversed process*. In some special cases, for example the birth and death process, the reversed process is stochastically identical to the original process, which is then called *reversible*. Reversibility arguments allow simple derivations of many interesting properties of stationary Markov processes. For example, we can relate the arrival process to a queueing system to the departure process from that system since departures correspond to arrivals in the reversed process. Moreover, we will also see how the balance equations of a Markov process can be solved using properties of its reversed process. This enables stationary distributions to be obtained with relative ease for quite complex processes such as queueing network models. An excellent account of reversibility with applications in stochastic modelling is Kelly (1979).

We begin by defining two of the above intuitive notions precisely. We say that a stochastic process $\{X_t | -\infty < t < \infty\}$ is

- **stationary** if $(X_{t_1}, X_{t_2}, \ldots, X_{t_n})$ and $(X_{t_1+\tau}, X_{t_2+\tau}, \ldots, X_{t_n+\tau})$ have the same distribution for all times $t_1, t_2, \ldots, t_n$ and τ;

- **reversible** if $(X_{t_1}, X_{t_2}, \ldots, X_{t_n})$ and $(X_{\tau-t_1}, X_{\tau-t_2}, \ldots, X_{\tau-t_n})$ have the same distribution for all times $t_1, t_2, \ldots, t_n$ and τ.

A reversible Markov process is irreducible, for otherwise certain reversed state sequences could not occur. Moreover, we take all stationary Markov processes to be irreducible – refer to the corollary to Proposition 4.8.

The arguments given in this section apply equally to irreducible Markov chains and Markov processes, but we just consider the latter. The conversion to the case of discrete time is straightforward. Although a stationary process need not be reversible, every reversible process is stationary. This follows since if the process $\{X_t\}$ is reversible, both $(X_{t_1}, X_{t_2}, \ldots, X_{t_n})$ and $(X_{t_1+\sigma}, X_{t_2+\sigma}, \ldots, X_{t_n+\sigma})$ have the same distribution as $(X_{-t_1}, X_{-t_2}, \ldots, X_{-t_n})$ for all σ; take $\tau = 0$ and σ respectively in the definition above. We can now give an equivalent definition of reversibility in terms of the balance conditions of a stationary Markov process.

Proposition 4.21

A stationary Markov process $\{X_t\}$ with generator matrix $Q = [q_{ij}]$ is reversible if and only if there exists a collection of positive real numbers $\{\pi_k | k \in S\}$ satisfying the **detailed balance equations** (or **conditions**)

$$\pi_i q_{ij} = \pi_j q_{ji} \qquad (i, j \in S)$$

such that $\sum_{k \in S} \pi_k = 1$. Such a solution π is the stationary distribution of the process. It is unique by the steady state theorem, Proposition 4.20.

Proof If the process is reversible, let $\pi_j = P(X_t = j)$ which is independent of t since the process is stationary. Then for all i, $j \in S$,

$$P(X_t = i, X_{t+\tau} = j) = P(X_{-t} = i, X_{-t-\tau} = j)$$

$$\text{by reversibility}$$

$$= P(X_{2t+\tau-t} = i, X_{2t+\tau-t-\tau} = j)$$

$$\text{by stationarity}$$

$$= P(X_t = j, X_{t+\tau} = i)$$

Thus we have

$$\pi_i \frac{P(X_{t+\tau} = j | X_t = i)}{\tau} = \pi_j \frac{P(X_{t+\tau} = i | X_t = j)}{\tau}$$

As $\tau \to 0$, we obtain the detailed balance equation $\pi_i q_{ij} = \pi_j q_{ji}$. The π_i define the stationary distribution by definition.

For the converse, suppose $\{\pi_k\}$ satisfy the detailed balance conditions. Clearly they constitute the stationary distribution by uniqueness and we have to prove reversibility. Consider the behaviour of the process in the interval $[-u, u]$. Suppose that $X_{-u} = i_0$, that X_t changes state to i_n at time τ_n for $1 \leq n \leq m$, $-u < \tau_1 < \ldots < \tau_m < u$ and that $X_t = i_m$ for all $t \in (\tau_m, u]$. In other words, during the interval $[-u, u]$ the process begins in state i_0, undergoes the state transitions $i_0 \rightarrow i_1 \rightarrow \ldots \rightarrow i_m$ and remains in state i_m up to time u. Let $T_k = \tau_{k+1} - \tau_k$ for $0 \leq k \leq m$ where we define $\tau_0 = -u$, $\tau_{m+1} = u$. Then, for $0 \leq k < m$, T_k is the holding time in state i_k which has exponential distribution with parameter q_{i_k} and $P(T_m > t_m) = e^{-q_{i_m} t_m}$. The joint probability density function of $(T_0, \ldots, T_m)$ together with the joint mass function of $(X_{\tau_0^+}, \ldots, X_{\tau_m^+})$ is therefore

$$f(t_0, \ldots, t_m, i_0, \ldots, i_m)$$

$$= \pi_{i_0} q_{i_0} e^{-q_{i_0} t_0} \left(\prod_{k=1}^{m-1} r_{i_{k-1} i_k} q_{i_k} e^{-q_{i_k} t_k} \right) r_{i_{m-1} i_m} e^{-q_{i_m} t_m}$$

$$= \pi_{i_0} e^{-q_{i_0} t_0} \left\{ \prod_{k=1}^{m} q_{i_{k-1} i_k} e^{-q_{i_k} t_k} \right\}$$

where $r_{ij} = q_{ij}/q_i$ is the probability of a state transition in state i leading to state j; see the previous section. Now, using the detailed balance equation m times for the pairs of states (i_{k-1}, i_k), $1 \leq k \leq m$, now yields

$$\pi_{i_0} \prod_{k=1}^{m} q_{i_{k-1} i_k} = \pi_{i_m} \prod_{k=1}^{m} q_{i_{m-k+1} i_{m-k}}$$

so that the above density f is equal to the corresponding density for the process starting in state i_m at time $-u$, passing through the sequence of states $i_m \rightarrow i_{m-1} \rightarrow \ldots \rightarrow i_0$ with holding time t_k in state i_k $(m \geq k \geq 1)$ and remaining in state i_0 until time u. Thus X_t behaves probabilistically as X_{-t} on $[-u, u]$ for all u and so $(X_{t_1}, \ldots, X_{t_m})$ has the same distribution as $(X_{-t_1}, \ldots, X_{-t_m})$ for all positive integers m. Finally, this distribution is the same as $(X_{\tau - t_1}, \ldots, X_{\tau - t_m})$ for all τ by stationarity. ∎

We can now use the aggregated balance equations of Section 4.3 to deduce the following sufficient condition for a stationary Markov process to be reversible.

Proposition 4.22

If the (undirected) state transition graph of a stationary Markov process is a tree, the process is reversible.

Proof Every state s in the graph other than the root has a unique parent s' since the graph is a tree. Let us define the subset A of states to contain all those *not* in the subtree with s at its root. Then the only probability flux going out of A is from s' to s and the only flux going into A is from s to s'.   ∎

We have already seen one important reversible Markov process: the birth and death process. Its state transition graph is linear, i.e. a tree with no branches, which proves its reversibility. We can also define reversible processes from other reversible processes. For example, if $\{X_t\}$ and $\{Y_t\}$ are reversible, so is their product $\{(X_t, Y_t)\}$, and similarly for any finite product of reversible processes. Also, if $\{X_t\}$ is reversible, then so is $\{f(X_t)\}$ for any function f. These results are clear if the original processes have trees for their transition graphs but require a little more work to establish (left as an exercise) if not.

As with the birth and death process, we can use the detailed balance equations to obtain the stationary distribution of a reversible Markov process by simply forming a product of ratios of instantaneous transition rates.

Proposition 4.23

The stationary distribution π of a reversible Markov process with generator matrix Q and state space S is given by

$$\pi_i = \frac{\alpha_i}{\sum_{k \in S} \alpha_k} \qquad (i \in S)$$

where

$$\alpha_i = \prod_{k=1}^{n} \frac{q_{i_{k-1}i_k}}{q_{i_k i_{k-1}}}, \; i_0, \ldots, i_n \in S, \, i_n = i \qquad \text{and} \quad \begin{array}{l} q_{i_{k-1}i_k} > 0, \\ q_{i_k i_{k-1}} > 0 \end{array}$$

$$\text{for } k = 1, 2, \ldots, n - 1$$

Proof The proof is straightforward, successively using the detailed balance equations $\pi_k = \pi_j q_{jk}/q_{kj}$ for $(j, k) = (i_0, i_1)$, $(i_1, i_2), \ldots, (i_{n-1}, i_n)$. We can choose the state i_0 arbitrarily as a reference state – cf. the state 0 which represented population 0 in the birth and death process. Notice that we can *always* find a chain of one-step transitions $i_0 \to i_1 \to \ldots \to i_{n-1} \to i$ (with $q_{i_{k-1}i_k} > 0$ for $k = 1, 2, \ldots, n$) in an irreducible Markov process.   ∎

4.4.1 Kolmogorov's criteria

Detailed balance is a necessary and sufficient condition for a Markov process to be reversible but it involves the unknown vector π, i.e. the sought after equilibrium state space probabilities. Since π is itself defined by the generators of a Markov process, we might hope to find a test for reversibility which involves *only* the generators. Such a test is provided by Kolmogorov's criteria for Markov processes; similar criteria exist for discrete Markov chains.

Proposition 4.24

A stationary Markov process with instantaneous transition rate matrix Q is reversible if and only if

$$q_{i_1i_2}q_{i_2i_3} \cdots q_{i_{n-1}i_n}q_{i_ni_1} = q_{i_1i_n}q_{i_ni_{n-1}} \cdots q_{i_3i_2}q_{i_2i_1} \tag{4.1}$$

for every finite sequence of states $i_1, i_2, \ldots, i_n$.

Proof If the process is reversible, detailed balance implies that $\pi_j q_{jk} = \pi_k q_{kj}$ for all $j, k \in S$. Taking $(j, k) = (i_1, i_2)$, (i_2, i_3), $\ldots$, (i_{n-1}, i_n), (i_n, i_1) in turn and multiplying then yields Equation (4.1).

Conversely, suppose that Equation (4.1) is satisfied. Now, for all $j, k \in S$, we can find a chain $j \to j_1 \to \ldots \to j_{n-1} \to k$ $(n \geq 1)$ of one-step transitions since the Markov process is irreducible. Suppose that $q_{kj} > 0$. Then there is a chain $j \to j_1 \to \ldots \to j_{n-1} \to k \to j$ and so by Equation (4.1) there is also a chain $j \to k \to j_{n-1} \to \ldots \to j_1 \to j$. Hence $q_{kj} > 0 \Rightarrow q_{jk} > 0$ for all $j, k \in S$.

Now pick an arbitrary state $i_0 \in S$ as a reference state and for state $i \in S$, let $i \to i_{n-1} \to \ldots \to i_0$ $(n \geq 1)$ be a chain of one-step transitions. Let

$$\pi_i = C \prod_{k=1}^{n} \frac{q_{i_{k-1}i_k}}{q_{i_ki_{k-1}}}$$

where $i_n = i$ and C is a positive constant. π_i is well defined since if $i = j_m \to j_{m-1} \to \ldots \to j_0 = i_0$ is another chain, Equation (4.1) ensures that

$$\prod_{k=1}^{m} \frac{q_{j_{k-1}j_k}}{q_{j_kj_{k-1}}} = \prod_{k=1}^{n} \frac{q_{i_{k-1}i_k}}{q_{i_ki_{k-1}}}$$

since

$$\prod_{k=1}^{m} q_{j_{k-1}j_k} \prod_{k=1}^{n} q_{i_ki_{k-1}} = \prod_{k=1}^{n} q_{i_{k-1}i_k} \prod_{k=1}^{m} q_{j_kj_{k-1}}$$

and $j_m = i_n = i$ and $j_0 = i_0$. Now suppose that $q_{ik} > 0$ for $k \in S$. Then,

$$\pi_k = C \frac{q_{ik}}{q_{ki}} \prod_{k=1}^{n} \frac{q_{i_{k-1}i_k}}{q_{i_ki_{k-1}}}$$

so that $\pi_k q_{ki} = \pi_i q_{ik}$ and so the detailed balance equations are satisfied. Hence the steady state equation is satisfied by π and, since the Markov process is stationary by hypothesis, $\sum_{i \in S} \pi_i < \infty$. Hence we can choose $C = [\sum_{i \in S} \pi_i]^{-1}$ to make the π_i sum to unity.   ∎

Kolmogorov's criteria imply that there can be no *net circulation* of transitions amongst the states of a Markov process and the name 'reversible' appears very apt.

We have shown how to detect reversible Markov processes and how to construct new reversible processes from old. There are also other such results, for example that a truncated reversible Markov process is reversible. (A truncated process is one with all transition rates into a subset of its state space set to zero.) Most Markov processes are not reversible, but we can still use a similar approach by defining the **reversed process** $X_{\tau-t}$ when X_t is a not necessarily a reversible Markov process. Of course, since the Markov property can be expressed as 'the past and future are independent when conditioned on the present', a reversed Markov process must also be a Markov process. The instantaneous transition rates of the reversed process are related to those of the original process through the stationary distribution π, which is the same for both processes. Indeed, the relationships are so simple that quantities satisfying them can often be found by inspection. Then, by uniqueness, the normalized vector chosen for π must be the actual stationary mass function. This procedure provides a viable methodology for determining this mass function and typically produces much shorter derivations. The basic results relating a stationary Markov process to its reversed process are the following.

Proposition 4.25

The reversed process of a stationary Markov process $\{X_t\}$ with generator matrix Q and stationary probabilities π is a stationary Markov process with transition rate matrix Q' defined by

$$q'_{ij} = \frac{\pi_j q_{ji}}{\pi_i} \qquad i, j \in S$$

and with the same stationary probabilities π.

Proof For $i \neq j$ and $h > 0$,

$$P(X_{t+h} = i) \, P(X_t = j | X_{t+h} = i)$$
$$= P(X_t = j) \, P(X_{t+h} = i | X_t = j)$$

Thus,

$$P(X_t = j | X_{t+h} = i) = \frac{\pi_j}{\pi_i} \, P(X_{t+h} = i | X_t = j)$$

by stationarity. Dividing by h and taking the limit $h \to 0$ yields the required equation for q'_{ij} when $i \neq j$. But, when $i = j$,

$$-q'_{ii} = \sum_{k \neq i} q'_{ik} = \sum_{k \neq i} \frac{\pi_k q_{ki}}{\pi_i} = \sum_{k \neq i} q_{ik}$$

since $\{X_t\}$ has stationary distribution π

$$= -q_{ii}$$

Finally,

$$-\pi_i q'_{ii} = \pi_i \sum_{k \neq i} q_{ik}$$

since $\{X_t\}$ has stationary distribution π

$$= \sum_{k \neq i} \pi_k q'_{ki}$$

so that π is the stationary distribution of the reversed process also. ∎

We can often use this result to obtain the equilibrium distribution of a stationary Markov process in the following way: *guess* possible transition rates $\{q'_{ij} | i, j \in S\}$ for the reversed process and a collection of positive real numbers $\{\pi_i | i \in S\}$ with finite sum G such that

- $q'_i = q_i$ for all $i \in S$
- $\pi_i q'_{ij} = \pi_j q_{ji}$ for all $i \neq j \in S$

Then it follows immediately that $\sum_{j \neq i} \pi_j q_{ji} = \pi_i q'_i = \prod_i q_i$. Thus, π satisfies the balance equations of the Markov process and so $\{\pi_i / G | i \in S\}$ *is* its equilibrium distribution by uniqueness. The reversed process has the same equilibrium distribution and $\{q'_{ij} | i, j \in S\}$ are its instantaneous transition rates by Proposition 4.25.

Of course, this methodology depends crucially on the ability to make the right guess; the same approach could be used to solve *any* set of simultaneous equations defined by a stochastic matrix. It is the intuition associated with a reversed process, together with the fact that it has the same equilibrium state space distribution, that induces 'good guesses'. We start out by literally imagining the physical system working backwards in time; for example, departures from a system become arrivals in the reversed process and vice versa. Moreover, it is plausible that the arrivals in the reversed process will have the same rate as the arrivals in the original process so that the equilibrium distributions are the same. Perhaps more importantly, an apparently reasonable, but

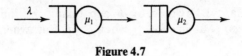

Figure 4.7

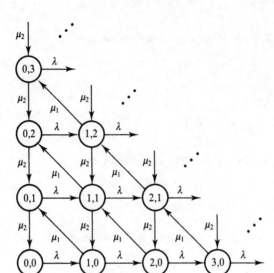

Figure 4.8

incorrect, guess can often be improved when the way in which the equations $\pi_i q'_{ij} = \pi_j q_{ji}$ fail to be satisfied can be understood. In this way, correct values might be determined iteratively. Remember that once the equations are satisfied, we know the unique solution has been found; it matters not *how* we got to it.

To illustrate the approach, we look at the simplest of queueing networks of the type considered in the forthcoming chapters.

Example 4.10 _____

Suppose we have two queues in tandem with Poisson arrivals to queue 1 at rate λ. On leaving queue 1, customers proceed immediately to queue 2 and on leaving queue 2 they depart the system. Customers are served in first come first served order in each queue and both queues' service times are exponential with parameters μ_1 and μ_2 (Figure 4.7); compare the birth and death process. The state space of this process is $\{(i, j) \mid i, j \geq 0\}$ where i and j denote the numbers of customers at queues 1 and 2 respectively. The process is clearly Markov and has the state transition graph shown in Figure 4.8, which shows the instantaneous transition rates q_{ij}. Since the graph has a pair of states that are connected by an arrow in only one direction, the Markov process is not

Figure 4.9

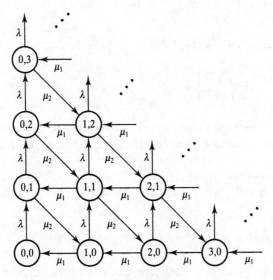

Figure 4.10

reversible – the detailed balance equations cannot be satisfied. (In fact no two states are connected by arrows in both directions.) We therefore set about looking for the reversed process. Imagining the system working backwards, we would expect arrivals to queue 2, probably with rate λ to produce the same steady state distribution. (However, we could always change this value if things were not to work out.) Next, customers leaving queue 2 will proceed to queue 1 and those leaving queue 1 will depart. Again we speculate: that the service rates of each queue should depend on their servers' characteristics and hence remain unchanged. The proposed reversed system is therefore that shown in Figure 4.9. The state transition graph of the reversed process, showing the transition rates q'_{ij}, is therefore as shown in Figure 4.10.

To check if the equations $\pi_i q'_{ij} = \pi_j q_{ji}$ have a solution, we observe that transitions are of three types: horizontal, vertical and diagonal.

Horizontal transitions
For $m \geq 0$, $n \geq 0$, $q_{(m,n),(m+1,n)} = \lambda$ and $q'_{(m+1,n),(m,n)} = \mu_1$. Thus we require

$$\pi_{(m+1,n)} = \left(\frac{\lambda}{\mu_1}\right)^{m+1} \pi_{(0,n)} \qquad m, n \geq 0$$

Vertical transitions

For $m \geq 0$, $n \geq 0$, $q_{(m,n+1),(m,n)} = \mu_2$ and $q'_{(m,n),(m,n+1)} = \lambda$. Thus we require

$$\pi_{(m,n+1)} = \left(\frac{\lambda}{\mu_2}\right)^{n+1} \pi_{(m,0)} \qquad m, n \geq 0$$

Combining these results, we have

$$\pi_{(m,n)} = \left(\frac{\lambda}{\mu_1}\right)^m \left(\frac{\lambda}{\mu_2}\right)^n \pi_{(0,0)} \qquad m, n \geq 0$$

So far, any choice of values for the q'_{ij} would be acceptable since the sets of transitions are orthogonal. The crucial test comes next:

Diagonal transitions

For $m \geq 0$, $n \geq 0$, $q_{(m+1,n),(m,n+1)} = \mu_1$ and $q'_{(m,n+1),(m+1,n)} = \mu_2$. Thus we require

$$\pi_{(m,n+1)}\mu_2 = \pi_{(m+1,n)}\mu_1$$

which is clearly true upon substitution of our expression for $\pi_{(m,n)}$.

We therefore conclude that the (full) balance equations hold and that the process is stationary if $\sum_{m=0}^{\infty}\sum_{n=0}^{\infty} \pi_{(m,n)}$ converges so that there is a solution which is a probability mass function. The stationarity condition is therefore $\lambda < \min(\mu_1, \mu_2)$, whereupon, normalizing our expression for $\pi_{(m,n)}$, the stationary distribution is

$$\pi_{(m,n)} = (1 - \rho_1)(1 - \rho_2)\rho_1^m \rho_2^n \qquad m, n \geq 0$$

where $\rho_1 = \lambda/\mu_1$ and $\rho_2 = \lambda/\mu_2$. In other words, the two queues are identical to two independent birth and death processes, i.e. independent simple queues. We will learn much more about queueing networks in the rest of this book. For example, we will show using reversibility arguments that the times spent by a given customer in each queue of a tandem series are also independent.

4.5 Renewal theory

In a Markov process, the times between state transitions are exponential random variables. We now relax this restriction and define a renewal process as follows. Let X_1, X_2, ... be the times of successive occurrences of some fixed phenomenon and let $Z_i = X_i - X_{i-1}$ (with $X_0 = 0$) be the time between the $(i - 1)$th and ith occurrence, $i \geq 1$. If

$\{Z_i | i \geq 1\}$ are independent and identically distributed, then the stochastic process $\{X_i | i \geq 0\}$ is called a **renewal process**. The times $\{X_i\}$ are called **renewal times** and the intervals $\{Z_i\}$ are called **renewal periods**. The occurrences themselves at each X_i are often just called **renewals**. The study of renewal processes is called **renewal theory** and forms a central part of probability theory as a general account of functions of independent, identically distributed random variables. Whole books have been written on the subject. Here we introduce the main ideas and show the role of renewal theory in modelling applications.

A renewal process therefore generalizes the notion of a Markov process but also specializes it in the sense that there is only one type of event, i.e. only one state, the occurrence of the said phenomenon. However, we can extend renewal theory to allow for any number of phenomena, each having its own independent, identically distributed renewal periods – measured up to the next renewal of any type. If the next renewals are selected according to a discrete time Markov chain, the renewal process is called a **semi-Markov process**. We will consider such processes briefly at the end of this section and model M/G/1 queues in this way in the next chapter.

Examples of renewal processes abound. In the world of computers and communications, the 'phenomenon' might be the arrival of a message at a node in a communication network. Then, if the message inter-arrival times Z_i are independent and identically distributed, $\{X_i\}$ is a renewal process. In the special case that the inter-arrival times are exponential, the renewal process will be a Poisson process. Similarly, the arrivals might be students handing in coursework at a departmental office or buses at a bus stop. The traditional application of renewal theory was in reliability modelling, which remains at least as important now in computer applications. The archetypal example is that of a light bulb installed at time 0, which burns continuously until it fails, whereupon it is replaced instantaneously and the process is repeated. If the lifetime of the ith bulb is Z_i, its installation time is $X_i = Z_1 + \ldots + Z_{i-1}$, where $X_0 = 0$. Assuming the Z_i to be independent and identically distributed, they form the renewal periods of the renewal process $\{X_i\}$.

From the definition of a renewal process, we can determine the joint distribution of any number of the renewal times solely from the distribution function of the renewal period, which we denote by F. In particular,

$$P(X_{m+n} - X_m \leq t | X_i = x_i, 0 \leq i \leq n) = F^{n*}(t)$$

where F^{n*} denotes the n-fold convolution of F with itself, $F*F*\ldots*F$ (with n occurrences of F). In addition, for $m < n$,

$$P(X_m \leq s, X_n \leq t) = \int_0^s P(X_n \leq t | X_m = u) \, dP(X_m \leq u)$$

$$= \int_0^s P(Z_{m+1} + \ldots + Z_n \leq t - u) \, dF^{m*}(u)$$

$$= \int_0^s F^{(n-m)*}(t - u) \, dF^{m*}(u)$$

Hence, the distribution function F of the renewal period is sufficient to characterize completely the renewal process $\{X_i\}$.

4.5.1 The renewal equation

Let us now consider the number of renewals N_t in the interval $(0, t]$, given that there was a renewal at time 0. Then $N_t = \max\{n | X_n \leq t\}$. Since the Markov property holds at renewal times, the number of renewals in an interval $(s, t]$ has the same distribution as N_{t-s}. Thus, given that the first renewal occurs at time $X_1 = s$,

$$N_t = \begin{cases} 0 & (s > t) \\ 1 + N_{t-s} & (s \leq t) \end{cases}$$

(see Figure 4.11). Now suppose that the renewal period has distribution function F and that the random variable S denotes the time of the first renewal. We also assume that F is differentiable, i.e. that the renewal period has a probability density function f, although we could proceed using Stieltjes integrals without this stronger assumption. We now have

$$E[z^{N_t}] = E[E[z^{N_t} | S]]$$

$$= \int_t^\infty E[z^0] f(s) \, ds + \int_0^t E[z^{1+N_{t-s}}] f(s) \, ds$$

$$= 1 - F(t) + z \int_0^t E[z^{N_{t-s}}] f(s) \, ds$$

Thus we have the following integral equation for $\Pi_t(z)$, the probability generating function of N_t:

$$\Pi_t(z) = 1 - F(t) + z \int_0^t \Pi_{t-s}(z) f(s) \, ds \tag{4.2}$$

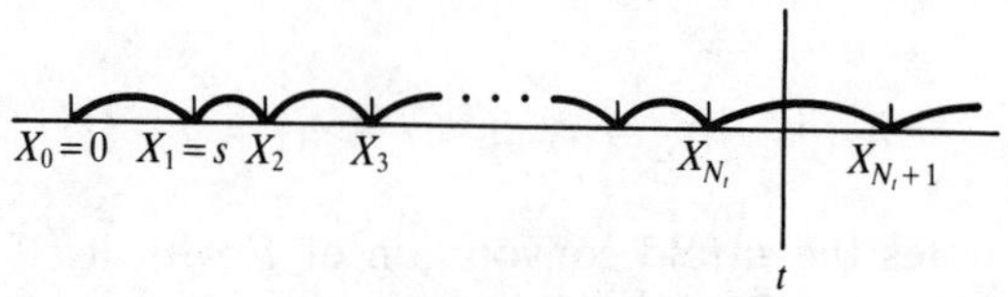

Figure 4.11

An integral equation of the form

$$A(t) = a(t) + \int_0^t A(t - s)\,dF(s) \tag{4.3}$$

where the function $a(t)$ and distribution function $F(s)$ are given, is called a **renewal equation**; so-called because of the renewal argument which leads to it, i.e. conditioning on a 'first renewal time'. In our case, for each z, Equation (4.2) is a renewal equation in $A(t) \equiv \Pi_t(z)$ with $a(t) = 1 - F(t)$ and $f(s) = zF'(s)$.

Renewal equations have unique solutions under quite mild conditions as we will see shortly. Moreover, the solution is given in terms of a function which is fundamental to the whole concept of renewal theory. This is the mean number of renewals in the interval $(0, t]$, which we denote by $R(t)$. Differentiating Equation (4.2) with respect to z and setting $z = 1$, we obtain another renewal equation

$$R(t) = \int_0^t \Pi_{t-s}(1)f(s)\,ds + \int_0^t \left.\frac{\partial \Pi_{t-s}(z)}{\partial z}\right|_{z=1} f(s)\,ds$$

$$= F(t) + \int_0^t R(t - s)f(s)\,ds \tag{4.4}$$

Of course, we could have derived this directly using the same renewal argument. $R(t)$ is called the **renewal function** and can also be obtained by the following simple argument. First, notice that the event 'there are at least n renewals in $(0, t]$' is the same as the event 'the nth renewal time is less than or equal to t'. Thus, $N_t \geq n \equiv X_n \leq t$ and so $P(N_t \geq n) = P(X_n \leq t)$. Hence,

$$R(t) = \sum_{k=1}^{\infty} kP(N_t = k)$$

$$= \sum_{k=1}^{\infty} k[P(N_t \geq k) - P(N_t \geq k + 1)]$$

$$= \sum_{k=1}^{\infty} k[P(X_k \leq t) - P(X_{k+1} \leq t)]$$

$$= \sum_{k=1}^{\infty} F^{k*}(t)$$

Thus, $F(t) + [F*R](t) = R(t)$, which is exactly what is stated by the renewal equation.

The solution of the general renewal equation is given by the renewal function as follows.

Proposition 4.26

If the function a is bounded, there is a *unique* function A, bounded on finite intervals, which satisfies the renewal equation $A(t) = a(t) + \int_0^t A(t - s) \, dF(s)$ defined by

$$A(t) = a(t) + \int_0^t a(t - s) \, dR(s)$$

Proof We just sketch a plausible argument. A full proof may be found in Karlin and Taylor (1975). Denoting by g^* the Laplace transform of a function g, we obtain from the renewal equation

$$A^* = a^* + A^*F^*$$

since the integral is a convolution. Similarly, from the renewal Equation (4.4) for R above,

$$R^* = F^* + R^*F^*$$

so that $F^* = R^*/(1 + R^*)$. Thus $A^* = a^*/(1 - F^*)$. But this is the Laplace transform of the solution to be proved. ■

If we differentiate Equation (4.4) for $R(t)$ with respect to t, defining $r(t) = dR(t)/dt$, we obtain

$$r(t) = f(t) + R(0)f(t) + \int_0^t r(t - s)f(s) \, ds$$

But since $N_0 = 0$, $R(0) = 0$ and so we have the renewal equation

$$r(t) = f(t) + \int_0^t r(t - s)f(s) \, ds$$

We call $r(t)$ the **renewal density** which is the *instantaneous renewal rate* in the sense that the probability of a renewal in $(t, t + h]$ is $r(t)h + o(h)$; see Exercise 4.15.

4.5.2 Asymptotic properties of the renewal function

Intuitively, the number of renewals occurring up to a large time t should be close to the ratio t/μ where μ is the mean renewal period.[1] Furthermore, after the process has been running for a long time t, we

---

[1]*Warning*: The use of μ to denote a mean time interval is conventional in renewal theory and many texts on statistics. In the later chapters μ will always denote a service *rate*, with dimension t^{-1}, which is also conventional.

might expect the number of renewals in the interval $(t, t + \tau]$ to be close to τ/μ for all $\tau > 0$. We formalize these ideas in the following collection of propositions which are central to renewal theory.

Proposition 4.27 (Arrival rate lemma)

If $\mu < \infty$, $N_t/t \to 1/\mu$ with probability 1 as $t \to \infty$.

Proof   For all $t > 0$, $X_{N_t} \leqslant t < X_{N_t+1}$ and so

$$\frac{X_{N_t}}{N_t} \leqslant \frac{t}{N_t} < \frac{X_{N_t+1}}{N_t + 1} \frac{N_t + 1}{N_t}$$

Now, by the strong law of large numbers, $X_n/n \to \mu$ as $n \to \infty$ and so, since $N_t \to \infty$ as $t \to \infty$, t/N_t is 'trapped' between two quantities which both converge to μ as $t \to \infty$. Thus $t/N_t \to \mu$ also. ∎

If we can take expectation within the limit, we can now immediately deduce that $R(t)/t \to 1/\mu$ as $t \to \infty$ since $R(t) = E[N_t]$. However, the result can be proved directly as follows.

Proposition 4.28 (Elementary renewal theorem)

If $\mu < \infty$, $R(t)/t \to 1/\mu$ as $t \to \infty$.

Proof   We prove that

$$1/\mu \leqslant \liminf_{t \to \infty} R(t)/t \leqslant \limsup_{t \to \infty} R(t)/t \leqslant 1/\mu$$

where the middle inequality always holds by definition. Now, $t < X_{N_t+1}$ for all t, and so $t < E[X_{N_t+1}]$. For the left-hand inequality, we claim that $E[X_{N_t+1}] = (R(t) + 1)\mu$ so that $R(t)/t > 1/\mu - 1/t$ for all $t > 0$ and the result follows. To prove the claim, we have, by the law of total probability,

$$E[X_{N_t+1}] = \int_0^\infty E[X_{N_t+1}|X_1 = s]f(s)\,ds$$

$$= \int_t^\infty sf(s)\,ds + \int_0^t \{s + E[X_{N_{t-s}+1}]\}f(s)\,ds$$

since, using the usual renewal argument,

$$E[X_{N_t+1}|X_1 = s] = \begin{cases} s & \text{if } s > t \text{ since then } N_t = 0 \\ s + E[X_{N_{t-s}+1}] & \text{if } s \leqslant t \end{cases}$$

Thus,

$$E[X_{N_t+1}] = \mu + \int_0^t E[X_{N_{t-s}+1}]f(s)\,ds$$

and we have a renewal equation with $A(t) = E[X_{N_t+1}]$, $a(t) = \mu$. By Proposition 4.26, the solution is

$$E[X_{N_t+1}] = \mu + \int_0^t \mu \, dR(s) = \mu(1 + R(t))$$

as required. For the right-hand inequality, we consider a related 'truncated' renewal process with renewal periods $\{Z_i^c\}$ defined by

$$Z_i^c = \begin{cases} Z_i & \text{if } Z_i \leq c \\ c & \text{if } Z_i > c \end{cases}$$

Superscripting the analogous quantities of the truncated process with c, we must have $t + c \geq X_{N_t^c+1}^c$ for all t so that $t + c \geq (R^c(t) + 1)\mu^c$ using the same claim. But since $X_i^c \leq X_i$, $N_t^c \geq N_t$ so that $R(t) \leq R^c(t)$ for all t. Thus we obtain

$$\frac{R(t)}{t} \leq \frac{1}{\mu^c} + \frac{1}{t}\left(\frac{c}{\mu^c} - 1\right)$$

and hence $\limsup_{t\to\infty} R(t)/t \leq 1/\mu^c$ for any $c > 0$. Finally, $\mu^c \to \mu$ as $c \to \infty$ and so the result follows. ∎

We now consider the asymptotic behaviour, as $t \to \infty$, of the solution $A(t)$ of the general renewal Equation (4.3). This is given by the following proposition, the **Key Renewal Theorem**, also called the **Basic Renewal Theorem**, which essentially allows us to take the limit under the integral sign in the expression for $A(t)$; see our apology for a proof. As its name indicates, this is a deep and fundamental result and to state it in reasonable generality requires two definitions.

Definition 4.4

The point x is a **point of increase** of a distribution function F if for all $\varepsilon > 0$, $F(x + \varepsilon) > F(x - \varepsilon)$. F is **arithmetic** if there exists $\lambda > 0$ such that F has points of increase only in the set $\{0, \pm\lambda, \pm 2\lambda, \ldots\}$. Thus, any distribution function with a continuous part is non-arithmetic.

Definition 4.5

A function g is **absolutely integrable** on $[0, \infty)$ if $\int_0^\infty |g(x)| \, dx < \infty$.

Proposition 4.29 (Key Renewal Theorem)

Let F be the non-arithmetic distribution function of a positive random variable with mean μ and suppose that the function a is monotonic and absolutely integrable. Then,

$$\int_0^t a(t-s)\,dR(s) \to \frac{1}{\mu} \int_0^\infty a(s)\,ds \qquad \text{as } t \to \infty$$

In other words, if A is the solution of the renewal equation $A(t) = a(t) + \int_0^t A(t-s)\,dF(s)$, then

$$A(t) \to \frac{1}{\mu} \int_0^\infty a(s)\,ds \qquad \text{as } t \to \infty$$

Proof A rigorous proof is long and laborious and the dedicated reader is referred to Feller (1971). Here we offer a plausible argument. By the elementary renewal theorem, we know that $R(t)/t \to 1/\mu$ and hence that $r(t) \to \mu^{-1}$ as $t \to \infty$. In addition, by hypothesis, $a(t) \to 0$ as $t \to \infty$. Thus, for fixed, sufficiently large t, we can choose τ large enough that $r(s) - \mu^{-1}$ is negligible for $s \geq \tau$ and $a(t-s)$ is negligible for $s \leq \tau$. Then,

$$\int_0^t [r(s) - \mu^{-1}] a(t-s)\,ds = \int_0^\tau [r(s) - \mu^{-1}] a(t-s)\,ds$$

$$+ \int_\tau^t [r(s) - \mu^{-1}] a(t-s)\,ds \approx 0$$

since both integrals on the right-hand side are negligible. Thus, as $t \to \infty$,

$$\int_0^t a(t-s)\,dR(s) = \int_0^t r(s) a(t-s)\,ds \to \int_0^t \mu^{-1} a(s)\,ds$$

by change of integration variable s to $t-s$. But the left-hand side is the solution of the renewal equation as $t \to \infty$ by Proposition 4.26. ∎

An equivalent statement of the Key Renewal Theorem is **Blackwell's theorem** which relates directly to the renewal function and is now presented as a corollary.

Corollary (Blackwell's theorem)

$$\lim_{t \to \infty} [R(t) - R(t-h)] = \frac{h}{\mu}$$

Proof Given $h > 0$, define a by

$$a(s) = \begin{cases} 1 & \text{if } 0 \leq s < h \\ 0 & \text{if } s \geq h \end{cases}$$

Then, by Proposition 4.26,

$$A(t) = a(t) + \int_{t-h}^{t} a(t - s)\,dR(s)$$

so that for $t > h$,

$$A(t) = \int_{t-h}^{t} dR(s) = R(t) - R(t - h)$$

The Key Renewal Theorem then yields $R(t) - R(t - h) \to \mu^{-1}h$ as $t \to \infty$.   ∎

The converse implication, that the Key Renewal Theorem follows from Blackwell's theorem, may be proved by approximating an integrable function with step functions. In fact, the condition that a be a monotonic, absolutely convergent function can be relaxed to a being directly Riemann integrable. An immediate corollary to Blackwell's theorem is the Renewal Density Theorem, $r(t) \to \mu^{-1}$ as $t \to \infty$. We conclude our discussion of asymptotic properties by finding the second-order term in the expansion of $R(t)$.

Proposition 4.30

If F is differentiable with density f, finite mean μ and variance σ^2,

$$R(t) - \frac{t}{\mu} \to \frac{\sigma^2 - \mu^2}{2\mu^2} \qquad \text{as } t \to \infty$$

Proof Let $f^*(\theta)$, $R^*(\theta)$, $r^*(\theta)$ be the Laplace transforms of $f(t)$, $R(t)$, $r(t)$ respectively. Then by the renewal Equation (4.4) for R and its derivative, $r^* = f^*/(1 - f^*)$. Thus, since

$$f^*(\theta) = E[e^{-\theta Z}] = 1 - \theta\mu + \frac{\theta^2}{2!}(\sigma^2 + \mu^2) + o(\theta^2)$$

and $r^*(\theta) = \theta R^*(\theta)$,[1] we have

$$\begin{aligned} R^*(\theta) &= \frac{f^*(\theta)}{\theta[1 - f^*(\theta)]} = \frac{1 - \mu\theta + o(\theta)}{\mu\theta^2[1 - (\theta/2\mu)(\sigma^2 + \mu^2) + o(\theta)]} \\ &= \frac{[1 - \mu\theta + o(\theta)][1 + (\theta/2\mu)(\sigma^2 + \mu^2) + o(\theta)]}{\mu\theta^2} \\ &= \frac{1}{\mu\theta^2} + \frac{1}{\theta}\left(\frac{\sigma^2 - \mu^2}{2\mu^2}\right) + O(1) \end{aligned}$$

[1] Let $g(t) = G'(t)$ and let $g^*(\theta)$, $G^*(\theta)$ be the Laplace transforms of $g(t)$, $G(t)$ respectively. Then, for reasonable g – certainly a density function,

$$-G(0) = \int_0^{\infty} \frac{d}{dt}[e^{-\theta t}G(t)]\,dt = \int_0^{\infty} \{-\theta e^{-\theta t}G(t) + e^{-\theta t}g(t)\}\,dt = -\theta G^*(\theta) + g^*(\theta)$$

The result follows since $R(0) = 0$.

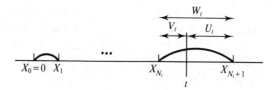

Figure 4.12

We now use the Tauberian theorem which states that if $g^*(\theta) = a\theta^{-2} + b\theta^{-1} + O(1)$ as $\theta \to 0$, then $g(t) = at + b + o(1)$ as $t \to \infty$. This yields

$$R(t) = \frac{t}{\mu} + \frac{\sigma^2 - \mu^2}{2\mu^2} + o(1)$$

as $t \to \infty$, as required.   ∎

4.5.2 Recurrence times

Another random variable of interest is the time remaining in a renewal period from the current time t up to the next renewal. This random variable is the **forward recurrence time** at time t, which we denote by U_t. It is often also called the **residual life**, corresponding to the time left before the failure of a component and its immediate replacement by another. Similarly, the **backward recurrence time** at time t, V_t, is the time elapsed since the most recent renewal. These times are illustrated in Figure 4.12. A related random variable is the sum $W_t = U_t + V_t$. This is the length of a renewal period, but not just any renewal period: the particular period is conditioned on its containing the observation time point, t. There is therefore no reason to believe that the distribution of W_t should be the same as that of the renewal period, namely F. Indeed, we would expect a random observation point to lie in a given renewal period with probability proportional to the length of that period. Thus, if W_t has density f_{W_t}, we would expect $f_{W_t}(x) \propto x$ and we shall verify this shortly.

We now obtain the probability densities of the forward and backward recurrence times, f_{U_t} and f_{V_t} respectively, as well as f_{W_t}, assuming that the renewal period has density f.

Using the renewal argument again, i.e. conditioning on the time of the first renewal, given that $X_1 = \tau$,

$$U_t = \begin{cases} \tau - t & \text{if } \tau \geq t, \text{ i.e. there are no renewals in } (0, t) \\ U_{t-\tau} & \text{if } \tau < t \end{cases}$$

Hence,

$$P(U_t > u | X_1 = \tau) = \begin{cases} 1 & \text{if } \tau > t + u \\ 0 & \text{if } t + u \geqslant \tau \geqslant t \\ P(U_{t-\tau} > u) & \text{if } 0 < \tau < t \end{cases}$$

Thus, by the law of total probability,

$$P(U_t > u) = \int_0^\infty P(U_t > u | X_1 = \tau) f(\tau) \, d\tau$$

$$= \int_{t+u}^\infty 1 \times f(\tau) \, d\tau + \int_t^{t+u} 0 \times f(\tau) \, d\tau$$

$$+ \int_0^t P(U_{t-\tau} > u) f(\tau) \, d\tau$$

$$= [1 - F(t + u)] + \int_0^t P(U_{t-\tau} > u) f(\tau) \, d\tau$$

This is a renewal equation of the form of Proposition 4.26 with $A(t) = P(U_t > u)$ and $a(t) = 1 - F(t + u)$. Thus,

$$P(U_t > u) = [1 - F(t + u)] + \int_0^t [1 - F(t + u - s)] \, dR(s)$$

and, differentiating with respect to u and negating, we obtain

$$f_{U_t}(u) = f(t + u) + \int_0^t f(t + u - s) \, dR(s)$$

Now consider the asymptotic behaviour of this density as $t \to \infty$. The conditions of the Key Renewal Theorem are satisfied, with $a(t) = f(t + u)$, so that, as $t \to \infty$,

$$f_{U_t}(u) \to f_U(u) = \frac{1}{\mu} \int_0^\infty f(s + u) \, ds$$

$$= \frac{1}{\mu} \int_u^\infty f(s) \, ds$$

i.e.

$$f_U(u) = \frac{1}{\mu} [1 - F(u)]$$

Using the same argument, we can determine the moments of forward recurrence time.

$$E[U_t^p] = \begin{cases} (\tau - t)^p & \text{if } \tau \geqslant t \\ E[U_{t-\tau}^p] & \text{if } \tau < t \end{cases}$$

given $X_1 = \tau$. This gives for the mean after careful consideration of the integration variables

$$E[U_t] = E[E[U_t|X_1]] = \mu[1 + R(t)] - t$$

As $t \to \infty$, by Proposition 4.30,

$$E[U_t] \to m = \mu \, \frac{\sigma^2 + \mu^2}{2\mu^2} = \frac{M_2}{2\mu}$$

where M_2 is the second moment of the renewal period distribution F. This result can also be obtained from the expression we derived above for $f_U(u)$ by integration by parts.

Now let us consider the backward recurrence time, V_t. In this case, if $X_1 = \tau$, $V_t = t$ if $t < \tau$ and $V_t = V_{t-\tau}$ if $t \geq \tau$. Thus, for $v \leq t$,

$$P(V_t \leq v) = \int_t^\infty I_{t \leq v} f(\tau) \, d\tau + \int_0^t P(V_{t-\tau} \leq v) f(\tau) \, d\tau$$

Thus, the backward recurrence time distribution is

$$F_{V_t}(v) = [1 - F(t)]I_{t \leq v} + \int_0^t F_{V_{t-\tau}}(v) f(\tau) \, d\tau$$

and, by Proposition 4.26,

$$F_{V_t}(v) = [1 - F(t)]I_{t \leq v} + \int_0^t [1 - F(t - s)]I_{t-s \leq v} \, dR(s)$$

The corresponding density is therefore

$$f_{V_t}(v) = [1 - F(t)]\delta(v - t)$$
$$+ \int_0^t [1 - F(t - s)]\delta(s - t + v) r(s) \, ds$$
$$= [1 - F(t)]\delta(v - t) + [1 - F(v)]r(t - v)$$

where δ is the Dirac delta function. The asymptotic density now follows from the renewal density theorem, $r(t) \to \mu^{-1}$ as $t \to \infty$:

$$f_V(v) = \lim_{t \to \infty} f_{V_t}(v) = [1 - F(v)]\mu^{-1}$$

Hence, $f_V = f_U$.

Now, for f_{W_t} we have,

$$F_{W_t}(w) = \begin{cases} \int_t^w 1 \times f(\tau) \, d\tau + \int_w^\infty 0 \times f(\tau) \, d\tau + \int_0^t F_{W_{t-\tau}}(w) f(\tau) \, d\tau \\ \hspace{8cm} \text{if } t < w \\ \int_0^t F_{W_{t-\tau}}(w) f(\tau) \, d\tau \hspace{3cm} \text{if } t \geq w \end{cases}$$

Thus,

$$F_{W_t}(w) = [F(w) - F(t)]I_{t<w} + \int_0^t F_{W_{t-\tau}}(w)f(\tau)\,d\tau$$

so that by Proposition 4.26,

$$F_{W_t}(w) = [F(w) - F(t)]I_{t<w} + \int_0^t [F(w) - F(t - s)]I_{t-s<w}\,dR(s)$$

$$= \int_{t-w}^t [F(w) - F(t - s)]\,dR(s)$$

when $w \leq t$. Differentiating with respect to w now gives

$$f_{W_t}(w) = \int_{t-w}^t f(w)r(s)\,ds - [F(w) - F(w)]r(t - w)$$

$$= f(w)[R(t) - R(t - w)]$$

Thus, by Blackwell's theorem,

$$f_W(w) = \lim_{t\to\infty} f_{W_t}(w) = \frac{w}{\mu} f(w)$$

for all $w > 0$. This is as expected since a point chosen 'at random' on the real line can be expected to lie in a renewal period of length w with probability density proportional to both w and the proportion of intervals of length w in the sample.

Finally, let us consider the joint distribution of U and V – the asymptotic case only. Now the event $U_t > u \cap V_t > v$ is the same as the event $N_{t-v,t+u} = 0$ $(v < t)$. Thus,

$$P(U_t > u \cap V_t > v) = P(U_{t-v} > u + v)$$

$$= [1 - F(t - v + u + v)]$$

$$+ \int_0^{t-v} [1 - F(t - v + u + v - s)]\,dR(s)$$

$$= [1 - F(t + u)]$$

$$+ \int_0^{t-v} [1 - F(t + u - s)]\,dR(s)$$

by the renewal argument used for forward recurrence times

$$\to \frac{1}{\mu} \int_0^\infty [1 - F(s + u + v)]\,ds$$

as $t \to \infty$ by the Key Renewal Theorem. Differentiating with respect to u and v now yields

$$f_{U_t, V_t}(u, v) = \frac{\partial^2}{\partial u \partial v} P(U_t > u \cap V_t > v) = f(u + v) r(t - v)$$

$$\rightarrow \frac{1}{\mu} f(u + v) \qquad \text{as } t \rightarrow \infty$$

We conclude this section by identifying some unique properties of the Poisson renewal process.

Proposition 4.31

The Poisson process is the only renewal process for which

(a)   The forward recurrence time, backward recurrence time and renewal time all have the same density;

(b)   The forward recurrence time and backward recurrence time are independent.

Proof

(a)   Asymptotically, $f_U(t) = f_V(t) = [1 - F(t)]\mu$ and so $f(t) = f_U(t)$ iff

$$\frac{dF}{dt} = \frac{1}{\mu} [1 - F(t)]$$

i.e.

$$\frac{d}{dt} (Fe^{t/\mu}) = \frac{e^{t/\mu}}{\mu}$$

Thus we require $Fe^{t/\mu} = e^{t/\mu} + C$ where C is a constant. Since $F(0) = 0$ (the first renewal cannot be at time 0), $C = -1$ and so $F(t) = 1 - e^{-t/\mu}$. Hence the renewal period is exponentially distributed. It therefore remains to prove that $f_{U_t}(x) = f_{V_t}(x) = \mu^{-1} e^{-x/\mu}$ at all t. Now, $f_{U_t}(x)$ is the unique solution of the renewal equation

$$f_{U_t}(x) = f(t + x) + \int_0^t f_{U_{t-s}}(x) f(s) \, ds$$

Trying the solution $f_{U_t}(x) = \mu^{-1} e^{-x/\mu}$ for all t, we get on the right-hand side

$$\mu^{-1} e^{-(t+x)/\mu} + \mu^{-1} e^{-x/\mu} \int_0^t \mu^{-1} e^{-s/\mu} \, ds$$

$$= \mu^{-1} e^{-(t+x)/\mu} - \mu^{-1} e^{-x/\mu} [e^{-t/\mu} - 1] = \mu^{-1} e^{-x/\mu}$$

which is the left-hand side. The result is therefore proved and the case of $f_{V_t}(x)$ is similar.

(b)   If U_t and V_t are independent in the limit $t = \infty$, $\mu^{-1}f(u + v) = \mu^{-1}[1 - F(u)]\mu^{-1}[1 - F(v)]$ for all u, v by the previous result. Letting $v = 0$, we obtain, as in part (a), $f(u) = (1/\mu)[1 - F(u)]$ so that f is the exponential density. It remains to prove that U_t and V_t are independent for the Poisson process for all t. This follows since

$$
\begin{aligned}
f_{U_t, V_t}(u, v) &= f(u + v)r(t - v) \\
&= \mu^{-1}[1 - F(u)][1 - F(v)]r(t - v) \\
&= \mu f(u)f(v)r(t - v) \\
&= f_{U_t}(u)f_{V_t}(v)[\mu r(t - v)]
\end{aligned}
$$

But $r(t) = \mu^{-1}$ at all t for the Poisson process; the proof of this is left as an exercise.   ∎

4.5.3   Generalized renewal processes

We now consider two variations of renewal processes. The first variation relaxes the assumption that there was a renewal at time 0, i.e. $X_0 = 0$. Thus we could analyse a process *in equilibrium*, which is observed from an arbitrary time point between two renewals. The time to the first renewal, X_1, then has density $f_{U_t} = \mu^{-1}[1 - F(u)]$. However, *any* distribution is allowed for X_1. Such a process is called a **delayed renewal process**.

Let us consider the renewal function $R_1(t)$ of the delayed process and suppose that X_1 has distribution function F_1. Now, relative to the time of the first renewal, the delayed process behaves in the same way as the ordinary one considered previously in this section. Denoting the number of renewals in the interval $(0, t]$ by N'_t, the familiar renewal argument now yields

$$
E[N'_t | X_1 = \tau] = \begin{cases} 0 & \text{if } \tau > t \\ 1 + E[N_{t-\tau}] & \text{if } \tau \leqslant t \end{cases}
$$

where $N_{t-\tau}$ refers to the ordinary process. Hence,

$$
\begin{aligned}
R'(t) &= E[E[N_t | X_1]] \\
&= \int_t^\infty 0 \times \mathrm{d}F_1(\tau) + \int_0^t [1 + R(t - \tau)]\,\mathrm{d}F_1(\tau)
\end{aligned}
$$

i.e.

$$
R'(t) = F_1(t) + \int_0^t R(t - \tau)\,\mathrm{d}F_1(\tau)
$$

As expected, the result is a simple modification of that of the ordinary process, based on the distribution of the first renewal time. Similarly we can obtain the generating function of N_t and recurrence time densities. A similar situation arises in the analysis of queues where the server may take a vacation when there is no work; see Section 5.2.3. A new arrival may then have to wait before the server returns to start service, giving an exceptional service time.

A second, more fundamental, generalization admits more than one type of phenomenon, or state, to occur. Suppose we have two states, 0 and 1, which might represent 'busy' and 'idle' for a communication channel or 'working' and 'being repaired' in a machine shop – the traditional example in operations research. In an **alternating renewal process** these states alternate and the times spent in each are positive, independent random variables with distribution functions F_0 and F_1 respectively. Suppose state 0 is entered at time 0, e.g. a new packet of data arrives at a channel at time 0. Of course, if this is not the case, we can devise a delayed process as above. Clearly, the times at which state 0 is entered form a renewal process with renewal period distribution F_0*F_1 since the sums of successive renewal periods are independent. Similarly, the times at which state 1 is entered form a delayed renewal process. We are interested in the probability mass function of the state at time t, in particular as $t \to \infty$, so that we can estimate such quantities as channel utilization or machine reliability. Let the random variable s_t denote the state at time t, i.e. the image of s_t is $\{0, 1\}$. We seek $\alpha(t) = P(s_t = 0)$, which we obtain by considering the following more general problem.

Suppose that associated with the ith renewal period in the ordinary renewal process, there is another random variable Y_i, which may depend on the renewal period Z_i, but such that the pairs (Z_1, Y_1), (Z_2, Y_2), ... are independent. For example, Y_i might be a portion of the renewal period, such as the first half. Alternatively it might be a cost function associated with the renewal period, for example the cost of the ith replacement of an electronic component. Let us consider the former case and write $t \sim Y_i$ to denote that the point t lies in the portion of the ith renewal period covered by Y_i. Then, if $p(t)$ is the probability that $t \sim Y_i$ for some i, we immediately obtain (with our now extensive experience) the renewal equation

$$p(t) = P(t \sim Y_1) + \int_0^t p(t - s)f(s)\,ds$$

Thus, by the Key Renewal Theorem,

$$\lim_{t \to \infty} p(t) = \mu^{-1}\int_0^\infty P(s \sim Y_1)\,ds$$

under the appropriate conditions on $P(t \sim Y_1)$ and F. Now $P(t \sim Y_1) = E[I_{t \sim Y_1}]$ and so

$$\int_0^\infty P(s \sim Y_1)\, ds = \int_{s=0}^\infty \int_{s \sim y} ds\, dF_{Y_1}(y) = \int_{y=0}^\infty \int_{s \sim y} ds\, dF_{Y_1}(y)$$

$$= \int_{y=0}^\infty y\, dF_{Y_1}(y) = E[Y_1]$$

$E[Y_1]$ is the mean length of the Y-portion of the renewal period, which we denote by v. Thus,

$$\lim_{t \to \infty} p(t) = \frac{v}{\mu} \tag{4.5}$$

Notice that Y_i cannot be the forward or backward recurrence time – why?

We now view the above alternating renewal process as a simple renewal process with transitions into state 0 as the renewals and let Y_i be the length of the time spent in state 0 in the ith renewal period. Then the probability $\alpha(t)$ is just the $p(t)$ of the preceding analysis with $\mu = \mu_0 + \mu_1$ and $v = \mu_0$, i.e.

$$\alpha(t) = \frac{\mu_0}{\mu_0 + \mu_1}$$

More generally, an alternating renewal process is a sequence X_1, X_2, ... of independent random variables where the $(nr + m)$th renewal period Z_{nr+m} has distribution function F_m, $1 \leq m \leq r$, $n \geq 0$. Here we have an r-state system that passes deterministically through states $1 \to 2 \to \ldots \to r \to 1 \to 2 \to \ldots \to r \to 1 \to \ldots$. Generalizing the previous result, the probability that the system is in state i at time t is

$$\alpha_i(t) = \frac{\mu_i}{\mu_1 + \ldots + \mu_r}$$

provided the convolution $F_1 * F_2 * \ldots * F_r$ is non-arithmetic so that the Key Renewal Theorem can be used.

Of course, transitions between states may not be deterministic. A **Markov renewal process** or **semi-Markov process** with state space S is a renewal process that passes through states in S at successive renewal points according to a *Markov chain*, with transition probability matrix $P = [p_{ij} | i, j \in S]$, say. The sojourn time spent in state i, given that the next state is j, has distribution function F_{ij} and, for a given sequence of states entered, all sojourn times are independent. The unconditional sojourn time distribution for state i is defined by

$$F_i(t) = \sum_{j \in S} p_{ij} F_{ij}(t)$$

which is assumed to have finite mean μ_i. It is also assumed that the Markov chain is ergodic with stationary distribution π. Now, given that the process starts in state i, let us consider the sequence of successive times that state i is entered. By the Markov property and independence of state sojourn times, this sequence defines a renewal process. Hence by Equation (4.5), the probability that the state is j at time t, $\alpha_j(t)$, is equal to the mean time spent in state j during a renewal period divided by the mean renewal period; recall the promise in the proof of Proposition 4.20. Thus it follows that

$$\alpha_j(t) = \frac{\pi_j \mu_j}{\sum_{k \in S} \pi_k \mu_k}$$

just as for a (full) Markov process.

The Markov renewal process subsumes both renewal processes and Markov processes in the following sense. If there is only one state in E, it is a renewal process and if F_i is exponential, it is a Markov chain with continuous time parameter. There is an extensive literature on Markov renewal processes; see for example Cinlar (1975).

4.5.4 Superposition of renewal processes

We saw in Proposition 4.15 that a superposition of independent Poisson processes is Poisson. However, it is not necessarily the case that a superposition of independent renewal processes is a renewal process. These properties are summarized in the following proposition which is stated without proof. The details can be found in Karlin and Taylor (1975).

> **Proposition 4.32**
>
> (a)   Let $N_t^{(1)}$ and $N_t^{(2)}$ be two independent renewal processes with the same renewal period distribution F of finite mean, and let $N_t = N_t^{(1)} + N_t^{(2)}$. Then N_t is a renewal process if and only if $N_t^{(1)}$ and $N_t^{(2)}$ are both Poisson (so that N_t is also Poisson).
>
> (b)   Let $N_t^{(1)}$ be a Poisson process and $N_t^{(2)}$ be a renewal process with finite mean renewal period such that $N_t^{(1)}$ and $N_t^{(2)}$ are independent. Then $N_t = N_t^{(1)} + N_t^{(2)}$ is a renewal process if and only if $N_t^{(2)}$ is Poisson.   ∎

However, things are actually better than they seem, since an infinite superposition of 'sparse' renewal processes tends to a Poisson process under appropriate conditions. We conclude this chapter with a statement of this result. For $n \geq 1$ and $1 \leq i \leq k_n$ where $k_n \to \infty$ as $n \to \infty$, let $N_t^{(ni)}$ be a renewal process with renewal period distribution F_{ni}. Suppose that $\{N_t^{(ni)} | 1 \leq i \leq k_n\}$ are independent for each n and define the superposition process $N_t^{(n)} = \sum_{i=1}^{k_n} N_t^{(ni)}$.

Proposition 4.33

Suppose that $\lim_{n \to \infty} \max_{1 \leq i \leq k_n} F_{ni}(t) = 0$ for all $t \geq 0$. Then

$$\lim_{n \to \infty} P(N_t^{(n)} = j) = e^{-\lambda t} \frac{(\lambda t)^j}{j!} \qquad \text{for } j \geq 0$$

if and only if

$$\lim_{n \to \infty} \sum_{i=1}^{k_n} F_{ni}(t) = \lambda t \qquad \text{for some } \lambda \qquad \blacksquare$$

As an example of this rather hard to interpret result, suppose F is a distribution function for which $F(0) = 0$ and $f(0) = F'(0) = \lambda > 0$. Then if we define $F_{ni}(t) = F(t/n)$ for $1 \leq i \leq n$, $n \geq 1$, it can be shown that the conditions of Proposition 4.33 are satisfied so that the superposition $N_t^{(n)}$ of identical renewal processes with renewal period distribution $F(t/n)$ does indeed approach a Poisson process with parameter λ as $n \to \infty$. The verification is a routine exercise. Notice the 'sparseness' in the distribution $F(t/n)$, i.e. the decreasing probability of short renewal periods.

SUMMARY

- Almost all analytical models of communication and computer systems, as well as others in operations research, are based on stochastic processes.

- Markov processes have an evolutionary structure with the minimum dependence and provide tractable models for many complex systems.

- The evolution of a Markov chain is given by the Chapman–Kolmogorov equations.

- The states of a Markov chain fall into equivalence classes of transient, periodic, null-recurrent and positive-recurrent states.

- Kolmogorov's theorem gives linear equations for the steady state probabilities of an irreducible, aperiodic positive-recurrent Markov chain.

- Continuous time Markov chains, or Markov processes, have a similar steady state theorem.

- The Poisson process is the simplest and most widespread Markov process and has the memoryless and random observer properties.

- Reversibility arguments allow many important properties of stationary Markov processes to be derived by simple probability and symmetry arguments.

- Renewal theory allows arbitrary, i.i.d. intervals between arrivals (or other occurrences), removing the exponential requirement of Markov processes.

- The asymptotic properties of renewal functions are fundamental to stochastic modelling; for example, the elementary renewal theorem.

- Forward and backward recurrence times in a steady state renewal process allow properties of random observations to be determined; cf. the random observer property.

- A Markov renewal process, or semi-Markov process, generalizes both renewal and Markov processes to allow arbitrary times between transitions amongst an arbitrary collection of states.

- The superposition of two renewal processes is not, in general, a renewal process but, under certain sparseness conditions, the superposition of a large number of renewal processes approaches a Poisson process asymptotically.

EXERCISES

4.1 (10 Transient states)

Let j be a transient state for some Markov chain and v_{jj} be the probability that after visiting j, the chain will eventually return to it. Show that, if the chain visits j at all, then the total number of such visits, K_j, is geometrically distributed with parameter v_{jj}:

$$P(K_j = k) = v_{jj}^{k-1}(1 - v_{jj}) \qquad k = 1, 2, \ldots$$

Hence deduce that K_j is finite with probability one.

4.2 (20 Random walk – non-negative integers)

A particle meanders among the non-negative integers. If, at time n, it is in position i ($i = 1, 2, 3, \ldots$), then at time $n + 1$ it can move to point $i - 1$ with probability α, or to point $i + 1$ with probability $1 - \alpha$ ($0 < \alpha < 1$). If it is at point 0, then it either remains there, with probability α, or moves to point 1 with probability $1 - \alpha$. Let X_n be the position of the particle at time n.

Draw the state diagram of the Markov chain $X = \{X_n; n = 0, 1, 2, \ldots\}$. Show that X is irreducible and aperiodic, and that the solution of the balance equations is of the form

$$p_j = \gamma^j p_0 \qquad \text{where } \gamma = \frac{1 - \alpha}{\alpha}$$

Hence show that X is recurrent non-null if and only if $\gamma < 1$ or $\alpha > \frac{1}{2}$. In that case, the steady state distribution of X is geometric, $p_0 = 1 - \gamma$.

4.3   (20 Random walk – 2 states)
A particle meanders over the integers on the number line. Suppose if at time point n, it is on an odd number, it moves to an even number at time point $n + 1$. If it is on an even number at time point n, it moves to anther even number with probability ω, otherwise it moves to an odd number. Define a two-state Markov chain model for this behaviour and determine:

(a)   the 4-step state transition matrix

(b)   the value of ω for which the chain is (i) aperiodic, (ii) recurrent

(c)   the long-term probability of finding the particle on an even number

4.4   (20 Finite synchronous buffer)
A communication buffer has space for M fixed-length messages and has the following operations that occur in a given cycle. When the buffer has messages, a message is removed in a given cycle with probability β. If during a cycle there are no messages removed and the buffer is not full, then a new message arrives with probability α. Consider the chain formed by observing the number of messages in the buffer at the end of each cycle. Show that this chain is irreducible and aperiodic, and hence find the probability that the buffer is full.

4.5   (20 Execution phases with failure)
In order to complete normally, a job has to go through M consecutive execution phases. The duration of phase i is exponentially distributed with parameter μ_i $(i = 1, 2, \ldots, M)$. After completing phase i, the job starts phase $i + 1$ with probability α_i (for $i < M$), or is aborted with probability $1 - \alpha_i$ $(0 < \alpha_i < 1)$. An aborted job, or one which completes phase M, is replaced immediately with a new job which starts phase 1.

Let X_t be the index of the phase that is being executed at time t. Show that $X = \{X_t; t \geq 0\}$ is an irreducible Markov process with state space $S = \{1, 2, \ldots, M\}$. Find the steady state distribution for X. Hence obtain the average number of jobs that complete normally, and the average number that are aborted, per unit time.

4.6   (20 Synchronous single buffer)

A buffer has a capacity for just one record. If on one clock pulse the buffer is empty, a record will have arrived before the next pulse with probability α, otherwise the buffer will remain empty. If on one clock pulse the buffer contains a record, this will have been removed at the next pulse with probability β, otherwise the buffer will remain full.

(a)   Describe how the buffer may be modelled by a Markov chain with two states 1 and 2, representing an empty and full buffer respectively. Define the chain's one-step transition probability matrix, P.

(b)   Given the matrix

$$M = \begin{pmatrix} 1 & \alpha \\ 1 & -\beta \end{pmatrix}$$

show that

$$PM = M \begin{pmatrix} 1 & 0 \\ 0 & \omega \end{pmatrix} \qquad \text{where } \omega = 1 - \alpha - \beta$$

Hence prove that

$$P^n M = M \begin{pmatrix} 1 & 0 \\ 0 & \omega^n \end{pmatrix} \qquad \text{for } n \geq 0$$

(c)   Verify that the inverse of M is

$$\frac{1}{\alpha + \beta} \begin{pmatrix} \beta & \alpha \\ 1 & -1 \end{pmatrix}$$

and hence show that

$$P^n = \frac{1}{\alpha + \beta} \begin{pmatrix} \beta + \alpha\omega^n & \alpha(1 - \omega^n) \\ \beta(1 - \omega^n) & \alpha + \beta\omega^n \end{pmatrix}$$

(d)   If $-1 < \omega < 1$ and P^∞ is the limit of P^n as $n \to \infty$, show that the rows of P^∞ are the same and satisfy $p = pP$ where $p_j = P_{1j}^\infty = P_{2j}^\infty$ $(j = 1, 2)$. For what values of α, β does P^n not converge as $n \to \infty$, and what property does the Markov chain then exhibit? What is the significance of the case in which $\omega = 1$?

4.7   (10 Clearing a buffer – Markov chain)

Packets arrive at a communication network's input buffer in m independent Poisson streams each with rate λ. The buffer never overflows and is cleared every t_0 seconds. Show that the number of packets in the buffer at the clearance instants defines a Markov chain. What is the probability that the buffer is empty immediately before a clearance instant?

4.8   (30 Eigenvalues of a stochastic matrix)
Show that 1 is always an eigenvalue of a stochastic matrix and that all other eigenvalues of a finite stochastic matrix have absolute value less than one. In other words, find the eigenvalues $1, \lambda_1, \ldots, \lambda_s$ of the one-step transition matrix P.
(Hint: consider $|\lambda||x_j|$ where $x_j \neq 0$ is the component of maximum magnitude in the eigenvector of λ.)

4.9   (30 Poisson process – superposition)
Give a proof of the superposition and decomposition properties of Poisson streams based on inter-arrival times.

4.10   (20 Poisson process – union)
Prove the union property of Poisson processes (using a direct method and interchanging λ, t).

4.11   (20 Markov process for buffer with 2 slots)
Consider a simple buffer of capacity 2 records. New records are added according to a Poisson process with rate λ when the buffer contains 0 or 1 records. A non-empty buffer is cleared at rate μ such that the time to the next clearance is exponentially distributed. Show that in the steady state, the buffer is full for a fraction $[\lambda/(\lambda + \mu)]^2$ of time. Why must a steady state always exist?

4.12   (40 Forward Kolmogorov equation)
Prove that q_i bounded implies uniform convergence with respect to j.

4.13   (30 Reversed process)
Prove that the reversed process of a non-stationary time-homogeneous Markov process is Markov but not time-homogeneous. (Hint: use

$$P(X_t = j)P(X_{t+s} = k | X_t = j) = P(X_{t+s} = k)P(X_t = j | X_{t+s} = k).)$$

4.14   (20 Poisson process – renewal function)
Find the renewal function $R(t)$ and the renewal density $r(t)$ for a Poisson process with parameter λ.

4.15   (30 Renewal equation)
Derive a renewal equation for the instantaneous renewal rate and hence show that the renewal density is the unique rate.

4.16   (30 Renewal equation)
Find the renewal equation for $E[N_t(N_t - 1)]$.

4.17 (30 Residual life)

An arrival process has inter-arrival time with mean m, probability density function $f(t)$, and distribution function $F(t)$. Show that

(a)   a randomly observed inter-arrival time has a density $f_O(s) = (1/m)sf(s)$

(b)   the residual life of the arrival process has density $f_R(u) = (1/m)(1 - F(u))$

(c)   the mean residual life is $M_2/(2m)$, where M_2 is the second moment of the inter-arrival time.

4.18 (30 Backward recurrence time density)

Obtain an expression for the probability that there is a renewal in the infinitesimal interval $(t - \tau - h, t - \tau)$ and that there are no further renewals in $(t - \tau, t)$ in terms of the renewal density function $r(t)$. Hence derive the backward recurrence time density.

Chapter 5
Queues

5.1 Simple Markovian
    queues   171

5.2 The M/G/1 queue   188
5.3 The G/G/1 queue   207

Queues of some sort are central in the majority of models of computer and other communication systems. This is because they represent *contention* for a resource. The servers associated with queues correspond to resources and the customers that enter queues correspond to the tasks, jobs, messages or packets that constitute the workload of the physical system. In general, a more explicit model is provided by a network of queues that represent the resources visited by actual tasks. Such networks will be considered in depth in the forthcoming chapters, but the single server queue is particularly important for a number of reasons. First, its underlying theory is highly developed and properties can be derived in great generality. For example, transient (i.e. time-dependent, non-equilibrium) solutions can be obtained for simple queues and, for a stationary queue, the arrival process and/or service time distribution can often be arbitrary. Thus, quite complex contention systems can often be recast as a single server queue. We will see applications later in this chapter, for example a token ring communication network and a fixed head disk. Another common (structurally equivalent) application is bus arbitration. Finally, the single server queue provides a building block for networks of queues and many of the techniques we introduce in this chapter will be applied extensively later in the book.

Any queue consists of three components: an *arrival process* which determines when customers arrive at the queue and possibly what their characteristics are, a *buffer* or *waiting room* (also often referred to as a *queue* itself) where customers wait to be served and a *service time*

164

requirement for each customer at the server serving the queue. By convention, the term **queue length** includes the customer currently being served, if any. Thus, if the queue is empty, i.e. the queue length is 0, the server must be idle. If the queue length is 1, there is just one customer in the system which is being served; there are none queueing, i.e. waiting for service. A customer's service time is often considered in two parts: the *demand* of the customer, expressed in some units of work, together with the *service rate* of the server, specified in work units performed in unit time. Service time is then the demand divided by the rate, either or both of which can be random variables; for example, the rate is often a function of queue length and the demand may be an exponential random variable.

Queues are classified according to **Kendall's notation** which, in its basic form, defines the class $A/S/m$ as follows:

- A describes the nature of the arrival process. For example, if the arrival process is Poisson, $A = M$ for *Markovian* or *memoryless*, and if inter-arrival times are constant, $A = D$ for *deterministic*. If the arrival process is arbitrary, $A = G$ since inter-arrival times have *general* distribution. Otherwise, we can introduce our own notation, such as $A = E_2$ if inter-arrival times have Erlang-2 distribution. The arrival rate is conventionally denoted by λ which is the reciprocal of the mean inter-arrival time. In general, λ may depend on the number of customers in the queue.

- Similarly, S describes the service time distribution. Again, we have M for a Markovian service time, i.e. one with exponential distribution, D for deterministic (constant) service times and G for a general service time distribution.

- m denotes the number of servers available to give service to customers in the queue.

There is one important aspect of queues we have not mentioned. How does the server decide which customer in the queue to pick next for service, and when is this decision made? This is determined by the **queueing discipline** of the server. Common disciplines are

- **First come first served (FCFS)** or **first in first out (FIFO)** under which customers are served in strict order of arrival.

- **Last come first served (LCFS)** or **last in first out (LIFO)** under which the most recent arrival is served next; i.e. the queue is a form of stack. There are three versions of this discipline, **pre-emptive resume**, **pre-emptive restart** and **non-pre-emptive**. In a pre-emptive discipline, the customer currently being served is replaced immediately upon the arrival of a new customer and, when reaching the front of the queue again (after any further new arrivals have also been served), may either resume service from the point at which it was pre-empted or else begin again. In the non-pre-emptive case, a new arrival has to wait until the current service ends – in which case later arrivals would be served first.

- **Processor sharing** (PS) under which the service capacity is equally divided amongst all customers in the queue; there is no queueing, just an increasing service time as the number of customers at the server increases. Considering service times as composed of a customer demand D and a service rate μ, each customer 'sees' an instantaneous service rate of μ/n when the queue length is n, keeping its demand at D. PS discipline is often used to model *round robin* time sharing in which a scheduler assigns the server for a fixed time quantum q to each task in the system in turn. The order of assignment is fixed and repeats when all tasks have received their quanta – hence the name 'round robin'. Assuming no switching overheads when the task being served changes – an approximation in practice – the round robin scheduling algorithm approaches PS as $q \to 0$. This is because in any small interval of length h, if there are n tasks in the system, each will receive $(h/n)\mu$ units of service from a server with rate μ. The instantaneous service rate experienced by any one task is therefore μ/n.

- **Infinite server** (IS) under which every customer in the queue receives the same service as if it were the only customer. It is as if a new 'clone' of the server were produced for each customer, with no limit to the number of clones available – hence the name 'infinite server'. There is no queueing and no service degradation as the number of customers increases – hence this type of server is sometimes called a **delay server**.

A queueing discipline is called **conservative** or **work conserving** if no work performed by the server is lost and the server is always busy when the queue length is non-zero. Thus, for example, LCFS with pre-emptive restart is not conservative whereas all the other disciplines listed above are. A server that 'takes a vacation' when its queue is empty is also non-conservative since a new arrival may find the server absent; see Section 5.2. Clearly, there are many other disciplines possible, such as **random**, where the next customer is selected from the queue at random, and various priority disciplines. We consider priority disciplines in Chapter 7 in the context of multiple customer classes.

Kendall's notation also has an extended form with two additional fields that define the capacity of the waiting room, c, and the population of the customer pool, i.e. the maximum number of customers, p. The queue is then specified as $A/S/m/c/p$. If c and p are unspecified they are assumed to be infinite, i.e. it is assumed that the queue is unbounded, e.g. that buffers do not overflow, and that there is an

unlimited pool of potential customers. Typically p appears as a parameter of the arrival process and is often related to c, as we shall soon
see.

Before embarking on studies of various types of queue, we first
give a ubiquitous result that applies to any queue or other contention
system in a steady state. It relates the mean number of customers
competing for a resource (here its queue length) with the mean time
that a customer waits in the system to complete service. This result is
called **Little's result**, **formula**, **law** or **theorem** by different authors. We
define a **queueing system** solely in terms of its relationship with a set of
entities called tasks – customers in the case of queues. Suppose a
queueing system is in equilibrium so that the following finite quantities
exist:

- the mean arrival rate of tasks, λ, i.e. the expected number of
  arrivals in unit time
- the mean (time-average) number of tasks in the system, L
- the mean time spent by a task in the system, W

Of course, more generally, there must exist a unique probability
distribution for the state of a system in equilibrium by definition, but we
will not use this fact. For such a system, Little's result states the
following.

Proposition 5.1 (Little's result)

$$L = \lambda W$$

Proof The number of tasks in the queueing system at time t is
equal to the number that arrive before t and depart after t. For
$0 \leqslant u < v \leqslant t$, let A_{uvt} be the number of arrivals in the interval
$(u, v]$ that depart after time t. Then, for $v < t$,

$$P(A_{0,v+dv,t} = n) = \sum_{i=0}^{n} P(A_{0vt} = n - i)P(A_{v,v+dv,t} = i)$$

Multiplying by n, summing over $0 \leqslant n \leqslant \infty$ and rearranging then
gives

$$L_{v+dv,t} = \sum_{i=0}^{\infty} \sum_{n=i}^{\infty} (n - i)P(A_{0vt} = n - i)P(A_{v,v+dv,t} = i)$$

$$+ \sum_{i=0}^{\infty} \sum_{n=i}^{\infty} iP(A_{0vt} = n - i)P(A_{v,v+dv,t} = i)$$

where L_{vt} is the expected number of arrivals in $(0, v]$ that remain in the system at time t. But $\sum_{n=i}^{\infty} s(n - i) P(A_{0vt} = n - i) = L_{vt}$ and $\sum_{i=0}^{\infty} s P(A_{v,v+dv,t} = i) = 1$. Thus, rearranging the second sum,

$$L_{v+dv,t} = L_{vt} + \sum_{i=0}^{\infty} i P(A_{v,v+dv,t} = i) \sum_{m=0}^{\infty} P(A_{0vt} = m)$$

$$= L_{vt} + \sum_{i=0}^{\infty} i P(A_{v,v+dv,t} = i)$$

But $\sum_{i=0}^{\infty} i P(A_{v,v+dv,t} = i)$ is the expected number of arrivals in an interval of length dv that leave the system after time t. Therefore, since the system is in equilibrium with mean number of arrivals λdv in an interval of length dv, we have[1]

$$L_{v+dv,t} - L_{vt} = \lambda[1 - F(t - v)] dv$$

where F is the distribution function of a task's waiting time in the steady state. Hence,

$$\frac{dL_{vt}}{dv} = [1 - F(t - v)]\lambda$$

Thus, the expected number of tasks in the system at time t is, since $L_{0t} = 0$,

$$L_{tt} = \int_0^t [1 - F(t - v)]\lambda \, dv = \lambda t[1 - F(t)] + \lambda \int_0^t u \, dF(u)$$

(changing the variable of integration to $u = t - v$). Now, since F has finite mean, $W = \int_0^{\infty} u \, dF(u)$ and $[1 - F(t)]t \to 0$ as $t \to \infty$.[2] Consequently $L_{tt} \to \lambda W$ as $t \to \infty$ as required. ∎

An alternative proof of Little's result, due to S. Stidham is given in King (1990). This is based on the following simple argument. Suppose each task is charged £1 per unit time spent in the queueing system. Then the total charge expected to be due in one unit of time is £L,

---

[1] In fact, this equation can be obtained from the following heuristic argument: the contribution dL_{ut} to the expected number of tasks arriving before time u and leaving after time t is equal to the expected number of arriving tasks in the interval $(u, u + du)$, λdu, multiplied by the probability that an arrival remains in the system longer than $t - u$ time units, $1 - F(t - u)$. This follows since arrivals are independent.

[2] This follows since $0 \leq t[1 - F(t)] \leq \int_t^{\infty} u \, dF(u) \to 0$ as $t \to \infty$ if the integral is finite. Indeed, if the kth moment of F is finite, $t^k[1 - F(t)] \to 0$ as $t \to \infty$ by a similar argument.

since there are, on average, L tasks in the system at any given time. The average cost to a task is £W since the mean time it spends in the system is W. Thus, if the charge is paid on arrival, an average of £λW will be collected in one time unit. Similarly, if the charge is paid on departure, an average of £λW will be collected in one time unit since the departure rate must be equal to the arrival rate in a steady state. Thus, the average rate at which revenue is generated is equal to both L and λW. Stidham's proof makes this intuitive argument rigorous, in particular showing that the average collection rates are the same at arrival and departure times in the long term.

The proof of Proposition 5.1 can be adapted to find a relation between higher moments than the mean. In general, this is somewhat complicated, but we can obtain a result quite simply when the arrivals are Poisson.

Proposition 5.2

For a queueing system with Poisson arrivals in equilibrium,

$$L_k^f = \lambda^k W_k$$

where W_k is the kth moment of a task's waiting time and L_k^f is the kth factorial moment of the number of tasks in the system, both assumed finite.

Proof The proof is an extension of our proof of Little's result, Proposition 5.1. For Poisson arrivals, the probability of more than one arrival in the interval $(v, v + dv]$ is $o(dv)$ and so we have, in the notation of the previous proof:

$$P(A_{0,v+dv,t} = n) = P(A_{0vt} = n - 1)P(A_{v,v+dv,t} = 1)$$
$$+ P(A_{0vt} = n)P(A_{v,v+dv,t} = 0)$$
$$+ o(dv)$$

Moreover, $P(A_{v,v+dv,t} = 1) = \lambda dv + o(dv)$ and $P(A_{v,v+dv,t} = 0) = 1 - \lambda dv + o(dv)$. Hence,

$$P(A_{0,v+dv,t} = n) - P(A_{0vt} = n)$$
$$= [P(A_{0vt} = n - 1) - P(A_{0vt} = n)]\lambda\, dv + o(dv)$$

and so, multiplying by $n(n - 1) \ldots (n - k + 1)$ and summing over $k \leqslant n < \infty$, after some rearrangement,

$$\frac{\mathrm{d}}{\mathrm{d}v} M_k^f(v) = \sum_{n=k}^{\infty} [(n-1)(n-2) \dots$$

$$(n-k)P(A_{0vt} = n-1) - n(n-1) \dots$$

$$(n-k+1)P(A_{0vt} = n)]\lambda + k\lambda \sum_{n=k}^{\infty}(n-1)$$

$$\dots (n-k+1)P(A_{0vt} = n-1)$$

where $M_k^f(v) = \sum_{n=k}^{\infty} n(n-1) \dots (n-k+1)P(A_{0vt} = n)$ is the kth factorial moment (assumed finite) of the number of arrivals in $(0, v]$ that remain in the system at time t. By cancellation between successive terms in the first sum, we now obtain

$$\frac{\mathrm{d}}{\mathrm{d}v} M_k^f = k\lambda M_{k-1}^f$$

since the leftover term in the partial sums $-n(n-1) \dots (n-k+1)P(A_{0vt} = n) \to 0$ as $n \to \infty$ since the number of arrivals in $(0, v]$ has a Poisson distribution. This differential difference equation is easily seen to have as a solution at $v = t$

$$M_k^f(t) = k!\lambda^k \int_{v_k=0}^{t} \int_{v_{k-1}=0}^{v_k} \dots$$

$$\int_{v_1=0}^{v_2} [1 - F(t-v_1)] \, \mathrm{d}v_k \, \mathrm{d}v_{k-1} \dots \mathrm{d}v_1 \to \lambda^k W_k$$

as $t \to \infty$. But $M_k^f(\infty) = L_k^f$. The proof that the multiple integral does indeed evaluate to $W_k/k!$ is (rigorously) by induction on k. The result is trivial for $k = 0$.

Let

$$I_k = \int_{v_k=0}^{t} \int_{v_{k-1}=0}^{v_k} \dots \int_{v_1=0}^{v_2} [1 - F(t-v_1)] \, \mathrm{d}v_k \, \mathrm{d}v_{k-1} \dots \mathrm{d}v_1$$

$$\text{for } k \geq 1$$

Then we can rewrite I_k in the form:

$$I_k = \int_{v_1=0}^{t} \int_{v_2=v_1}^{t} \dots \int_{v_k=v_{k-1}}^{t} [1 - F(t-v_1)] \, \mathrm{d}v_1 \, \mathrm{d}v_2 \dots \mathrm{d}v_k$$

$$= \int_{v_1=0}^{t} \dots \int_{v_{k-1}=v_{k-2}}^{t} [1 - F(t-v_1)](t-v_{k-1}) \, \mathrm{d}v_1 \mathrm{d}v_2 \dots \mathrm{d}v_{k-1}$$

$$= \int_{v_1=0}^{t} \dots \int_{v_{k-2}=v_{k-3}}^{t} [1 - F(t-v_1)] \frac{(t-v_{k-2})^2}{2!} \, \mathrm{d}v_1 \, \mathrm{d}v_2 \dots \mathrm{d}v_{k-2}$$

$$= \int_{v_1=0}^{t} [1 - F(t - v_1)] \frac{(t - v_1)^{k-1}}{(k-1)!} dv_1$$

$$= \left[-[1 - F(t - v_1)] \frac{(t - v_1)^k}{k!} \right]_0^t + \int_0^t \frac{x^k}{k!} dF(x)$$

(changing the integration variable v_1 to $t - x$)

$$= [1 - F(t)] \frac{t^k}{k!} + \frac{W_k}{k!}$$

As $t \to \infty$, the first term approaches zero if the kth moment is finite and so the result follows. ∎

We will see numerous applications of Little's formula (for means) later in the book, mainly relating directly to a physical queue. First, let us consider a slightly different situation, in which the server alone comprises the 'queueing system' (Figure 5.1). Here we ignore the queue of *waiting* customers. In the steady state, the mean arrival rate to the server must be the same as the mean external arrival rate to the whole queue, λ say; and the same as the mean *departure rate* for that matter. Now, the server is either idle, serving no customer, or else busy, serving exactly one customer. Suppose that in equilibrium, the utilization of the server, i.e. the probability that it is busy, is U. Then the mean number of customers in the system in the steady state is $U \times 1 + (1 - U) \times 0 = U$. But the mean time spent by a customer at the server is just the mean service time, μ^{-1} say if the server has constant rate μ. Hence Little's result yields $U = \lambda/\mu$. This is exactly what we expect since now $\lambda = U\mu$, which has the reading

$$\text{mean arrival rate} = \frac{\text{mean service}}{\text{rate}} \times \frac{\text{probability that}}{\text{the server is not idle}}$$

This follows directly from the condition that the system is in equilibrium. We will see this simple argument repeated several times to derive a model of a crossbar switch and then a multistage interconnection network in Chapter 11. The situation is a little more complicated when the service rate depends on the queue length, since the mean service time, the reciprocal of the mean service rate, then depends on the stationary distribution of the queue length.

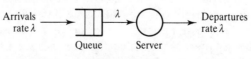

Figure 5.1

5.1 Simple Markovian queues

The M/M/1 queue is a birth and death process of the kind considered in Example 4.9. The 'births' are arrivals of new customers and 'deaths' are departures of customers who have completed their service. We consider the M/M/1 queue in equilibrium (in common with other types of queue), only looking very briefly at how to obtain its time-dependent behaviour at the end of this section. Suppose that the arrival rate and service rate are respectively $\lambda(n)$ and $\mu(n)$ when the queue length is n (we sometimes say 'the state is n'). Then from Example 4.9, letting

$$\rho(j) = \prod_{k=1}^{j} \frac{\lambda(k-1)}{\mu(k)} \qquad \text{for } j > 0$$

the stationarity condition and steady state probabilities are the following:

- the queue is stationary if and only if $\sum_{k=0}^{\infty} \rho(k) < \infty$
- the equilibrium probability $\pi(n)$ for state $n \geqslant 0$ in a stationary queue is

$$\rho(n)/\sum_{k=0}^{\infty} \rho(k)$$

When the arrival and service rates are *constant*, λ and μ respectively at every state n say, we have the classical M/M/1 queue. Then $\rho(k) = \rho^k$ where $\rho = \lambda/\mu$ and the equilibrium probability of state n is

$$\pi(n) = \frac{\rho^n}{\sum_{k=0}^{\infty} \rho^k} = (1 - \rho)\rho^n$$

This is a geometric probability mass function and it is easy to show that, for example, the mean queue length in equilibrium is $\rho/(1 - \rho)$. Notice that the utilization of the server is $U = 1 - \pi(0) = \rho$, as required in the steady state to make the mean arrival rate (λ) equal to the mean departure rate ($U\mu$). Of course, this is exactly what we also proved above using Little's result.

We have not assumed anything about the queueing discipline: only that customers arrive at rate $\lambda(n)$ and the server works at rate $\mu(n)$ when there are n customers in the queue, including any in service. Both the arrival and (instantaneous) service-completion (departure) processes are, of course, Poisson. Thus, the steady state conditions and queue length probability distribution are the same for all other disciplines consistent with these assumptions, for example all those listed at the beginning of this chapter. Notice, that the pre-emptive LCFS disciplines with restart and resumption of a pre-empted customer are indistinguishable in an $M/M/1$ queue. This is because the distributions of a whole service time and of a remaining service time after pre-emption are the same for exponential service times, the latter being the forward recurrence time – see Section 4.5.2. However, the result is a little surprising in view of the operational differences between the disciplines; recall that one is conservative and the other not. We will see in the next chapter that a similar result holds for *networks* of queues, even when the service times are not exponential in the case of some (non-FCFS) disciplines.

One application of the $M/M/1$ queue is to describe a single queue served by more than one identical servers, i.e. the $M/M/m$ queue. For this queue, suppose that each of the m servers has constant rate μ (with exponential service times) and that the Poisson arrival process has rate $\lambda(n)$ when the queue length is n. Then, when the queue has more than m customers, all m servers are busy. When the queue length is $n < m$, only n servers are busy, and it matters not which of the m they are since all are identical. Now, when $n \geq 1$ servers are busy, the time to the next service completion (from the time of either a new arrival or a service completion) is the minimum of n exponential random variables, each with parameter μ. This time is the service time random variable, S say, of an equivalent single server queue. Now,

$$P(S > t) = P(S_1 > t \cap \ldots \cap S_n > t)$$

where the S_i are independent exponential random variables with parameter $\mu (1 \leq i \leq n)$. Thus,

$$P(S > t) = P(S_1 > t) \ldots P(S_n > t) = e^{-\mu t} \ldots e^{-\mu t} = e^{-(n\mu)t}$$

In other words, the equivalent single server queue has exponential service times with parameter $n\mu$.[1] Since its arrival process is also Poisson, namely the arrival process of the original $M/M/m$ queue, the equivalent single server queue is $M/M/1$; it is often called a **multi-server** or, more specifically, an **m-multi-server**. A similar result holds when the service rates of the m identical servers in an $M/M/m$ queue depend on the queue length.

Example 5.1 (Erlang's loss formula) ——————————————

Suppose a telephone exchange has m lines which can each connect any pair of (distinct) subscribers. Suppose further that subscribers dial non-engaged callees (those not already connected to another subscriber)

---

[1] We could also have deduced this by observing that the instantaneous departure process when n servers are busy is the superposition of n independent Poisson processes, each with parameter μ. By Proposition 4.15, this is a Poisson process with rate $n\mu$ so that inter-departure time is exponential with parameter $n\mu$.

at rate λ according to a Poisson process, i.e. the number of calls attempted to non-engaged callees in a given time interval has a Poisson distribution with parameter λ. Calls made when there are currently m calls already in progress are lost – the exchange has no 'hold' facility. Assuming that the length of a call has exponential distribution with mean μ^{-1}, this system can be modelled as an $M/M/m/m$ queue with FCFS queueing discipline – or equivalently IS discipline since there is never any queueing. The arrival rate function at queue length (number of calls in progress) n is

$$\lambda(n) = \begin{cases} \lambda & \text{if } 0 \leqslant n < m \\ 0 & \text{if } n \geqslant m \end{cases}$$

and the corresponding service rate function is

$$\mu(n) = n\mu$$

for $0 \leqslant n \leqslant m$; clearly we can never have $n > m$. In the above terminology, $\rho(j) = \lambda^j/j!\mu^j$ for $0 \leqslant j \leqslant m$ so that the steady state probability that there are n calls in progress is

$$\pi(n) = \frac{\lambda^n/n!\mu^n}{\sum_{k=0}^{m} \lambda^k/k!\mu^k} \qquad (0 \leqslant n \leqslant m)$$

Since this is a finite system, i.e. one with finite state space, the stationarity condition holds for all positive λ, μ – the denominator is always finite. In particular, the probability that a call is lost, i.e. the probability that a subscriber finds all m lines in use when dialling, is

$$\pi(m) = \frac{\lambda^m/m!\mu^m}{\sum_{k=0}^{m} \lambda^k/k!\mu^k} \qquad (0 \leqslant n \leqslant m)$$

by the Random Observer Property. This result is known as **Erlang's loss formula**. Many other useful performance measures can be obtained from the queue length distribution $\pi(n)$. For example, the throughput of the system can be obtained as $\sum_{k=1}^{m} \pi(k)k\mu$. However, in the steady state, this must be the same as the mean *arrival rate* which is easier to compute since the arrival rate is λ at all queue lengths less than m. Thus, throughput is equal to $\sum_{k=0}^{m-1} \pi(k)\lambda = [1 - \pi(m)]\lambda$ where $\pi(m)$ is given by Erlang's loss formula.

Example 5.2 (Multi-access system)

A terminal system connected to a multiprocessing computing facility can be modelled as an $M/M/m/N$ queue as follows. Suppose that N terminals are logged on. Then a user at a terminal is either in 'think mode' when he or she has no task currently submitted to the computer system or else is in 'processing mode' when the user is awaiting the response from a command issued to the system (Figure 5.2). A user's

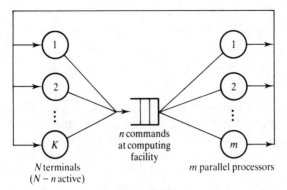

Figure 5.2

command processing time is defined to be the time elapsed between the input of a command and the receipt of the corresponding response from the system. Similarly, **think time** is defined to be the time elapsed between the receipt of a response and the issue of the next command. Of course, a user will generally be thinking whilst the system is processing a command, but we do not represent this explicitly in our model. Essentially we consider the 'residual' think time still required after a response has arrived at the terminal, but in this simplest of models this is only a secondary approximation.

We can model this system as an $M/M/m/N$ queue, corresponding to the computing facility, by treating each of the N customers as a logged-on user. If we assume that (residual) think times are exponentially distributed with mean λ^{-1}, we can represent the terminals as a state-dependent Poisson process. The rate parameter $\lambda(n)$ is defined by

$$\lambda(n) = \begin{cases} (N-n)\lambda & (n \leqslant N) \\ 0 & (n \geqslant N) \end{cases}$$

The computing facility is represented by an m-multi-server where we assume that command processing times are exponentially distributed with mean μ^{-1}. The service rate function of the multi-server is therefore

$$\mu(n) = \begin{cases} n\mu & (0 \leqslant n \leqslant m) \\ m\mu & (n \geqslant m) \end{cases}$$

Under these Markovian assumptions, we can write down the steady state solution for the distribution of queue length at the computing facility, $\pi(n)$, as follows. Let $\rho = \lambda/\mu$. Then, in the above terminology,

$$\rho(n) = \begin{cases} \dfrac{N(N-1)\ldots(N-n+1)}{n!}\rho^n & (0 \leqslant n \leqslant m) \\[2ex] \dfrac{N(N-1)\ldots(N-n+1)}{m!m^{n-m}}\rho^n & (m \leqslant n \leqslant N) \end{cases}$$

that is,

$$\rho(n)=\begin{cases}\binom{N}{n}\rho^n & (0 \leqslant n \leqslant m)\\[2mm]\dfrac{N!}{(N-n)!m!m^{n-m}}\rho^n & (m \leqslant n \leqslant N)\end{cases}$$

As before, the queue is stationary for all λ, μ since the state space is finite and the equilibrium queue length distribution is $\pi(n) = \rho(n)/\sum_{k=0}^{N}\rho(k)$. In particular, system throughput, i.e. the mean number of commands processed in unit time, is $\sum_{n=0}^{N}\pi(n)\mu(n)$. It is a bit simpler to compute the mean arrival rate, $\sum_{n=0}^{N}\pi(n)(N-n)\lambda = N\lambda - \sum_{n=0}^{N}\pi(n)n\lambda$, which is the same in the steady state.

We will see in the next chapter that we could model this system as a closed queueing network of two queues: one representing the computing facility as here and the other an IS server representing the terminals. The use of an IS server reflects the fact that there is no queueing at a terminal, which is either 'idle' (when the user has a command being processed) or else 'has a queue of length one' (whilst its user is in think mode). We will also see that a consequence of this is that we do not need think times to be exponential – *any* service time distribution at a server with IS discipline gives the same equilibrium queue length probabilities.

5.1.1 Bulk arrivals

There are many variants of the M/M/1 queue, most of which can be handled with the greater generality of the M/G/1 or even G/G/1 queue. We therefore defer our main discussion of variants to Section 5.2, but here we consider the situation in which the arrivals to a Markovian queue occur in batches of more than one, i.e. 'in bulk'. The arrival *instants* still occur as a Poisson process, with constant rate λ say, but immediately after each arrival, the state may jump by more than one. First, suppose batch sizes are fixed at $b \geqslant 1$ customers. Then the only transitions that can occur are $n \to n+b$ and $n+1 \to n$ for $n \geqslant 0$. Assuming that a stationary solution π exists, the balance equation for state n yields, for $n \geqslant 1$,

$$(\lambda + \mu)\pi(n) = \mu\pi(n+1) + \lambda\pi(n-b)$$

where we define $\pi(x) = 0$ for $x < 0$. For $n = 0$, we have similarly

$$\lambda\pi(0) = \mu\pi(1)$$

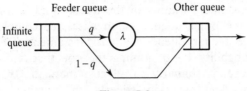

Figure 5.3

If we now define the generating function $\Pi(z) = \sum_{i=0}^{\infty} \pi(n)z^n$, multiplying the balance equation for state n by z^n and summing gives

$$(\lambda + \mu)\Pi(z) - \mu\pi(0) = \mu z^{-1}\Pi(z) - \mu z^{-1}\pi(0) + \lambda z^b\Pi(z)$$

Thus,

$$\Pi(z) = \frac{\mu\pi(0)(1 - z^{-1})}{\mu(1 - z^{-1}) + \lambda(1 - z^b)} = \frac{(1 - \rho)(1 - z)}{(1 - z) - (\lambda/\mu)z(1 - z^b)}$$

where $\rho = 1 - \pi(0)$. But in the steady state, we must have $\lambda b = [1 - \pi(0)]\mu$ so that the average arrival and departure rates balance (or by Little's law as we saw above). Hence, $\rho = \lambda b/\mu$ and so

$$\Pi(z) = \frac{(1 - \rho)(1 - z)}{(1 - z) - (\rho/b)z(1 - z^b)}$$

More generally, if the batch size is a random variable $B \geq 1$ with probability mass function $r_i \, (i \geq 1)$, expectation b and probability generating function $G(z) = \sum_{i=1}^{\infty} r_i z^i$, we obtain by the same method

$$\Pi(z) = \frac{(1 - \rho)(1 - z)}{(1 - z) - (\rho/b)z(1 - G(z))}$$

where $\rho = \lambda b/\mu$ as before. This result will be obtained in greater generality when we consider the M/G/1 queue in Section 5.2.

An important example of bulk arrivals has a *geometrically distributed* batch size. In this case, $r_i = q(1 - q)^{i-1}$ for some q, $0 < q < 1$, $G(z) = qz/[1 - (1 - q)z]$ and $b = 1/q$. Thus,

$$\Pi(z) = \frac{(1 - \rho)(1 - z + qz)}{(1 - z) + qz(1 - \rho)}$$

Geometric batch sizes occur when one queue is fed by another queue that has FCFS queueing discipline and at which customers *skip* the server with fixed, independent probability $1 - q$ (Figure 5.3). We assume that the feeder has an infinite queue and so constitutes an arrival process for the other queue. A customer in service at the feeder holds up any customers waiting in the queue until it completes service and passes to the other queue. Upon a service completion, the next customer in the feeder queue will pass instantaneously to the other queue with probability $1 - q$, joining the one that had just completed service. This extends similarly to all customers that wish to skip the server until one does not skip. Clearly, the number of simultaneous arrivals at the second queue is geometric with parameter q and the arrival instants form a Poisson process if the service times of the feeder server are exponential. In fact, instead of having 'skipping', we could just define the service time distribution function F of the feeder server to be

$$F(t) = (1 - q) + q(1 - e^{-\lambda t}) = 1 - qe^{-\lambda t}$$

since this has zero service time with probability $1 - q$. F is called the **generalized exponential** distribution function and we denote an arrival process with inter-arrival times that have this distribution by GE in Kendall's notation. Generalized exponential service times are also denoted by GE. Thus, GE/G/1 denotes a queue with batch arrivals. In particular, the stationary queue with probability generating function $[(1 - \rho)(1 - z + qz)]/[(1 - z) + qz(1 - \rho)]$ obtained above is a GE/M/1 queue. We will see the GE distribution arise again when we consider approximate methods in queueing network analysis – specifically the maximum entropy method. It arises for quite separate reasons and its ability to represent a class of bulk arrivals strengthens the argument for the use of the maximum entropy method.

Bulk arrivals are important since in many communication systems the traffic is *bursty*, with little traffic over long periods and interspersed periods, or 'bursts', of heavy traffic. The arrival rate of traffic in a burst might well be much greater than the service rate of the communication system, a situation that would lead to non-stationarity if allowed to persist. However, the long-term average arrival rate will in general be less than the service rate. Bursty traffic is the norm in modern integrated services digital network (ISDN) telecommunication systems which handle the transmission of data, voice and video on the same medium. The burstiness arises since, in the case of video for example, a considerable amount of time is spent packetizing images into digital form, whereupon a large block of data is transmitted. No data is transmitted during the packetizing process and the representation of a burst of packets over a short period by a batch of arrivals at a single point in time can provide a good approximation. The transmission of voice is similar. Before leaving this subject, we note that such a telecommunication system will normally be handling a large number of transmissions simultaneously. Hence we really need to consider a superposition of bursty arrival processes, which we may take to be sparse in the sense of Section 4.5. Under appropriate conditions, which we make no attempt to justify, the superposition could be approximately Poisson (cf. Proposition 4.34) and we would not need to consider bulk arrivals after all.

5.1.2 Waiting time distributions

In this section we investigate the time interval between the instants at which a given customer arrives at an M/M/1 queue and departs after completing service. This random variable is called the customer's **waiting time** and is denoted by T_W; it *includes* the time spent being served. The corresponding interval from the arrival instant to the instant at which the customer first enters service is called the **queueing time**, denoted T'; it *excludes* the service time. We consider the classical M/M/1 queue with arrival rate λ and service rate μ independent of the queue length. First, we can calculate the mean waiting time (and queueing time) quite easily using Little's result as follows. We have already seen that the mean equilibrium queue length is $\rho/(1 - \rho)$, where $\rho = \lambda/\mu$, and we know that the mean arrival rate is λ. Hence, mean waiting time W is the ratio of these quantities, $1/(\mu - \lambda)$. For an FCFS queueing discipline, we can now find the expected queueing time, Q, from the relation $T_W = T' + S$ where S is the service time random variable, i.e. exponential with parameter μ. Taking expectations gives

$$(\mu - \lambda)^{-1} = E[T_W] = E[T'] + E[S] = Q + \mu^{-1}$$

so that $Q = \rho/(\mu - \lambda)$. Notice that the result for W holds regardless of the queueing discipline. However, we no longer have this invariance when we consider the probability distribution of waiting time.

First, suppose the queueing discipline is FCFS and that immediately after a new arrival, the queue length is $n + 1$; i.e. the arrival 'faces' a queue of length $n \geq 0$. The arriving customer's waiting time is now a sum of $n + 1$ random variables:

$$T_W = \begin{cases} U + S_1 + S_2 + \ldots + S_n & \text{if } n \geq 1 \\ S_1 & \text{if } n = 0 \end{cases}$$

Each S_i is distributed as the service time, i.e. exponential with parameter μ, and U is the residual service time of the customer being served at the arrival instant. But we saw in Section 4.5 that U has the same exponential distribution as service time. Thus, T_W is a sum of $n + 1$ independent exponential random variables with parameter μ when the queue length faced on arrival is $n \geq 0$. Similarly, T' is a sum of n such random variables. Since the arrival process is Poisson, by the Random Observer Property of Section 4.3, the probability that the queue length faced by an arrival is n is the same as the equilibrium probability that the queue length is n, here $(1 - \rho)\rho^n$. Thus, by the law of total probability,

$$P(T_W \leqslant t) = \sum_{n=0}^{\infty} (1 - \rho)\rho^n F^{(n+1)*}(t)$$

where $F(t) = 1 - e^{-\mu t}$ is the service time distribution function and $F^{k*}(k \geqslant 1)$ denotes the k-fold convolution of F with itself; recall Section 4.5. By Proposition 2.3, $F^{(n+1)*}$ is the Erlang-$(n + 1)$ distribution with parameter μ and so the waiting time density function f_W is defined by

$$f_W(t) = \sum_{n=0}^{\infty} (1 - \rho)\rho^n \mu \frac{(\mu t)^n}{n!} e^{-\mu t}$$

$$= (1 - \rho)\mu e^{-\mu t} \sum_{n=0}^{\infty} \frac{(\rho \mu t)^n}{n!}$$

$$= (\mu - \lambda)e^{-(\mu - \lambda)t}$$

Waiting time is therefore exponential with parameter $\mu - \lambda$, as expected from our derivation of the mean waiting time. The fact that waiting time is exponential can actually be deduced by a purely probabilistic argument, using the memoryless properties of both the geometric distribution (of the queue length) and the exponential distribution. We then need only the mean waiting time, which we have already determined, to characterize completely the waiting time random variable. This approach is taken by Mitrani (1987).

We can obtain waiting time distributions for variants of the M/M/1 queue, revealing the sensitivity to different queueing disciplines, for example. If we have a load-dependent server, i.e. one with rate depending on the instantaneous queue length, waiting time distribution is much more difficult to obtain. In particular, the derivation of the result for PS discipline is lengthy, even when the arrival and (total) service rates are both constant; we consider this problem below. However, we can quite easily find the waiting time density for the multi-server queue, i.e. the M/M/m queue. In this case, a new arrival has to queue iff the queue length faced on arrival is at least m. Waiting time is now given by:

$$T_W = \begin{cases} X_1 + \ldots + X_{n-m+1} + S & \text{if } n \geqslant m \\ S & \text{if } n < m \end{cases}$$

where X_i $(1 \leqslant i \leqslant n - m + 1)$ is distributed as the service time *of an exponential server with rate $m\mu$* and S is distributed as an exponential server with rate μ. This follows because when the number of customers ahead of the customer being traced is $n, n - 1, \ldots, m$, there are m

parallel servers active and their superposition is a Poisson process with rate $m\mu$ (i.e. the time to the next service completion is exponential with parameter $m\mu$). But this is exactly the situation with an M/M/1 queue with service rate $m\mu$. When there are fewer than m customers ahead of the customer being traced, including when the queue length faced on arrival is $n < m$, the remaining waiting time is just one service time, S. By the Random Observer Property, the probability of not having to queue is

$$\alpha = Z^{-1} \sum_{n=0}^{m-1} \frac{\rho^n}{n!}$$

where $\rho = \lambda/\mu$ and

$$Z = \sum_{n=0}^{m-1} \frac{\rho^n}{n!} + \sum_{n=m}^{\infty} \frac{\rho^n}{m! m^{n-m}} = \sum_{n=0}^{m-1} \frac{\rho^n}{n!} + \frac{\rho^m}{(m-1)!(m-\rho)}$$

is the normalizing constant of the equilibrium queue length probability distribution. Hence the queueing time distribution is

$$P(T' \le t) = Z^{-1} \sum_{n=m}^{\infty} \frac{\rho^n}{m! m^{n-m}} F_X^{(n-m+1)*}(t) + \alpha$$

$$= Z^{-1} \frac{\rho^m}{m!} \sum_{n=0}^{\infty} \left(\frac{\rho}{m}\right)^n F_X^{(n+1)*}(t) + \alpha$$

$$= Z^{-1} \frac{\rho^m}{(m-1)!(m-\rho)} (1 - \rho/m) \sum_{n=0}^{\infty} \left(\frac{\rho}{m}\right)^n F_X^{(n+1)*}(t) + \alpha$$

But the first term is recognized as $1 - \alpha$ multiplied by the waiting time distribution for an M/M/1 queue with service time distribution function F_X, this being exponential with parameter $m\mu$. We therefore conclude that

$$F_Q(t) = \alpha + (1 - \alpha)[1 - e^{-(m\mu-\lambda)t}] = 1 - (1 - \alpha)e^{-(m\mu-\lambda)t}$$

Example 5.3 _____

A telephone exchange with holding facilities is modelled as an M/M/m queue, cf. Example 4.1. How many lines are necessary such that the probability of a caller being 'on hold' for more than 1 minute is less than 10 per cent? We can simply use the above formula for $F_Q(t)$ since the probability of holding time exceeding 1 minute is $1 - F_Q(1)$. Thus we require

$$(1 - \alpha)e^{-(m\mu-\lambda)} < 0.1$$

i.e.

$$(m\mu - \lambda) > \ln 10(1 - \alpha)$$

i.e.

$$m > \frac{\ln 10(1 - \alpha) + \lambda}{\mu}$$

Of course, α is a non-trivial function of m, and numerical methods are needed to obtain particular solutions. However, the naïve approach of successively testing the cases $m = 1, 2, \ldots$ until the inequality is satisfied is quite practicable.

As we have seen, work-conserving queueing disciplines all produce the same equilibrium queue length probability distributions and so, by Little's law, the same *mean* waiting time. In order to compare the performance of different queueing disciplines with respect to a particular customer, we must consider the distribution of waiting time, or at least moments higher than the first. Moreover, we are often more interested in the *conditional* waiting time, given the service time required by a customer. Then we can assess the effect of different disciplines on tasks of various 'sizes', for example whether small tasks are favoured. Clearly, in the case of FCFS discipline, a customer's queueing time is independent of its service time. Hence, the variation in a customer's waiting time is exactly the same as the variation in its service time and no class of customer is favoured.

As far as a given customer is concerned, PS discipline involves a state-dependent service rate but the problem is not as straightforward as in the multi-server case. This is because it does not split into two parts so conveniently: there is no queueing phase and the service phase involves a variable rate. However, in Chapter 9 we obtain the Laplace transform $W^*(s|x)$ of the waiting time distribution, conditioned on a customer's service requirement x, by considering the possible state transitions in an initial infinitesimal interval of the waiting time and then using the Random Observer Property twice. This leads to a first-order partial differential equation and the result:

$$W^*(s|x) = \frac{(1 - \rho)(1 - \rho r^2)e^{-[\lambda(1-r)+s]x}}{(1 - \rho r)^2 - \rho(1 - r)^2 e^{-(\mu/r - \lambda r)x}}$$

where r is the smaller root of the equation $\lambda r^2 - (\lambda + \mu + s)r + \mu = 0$. Differentiation of this equation with respect to s gives

$$2\lambda r r' - (\lambda + \mu + s)r' - r = 0$$

so that at $s = 0$, $r' = 1/(\lambda - \mu)$. The derivative of $W^*(s|x)$ with respect to s at $s = 0$ then simplifies to $x/(\rho - 1)$ so that the mean waiting time is

$x/(1 - \rho)$. In fact this result also holds for the M/G/1 queue (Kleinrock 1976). It shows that mean waiting time is linear in the service time requirement of a customer. Hence, short tasks are favoured and the discipline is 'fair' in the sense that mean waiting time is proportional to service time requirement. (Remember that a task with *average* service time has the same mean waiting time under any work-conserving discipline.) Moreover, for the M/G/1 case, mean waiting time is independent of the distribution of service time, depending only on its mean through ρ. Thus, in particular, if $\rho < 1$ and the average service time requirement is finite, then mean waiting time will also be finite. In contrast, we will see in Section 5.2 that for an M/G/1 queue with FCFS discipline, mean waiting time diverges to infinity with the second moment of the service time.

We consider LCFS disciplines for the more general M/G/1 queue in Chapter 9. The proof is based upon the distribution of the busy period of the server, i.e. the interval between an arrival during an idle period and the server next becoming idle again. The same argument is used for the M/M/1 case and we do not repeat it here.

5.1.3 The output of the M/M/1 queue and reversibility

Given the input process to an M/M/1 queue, namely Poisson with rate λ, we might be interested in determining the output process, characterized by the probability distribution of inter-departure times. Of course, when the server is busy, this would be the same as the service time distribution, giving a Poisson departure process of rate μ. When it is idle, there are no departures and it is tempting to conjecture that we have a superposition of Poisson processes of rates μ and 0, giving a Poisson departure process. The rate of this process must be λ in the steady state and this does indeed follow by taking the probability weight of the rate μ component in the superposition equal to the utilization ρ. Of course, there is no rigour in this argument since we do not have a superposition of simultaneous processes, but its conclusion is valid for the M/M/1 queue, as we will now see by two different methods.

First, let the sequence of arriving customers be C_1, C_2, ... and U_{n+1} be the interval between the departures of C_n and C_{n+1}. Then,

$$U_{n+1} = \begin{cases} S_{n+1} & \text{if } C_{n+1} \text{ was in the queue on } C_n\text{'s departure} \\ A_{n+1} + S_{n+1} & \text{otherwise} \end{cases}$$

where S_{n+1} is the service time of the $(n + 1)$th customer and A_{n+1} is the interval between C_n's departure and the next arrival. A_{n+1} is a forward recurrence time of the arrival process and so is distributed exponentially with parameter λ. Thus,

$$P(U_{n+1} \leqslant u) = \rho_{n+1} P(S_{n+1} \leqslant u)$$
$$+ (1 - \rho_{n+1}) \int_0^u P(S_{n+1} \leqslant u - v) \lambda e^{-\lambda v} \, dv$$

where ρ_{n+1} is the probability that the queue is not empty just after C_n's departure. Now, S_{n+1} is an exponential random variable with parameter μ and the integral is just a convolution. Moreover, in equilibrium, $\rho_{n+1} = \rho$ since the state existing at departure times has the same stationary distribution as the state existing at arrival times; we show this in the next section. By the Random Observer Property applied to the arrival process, this is the same as the equilibrium distribution. We therefore have

$$P(U_{n+1} \leqslant u) = \rho(1 - e^{-\mu u})$$
$$+ (1 - \rho)\left[1 - e^{-\lambda u} - \int_0^u e^{-\mu(u-v)} \lambda e^{-\lambda v} \, dv\right]$$
$$= 1 - \rho e^{-\mu u} - (1 - \rho) e^{-\lambda u}$$
$$- \frac{(1 - \rho)\lambda}{\mu - \lambda} e^{-\mu u}[e^{(\mu-\lambda)u} - 1]$$
$$= 1 - \rho e^{-\mu u} - (1 - \rho) e^{-\lambda u} - \rho[e^{-\lambda u} - e^{-\mu u}]$$
$$= 1 - e^{-\lambda u}$$

Thus the output process of the M/M/1 queue is indeed Poisson with rate λ, a result often known as Burke's theorem. However, our proof was not simple and relied on the property that the queue length distribution at departure times is the same as at arrival times. There is a much easier way to establish a more general result by using reversibility to relate the arrival and departure processes directly.

Proposition 5.3 (Burke's theorem, extended)

In equilibrium, the departure process from an M/M/m queue ($m \geqslant 1$) is a Poisson process and the number of customers in the queue at any given time is independent of the departure process before that time.

Proof Since the M/M/m queue is a birth and death process, it is reversible by Proposition 4.22. Consider the process N_t denoting the number of customers in the queue at time t. The instants at which N_t jumps upwards by one correspond to arrivals and so define a Poisson process. Thus, the instants at which N_{-t} jumps upwards by one define an identical Poisson process by reversibility. But an upward jump in N_{-t} is a downward jump in N_t and so the departure instants also form an identical Poisson process.

Now let τ be a fixed point in time. For N_{-t}, the arrival (i.e. upward jumping) process after time $t = -\tau$ is independent of the queue length at time $-\tau$. Hence the departure process of N_t before time τ is independent of the queue length at time τ as required. In fact, by the same reasoning, the joint distribution of the queue length at τ and the inter-departure periods before τ is the same as the joint distribution of the queue length at τ and the inter-arrival periods after τ.   ∎

Proposition 5.3 is more general than the result we obtained before it in that it includes the extra independence property, there may be more than one server, and the service rate may depend on the queue length. Moreover, the same reasoning applies to any reversible process with Poisson arrivals, provided an arrival causes a state transition and the reverse transition represents a departure in the reversed process (which is stochastically identical to the original process).

We can generalize still further by observing that we only used the property of reversibility to deduce that the arrival process of N_{-t} was the same as that of N_t. Suppose now that we have a non-reversible, stationary Markov process but that we know something about the reversed process. Each event causing a change of state in the original process *corresponds* to an event in the reversed process with a known interpretation. The inter-occurrence times of the respective sequences of events have the same joint distribution by construction – it matters not how we interpret the reversed process for this. However, if the event sequence in the reversed process can be *interpreted* as some event sequence in the original process, we can identify stochastically two sequences of events in the same, original process. For example, if the process *were* reversible, the reversed process is the same as the original one. Hence, arrivals in the reversed process can be interpreted as arrivals in the original process, but they also correspond to departures in the original process, using the above italicized terminology. There are also non-reversible processes that possess the same kind of duality.

Example 5.4

Consider a two-server queue with Poisson arrivals where the servers are exponential with different rates and an arrival to an empty queue is served by the server that has been idle longest. This process is non-reversible for the following reason. Let the servers be labelled s and s' and the state space be $\{0, 0', 1, 1', 2, 3, \ldots\}$ where $0, 0'$ denote an empty queue in which s, s' respectively have been idle longest and $1, 1'$ denote a queue of length 1 with the customer being served by s, s' respectively. Then there is a transition from 1 to $0'$ but no transition

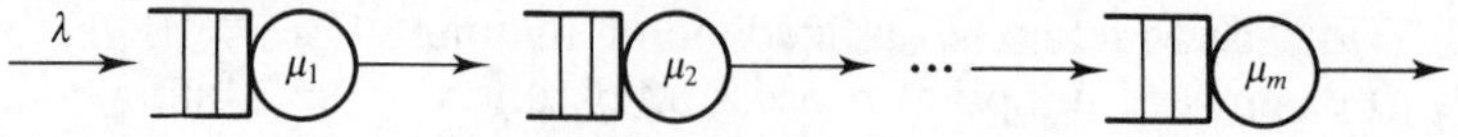

Figure 5.4

from $0'$ to 1 because an arrival in state $0'$ causes a transition to state $1'$. However, the reversed process is a similar two server queue in which the states $0, 0'$ are interchanged. The proof of this is left as an exercise. Now, the arrival processes in both the original and the reversed processes are the same and so Burke's theorem still holds since always arrivals in the reversed process correspond to departures in the original process.

An important motivation for studying the output process of a queue is in *networks of queues*, where the input to one queue is the output from another. We will consider such networks extensively in this book and look now at the simplest case – the tandem queueing network, i.e. a *series* of queues. Suppose we have a series of m queues in equilibrium with rates $\mu_1, \ldots, \mu_m$ and Poisson arrivals to queue 1 with rate λ (Figure 5.4). It is clear from Proposition 5.3 that the arrival process to any queue in the series is Poisson with rate λ, so that the nth queue, taken in isolation, behaves as an M/M/1 queue with service rate μ_n. However, we can deduce more. Let $N_i(t)$ be the number of customers in queue i at time t. Now, by Proposition 5.3, for all t, $N_1(t)$ is independent of the departure process from queue 1 before t. Thus, $N_1(t)$ is independent of $(N_2(t), \ldots, N_m(t))$. Similarly, $N_j(t)$ is independent of $(N_{j+1}(t), \ldots, N_m(t))$ for $j \geq 1$ and so $N_1(t), \ldots, N_m(t)$ are independent. Thus, in equilibrium,

$$P(n_1, \ldots n_m) = \prod_{i=1}^{m} \left(1 - \frac{\lambda}{\mu_i}\right)\left(\frac{\lambda}{\mu_i}\right)^{n_i}$$

As we will see in later chapters, a similar simple form of solution can be obtained for the joint distribution of queue lengths in much more complex networks. For now we just observe that we need not be restricted to M/M/1 queues (any reversible queues are eligible), that we could allow the network to 'fan out' into a tree with fixed probabilities of selecting each branch, and that queues could be skipped with fixed probability. However, to handle queueing networks with feedback, i.e. with the output of queue j going to a queue $i < j$ $(1 \leq i, j \leq m)$, requires further work – see Chapters 6 and 7. Finally, we note that reversibility provides a very elegant way to find the probability distribution of the delay of a given customer passing through a series of queues. This will be covered in Chapter 9.

5.1.4   Time-dependent solution

The M/M/1 queue is the simplest of all queues and its time-dependent solution, also called its transient solution, can be obtained with some effort; see for example Kleinrock (1975). We will not develop the transient solution here, but it is simple to obtain the differential difference equation it satisfies. We will find the reasoning useful later in this chapter, also providing a direct route to the balance equations of the stationary queue. As before, suppose that the arrival and service rates are $\lambda(n)$ and $\mu(n)$ respectively when the queue length is n. At time t, suppose that the queue length is n and consider the small interval $(t, t + h)$ where h is small. The probability that there is an arrival in $(t, t + h)$, causing the state transition $n \to n + 1$, is $\lambda(n)h + o(h)$. Similarly, if $n > 0$, the probability that there is a departure, causing the state transition $n \to n - 1$, is $\mu(n)h + o(h)$. The probability that there is no transition is $1 - [\lambda(n) + \mu(n)]h + o(h)$, again for $n > 0$. (This follows by subtraction or by noting that the superposed arrival and departure processes form a Poisson process with rate $\lambda(n) + \mu(n)$.) Let $p_n(t)$ denote the probability that the state at time t is n. Then, by the law of total probability, for $n > 0$,

$$p_n(t + h) = p_{n-1}(t)\lambda(n - 1)h + p_{n+1}(t)\mu(n + 1)h$$
$$+ p_n(t)\{1 - [\lambda(n) + \mu(n)]h\} + o(h)$$

Thus,

$$\frac{p_n(t + h) - p_n(t)}{h} = p_{n-1}(t)\lambda(n - 1) + p_{n+1}(t)\mu(n + 1)$$
$$- p_n(t)[\lambda(n) + \mu(n)] + o(1)$$

In the limit that $h \to 0$, we therefore obtain

$$\frac{\partial p_n}{\partial t} = -[\lambda(n) + \mu(n)]p_n + \lambda(n - 1)p_{n-1}$$
$$+ \mu(n + 1)p_{n+1} \quad (n > 0)$$

The corresponding equation for $n = 0$ is easily seen to be

$$\frac{\partial p_0}{\partial t} = -\lambda(0)p_0 + \mu(1)p_1$$

This system of differential equations has a fairly complicated solution which we will not pursue. However, notice that if we can assume a steady state, the derivatives vanish and we are left with the balance equations of the birth and death process; cf. Example 4.9.

5.2   The M/G/1 queue

We now consider the next simplest form of queue in which we still require Poisson arrivals but allow arbitrary service times. We can still make use of Markovian methods because we still have the Random Observer Property, but we introduce some more general techniques which are necessary for the G/G/1 queue and useful elsewhere. When the queue is in equilibrium, we can obtain the mean queue length L and the mean waiting time W using only Little's result and the Random Observer Property as follows.

First, from Little's result applied to the server only (as at the beginning of the chapter) – or directly from the assumption that we have a steady state – the probability that the queue is non-empty is $\lambda\mu^{-1}$ where μ^{-1} is the mean service time of the server, i.e. μ is its service rate. In fact the condition for the queue to have a steady state is that $\lambda\mu^{-1} < 1$. Now let the random variables T_W and T' denote respectively the waiting time and queueing time of a customer in the steady state. Let further N and N' denote the queue length and the number of queueing customers waiting to commence service respectively. Then we have, by Little's result applied to the whole queue

$$L = \lambda W$$

where λ is the rate of the Poisson arrival process. Similarly, considering just the queueing customers as a subsystem,

$$L' = \lambda W'$$

where L', W' are the expected values of N' and T' respectively. Now,

$$T_W = T' + S$$

where S is the service time of the tagged customer. Taking expectations, we have

$$W = W' + \mu^{-1}$$

We now have three equations in four unknowns and obtain a fourth equation by considering the queueing time in terms of the number of queueing customers A found at the arrival instant. Given that $A = n$ for some $n \geqslant 0$,

$$T' = S_1 + \ldots + S_n + R$$

where each S_i denotes a full service time and R denotes the residual service time of the customer in service at the arrival instant, if any. Thus,

$$E[T'|A = n] = n\mu^{-1} + E[R]$$

But if the server is busy at the arrival instant, $E[R] = M_2\mu/2$ by the result obtained for forward recurrence times in Section 4.5, and $E[R] = 0$ otherwise. Thus,

$$W' = E[T'] = E[E[T'|A]]$$

$$= \mu^{-1}E[A] + P(\text{server busy at arrival instant})\frac{M_2\mu}{2}$$

and so, by the Random Observer Property,

$$W' = L'\mu^{-1} + \rho\frac{M_2\mu}{2} = L'\mu^{-1} + \frac{M_2\lambda}{2}$$

Thus, $W' = W'\rho + M_2\lambda/2$ so that

$$W' = \frac{M_2\lambda}{2(1 - \rho)}$$

and so

$$W = \mu^{-1} + \frac{M_2\lambda}{2(1 - \rho)} \qquad L = \rho + \frac{M_2\lambda^2}{2(1 - \rho)}$$

These results are called the **Pollaczek–Khintchine formulae** for mean queue length and mean waiting time; we will see a formula of the same name for the probability generating function of queue length in the next section.

What has become the classical example to illustrate the use of M/G/1 queues in performance modelling is the fixed head disk storage device.

Example 5.5 _____

Certain storage devices consist of a rotating disk (or drum in days gone by) which contains blocks of data in sectors. Sensors called heads are located close to the rotating surface and read or write data blocks at some predetermined sector. All blocks begin on a sector boundary. In this example, we consider a disk with a single head (Figure 5.5), although the case of multiple independent heads can be analysed in the same way. Similarly we could apply our analysis to fixed head disks with several surfaces. Suppose that read/write requests arrive at the head as a Poisson process with parameter λ, requiring blocks of data of fixed length b sectors, beginning at a random sector boundary. We require the mean waiting time for a disk access, given that the disk spins at rate r revolutions per second and has s sectors.

We make the approximation that the next request to be served always finds the head at a boundary between two sectors. This is

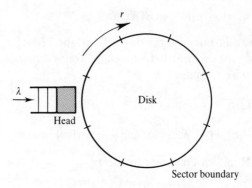

Figure 5.5

certainly the case when the request enters service immediately after the previous one has completed (for integer b), but not in general when an arriving request finds an empty queue. We consider such 'exceptional first service times' in Section 5.2.3; see Example 5.8 in particular. The distance along the circumference between the beginning of a given block and the beginning of the required block is N sectors with probability $1/s$ ($0 \leqslant N \leqslant s - 1$). Thus, the mean circumferential distance to be traversed to the end of the required block is

$$b + \sum_{i=1}^{s-1} \frac{i}{s} = \frac{s + 2b - 1}{2}$$

and so the mean service time is $(s + 2b - 1)/2sr$. Similarly, the second moment of the service time is

$$\frac{1}{s^2 r^2} \sum_{i=0}^{s-1} \frac{(b + i)^2}{s} = \frac{1}{s^2 r^2} \left(b^2 + b(s - 1) + \frac{(s - 1)(2s - 1)}{6} \right)$$

To simplify the notation, we now take $b = 1$. We therefore model the system as an M/G/1 queue with service rate $\mu = 2sr/(s + 1)$ and second moment of service time $M_2 = (s + 1)(2s + 1)/6s^2 r^2$. The system is therefore stationary if and only if

$$\lambda < \frac{2sr}{s + 1}$$

whereupon the mean queue length and mean waiting time are respectively

$$L = \frac{\lambda(s + 1)[(6r - \lambda)s - 2\lambda]}{6rs[(2r - \lambda)s - \lambda]}$$

$$W = \frac{(s + 1)[(6r - \lambda)s - 2\lambda]}{6rs[(2r - \lambda)s - \lambda]}$$

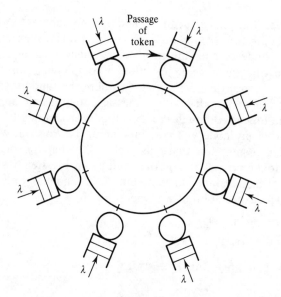

Figure 5.6

In particular, if the number of sectors is large, i.e. as $s \to \infty$,

$$W \to \frac{6r - \lambda}{6r(2r - \lambda)}$$

This can be written as $(1/2r) + \lambda/[3r(2r - \lambda)]$ where the second term is the mean time spent by a disk request waiting in the head's queue before entering service.

Example 5.6

A similar common system is the **token ring network**. Such a network uses a transmission medium that supports no more than one transmission at any given time. To resolve conflicts, a token is passed from one node to another on the network in round robin order and a node has control of the medium, i.e. can transmit, only whilst it holds the token. Suppose that the time to pass the token between any pair of adjacent nodes is x and that the transmission time of any message, i.e. the time a node holds the token if it has a message to transmit, is y. In this example, x and y are constants, but the analysis generalises simply to the case where they are replaced by random variables X and Y with known distributions. We require the mean time required for a message to be transmitted from the instant it arrives at some node in an n-node ring, assuming messages arrive at the nodes as n independent Poisson streams with rate λ (see Figure 5.6). We model this system as n independent M/G/1 queues and consider one (arbitrary) such queue.

Let its service time have mean m and second moment M_2. Then its utilization is $\rho = \lambda m$. Assuming, as in the previous example, that a message at a node reaches the front of its queue immediately after the node releases the token, e.g. just after a completed transmission from that node, its service time $S = nx + Ky$ where the random variable K is the number of other nodes with a message to transmit at the time of arrival of the token. Although the arrival process defined by the arrivals of the *token* at any node will not, in general, be Poisson, we make the approximating assumption that the probability that the queue is non-empty at a token-arrival time is the same as in the steady state, i.e. ρ. Thus, since the nodes are independent, K is binomial with parameters $(n - 1, \rho)$. The expectation of S is therefore

$$m = nx + (n - 1)\rho y$$

and its second moment is

$$\begin{aligned} M_2 &= E[n^2x^2 + 2nxyK + y^2K^2] \\ &= n^2x^2 + 2xyn(n - 1)\rho \\ &\quad + (n - 1)y^2\{\rho(1 - \rho) + (n - 1)\rho^2\} \end{aligned}$$

This is most easily computed by noting that $\mathrm{Var}[S] = y^2\mathrm{Var}[K] = y^2(n - 1)\rho(1 - \rho)$. Of course, we can obtain this variance directly, without using properties of the binomial distribution, by noting that the second moment of the time spent at a node is $\rho y^2 + (1 - \rho)0^2 = \rho y^2$ so that its variance is $\rho(1 - \rho)y^2$. By the independence assumption, the total variance is then as above.

We can now compute ρ from the equation

$$\rho = \lambda m = \lambda[nx + (n - 1)\rho y]$$

so that $\rho = \lambda nx/[1 - \lambda y(n - 1)]$. Mean queue length and waiting time are then obtained by substituting for ρ and M_2 in the Pollaczek–Khintchine formula.

5.2.1   The distribution of the queue length

There are a number of ways of solving for the queue length distribution in an M/G/1 queue, and we consider two. The difference with the M/M/1 queue is that the time to the next transition at an arbitrary time t does not have a known distribution – let alone an exponential distribution. In other words, we do not have a Markov process and so cannot write down a set of balance equations as we might be tempted to do intuitively. (This is a major reason for our exposition of the theory of Markov processes in the previous chapter: not to derive results which are intuitively obvious, but to find the conditions under which our intuition is valid.) Thus, one approach here is to extend the state of the system to include the time since the last state transition; or at least the time a customer being served has spent in service so far since the time to the next arrival is *always* exponential. This is the 'method of supplementary variables' and is considered in Section 5.2.4.

There is a simpler approach, however, which exploits the Markovian component of our model: the Poisson arrival process with its Random Observer Property and exponential interarrival times. Thus, if we consider the state of the system at a departure instant, we know the distribution of the time interval to the next state transition and hence to the next departure instant. This follows because the time to the next arrival (measured from *any* instant) is negative exponential with parameter λ and the time to the next departure, assuming the queue is non-empty, is a complete service time, the distribution of which is given. Thus, the sequence of queue lengths immediately after departure instants satisfies the Markov property and so defines a discrete time Markov chain – an embedded Markov chain. We solve for the equilibrium probability distribution of this chain, under the appropriate stability condition, and hence for the equilibrium distribution of the continuous time stochastic process, which we show is the same in Proposition 5.4.

Suppose that at time $t = 0$ the queue has customers C_1, C_2, ..., C_{x_0} and that arrivals after time 0 are denoted by C_{x_0+1}, C_{x_0+2}, ... For $n \geq 1$, let X_n denote the queue length immediately after C_n completes service and leaves the system – i.e. the number of customers C_n 'leaves behind in the queue'. Also, let Z_n denote the number of arrivals during the interval in which C_{n+1} is being served ($n \geq 0$). Then we have, taking $X_0 = x_0$,

$$X_{n+1} = \begin{cases} X_n - 1 + Z_n & \text{if } X_n > 0 \\ Z_n & \text{if } X_n = 0 \end{cases}$$

since if the queue was non-empty on the departure of C_n, there will have been Z_n new arrivals up to the departure of C_{n+1}, whereupon the queue will reduce by one (namely C_{n+1}). In the case that C_n leaves behind an empty queue, we first have to wait for a new arrival to be the next departure and so $X_{n+1} = 1 + Z_n - 1$. Now, the Z_n are i.i.d. random variables and so $\{X_n | n \geq 0\}$ is indeed a (embedded) Markov chain. Suppose Z_n ($n \geq 0$) has probability mass function $p_j = P(Z_n = j)$ ($j \geq 0$) and probability generating function

$$G(z) = E[z^{Z_n}] = \sum_{j=0}^{\infty} p_j z^j$$

We now need the transition probabilities of the embedded Markov chain for which we have to determine the p_j. Denoting the service time random variable of C_n by S_n and the service time distribution function of the server by F_S, we have

$$P(Z_n = j | S_{n+1} = x) = \frac{(\lambda x)^j}{j!} e^{-\lambda x} \qquad (j \geq 0)$$

since the arrival process is Poisson with rate λ. Thus, by the Law of Total Probability,

$$p_j = \int_0^\infty \frac{(\lambda x)^j}{j!} e^{-\lambda x} \, dF_S(x)$$

and so

$$G(z) = \int_0^\infty e^{\lambda xz} e^{-\lambda x} \, dF_S(x) = B^*[\lambda(1 - z)]$$

where B^* is the Laplace–Stieltjes transform of the distribution function F_S. The reader may find it easier to work with the *density* function f_S, assuming this exists, and its ordinary Laplace transform B^*. The result is the same, although slightly less general. However, the most elegant method, which we will make use of below, uses conditional expectations as follows:

$$G(z) = E[z^Z] = E[E[z^Z | S]] = E[e^{-\lambda S(1-z)}]$$

since Z (conditioned on S) is Poisson with mean λS. But this is just the definition of $B^*[\lambda(1 - z)]$.

The embedded Markov chain therefore has transition matrix $Q = (q_{ij} | i, j \geq 0)$ given by

$$q_{0j} = P(X_{n+1} = j | X_n = 0) = P(Z_n = j) = p_j$$
$$q_{ij} = P(X_{n+1} = j | X_n = i) = P(X_n - 1 + Z_n = j | X_n = i) = P(Z_n = j - i + 1)$$
$$(i > 0)$$
$$= \begin{cases} p_{j-i+1} & (j \geq i - 1 \geq 0) \\ 0 & (0 \leq j \leq i - 2) \end{cases}$$

i.e.

$$Q = \begin{bmatrix} p_0 & p_1 & p_2 & p_3 & p_4 & \cdots \\ p_0 & p_1 & p_2 & p_3 & p_4 & \cdots \\ 0 & p_0 & p_1 & p_2 & p_3 & \cdots \\ 0 & 0 & p_0 & p_1 & p_2 & \cdots \\ \vdots & \vdots & \vdots & \vdots & \vdots & \ddots \end{bmatrix}$$

The steady state equations for the Markov chain, $\pi = \pi Q$, are

$$\pi_i = \pi_0 p_i + \sum_{j=0}^{i} \pi_{j+1} p_{i-j}$$

and so, if it exists, the generating function $\Pi(z) = \sum_{i=0}^{\infty} \pi_i z^i$, satisfies

$$\Pi(z) = \pi_0 G(z) + \sum_{i=0}^{\infty} \sum_{j=0}^{i} \pi_{j+1} p_{i-j} z^i$$

$$= \pi_0 G(z) + \sum_{j=0}^{\infty} \sum_{i=j}^{\infty} \pi_{j+1} p_{i-j} z^i$$

since the summation domain is $\{(i, j) | 0 \le j \le i < \infty\}$. Thus

$$\Pi(z) = \pi_0 G(z) + \sum_{j=0}^{\infty} \pi_{j+1} z^j \sum_{i=0}^{\infty} p_i z^i$$

by changing the second summation variable and rearranging, which yields

$$\Pi(z) = \pi_0 G(z) + z^{-1}[\Pi(z) - \pi_0] G(z)$$

Thus,

$$\Pi(z) = \frac{\pi_0(1 - z)G(z)}{G(z) - z}$$

if the chain is stationary. The stationarity condition is that $\Pi(1) = 1$ and we note that both the numerator and denominator of our expression for $\Pi(z)$ approach 0 as $z \to 1$, since $G(1) = 1$, G being a probability generating function. We therefore apply L'Hôpital's rule to obtain (where $G'(z) = dG/dz$):

$$\Pi(1) = \lim_{z \to 1} \frac{\pi_0(1 - z)G(z)}{G(z) - z} = \lim_{z \to 1} \frac{\pi_0(1 - z)G'(z) - \pi_0 G(z)}{G'(z) - 1}$$

$$= \frac{\pi_0}{1 - G'(1)}$$

Thus, for the chain to be positive recurrent and hence stationary, we require $G'(1) < 1$ whereupon we have $\pi_0 = 1 - G'(1)$. But, $G'(1) = E[Z]$ where Z is distributed as any of the Z_n, the number of arrivals during a service period. Thus,

$$G'(1) = E[E[Z|S]] = E[\lambda S]$$

since the number of arrivals in an interval of length S has expectation λS. But the service time random variable S has mean μ^{-1} by hypothesis and so $G'(1) = \rho = \lambda/\mu$. To summarize, the embedded Markov chain is stationary if and only if $\rho < 1$ and in this case, $\pi_0 = 1 - \rho$. Next, we will show that the continuous time process describing the queue length at positive real times has the same stationarity condition and equilibrium distribution. First, however, we recall that, *assuming* stationarity, we have already obtained, by Little's result, this formula since $1 - \pi_0$ is the utilization of the server. We also note without proof that the Markov chain is null-recurrent and transient in the cases $\rho = 1$ and $\rho > 1$ respectively.

We could obtain the solution for the continuous time process immediately if we had solved for the steady state of the Markov chain defined by the sequence of states *immediately before each arrival*; by the Random Observer Property, this Markov chain has the same steady state distribution. In fact it also has the same steady state as the chain we have been considering, as we now prove in the following proposition.

Proposition 5.4

For any stationary queueing system in which all transitions may only cause the discrete state to change by ±1 unit, the equilibrium probability that the queue length is k immediately before an arrival is equal to the equilibrium probability that the queue length is k immediately after a departure.

Proof Let the positive real random variables $A_1 \le A_2 \le \ldots$ denote the arrival instants of the queueing system after time 0 and $D_1 \le D_2 \le \ldots$ denote the departure instants. Suppose the initial queue length is $h \ge 0$, and let the length of the queue at time t be $X(t)$, so that $X(0) = h$. Now, suppose that the dth departure (at instant D_d) leaves behind a queue of j customers. Then the number of arrivals, a say, up to the instant of this departure satisfies

$$j = h + a - d$$

so that the most recent arrival before the dth departure is the $(d + j - h)$th. This arrival will see the same queue length j and so we have, for all $j \ge 0$, $d \ge 1$,

$$X(D_d^+) = j \Leftrightarrow X(A_{d+j-h}^-) = j$$

Thus,

$$P(X(D_d^+) = j) = P(X(A_{d+j-h}^-) = j) = P(X(A_d^-) = j)$$

by stationarity – or letting $d \to \infty$ for the equilibrium distributions. ∎

To summarize, in the notation of the preceding proof, the two discrete processes $\{X(A_n^-)|n \ge 1\}$, $\{X(D_n^+)|n \ge 1\}$ and the continuous time process $\{X(t)|t \ge 0\}$ all have the same steady state properties. In particular, the equilibrium probability generating function of the queue length is

$$\Pi(z) = \frac{(1 - \rho)(1 - z)G(z)}{G(z) - z} = \frac{(1 - \rho)(1 - z)B^*[\lambda(1 - z)]}{B^*[\lambda(1 - z)] - z}$$

This is known as the **Pollaczek–Khintchine transform equation** and from it any moment of the queue length can be obtained. In particular, $\Pi'(1)$ reduces to the same formula for the mean queue length as we obtained above by Little's result, using multiple applications of L'Hôpital's rule. It is left as an exercise to obtain higher moments and compare them with the formulae obtained from the generalized form of Little's result.

5.2.2 Waiting time distribution

The waiting time distribution for the FCFS discipline is readily obtained from the following observation. For $n \geqslant 1$, the queue, of length X_n, existing on the departure of customer C_n comprises precisely the customers that arrived during that customer's waiting time. In equilibrium, denoting the waiting time distribution of each customer C_n by F_W, the generating function for the queue length is, by the argument we used in the previous section,

$$\Pi(z) = \int_0^{\infty} e^{\lambda xz - \lambda x} \, dF_W(x) = W^*[\lambda(1 - z)]$$

where W^* is the Laplace–Stieltjes transform of F_W. An equivalent derivation uses conditional expectations to give, with X and W denoting the queue length and waiting time random variables respectively:

$$\Pi(z) = E[E[z^X|W]] = E[e^{-\lambda W(1-z)}] = W^*[\lambda(1 - z)]$$

since X, conditional on W, has a Poisson distribution.

Writing $\theta = \lambda(1 - z)$ so that $z = (\lambda - \theta)/\lambda$, we now have

$$W^*(\theta) = \Pi[(\lambda - \theta)/\lambda] = \frac{(1 - \rho)\theta B^*(\theta)}{\theta - \lambda[1 - B^*(\theta)]}$$

We can now easily demonstrate Little's result for the M/G/1 queue since

$$-W^{*'}(0) = -\lambda^{-1}\Pi'(1)$$

Notice too that we get the required exponential distribution in the case of an M/M/1 queue where Π is the generating function of the geometric random variable with parameter ρ; this is left as an exercise.

Example 5.7 _____

For the rotating disk defined in Example 5.5 and modelled by the same
$M/G/1$ queue, what is the probability that a request takes more than r
time units to complete? There are essentially two problems: to find the
Laplace transform $B^*(\theta)$ – previously we computed only the second
moment of service time – and then to invert the resulting expression for
$W^*(\theta)$. To obtain the solution requires numerical methods and we just
give the analysis. Again, we assume that the block size (b) is 1 sector.

First, the service time distribution function F_S is defined by

$$F_S(t) = \begin{cases} \dfrac{n}{s} & \text{if } n \leqslant rst < n + 1 \ (0 \leqslant n \leqslant s - 1) \\ 1 & \text{if } t \geqslant 1/r \end{cases}$$

so that the density function is

$$f_S(t) = \frac{1}{s} \sum_{n=1}^{s} \delta\left(t - \frac{n}{sr}\right)$$

The Laplace transform of this density is therefore

$$B^*(\theta) = \frac{1}{s} \sum_{n=1}^{s} e^{-n\theta/sr}$$

from which the Laplace transform of the required waiting time density is

$$W^*(\theta) = \frac{(1 - \rho)\theta \sum_{n=1}^{s} e^{-n\theta/sr}}{s\theta - \lambda(s - \sum_{n=1}^{s} e^{-n\theta/sr})}$$

by substitution into the above formula. Clearly we cannot invert this by
inspection to find the waiting time density function, from which the
90-percentile would follow. One way to proceed is to try to find the
zeros of the denominator and hence the residues at the poles of $W^*(\theta)$.
The inversion of the Laplace transform is then given by a contour
integral, the Bromwich integral. For an introduction to the methods of
complex analysis used here, the reader might consult Priestley (1985).
The zeros of the denominator are given by the intersections between a
straight line with gradient s and a polynomial curve of degree s in
$e^{-\theta/sr}$. Numerical methods are needed for this and an alternate method
of solution is to do the whole inversion by a more general numerical
method.

5.2.3 Variants of the M/G/1 queue

There are many extensions that can be made to the $M/G/1$ model. Here
we consider just two, queues with exceptional first service times and
queues with bulk arrivals. The former queue is important since it models

a server that takes vacations in the sense that an arrival to an empty queue has to wait a random time for its service to begin, i.e. for the server to return from vacation. The server never takes a vacation when there is work outstanding, i.e. when the queue is non-empty. This is exactly what we need to handle the disk and token ring problems of Examples 5.5 and 5.6. The analysis of bulk arrivals will generalize that given for M/M/1 queues in Section 5.1.1. Other extensions include queues with a 'walking server', where there is a random delay between completing the service of one customer and beginning the next, server breakdowns and priorities. A thorough and mathematically rigorous treatment is given for these and many more variants in Cohen (1982).

Servers with exceptional first service times

We can solve for the equilibrium queue length probability generating function by modifying the argument used in Section 5.2.1. We again consider the embedded Markov chain defined by the queue length at departure instants, i.e. just after a customer completes service. Given the queue length at these instants, the distribution of the time to the next state transition is known independently of past history, and so the Markov property holds. Let R denote the probability distribution function of the *first* service time, i.e. the time interval between a customer's arrival at an empty queue and its completion of service. As before, all other, *ordinary* service times have distribution function B. The argument of Section 5.2.1 now gives the following equation for the equilibrium probabilities π, when they exist, of the embedded Markov chain

$$\pi_i = \pi_0 u_i + \sum_{j=0}^{i} \pi_{j+1} p_{i-j} \quad (i \geq 0)$$

where u_i and p_i are the probabilities that there are i arrivals during a first service period and an ordinary service period respectively $(i \geq 0)$. The only change we have made to the previous argument is the replacement of p_i by u_i in the first term on the right-hand side. Hence we can derive the generating function $\Pi(z)$ of π in the same way to obtain

$$\Pi(z) = \frac{\pi_0[G_P(z) - zG_U(z)]}{G_P(z) - z}$$

where G_U and G_P are the generating functions of $\{u_i\}$ and $\{p_i\}$ respectively. But we know that $G_P(z) = B^*[\lambda(1-z)]$ and, similarly, $G_U(z) = R^*[\lambda(1-z)]$ where an asterisk denotes the Laplace–Stieltjes transform, as before. We determine π_0 by imposing $\Pi(1) = 1$ and so, by L'Hôpital's rule again,

$$1 = \pi_0 \frac{\rho - 1 - \lambda m_R}{\rho - 1}$$

so that $\pi_0 = (1 - \rho)/(1 + \lambda m_R - \rho)$, where m_R is the mean first service time. In particular, the stability condition given by $0 < \pi_0 \leqslant 1$ is $\rho < 1$, i.e. the same as for the standard M/G/1 queue. Informally, this is because there is no difference between the queues when the queue length is greater than zero. Thus, the divergence conditions, which relate to large queue lengths, are also the same.

The most common case of an exceptional first service time arises when a server 'takes vacations' when the queue becomes empty, so that an arrival to an empty queue suffers an elongated service period since it first has to wait for the server to return from vacation. We consider the case where the server immediately takes another vacation if the queue is still empty on return from the previous one. We assume that vacation periods are independent and identically distributed, with probability distribution function V. In this case, u_i is the probability that there are $i + 1$ arrivals in the interval between the beginning of a vacation and the end of the next service period. Thus,

$$u_i = v_0 u_i + \sum_{j=1}^{i+1} v_j p_{i-j+1}$$

where v_i is the probability that there are i arrivals during a vacation $(i \geqslant 0)$. We therefore obtain, using manipulations similar to those of Section 5.2.1,

$$
\begin{aligned}
G_U(z) &= \frac{1}{1 - v_0} \left(\sum_{i=0}^{\infty} \sum_{j=1}^{i+1} v_j p_{i-j+1} z^i \right) \\
&= \frac{z^{-1}}{1 - v_0} \left(\sum_{j=0}^{\infty} \sum_{i=j}^{\infty} v_{j+1} z^{j+1} p_{i-j} z^{i-j} \right) \\
&= \frac{z^{-1} G_P(z)[G_V(z) - v_0]}{1 - v_0}
\end{aligned}
$$

where G_V is the probability generating function of $\{v_i\}$. But $G_V(z) = V^*[\lambda(1 - z)]$ by the usual argument and so

$$G_U(z) = \frac{z^{-1} B^*[\lambda(1 - z)]\{V^*[\lambda(1 - z)] - v_0\}}{1 - v_0}$$

Thus, omitting the $\lambda(1 - z)$ arguments of the transforms,

$$\Pi(z) = \frac{\pi_0[(1 - v_0)B^* - (V^* - v_0)B^*]}{(1 - v_0)(B^* - z)} = \frac{\pi_0}{1 - v_0} \frac{B^*(1 - V^*)}{B^* - z}$$

To have $\Pi(1) = 1$, we require, using L'Hôpital's rule again,

$$1 = \frac{\pi_0}{1 - v_0} \frac{B^*(0)[\lambda V^{*\prime}(0)]}{-\lambda B^{*\prime}(0) - 1} = \frac{\pi_0}{1 - v_0} \frac{\lambda m_V}{1 - \rho}$$

where m_V is the mean length of a vacation. Hence, we finally obtain

$$\Pi(z) = \frac{(1 - \rho) B^*(1 - V^*)}{\lambda m_V (B^* - z)}$$

This is also the generating function for the equilibrium queue length probabilities in continuous time by Proposition 5.4 and the Random Observer Property – exactly as for the standard queue.

Example 5.8

Let us now reconsider the paging disk example, where we now take into account the fact that requests arriving to find the head free have to wait until the head comes under a sector boundary before the service time begins to be measured. To determine the mean queue length in the steady state, and hence the mean waiting time by Little's result, we differentiate the above expression for $\Pi(z)$ at $z = 1$ and then use L'Hôpital's rule to obtain (after significant algebraic manipulation)

$$L = \rho + \frac{M_{2S} \lambda^2}{2(1 - \rho)} + \frac{\lambda M_{2V}}{2 m_V}$$

where M_{2S} and M_{2V} are the second moments of service time (as in the standard M/G/1 queue) and vacation time respectively. This represents an increase in mean queue length of $\lambda M_{2V}/2 m_V$ over the model of Example 5.5. Now, the 'vacation' in this case is the time for the head to reach the next sector boundary after an arrival to an empty queue. Assuming a random position at the arrival instant, the distance to the next boundary is uniformly distributed over $[0, 1]$ sectors. Thus, the mean of the distance is $\frac{1}{2}$ sector and its second moment is $\int_0^1 x^2 \, dx = \frac{1}{3}$. The corresponding mean and second moment of vacation time are therefore $1/2sr$ and $1/3s^2 r^2$ respectively. The increase therefore becomes $\lambda/3sr$ which decreases linearly to zero as $s \to \infty$, justifying the claim made in Example 5.5.

Other types of vacation-taking can be represented similarly, for example when a server does not take multiple vacations. The analysis also extends simply to cases where there is a random delay between service periods, for example due to a 'walking server', 'set-up' or 'shut-down' time.

Bulk arrivals

We considered the M/M/1 queue with bulk arrivals in Section 5.1.1, and discussed its importance in the modelling of 'bursty traffic' which is typical in ISDN communication systems. In this section we generalize that analysis to the M/G/1 queue. We again use the embedded Markov chain method to derive the equilibrium queue length probability generating function at departure instants. Unfortunately, however, the condition of Proposition 5.4 that all state transitions are of ±1 unit is not satisfied by bulk arrivals. Thus, the equilibrium generating function we derive is not that of the continuous time process, although the latter can be derived from it.

The modification of the embedded chain method is more profound than in the extension to exceptional first service times. We begin with the definition of the queue length X_n ($n \geqslant 0$) at departure instants, using the notation of Section 5.2.1:

$$X_{n+1} = \begin{cases} X_n - 1 + Z_n & \text{if } X_n > 0 \\ B_n - 1 + Z_n & \text{if } X_n = 0 \end{cases}$$

where Z_n is the number of arrivals during the service of customer C_{n+1} and B_n is the number of customers in the batch of which C_{n+1} is the first. We assume that the Z_n are i.i.d. with probability generating function G_Z, the B_n are i.i.d. with probability generating function G_B and that the B_n are independent of the Z_n and X_n. Let X_n have probability generating function Π_n. Now,

$$X_{n+1} = X_n - 1 + Z_n + I_{X_n=0}B_n$$

where I is the indicator function that evaluates to 1 or 0 when its subscript is true or false respectively. Thus we have

$$E[z^{X_{n+1}}] = z^{-1}G_Z(z)E[z^{X_n+I_{X_n=0}B_n}]$$

But

$$E[z^{X_n+I_{X_n=0}B_n}] = E[E[z^{X_n+I_{X_n=0}B_n}|X_n]]$$

$$= P(X_n = 0)G_B(z) + \sum_{k=1}^{\infty} P(X_n = k)z^k$$

$$= \Pi_n(0)G_B(z) + [\Pi_n(z) - \Pi_n(0)]$$

Hence,

$$\frac{z}{G_Z(z)}\Pi_{n+1}(z) = \Pi_n(z) + \Pi_n(0)[G_B(z) - 1]$$

This recurrence relation allows, in principle, $\Pi_n(z)$ to be computed at any z for $n = 1, 2, \ldots$ from $\Pi_0(z)$ and $\Pi_0(0)$. Of more interest, however, is the equilibrium case (when it exists). As $n \to \infty$, suppose $\Pi_n \to \Pi$ so that

$$\frac{z}{G_Z(z)} \Pi(z) = \Pi(z) + \Pi(0)[G_B(z) - 1]$$

i.e.

$$\Pi(z) = \frac{\pi_0 G_Z(z)[1 - G_B(z)]}{G_Z(z) - z}$$

where $\pi_0 = \Pi(0)$ is the equilibrium probability that the queue is empty just after a departure. We can determine π_0 by setting $\Pi(1) = 1$ and using L'Hôpital's rule or by noting that

$$E[X_{n+1}] = E[X_n] - 1 + E[Z_n] + \pi_0 E[B_n]$$

This gives $\pi_0 = (1 - m_Z)/m_B$ where m_Z and m_B are the means of Z_n and B_n respectively (for any $n \geq 0$).

Now, G_B characterizes the batch sizes and is given but we can compute $G_Z(z)$ in terms of the Laplace–Stieltjes transform of the service time distribution, B^*, as follows. Suppose batches arrive according to a Poisson process with rate λ. Then, conditioning on the number of *batches*, A say, that arrive during a service time S, we have

$$\begin{aligned}
G_Z(y) &= E[E[E[y^Z|A]|S]] \\
&= E[E[E[y^{B_1 + B_2 + \ldots + B_A}]|S]] \\
&= E[E[\{G_B(y)\}^A|S]] \\
&= E[e^{-\lambda S\{1 - G_B(y)\}}] \\
&= B^*\{\lambda[1 - G_B(y)]\}
\end{aligned}$$

Finally, $m_Z = G_Z'(1) = B^{*'}(0)[-\lambda G_B'(1)] = \lambda m_B/\mu = \rho$, the 'load', since the mean *customer* arrival rate is λm_B. Hence we conclude that

$$\Pi(z) = \frac{(1 - \rho)[1 - G_B(z)]B^*\{\lambda[1 - G_B(z)]\}}{m_B(B^*\{\lambda[1 - G_B(z)]\} - z)}$$

As we observed above, this is *not* the generating function of the equilibrium continuous time process, $\lim_{t\to\infty} X_t$. We can see this by noting that we have $\pi_0 = (1 - \rho)/m_B$ rather than the $1 - \rho$ which we know we must have for the continuous time process. To obtain this generating function requires results from the theory of semi-Markov processes (of which the M/G/1 queue is one) which is outside the scope of this book.

5.2.4 The use of supplementary variables

The trouble with the M/G/1 queue as distinct from the M/M/1 queue is that it is not a continuous time Markov chain. The embedded Markov chain method exploits the remaining Markovian properties to derive a solution. However, an alternative method is to observe that, if we knew how long a customer had been in service at any time, the distribution of the time to the next state transition, together with the probabilities of the next possible states, would be known. Thus, if we included in the state the time elapsed since the current customer being served (if any) entered service, we would indeed have the Markov property at all times and hence a continuous time Markov chain. The price to pay is that the state space is no longer discrete. However, the method is viable, as we are about to find out, and it can also be generalized to many other stochastic processes. For example, in the case of the G/G/1 queue, if we record in the state the intervals since the current customer (if any) entered service *and* since the most recent arrival, we would again have a Markov process.

Let V_t denote the amount of service a customer being served at time t has had already and define an augmented state space as follows:

- 0 denotes an empty queue
- (k, v) denotes a queue of length $k > 0$ in which the customer being served has already received v units of service

We first introduce the **hazard function** for a random variable X, η_X, defined by (dropping the subscript X for brevity):

$$\eta(x)\,dx = P(x < X \leqslant x + dx \mid X > x)$$

$$= \frac{f_X(x)}{1 - F_X(x)}\,dx$$

Thus, $\eta(x) = -(d/dx)\ln[1 - F_X(x)]$ so that $F_X(x) = 1 - \exp[-\int_0^x \eta(u)\,du]$ provided $F_X(0) = 0$. In particular, if $\eta(x) = \lambda$ for all x, X is exponential with parameter λ.

Now define $p_j(t) = P(X_t = j)$ and $p_k(v, t)\,dv = P(X_t = k \cap v < V_t \leqslant v + dv)$ for $j \geqslant 0$, $k \geqslant 1$. Then, taking η to be the hazard function for the service time random variable S, we have the following equations as t increases by the infinitesimal amount h. First,

$$p_0(t + h) = (1 - \lambda h)p_0(t) + \int_0^\infty \eta(v)h p_1(v, t)\,dv + o(h)$$

Next,

$$p_k(v + h, t + h) = \lambda h p_{k-1}(v, t) + [1 - \lambda h - \eta(v)h]p_k(v, t)$$
$$+ o(h) \qquad (k > 1)$$

since a service completion at time t must lead to a state $(k, 0)$ or 0 at time t^+ ($k \geq 1$). Hence there is no transition from any state $(k + 1, u)$ on the right-hand side. Similarly,

$$p_1(v + h, t + h) = [1 - \lambda h - \eta(v)h]p_1(v, t) + o(h)$$

There is no transition due to an arrival in state 0 since this too would produce the state $(1, 0)$. The corresponding equations with $v = 0$, corresponding to a new service period starting at time t, are, for $k > 1$,

$$p_k(0, t + h)h = P(X_{t+h} = k \cap V_{t+h} \in (0, h))$$
$$= P(X_t = k + 1 \cap \text{departure in } (t, t + h))$$
$$+ o(h)$$
$$= \int_0^\infty \eta(v)hp_{k+1}(v, t)\,dv + o(h) \qquad (k > 1)$$

$$p_1(0, t + h)h = P(X_t = 2 \cap \text{departure in } (t, t + h))$$
$$+ P(X_t = 0 \cap \text{arrival in } (t, t + h)) + o(h)$$
$$= \lambda hp_0(t) + \int_0^\infty \eta(v)hp_2(v, t)\,dv + o(h)$$

Rearranging these equations, dividing by h in the first three and letting $h \to 0$ we now obtain the five equations

$$\frac{\partial p_0(t)}{\partial t} = -\lambda p_0(t) + \int_0^\infty p_1(v, t)\eta(v)\,dv$$

$$\frac{\partial p_k(v, t)}{\partial t} + \frac{\partial p_k(v, t)}{\partial v} = \lambda p_{k-1}(v, t) - [\lambda + \eta(v)]p_k(v, t)$$
$$(k > 1)$$

$$\frac{\partial p_1(v, t)}{\partial t} + \frac{\partial p_1(v, t)}{\partial v} = -[\lambda + \eta(v)]p_1(v, t)$$

$$p_k(0, t) = \int_0^\infty p_{k+1}(v, t)\eta(v)\,dv \qquad (k > 1)$$

$$p_1(0, t) = \lambda p_0(t) + \int_0^\infty p_2(v, t)\eta(v)\,dv$$

For the equilibrium solution, if it exists, we define, for $j \geq 0$, $k \geq 1$, $\pi_j = \lim_{t \to \infty} p_j(t)$ and $\pi_k(v) = \lim_{t \to \infty} p_k(v, t)$. The above equations then become

$$\lambda\pi_0 = \int_0^\infty \pi_1(v)\eta(v)\,dv \qquad (5.1)$$

$$\frac{\partial \pi_k(v)}{\partial v} = \lambda \pi_{k-1}(v) - [\lambda + \eta(v)]\pi_k(v) \qquad (k > 1) \tag{5.2}$$

$$\frac{\partial \pi_1(v)}{\partial v} = -[\lambda + \eta(v)]\pi_1(v) \tag{5.3}$$

$$\pi_k(0) = \int_0^\infty \pi_{k+1}(v)\eta(v)\,dv \qquad (k > 1) \tag{5.4}$$

$$\pi_1(0) = \lambda \pi_0 + \int_0^\infty \pi_2(v)\eta(v)\,dv \tag{5.5}$$

Now let $R(z, v) = \sum_{k=1}^\infty \pi_k(v)z^k$. Then, multiplying Equation (5.3) by z and Equation (5.2) by z^k and summing, we obtain

$$\frac{\partial R(z, v)}{\partial v} = [\lambda z - \lambda - \eta(v)]R(z, v) \tag{5.6}$$

Similarly, from Equations (5.5) and (5.4),

$$R(z, 0) = \lambda z \pi_0 + z^{-1}\int_0^\infty [R(z, v) - \pi_1(v)z]\eta(v)\,dv$$

$$= z^{-1}\int_0^\infty R(z, v)\eta(v)\,dv + \lambda(z - 1)\pi_0 \tag{5.7}$$

by Equation (5.1). Integrating Equation (5.6) yields

$$\ln R(z, v) = -\lambda(1 - z)v - \int_0^v \eta(u)\,du + C(z)$$

where $C(z)$ is some function of z. Thus, since η is the hazard function of the service time random variable S,

$$R(z, v) = A(z)e^{-\lambda(1-z)v}[1 - F_S(v)]$$

where A is a positive function of z. At $v = 0$, this gives $A(z) = R(z, 0)$ for service time distribution function with $F_S(0) = 0$. We can now obtain $R(z, 0)$ by substituting into Equation (5.7) to get

$$R(z, 0) = z^{-1}\int_0^\infty R(z, 0)e^{-\lambda(1-z)v}[1 - F_S(v)]\eta(v)\,dv$$

$$+ \lambda(z - 1)\pi_0$$

$$= z^{-1}R(z, 0)\int_0^\infty e^{-\lambda(1-z)v}f_S(v)\,dv + \lambda(z - 1)\pi_0$$

by definition of the hazard function. Thus

$$R(z, 0) = \frac{\lambda z(z - 1)\pi_0}{z - B^*(\lambda - \lambda z)}$$

Now, the required generating function $\Pi(z) = \sum_{k=0}^{\infty} \pi_k z^k = \pi_0 + \int_0^{\infty} R(z, v)\,dv$. But, integrating by parts,

$$\int_0^{\infty} e^{-\lambda(1-z)v}[1 - F_S(v)]\,dv$$

$$= -\left[\frac{e^{-\lambda(1-z)v}}{\lambda(1-z)}\right]_0^{\infty} - \int_0^{\infty} \frac{e^{-\lambda(1-z)v}}{\lambda(1-z)} f_S(v)\,dv$$

$$= \frac{1 - B^*[\lambda(1-z)]}{\lambda(1-z)}$$

Hence,

$$\Pi(z) = \pi_0 + \frac{\lambda z(z-1)\pi_0}{z - B^*[\lambda(1-z)]} \frac{1 - B^*[\lambda(1-z)]}{\lambda(1-z)}$$

$$= \frac{\pi_0(1-z)B^*[\lambda(1-z)]}{B^*[\lambda(1-z)] - z}$$

which, at long last, is the continuous time result we got using the embedded Markov chain method, the Random Observer Property and Proposition 5.4. The stationarity condition and value for π_0 are obtained, as before, by imposing $\Pi(1) = 1$.

5.3   The G/G/1 queue

The dual to the M/G/1 queue we have been considering is the G/M/1 queue which has arbitrary inter-arrival time distribution and exponential service times. It can be solved in an analogous manner to the M/G/1 case, for example by analysing the embedded Markov chain defined by the queue length immediately after an arrival. Then the time to the next arrival is a whole inter-arrival time, with known distribution. But the time to the next service completion is distributed as a whole service time, by the residual life property of the exponential distribution in the case that a customer is being served at the time of arrival. The analysis follows that of the M/G/1 queue closely and is the subject of an exercise.

More generally, in a G/G/1 queue, both inter-arrival time and service time have arbitrary distributions. The arrivals form a renewal process (so that inter-arrival times are i.i.d.) and the service times are also i.i.d. For these reasons, the queue is more correctly known as the GI/GI/1 queue. (For that matter, we could call the M/G/1 queue an M/GI/1 queue as well.) Surprisingly, many properties can be derived even for such a generally specified queue and we describe the best known approach. We assume that service time distribution is independent of queue length and that the queueing discipline is FCFS. As with the $M/G/1$ queue, we look for some embedded Markov chain but the queue length at departure times is not Markovian since the distribution of time to the next arrival is no longer known independently of past history. Of course, the instants at which arrivals find an empty queue are Markov times since there the distributions of the times to the next arrival and departure are known.[1] Unfortunately, since the queue length is always zero at these instants, little can be deduced about the continuous time process. However, the *queueing times* $\{Q_n | n \geqslant 1\}$ of successive arrivals also define a discrete time, continuous state space Markov chain. This is because, given the queueing time of one customer, the queueing time of the next customer is determined by the first customer's service time and the time interval between the arrival instants. We now proceed to analyse this process.

The nth customer C_n has waiting time $W_n = Q_n + S_n$ where S_n is a service time random variable ($n \geqslant 1$). Now let A_n be the interval between the arrivals of C_n and C_{n+1}. Then we have

$$Q_{n+1} = \begin{cases} 0 & \text{if } A_n > W_n \\ W_n - A_n & \text{if } A_n \leqslant W_n \end{cases}$$

$$= \max(0, W_n - A_n)$$

$$= \max(0, Q_n + T_n)$$

where the $T_n = S_n - A_n$ are i.i.d. with distribution function F_T say. From this simple equation, we can prove the following result.

Proposition 5.5

For $n \geqslant 1$,

$$F_{Q_{n+1}}(t) = \begin{cases} 0 & \text{if } t < 0 \\ \int_{-\infty}^{t} F_{Q_n}(t-u) \, dF_T(u) & \text{if } t \geqslant 0 \end{cases}$$

Proof Q_{n+1} is never negative, and so the result for $t < 0$ is immediate. For $t \geqslant 0$,

$$F_{Q_{n+1}}(t) = P(Q_n + T_n \leqslant t \cap 0 \leqslant t)$$

$$= \int_{-\infty}^{\infty} P(Q_n \leqslant t - u \,|\, T_n = u) \, dF_T(u)$$

$$= \int_{-\infty}^{\infty} F_{Q_n}(t - u) \, dF_T(u)$$

---

[1] In fact these instants are **regeneration points**. The evolution of a regenerative process after one regeneration point is a probabilistic replica of its evolution after any other. Regenerative processes are important in discrete event simulation since they have laws of large numbers that enable unbiased estimates to be made for functions of the state within prescribed confidence bands.

since T_n and Q_n are independent. The result then follows since $F_{Q_n}(t - u) = 0$ for $u > t$.   ∎

Since we are interested in the stationary queue, we now investigate the limit of $F_{Q_n}(t)$ as $n \to \infty$. In fact this always exists but is not necessarily a proper distribution, i.e. it may be that $\lim_{n \to \infty} F_{Q_n}(\infty) < 1$. This is stated in the following:

Proposition 5.6

As $n \to \infty$, $F_{Q_n}(t) \to F_Q(t)$ which satisfies

$$F_Q(t) = \int_{-\infty}^{t} F_Q(t - u)\, dF_T(u)$$

This equation is called **Lindley's integral equation**.

Proof We show that $F_{Q_{n+1}}(t) \leqslant F_{Q_n}(t)$ for all t and $n \geqslant 1$. The result is trivial for $t < 0$. Assuming without loss of generality that the first customer C_1 finds an empty queue, so that $Q_1 = 0$, $F_{Q_1}(t) = 1$ for all $t \geqslant 0$ and so the result follows for $n = 1$. For $n \geqslant 2$, the inductive step is now

$$F_{Q_{n+1}}(t) - F_{Q_n}(t)$$

$$= \int_{-\infty}^{t} \{F_{Q_n}(t - u) - F_{Q_{n-1}}(t - u)\}\, dF_T(u) \geqslant 0$$

by the inductive hypothesis.

Thus for each t, $\{F_{Q_n}(t) | n \geqslant 0\}$ is bounded below (by 0) and decreasing and so has a limit. This limit satisfies the given equation by monotone convergence.   ∎

One important question now is, under what conditions is F_Q a proper distribution? We would expect this to be the case if and only if the queue is *stable*, i.e. has a steady state. From our analysis of other queues, we expect the stability condition to depend on the traffic intensity or load, $\rho = E[S]/E[A]$ where S is a service time random variable, distributed as each S_n, and A is an inter-arrival time, distributed as each A_n. We know that if there is a stationary solution, the equilibrium probability that the queue length is zero, π_0, is $1 - \rho$, which follows, for example, by Little's result. The following proposition is therefore not surprising.

Proposition 5.7

Let $T = S - A$. Then

(a) F_Q is a proper distribution if $E[T] < 0$

(b) $F_Q(t) = 0$ for all t if $E[T] > 0$

(c) $F_Q(t) = 0$ for all t if $E[T] = 0$

In case (a) the queue is stable and in the other cases it is unstable. Notice that $E[T]$ is negative, positive or zero when ρ is less than 1, greater than 1 or equal to 1 respectively.

Proof First we observe that

$$Q_{n+1} = \max(0, Q_n + T_n)$$
$$= \max[0, \max(0, Q_{n-1} + T_{n-1}) + T_n]$$
$$= \max[0, T_n, T_n + T_{n-1} + \max(0, Q_{n-2} + T_{n-2})]$$

and so on, so that, for $n \geq 1$,

$$Q_{n+1} = \max(0, T_n, T_n + T_{n-1}, \ldots, T_n + \ldots + T_1 + Q_1)$$

as may be proved by an easy induction. But $Q_1 = 0$ and $(T_n, \ldots, T_1)$ has the same joint distribution as $(T_1, \ldots, T_n)$ since $T_1, \ldots, T_n$ are i.i.d. Thus, replacing T_i by T_{n-i+1}, we have that Q_{n+1} has the same distribution as

$$Q'_{n+1} = \max(0, U_1, U_2, \ldots, U_n)$$

where $U_j = \sum_{i=1}^{j} T_i$. Now let $Q' = \lim_{n \to \infty} Q'_n$ which always exists (almost surely) if we allow $Q' = \infty$, since $Q'_{n+1} \geq Q'_n$ for $n \geq 1$. Thus, $F_Q(t) = P(Q' \leq t) = P(U_n \leq t, n = 1, 2, \ldots)$ for $t \geq 0$.

Case (a)
For $E[T] < 0$,

$$P(U_j > 0 \text{ for infinitely many } j)$$

$$= P\left(\frac{U_j}{j} - E[T] > |E[T]| \text{ for infinitely many } j\right)$$

$$= 0$$

by the strong law of large numbers applied to the T_i. Thus, Q' is the maximum of finitely many U_j with probability 1. But U_j is finite with probability 1 for any finite j, since the distributions F_S and F_A are proper. Consequently, $P(Q' < \infty) = 1$ so that $F_{Q'}$ and hence F_Q are proper.

Case (b)
For any $t \geq 0$, $j \geq 1$

$$P(U_j > t) = P\left(\frac{U_j}{j} - E[T] > \frac{t}{j} - E[T]\right)$$

$$\geqslant P\left(\frac{U_j}{j} - E[T] > - \frac{E[T]}{2}\right)$$

for sufficiently large j since $E[T] > 0$. Thus, $P(U_j > t) \to 1$ as $j \to \infty$ by the weak law of large numbers. But $P(Q' \geqslant t) \geqslant P(U_j \geqslant t)$ for all $j \geqslant 1$ and so $P(Q' \geqslant t) = 1$. Since t was arbitrary, we must therefore have $P(Q' < \infty) = 0$ and F_Q improper.

Case (c)
Here we use the Law of the Iterated Logarithm (see Section 3.3.1) to show that, when $\text{Var}[T] > 0$, given any $t > 0$, $P(U_j \geqslant t$ for some $j) = 1$. We then proceed as in case (b). It is always possible to find an n and $c < 1$ such that $t \leqslant c\{2n \ln[\ln(n)]\text{Var}[T]\}^{1/2}$. Then,

$$U_j \geqslant c\{2j \ln[\ln(j)]\text{Var}[T]\}^{1/2}$$

$$\geqslant c\{2n \ln[\ln(n)]\text{Var}[T]\}^{1/2} \geqslant t$$

for infinitely many $j \geqslant n$, as required.   ∎

One way of finding the distribution F_Q is to solve Lindley's integral equation. This can be done in terms of transforms, using results from the theory of complex variables. A good summary of this method is given in Kleinrock (1975). Here we analyse the random walk defined by the sequence of random variables $\{U_j | j \geqslant 0\}$ where $U_0 = 0$ and $U_j = \sum_{i=1}^{j} T_i$ for $j \geqslant 1$. This random walk jumps (up or down) by T_n at the nth step and a number of its properties relate to the G/G/1 queue directly. In particular, Q_n is distributed as the maximum of the first n positions of the walk, since Q'_n was defined to be equal to this maximum.

Since we are considering a cumulative maximum, let us define a **ladder point** to be a time instant at which the position of the walk is greater than any previous position, i.e. the nth ladder point L_n is defined by

$$L_0 = 0$$

$$L_{n+1} = \min(i | i > L_n, U_i > U_{L_n})$$

An equivalent statement to Proposition 5.7 is now that for a stable queue $(E[T] < 0)$ there are only finitely many ladder points with probability one. Excluding L_0, let the total number of ladder points be N and let q be the probability that there is at least one ladder point. Then,

$$P(N \geqslant n + 1 | N \geqslant n) = q$$

since the joint probability distribution of the jumps that occur after any step, in particular a ladder point, is always the same. Thus, for $n \geqslant 1$,

$$P(N \geqslant n + 1) = qP(N \geqslant n) = \ldots = q^n P(N \geqslant 1) = q^{n+1}$$

and so $P(N = n) = q^n - q^{n+1} = (1 - q)q^n$. Thus the queue is stable if and only if $q < 1$.

We now consider the distance between the positions of the walk at successive ladder points, letting $D_n = U_{L_n} - U_{L_{n-1}}$ for $1 \leqslant n \leqslant N$. Then, since the random walk has the Markov property at all steps, the D_n are i.i.d. with distribution function F_D. From F_D we can obtain the distribution of queueing time, F_Q, as in the following.

Proposition 5.8

For a stable G/G/1 queue, $Q^*(s) = (1 - q)/[1 - qD^*(s)]$ where Q^* and D^* denote the Laplace–Stieltjes transforms of F_Q and F_D respectively.

Proof   First we observe that $Q' = \sum_{i=1}^{N} D_i$. Hence,

$$Q^*(s) = E[e^{-sQ'}] = E[E[e^{-sQ'}|N]] = E[\{E[e^{-sD}]\}^N]$$
$$= E[\{D^*(s)\}^N]$$

since the D_i are i.d.d., where D is distributed as any of the D_i. This expectation is just the probability generating function of N, $G_N(z)$ say, evaluated at $z = D^*(s)$. Now,

$$G_N(z) = \sum_{n=0}^{\infty} P(N = n)z^n$$

$$= \sum_{n=0}^{\infty} (1 - q)q^n z^n$$

$$= \frac{1 - q}{1 - qz}$$

and so the result follows.   ∎

Although all these results look very promising, unfortunately the distribution F_D is hard to obtain. A further development of the theory considers a dual queue, in which the inter-arrival time and service time distributions are interchanged, and idle period distributions. A server's idle period is an interval between successive busy periods, which are better understood. In fact, it can be shown that the idle period of the dual queue has the same distribution as D.

SUMMARY

- Queues represent contention systems and are central in many models of communication and computer systems.
- A queue is characterized by its arrival process, service time distribution and queueing discipline. Kendall's notation summarizes these characteristics.
- Little's result relates the means of random variables associated with a queueing system in equilibrium. A similar result relates higher moments when the arrival process is Poisson.
- Markovian (M/M/m) queues can model various communication systems but require exponential service times and Poisson arrivals.
- Queues with bulk arrivals can model burstiness in telecommunication systems.
- Burke's theorem shows that the output process of an M/M/m queue is Poisson and independent of the arrival process. It can be proved elegantly using reversibility.
- The M/G/1 queue has service times with arbitrary distribution and can model many realistic systems. Two methods of analysing it use an embedded Markov chain and supplementary variables.
- The Pollaczek–Khintchine equations relate the queue length, waiting time and service time distributions through transforms.
- Lindley's integral equation for the G/G/1 queue relates the distributions of queueing time and the difference between service time and inter-arrival time.
- The Laplace–Stieltjes transform of the queueing time distribution in a G/G/1 queue can be found by considering the ladder points in a certain random walk.

EXERCISES

5.1 (20 M/M/1 with discouragement)
Consider an M/M/1 queue where a job's willingness to join the queue is influenced by the queue size. More precisely, a job which finds j $(j = 0, 1, \ldots)$ other jobs in the system joins the queue with probability $1/(j + 1)$ and departs immediately otherwise. Draw the state transition diagram for this system with arrival rate λ and mean service time $1/\mu$. Write down and solve the balance equations for the equilibrium probabilities p_j $(j = 0, 1, \ldots)$. Show that a steady-state distribution always exists. Find the utilization of the server, the throughput, the average number of jobs in the system and the average response time for a job that decides to join. Note that the form of distribution is the same as that of the M/M/∞ queue.

5.2 (20 M/M/1 with pressure and discouragement)
Consider an M/M/∞ system with discouraged arrivals that have

the following birth and death coefficients:

$$\lambda(j) = \frac{\lambda}{(j + 1)^b} \quad \text{and} \quad \mu(j) = j^c \mu$$

where c is the *pressure coefficient* – a constant that indicates the degree to which the service rate of the system is affected by the system state. Similarly, b is the *discouraging coefficient*. Obtain the equilibrium probabilities p_j for this birth and death process. What is the distribution when $b + c = 1$?

5.3   (20 M/M/1 departure process)
Let D be a random interval between two consecutive departures from the M/M/1 queue in the steady state with arrival rate λ and service rate μ. If, after the last departure, the queue was not empty, then D coincides with the service time of the next job. If the queue was empty, then D consists of the period until the next arrival, as well as the service time of the new job. Arguing that the probability of a non-empty system just after a departure is the same as the utilization (U), show that D is exponentially distributed with parameter λ.

5.4   (20 M/M/n reverse transition rates)
Consider an M/M/n system in the steady state, from the point of view of an observer looking backwards in time. Show that the instantaneous transition rates from state j to states $j + 1$ and $j - 1$ in reverse time (e.g. $q'(j, j + 1)$ and $q'(j, j - 1)$) are the corresponding rates in forward time (i.e. $q(j, j + 1) = \lambda$ and $q(j, j - 1) = \mu$), i.e. $P(\text{state } j + 1 \text{ at time } t - h | \text{state } j \text{ at time } t) = \lambda h + o(h), j = 0, 1, 2, \ldots$.
This shows that the reversibility property holds for the M/M/n queue, i.e. the behaviour of the system with time reversed in indistinguishable from its behaviour in forward time.

5.5   (20 Burke's theorem and reversibility)
Burke's theorem states that for an M/M/n queue the departure process is statistically identical to the arrival process (i.e. Poisson with same rate) and its past history is independent of the current system state.
      Show that Burke's theorem is a consequence of the reversibility property.
      (Note that the arrival process in forward time is Poisson and is statistically identical to the arrival process in reverse time which corresponds with the departure process in forward time.)

5.6   (30 M/G/1 token ring)
A token ring communication network operates as follows. There are M stations and a token continually circulates amongst them in

a fixed order (round robin). The time to pass between stations is x seconds and the time required for a station to transmit (a delay on the token's passage) is d seconds: there is no delay if a station has no message to transmit.

Messages arrive at each station in a Poisson stream with rate λ. Assuming that the system is in equilibrium and heavily loaded so that a message arriving at any station is unlikely to encounter an empty queue, model this system as M independent, identical M/G/1 queues. Hence find the expected time required for a complete message transmission to take place (i.e. including all queueing time). How could random message transmission times be handled?

5.7 (20 M/G/1 mean queue length using Little's result)
For an M/G/1 queue in equilibrium with constant arrival rate λ and constant service rate μ, prove that the mean queue length is $L = (\lambda/\mu) + \lambda^2 r/(\mu - \lambda)$ where r is the mean residual service time of the task in service (if any) at an arrival instant. (Hint: consider both the whole queue and the collection of customers waiting to be served in separate applications of Little's result.)

5.8 (20 M/G/1 polling system – round robin)
A polling system services n stations repeatedly in round robin order. The times required at each station are independent, identically distributed random variables and the time taken to pass between successive stations is constant. Explain how an M/G/1 queue can be used to approximate the behaviour of such a system when tasks arrive at each station as independent Poisson processes.

5.9 (30 Mean waiting time for M/G/1)
Show that the mean waiting time in an LCFS-PR M/G/1 queue is equal to the mean waiting time in the M/M/1 queue. Why?

5.10 (40 M/G/1's outstanding service demand)
Suppose O_t is the amount of 'outstanding work' at time t in an M/G/1 queue, i.e. the sum of all the service times of the queueing customers (if any) and the residual service time of the customer being served (if any) at time t. Show that $\{O_t | t \geq 0\}$ defines a continuous time, continuous state space Markov chain.

5.11 (30 M/G/1 higher moments)
Using the Pollaczek–Khintchine transform equations for the M/G/1 queue, find the second moment of the queue length and the second factorial moment of the waiting time. Compare with the generalized Little's result.

Chapter 6
Single Class Queueing Networks

6.1 Introduction	216	6.5 Performance measures	
6.2 Open queueing		for the state-dependent	
networks	218	case	245
6.3 Closed queueing		6.6 The flow equivalent	
networks	231	server method	249
6.4 Mean value analysis	238		

6.1 Introduction

So far we have been analysing single servers to model single or collections of resources. In this chapter, we consider systems with multiple resources that can be modelled by a network of servers. A queueing network is a directed graph $G = (V, E)$ consisting of a set of nodes or vertices $V = (1, 2, \ldots, M\}$ and a set of arcs or edges $E \subseteq V \times V$ as shown in Figure 6.1. Each node is a service centre representing some active resource in the physical system. The service centre has a single queue and one or more servers. For example, the node may model a processing element in a computer (central processing unit or input/output device) or some node in a communication network. Such nodes may have wide geographic separation, but we assume that transfer times from node to node are zero (for now). The arcs define the topology of the network and represent the possible paths taken by customers.

The workload of the system of resources defines the characteristics given to each task or customer in the network. Typically, we characterize the workload by the service time at each node and the

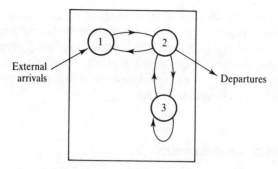

Figure 6.1   A simple queueing network.

routing probabilities between nodes. We will begin by considering the single class case in which all customers have identical characteristics. More generally, there may be several different types of customers (e.g. CPU bound customers and i/o bound customers) in the same network. Indeed, a customer may initially be CPU bound but become i/o bound as it progresses through the network. This gives a multi-class or multi-chain network in which customers may have different service requirements at each node and different routing behaviour through the network. Analysis of such networks is, in principle, a straightforward generalization of single class networks but with more complex notation; see Chapter 7.

6.1.1   Types of network

We can classify queueing networks into three basic types: open, closed and mixed networks. In **open networks** there is at least one arc coming from outside and at least one arc going out. The incoming arc comes from some infinite source of customers and the outgoing arc goes to some external sink. For example, Figure 6.1 shows a network with three nodes and two external arcs (one incoming arc and one outgoing arc). If all external arcs are incoming then the network will saturate in finite time, i.e. have no equilibrium state. On the other hand, if all external arcs are outgoing then the network will be eventually null (or empty). In **closed networks**, there are no external arcs and so the network population is constant and all customers are forever circulating. For example, Figure 6.1 with external arcs removed from nodes 1 and 2 is a closed network. Multi-class networks that are closed with respect to some customer types and open with respect to others are said to be **mixed networks**. For example, Figure 6.1 with one class that circulates between nodes 1 and 2 only and another class that uses all nodes is a mixed network with 2 classes.

These three types of queueing networks relate to computer and communication systems in a very simple way. The open network can represent a transaction system with external arrivals and departures. The closed network is typically used for modelling batch type workloads where the multiprogramming level is held constant. Of course, the mixed network can represent both transaction and batch type workloads simultaneously in a computer system.

6.1.2 Types of service centre

Generally, a node in the queueing network is defined by the service discipline (or queueing discipline) and the service time distribution for each class of customer. We can view the queue as ordered by arrival time, but the service discipline dictates how and when the customers are served. We will assume that the service time distribution is negative exponential at FCFS nodes. At other types of nodes, we will later allow general service time distributions:

- Processor sharing (PS) nodes at which service is shared equally amongst all customers in the queue;
- Last come first served pre-emptive resume (LCFS-PR) nodes at which new arrivals displace the customer in service (if any) to obtain immediate service;
- Infinite server (IS) or delay nodes, which provide immediate service to all customers in its queue and so independently delay all customers for some random time.

Suppose each node has a state dependent service rate $\mu_i(n)$ when there are n customers in the queue ($\mu_i(0) = 0$ and $\mu_i(n) > 0$ for $n > 0$). In the following sections we assume that all service centres belong to one of three types of node:

(a)   single server fixed rate (SSFR) with fixed rate $\mu_i(n) = \mu_i$
(b)   infinite server (IS), i.e. a delay node with no queueing and rate $\mu_i(n) = n\mu_i$
(c)   queue length dependent (QLD) with service rate $\mu_i(n)$

We separate node types (a) and (b), though they are special cases of (c), because they often give simpler analysis. Also for simplicity, the default queueing discipline is FCFS and the default service time distribution is exponential.

6.2 Open queueing networks

We begin by analysing open networks with various topologies, since these are the easiest to analyse. The simplest type of network is a series of nodes in tandem labelled $i = 1, 2, \ldots, M$ with arrivals at node 1 only and departures from node M only. Generalizing the linear structure further we obtain **tree-like networks**, which consist of a series of nodes forming a trunk and a hierarchy of nodes forming a tree so that each internal node has a unique parent node. As we will see in Chapter 9, tree networks have arrivals only at node 1 and departures only at the leaf nodes. These are all examples of **feedforward networks** since no customer visits a node more than once. In practical applications there is typically much feedback and often this is crucial to the performance of the system under consideration. The first breakthrough appeared in Jackson (1957) and (1963) and the class of networks described in these papers has become known as **Jackson networks**.

Definition 6.1 (Jackson network)

A Jackson network with M nodes (labelled $i = 1, 2, \ldots M$, say) is defined as follows:

- node i is QLD with rate $\mu_i(n)$ when it has n customers
- a customer completing service at a node makes a probabilistic choice of either leaving the network or entering another node, independent of past history
- the network is open and any external arrivals to node i form a Poisson stream

Consider an open Jackson network with M nodes and state space given by

$$S = \{(n_1, \ldots, n_M) | n_i \geq 0\}$$

where n_i is the queue length at node i.

Suppose the queue length vector random variable is $(N_1, \ldots, N_M)$ so we can define

$$\pi(n) = \pi(n_1, \ldots, n_M) = P(N_1 = n_1, \ldots, N_M = n_M)$$

as the steady state probability (if this exists) that the network is in state n.

The routing behaviour of customers in the network is defined by the routing probability matrix $Q = (q_{ij} | i, j = 1, \ldots, M)$ where q_{ij} is the constant probability that on leaving node i a customer next goes to node j (independently of past history). If this routing probability is state dependent then we have adaptive routing (see Kelly 1979) but we assume it is constant. The probability of an external departure from node i is given by:

$$q_{i0} = 1 - \sum_{j=1}^{M} q_{ij} \tag{6.1}$$

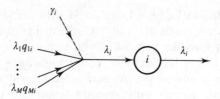

Figure 6.2 Traffic flow through nodes.

Since the network is open there is at least one node i with $q_{i0} > 0$, and so at least one row of Q sums to less than one. We can think of an imaginary node 0 that acts as an external source and sink of customers. The total external arrivals to the open network form a Poisson stream with rate $\gamma > 0$ and each external arrival joins node $i = 1, 2, \ldots M$ with probability $q_{0i} \geqslant 0$. The external arrivals into node i form a Poisson stream with rate $\gamma_i = \gamma q_{0i}$ (by the decomposition property of the Poisson process). Thus we have $\gamma = \sum_{i=1}^{M} \gamma_i$.

All the centres in the network are QLD nodes with exponential service times. The service rate of node i is $\mu_i(n_i)$ when its queue length is n_i, so the service rates depend on the local state. More generally, the service rate could depend on the global network state $\mu_i(\mathbf{n})$. This would allow the rate at one node to depend on the state of another so that blocking can be represented. For example, the rate becomes zero when the finite capacity queue at the next node is full. Here, we will only consider local state dependent service rates (and infinite buffer sizes) because this case is considerably easier to analyse than global state dependence. However, in Chapter 10 we will consider queueing networks with finite buffers and hence blocking.

6.2.1 Traffic equations

We now use the traffic routing behaviour to determine mean arrival rates λ_i to each node i in the network. In unit time, the mean number of arrivals to node i is the sum of the mean external arrivals (i.e. γ_i) and the mean number of arrivals from all nodes j (i.e. $\lambda_j q_{ji}$) as shown in Figure 6.2. Thus the traffic equation for node $i = 1, 2, \ldots, M$ is given by:

$$\lambda_i = \gamma_i + \sum_{j=1}^{M} \lambda_j q_{ji} \tag{6.2}$$

In the steady state, we also have a traffic equation for the network as a whole:

$$\gamma = \sum_{i=1}^{M} \lambda_i q_{i0}$$

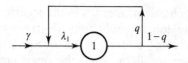

Figure 6.3   Example of a network with feedback.

Because of the properties of the matrix Q, there is a unique solution for the set of unknowns $\{\lambda_i\}$ since in vector form the traffic equation is $\lambda(I - Q) = \gamma$ and $I - Q$ is non-singular (cf. the Markov process analysis in Chapter 4). Note that the traffic Equation (6.2) assumes only the existence of a steady state and is independent of the Poisson assumption since we are considering mean numbers of arrivals in unit time.

Example 6.1 _____

Let us consider the simple network shown in Figure 6.3. This models a data transmission channel with probability q that a message is transmitted unsuccessfully and requires retransmission. The traffic equation for this network is $\lambda_1 = \gamma + \lambda_1 q$, so $\lambda_1 = \gamma/(1 - q)$.

Though external arrivals to the network are Poisson, arrivals to a node are not generally Poisson (e.g. the example above). Still, if there is no feedback then all arrival processes are Poisson because from Burke's theorem the departure process of an M/M/1 queue is Poisson and the superposition of independent Poisson processes is also Poisson. Note that in the example above the processes being superposed are not independent because of the feedback.

6.2.2   Jackson's theorem

Jackson's theorem (Jackson 1963) provides the steady state joint probability distribution for states.

Proposition 6.1 (Jackson's theorem)

For a Jackson network in the steady state with arrival rate λ_i to node i:

(a)   The number of customers at any node is independent of the number of customers at every other node.

(b)   Node i behaves stochastically *as if* it were subjected to Poisson arrivals, rate λ_i.

Proof All stochastic properties in the steady state are implied by the joint queue length probability distribution $\pi(n)$ where state $n = (n_1, n_2, \ldots, n_M)$ and n_i is the queue length at node i. We prove the above result by using the open network's steady state global balance equations:

$$\pi(n) \sum_{n'} q(n, n') = \sum_{n'} \pi(n')q(n', n) \tag{6.3}$$

where $q(n, m)$ is the instantaneous transition rate from state n to state m. The term $\pi(n)q(n, m)$ is often called the probability flux from state n to state m, so in words these balance equations are:

$$\begin{array}{l}\text{total probability} \\ \text{flux out of state } n\end{array} = \begin{array}{l}\text{total probability flux} \\ \text{from all states into state } n\end{array}$$

To obtain the transition rates, we define the following notation:

$$n_i = (n_1, \ldots, n_i - 1, \ldots, n_M)$$
$$n^i = (n_1, \ldots, n_i + 1, \ldots, n_M)$$
$$n_i^j = (n_1, \ldots, n_i - 1, \ldots, n_j + 1, \ldots, n_M) \qquad (i \neq j)$$
$$n_i^i = n$$

Note that if $i \neq j$ $(n_i^j)_j = n_j + 1$ and $(n_i^j)_i = n_i - 1$.

The process goes out of state n by a departure from some node or an external arrival to some node. So the total probability flux out of state n is given by:

$$\pi(n) \sum_{i=1}^{M} [\mu_i(n_i)I_{(n_i>0)} + \gamma_i]$$

Recall that $I_B = 1$ if the Boolean expression B is true and 0 otherwise. Similarly, the total probability flux into state n is given by:

$$\sum_{i=1}^{M} \Bigg(\pi(n_i)I_{(n_i>0)}\gamma_i + \pi(n^i)\mu_i((n^i)_i)q_{i0}$$

$$+ I_{(n_i>0)} \sum_{j=1}^{M} \pi(n_i^j)\mu_j((n_i^j)_j)q_{ji} \Bigg)$$

The global balance equations can be written as follows after isolating the term where $j = i$.

$$\pi(n) \sum_{i=1}^{M} (\mu_i(n_i) I_{(n_i>0)} + \gamma_i)$$

$$= \sum_{i=1}^{M} \left(\pi(n_i) I_{(n_i>0)} \gamma_i + \pi(n^i) \mu_i(n_i + 1) q_{i0} \right.$$

$$+ I_{(n_i>0)} \sum_{j=1,j\neq i}^{M} \pi(n_i^j) \mu_j(n_j + 1) q_{ji}$$

$$\left. + \pi(n) \mu_i(n_i) I_{(n_i>0)} q_{ii} \right) \tag{6.4}$$

Groups of terms on either side of the global balance equations sometimes cancel. In such cases we can partition the global balance equations into a set of local balance equations (also called independent balance equations or partial balance equations). Here each local balance equation simply equates the rate of transitions that cause a departure from node i (going out of state n) with the rate of transitions that cause an arrival to node i (going into state n). This amounts to removing the outer summations in the global balance equations for certain terms. The local balance equation for node i when $n_i > 0$ is:

$$\pi(n)\mu_i(n_i) = \pi(n_i)\gamma_i + \sum_{j=1,j\neq i}^{M} \pi(n_i^j)\mu_j(n_j + 1)q_{ji}$$

$$+ \pi(n)\mu_i(n_i)q_{ii} \tag{6.5}$$

The remaining terms in the global balance equation give the following equation (which we can think of as the local balance equation for the imaginary external node):

$$\sum_{i=1}^{M} \pi(n)\gamma_i = \sum_{i=1}^{M} \pi(n^i)\mu_i(n_i + 1)q_{i0}$$

Clearly, a solution that satisfies all the local balance equations also satisfies the global balance equations, although the converse does not necessarily hold. Moreover, the solution is unique by the steady state theorem of Markov processes.

Since we are looking for a product of M/M/1 queue solutions let us try the following for the solution of the local balance equations:

$$\pi(n) = c \prod_{i=1}^{M} \left(\frac{\lambda_i^{n_i}}{\prod_{j=1}^{n_i} \mu_i(j)} \right)$$

where c is a constant. Note that this solution implies the following relationships (recalling that $\mu_i(0) = 0$):

$$\pi(\boldsymbol{n}_i)I_{(n_i>0)} = \pi(\boldsymbol{n}) \frac{\mu_i(n_i)I_{(n_i>0)}}{\lambda_i}$$

$$\pi(\boldsymbol{n}^i) = \pi(\boldsymbol{n}) \frac{\lambda_i}{\mu_i(n_i + 1)}$$

so that

$$\pi(\boldsymbol{n}_i^j)I_{(n_i>0)} = \pi(\boldsymbol{n}) \frac{\lambda_j}{\mu_j(n_j + 1)} \frac{\mu_i(n_i)I_{(n_i>0)}}{\lambda_i}$$

Dividing the local balance equation for node i by $\pi(\boldsymbol{n})$, we require:

$$\mu_i(n_i) = \frac{\mu_i(n_i)}{\lambda_i} \gamma_i + \sum_{j=1,j\neq i}^{M} \frac{\lambda_j}{\mu_j(n_j + 1)} \frac{\mu_i(n_i)}{\lambda_i} \mu_j(n_j + 1)q_{ji}$$

$$+ \mu_i(n_i)q_{ii}$$

$$= \frac{\mu_i(n_i)}{\lambda_i} \gamma_i + \frac{\mu_i(n_i)}{\lambda_i} \sum_{j=1,j\neq i}^{M} \lambda_j q_{ji} + \mu_i(n_i)q_{ii}$$

which simplifies to the traffic equations (Equation 6.2):

$$\lambda_i = \gamma_i + \sum_{j=1}^{M} \lambda_j q_{ji}$$

With our choice for $\pi(\boldsymbol{n})$, the remaining terms in the global balance equations become

$$\sum_{i=1}^{M} \gamma_i = \sum_{i=1}^{M} \lambda_i q_{i0}$$

which holds in the steady state, since the rate of external arrivals to the network is the same as the rate of departures from the network.

As we have noted, since the solution $\pi(\boldsymbol{n})$ satisfies the local balance equations, it must also satisfy the global balance equations. Thus we obtain the following result for the steady state probabilities:

$$\pi(n_1, \ldots, n_M) = \prod_{i=1}^{M} \pi_i(n_i)$$

$$\text{where} \quad \pi_i(n_i) = \pi_i(0) \left(\frac{\lambda_i^{n_i}}{\prod_{j=1}^{n_i} \mu_i(j)} \right) \quad \textbf{(6.6)}$$

The $\pi_i(n_i)$ comes from the M/M/1 result and $\pi_i(0)$ is found by normalizing these probabilities.

Part (a) now follows from the product form (by the definition of independence) and part (b) from the form of the ith term in the product.   ∎

Intuitively we may expect that a large queue at one node may suggest large queues nearby, but this is not so according to Jackson's theorem. Part (b) of the theorem allows us to treat the system as if it were a collection of M independent M/M/1 queues, though arrivals are not necessarily Poisson.

In open networks with all SSFR nodes and fixed service rate μ_i at node i, the factor $\prod_{j=1}^{n_i} \mu_i(j)$ becomes $\mu_i^{n_i}$ and $\pi_i(0) = 1 - \rho_i$ where $\rho_i = \lambda_i/\mu_i$. Thus the joint probability becomes

$$\pi(n_1, \ldots, n_M) = \prod_{i=1}^{M}(1 - \rho_i)\rho_i^{n_i} \tag{6.7}$$

From the steady state probabilities the usual performance measures such as mean queue lengths, utilizations and throughput can be readily obtained. The mean waiting times are also easy to find using Little's result.

6.2.3 Performance measures for open networks

We can exploit Jackson's theorem directly and use Little's result to derive many performance measures provided we require only average quantities. For networks with SSFR nodes only (with fixed rates μ_i) the traffic intensity $\rho_i = \lambda_i/\mu_i$. The utilization of node i is given by $U_i = P(N_i \geqslant 1) = \rho_i$.

Mean queue length

The mean queue lengths, $L_i = E(N_i)$, are those for isolated M/M/1 queues with arrival rates λ_i:

$$L_i = \frac{\rho_i}{1 - \rho_i} \tag{6.8}$$

So the total average number of customers in the network is given by

$$
\begin{aligned}
L &= E(N_1 + N_2 + \ldots + N_M) \\
  &= E(N_1) + E(N_2) + \ldots + E(N_M) \\
  &= \sum_{i=1}^{M} L_i = \sum_{i=1}^{M} \frac{\rho_i}{1 - \rho_i}
\end{aligned}
\tag{6.9}
$$

Mean waiting time

Mean waiting times are just as easy to figure out. The average waiting time in the network $W = L/\gamma$ by Little's result, where $\gamma = \Sigma_i \gamma_i$ is the total arrival rate. The average time spent at node i during each visit is given by

$$W_i = \frac{L_i}{\lambda_i} = \frac{1}{\mu_i(1 - \rho_i)} \qquad\qquad (6.10)$$

The average time spent queueing on a visit to node i (i.e. excluding service time) is given by

$$W_i' = \frac{L_i'}{\lambda_i} = \frac{\rho_i}{\mu_i(1 - \rho_i)} \qquad \text{(since } L_i' = L_i - U_i) \qquad (6.11)$$

where L_i' is the average number of customers in the queue but not in service (i.e. equal to the average number L_i in the queue minus the average number U_i in service).

Let $W_{i,0}$ be the average interval between a customer's arrival at node i and its departure from the network (i.e. the average remaining sojourn time). Using an argument similar to that used for deriving the traffic equations we have

$$W_{i,0} = W_i + \sum_{j=1}^{M} q_{ij} W_{j,0} \qquad\qquad (6.12)$$

This determines $W_{i,0}$ uniquely because $(I - Q)$ is non-singular.

6.2.4 An alternate formulation

We now describe an alternate way of describing the network traffic so that the traffic equations do not need to be solved. Let v_i be the average number of visits made by a customer to node i during its stay in the network. Suppose that on each visit to node i the customer incurs a charge of 1 unit of currency. The amount due may be collected either upon arrival at the node or upon arrival to the network. The amount collected in unit time by the first method is λ_i and by the second method it is γv_i, since γ customers arrive from outside in unit time, each requiring v_i visits (on average) to node i. Since both these methods collect the same amount, $\lambda_i = \gamma v_i$ and we have

$$v_i = \frac{\lambda_i}{\gamma} \qquad\qquad (6.13)$$

The visit count v_i of node i is relative to the number of visits to the imaginary external node (labelled 0) and so can be referred to as a **visit ratio** if we define $v_0 = 1$. The visit ratios are simply another way of describing the routing in the network: given the routing probabilities we can determine the visit ratios. Often the visit ratios can be measured most easily (simply by counting arrivals) whereas for routing probabilities we have to monitor departures and their destinations. Suppose we divide the traffic equations (Equation 6.2) by γ and introduce visit ratios using Equation (6.13); then we obtain

$$v_i = q_{0i} + \sum_{j=1}^{M} v_j q_{ji}$$

So we can convert routing probabilities to visit ratios using the following equations:

$$v_0 = 1$$

$$v_i = \sum_{j=0}^{M} v_j q_{ji} \qquad (i = 0, 1, \ldots, M)$$

where $q_{00} = 0$. Note that the probabilities q_{0i} are obtained immediately from the external arrival rates γ_i.

Let D_i be the total average service demand on node i from one customer. Since each customer requires service time $(1/\mu_i)$ per visit to node i, for v_i visits its service demand is given by $D_i = v_i(1/\mu_i) = \rho_i/\gamma$, which implies that $\rho_i = \gamma D_i$. This appears reasonable since ρ_i is the average work for node i arriving from outside the network in unit time. Often we may want to specify a queueing network directly in terms of $\{D_i | i = 1, 2, \ldots, M\}$ and γ (which gives ρ_i), so there is no need to solve the traffic equations. In practical cases, the total service demand at each node is normally easier to obtain than the individual service times per visit from measurements.

Performance measures

Many performance measures can be derived readily in the alternate formulation. For example, the mean queue length is given by

$$L_i = \frac{\rho_i}{1 - \rho_i} = \frac{\gamma D_i}{1 - \gamma D_i} \tag{6.14}$$

and so L and W can be determined as before.

Suppose on each of the v_i visits a customer spends W_i units of time at node i on average. Then the total average time a customer spends at node i, i.e. the total units of time spent in the queue at node i, Q_i, is given by

$$Q_i = v_i W_i = \mu_i D_i \left(\frac{1}{\mu_i (1 - \rho_i)} \right) = \frac{D_i}{1 - \gamma D_i} \qquad (6.15)$$

Alternatively, we can apply Little's result to node i with the external arrival process directly giving the same result since $Q_i = L_i/\gamma$. But D_i and γ cannot be used to find μ_i, so using this approach we lose per visit information such as W_i and $W_{i,0}$.

The alternate formulation can be extended easily to include IS (delay) nodes also. For an IS node i, we specify the parameters as follows:

$$L_i = \rho_i = \gamma D_i$$

$$Q_i = D_i \qquad \text{(since there is no queueing)}$$

$$W_i = 1/\mu_i$$

$$D_i = v_i/\mu_i$$

6.2.5 Random Observer Property

Though arrivals at each node are not generally Poisson, the Random Observer Property (ROP) still holds as we prove in Proposition 6.2 below. In other words, customers arriving at a node in an open network 'see' the same distribution of number of customers at a queue as a random observer in the steady state. This implies that the waiting time distribution at node i is exponential with parameter $\mu_i - \lambda_i$. Notice that this does not follow from Jackson's theorem above. Jackson's theorem considers the steady state in continuous time, whereas here we are concerned with the steady state at particular points in time, namely arrival instants. The original proof of this proposition appears in Sevcik and Mitrani (1981).

Proposition 6.2 (Random Observer Property)

For an open Jackson queueing network, suppose $\pi(n)$ is the stationary probability that the network is in state n. Then the probability that the network is in state n immediately before an arrival to any node is also $\pi(n)$.

Proof First, we define the following notation:

• $A_i(n)$ is the probability that an arrival at node i sees the network in state n

- $\eta_i(n)$ is the expected number of arrival instants at node i that see state n in unit time
- $q(n^j, n^i)$ is the instantaneous transition rate from state n^j to state n^i (i.e. a transfer from node j to node i)
- $\mu_j(n^j)$ is the service rate of node j when the network state is n^j (although only local queue length dependence is allowed for a product form solution to exist)

For internal customer transitions, note that the network state n seen by an arrival will have one less customer because the arriving customer cannot see itself. Therefore we consider compound state transitions of the form

$$n^j \to n \to n^i$$

The expected number of transitions per unit time (i.e. the probability flux) from state n^j to n^i is

$$\pi(n^j)q(n^j, n^i)$$

where $q(n^j, n^i) = \mu_j(n^j)q_{ji}$. The total expected number of state transitions that pass through internal state n in unit time before entering state n^i is

$$\eta_i(n) = \sum_{j=1}^{M} \pi(n^j)\mu_j(n^j)q_{ji} + \pi(n)\gamma_i$$

From the product form solution we have

$$\pi(n^j)\mu_j(n^j) = \pi(n)\lambda_j \qquad \text{(see Proposition 6.1)}$$

and so

$$\eta_i(n) = \pi(n)\left(\sum_{j=1}^{M} \lambda_j q_{ji} + \gamma_i\right) = \lambda_i \pi(n)$$

using the traffic Equation (6.2) for node i. But for a stationary process, $A_i(n)$ can be expressed as the ratio of the expected number of transitions giving an arrival to node i with internal state n and the expected number with any internal state. (Chapter 4 explores this result in more detail.) Hence, we have

$$A_i(n) = \frac{\eta_i(n)}{\sum_n \eta_i(n)} = \pi(n)$$

A simpler proof by quasi-reversibility arguments is also possible (see Chapter 7). ∎

A related performance measure of considerable interest is the time taken for a customer to traverse a particular route through a network. The mean sojourn time for any route is always easy to obtain because the mean of a sum of random variables is the sum of the means of those random variables, whether or not they are independent. We therefore only have to add the mean sojourn times at each queue in the route. The distribution of this time delay on any route can be determined in networks with no overtaking (e.g. tree networks) as shown in Chapter 9. In more general networks, however, it is more difficult and remains an open problem.

Jackson's theorem does not apply here because it is concerned only with steady state probabilities (i.e. the asymptotic behaviour of $\pi_t(n)$ at time t as $t \to \infty$). Here we consider the progress of a particular customer through the network, so past events can affect the future. Yet many approximate methods have been developed to determine time delay distributions in general networks.

6.2.6 Optimal allocation

Consider an open network of SSFR nodes with arrival rate λ_i and service rate μ_i for node i $(i = 1, 2, \ldots, M)$. From Jackson's theorem, the queue length distribution at node i is independent of the state of the other nodes and is given by

$$\pi(n_i) = \left(1 - \frac{\lambda_i}{\mu_i}\right)\left(\frac{\lambda_i}{\mu_i}\right)^{n_i}$$

The mean queue length at node i is given by

$$L_i = \frac{\lambda_i}{\mu_i - \lambda_i}$$

Suppose we have control over the service rates $\mu_1, \mu_2, \ldots \mu_M$ but with a constraint that fixes the total service capability to some constant value C, as follows

$$\sum_{i=1}^{M} \mu_i = C$$

For a given set of arrival rates $\{\lambda_i\}$, we want to find the optimal set $\{\mu_i\}$ that minimizes the average network population $L = \sum_{i=1}^{M} L_i$. Using the method of Lagrangian multipliers, we define

$$H = \sum_{i=1}^{M} \frac{\lambda_i}{\mu_i - \lambda_i} + y\left(\sum_{i=1}^{M} \mu_i - C\right)$$

If we differentiate H w.r.t. μ_i, we obtain

$$\frac{\partial H}{\partial \mu_i} = \frac{-\lambda_i}{\mu_i - \lambda_i} + y$$

Setting the derivative to zero, we find that H is minimized by

$$\mu_i = \lambda_i + (\lambda_i/y)^{1/2}$$

Substituting this expression for μ_i into the constraint $\sum_{i=1}^{M} \mu_i = C$, we find that

$$\frac{1}{\sqrt{y}} = \frac{C - \sum_{j=1}^{M} \lambda_j}{\sum_{j=1}^{M} \sqrt{\lambda_j}}$$

Hence the optimal allocation, obtained by substituting y into the optimal value of μ_i, gives

$$\mu_i = \lambda_i + \frac{\sqrt{\lambda_i}}{\sum_{j=1}^{M} \sqrt{\lambda_j}} \left(C - \sum_{j=1}^{M} \lambda_j \right)$$

This result has an interesting interpretation, as follows. Each node is given just enough service capacity to handle its arrival rate (λ_i) and the surplus $(C - \sum_{j=1}^{M} \lambda_j)$ is distributed in proportion to the square root of the arrival rates.

6.3 Closed queueing networks

In this section we analyse closed queueing networks, which have no external arrivals or departures. They are often more useful than open networks in modelling computer and communication networks because network population is normally limited by the resource capacity. Since closed networks have no external arcs, the number of customers in the network is constant. Much of the early work in closed networks was done by Gordon and Newell (1967).

Definition 6.2 (Gordon–Newell network)

A Gordon–Newell network with M nodes (labelled $i = 1, 2, \ldots, M$, say) is defined as follows:

- node i is QLD with rate $\mu_i(n)$ when it has n customers
- a customer completing service at a node chooses a node to enter next probabilistically, independent of past history
- the network is closed and has fixed population K

Suppose there are M nodes and the network population is a positive integer $K > 0$; then the state space is finite and given by

$$S = \left\{ (n_1, \ldots, n_M) | n_i \geq 0, \sum_{i=1}^{M} n_i = K \right\} \tag{6.16}$$

The number of elements in the set S can be determined by simple combinatorial arguments. For example, $|S|$ is the same as the number of ways of putting K balls into M bags, which is given by:

$$|S| = \binom{K + M - 1}{M - 1}$$

where the binomial coefficient

$$\binom{n}{r} = \frac{n!}{(n - r)!r!}$$

Recall from Chapter 4 that if the network can be represented by an irreducible positive recurrent Markov process then the finiteness of S implies that a steady state always exists. We assume that all nodes are QLD with exponentially distributed service times.

Since there are no external arrivals or departures (no γ_i terms), the routing probabilities q_{ij} satisfy

$$\sum_{j=1}^{M} q_{ij} = 1 \qquad i = 1, 2, \ldots, M$$

Thus the traffic equations are

$$\lambda_i = \sum_{j=1}^{M} \lambda_j q_{ji} \qquad i = 1, 2, \ldots, M \tag{6.17}$$

These form a set of homogeneous linear equations that have the form $\lambda(I - Q) = 0$ where I is the identity matrix. Since all rows of Q sum to zero, $|I - Q| = 0$. The number of solutions $\{\lambda_i\}$ that satisfy the traffic equations is infinite and, in fact, all solutions differ by a multiplicative factor because of the structure of Q. Suppose we let $(e_1, e_2, \ldots, e_M)$ be any non-zero solution; then e_i is proportional to the arrival rate at node i, λ_i (say $e_i = c\lambda_i$ for some constant c). For SSFR nodes, we can define $x_i = e_i/\mu_i$ which is proportional to the load at node i, $\rho_i = \lambda_i/\mu_i$ (i.e. $x_i = c\rho_i$).

Typically, $(e_1, e_2, \ldots, e_M)$ is chosen by fixing one component to a convenient value, such as $e_1 = 1$. This means that for every visit to node 1, a customer makes e_i visits to node i, on average. Thus e_i is called the relative visitation rate of node i. Another way of fixing $(e_1, e_2, \ldots e_M)$ is by normalizing the components to a probability distribution, i.e. by making $\sum_{i=1}^{M} e_i = 1$. For this case, we can think of a network with population one where the individual customer does a random walk on the set of nodes. Then e_i is the probability that a customer is at node i of the network (i.e. the Markov chain is in state i). For our purposes now, we will not need to know the exact value of $(e_1, e_2, \ldots, e_M)$ provided it satisfies the traffic Equation (6.17).

6.3.1 Steady state probability distribution

We cannot apply the open network solution to closed networks because the queue length at a node in the closed network is limited by the network population. Still, suppose we do use the open network solution and eliminate the infeasible states by renormalizing the probabilities. We find that this informal approach gives us the correct answer. Gordon and Newell (1967) extended Jackson's theorem to closed networks of exponential servers giving a product form solution as follows.

> ### Proposition 6.3 (Gordon–Newell theorem)
>
> Suppose $\mu_i(j)$ is the service rate of QLD node i when its queue length is j in a Gordon–Newell network of M nodes and K customers. Then the steady state joint queue length probability distribution is given by
>
> $$\pi(n_1, \ldots, n_M) = \frac{1}{G} \prod_{i=1}^{M} x_i(n_i) \qquad (6.18)$$
>
> where
>
> $$x_i(n_i) = \left(\frac{e_i^{n_i}}{\prod_{j=1}^{n_i} \mu_i(j)} \right) \qquad \sum_{i=1}^{M} n_i = K \qquad (6.19)$$
>
> and G is the normalizing constant defined by:
>
> $$G = \sum_{n \in S} \prod_{i=1}^{M} x_i(n_i) \qquad (6.20)$$
>
> *Proof* As for the open network (Proposition 6.1), we prove the above result by using the network's steady state global balance equations:
>
> $$\begin{array}{l} \text{Total probability} \\ \text{flux out of state } n \end{array} = \begin{array}{l} \text{Total probability flux} \\ \text{from all states } n_i^j \to n \end{array}$$
>
> $$\sum_{i=1}^{M} \pi(n)\mu_i(n_i)I_{(n_i>0)} = \sum_{i=1}^{M} \sum_{j=1}^{M} \pi(n_i^j)\mu_j((n_i^j)_j)q_{ji}I_{(n_i>0)} \qquad (6.21)$$
>
> As in the proof for open networks, we remove the outer summations in the global balance equations to get the local

balance equations. A solution that satisfies all the local balance equations also satisfies the global balance equations and is unique by the steady state theorem of Markov processes. For node i the local balance equation is given by

$$\pi(\boldsymbol{n})\mu_i(n_i)I_{(n_i>0)} = \sum_{j=1}^{M}\pi(\boldsymbol{n}_i^j)\mu_j((\boldsymbol{n}_i^j)_j)q_{ji}I_{(n_i>0)} \qquad (6.22)$$

We can split the summation on the RHS by considering two cases: $j = i$ and $j \neq i$:

$$\pi(\boldsymbol{n})\mu_i(n_i)I_{(n_i>0)} = \pi(\boldsymbol{n})\mu_i(n_i)q_{ii}I_{(n_i>0)}$$
$$+ \sum_{\substack{j=1 \\ j \neq i}}^{M}\pi(\boldsymbol{n}_i^j)\mu_j(n_j+1)q_{ji}I_{(n_i>0)}$$

Let us try

$$\pi(\boldsymbol{n}) = \frac{1}{G}\prod_{i=1}^{M}\left\{\frac{e_i^{n_i}}{\prod_{j=1}^{n_i}\mu_i(j)}\right\}$$

for a solution of the local balance equations. Dividing the local balance equations by $\pi(\boldsymbol{n})$, we require

$$\mu_i(n_i)I_{(n_i>0)} = \mu_i(n_i)q_{ii}I_{(n_i>0)}$$
$$+ \sum_{\substack{j=1 \\ j \neq i}}^{M}\frac{e_j}{e_i}\frac{\mu_i(n_i)}{\mu_j(n_j+1)}\mu_j(n_j+1)q_{ji}I_{(n_i>0)}$$

i.e.

$$\mu_i(n_i)I_{(n_i>0)} = \mu_i(n_i)I_{(n_i>0)}\left(\frac{\sum_j e_j q_{ji}}{e_i}\right)$$

Thus we require that the visitation rates e_i satisfy the traffic equations, which they do by definition. Since the local balance equations are satisfied by $\pi(\boldsymbol{n})$ then the global balance equations are also satisfied by $\pi(\boldsymbol{n})$. ∎

Note that if $e_i' = ce_i$ (for $i = 1, 2, \ldots, M$), the corresponding probabilities $\pi'(\boldsymbol{n})$ (with normalizing constant G') are given by

$$\pi'(\boldsymbol{n}) = \frac{1}{G'}Gc^{\sum n_i}\pi(\boldsymbol{n})$$

Summing over the entire state, we obtain $G' = Gc^K$. Thus we have $\pi'(\boldsymbol{n}) = \pi(\boldsymbol{n})$, which confirms the arbitrariness of $\{e_i\}$ up to a multiplicative factor.

The normalizing constant is important in its own right for calculating performance measures such as mean queue lengths, throughputs and mean response times. However, direct computation of this normalizing constant is inefficient because of the summation over such a large domain. Moreover, the numerical errors introduced by the floating point number representation on the computer may accumulate and prove too inaccurate. In the next section, we describe more tractable methods.

6.3.2 Computation of the normalizing constant

Initially we consider a closed network with SSFR nodes only since this leads to efficient algorithms for computing the normalizing constant. Other algorithms can handle more general types of node. For example, the convolution algorithm can have QLD nodes and the mean value analysis (MVA) algorithm can have both SSFR and IS nodes (we will consider MVA in detail in Section 6.4). Both algorithms have the same computational requirements, but MVA avoids some floating point problems inherent in the convolution algorithm.

To make the number of nodes (M) and population (K) explicit in the normalizing constant, let $G = G(M, K)$ and $S = S(M, K)$, where

$$S(m, n) = \left\{ (n_1, \ldots, n_m) | n_i \geq 0, \sum_{i=1}^{m} n_i = n \right\} \tag{6.23}$$

$$G(m, n) = \sum_{n \in S(m,n)} \prod_{i=1}^{m} x_i^{n_i} \quad \text{where} \quad x_i = \frac{e_i}{\mu_i}$$

For $m, n > 0$ we can split the summation into cases when $n_m = 0$ and when $n_m > 0$:

$$G(m, n) = \sum_{\substack{n \in S(m,n) \\ n_m=0}} \prod_{i=1}^{m} x_i^{n_i} + \sum_{\substack{n \in S(m,n) \\ n_m>0}} \prod_{i=1}^{m} x_i^{n_i}$$

$$= \sum_{n \in S(m-1,n)} \prod_{i=1}^{m-1} x_i^{n_i} + x_m \sum_{\substack{n \in S(m,n) \\ k_i=n_i(i \neq m) \\ k_m=n_m-1}} \prod_{i=1}^{m} x_i^{k_i}$$

Since the second summation domain is $\{k | k_i \geq 0; \ \Sigma_i k_i = n - 1\} = S(m, n - 1)$, we have the following recurrence:

$$G(m, n) = G(m - 1, n) + x_m G(m, n - 1) \qquad m, n > 0 \tag{6.24}$$

The boundary conditions can be determined from the definitions:

$$G(m, 0) = 1 \qquad m > 0$$
$$G(0, n) = 0 \qquad n \geq 0 \tag{6.25}$$

The recursive method to compute the normalizing constant is called the convolution algorithm. We will see more of this approach later in Section 6.5.1.

6.3.3 Performance measures

The fact that the factors in the expression for $\pi(k)$ are from the M/M/1 result is just a serendipitous mathematical property and has no probabilistic interpretation, so performance measures for a single node in closed networks are not as easy to find as in open networks. Many performance measures can be determined by summing the product form solution over a subspace of the state space given by some restricting condition. Often this partial or conditional summation can be replaced by a normalizing constant for a 'smaller' queueing network. Thus we find that the performance measures of interest can be expressed in terms of normalizing constants. In this way, we can develop efficient algorithms that avoid summation over the entire state space.

The probability that node M is idle can be determined directly by summing the joint probability distribution over all states with $n_M = 0$, as follows:

$$P(N_M = 0) = \frac{1}{G(M, K)} \sum_{\substack{n \in S(M,K) \\ n_M = 0}} \prod_{i=1}^{M-1} x_i^{n_i} = \frac{G(M - 1, K)}{G(M, K)}$$

In general, for node i the idle probability is given by

$$P(N_i = 0) = \frac{G(M \backslash i, K)}{G(M, K)} \qquad i = 1, 2, \ldots, M$$

where $G(M \backslash i, K)$ is the normalizing constant for an M-node network with node i removed and population K. More formally:

$$G(M \backslash i, K) = \sum_{n \in S(M-1,K)} \prod_{j=1}^{M-1} y_j^{n_j}$$

where

$$y_j = \begin{cases} x_j & j = 1, \ldots, i - 1 \\ x_{j+1} & j = i, \ldots, M - 1 \end{cases}$$

Thus the utilization of node i is given by

$$U_i = 1 - \frac{G(M \backslash i, K)}{G(M, K)} \tag{6.26}$$

6.3.4 Cumulative probabilities

Instead of considering the marginal queue length probabilities, we may consider the cumulative marginal queue length probabilities: more precisely its complement. For $k = 1, \ldots, K$, we have

$$P(N_i \geq k) = \frac{1}{G(M, K)} \sum_{\substack{n \in S(M,K) \\ n_i \geq k}} \prod_{j=1}^{M} x_j^{n_j}$$

$$= \frac{x_i^k}{G(M, K)} \sum_{\substack{m_j = n_j (j \neq i) \\ m_i = n_i - k \\ n \in S(M,K) \\ n_i \geq k}} \prod_{j=1}^{M} x_j^{m_j}$$

The summation domain is $m \in S(M, K - k)$, so we obtain the following result:

$$P(N_i \geq k) = x_i^k \frac{G(M, K - k)}{G(M, K)} \qquad i = 1, \ldots, M \tag{6.27}$$

When $k = 1$, we obtain the node utilization

$$U_i = x_i \frac{G(M, K - 1)}{G(M, K)} \tag{6.28}$$

Equating the two expressions for U_i (Equations 6.26 and 6.28) yields a recurrence relation similar to the one obtained for $G(M, K)$ previously (Equation 6.24):

$$G(M, K) = G(M \backslash i, K) + x_i G(M, K - 1) \qquad M, K > 0$$

The throughput of node i is given by:

$$\lambda_i = \mu_i U_i = e_i \frac{G(M, K - 1)}{G(M, K)} \tag{6.29}$$

As expected, the throughput at node i is proportional to its visitation rate.

Let us denote the steady state queue length distribution at node i by $\pi_i(k)$. This is easy to determine from the cumulative probabilities:

$$\pi_i(k) = P(N_i \geq k) - P(N_i \geq k + 1)$$

$$= x_i^k \left(\frac{G(M, K - k) - x_i G(M, K - k - 1)}{G(M, K)} \right)$$

$$k = 0, \ldots, K; i = 1, \ldots, M \quad (6.30)$$

where $G(M, -1) = 0$ by definition.

Notice, however, that the previous formulation gives a neater expression for $\pi_i(k)$:

$$\pi_i(k) = \frac{1}{G(M, K)} \sum_{\substack{n \in S(M,K) \\ n_i = k}} \prod_{j=1}^{M} x_j^{n_j} = \frac{x_i^k}{G(M, K)} \sum_{\substack{n \in S(M,K-k) \\ n_i = 0}} \prod_{j=1}^{M} x_j^{n_j}$$

$$\pi_i(k) = x_i^k \frac{G(M \backslash i, K - k)}{G(M, K)} \qquad i = 1, \ldots, M; k = 0, \ldots, K$$

$$(6.31)$$

Suppose we denote the mean queue length at node i by $L_i(K)$ when the network population is K. Then we have the triangular summation of the cumulative probabilities:

$$L_i(K) = \sum_{j=1}^{K} j P(N_i = j) = \sum_{j=1}^{K} \sum_{k=1}^{K} P(N_i = j) I_{(k \leq j)}$$

$$= \sum_{k=1}^{K} \sum_{j=k}^{K} P(N_i = j) = \sum_{k=1}^{K} P(N_i \geq k)$$

Thus, using the expression for the cumulative probabilities we obtain the following expression for the mean queue length.

$$L_i(K) = \frac{1}{G(M, K)} \sum_{k=1}^{K} x_i^k G(M, K - k) \qquad i = 1, 2, \ldots, M$$

$$(6.32)$$

6.4 Mean value analysis

In this section we describe the mean value analysis (MVA) algorithm; this provides another way of deriving performance measures for a closed network. It is based merely on simple applications of Little's result. This time we will only determine mean values and try to avoid manipulation of the steady state probabilities directly. First we convert a closed network into an equivalent open network that has all the characteristics of the closed network.

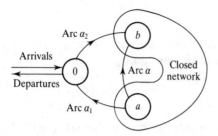

Figure 6.4 Equivalent open network.

6.4.1 The equivalent open network

We assume that the closed network can be represented by an irreducible positive recurrent Markov process with finite state space. Thus every arc is traversed within finite time with probability one and we introduce a new node labelled 0 in one of the arcs as shown in Figure 6.4. Suppose we choose to replace some arc α by arc α_1, node 0 and arc α_2, so that the source of α_1 is the source of α and the destination of α_2 is the destination of α. Whenever a customer arrives at node 0 (along arc α_1), it departs from the network and is immediately replaced by a stochastically identical customer that immediately leaves node 0 along arc α_2. All customers have infinite total service requirements at every node. We only need the new customer to have the same routing probabilities since all customers place infinite service demands. Since customers are simply substituted by node 0 and immediately replaced, the open network behaves exactly as the closed one (except node 0).

Now that the network is open, the parameters throughput, visit ratio and response time acquire meaning and interest. Note, however, that the values of these parameters depend on the arc chosen to be replaced. We can define the network's throughput, T, as the average rate at which customers pass along arc α in the steady state, i.e. the mean number of customers traversing arc α in unit time. Therefore, T corresponds to the external arrival rate (γ) in the open network. All external arrivals go to a single node, here b.

Suppose that for node i $(i = 1, \ldots, M)$, the average number of visits to it made by a customer is v_i and the average arrival rate is λ_i. As before, we have the relationship $\lambda_i = Tv_i$, which implies that the set $\{v_i\}$ satisfies the traffic equations. Thus we will refer to v_i as the visitation rate for node i. Note that the set $\{v_i\}$ can be determined uniquely if we know the value of one member of the set because of the traffic equation for λ_i, which is the same for v_i. We will continue to use $\{e_i\}$ as any solution of the traffic equations and use $\{v_i\}$ when we have a particular solution in mind.

Since arc α connects node a to node b in the closed network, all traffic from a to b goes through node 0 in the open network. So we have

$$v_0 = v_a q_{ab}$$

But we know that every customer enters node 0 exactly once (i.e. $v_0 = 1$), from which we can find v_a:

$$v_a = \frac{1}{q_{ab}}$$

Since one visitation rate is known the set $\{v_i | i = 1, \ldots, M\}$ can be determined uniquely.

Applying Little's result to node i ($L_i = \lambda_i W_i$) now yields

$$L_i = T v_i W_i \qquad i = 1, 2, \ldots, M$$

Since the sum of individual queue lengths is exactly K in the closed network, we have

$$\sum_{i=1}^{M} L_i = K = T \sum_{i=1}^{M} v_i W_i$$

This gives us another relationship between the unknown performance measures T and W_i:

$$T = \frac{K}{\sum_{i=1}^{M} v_i W_i}$$

If node i is an IS node then the mean waiting time is the same as the mean service time (i.e. $W_i = 1/\mu_i$). But for SSFR nodes the waiting time is the sum of the queueing time and the service time. Suppose we let Y_i be the mean number of customers seen by an arrival to node i, so that its mean waiting time is the sum of the service times of those customers and its own service time, i.e.

$$W_i = \frac{1}{\mu_i} (Y_i + 1)$$

In open networks, $Y_i = L_i$ because of the Random Observer Property. But in closed networks this property does not hold, i.e. the number of customers seen by an arrival does not have the same steady state distribution as the continuous time queue length. For example, the arrival cannot 'see' itself, so K customers are never seen by an arrival. Fortunately, we do have the analogous customer or job observer property that is often called the **arrival theorem.** Informally, this says that the state of a stationary closed queueing network with population K seen by an arrival at any node has the same distribution as the stationary distribution of the same network with the arriving customer removed. More formally, we have:

Proposition 6.4 (Arrival theorem)

For a closed queueing network, suppose $\pi(k, n)$ is the equilibrium probability that the network is in state n when the population is $k = \Sigma_i n_i$ (the number of customers in the network k is made explicit in the expression for clarity). Then, when the network population is K, the equilibrium probability that the network is in state n immediately before an arrival at node i is:

$$A_i(n) = \pi(K - 1, n)$$

Proof The proof is analogous to that of Proposition 6.2. First, we define the following notation:

- $\eta_i(n)$ is the expected number of arrival instants at node i that see state n in unit time
- $q(n^j, n^i)$ is the instantaneous transition rate from state n^j to state n^i (i.e. a transfer from node j to node i)
- $\mu_j(n^j)$ is the service rate of node j when the network state is n^j (although only local queue length dependence is allowed for a product form solution to exist)

Note that the network state n seen by an arrival will have $K - 1$ customers because the arriving customer cannot see itself. Therefore we consider compound state transitions of the form

$$n^j \rightarrow n \rightarrow n^i$$

In other words, a customer at node j moves to node i so states n^j and n^i have K customers and internal state n has $K - 1$ customers. This is the state that interests us. The expected number of transitions per unit time from state n^j to n^i is

$$\pi(K, n^j)q(n^j, n^i)$$

where $q(n^j, n^i) = \mu_j(n^j)q_{ji}$. The total expected number of state transitions that pass through internal state n in unit time before entering state n^i is:

$$\eta_i(n) = \sum_{j=1}^{M} \pi(K, n^j)\mu_j(n^j)q_{ji}$$

From the product form solution we have

$$G(M, K)\pi(K, n^j) = G(M, K - 1)\pi(K - 1, n) \frac{e_j}{\mu_j(n^j)}$$

and so

$$\pi(K, n^j)\mu_j(n^j) = ce_j\pi(K - 1, n)$$

where $c = G(M, K - 1)/G(M, K)$ is a constant ratio of normalizing constants. So now,

$$\eta_i(n) = \sum_j ce_j\pi(K - 1, n)q_{ji}$$

and after using the traffic equation for e_i, we have

$$\eta_i(n) = ce_i\pi(K - 1, n)$$

But for a stationary process, $A_i(n)$ can be expressed as the ratio of the expected number of transitions giving an arrival to node i with internal state n and the expected number with any internal state and so

$$A_i(n) = \frac{\eta_i(n)}{\sum_n \eta_i(n)} = \pi(K - 1, n) \qquad \blacksquare$$

The arrival theorem tells us that the arriving customer behaves as a random observer in a network with population reduced by one. This is intuitively appealing since we can think of the removed customer as the arriving customer itself. The job observer property yields $Y_i(K) = L_i(K - 1)$ for $K > 0$, after the dependence on the network population K is made explicit.

Therefore, we obtain the following recurrence relations for $i = 1, 2, \ldots, M$ and $K > 0$:

$$W_i(K) = \frac{1}{\mu_i} [L_i(K - 1) + 1] \qquad (6.33)$$

$$T(K) = \frac{K}{\sum_{i=1}^{M} v_i W_i(K)} \qquad (6.34)$$

$$L_i(k) = T(K)v_i W_i(K) \qquad (6.35)$$

with initial conditions $L_i(0) = 0$. We can compute the values of $W_i(K)$, $T(K)$ and $L_i(K)$ by a simple iteration as follows. Starting with the base case $L_i(0) = 0$ we obtain the values of $W_i(1)$, $T(1)$ and $L_i(1)$ for $1 \leq i \leq M$ from which we derive the next population level, and so on until the iteration reaches the desired population. On each iteration, we compute $2M + 1$ quantities since i takes M values. Thus for K iterations, we need $O(MK)$ operations to compute the performance measures.

6.4.2 Alternate formulation

As for open networks, we now describe an alternate formulation of the mean value analysis algorithm by introducing two new parameters for $i = 1, 2, \ldots, M$. Let $Q_i(K)$ denote the total average time spent at node i when the population is K and let D_i denote the total average service time (demand) a customer requires from node i. Often it is easier to obtain D_i from measurements than the service demand required on each visit $1/\mu_i$. For example, a simple counting monitor can easily measure the total demand at some physical resource whereas the demand per visit is much harder to obtain.

In terms of our previous formulation these parameters can be defined as follows: $Q_i(K) = v_i W_i(K)$ and $D_i = v_i/\mu_i$. Thus the recurrence relations now become

$$Q_i(K) = D_i[L_i(K - 1) + 1] \tag{6.36}$$

$$T(K) = \frac{K}{\sum_{i=1}^{M} Q_i(K)} \tag{6.37}$$

$$L_i(K) = T(K)Q_i(K) \tag{6.38}$$

The total average time spent by a customer in the network is thus given by

$$W(K) = \sum_{i=1}^{M} v_i W_i(K) = \sum_{i=1}^{M} Q_i(K) = \frac{K}{T(K)}$$

as expected from Little's result.

The utilization of node i, U_i, is given by:

$$U_i = \frac{\lambda_i}{\mu_i} = \frac{T(K)v_i}{\mu_i} = T(K)D_i \leq 1$$

This gives us a bound on the throughput $T(K) \leq \min_i (1/D_i)$. Thus the maximum throughput is dictated by a bottleneck node (or nodes), namely the node with maximum service demand D_i.

Example 6.2 (Multiprogramming computer system) ————————

We now apply the MVA algorithm to a queueing network model of a multiprogramming computer system. The multiprogramming level is fixed and represented by the number of customers in the network, K, as shown in Figure 6.5. Each customer spends a random time (exponentially distributed with mean $1/\mu_1$) at the CPU (node 1) before doing i/o

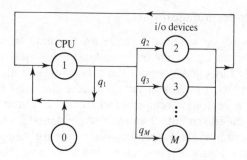

Figure 6.5   Multiprogramming computer system.

at one of the i/o devices (nodes $2, 3, \ldots, M$). The i/o times are also exponentially distributed with mean $1/\mu_i$ for node i. On leaving the CPU, a customer makes a probabilistic choice about its next destination. With probability q_1 it leaves the network and is immediately replaced by a new customer and with probability q_i $(i = 2, 3, \ldots, M)$ it visits i/o device i.

Suppose we insert a node labelled 0 in the arc from the CPU back to itself. This is an arbitrary choice but models the idea that customers do change, although their probabilistic characteristics remain the same. Thus in the equivalent open network, the throughput is the rate at which customers leave the network. The visitation rates v_i $(i = 1, 2, \ldots, M)$ now have to satisfy the following equations:

$$v_1 = q_1 v_1 + v_2 + \ldots + v_M \quad \text{and} \quad v_i = q_i v_1, \quad i = 2, 3, \ldots, M$$

With our choice of the position of node 0, $q_1 v_1 = v_0 = 1$, and these equations are satisfied by

$$v_1 = 1/q_1 \quad \text{and} \quad v_i = \frac{q_i}{q_1} \quad i = 2, 3, \ldots, M$$

Thus the service demand for the CPU and for i/o devices $i \geqslant 2$ are given by

$$D_1 = \frac{1}{q_1 \mu_1} \quad \text{and} \quad D_i = \frac{q_i}{q_1 \mu_i}$$

The throughput $T(K)$ can be obtained by solving the recurrence relations of the MVA algorithm. A fraction q_1 of the customers leaving the CPU actually leaves the open network (i.e. $T(K)$ is q_1 of the CPU throughput) so the CPU throughput is $T(K)/q_1$.

6.5 Performance measures for the state-dependent case

Now let us derive some performance measures for a closed product form network with M QLD nodes. This time we use generating functions to derive some general results. We begin by deriving an algorithm for determining the normalizing constant $G(M, K)$. This is commonly called the convolution algorithm.

6.5.1 Convolution algorithm

Suppose we define the main generating function as

$$f(z) = f_1(z)f_2(z) \ldots f_M(z) \quad \text{where} \quad f_i(z) = \sum_{k=0}^{\infty} x_i(k)z^k$$

This infinite power series in z has coefficients of z^k that are sums of products of the form $x_1(n_1)x_2(n_2) \ldots x_M(n_M)$ in which $\Sigma_i n_i$ is k. Thus $f(z)$ has the form

$$1 + G(M, 1)z + G(M, 2)z^2 + \ldots + G(M, K)z^K + \ldots$$

where $G(M, K)$ is the required normalizing constant for population K. We can build up the function $f(z)$ from the following partial products $g_i(z)$ so that $G(i, k)$ is the coefficient of z^k in $g_i(z)$:

$$g_1(z) = f_1(z)$$
$$g_i(z) = g_{i-1}(z)f_i(z) \quad i = 2, 3, \ldots, M$$

Equating coefficients of z^k in these equations gives

$$G(1, k) = x_1(k) \tag{6.39}$$

$$G(i, k) = \sum_{j=0}^{k} G(i - 1, j)x_i(k - j) \tag{6.40}$$

This convolution gives us an algorithm to calculate $G(M, K)$ recursively, which is much faster than summing over the entire state space.

If node i is an SSFR node, $x_i(n_i) = x_i^{n_i}$ where $x_i = e_i/\mu_i$ and $f_i(z)$ is a geometric sum which has a closed form when $|x_i z| < 1$:

$$f_i(z) = \sum_{k=0}^{\infty} (x_i z)^k = \frac{1}{1 - x_i z}$$

Substituting this in the definition of $g_i(z)$ we obtain the following recurrence:

$$g_i(z) = g_{i-1}(z) + x_i z g_i(z)$$

Equating coefficients of z^k now gives the result derived in Section 6.3.3, by explicitly manipulating the product form solution,

$$G(i, k) = G(i - 1, k) + x_i G(i, k - 1)$$

Together with the boundary conditions this recurrence suggests an algorithm to calculate $G(M, K)$ in $O(MK)$ arithmetic operations.

Let us now use the generating function approach to determine the utilization of node i when the network population is K.

$$U_i(K) = P(N_i \geq 1)$$

$$= \frac{1}{G(M, K)} \sum_{\substack{n \in S(M,K) \\ n_i \geq 1}} x_1(n_1) x_2(n_2) \ldots x_M(n_M)$$

We can obtain the same sum of terms by manipulating the generating function $f(z)$ as follows. Since $f_i(z) = 1 + x_i(1)z + x_i(2)z^2 + \ldots$ if, for one i, we replace $f_i(z)$ by $f_i(z) - 1$ in $f(z)$ there will be no term corresponding to $n_i = 0$ in the generating function $f(z)$. This results in the modified generating function

$$h_i(z) = f(z) \frac{f_i(z) - 1}{f_i(z)} = f(z)[1 - (f_i(z))^{-1}]$$

Now the coefficient of z^K in $h_i(z)$ is the sum of all products of type $x_1(n_1) x_2(n_2) \ldots x_M(n_M)$ with $\Sigma_k n_k = K$ but with $n_i \geq 1$, so the coefficient is $U_i(K)G(M, K)$ by the analysis above. If we let $H(i, k) = U_i(k)G(M, k)$ be the coefficient of z^k in $h_i(z)$ and equate those coefficients in the equation above, we obtain

$$H(i, k) = G(M, k) - \sum_{j=0}^{k} G(M, j)R(i, k - j)$$

where $R(i, k)$ is the coefficient of z^k in $(f_i(z))^{-1}$ and can be obtained from the identity

$$(f_i(z))^{-1} f_i(z) = 1$$

Equating constant terms gives $R(i, 0) = 1$ and equating coefficients of z^k gives

$$\sum_{j=0}^{k} R(i, j) x_i(k - j) = 0$$

i.e.

$$R(i, k) + \sum_{j=0}^{k-1} R(i, j)x_i(k - j) = 0$$

since $x_i(0) = 1$, by definition. This gives a recurrence to calculate $R(i, k)$ and hence $H(i, k)$, which gives the node utilization $U_i(K) = H(i, K)/G(M, K)$.

If node i is an SSFR node then the modified generating function $h_i(z)$ simplifies because $1/f_i(z) = 1 - x_i z$:

$$h_i(z) = f(z)[1 - (f_i(z))^{-1}] = f(z)x_i z$$

Equating coefficients of z^K gives

$$H(i, k) = x_i G(M, K - 1)$$

This gives node utilization

$$U_i(K) = x_i \frac{G(M, K - 1)}{G(M, K)} \tag{6.41}$$

as before.

The cumulative probabilities $P(N_i \geqslant k)$ can also be determined in a similar way by extending the method for finding U_i. Instead of replacing $f_i(z)$ by $f_i(z) - 1$ we replace it by

$$f_i(z) - [1 + x_i(1)z + x_i(2)z^2 + \ldots + x_i(k - 1)z^{k-1}]$$

and obtain a more complex relation for a generating function analogous to $h_i(z)$. When all nodes in the network are SSFR, the modified generating function becomes

$$f(z)\left(\frac{f_i(z) - 1}{f_i(z)}\right)^k$$

In the general case this method is not tractable, and so we use a direct method to find the marginal queue length probabilities. As in the constant rate case, we have

$$\pi_i(k) = P(N_i = k)$$

$$= \frac{1}{G(M, K)} \sum_{\substack{n \in S(M,K) \\ n_i = k}} x_1(n_1)x_2(n_2) \ldots x_M(n_M)$$

$$= x_i(k) \frac{G(M \backslash i, K - k)}{G(M, K)} \tag{6.42}$$

The throughput λ_i of node i can then be expressed as

$$\lambda_i = \sum_{k=1}^{K} \pi_i(k)\mu_i(k) = \sum_{k=1}^{K} x_i(k) \frac{G(M\backslash i, K - k)}{G(M, K)} \mu_i(k)$$

but $x_i(k)\mu_i(k) = e_i x_i(k - 1)$ and so

$$\lambda_i = \frac{e_i}{G(M, K)} \sum_{k=1}^{K} x_i(k - 1)G(M\backslash i, K - k)$$

Replacing the summation variable k by $j = K - k$ gives the normalizing constant for population $K - 1$ (from the recurrence for determining normalizing constants). Thus we have

$$\lambda_i = e_i \frac{G(M, K - 1)}{G(M, K)} \tag{6.43}$$

Thus, even when we have a state-dependent service rate at node i, the arrival rate is proportional to the visitation rate at node i, as we would hope.

6.5.2 Mean value analysis

The MVA algorithm described earlier in Section 6.4 can be extended to handle state-dependent service rates. Here, we give a very informal proof of the extension. The equation for the system throughput remains unchanged:

$$T(K) = \frac{K}{\sum_{i=1}^{M} v_i W_i(K)} \tag{6.44}$$

Let $\pi_i(j|K)$ be the proportion of time that node i has j customers when the entire network has K customers in equilibrium. Intuitively, we can imagine that an arrival finding $j - 1$ customers in the queue at node i will have a mean response time of $j/\mu_i(j)$. Thus we can write down the mean waiting time at node i, as follows:

$$W_i(K) = \sum_{j=1}^{K} \pi_i(j - 1|K - 1) \frac{j}{\mu_i(j)} \tag{6.45}$$

The mean queue length at node i is given by

$$L_i(K) = \sum_{j=1}^{K} j\pi_i(j|K) \tag{6.46}$$

By definition, $\pi_i(0|0) = 1$, and for $K > 0$, we can determine the distribution $\pi_i(j|K)$ as follows:

$$
\pi_i(j|K) = \begin{cases} \dfrac{v_i T(K)}{\mu_i(j)} \, \pi_i(j-1|K-1) & j = 1, 2, \ldots, K \\[2ex] 1 - \displaystyle\sum_{k=1}^{K} \pi_i(k|K) & j = 0 \end{cases} \tag{6.47}
$$

This recurrence can be verified by substituting the marginal probabilities (Equation 6.31). As before we can omit the visit ratios and consider only total customer demands at each node. However, we need to introduce a service time multiplier:

$$
\alpha_i(j) = \frac{\mu_i(j)}{\mu_i(1)}
$$

This allows us to replace $\mu_i(j)$ by $\alpha_i(j)\mu_i(1)$ in Equations (6.45) and (6.47). The demand for node i is then given by $D_i = v_i/\mu_i(1)$ and the total time spent at node i on average is $Q_i(K) = v_i W_i(K)$. These state-dependent service rates are particularly important for the flow equivalent server method, which we now consider.

6.6   The flow equivalent server method

The flow equivalent server (FES) method is a popular divide-and-conquer method used to solve product form queueing networks efficiently. It does this by reducing the number of nodes through aggregating sub-networks into single, more complex nodes. This is particularly efficient when a large number of nodes can be grouped together and information on the internal distribution of customers is not needed.

The basic idea in the FES method is to decompose the queueing network into several sub-networks (i.e. subsets of nodes). Normally, we only need to consider successively splitting the network into two: the **FES sub-network** and the **complement sub-network**. We then short-circuit the complement sub-network (i.e. the remaining nodes) to form a closed network. Essentially, shorting the complement sub-network is done by setting all the service times of its nodes to zero. In this way, we can analyse the FES sub-network in isolation to obtain the throughput $T(k)$ across the short-circuit for various populations $k = 1, 2, \ldots, K$. We can then replace the sub-network in the original network by a single QLD node (the FES node) with service rate function $\mu(k) = T(k)$. Finally we can solve the FES-transformed network that consists of the FES node and the complement sub-network.

What do we mean precisely by short-circuiting a sub-network of nodes? For each node i in the complement sub-network, we make $x_i(n) = 1$ if $n = 0$ and 0 otherwise so that node i is ignored in the calculation of the normalizing constant. The actual connections of these nodes to other nodes, i.e. the routing probabilities, do not matter. This is because the stationary state space probability distribution of the closed queueing network is defined solely by the quantities $\{e_i\}$ and $\{\mu_i(n_i)\}$, i.e. through the terms $x_i(n_i)$ in the product form solution.

This decomposition is in fact exact for product form networks, by the following theorem:

Proposition 6.5 (Norton's theorem)

The joint stationary probability distribution for the number of customers in the FES sub-network and queue lengths in the complement sub-network is the same in the original and the FES-transformed network. The FES sub-network in the FES-transformed network is just the new FES node.

Proof Without loss of generality the FES sub-network is formed by nodes $1, 2, \ldots, m$ and the complement sub-network is formed by nodes $m + 1, m + 2, \ldots, M$. So we replace the first m nodes with a FES node that has service rate function $\mu(k) = T(k)$ when its queue length is k and T is the throughput function of the FES sub-network. Suppose we give the FES node the label 0 so that we form the FES-transformed network shown in Figure 6.6. Although it may appear as if customers visit the FES sub-network once for every visit to the complement sub-network, this is not necessarily the case. The visitation rates to the two sub-networks are in general different, and the equations will represent this.

Let $\pi(n_{m+1}, n_{m+2}, \ldots, n_M)$ and $\pi'(n_{m+1}, n_{m+2}, \ldots, n_M)$ be the marginal joint queue length probabilities at nodes $m + 1, m + 2, \ldots, M$ in the original and FES-transformed networks respectively. In the original network with population K and n_0 customers in the FES sub-network, we have

$$\pi(n_0, n_{m+1}, n_{m+2}, \ldots, n_M)$$

$$= \sum_{n_1+n_2+\ldots+n_m=n_0} \pi(n_1, n_2, \ldots, n_m, n_{m+1}, n_{m+2}, \ldots, n_M)$$

$$= \frac{1}{G(M, K)} x(n_{m+1})x(n_{m+2}) \cdots$$

$$x(n_M) \sum_{n_1+n_2+\ldots+n_m=n_0} x(n_1)x(n_2) \ldots x(n_m)$$

$$= \frac{1}{G(M, K)} x(n_{m+1})x(n_{m+2}) \cdots x(n_M)G(m, n_0)$$

We now prove that this distribution is identical to $\pi'(n_0, n_{m+1}, n_{m+2}, \ldots, n_M)$ in the FES-transformed network. Let

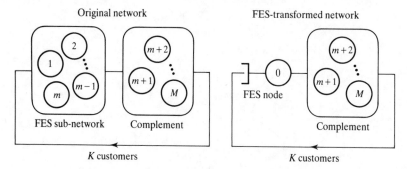

Original network

FES-transformed network

FES sub-network   Complement

Complement

K customers

K customers

Figure 6.6 Flow equivalent server method.

e_0 be the total visitation rate for the FES sub-network in the original network:

$$e_0 = \sum_{\substack{m < i \le M \\ 1 \le j \le m}} e_i q_{ij}$$

By definition, e_0 is also the visitation rate of the FES node in the FES-transformed network.

When the complement sub-network is short-circuited, the throughput along the short-circuiting arc of the FES sub-network with population k is given by

$$T(k) = e_0 \frac{G(m, k - 1)}{G(m, k)} \quad \text{for } k = 1, 2, \ldots, K$$

This gives us the service rate function for the FES node.

Now the $(M - m + 1)$-node FES-transformed queueing network also has a product form as follows:

$$\pi'(n_0, n_{m+1}, n_{m+2}, \ldots, n_M)$$

$$\propto x_0(n_0) x(n_{m+1}) x(n_{m+2}) \ldots x(n_M)$$

$$\propto x(n_{m+1}) x(n_{m+2}) \ldots x(n_M) \prod_{k=1}^{n_0} \frac{e_0}{T(k)}$$

Substituting the FES service rate function thus gives

$$\pi'(n_0, n_{m+1}, n_{m+2}, \ldots, n_M)$$

$$\propto x(n_{m+1}) x(n_{m+2}) \ldots x(n_M) \prod_{k=1}^{n_0} \frac{G(m, k)}{G(m, k - 1)}$$

$$\propto x(n_{m+1}) x(n_{m+2}) \ldots x(n_M) G(m, n_0)$$

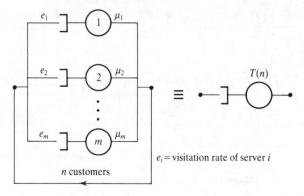

Figure 6.7   Multiple server aggregation.

Thus $\pi'(n_0, n_{m+1}, n_{m+2}, \ldots, n_M) = \pi(n_0, n_{m+1}, n_{m+2}, \ldots, n_M)$, since π' is a probability distribution, which completes the proof. ∎

This result was first proved by Chandy *et al*. (1975), and is related to Norton's theorem in electrical circuit theory. The customers are analogous to electric charge and so throughput is analogous to electric current.

Example 6.3 (Multiple parallel servers) _____

We use Norton's theorem to find the flow equivalent server for a set of m parallel servers each with the same utilization, as shown in Figure 6.7. According to the FES method we have short-circuited the remainder of the product form network and formed a closed network. We assume that server i has a fixed service rate μ_i and visitation rate e_i. Given these parameters we require the throughput $T(n)$ of the sub-network when the population is n. The state space of this sub-network is described by:

$$S(m, n) = \left\{ (k_1, k_2, \ldots, k_m) \mid \sum_{i=1}^{m} k_i = n \right\}$$

For FCFS and PS disciplines at the servers, this network has a product form solution for the steady state distribution given by

$$\pi(k) = \frac{1}{G(m, n)} \prod_{i=1}^{m} \left(\frac{e_i}{\mu_i} \right)^{k_i}$$

where $G(m, n)$ is the normalizing constant for an m-server network with population n. If all servers are equally utilized we can take $e_i = \mu_i$, which gives

$$\pi(k) = \frac{1}{G(m, n)} \qquad \text{for all } k \in S(m, n)$$

Thus all states are equi-probable in equilibrium and the normalizing constant is the same as the size of the state space $|S(m, n)|$. Thus the normalizing constant is the number of arrangements of n balls in m urns:

$$G(m, n) = \binom{n + m - 1}{m - 1}$$

as shown in Section 6.3.

The probability that server i has a non-empty queue is therefore given by the ratio of the number of states with queue i non-empty and the total number of states. The number of states with a non-empty queue at server i is the same as the number of arrangements of $n - 1$ customers on the m queues (since all these arrangements have the nth customer at least in node i). Thus the utilization of server i ($i = 1, 2, \ldots, m$) is given by:

$$U_i = \frac{G(m, n - 1)}{G(m, n)} = \frac{n}{m + n - 1}$$

So the throughput of server i is $\mu_i U_i$. Summing over all parallel servers gives the throughput function

$$T(n) = \frac{n \sum_{i=1}^{m} \mu_i}{m + n - 1}$$

This is just one of the ways to derive this result. We can now use $T(n)$ as our service rate function for the FES node in the original network.

The FES method is often also applied when the network does not have a product form solution to give an approximate solution for the closed queueing network. We will consider this approach to solve queueing networks with blocking in Chapter 10. We also use it for modelling switching networks in Chapter 11.

We have presented the classical approach to the analysis of single class queueing networks. However, many of the classical results can be obtained by a complementary approach called **operational analysis**, as shown by the early work in Buzen (1973) and Denning and Buzen (1978). This approach derives relationships (operational laws) between observable variables during a finite period of operation and so often does not require distribution assumptions (cf. Little's result). More recently, Dallery and Cao (1992) have extended this approach for closed networks and provided simpler proofs for the product form solution, the arrival theorem and Norton's theorem as well as approximate analysis of general queueing networks.

This completes our survey of single class queueing networks. To model more general situations we have to consider queueing networks with several different classes of customer. This is the subject of the next chapter.

SUMMARY

- Open Jackson networks have a product form solution for the joint queue length distribution in the steady state. This makes it easy to derive many performance measures of interest because nodes can be treated independently.

- An important result for Jackson networks is the Random Observer Property, which states that an arrival to a node in the network sees a given network state as if it were a random observer.

- Jackson networks with no external arrivals or departures (i.e. closed networks) are sometimes called Gordon–Newell networks. This type of network also has a product form solution for the steady state joint queue length distribution.

- The convolution algorithm provides an efficient way of computing the normalizing constant in the product form solution for nodes with state-dependent service rates. The performance measures of interest are then easy to determine since they can be expressed in terms of normalizing constants.

- The arrival theorem for closed networks states that an arrival sees the equilibrium state with one less customer.

- The mean value analysis algorithm derives relationships between various performance measures by applications of Little's result and the arrival theorem. The algorithm can be extended to allow state-dependent service rates, and the resulting set of recursive equations are intuitively appealing and easy to solve.

- Product form networks exhibit the aggregation property (Norton's theorem), which states that a group of nodes can be replaced by a flow equivalent server without affecting queues at the other nodes.

- Operational analysis provides a complementary way of deriving many classical results of product form networks.

EXERCISES

6.1   (10/20 Jackson network with 3 nodes – mean waiting time)
Consider a steady state open network with three exponential
nodes (with parameters μ_1, μ_2, μ_3) and Poisson arrivals (with rate
γ) to node number 1. Customers follow one of two routes through
the network: node 1 to node 2 (with probability p) and node 1 to
node 3 (with probability $q = 1 - p$). Write down the arrival rates
λ_i at node i ($i = 1, 2, 3$). Use Little's result and Jackson's theorem
to obtain the mean waiting time spent by a customer in the
network and show that if $\mu_2 = \mu_3$, this is least when $p = q = \frac{1}{2}$.

6.2   (20 Number of states for a closed network)
The state of a closed network with m nodes (numbered 1, 2, . . .,
m) and population n can be encoded by a string of m zeros and n
ones. Each node, starting with node 1, contributes to the string a
0 followed by as many 1s as there are customers present at that
node. For example, the string 01001111 represents the state where
there is 1 customer at node 1, no customers at node 2 and 4
customers at node 3. Using this representation, show that the
number of feasible states for the network is given by

$$\binom{m + n - 1}{m - 1} \quad \text{where} \quad \binom{n}{r} = \frac{n!}{(n - r)!r!}$$

is the binomial coefficient. Hence show that the number of
arrangements of n customers on m non-empty queues is given by

$$\binom{n - 1}{m - 1}$$

6.3   (20 Conditional queue length of closed network)
Let $G(K)$ be the normalizing constant for a Gordon–Newell
network of M servers with constant service rates $\mu_1, \ldots, \mu_M$,
visitation rates $e_1, \ldots, e_M$ and population K. Prove that in the
steady state:

(a) $P(N_i = k | N_j \geq h) = \left(\frac{e_i}{\mu_i}\right)^k \dfrac{G_i(K - k - h)}{G(K - h)}$

$$(1 \leq i \neq j \leq M)$$

(b) $P(N_i = k | N_j = h) = \left(\frac{e_i}{\mu_i}\right)^k \dfrac{G_{ij}(K - k - h)}{G_j(K - h)}$

$$(1 \leq i \neq j \leq M)$$

where N_i is the random variable for the queue size at server i and G_i, G_{ij} are the normalizing constants for the network with servers i, i and j respectively removed.

6.4　(30 Mean queue lengths in a closed network)
For a Gordon–Newell network, prove that

$$L_i(n) = U_i(n)(1 + L_i(n - 1))$$

where $L_i(n)$, $U_i(n)$ are the mean queue length and utilization respectively of server i when the population of the network is n $(1 \leqslant i \leqslant M)$.
　　Hence prove that if $u = \lim_{n \to \infty} U_i(n)$,

$$L_i(n) \to \frac{u}{1 - u} \qquad \text{as } n \to \infty \text{ if } u < 1$$

$$L_i(n) \to \infty \qquad \text{as } n \to \infty \text{ if } u = 1$$

6.5　(20 Normalizing constants for closed network)
Suppose A is a Gordon–Newell queueing network with M nodes with constant service rates such that x_i is the visitation rate to service rate ratio for node i. $G(N)$ is the normalizing constant for A with population N and $G_{i,j}(N)$ is the normalizing constant for A with nodes $i, i + 1, \ldots, j$ removed $(1 \leqslant i \leqslant j \leqslant M)$.

(a)　Show that the mean total number of customers in queues 1, 2, ..., m is

$$\sum_{k=1}^{N} \frac{G_{1,m}(N - k)G_{m+1,M}(k)k}{G(N)} \qquad (1 \leqslant m \leqslant M)$$

(b)　By considering the mean of the sum of queue length random variables, show that

$$\sum_{i=1}^{m} \sum_{k=1}^{N} G_{i,i}(N - k)kx_i^k = \sum_{k=1}^{N} G_{1,m}(N - k)G_{m+1,M}(k)k$$

6.6　(20 Parallel computer as a closed network)
A parallel computer architecture has a collection A of m_1 processors that share a single queue connected bidirectionally to a collection B of m_2 processors, each with their own queue. All processors are identical. You may assume that the transmission times between collections can be neglected and the buffer space is sufficient to avoid overflow. A fixed set of N tasks pass between collections A and B successively forever in a closed system, choosing a particular processor in each collection at random.

(a)   By using the decomposition method, model this as a 2-node cyclic Markovian queueing network and give the service rate functions.

(b)   Hence show that in the steady state, the probability that there are n tasks in collection A is proportional to $p(n)q(N - n)$, where

$$p(i) = \begin{cases} \dfrac{1}{i!} & (i \leqslant m_1) \\[2ex] \dfrac{1}{m_1^{i-m} m_1!} & (i \geqslant m_1) \end{cases}$$

and

$$q(i) = \frac{(m_2 + i - 1)!}{(m_2 - 1)! m_2^i i!} \qquad (i \geqslant 1)$$

6.7   (30 FES for a multi-server)

Consider a closed network, with population n, consisting of m parallel servers each with service rate μ. By arguing that a new arrival can be placed in a queue of length q in $q + 1$ different positions (so the nth arrival is equally likely to be placed in any of the $m + n - 1$ positions), show that

$$(m + n - 1)v_{b|n} = (m - b + 1)v_{b-1|n-1}$$
$$+ (b + n - 1)v_{b|n-1}$$

where $v_{b|n} = P(b$ servers are busy$|$population $= n)$.

By using appropriate generating functions, derive a recurrence for $A(n)$, the expected number of busy servers when the population is n. Hence show that the sub-network can be replaced by an FES with rate

$$T(n) = \frac{mn\mu}{m + n - 1}$$

6.8   (30 Parallel servers)

Show that the maximum throughput for a set of parallel servers with service rates μ_i and visitation rates e_i occurs when $e_i \propto \mu_i$.

Chapter 7
Multi-class Queueing Networks

7.1 Service time distributions 259

7.2 Types of service centre 262

7.3 Multi-class traffic model 270

7.4 BCMP theorem 271

7.5 Properties and extensions of BCMP networks 275

7.6 Computational algorithms for BCMP networks 276

7.7 Priority disciplines 281

7.8 Quasi-reversibility 288

So far we have assumed that all customers have identical characteristics. In order to model more complex systems we need to refine this and allow customers of different class to have different characteristics, such as routing behaviour and service requirements. For example, in modelling computer systems there may be certain i/o bound customers and others that are processor bound. The need to model such characteristics led to the BCMP theorem (Baskett *et al.* 1975) which was the amalgamation of the work of several authors. Kelly's work (Kelly 1975) also considers multi-class networks with adaptive routing. This type of routing is dynamic in that it can depend on the state of the system, and so is useful for load balancing applications. The BCMP theorem also includes the possibility of customers changing class from node to node and general service times at certain types of nodes. We first consider how to have general service times and still remain within the realms of Markov models.

7.1 Service time distributions

In practical applications of queueing networks, we often encounter cases where the exponential distribution does not adequately model the observed service time. However, to maintain the Markov property in the underlying process, we need to preserve a memoryless property in service times. As we have seen, the negative exponential distribution is the only continuous distribution with this property. Hence if we consider *some* network of exponential servers we will still maintain the Markov property, and the state holding time will consist of some combination of exponential random variables. We now consider several alternatives to the exponential distribution and assess their generality. Note that the networks of exponential servers we will consider just prescribe a method of constructing the service time at a particular node for one customer, so no queueing is involved; they are delay networks.

Let the random variable X be the service time constructed from the exponential delay network. The variability of X can be assessed by the value of the variation coefficient c, which is defined by

$$c^2 = \frac{\text{Var}[X]}{E[X]^2}$$

The square of the variation coefficient $\text{svc}[X]$ is often used instead of the variance in queueing theory literature. For the exponential distribution, it is easy to verify that $\text{svc}[X] = 1$. We will use this as a measure of the generality of the delay network construct.

7.1.1 Erlang-*k* distribution

Suppose the random variable X is the time taken by a customer to pass through k identical exponential delays in tandem (as shown in Figure 7.1). Then X has the Erlang-k distribution, as we saw in Chapter 2. Note that customers do not need to queue at any server. The Erlang-1 is the exponential distribution with parameter μ and the Erlang-k ($k > 1$) is the convolution of k exponential distributions with parameter μ. The probability density function of X and its Laplace transform are given by

$$f(x) = \frac{\mu(\mu x)^{k-1}}{(k-1)!}\, e^{-\mu x} \quad \text{and} \quad f^*(s) = \left(\frac{\mu}{\mu + s}\right)^k \tag{7.1}$$

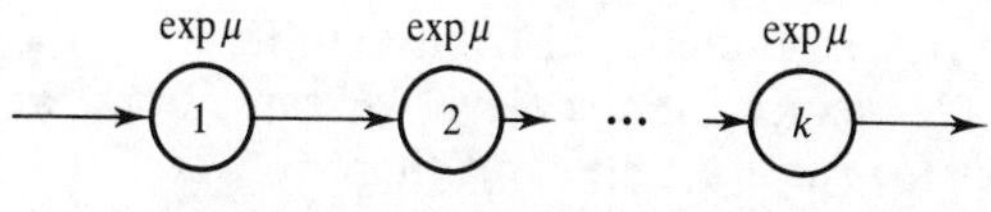

Figure 7.1 Erlang-k model.

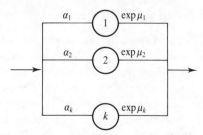

Figure 7.2   Hyperexponential model.

By differentiating $f^*(s)$ at $s = 0$, it can be shown that the square of the variation coefficient c of the Erlang-k distribution is $1/k$. Thus we see that $c \leqslant 1$, with equality if and only if $k = 1$. We note that the Erlang-k distribution is a special case of the gamma distribution which can have $c > 1$.

7.1.2 Hypoexponential distribution

Suppose the servers in the Erlang-k model can have different rates (say the ith delay is exponential with rate μ_i). This gives the hypoexponential distribution, which has Laplace transform

$$f^*(s) = \prod_{i=1}^{k} \frac{\mu_i}{\mu_i + s} \tag{7.2}$$

Again we find that the variation coefficient $c < 1$, i.e. less variability than the exponential distribution (hence the name hypoexponential).

7.1.3 Hyperexponential distribution

Suppose X is the service time of a customer going through k parallel exponential delays as shown in Figure 7.2. In other words, the service time is exponential with rate μ_i with probability α_i where $\Sigma_i \alpha_i = 1$. This gives the hyperexponential distribution with density function of X and its Laplace transform given by

$$f(x) = \sum_{i=1}^{k} \alpha_i \mu_i e^{-\mu_i x} \quad \text{and} \quad f^*(s) = \sum_{i=1}^{k} \alpha_i \frac{\mu_i}{\mu_i + s} \tag{7.3}$$

Now we have $c \geqslant 1$, with equality if and only if $k = 1$, i.e. more variability than the exponential distribution. Thus with a combination of series and parallel exponential delays we can obtain any desired variation coefficient for service time. But there is a better, less complicated, way to achieve the same result, which we now describe.

7.1.4 Coxian distribution

This model was first described by Cox (1955) and is referred to as the **Coxian model** or the **method of stages** (Barbour 1976). Suppose X is the time taken for a customer to go through a series of exponential delays (called stages) but with the possibility of leaving the network before entering any stage of service, as shown in Figure 7.3. Let b_i ($i = 0, 1, \ldots, k - 1$) be the probability of a customer entering stage $i + 1$ having gone through i stages already. Note that it is possible for a customer to leave the network without receiving any service at all (i.e. $P(X = 0) = 1 - b_0$). Often we may want to avoid this by making $b_0 = 1$ and henceforth $b_0 = 1$ unless stated otherwise. Let A_i be the probability that a customer enters stage i (i.e. $A_i = b_0 b_1 \ldots b_{i-1}$). We also define $b_k = 0$, so that $A_{k+1} = 0$.

With probability $A_i(1 - b_i)$, the Coxian random variable is the sum of the first i exponential delays. The Laplace transform of the density of the random variable X is therefore given by

$$f^*(s) = 1 - b_0 + \sum_{i=1}^{k} A_i(1 - b_i) \prod_{j=1}^{i} \frac{\mu_j}{\mu_j + s} \qquad (7.4)$$

The mean of X is derived as follows:

$$E(X) = \sum_{i=1}^{k} A_i(1 - b_i) \sum_{j=1}^{i} \frac{1}{\mu_j} = \sum_{j=1}^{k} \frac{1}{\mu_j} \sum_{i=j}^{k} A_i(1 - b_i)$$

$$= \sum_{j=1}^{k} \frac{1}{\mu_j} \sum_{i=j}^{k} (A_i - A_{i+1}) = \sum_{j=1}^{k} \frac{A_j}{\mu_j} \qquad (7.5)$$

All the distributions described above (Erlang-k, hypoexponential, hyperexponential) are Coxian distributions. We obtain the Erlang-k and the hypoexponential distributions by using $b_i = 1$ for $i = 0, 1, \ldots, k - 1$ in the Coxian model. For the hyperexponential distribution we show that it is Coxian for the $k = 2$ case.

Example 7.1 _____

In this example we parameterize the Coxian distribution so that it is the hyperexponential-2 distribution. The Laplace transform of the hyperexponential-2 distribution is

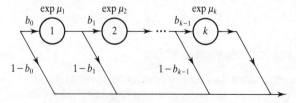

Figure 7.3 Coxian model.

$$f^*(s) = \frac{\alpha_1 \mu_1}{s + \mu_1} + \frac{\alpha_2 \mu_2}{s + \mu_2} \qquad \text{where } \alpha_1 + \alpha_2 = 1$$

The Laplace transform of a Coxian distribution with two stages is

$$f^*(s) = \frac{(1 - b_1)\mu_1}{s + \mu_1} + \frac{b_1 \mu_1 \mu_2}{(s + \mu_1)(s + \mu_2)}$$

Equating these Laplace transforms and multiplying throughout by $(s + \mu_1)(s + \mu_2)$ gives

$$\alpha_1 \mu_1 (s + \mu_2) + \alpha_2 \mu_2 (s + \mu_1) = (1 - b_1)\mu_1 (s + \mu_2) + b_1 \mu_1 \mu_2$$

Equating coefficients of s gives

$$\alpha_1 \mu_1 + \alpha_2 \mu_2 = (1 - b_1)\mu_1$$

This gives $b_1 = (1 - \mu_2/\mu_1)(1 - \alpha_1)$ and it is easy to verify that the constant terms on each side are equal. Since b_1 is a probability we require $\mu_2 \leqslant \mu_1$. However, if $\mu_1 \leqslant \mu_2$, we can simply invert the stages in the Coxian model, i.e. interchange μ_2 and μ_1. Notice that when $\mu_1 = \mu_2$ or $\alpha_1 = 1$ we get $b_1 = 0$ in the Coxian model, which effectively removes the second stage since only one exponential delay is required.

For the hyperexponential distribution with more than two parallel exponential delays the same method can be used – essentially expanding the Laplace transform of the corresponding Coxian distribution in partial fractions.

Coxian distributions are very general. The sum of Coxian distributions is also Coxian. In fact, Coxian distributions are equivalent to the set of distributions with rational Laplace transforms. Furthermore, a Coxian distribution can be constructed so that its Laplace transform approaches that of any distribution (even without a rational Laplace transform) as closely as required. Cox also showed that allowing customers to loop back probabilistically to a previous stage or skip some stages does not increase the generality of this distribution. The single stage Coxian with $b_0 < 1$ is sometimes called the **generalized exponential** and arises in maximum entropy methods (see Chapter 8 on approximate methods).

7.2   Types of service centre

As well as extending Jackson networks to general service time distributions, we also want to analyse the properties of queueing disciplines other than first come first served. For now we will consider a service node in isolation and later combine our results to obtain a product form solution for the entire queueing network. We assume that customers of class r arrive at the node in a Poisson stream with rate λ_r, and that there are R classes: $1, 2, \ldots, R$.

The service time for class r customers has a Coxian distribution with J_r stages and for $s = 1, 2, \ldots, J_r$ we define the following parameters:

μ_{rs} = parameter for the exponential server in stage s

b_{rs} = probability of continuing to stage $s + 1$ after service from stage s

$A_{rs} = \prod\limits_{i=0}^{s-1} b_{ri}$ = probability of entering stage s

Note that when $s = J_r$, $b_{rs} = 0$ by definition.

The mean service time for a class r customer is denoted by $1/\mu_r$, and so by Equation (7.5) we have

$$\frac{1}{\mu_r} = \sum_{s=1}^{J_r} \frac{A_{rs}}{\mu_{rs}} \tag{7.6}$$

We also denote the traffic intensity for class r customers by $\rho_r = \lambda_r/\mu_r$ and define $\rho = \sum_{r=1}^{R} \rho_r$.

In the following sections, we shall derive the pertinent properties of certain types of node. Each type of node is defined by the number of queues and servers as well as the queueing discipline and service time distribution. We will then define a state space and obtain the steady state probabilities. In some cases, we will need to aggregate states in order to obtain more useful steady state solutions. For aggregating states, we will find the multinominal theorem particularly useful.

Proposition 7.1 (Multinomial theorem)
Suppose $S(m, n) = \{(k_1, k_2, \ldots, k_m) | \sum_{i=1}^{m} k_i = n, \ k_i \geqslant 0\}$, then

$$\sum_{k \in S(m,n)} \prod_{i=1}^{m} \frac{x_i^{k_i}}{k_i!} = \frac{(x_1 + x_2 + \ldots + x_m)^n}{n!}$$

where x_i ($i = 1, 2, \ldots, m$) is a real number.

Proof We prove this result by induction on m. For the base case, $m = 1$, the result is trivially true. Note that when $m = 2$ it is the binomial theorem. For the inductive step, let us consider the following:

$$(x_1 + x_2 + \ldots + x_{m-1} + x_m)^n$$
$$= \sum_{r=0}^{n} \binom{n}{r} (x_1 + x_2 + \ldots + x_{m-1})^r x_m^{n-r}$$

by the binomial theorem

$$= \sum_{r=0}^{n} \frac{n!}{(n-r)!} \sum_{k \in S(m-1,r)} \left[\prod_{i=1}^{m-1} \frac{x_i^{k_i}}{k_i!} \right] x_m^{n-r}$$

by the inductive hypothesis

$$= n! \sum_{r=0}^{n} \frac{x_m^{n-r}}{(n-r!)} \sum_{k \in S(m-1,r)} \left[\prod_{i=1}^{m-1} \frac{x_i^{k_i}}{k_i!} \right]$$

$$= n! \sum_{k \in S(m,n)} \prod_{i=1}^{m} \frac{x_i^{k_i}}{k_i!}$$

as required ∎

We now analyse four types of node that we will allow in the multi-class network:

Type 1: First come first served (FCFS) node
Type 2: Processor sharing (PS) node
Type 3: Infinite server (IS) node
Type 4: Last come first served pre-emptive resume (LCFS-PR) node

7.2.1 Type 1: FCFS node

The FCFS node has a single queue and a single server. All customers, regardless of class, have identical exponential service time distributions with parameter $\mu(n)$ when the queue length is n. As in Chapter 5, we can define $\mu(n)$ appropriately to model multiple servers. The FCFS discipline has already been analysed in Chapter 5, and for a fixed rate server (for example) with rate μ and arrival rate λ, the standard M/M/1 result for the steady state queue length distribution is

$$p(n) = (1 - \rho)\rho^n \quad \text{where } \rho = \lambda/\mu \tag{7.7}$$

Note that we do not allow a Coxian service time distribution at FCFS nodes because otherwise arriving customers can become blocked.

7.2.2 Type 2: PS node

As with the FCFS node, the PS node also has a single queue and single server. However, when the queue length is $n > 0$, each customer in the queue is served at a fraction $1/n$ of the server's service capacity, $\mu(n)$.

The classic application of this type of node is for modelling round robin scheduling at a processor. Each customer in the processor queue receives a quantum of service and so, as the time quantum tends to zero, all customers are served simultaneously. In this case, we can allow distinct Coxian distributions for each class of customer.

In the node, let $n_{rs} \geq 0$ be the number of class r customers in stage s of Coxian service $(1 \leq r \leq R, 1 \leq s \leq J_r)$. The state space can be described by the vector $n = (n_1, n_2, \ldots, n_R)$ where $n_r = (n_{r1}, n_{r2}, \ldots, n_{rJ_r})$. We also define the following abbreviations:

$$n_r = \sum_{s=1}^{J_r} n_{rs} \quad \text{(i.e. the number of customers of class } r \text{ at the node)}$$

$$n = \sum_{r=1}^{R} n_r \quad \text{(i.e. the total number of customers at the node)}$$

State transitions into state n are caused by:

(a)   a customer of class r arriving: $n_{r1} - 1 \rightarrow n_{r1}$, which occurs at rate $\lambda_r b_{r0}$ $(n_{r1} > 0)$

(b)   a customer leaving stage s of service:
either $n_{rs} + 1 \rightarrow n_{rs}$ and $n_{r,s+1} - 1 \rightarrow n_{r,s+1}$, which occurs at rate $\mu_{rs} b_{rs}/n$ $(1 \leq s \leq J_r - 1, n_{r,s+1} > 0)$
or $n_{rs} + 1 \rightarrow n_{rs}$ only, which occurs at rate $\mu_{rs}(1 - b_{rs})/n$ $(1 \leq s \leq J_r)$

Note that the division by n in case (b) is required because for the PS discipline the server's capacity is shared by all the customers in the queue.

By construction, the times between state transitions are exponential, and so define a Markov process. The balance equations for this process have the following solution, which is obtained by routine analysis:

$$p(n) = p(n_1, n_2, \ldots, n_R) = (1 - \rho)n! \prod_{r=1}^{R} \prod_{s=1}^{J_r} \left[\frac{1}{n_{rs}!} \left(\frac{\lambda_r A_{rs}}{\mu_{rs}} \right)^{n_{rs}} \right]$$

(7.8)

Normally, we do not require such a detailed solution and remove the information about stages. By summing Equation (7.8) over all stages and using the multinomial theorem we obtain

$$p(n_1, n_2, \ldots, n_R) = (1 - \rho)n! \prod_{r=1}^{R} \frac{\rho_r^{n_r}}{n_r!}$$

(7.9)

By summing Equation (7.9) over all vectors $(n_1, n_2, \ldots, n_R)$ with the same number of customers, we can apply the multinomial theorem again to obtain:

$$p(n) = (1 - \rho)\rho^n \tag{7.10}$$

Thus the queue length distribution is the same as for the FCFS node with exponential service times for all customers. The PS node is actually much more complex with distinct Coxian distributions for different customer classes and yet gives the same simple result for queue length as the M/M/1 queue. This is quite remarkable, since it shows that the queue length depends only on the mean of the service time and not on any higher moments.

7.2.3   Type 3: IS node

As with the PS node, the IS node provides immediate service to all customers in the queue. But for the IS node there are enough servers to serve all the customers, so that each customer is delayed only by a service time. Each class of customer can have distinct Coxian distribution of service time. Typically this node is used to model delays of some random time interval (e.g. think times in terminal systems).

The state space can be described by $n = (n_1, n_2, \ldots, n_R)$ as for the PS node. The state transitions are also very similar since state transitions into state n are caused by:

(a)   a customer of class r arriving: $n_{r1} - 1 \to n_{r1}$, which occurs at rate $\lambda_r b_{r0}$ $(n_{r1} > 0)$

(b)   a customer leaving stage s of service
either $n_{rs} + 1 \to n_{rs}$ and $n_{r,s+1} - 1 \to n_{r,s+1}$, which occurs at rate $\mu_{rs} b_{rs}$ $(1 \leq s \leq J_r - 1, n_{r,s+1} > 0)$
or $n_{rs} + 1 \to n_{rs}$ only, which occurs ar rate $\mu_{rs}(1 - b_{rs})$ $(1 \leq s \leq J_r)$

These state transition rates can be used to define a Markov process whose balance equations have the solution:

$$p(n_1, n_2 \ldots, n_R) = e^{-\rho} \prod_{r=1}^{R} \prod_{s=1}^{J_r} \left[\frac{1}{n_{rs}!} \left(\frac{\lambda_r A_{rs}}{\mu_{rs}} \right)^{n_{rs}} \right] \tag{7.11}$$

We can aggregate all states with the same number of customers (n_r) in each class r by summing Equation (7.11) over all stages. Applying the multinomial theorem leads to the following result:

$$p(n_1, n_2, \ldots, n_R) = e^{-\rho} \prod_{r=1}^{R} \frac{\rho_r^{n_r}}{n_r!} \tag{7.12}$$

This can be simplified further by aggregating all states $(n_1, n_2, \ldots, n_R)$ with the same number of customers (n) in service. Applying the multinomial theorem then gives

$$p(n) = e^{-\rho} \frac{\rho^n}{n!} \tag{7.13}$$

As for the PS node, we find that the queue length at an IS node only depends on the mean of the service time and not on higher moments. Again the aggregated result is the same as for an exponential IS node.

7.2.4   Type 4: LCFS-PR node

The LCFS-PR node has a single queue and a single server. As with the PS and IS nodes, the LCFS-PR node also immediately starts serving customers on arrival. The arriving customer goes directly into service, pre-empting (i.e. displacing) any customer in service (if any). After the new customer finishes, the displaced customer resumes service from the point of interruption. Each customer class can have a distinct Coxian service time distribution so the queue is of type $M/G/1$.

Suppose we label the customers according to their arrival order; so customer i is the $(n - i + 1)$th most recent arrival when the queue length is n. So customer 1 has been in the queue longest and customer n was the last one to arrive. For customer i, let r_i denote its class and s_i denote its current stage of service in the Coxian model. The state space for this node is $((r_1, s_1), (r_2, s_2), \ldots, (r_n, s_n))$ when there are n customers in the queue and the last customer to arrive (of class r_n) is in service at stage s_n.

State transitions into state $((r_1, s_1), (r_2, s_2), \ldots, (r_n, s_n))$ can be of three types:

(a)   by a customer completing service and leaving:

$$((r_1, s_1), (r_2, s_2), \ldots, (r_n, s_n), (r_{n+1}, s_{n+1})) \rightarrow$$

$$((r_1, s_1), (r_2, s_2), \ldots, (r_n, s_n))$$

which occurs at rate $(1 - b_{rs})\mu_{rs}$ where $r = r_{n+1}$ and $s = s_{n+1}$

(b)   by a customer completing a stage of service:

$$((r_1, s_1), (r_2, s_2), \ldots, (r_n, s_n - 1)) \rightarrow$$

$$((r_1, s_1), (r_2, s_2), \ldots, (r_n, s_n)) \ (s_n > 1)$$

which occurs at rate $b_{rs}\mu_{rs}$ where $r = r_n$ and $s = s_n - 1$

(c)   by a new arrival where $s_n = 1$:

$$((r_1, s_1), (r_2, s_2), \ldots, (r_{n-1}, s_{n-1})) \rightarrow$$

$$((r_1, s_1), (r_2, s_2), \ldots, (r_{n-1}, s_{n-1}), (r_n, 1))$$

which occurs at rate $b_{r0}\lambda_r$ where $r = r_n$

The transition rate out of state $((r_1, s_1), (r_2, s_2), \ldots, (r_n, s_n))$ is $\Sigma_r \lambda_r + \mu_{r_n s_n}$.

The balance equations corresponding to these transition rates are easy to write down and have solution given by

$$p((r_1, s_1), (r_2, s_2), \ldots, (r_n, s_n)) = (1 - \rho) \prod_{j=1}^{n} \left[\lambda_{r_j} \frac{A_{r_j s_j}}{\mu_{r_j s_j}} \right] \qquad (7.14)$$

Aggregating states with the same ordering of customer classes by summing Equation (7.14) over all stages gives

$$p((r_1, r_2, \ldots, r_n)) = (1 - \rho) \prod_{j=1}^{n} \rho_{r_j} \qquad (7.15)$$

Aggregating states with the same number of customers of each class by summing Equation (7.15) over all orderings (i.e. all $n!$ permutations) we obtain

$$p(n_1, n_2, \ldots, n_R) = (1 - \rho)n! \prod_{r=1}^{R} \frac{\rho_r^{n_r}}{n_r!} \qquad (7.16)$$

This is the same as for the PS node and so by summing Equation (7.16) over all vectors $(n_1, n_2, \ldots, n_R)$ with the same number of customers, we can apply the multinomial theorem again to obtain

$$p(n) = (1 - \rho)\rho^n \qquad (7.17)$$

Thus we again arrive at the M/M/1 result even though we have general service times and different queueing discipline.

Remarks

Note that in all four cases above, the number of customers in the queue at equilibrium depends only on the means of the service time distributions (i.e. it is insensitive to higher moments). For the FCFS node this is expected because the first moment of the exponential distribution defines all other moments. We also found that the PS and LCFS-PR nodes have the same probability distribution for the number of customers of each class. In fact, a large class of queueing disciplines have the same queue length distribution. They are often called symmetric queueing disciplines, or symmetric scheduling strategies.

7.2.5 Symmetric queueing disciplines

Symmetric queueing disciplines can be described by numbering the positions in the queue. Suppose customers occupy a numbered 'seat' in the queue, such that when j customers are present, they occupy seats $1, 2, \ldots, j$. A new arrival finding this state sits in seat $k = 1, 2, \ldots, j + 1$ with probability $\alpha(k, j + 1)$. This means that customers in seats $k, k + 1, \ldots, j$ move up one to $k + 1, k + 2, \ldots, j + 1$ respectively. The server devotes different processing capacity to each seat. Let us suppose that a fraction $\beta(k, j)$ of capacity is given to seat k when there are j customers in the queue. Now a departure from seat k leaves a gap and so customers in seats $k + 1, k + 2, \ldots, j$ move down one to $k, k + 1, \ldots, j - 1$ respectively. In a symmetric queueing discipline: $\alpha(k, j) = \beta(k, j)$. Also suppose the server has a total service rate of $\mu(n)$ when there are n customers in the queue and that each class of customers can have arbitrary service time distribution.

For example, for processor sharing (PS), we have

$$\alpha(k, j) = \beta(k, j) = 1/j \quad \text{for } k = 1, 2, \ldots, j$$

For a stack discipline (LCFS-PR), we have

$$\alpha(1, j) = \beta(1, j) = 1, \; \alpha(k, j) = \beta(k, j) = 0 \quad \text{for } k > 1$$

For the infinite server discipline (IS), we have

$$\alpha(k, j) = \beta(k, j) = 1/j \quad \text{and} \quad \mu(j) = j\mu$$

Note that the FCFS discipline is not symmetric because we have

$$\alpha(k, j) = 1 \text{ if } k = j \text{ and } 0 \text{ otherwise}$$

$$\beta(k, j) = 1 \text{ if } k = 1 \text{ and } 0 \text{ otherwise}$$

so we have $\alpha(k, j) \neq \beta(k, j)$ for $k > 1$, $j > 1$.

In fact, all symmetric queues with general service time distributions have the quasi-reversible property, which we consider in Section 7.8. By a similar analysis as for the LCFS-PR node, it can be shown that all symmetric queueing disciplines have the same equilibrium queue length probabilities. For arbitrary service time requirements, the analysis requires continuous state space Markov processes, which is beyond the scope of this book (see Kelly (1979) for a discussion). Here, we present some of the interesting results (without proof). Suppose class r customers arrive according to a Poisson stream with rate λ_r and have a service time requirement with an arbitrary distribution with mean $1/\mu_r$. Then the average amount of service requirement arriving per unit time is given by

$$\rho = \sum_{r=1}^{R} \lambda_r \frac{1}{\mu_r}$$

Now the probability that the queue contains n customers is given by

$$p(n) = \frac{1}{G} \frac{\rho^n}{\prod_{k=1}^{n} \phi(k)} \tag{7.18}$$

where G normalizes the probabilities and $\phi(k)$ is the service rate multiplier when there are k customers in the queue (for a proof see Kelly (1979)). The service rate multiplier indicates how much faster a server works when the queue length is k than when there is a single customer. Thus for an IS node, $\phi(k) = k$, which turns Equation (7.18) into Equation (7.13). For the PS and LCFS-PR nodes, $\phi(k) = 1$ which turns Equation (7.18) into the standard M/M/1 result (Equations 7.10 and 7.17).

However, waiting time distributions may be different for the different symmetric disciplines. Although symmetric queues form a large class of quasi-reversible queues that allow arbitrary service time distributions, they are not the only ones.

7.3   Multi-class traffic model

We now extend our notation for nodes to entire queueing networks. Each customer still belongs to a class r ($r = 1, 2, \ldots, R$) but now customers traverse a network of M nodes labelled $1, 2, \ldots, M$. The node transition probabilities are defined by the set $\{q_{ir;js}\}$, which describes the probability that a class r customer at node i goes next to node j as a class s customer. If there is a non-zero probability that a customer of class r can change to class s and a customer of class s can change to class r then r and s are said to be **interchangeable**. The interchangeable relation is an equivalence relation (i.e. reflexive, symmetric and transitive) and so it can partition the set of classes $\{1, 2, \ldots, R\}$ such that two customer classes belong to the same subset if and only if they are interchangeable.

Some customer classes do not visit the entire set of nodes $\{1, 2, \ldots, M\}$ and so we want to know only about those nodes that are visited by a given class. In particular, we want to consider the nodes visited by any class in a subset P of the class partition. Thus we define a **routing chain** for subset P as a set of pairs (i, r) where node i is reachable by class r customers, that is,

$$\{(i, r) | i \text{ reachable by class } r \in P\}$$

Thus, the routing chain contains information about all the nodes that a given customer class can visit, as well as all the classes that a customer can change into. We can think of a routing chain as a separate queueing network, but with interference from other routing chains that share the same nodes. Just like a simple queueing network, a routing chain is said to be closed if the number of customers in it remains constant. Open routing chains allow external arrivals and departures.

Arrival process

For open networks, customers arrive at the network according to a Poisson process whose rate can depend on the state of the network. We consider two cases:

(1)   rate $\gamma(K)$ where K is the number of customers in the network

(2)   rate $\gamma_c(K_c)$ where K_c is the number of customers in chain c

If the arrival rates are state independent, then we have $\gamma(K) = \gamma$ and $\gamma_c(K_c) = \gamma_c$. For simplicity, we will use state-independent arrival rates, unless otherwise stated.

Traffic equations

Suppose e_{ir} is the relative frequency of visits to node i by class r customers in chain c. Then for node i and class r, $(i, r) \in c$, we can write the following traffic equations:

$$\sum_{(j,s)\in c} e_{js}q_{js;ir} + q_{0;ir} = e_{ir} \tag{7.19}$$

where $q_{0;ir}$ is the probability that an external arrival is for node i and class r.

If $q_{0;ir} = 0$ for all $(i, r) \in c$ then c is a closed chain and so $\{e_{ir}|(i, r) \in c\}$ can be determined up to a multiplicative constant and e_{ir} is the relative arrival rate (or visitation rate) of class r customers to node i. However, if $q_{0;ir} > 0$ for some $(i, r) \in c$ then c is an open chain and so the traffic equations have a unique solution for $\{e_{ir}\}$. For an open chain c, let γ_c be the external arrival rate. Then $\gamma_c q_{0;ir}$ (with $(i, r) \in c$) is the external arrival rate at node i of class r customers. Furthermore, $\gamma_c e_{ir}$ is the actual total arrival rate of class r customers to node i.

7.4 BCMP theorem

The BCMP theorem states that queueing networks with nodes of type 1, 2, 3 and 4 (as defined in Section 7.2) and multi-class traffic (as defined in Section 7.3) have a product form solution for the steady state joint probability distribution of the node states (cf. Jackson's theorem). We will consider simple cases of the theorem (without proof) before presenting the general case and its extensions. The state space for the BCMP network will be different depending on the assumptions made and the level of detail required.

We extend our notation for nodes by introducing a subscript (to indicate the node number) to all parameters defined in Section 7.2. The meanings of all parameters remain the same unless they are redefined. The first subscript is the node number, the second is the class and the third is the stage number of the Coxian model. Not all subscripts are required in some cases (e.g. the Coxian stage number is not needed when the service time is exponential). Thus we have for node i:

J_{ir} = the number of stages in the Coxian model for class r
A_{irs} = the probability of a class r customer entering stage s of service
μ_{irs} = the service rate for class r customers at stage s
μ_{ir} = the service rate for class r customers
n_{irs} = the number of customers of class r in stage s of service
n_{ir} = the number of customers of class r
n_i = the number of customers at the node

Case 1: Open network with state-independent arrival rates and fixed rate servers

If we are not interested in the behaviour of individual classes, the state space can be described by the vector $n = (n_1, n_2, \ldots, n_M)$ where n_i is the number of customers at node i $(i = 1, 2, \ldots, M)$. The steady state probability distribution is given by

$$p(n_1, n_2, \ldots, n_M) = p_1(n_1)p_2(n_2) \ldots p_M(n_M) \qquad (7.20)$$

where

$$p_i(n_i) = \begin{cases} (1 - \rho_i)\rho_i^{n_i} & \text{for FCFS, PS and LCFS-PR nodes } (7.21) \\ e^{-\rho_i} \dfrac{\rho_i^{n_i}}{n_i!} & \text{for IS nodes} \qquad (7.22) \end{cases}$$

$$\rho_i = \sum_{r=1}^{R} \frac{\gamma e_{ir}}{\mu_{ir}}$$

and γ is the external arrival rate.

Case 2: Mixed multi-class network with fixed rate servers

The state space can be described by the vector $n = (n_1, n_2, \ldots, n_M)$ where $n_i = (n_{i1}, n_{i2}, \ldots, n_{iR})$ and n_{ir} is the number of customers of class r at node i $(i = 1, 2, \ldots, M; r = 1, 2, \ldots, R)$. The steady state probability distribution is given by:

$$p(\boldsymbol{n}_1, \boldsymbol{n}_2, \ldots, \boldsymbol{n}_M) = \frac{d(K)p_1(\boldsymbol{n}_1)p_2(\boldsymbol{n}_2) \cdots p_M(\boldsymbol{n}_M)}{G} \qquad (7.23)$$

where G is the normalizing constant,

$$d(K) = \begin{cases} \displaystyle\prod_{k=0}^{K-1} \gamma(k) & \text{if the network is open and has only 1 chain} \\ \displaystyle\prod_{c=1}^{m} \prod_{k=0}^{K_c-1} \gamma_c(k) & \text{if the network is open and has } m \text{ chains} \\ & \text{(chain } c \text{ has population } K_c) \\ 1 & \text{if the network is closed} \qquad (7.24) \end{cases}$$

$$p_i(\boldsymbol{n}_i) = n_i! \prod_{r=1}^{R} \left[\frac{1}{n_{ir}!} \left(\frac{e_{ir}}{\mu_{ir}} \right)^{n_{ir}} \right]$$

$$\text{for types 1 (FCFS), 2 (PS) and 4 (LCFS-PR)} \qquad (7.25)$$

$$p_i(\boldsymbol{n}_i) = \prod_{r=1}^{R} \left[\frac{1}{n_{ir}!} \left(\frac{e_{ir}}{\mu_{ir}} \right)^{n_{ir}} \right] \qquad \text{for type 3 (IS)} \qquad (7.26)$$

and

$$n_i = \sum_r n_{ir}$$

Note that for FCFS nodes μ_{ir} has the same value for all customer classes r.

Case 3: Mixed multi-class network with state-dependent servers

This is a simple extension of case 2 with service rates that depend on the queue length for certain node types. If at some node i the mean service time is the same for all customer classes we can introduce a local state-dependent server as follows. For example, in case 2, at FCFS nodes we have mean service time $1/\mu_i$ for all customer classes. We can therefore replace a factor as follows since it is independent of the customer class:

$$\prod_{r=1}^{R} \left(\frac{1}{\mu_{ir}} \right)^{n_{ir}} = \left(\frac{1}{\mu_i} \right)^{n_i}$$

This suggests we can extend the result to the state-dependent server case by replacing such factors in $p_i(n_i)$ by

$$\prod_{j=1}^{n_i} \frac{1}{\mu_i(j)}$$

where $\mu_i(j)$ is the rate of the state-dependent server when its queue length is j. The other factors remain the same as in case 2 above and the argument can be shown to be valid.

All of these cases are instances of the BCMP theorem that follows and can be proved by aggregating states, as in Section 7.2.

Proposition 7.2 (BCMP theorem)

In a general mixed multi-class queueing network let the state space be denoted by $n = (n_1, n_2, \ldots, n_M)$ where n_i depends on the type of node and n_i is the number of customers at node i.

For type 1 (FCFS) nodes, $n_i = (r_{i1}, r_{i2}, \ldots, r_{i,n_i})$, where r_{ij} is the class of the jth customer waiting in FCFS order at node i.

For type 2 (PS) and type 3 (IS) nodes, $n_i = (n_{i1}, n_{i2}, \ldots, n_{iR})$ and $n_{ir} = (n_{ir1}, n_{ir2}, \ldots, n_{irJ_i})$, where n_{irs} is the number of customers at node i of class r and in stage s of their service.

For type 4 (LCFS-PR) nodes, $n_i = ((r_{i1}, s_{i1}), (r_{i2}, s_{i2}), \ldots, (r_{i,n_i}, s_{i,n_i}))$ where r_{ij} is the class of the jth customer waiting in arrival order at node i and s_{ij} is its stage of service.

Then the steady state probability distribution of n is

$$p(n_1, n_2, \ldots, n_M) = G^{-1} d(K) p_1(n_1) p_2(n_2) \ldots p_M(n_M) \tag{7.27}$$

where G is the normalizing constant and $d(K)$ is defined as for case 2 (Equation 7.24):

$$p_i(n_i) = \prod_{j=1}^{n_i} \frac{e_{ir_{ij}}}{\mu_i(j)} \qquad \text{if } i \text{ is type 1 (FCFS)} \tag{7.28}$$

$$p_i(n_i) = n_i! \prod_{r=1}^{R} \prod_{s=1}^{J_{ir}} \left[\frac{1}{n_{irs}!} \left(\frac{e_{ir} A_{irs}}{\mu_{irs}} \right)^{n_{irs}} \right] \qquad \text{if } i \text{ is type 2 (PS)} \tag{7.29}$$

$$p_i(n_i) = \prod_{r=1}^{R} \prod_{s=1}^{J_{ir}} \left[\frac{1}{n_{irs}!} \left(\frac{e_{ir} A_{irs}}{\mu_{irs}} \right)^{n_{irs}} \right] \qquad \text{if } i \text{ is type 3 (IS)} \tag{7.30}$$

$$p_i(n_i) = \prod_{j=1}^{n_i} \left[e_{ir_{ij}} \frac{A_{ir_{ij}s_{ij}}}{\mu_{ir_{ij}s_{ij}}} \right] \qquad \text{if } i \text{ is type 4 (LCFS-PR)} \tag{7.31}$$

Proof The global balance equations may be expressed as

$$p(n)[\text{rate of leaving state } n]$$

$$= \sum_{n'} p(n')[\text{rate of transitions } n' \to n]$$

As before with the proof of Jackson's theorem, these equations can be decomposed into local balance equations. For each node i (except FCFS), class r, stage s:

$p(n)$[rate of class r customers leaving stage s in node i
(from state n)]

$$= \sum_{n'} p(n')[\text{rate of class } r \text{ customers entering stage } s \text{ in node } i \text{ (from } n' \rightarrow n)]$$

and for each node i, class r:

$p(n)$[rate of class r customers leaving node i
(from state n)]

$$= \sum_{n'} p(n')[\text{rate of class } r \text{ customers entering node } i \text{ (from } n' \rightarrow n)]$$

Each global balance equation is a sum of local balance equations, so a solution of the local balance equations must also be a solution of the global balance equations. Substituting the product form solution into the local balance equations reduces them to the defining equations for the e_{ir}, showing that the solution is indeed correct and unique by the steady state theorem.   ∎

7.5 Properties and extensions of BCMP networks

BCMP networks have a number of interesting properties that give us a clue as to why the steady state probabilities have a product form solution. Furthermore, better understanding of some of these properties has given rise to good computational algorithms for finding performance measures of interest. The local balance property plays an important part in giving compact solutions. In fact, it can be shown that any Markovian queueing network with a product form solution has satisfiable local balance equations.

Another observation is that all nodes in a BCMP network preserve the Markov property. When a node is subjected to Poisson arrivals then the departure process is also Poisson and independent of the arrival process (see Section 7.8 for more details). This is called the $M \Rightarrow M$ property and holds for all four types of nodes in BCMP networks. It can be shown that if a Markovian queueing network has the local balance property then the $M \Rightarrow M$ property holds for all nodes in the network.

In general, arrival processes at nodes in BCMP networks are not Poisson. However, actual arrival processes do have Poisson-like properties, since the arrival theorem for single class networks extends to

BCMP networks. In an open network, when a customer leaves a queue (or enters a new queue) it 'sees' the network in equilibrium. In a closed network, the departing customer 'sees' the network in equilibrium, but with one fewer customer in its own class. This theorem is crucial in the mean value analysis of BCMP networks and the proof is an extension of that of Proposition 6.4.

Since the first paper on multi-class networks was published, many extensions have been proposed. At about the same time Kelly (1975) showed how arbitrary routes across the BCMP network can also be analysed and Barbour (1976) showed that general service time distributions could be used in place of Coxian distributions. Specialized state-dependent routing was also analysed where customers entered either of two parallel disjoint sub-networks before going to a common node with probability dependent on the number of customers in each sub-network (Towsley 1980; Hordijk and van Dijk 1983). Other service disciplines have also been considered, such as random order service with exponential service times and load balancing nodes. These nodes have several servers and several queues so that idle servers select a queue depending on its length and attempt to keep all queues the same length. Many of these extensions to BCMP networks can be found in Disney and Konig (1985) and Bard (1979). More recently, qualitative properties of these networks have received much attention (Lin and Nain 1991). These properties include the sensitivity of various performance measures (such as throughput and mean queue length) with respect to particular parameters such as arrival rates and service rates.

7.6 Computational algorithms for BCMP networks

All the standard algorithms for single class networks extend, quite naturally, to multi-class BCMP networks. The convolution algorithm recurrence for computing normalizing constants is virtually identical, but the summation is over a domain of vectors rather than a domain of scalars representing the numbers of customers at nodes. The vector indicates the number of customers of each class present at the node. Mean value analysis of BCMP networks gives rise to three sets of equations as for the single class case because Little's result can be applied to any given class of customers at a node. As for the single class case, approximations to break the recursion in these equations are also applicable and give a much more efficient algorithm. Clearly the summation domain of vectors or the recursion involving vectors can be very large and complex. Consequently, very large networks cannot be solved exactly in reasonable time. We look at some of these below.

However, several other algorithms have been developed to solve particular types of multi-class networks. For example, the linearizer algorithm can solve large networks approximately with 1% error. Other approximate methods are applicable to particular applications, such as in the modelling of local area networks, which requires hundreds of classes. Exact methods, such as tree convolution and tree MVA, are useful when customers of any given class visit only a small number of nodes. RECAL (recursion by chain) and MVAC (MVA by chain; Conway *et al.* 1989) are good for a small number of nodes but many chains.

We now consider closed chains in the multi-class networks described in case 3, since they are frequently used in practical applications. The fully general case is similar, but much more involved algebraically. The closed chain can have SSFR (i.e. single server with fixed rate), IS or QLD (i.e. queue length dependent) nodes. For simplicity, we assume that there are no class transitions, so the number of chains is the same as the number of classes and the number of customers of each class remains fixed. The state space of such a network with M nodes is

$$S(M, K) = \{(n_1, n_2, \ldots, n_M) | n_1 + n_2 + \ldots + n_M = K)\}$$

where $K = (K_1, K_2, \ldots, K_R)$ and K_r is the number of class r customers in the network – vectors are added component-wise.

From the BCMP theorem (Equation 7.23), the steady state distribution is given by:

$$p(n_1, n_2, \ldots, n_M) = \frac{x_1(n_1)x_2(n_2) \ldots x_M(n_M)}{G(M, K)} \tag{7.32}$$

where $G(M, K)$ is the normalizing constant and the terms $x_i(n_i) = p_i(n_i)$ are given by Equations (7.25) and (7.26).

$$G(M, K) = \sum_{(n_1, n_2, \ldots, n_M) \in S(M, K)} x_1(n_1)x_2(n_2) \ldots x_M(n_M) \tag{7.33}$$

Direct computation of the normalizing constant requires summing over the entire state space. The number of states is the same as the number of ways of arranging K_r customers over M queues (for each class r). Thus direct computation requires

$$\prod_{r=1}^{R} \binom{K_r + M - 1}{M - 1} \text{ steps}$$

7.6.1 Convolution algorithm

The generating function approach for computing the normalizing constant extends to the multi-class case. The base case and recurrence are given by:

$$G(1, k) = x_1(k)$$

$$G(i, k) = \sum_{j=0}^{k} G(i - 1, j)x_i(k - j) \qquad i > 1 \qquad (7.34)$$

If all nodes in the network are SSFR, the recurrence simplifies to

$$G(i, k) = G(i - 1, k) + \sum_{r=1}^{R} \frac{e_{ir}}{\mu_{ir}} G(i, k - 1_r) \qquad i > 1 \qquad (7.35)$$

where 1_r is the rth unit vector $(1 \leqslant r \leqslant R)$, i.e. $(1_r)_i = 1$ if $i = r$ and 0 otherwise.

As before, the normalizing constant allows efficient computation of throughputs and mean queue lengths, and so (by using Little's result) mean waiting times. The marginal queue length distributions are also easy to determine.

7.6.2 Mean value analysis

The MVA algorithm (Reiser and Lavenburg 1980) is also easy to extend to the multi-class case. Here we will consider networks with SSFR nodes and IS nodes only, but the algorithm has been extended to accommodate QLD nodes also. The queueing discipline at SSFR nodes can be FCFS, PS or LCFS-PR. We will briefly consider both open and closed multi-class networks with M nodes. Node i has a fixed service rate of μ_{ir} and relative visit frequency of v_{ir} for class r customers. At nodes with the FCFS discipline, we require that the service time is independent of the class (so, $1/\mu_{ir} = 1/\mu_i$ for all classes r). For open networks, v_{ir} is the average number of times that a class r customer visits node i before leaving the network. For closed networks, we assume that an equivalent open network has been created by introducing an external node at a particular arc for each class (as in Section 6.4). The system resources are described by the total service demand of a class r customer at node i:

$$D_{ir} = v_{ir} \frac{1}{\mu_{ir}}$$

We will consider total demands here, but note that the per visit performance measures can be obtained if the relative visit frequency is known.

For open multi-class networks, the workload is described by the external arrival rate of each class r (γ_r for $r = 1, 2, \ldots, R$). We are interested in the following performance measures:

T_r denotes the throughput of class r customers

U_{ir} denotes the utilization of node i by class r customers

U_i denotes the utilization of node i

W_{ir} denotes the mean waiting time of a class r customer at node i (i.e. for each visit)

Q_{ir} denotes the mean time that a class r customer spends at node i during its stay in the network (i.e. the mean residence time at node i for class r)

Q_r denotes the mean time that a class r customer spends in the network (i.e. the system response time for class r)

L_{ir} denotes the mean number of class r customers at node i

In the steady state, the throughput of class r is $T_r = \gamma_r$. Applying Little's result to a server at node i for class r, we find $U_{ir} = \gamma_r D_{ir}$ and so $U_i = \sum_{r=1}^{R} \gamma_r D_{ir}$. The BCMP theorem for open multi-class networks implies that we can analyse individual nodes in isolation (and so use our results from Section 7.2). Hence the mean waiting time of a class r customer at node i is given by:

$$
W_{ir} = \begin{cases} \dfrac{1/\mu_{ir}}{1 - U_i} & \text{if node } i \text{ is SSFR} \\[2mm] 1/\mu_{ir} & \text{if node } i \text{ is IS} \end{cases}
$$

This also gives the mean residence time: $Q_{ir} = v_{ir} W_{ir}$. The system response time for class r is then found from $Q_r = \sum_{i=1}^{M} Q_{ir}$. Applying Little's result to node i for class r customers, we obtain

$$
L_{ir} = \gamma_r Q_{ir}
$$

For a closed multi-class network, let the workload be described by the network population $k = (k_1, k_2, \ldots, k_r \ldots k_R)$, where k_r is the number of class r customers. We first need the following definitions of the main variables, which are similar to the variables for the open network case but explicitly state the network population:

$L_{ir}(k)$ denotes the mean number of class r customers at node i

$W_{ir}(k)$ denotes the mean waiting time of class r customers at node i

$Q_{ir}(k)$ denotes the mean residence time of class r customers at node i

$T_r(k)$ denotes the throughput of the network along a specified arc (chosen as in Section 6.4 by introducing a new node 0)

Note that the arc chosen may be different for each class r, since class r customers must pass through it. The same analysis as before (Section 6.4) leads to the following set of equations:

$$W_{ir}(k) = \begin{cases} \dfrac{1}{\mu_{ir}} \left(\sum_{s=1}^{R} L_{is}(k - 1_r) + 1 \right) & \text{if node } i \text{ is SSFR} \\[4mm] \dfrac{1}{\mu_{ir}} & \text{if node } i \text{ is IS} \end{cases}$$

$$T_r(k) = \frac{k_r}{\sum_{i=1}^{M} v_{ir} W_{ir}(k)} \tag{7.36}$$

$$L_{ir}(k) = T_r(k) v_{ir} W_{ir}(k)$$

Note that $k - 1_r$ is the network state with one fewer class r customers than state k. As before, the arrival theorem is crucial to the analysis.

Using the alternate formulation (total demands), we obtain the following recurrences:

$$Q_{ir}(k) = \begin{cases} D_{ir} \left(\sum_{s=1}^{R} L_{is}(k - 1_r) + 1 \right) & \text{if node } i \text{ is SSFR} \\[4mm] D_{ir} & \text{if node } i \text{ is IS} \end{cases}$$

$$T_r(k) = \frac{k_r}{\sum_{i=1}^{M} Q_{ir}(k)} \tag{7.37}$$

$$L_{ir}(k) = T_r(k) Q_{ir}(k)$$

The analysis above assumes that the customers do not change class in the network, so the number of routing chains in the network is the same as the number of classes. We can represent class transitions by considering multiple classes within the same routing chain. Suppose we have C routing chains $\{1, 2, \ldots, C\}$ and R classes as before. Routing chain c only contains classes that are interchangeable and is closed if its population k_c remains fixed (although the mix of customer classes within chain c changes). The workload of a closed queueing network is described by the population vector $k = (k_1, k_2, \ldots, k_C)$. The recurrence equations now become

$$W_{ir}(k) = \begin{cases} \dfrac{1}{\mu_{ir}} \left(\sum_{s=1}^{R} L_{is}(k - 1_c) + 1 \right) & \text{if node } i \text{ is SSFR} \\[4mm] \dfrac{1}{\mu_{ir}} & \text{if node } i \text{ is IS} \end{cases}$$

$$L_{ir}(k) = v_{ir} T_c(k) W_{ir}(k)$$

$$T_c(k) = \frac{k_c}{\sum_{i=1}^{M} \sum_{r \in c} v_{ir} W_{ir}(k)}$$

where class r belongs to routing chain c. The alternate formulation using total demands can be obtained in the same way as before (i.e. replace $v_{ir} W_{ir}(k)$ by $Q_{ir}(k)$ and replace v_{ir}/μ_{ir} by D_{ir}).

Mixed workloads (i.e. a mixture of open and closed classes) can

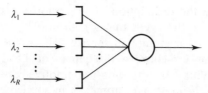

Figure 7.4   Queueing system with priorities.

also be handled exactly by the MVA algorithm. As we observed for the single class case, the MVA algorithm can also be used for QLD nodes in a multi-class network (see Lazowska *et al.* (1984) for a description of these extensions). This reference also considers approximate MVA analysis by changing the waiting time equation to an intuitively appealing form. With further modifications, we can approximate the analysis of networks with class dependent service times at nodes with the FCFS discipline. We will also consider some MVA approximations, later in Chapter 8.

7.7 Priority disciplines

Computer and communication systems are sometimes required to give faster service to certain users, e.g. signalling is favoured over data and voice in telecommunications. Typically, this priority treatment not only reduces the waiting times for these users, but can also improve the overall throughput and resource utilization. For example, giving priority to customers requiring short service time improves throughput. Such priority schemes have been successfully applied to CPU scheduling. Thus we need to analyse queueing systems with priority given to certain classes of customer. The analysis of customer priorities in queueing networks is a hard problem to analyse exactly; here we just consider a single queue.

Suppose the customer classes are labelled $1, 2, \ldots, R$ and each class is assigned a priority such that class r customers have priority over class s customers if $r > s$. Then the priority ordering is such that class R customers have the highest priority and class 1 customers have lowest priority.

Customers of class r arrive according to a Poisson stream with rate λ_r and have service times with distribution function $F_r(x)$ which has mean $1/\mu_r$ and second moment M_{2r}. We consider a single server queueing system with R FCFS queues (one for each customer class) as shown in Figure 7.4. After a service completion the next customer chosen for service is the one with the highest priority. Thus class r customers can only start service when all queues $r + 1, r + 2, \ldots, R$ are empty.

To complete the description of this priority discipline we need to specify what to do in the event that a high priority customer arrives and finds a lower priority customer in service. There are two main types of disciplines: the **non-pre-emptive discipline** (or head of line) and the **pre-emptive discipline**. In the non-pre-emptive case, a high priority arrival has to wait if another customer is in service even if the arriving customer has higher priority. However, in a pre-emptive discipline, the high priority arrival can displace a customer in service with lower priority. We also need to specify how to restart the service of an interrupted customer. For the pre-emptive resume discipline, the interrupted customer restarts from the point of interruption. For the pre-emptive repeat without re-sampling discipline the interrupted customer starts again with the original service time. For the pre-emptive repeat with re-sampling strategy, the interrupted customer starts again with a new service time. Note that for exponential service times, the pre-emptive resume and pre-emptive repeat with re-sampling disciplines are equivalent because of the memoryless property of the exponential distribution. However, the pre-emptive repeat without re-sampling discipline is different because a long service time is more likely to be interrupted and the system is clearly not memoryless.

Here, we will analyse the non-pre-emptive and the pre-emptive resume disciplines in the steady state. Our main aim is to determine the mean response time for each class of customer. We use the following notation:

$\rho_r = \lambda_r/\mu_r$ (i.e. the load for class r)
$U_r =$ probability that a class r customer is in service
$L_r =$ mean number of class r customers
$W_r =$ mean response time or mean waiting time for class r customers (i.e. the mean time that a class r customer spends in the system)
$L'_r =$ mean number of class r customers waiting for service
$W'_r =$ mean queueing time for class r customers (i.e. mean time that a class r customer spends queueing before entering service)

For non-saturation of any queue we require: $\rho_1 + \rho_2 + \ldots + \rho_R < 1$.

When a class r customer is in service, the departure rate is μ_r and so the overall departure rate of class r customers is $U_r\mu_r$ which must equal the arrival rate λ_r in the steady state. Thus we have $U_r = \rho_r$ and the probability that the server is idle is $1 - \rho_1 - \rho_2 - \ldots - \rho_R$.

By applying Little's result to class r customers we obtain two simple relationships between these variables, as in Chapter 5 for the M/G/1 queue:

$$L_r = \lambda_r W_r \tag{7.38}$$

$$L'_r = \lambda_r W'_r \tag{7.39}$$

Since the response time is the sum of the queueing time and the service time, we have

$$W_r = W'_r + 1/\mu_r \tag{7.40}$$

Suppose we let L denote the total number of customers in the system and λ denote the total arrival rate. Then $L = \sum_{r=1}^{R} L_r$ and $\lambda = \lambda_1 + \lambda_2 + \ldots + \lambda_R$. Applying Little's result to the system as a whole yields

$$W = \frac{L}{\lambda} = \sum_{r=1}^{R} \frac{L_r}{\lambda} = \sum_{r=1}^{R} \frac{\lambda_r W_r}{\lambda}$$

i.e.

$$W = \sum_{r=1}^{R} p_r W_r \tag{7.41}$$

where $p_r = \lambda_r / \lambda$ is the probability that an arrival is of class r (because the system is in the steady state with Poisson arrival streams). Thus the overall response time is the weighted sum of response times for each class.

These relationships apply to both non-pre-emptive and pre-emptive disciplines. First we consider the non-pre-emptive case.

7.7.1 Non-pre-emptive discipline

The total time that a class r customer spends in the system consists of a queueing time (mean W'_r) and a service time ($1/\mu_r$). For the non-pre-emptive discipline both of these times are contiguous because once a customer begins service it is not interrupted. The mean queueing time for a class r customer consists of three components whose means we define as:

(1) W_0: mean time spent waiting for the departure of the customer in service at the time of arrival

(2) A_r: mean time spent waiting for the departure of customers found waiting at the time of arrival and having higher or same priority (i.e. priorities $s = r, r + 1, \ldots, R$)

(3) B_r: mean delay caused by higher priority customers (i.e. priorities $s = r + 1, r + 2, \ldots, R$) arriving during the customer's queueing time (mean W'_r)

For each of these wait components we now derive expressions in terms of other variables.

(1) When a class r customer arrives it sees the system in equilibrium because the arrival stream is Poisson, and so we can invoke the Random Observer Property. Thus the probability that it finds a class s customer in service is $U_s = \rho_s$. The mean residual service time of the class s customer is $\mu_s M_{2s}/2$ and so wait component (1) is

$$W_0 = \sum_{s=1}^{R} \rho_s \mu_s M_{2s}/2 = \frac{1}{2} \sum_{s=1}^{R} \lambda_s M_{2s} \qquad (7.42)$$

(2) Again by the Random Observer Property, a class r arrival sees an average of L'_s class s customers waiting for service. Each class s customer requires a mean service time of $1/\mu_s$ time units. Waiting customers of class $1, 2, \ldots, r - 1$ are overtaken by class r customers, so we have

$$A_r = \sum_{s=r}^{R} \frac{1}{\mu_s} L'_s = \sum_{s=r}^{R} \rho_s W'_s \qquad (7.43)$$

using Equation (7.39) $L'_s = \lambda_s W'_s$.

(3) During the queueing time (mean W'_r) of a class r customer an average of $\lambda_s W'_r$ customers of class s arrive, each taking a mean of $1/\mu_s$ time units to serve. Arrivals of class $1, 2, \ldots, r$ do not affect the class r customer, and so we have

$$B_r = \sum_{s=r+1}^{R} \frac{1}{\mu_s} \lambda_s W'_r = W'_r \sum_{s=r+1}^{R} \rho_s \qquad (7.44)$$

Combining these results (Equations 7.42, 7.43 and 7.44), we obtain the following fixed point equation:

$$W'_r = W_0 + \sum_{s=r}^{R} \rho_s W'_s + W'_r \sum_{s=r+1}^{R} \rho_s$$

For the highest priority customers $(r = R)$, this becomes $W'_R = W_0 + \rho_R W'_R$ and so

$$W'_R = \frac{W_0}{1 - \rho_R}$$

For the next highest priority customers $(r = R - 1)$ the expression only involves W'_R and W'_{R-1}, and since we have a simple form for W'_R we can make W'_{R-1} the subject to obtain

$$W'_{R-1} = \frac{W_0}{(1 - \rho_R)(1 - \rho_R - \rho_{R-1})}$$

Successive substitution leads to **Cobham's formula** (Cobham 1954):

$$W'_r = \frac{W_0}{(1 - \sum_{s=r+1}^{R} \rho_s)(1 - \sum_{s=r}^{R} \rho_s)} \tag{7.45}$$

Once W'_r is known, the other performance measures are easy to determine by Little's result, i.e. Equations (7.38)–(7.40).

Cobham's formula shows that the waiting times for class r customers are influenced by lower priorities only through the mean residual service time (expressed through W_0). In addition, they are influenced by higher priorities through their total load $(\rho_{r+1} + \rho_{r+2} + \ldots + \rho_R)$.

As far as queueing times are concerned, class r customers effectively 'see' three types of customer: lower class $(1, 2, \ldots, r-1)$, same class (r) and higher class $(r+1, r+2, \ldots, R)$. The ordering of priorities within these types is immaterial to class r since only total load and W_0 are present in Cobham's formula.

The condition for non-saturation can be relaxed somewhat if we neglect those queues that are saturated. Suppose $\rho_v + \rho_{v+1} + \ldots + \rho_R < 1$ but $\rho_{v-1} + \rho_v + \ldots + \rho_R \geq 1$. Then in the steady state, the $R - v + 1$ high priority queues $(v, v+1, \ldots, R)$ are non-saturated and the remaining queues $(1, 2, \ldots, v-1)$ are saturated; they have infinite queues, so new arrivals are never served with probability one. Customers of class $v - 1$ that are at the front of the infinite queue do get served but customers of lower priority never get served (with probability one in each case). Cobham's formula still holds for the first $R - v + 1$ classes provided we alter the probability of class s being in service (U_s) as follows:

$$U_s = \rho_s \qquad\qquad s = v, v+1, \ldots, R$$
$$U_{v-1} = 1 - \rho_v - \rho_{v+1} - \ldots - \rho_R \tag{7.46}$$
$$U_s = 0 \qquad\qquad s = 1, 2, \ldots, v-2$$

So in Cobham's formula we only require the residual service time to be changed to

$$W_0 = \sum_{s=v-1}^{R} U_s \mu_s M_{2s}/2 \tag{7.47}$$

where U_s is defined as above, and the formula holds for $r = v$, $v + 1, \ldots, R$.

Example 7.2 (Shortest processing time first) ——————————

Suppose customers arrive at a queueing system as a Poisson stream with rate λ. The required service time for an arrival is x_1 with probability p and x_2 with probability q where $x_1 > x_2$ and $p + q = 1$. The queueing system gives non-pre-emptive priority to customers with the shorter service time. This is commonly called the non-pre-emptive shortest processing time first (SPT) discipline. We wish to find the condition for non-saturation for this system and the mean waiting time for customers requiring the different service times.

Let customers with service time x_1 be class 1 and customers with service time x_2 be class 2 so that class 2 customers have higher priority than class 1. Using the decomposition property (Proposition 4.15), class 1 and class 2 customers arrive as Poisson streams with rates $p\lambda$ and $q\lambda$ respectively. Thus the loads for class 1 and class 2 are $p\lambda x_1$ and $q\lambda x_2$, respectively, and for non-saturation we require

$$\lambda(px_1 + qx_2) < 1$$

Since class r service time is constant, its second moment is x_r^2 ($r = 1, 2$). Thus in the steady state the average residual service delay is given by

$$W_0 = \frac{\lambda}{2} M_2$$

where $M_2 = (px_1^2 + qx_2^2)$ is the second moment of overall service time.

Using Cobham's formula, we can write down an expression for the average waiting time for class 1 and class 2 customers:

$$W_2' = \frac{\lambda}{2} M_2/(1 - \lambda qx_2)$$

$$W_1' = \frac{\lambda}{2} M_2/\{(1 - \lambda qx_2)[1 - \lambda(qx_2 + px_1)]\}$$

This example can be extended easily to allow any number of classes with an arbitrary discrete distribution for the service times. In fact, it can be extended to the continuous case in the limit when there are continuous distribution functions for service times. In this case, the summation symbols in Cobham's formula become integrals.

7.7.2 Pre-emptive resume

We now turn our attention to the pre-emptive resume discipline. Unlike the non-pre-emptive case, the waiting times and service times are not, in general, contiguous (except for class R customers) because of interruptions caused by higher priority arrivals. However, we can dissect the total sojourn time for class r customers as follows:

average initial waiting time I_r = mean interval between arrival and start of service

average attendance time A_r = mean interval between start of service and completion

The average initial waiting time I_r can be derived easily by some simple observations. First, we can ignore customers of class $1, 2, \ldots, r - 1$ when analysing the performance of class r because class r customers always pre-empt any customers of lower priority. Furthermore, during the initial waiting time, it does not matter whether classes $r + 1, r + 2, \ldots, R$ are pre-emptive or not. This is because a class r customer starts service when there are no other class r customers in front and no higher priority customers in the system. Thus I_r in a pre-emptive system is the same as the W'_r in a non-pre-emptive system that has no classes $1, 2, \ldots, r - 1$. Thus from Cobham's formula (Equation 7.45) we have

$$I_r = \frac{W_{0r}}{(1 - \sum_{s=r+1}^{R} \rho_s)(1 - \sum_{s=r}^{R} \rho_s)} \tag{7.48}$$

where W_{0r} represents the residual service delay for classes $r, r + 1, \ldots, R$ only, i.e.

$$W_{0r} = \frac{1}{2} \sum_{s=r}^{R} \lambda_s M_{2s} \tag{7.49}$$

The attendance time for a class r customer is the sum of its service time and the service times of all higher priority customers that arrive during the attendance time. During this interval an average of $\lambda_s A_r$ class s ($s = r + 1, r + 2, \ldots, R$) customers arrive. Each of these higher priority customers requires an average service time of $1/\mu_s$ units. Thus the average attendance time is given by

$$A_r = \frac{1}{\mu_r} + \sum_{s=r+1}^{R} \frac{\lambda_s A_r}{\mu_s}$$

which simplifies to give

$$A_r = \frac{1}{\mu_r(1 - \sum_{s=r+1}^{R} \rho_s)} \tag{7.50}$$

These results give us enough information to obtain the mean waiting time since $W_r = I_r + A_r$ and $W'_r = I_r + A_r - 1/\mu_r$. The mean queue lengths are then also easy to determine using Little's result.

7.8   Quasi-reversibility

In Chapters 4 and 5 we looked at the properties of reversible systems, which have identical stochastic behaviour in both forward and reverse time. An analogous concept is **quasi-reversibility**, which applies to networks of queues and multi-class queues in a similar manner to that in which reversibility applies to single queues. We first consider a multi-class queue in isolation with customers of classes $r = 1, 2, \ldots, R$ and a state that follows a Markov process $X(t)$. At the very least, the state allows us to deduce the number of customers of each class in the queue, but may convey extra information. We treat this queueing system as a black box in a steady state with arrivals and departures that alter this state. Observe that given a realization of the process $X(t)$ over all t, we can determine the arrival times and departure times of all class r customers (i.e. the input and output processes for class r). We can do this because each arrival causes a state transition (upward jump in the number of customers) and similarly a departure causes the number of customers to drop by one. Such a queueing system is **quasi-reversible** if $X(t)$ is a stationary Markov process such that for all times t_0, the state $X(t_0)$ is independent of

(1)   the input process (or arrival times of class r) after t_0

(2)   the output process (or departure times of class r) before t_0

for all classes $r = 1, 2, \ldots, R$.

Thus for an M/M/1 queue with state-independent service rates, reversibility of the queue length process implies quasi-reversibility of the queue by Burke's theorem. However, in general, reversibility and quasi-reversibility are independent properties of stochastic processes in that neither property implies the other: despite the terminology, a reversible process is not necessarily quasi-reversible. For example, an M/M/1 queue, with state-dependent arrival rates and state-dependent service times, is reversible but not quasi-reversible. However, just as for reversible systems, a quasi-reversible system has the quasi-reversible property in both forward and reverse time (this follows directly from the definition). Also, we recall from Section 4.4 that a stochastic process is reversible if and only if the detailed balance equations hold. Similarly, if a queueing system is quasi-reversible then the local balance equations hold, as we are about to see.

7.8.1   Properties of quasi-reversible systems

Let $q(x, x')$ be the instantaneous transition rate from state x to state x' in forward time. Similarly, let $q'(x, x')$ be the instantaneous transition rate of the reversed process (i.e. from state x to state x' in reverse time). For a multi-class queue, let $S(r, x)$ be the set of all states with one more class r customer than in state x. Thus any state transition of the form $x \to x' \in S(r, x)$ indicates an arrival of a class r customer. Also, any state transition of the form $x' \to x$ where $x' \in S(r, x)$ indicates a departure of a class r customer.

Proposition 7.3

If a queueing system is quasi-reversible, then the following properties hold:

(1)   the input processes for the set of classes are independent Poisson processes

(2)   the output processes for the set of classes are independent Poisson processes

Proof For a quasi-reversible queue, the probability of a class r arrival in the small interval $(t_0, t_0 + h)$ is independent of the state $X(t_0)$ and so the instantaneous class r arrival rate, i.e. the probability intensity, $\alpha(r)$ say, of a class r arrival when the state is x, depends only on r, and not on x:

$$\alpha(r) = \sum_{x' \in S(r,x)} q(x, x') \tag{7.51}$$

Since $X(t)$ is a Markov process, the realization of $X(t)$ up to time t_0 (and hence all arrival times before t_0) tells us nothing more than what the state $X(t_0)$ tells us about the process $X(t)$ after time t_0. The probability intensity of a class r arrival is, therefore, $\alpha(r)$ even if we know all the class r arrival times before time t_0. Thus the time to the next class r arrival after time t_0 is memoryless and so must have the exponential distribution with mean $1/\alpha(r)$. Hence the arrival times of class r customers form an independent Poisson process. This proves part (1).

Now consider the reversed process $X(-t)$. Since the queue $X(t)$ is quasi-reversible, so is the reversed queue $X(-t)$. Thus by (1), the arrival times of class r customers at the queue $X(-t)$ form an independent Poisson process. The arrivals at the reversed queue $X(-t)$ after time $-t_0$ correspond to departures from queue $X(t)$ before time t_0. Thus the departure times of class r customers at the queue $X(t)$ form an independent Poisson process. ∎

How can we tell if a given queue is quasi-reversible? The Poisson input and output processes give a clue, but they do not guarantee that the queue is quasi-reversible. The state of the queue must be described by a Markov process $X(t)$. Often it is best to prove quasi-reversibility directly from the definition. First, by the definition of $X(t)$ we can show that $X(t_0)$ is independent of arrivals after t_0. Then we consider the reversed queue $X(-t)$ and try to show that $X(t_0)$ is independent of departures before t_0. This would then show quasi-reversibility. For example, consider a single class queue with Poisson arrivals. Suppose the state of the queue is a reversible Markov process that is independent of future arrivals (like an M/M/1 queue with state-independent rates). In reverse time, $X(-t_0)$ is independent of arrivals after $-t_0$, and so the queue is quasi-reversible.

Proposition 7.4

A quasi-reversible Markov queue $X(t)$ satisfies the local balance equations.

Proof In the steady state, the class r departure rate of the reversed queue $X(-t)$ is the same as the class r arrival rate at the queue $X(t)$, which we have already shown (Equation 7.51):

$$\alpha(r) = \sum_{x' \in S(r,x)} q(x, x')$$

Similarly, the arrival rate of the reversed queue $X(-t)$ is given by

$$\alpha(r) = \sum_{x' \in S(r,x)} q'(x, x') \tag{7.52}$$

The Equations (7.51) and (7.52) characterize the quasi-reversibility property of a Markov process. Let $\pi(x)$ be the equilibrium probability that the queueing system $X(t)$ is in state x. Then the transition rates $q'(x, x')$ of the reversed queue $X(-t)$ are given by (from Section 4.4)

$$\pi(x)q'(x, x') = \pi(x')q(x', x) \tag{7.53}$$

Summing over $x' \in S(r, x)$ we obtain the local balance equations:

$$\pi(x) \sum_{x' \in S(r,x)} q(x, x') = \sum_{x' \in S(r,x)} \pi(x')q(x', x) \tag{7.54}$$

■

The local balance equations for a set A (also called the partial balance equations) are defined as

$$\pi(x) \sum_{x' \in A} q(x, x') = \sum_{x' \in A} \pi(x')q(x', x) \qquad \text{for all states } x \qquad (7.55)$$

For a multi-class queue, we normally have $A = S(r, x)$ but this definition is more general. Here are some properties of local balance:

(1)   In terms of probability fluxes, satisfying the local balance equations means that the probability flux out of state x caused by a class r arrival is the same as the probability flux into state x caused by a class r departure. This shows that a class r arrival 'sees' the same distribution of states as that left behind by a class r departure.

(2)   Suppose we increase the transition rates for certain transitions by a factor $a > 0$, as follows:

$$q_a(x, y) = aq(x, y) \qquad x \in A \text{ and } y \in S - A$$

where S is the set of all states. Then (with normalizing constant G):

$$\pi_a(x) = \pi(x)/G \qquad \text{for } x \in A$$
$$\pi_a(x) = a\pi(x)/G \qquad \text{for } x \in S - A$$

if and only if local balance is satisfied for the set A.

(3)   Suppose X_A is the Markov chain formed by observing the process just before leaving A and let Y_A be the corresponding chain formed by observing the process just after entering A. Then X_A and Y_A have the same distribution if and only if local balance is satisfied for the set A.

These properties of local balance, which we stated without proof, provide a basis for many useful properties of product form queueing networks, such as the arrival theorem for BCMP networks.

7.8.2 Open networks of quasi-reversible queueing nodes

Many properties of open product form queueing networks are based on the underlying quasi-reversible property of the queues. For a queueing network of nodes, we introduce a subscript i to the variables used for the quasi-reversible queue to indicate the node label. For example, we have for node i in isolation:

$\pi_i(x_i) = $ the steady state probability that node i is in state x_i

$q_i(x_i, x_i') = $ probability intensity of a transition from state x_i to state $x_i' \in S(r, x_i)$ caused by class r arrival at node i

$\alpha_i(r) = $ probability intensity of class r arrivals at node i (given by Equation 7.51)

Customers of type c pass along a given route over the network with rate $\lambda(c)$, and at stage s of the route have class $r = (c, s)$. For Poisson external arrivals, the state of a network of quasi-reversible nodes forms a Markov process $X(t) = (x_1(t), x_2(t), \ldots, x_M(t))$. Note that when the nodes are put into a network, they may lose their quasi-reversible property. Below we obtain some of the properties that can be proved by the quasi-reversible property of nodes in isolation. The standard method of deriving many queueing theory results using quasi-reversible properties follows these steps:

(1)   consider a particular node i in isolation

(2)   assume that when it is put into a network of queueing nodes, it behaves as if all the nodes are in isolation

(3)   under the isolation assumption, guess the transition rates $q'(x, x')$ for the reversed process for the network of nodes

(4)   hence guess a product form solution and show Proposition 4.25 holds

Recall, for step (4), that we need to show for state space S:

(i)   for $x \in S$, $q'(x) = q(x)$, where $q'(x) = \sum_{x' \neq x} q'(x, x')$ and $q(x) = \sum_{x' \neq x} q(x, x')$

(ii)   for $x, x' \in S$, $\pi(x)q(x, x') = \pi(x')q'(x', x)$

Proposition 7.5

For multi-class open networks of quasi-reversible queueing nodes, the following properties hold:

(a)   the states of the individual nodes are independent

(b)   the stationary state distribution has a product form

(c)   the distribution of states seen by an arrival is the equilibrium state distribution and is the same as if the node were in isolation with Poisson inputs

(d)   the open network as a whole is quasi-reversible, which implies that departures are also Poisson

Proof We have proved (a), (b) and (c) directly for the single class queueing networks in Chapter 6. Here we provide an outline; for a more detailed proof see Kelly (1979). The arrivals to a node are external arrivals (i.e. from an external Poisson source) or internal arrivals (caused by a departure at some other node). Whereas in the isolated node, the arrivals are triggered by a Poisson process, for the node in a network the internal arrivals are caused by a more general stochastic process that is not necessarily Poisson. The probability intensity that a class r' customer leaves node i and joins node j causing state transition $x_i' \in S(r', x_i)$ to x_i for node i and x_j to $x_j' \in S(r, x_j)$ for node j is

$$q_i(x_i', x_i) \frac{q_j(x_j, x_j')}{\sum_{x' \in S(r, x_j)} q_j(x_j, x')} = \frac{q_i(x_i', x_i) q_j(x_j, x_j')}{\alpha_j(r)}$$

by using Equation (7.51).

Now we consider the reversed process and guess that customers enter the system backwards along their routes. In reverse time, the probability intensity that a customer of class r moves from node j to node i causing state transition $x_j' \in S(r, x_j)$ to x_j for node j and x_i to $x_i' \in S(r', x_i)$ at node i is

$$q_j'(x_j', x_j) \frac{q_i'(x_i, x_i')}{\sum_{x' \in S(r', x_i)} q_i'(x_i, x')} = \frac{q_j'(x_j', x_j) q_i'(x_i, x_i')}{\alpha_i(r')}$$

by using Equation (7.52).

This is suggested by a product form solution for the equilibrium probabilities:

$$\pi(x_1, x_2, \ldots, x_M) = \pi(x_1)\pi(x_2) \ldots \pi(x_M)$$

To show part (ii) of step (4) we need to show

$$\pi_i(x_i')\pi_j(x_j) \frac{q_i(x_i', x_i) q_j(x_j, x_j')}{\alpha_j(r)} =$$

$$\pi_i(x_i)\pi_j(x_j') \frac{q_j'(x_j', x_j) q_i'(x_i, x_i')}{\alpha_i(r')}$$

This holds by Equation (7.53) and the fact that $\alpha_j(r) = \alpha_i(r') = \lambda(c)$ where $r = (c, s + 1)$ and $r' = (c, s)$, i.e. node i is at stage s and node j is at stage $s + 1$. The condition (ii) also holds for external arrivals and departures.

It is easy to show that condition (i) also holds and so the product form solution is correct.

The form of the reversed process can be used to derive the arrival theorem for open networks as follows. The probability flux that a customer of class r' leaves node i in state x_i is

$$\sum_{x_i' \in S(r', x_i)} \pi_i(x_i') q_i(x_i', x_i) = \pi_i(x_i) \alpha_i(r')$$

by using Equations (7.53) and (7.52). Thus class r' customers leave a node in state x_i with probability $\pi_i(x_i)$. Similarly, by considering the reversed process, we can show that customers arriving at a node see the node in state x_i with probability $\pi_i(x_i)$.

∎

7.8.3 Closed networks of quasi-reversible queueing nodes

For closed networks, the number of customers in the network remains fixed, but customers can change class as they move from one node to the next. The traffic model is similar to the one for open networks, only that when a customer completes service at the last node on its route, it recycles to start at the first node on its route. General routing is achieved by allowing a customer to change routes with some fixed probability, but still remain within the same routing chain. Then the number of customers in a closed routing chain remains fixed. As we have seen, the traffic equations for a closed network do not have a unique solution, so we have to use visitation rates (to solve for the isolated nodes).

Proposition 7.6

For closed networks of quasi-reversible nodes, the following properties hold:

(a)   the stationary state distribution is a product form:

$$\pi(x_1, x_2, \ldots, x_M) = \pi(x_1)\pi(x_2) \ldots \pi(x_M)/G$$

(b)   the distribution of states seen by an arrival is the equilibrium state distribution of the network obtained with the arrival removed from the system. This is the arrival theorem.

(c)   under time reversal, the system becomes another closed network of quasi-reversible nodes.

Proof These properties can be derived in a similar way to the open network case. The probability intensities for the open network are unchanged for the closed network (since now all arrivals to a node are internal arrivals) and so the product form solution is just as easy to prove. Similar arguments hold for the arrival theorem but now the state seen by arrivals has one fewer customer, since the network is closed. For a detailed proof see Kelly (1979).

∎

The BCMP nodes (IS, PS, LCFS-PR, etc.) are quasi-reversible and so give a product form solution. Also, all symmetric queueing disciplines are quasi-reversible. Some of the assumptions made here can be relaxed without losing these properties. Many of these extensions and derivations of the properties are described in Kelly (1979).

SUMMARY

- There are a number of alternatives to the exponential service time distribution (such as the hyperexponential, hypoexponential and Coxian distributions), which allow us to specify higher moments but still maintain the memoryless property.

- Nodes with various service disciplines (including FCFS, PS, IS and LCFS) have similar steady state behaviour when an isolated node is subjected to a Poisson arrival stream with multiple classes. BCMP networks are constructed from these types of nodes and certain nodes (PS, IS and LCFS) can have general service time distributions (which can be distinct for each class).

- For multiple class networks, quite general routing behaviour can be represented by using the notion of routing chains. BCMP networks can have multiple routing chains (some open and others closed) and customers within a routing chain can change class probabilistically.

- The BCMP theorem states that BCMP networks have a product form solution. Many extensions have been proposed for the original BCMP theorem.

- There are many computational algorithms to solve BCMP networks, including the convolution algorithm and the mean value analysis algorithm.

- The BCMP theorem does not handle classes with priority, but a mean value analysis of isolated nodes with priority classes provides some useful results.

- Many of the classical results of product form queueing networks follow from the quasi-reversibility properties of isolated nodes. The proofs are often more succinct and more general than in the standard approach. Moreover, they provide many valuable insights that suggest ways of relaxing some assumptions and extending some of the classical results.

EXERCISES

7.1   (20 Overall service time distribution)
Consider a multi-class queue with arrivals of class r ($r = 1, 2, \ldots, R$) that form a Poisson stream with rate λ_r and service time with mean $1/\mu_r$ and variance v_r. Suppose we want to

approximate this by a single class M/G/1 queue by finding the mean and variance of the service time. Let X_r be the service time for a class r customer and let Z be the overall service time. Show that if

$$p_r = \lambda_r \left(\sum_{r=1}^{R} \lambda_r \right)^{-1}$$

then

(a) $E[Z^n] = \sum_{r=1}^{R} p_r E[X_r^n]$

(b)   For $R = 2$, $\mathrm{Var}[Z] = p_1 v_1 + p_2 v_2 + p_1 p_2 (1/\mu_1 - 1/\mu_2)^2$

7.2   (30 Gamma distribution)
The probability density function for the gamma distribution with parameters $\beta > 0$ and $\alpha > 0$ is

$$f(x) = \frac{\alpha(\alpha x)^{\beta-1} e^{-\alpha x}}{\Gamma(\beta)} \qquad \text{for } x \geq 0 \text{ and } 0 \text{ otherwise}$$

where $\Gamma(\beta)$ is the gamma function

$$\Gamma(\beta) = \int_0^\infty x^{\beta-1} e^{-x} \, dx$$

(a)   Show that $\Gamma(k) = (k-1)!$ for $k = 1, 2, \ldots$ and hence, by looking at density functions, show that the Erlang-k distribution is a special form of the gamma distribution. (Hint: show that $\Gamma(k+1) = k\Gamma(k)$ for $k > 0$.)

(b)   A random variable Y has mean $m_Y > 0$ and square of variation coefficient (svc) $c_Y^2 > 0$. Show how to set the parameters of the gamma distribution to give the same mean and svc.

     (Note that the Laplace transform for the gamma density is $L(s) = [\alpha/(\alpha + s)]^\beta$.)

(c)   If $c_Y^2 > 1$, show how an Erlang distribution with parameters k and μ can approximate the mean and svc of the random variable Y.

7.3   (20 Coxian distribution)
Consider a random variable Y with mean $1/\mu$ and square of variation coefficient $c^2 \geq \frac{1}{2}$. Marie's method suggests that Y can be approximated by X, the random variable for the two-stage Coxian model with parameters $\mu_1 = 2\mu$, $\mu_2 = \mu/c^2$, and probability of entering the second stage $b_1 = 1/(2c^2)$. Show that $E[X] = 1/\mu$ and svc $(X) = c^2$.

7.4   (30 PS node)

Show that the equilibrium probability given by Equation (7.9) satisfies the corresponding balance equations for a multi-class PS node in isolation with independent Poisson arrival streams and distinct exponential service time distributions.

7.5   (30 IS node)

Show that the equilibrium probability given by Equation (7.12) satisfies the corresponding balance equations for a multi-class IS node in isolation with independent Poisson arrival streams and distinct exponential service time distributions.

Chapter 8
Approximate Methods

8.1 Decomposition   300   8.3 Diffusion approximation   328
8.2 Fixed point methods   322   8.4 Maximum entropy
                                           methods   337

Modellers of a computer or communication system have several tools available, based on either analytical or simulation modelling techniques. On the one hand, they may use a product form queueing network model, or perhaps they may attempt an original mathematical model. For today's complex systems, they are likely to encounter problems that make the model either mathematically or computationally intractable. On the other hand, if a detailed model of a complex system were required, a modeller could write a simulation program. This gives a very general model, but the simulation results are approximate and need to be given with confidence intervals because they are based on actual sample paths. We can view simulation and analytical methods as complementary techniques. The modelling technique chosen depends on the system being modelled and the type of questions that need answering.

Once an analytical model is defined by abstracting away the less important details of the system (i.e. once the normal abstraction approximations are made), we normally need to make further approximations to permit a solution (i.e. make the model more mathematically tractable). If a solution is possible but computationally intractable, we make further approximations to the algorithm to get a faster solution. For example, approximate models are required when we want to model explicitly certain features that make a queueing network non-product form or when we want to reduce the computation time for obtaining a solution. Such models give insight into the problem at an early stage and so are vital tools to the modeller. In this chapter, we focus on the approximate methods that make analytical models more mathematically or computationally tractable.

Certain features prevent a queueing network from having a product form solution and we now highlight some of the more important problem areas. One common feature that we want to represent explicitly in our model is the effect of **passive resources**. A resource that actively serves customers in the sense of completing some of their service demand is called an **active resource** (e.g. a processor). On the other hand, a resource that must be held by a customer at an active resource before that resource can provide service, is called a passive resource. Memory is the most obvious example of a passive resource that is needed by the processor, the active resource. A similar phenomenon is **simultaneous resource possession** in which a customer holds more than one resource at the same time; for example, a disk and a channel. Finite buffers at queues cause blocking or lost customers and can also be considered as passive resources, but are generally treated separately (see Chapter 10). Priority scheduling disciplines can greatly affect the performance of a system, but they too make networks have non-product form. We sometimes want to relax the distributional assumptions and allow FCFS service centres with a general service time distribution or exponential service time distribution with class-dependent rates. The resulting networks again have no product form solution.

How can we justify the use of approximate methods? Generally it is difficult to get bounds on errors or to do much error analysis, often because the method is *ad hoc*. More fundamentally, a precise error analysis would facilitate better approximation in the first place. Approximate performance prediction can range from first order approximations to highly accurate results. For some methods, a degree of formal justification is possible in terms of problem structure (e.g. decomposition methods). Generally, however, we just appeal to intuition or rely on the success of the method in other areas of applied science. In many cases, we can use simulation to validate certain parameterized models of interest but this cannot give precise error bounds for a wide range of parameters. So the modelling methodology is iterative; each iteration starts with an approximate analytical model and ends with validation with respect to simulation. Ultimately, validation of any model must be with respect to the operational system it represents.

The remainder of this chapter is organized as follows. The first part considers the decomposition method and an interactive system with paging is used as an example. We then consider fixed point methods, in particular iterative methods based on the MVA algorithm. This is followed by diffusion approximations for heavy traffic and transient behaviour of systems. Finally, we look at maximum entropy methods for solving a variety of general queueing networks.

8.1 Decomposition

Decomposition is one of the most widely used approximate methods and is sometimes called the hierarchical method or the flow-equivalence method. One reason for its popularity is that intuitive justification is often clear when the model is a Markovian non-product form queueing network, as we will see later. The method is particularly useful when isolated features cannot be represented in product form networks, such as networks with global state dependence, contention for passive resources or blocking. Typically, the decomposition method gives a good approximation when the network is almost product form. It also gives surprisingly good results even when many product form criteria are violated. In product form networks, the decomposition is exact as we saw in the FES method. We will use single class networks as examples, but the method extends to the multi-class case.

The decomposition method is analogous to the divide-and-conquer technique that is popular with software engineers. The general approach of decomposition methods for queueing networks follows these steps:

(1)   decompose the network into appropriate sub-networks

(2)   solve each sub-network independently

(3)   aggregate the sub-network solutions to form an approximate solution of the entire network

(4)   validate the aggregate solution with a simulation model

Note that we are validating the model with respect to a simulation model to determine the accuracy of the approximation. We assume that the model already captures the essential features of the real system, so the approximations made in the abstraction are validated with respect to the actual system. Here we are really validating the approximations made in decomposing the network.

How can we separate the network into appropriate sub-networks? There are two extreme cases: each sub-network has one node or the entire network has just one sub-network (itself). Neither one makes any progress. Informally, we identify groups of service centres that are tightly coupled amongst themselves and loosely coupled with the rest of the network. By this we mean that when a customer enters a sub-network it stays in the service centres within the sub-network for a large expected time before leaving; this is enough time for the sub-network to approach a steady state. More precisely, we require a mean time between transitions that keep a customer in a sub-network to be much smaller than for transitions between different sub-networks. So within the sub-network we capture the short-term dynamics and between sub-networks we capture the long-term dynamics. Now we can decompose a network along those boundaries of the loosely coupled sub-networks and treat the sub-networks independently.

8.1.1 Decomposition of a Markov process

Decomposition is one of the few approximation techniques for queueing networks with a sound theoretical basis. First we will justify the method informally in terms of a Markov process before presenting a more rigorous version. This gives a theoretical basis in cases where the underlying process is Markovian. Sometimes the model cannot be represented as a finite state Markov process, but the decomposition method can sometimes still be applied. So even for more general situations that are non-Markovian, decomposition can give valuable insights. Much of this material is based on the general theory of decomposition presented by Courtois (1977).

First, let us informally define the term **nearly completely decomposable** (NCD). A Markov process is NCD if its transition rate matrix is almost block diagonal (after identical permutations of rows and columns). In other words, the off-block diagonal elements are small compared to block diagonal elements. Thus transitions between intra-block states occur more frequently than between inter-block states.

Suppose the queueing network model has an underlying Markov process that is NCD. We first make the rate matrix block diagonal, which corresponds to splitting the network into sub-networks. This is done by omitting the off-block diagonal elements in the rate matrix. Then we modify each block submatrix separately to obtain legitimate transition rate matrices with row sums of zero. This means that any state transition out of a block immediately enters the same block again. Note that it is difficult to find exactly which state to re-enter without solving for the exact steady state probabilities, but some good heuristics are possible. We look at one such method in Example 8.1.

Now we can solve the modified Markov process using the following steps. We compute the stationary distribution for each submatrix (i.e. block). Suppose this gives us the intra-block stationary probabilities, $\pi(m|n)$ for submatrix n (i.e. block n) with state m. This shows the short-term dynamics of customers in the network. Now we reinstate the original off-block diagonal elements to construct an approximate inter-block transition rate matrix. The resulting process has one state for each block. We compute the stationary distribution for the aggregated process and let $\pi(n)$ be the equilibrium probability for block n. This shows the long-term behaviour of customers in the network. The approximate complete solution is then given by $\pi(m|n)\pi(n) = \pi(m, n)$. We will show that the error tends to 0 as all off-block diagonal entries tend to 0.

Justification of decomposition

We now turn our attention to a more rigorous justification of decomposition (as described in Gelembe and Mitrani (1980)) than the one just described. Throughout this section we will be analysing the Markov chain with state space S and state transition matrix $P = (p(n, m)|n, m \in S)$ where $p(n, m)$ is the probability of a state transition from state n to state m. Elements of S are state vectors of the form $n = (n_1, n_2, \ldots, n_M)$ and describe the state of a closed queueing network with M service centres and population K. The vector n_i describes the state of service centre i (cf. the state of a multi-class queueing network in the previous chapter). The number n_i of customers at centre i can be deduced from the state of the centre (i.e. $n_i = f(n_i)$ for some function f). We assume the underlying Markov chain is aperiodic, irreducible and positive recurrent.

Let $\tau = \{\tau_1, \tau_2, \ldots, \tau_l\}$ be a partition of the service centres $\{1, 2, \ldots, M\}$ for some $l = 2, 3, \ldots, M - 1$. For example, for $M = 3$ and $l = 2$ we can have $\tau = \{\{1, 2\}, \{3\}\}$.

Definition 8.1 (τ-equivalence)

Two state vectors n and m are **τ-equivalent**, or **n-τ-m**, if and only if

$$\forall \text{ partitions } j: \sum_{i \in \tau_j} n_i = \sum_{i \in \tau_j} m_i$$

In words, **n-τ-m** means that in each subset τ_i in the partition τ, the number of customers is the same for states n and m (the distribution of customers within each subset is ignored). For example, for $\tau = \{\{1, 2\}, \{3\}\}$, the states $(1, 2, 3)$ and $(0, 3, 3)$ are τ-equivalent, but the states $(1, 2, 3)$ and $(1, 1, 4)$ are not τ-equivalent. The relation τ is an equivalence relation over states. Thus τ induces a partition t of the set of states n in $S:\{t_1, t_2, \ldots, t_k\}$ for some $k \geqslant 1$, defined by:

$$n, m \in t_i \text{ for some } i = 1, 2, \ldots, k \text{ iff } n\text{-}\tau\text{-}m$$

If two state vectors n and m are not τ-equivalent then they must be in different subsets t_i and t_j $(i \neq j)$ of the partition t. Each state belongs to exactly one subset of the partition, so for state n, we define a mapping function t that returns the subset t_i for some i:

$$t(n) = t_i \text{ iff } \forall m \in t_i: n\text{-}\tau\text{-}m$$

We refer to all states in the subset t_i of the partition t as a block of states, or block i.

Definition 8.2 (Nearly completely decomposable)

A Markov chain with transition matrix P is **nearly completely decomposable** (NCD) on a partition t if for each pair of states (n, m) in a subset t_i

$$p(n, m) \gg \sum_{m' \notin t_i} p(n, m')$$

In words, state transitions within a block of states are much more likely than others. For a closed queueing network, each block represents a fixed number of customers at each group of service centres given by τ. For simplicity, we assume the probability of a transition from state n to m (where $n, m \in t_i$), without passing through some other state $m' \notin t_i$, is non-zero.

Example 8.1(a) (NCD matrix) ────────────────────────────

Consider the following state transition matrix for a simple Markov chain with states $\{1, 2, 3, 4\}$.

$$P = \begin{bmatrix} \frac{1}{2} & \frac{3}{8} & \frac{1}{16} & \frac{1}{16} \\ \frac{7}{16} & \frac{7}{16} & 0 & \frac{1}{8} \\ \frac{1}{16} & 0 & \frac{1}{2} & \frac{7}{16} \\ 0 & \frac{1}{16} & \frac{3}{8} & \frac{9}{16} \end{bmatrix}$$

For the partition $t = \{\{1, 2\}, \{3, 4\}\}$, P is NCD because the within-block transition probabilities are all close to $\frac{1}{2}$ and the out of block transition probability is at most $\frac{1}{8}$. The block matrix P' is obtained by omitting the off-block diagonal elements:

$$P' = \begin{bmatrix} \frac{1}{2} & \frac{3}{8} & 0 & 0 \\ \frac{7}{16} & \frac{7}{16} & 0 & 0 \\ 0 & 0 & \frac{1}{2} & \frac{7}{16} \\ 0 & 0 & \frac{3}{8} & \frac{9}{16} \end{bmatrix}$$

Since the row elements do not sum to one, we have to modify them to get a stochastic matrix. This is the main approximation in the decomposition method.

───

Definition 8.3 (Block diagonal matrix)

For a Markov chain with transition matrix P, a **block diagonal matrix**, $B = (b(n, m)|n, m \in S)$ with respect to partition mapping t is a stochastic matrix over the state space where

$$b(n, m) = 0 \quad \text{if } m \notin t(n)$$

$$\sum_{m \in t(n)} b(n, m) = 1$$

The block diagonal matrix B has the following form when the states are enumerated appropriately:

$$B = \begin{bmatrix} B_1 & & & 0 \\ & B_2 & & \\ & & \ddots & \\ 0 & & & B_k \end{bmatrix}$$

since $b(n, m) \neq 0$ iff $m \in t(n)$ and B_i corresponds to state transitions within subset t_i. One way of modifying the transition matrix P to obtain a block diagonal matrix B is as follows:

$$b(n, m) = \begin{cases} p(n, m)\left(\sum_{m' \in t(n)} p(n, m') \right)^{-1} & \text{if } m \in t(n) \\ 0 & \text{if } m \notin t(n) \end{cases} \qquad (8.1)$$

i.e. we just renormalize the rows of P'.

We need to solve for p in $p = pP$ with $\sum_n p_n = 1$ where p_n is the element in p that corresponds to state n. Our approximation is given by a solution for b in:

$$b = bB$$

$$\sum_{n \in S} b_n = 1 \qquad (8.2)$$

where $b = (b_n | n \in S)$.

Since B is block diagonal, there is no unique solution for this system of equations. We need k more equations to be able to get an approximation b. This we can do in the next phase of the approximation by relating the inter-block elements. However, each submatrix B_i is a stochastic matrix by construction, so we can solve for each submatrix separately. This gives us an approximation for the steady state probabilities conditional on being in a particular block. Let b'_n be the equilibrium state probability of state $n \in t_i$ given that the chain is in the subset t_i. Let $b' = (b'_n | n \in S)$ so that we have the following set of equations:

$$b' = b'B$$

$$\sum_{n \in t_i} b'_n = 1 \quad \text{for } i = 1, 2, \ldots, k \qquad (8.3)$$

These equations have a unique solution; cf. the steady state theorem.

Example 8.1(b) (Block diagonal matrix) _____

Consider the matrix in Example 8.1(a) under the partition $t = \{\{1, 2\}, \{3, 4\}\}$. The partial sums of the first row of P are $\frac{7}{8}$ and $\frac{1}{8}$, and the same for the second row. The partial sums of the third row are $\frac{1}{16}$ and $\frac{15}{16}$, and the same for the last row. Omitting the off-block diagonal elements of P and dividing by the partial row sum gives the corresponding block diagonal matrix according to the definition above:

$$B = \begin{bmatrix} \frac{4}{7} & \frac{3}{7} & 0 & 0 \\ \frac{1}{2} & \frac{1}{2} & 0 & 0 \\ 0 & 0 & \frac{8}{15} & \frac{7}{15} \\ 0 & 0 & \frac{2}{5} & \frac{3}{5} \end{bmatrix}$$

This is one way of constructing a block diagonal matrix. What we are effectively doing to each row is taking the sum of the off-block probabilities (states 3 and 4 for row 1) and distributing them over the within-block probabilities (states 1 and 2 for row 1). It is this modification that is approximate in the decomposition technique.

Now the solution for $b' = b'B$ with normalizing condition $b_1' + b_2' = 1$ and $b_3' + b_4' = 1$ has a unique solution $b' = (\frac{7}{13}, \frac{6}{13}, \frac{6}{13}, \frac{7}{13})$. So the stationary probability that the chain is in state 1, given that the chain is in subset $t_1 = \{1, 2\}$, is $\frac{7}{13}$. We refer to the elements in b' as the conditional probabilities.

_____

This gives us only the conditional probabilities; we still need k more equations to obtain b. First we need to define some more terms.

Definition 8.4 (Lumpable matrix)

A stochastic matrix $A = (a(n, m) | n, m \in S)$, with same dimension as P, is a **lumpable matrix** on a partition $t = \{t_1, t_2, \ldots, t_k\}$ if $\forall 1 \leq i, j \leq k$, $n, n' \in t_i$,

$$\sum_{m \in t_j} a(n, m) = \sum_{m \in t_j} a(n', m)$$

In words, this means that all the rows n of A, restricted to a particular set of states t_i, have the same partial sums with respect to all sets in the partition. If A has this property then we can construct the **lumped matrix** A_t from A such that $A_t = (\alpha(i, j) | 1 \leq i, j \leq k)$ is a $k \times k$ stochastic matrix defined by

$$\alpha(i, j) = \sum_{m \in t_j} a(n, m) \qquad \text{for any } n \in t_i \tag{8.4}$$

Example 8.1(c) (Lumped matrices) ──────────────────────────

Consider the matrix P in Example 8.1(a), which is lumpable on
$t = \{(1, 2), (3, 4)\}$:

$$
P = \begin{bmatrix}
\frac{1}{2} & \frac{3}{8} & \frac{1}{16} & \frac{1}{16} \\
\frac{7}{16} & \frac{7}{16} & 0 & \frac{1}{8} \\
\frac{1}{16} & 0 & \frac{1}{2} & \frac{7}{16} \\
0 & \frac{1}{16} & \frac{3}{8} & \frac{9}{16}
\end{bmatrix}
$$

The partial sums of each row in a block are the same, so we get another
stochastic matrix:

$$
P_t = \begin{bmatrix}
\frac{7}{8} & \frac{1}{8} \\
\frac{1}{16} & \frac{15}{16}
\end{bmatrix}
$$

P_t is called the lumped matrix of P on t.

──

Now let us consider the block diagonal matrix B. This is lumpable on
$t = \{t_1, t_2, \ldots, t_k\}$ because all the non-zero elements in each row are in
the same block and these elements sum to one, by construction. Thus B_t
is the $k \times k$ identity matrix.

In the following analysis we assume P is lumpable on t with
lumped matrix P_t. When it is not lumpable we can split it into lumpable
and non-lumpable parts and follow a similar analysis. We will not
pursue the non-lumpable case (since this involves further splitting into
lumpable and non-lumpable matrices until the non-lumpable matrix is
small) and refer the interested reader to Courtois (1977). Let p^t be the
probability row vector that is a solution of

$$
p^t P_t = p^t
$$
$$
\sum_{i=1}^{k} p_i^t = 1 \tag{8.5}
$$

These are the balance equations for the process with k aggregate states.
The ith element of p^t, p_i^t is the equilibrium probability of finding the
chain in a state $n \in t_i$. Thus we can use the following to obtain the
additional k equations:

$$
p_i^t = \sum_{n \in t_i} b_n \tag{8.6}
$$

Thus we can find a solution for b in $b = bB$ (i.e. Equation 8.2). The solution must be unique because each submatrix B_i in B is a stochastic matrix and Equation (8.6) provides the normalizing condition.

Since the lumped matrix gives us the stationary probability (p_i^t) that the chain is in a particular block, we can simply multiply this by the conditional probability (b_n') that was obtained from Equation (8.3) and thereby obtain b. This approach gives

$$b_n = p_i^t b_n' \quad \text{where } n \in t_i \tag{8.7}$$

Example 8.1(d) (Approximate solution) ─────────────────────────

Solving $p^t P_t = p^t$ for our running example gives solution $p^t = (\frac{1}{3}, \frac{2}{3})$ after normalizing. So combining with the conditional probability $b' = (\frac{7}{13}, \frac{6}{13}, \frac{6}{13}, \frac{7}{13})$ gives the following solution: $b = (\frac{7}{39}, \frac{2}{13}, \frac{4}{13}, \frac{14}{39})$ as an approximation for p.

───

Errors are introduced when we estimate p by b using the k additional equations. Clearly, we can write P in terms of B and $E = (e(n, m) | n, m \in S)$ as

$$P = B + \varepsilon E \tag{8.8}$$

where

$$e(n, m) = [p(n, m) - b(n, m)]/\varepsilon \tag{8.9}$$

for any $\varepsilon > 0$. So E is the matrix of relative differences between P and B, with respect to some ε.

Suppose we let $\varepsilon = \max_{n,m} |p(n, m) - b(n, m)|$. Because P and B are stochastic matrices, the rows of E must sum to 0 and, by definition, $|e(n, m)| \leqslant 1$ for all n, m. Now we have (for all ε):

$$p = pP = p(B + \varepsilon E) = pB + \varepsilon pE$$

Let $p = b + \delta$ where δ is the error vector. Then we have

$$b + \delta = (b + \delta)B + \varepsilon pE$$

Since $b = bB$, this becomes

$$\delta = \delta B + \varepsilon pE \tag{8.10}$$

Consider the equation $B = P - \varepsilon E$ (from Equation 8.8). We think of a fixed P and a fixed E and see how B varies with ε. Clearly, $B \to P$ as $\varepsilon \to 0$, so the approximate solution becomes exact as the maximum difference tends to zero. Now let us consider the error vector δ as a function of ε (by substituting B into Equation 8.10):

$$\delta = \delta(P - \varepsilon E) + \varepsilon pE \tag{8.11}$$

For each value of ε, this system of equations has a unique solution for δ because both p and b are unique. Unfolding the recurrence once gives

$$\delta = [\delta(P - \varepsilon E) + \varepsilon pE](P - \varepsilon E) + \varepsilon pE$$

By expanding this recurrence further, we can show that the solution has the form

$$\delta = \sum_{i=1}^{\infty} a_i \varepsilon^i \tag{8.12}$$

for some set of vectors a_i, $i = 1, 2, \ldots$.

Substituting for δ in Equation (8.11) gives

$$\sum_{i=1}^{\infty} a_i \varepsilon^i = \sum_{i=1}^{\infty} a_i \varepsilon^i (P - \varepsilon E) + \varepsilon pE$$

Since this equation holds for all ε, we may equate coefficients of ε and coefficients of ε^{i+1} for $i = 1, 2, \ldots$ respectively to obtain:

$$a_1 = a_1 P + pE$$

$$a_{i+1} = a_{i+1} P - a_i E \tag{8.13}$$

These equations allow us to determine the vectors a_i independently of ε (given P and E), and for very small ε

$$\delta \approx a_1 \varepsilon$$

Suppose for some given P and E we vary ε, the maximum difference. We find that the error vector (δ) varies as $a_1 \varepsilon$ for small ε where a_1 is independent of ε. So the error vector varies linearly with the maximum difference.

Example 8.1(e) (Error analysis)

For our running example, the maximum absolute difference between P and B is $\varepsilon = \frac{1}{8}$, and this gives the relative error matrix

$$E = \begin{bmatrix} -\frac{4}{7} & -\frac{3}{7} & \frac{1}{2} & \frac{1}{2} \\ -\frac{1}{2} & -\frac{1}{2} & 0 & 1 \\ \frac{1}{2} & 0 & -\frac{4}{15} & -\frac{7}{30} \\ 0 & \frac{1}{2} & -\frac{1}{5} & -\frac{3}{10} \end{bmatrix}$$

The exact solution for our simple example is $p = (\frac{10}{57}, \frac{3}{19}, \frac{17}{57}, \frac{7}{19})$ and our approximation gives $b = (\frac{7}{39}, \frac{2}{13}, \frac{4}{13}, \frac{14}{39})$, so the error is $\delta = (\frac{1}{247}, -\frac{1}{247}, \frac{7}{741}, -\frac{7}{741})$. To three decimal places these vectors are:

$$b = (0.179, 0.154, 0.308, 0.359)$$

$$p = (0.175, 0.158, 0.298, 0.368)$$

$$\delta = (0.004, -0.004, 0.009, -0.009)$$

So the relative errors are less than 1%. Had we modified the elements in P differently to obtain B, we get a different result. Suppose we chose the following block diagonal matrix:

$$B^* = \begin{bmatrix} \frac{10}{19} & \frac{9}{19} & 0 & 0 \\ \frac{10}{19} & \frac{9}{19} & 0 & 0 \\ 0 & 0 & \frac{17}{38} & \frac{21}{38} \\ 0 & 0 & \frac{17}{38} & \frac{21}{38} \end{bmatrix}$$

Then the solution for the conditional probabilities is given by $b^* = (\frac{10}{19}, \frac{9}{19}, \frac{17}{38}, \frac{21}{38})$ and this gives the exact result for p.

We have been considering an NCD Markov chain, but a similar analysis holds for a Markov process. Moreover, we can think that the above analysis concerns the embedded Markov chain of a Markov process. Then all the properties that we defined for the chain become corresponding properties of the Markov process. For example, an NCD Markov process has an NCD embedded Markov chain.

Now we can justify the flow equivalent server (FES) method using the underlying NCD Markov process. The FES method can be applied to models that do not have a finite state space Markov process representation, but the NCD approximation gives insight into why the method is generally very accurate. The underlying Markov process has a state vector representing the queue size at each centre and we assume this is NCD. Thus we can apply decomposition to get a rate matrix that is almost block diagonal. Each block represents a sub-network with a fixed population. Intuitively, we can see that a customer spends a relatively long time in a sub-network before moving on to another sub-network. Thus the transition rates between sub-networks are small when compared to transition rates within a sub-network.

Consider the network used in Section 6.6 to prove Norton's theorem for a closed network with M service centres. As before, we decompose this into two sub-networks comprising centres $\{1, 2, \ldots, m\}$ and centres $\{m + 1, m + 2, \ldots, M\}$ respectively. Each block corresponds to a set of states with a fixed number of customers in the first

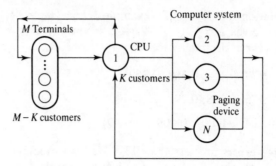

Figure 8.1 Computer system with terminals.

sub-network and the rest of the network (the second sub-network). The aggregated Markov process has a two-dimensional state space representing the numbers of tasks in these sub-networks. One way of modifying the block submatrices corresponds to the FES method and so the underlying NCD Markov process justifies the FES method. It turns out that the FES method is exact when applied to a product form network (by Norton's theorem), even though the transition matrix is not NCD.

Example 8.2(a) (Interactive system with paging)

Consider the classic model for representing an interactive computer system with paging, as shown in Figure 8.1. There are two subsystems: a terminal system and a computer system that consists of a single CPU and many i/o devices. One of the i/o devices provides support for virtual memory (i.e. a paging device to store pages swapped out of memory). Essentially, the multiprogrammed computer system is similar to the one analysed in Example 6.2, but now there is paging and the multiprogramming level can vary because tasks can enter and leave the computer system. Since the population of the entire closed system is M there is no queueing at the terminals. The terminal system is modelled by M identical parallel servers, each with rate γ (so mean 'think time' is $1/\gamma$). A 'departure' represents 'submission of a task to the computer system'. Thus the terminal system is an IS node because there are always enough terminals for the M tasks.

The computer system consists of the following: a CPU represented by node 1, i/o devices (disks etc.) represented by nodes 2, 3, ..., $N - 1$ and a paging device represented by node N. If a page fault occurs, the CPU is interrupted and the task goes to node N. Suppose we have P pages of main store and the total demand on node N is a function of the number of tasks in the computer system; this is reasonable because only the active tasks will be needing paging i/o. The paging device is not used exclusively for paging, so part of its traffic will be non-paging i/o. Let D_i be the average total service requirement of a

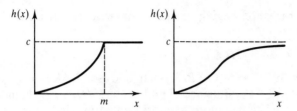

Figure 8.2   Lifetime functions.

task from node i, so that $D_1, D_2, \ldots, D_{N-1}$ are model parameters and the paging behaviour of the tasks determines D_N together with the non-paging requirement specified as a parameter. Suppose the paging demand for node N is $H(K)$ where K is the number of tasks in the computer system (i.e. at nodes $1, 2, \ldots, N$) and H is the monotonically increasing function representing the paging behaviour and memory constraints. The multiprogramming level is $K = M - n_0$ where n_0 is the number of terminals in 'think mode'.

The paging behaviour is represented by a lifetime function $h(x)$: the average CPU time between consecutive page faults when a task has amount x of main memory. This is some increasing function of x since, on average, more memory generates less frequent page faults. Suppose the first instruction causes a page fault (demand paging). Then we require $h(0) \approx 0$. If m is the maximum amount of memory needed by a task, then $h(x) \approx c$ for $x \geq m$ and a constant c (the total CPU time for the task). Typical formulae that are used include

$$h(x) = \begin{cases} ax^b & \text{for } x \leq m \\ c & \text{otherwise} \end{cases}$$

and

$$h(x) = \frac{c}{1 + (a/x)^2}$$

The values of a, b and c are chosen by analysing measurement data. These functions are plotted in Figure 8.2 to illustrate the initial rise and gradual flattening of the curve. Let each task have P/K pages of memory, so the average CPU time between faults is $h(P/K)$. The average number of page faults during the life of a task is $D_1/h(P/K)$ and for each fault the average time in service at node N is $1/\mu_N$ (the time to service a page fault). So the total average paging time of a task is given by

$$H(K) = \frac{D_1}{\mu_N h(P/K)}$$

If the average non-paging requirement of a task from node N is d_N, then we have

$$D_N = d_N + H(K)$$

Note that as $K \to \infty$, $h(P/K) \to 0$ and so $H(K) \to \infty$, causing the throughput $T(K) \to 0$ (since $T(K) \leq \min(1/D_i)$). A higher multiprogramming level causes more memory contention and so more paging i/o. Eventually, this leads to severe throughput degradation: an effect known as **thrashing**, when little useful work gets done.

The variation in the multiprogramming level causes global state dependence because the rate of visits to node N depends on the number of active jobs (i.e. the non-local network state). In other words, we have state-dependent routing from node 1 to node N and so also to nodes $2, 3, \ldots, N - 1$. Moreover, at node 1 we have a state-dependent service rate that depends on the number of active jobs, K. However, in terms of demands D_i, only D_N is state-dependent. This contrasts with the closed computer system model (Example 6.2) where K was the total population; a constant independent of every individual queue length. As a result, the present model has no simple exact solution (global state dependence implies no product form solution exists) and we need an approximate solution.

Example 8.2(b) (Short-circuited network) _____

Let us first consider the computer system in isolation with some fixed population K (i.e. the short-circuited network, without the terminals). In the embedded Markov chain, we are effectively creating a block in the state transition matrix for each population level in the computer system. For the short-circuited network, the transition probability of entering the terminals is reduced to zero (off-block diagonal elements) and the block elements are modified so that the matrix rows each sum to one. Each block is then a stochastic matrix, so with the normalizing condition we can obtain an approximation for the conditional probability (say $\pi(m|n)$ for n customers in the computer system and where m represents the internal state of the computer system) of being in any given state. Since the short-circuited network has a product form, we just use the MVA algorithm to compute the throughput function directly. For a given population K, the recurrence relations are

$$Q_N(k) = (d_N + H(K))[1 + L_N(k - 1)] \quad k = 1, \ldots, K$$

$$Q_i(k) = D_i[1 + L_i(k - 1)] \qquad\qquad i \neq N, k = 1, \ldots, K$$

$$T(k) = \frac{k}{\sum_{i=1}^{M} Q_i(k)} \qquad\qquad k = 1, \ldots, K$$

$$L_i(k) = T(k)Q_i(k) \qquad\qquad i = 1, \ldots, M; k = 1, \ldots, K$$

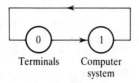

Figure 8.3   FES-transformed network.

where $Q_i(k)$ is the total average time spent at node i when the population is k, $L_i(k)$ is the average queue length at node i when the population is k and $T(k)$ is the throughput of the short-circuited network when the population is k.

Note that the service requirement $H(K)$ at node N is constant in the recurrence. However, the computation requires two nested loops: the outer loop for $K = 1, 2, \ldots, K_0$ (where the population K_0 is the required multiprogramming level) and the inner loop for $k = 1, 2, \ldots,$ K. More precisely, we have $Q_i(K, k)$, $L_i(K, k)$ and $T(K, k)$ for $k = 0,$ $\ldots, K$ and $K \geq 0$. Hence we need a new value of $H(K)$ each time round the outer loop. This will give us the throughput function $T(K_0)$ of the computer system at any multiprogramming level K_0.

Example 8.2(c) (Approximate model)

Let us apply the decomposition method to obtain an approximation. In this case it is easy to identify the sub-networks as the terminal system and the computer system. We isolate the computer system to get the throughput function $T(n)$ for $n = 1, \ldots, K$ (as in Example 8.2(b)). We can now replace the computer system by an FES with variable service rate $T(n)$. Thus the aggregated network has two QLD nodes, as shown in Figure 8.3. The service rates for the 2 nodes are:

$$\mu_0(j) = j\gamma \qquad j = 1, 2, \ldots, M$$
$$\mu_1(j) = T(j)$$

We need to find the stationary probability $\pi(n)$ that n tasks are at the computer system. In Example 8.1, we calculated the equivalent aggregate state probability exactly from the lumped matrix. This is not always possible in general and so further approximations are normally required. Here, we use the conditional throughput $T(n)$ (also derivable from the conditional probabilities $\pi(m|n)$) to obtain the probability $\pi(n)$.

Note that this is not an exact decomposition because of the global state dependence in the original network. However, it would be very accurate if the computer system sub-network reached its steady state very soon after the degree of multiprogramming changed. We expect

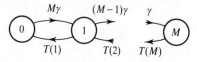

Figure 8.4   State transition diagram for process.

this to be a good approximation if the task transitions within the computer system occur much more frequently than the task transitions between the computer system and the terminals. Since the think time and total response time are measured in seconds and i/o time and time between page faults are measured in milliseconds, we expect accurate predictions from this model with respect to the underlying Markov process. This is because these different relative rates give a small maximum relative error ε between the transition matrix and the block diagonal matrix.

We can solve this network using standard queueing results (directly from Jackson's theorem for closed networks) since it is a closed network with just two QLD nodes. However, we present the solution from first principles to demonstrate the general method. The underlying Markov process for the FES-transformed network has integer state representing the number of tasks at the computer system. In fact, it is a simple birth–death process with the state diagram shown in Figure 8.4.

The balance equations are:

$$(M - j + 1)\gamma\pi(j - 1) = T(j)\pi(j) \qquad j = 1, 2, \ldots, M$$

where $\pi(j)$ is the steady state probability that j tasks are being multiprogrammed. This recurrence is by now very familiar and has the solution given in Chapter 4.

Once we know $\pi(j)$ we can derive several other performance measures. The throughput is given by

$$T = \sum_{j=1}^{M}\pi(j)T(j)$$

where the $\pi(j)$ are obtained from the balance equations and $T(j)$ from the paging model. Applying Little's result to the entire network gives

$$M = T(W + 1/\gamma)$$

where W is the time spent by a task in the computer system, perhaps the most important performance measure for the user. Thus the mean response time is given by

$$W = M/T - 1/\gamma$$

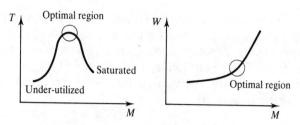

Figure 8.5 Thrashing curves.

Numerically, these equations typically yield thrashing curves similar to the ones in Figure 8.5 for the throughput and the mean response time as a function of the number of terminals in use.

8.1.2 Other forms of decomposition

There are a variety of decomposition methods that are applicable to non-separable queueing networks. **Hierarchical decomposition** methods consist of decomposition at a number of levels. At the lowest level, parts of a subsystem are isolated and replaced by FESs. At the next level, the subsystem is isolated and solved using the FESs at the lower level. This then defines the FESs at a higher level that can be used at yet another higher level. Finally, at the highest level (numbered 0, say), the entire system can be represented by FESs representing subsystems at level 1. Such a technique is particularly useful in making large queueing networks computationally tractable as well as isolating non-product form features for more precise treatment.

Another type of decomposition decomposes the queueing network as before but then considers the input and output processes of the related sub-networks. This method was first proposed by Kuehn (1979) and involves the following steps:

(1) decompose the network into sub-networks, some of which can be single service centres;

(2) analyse each sub-network in isolation in terms of arrival (input) and departure (output) processes of each sub-network;

(3) approximate all non-renewal processes by stationary renewal processes;

(4) consider the first two moments of the inter-arrival times of all processes, namely the mean and coefficient of variation (cf. the generalized exponential for the maximum entropy method in Section 8.4 and teletraffic results in Chapter 11);

(5) produce a computational algorithm to solve the entire model (for example, Whitt's work (Whitt 1983) on the superposition and decomposition of renewal processes).

Note that even for separable queueing networks (i.e. with product form solution), the internal processes are in general neither Poisson nor renewal. Nevertheless, decomposition gives a good approximation to the internal processes if the partitioning is done well. Of course, the final steady state queue length distribution for the decomposed network is exact for a separable network.

8.1.3   Decomposing queueing networks

Here we give some guidelines on decomposing general closed queueing networks into a number of sub-networks. Once the sub-networks in a queueing network are identified, each sub-network is analysed in isolation and replaced by an equivalent node. The resulting network with all sub-networks replaced by equivalent nodes is then called the equivalent network. We assume that the equivalent network has a product form solution. This assumption is clearly an approximation in general, but the results are reasonably accurate if we make the following assumptions.

Assumption 1: Transitions between sub-networks are single-step transitions; they only involve single customers. Thus if a node provides bulk service that simultaneously releases more than one customer, then the destination node must be in the same sub-network.

Assumption 2: The sub-network behaviour depends only on the sub-network state and is independent of the state of the other sub-networks. Thus nodes with a destination node that has a finite queue must be in the same sub-network as this destination (provided its limited capacity could cause blocking). In other words, the nodes that connect to a blocking node must be in the same sub-network; the blocking effect is all contained within a sub-network.

Assumption 3: The input/output behaviour of a customer (i.e. arrival and departure processes) through each sub-network is independent of the state-dependent routing decisions during its time in the sub-network.

Assumption 4: Transitions between sub-networks involving customers do not depend on the behaviour of any other *particular* customer (although they do depend on customers in general because of contention). For example, if a fork node generates a number of children customers that later synchronize with the parent at a join node, then both these nodes and the intermediate nodes must be in the same sub-network.

Under these assumptions the product form solution of the equivalent network has been found reasonably accurate. Suppose sub-network k is characterized by the visitation rate e_k and the service rate (conditional throughput) $\mu_k(n)$ when n customers are in the sub-network. The visitation rate e_k is easy to determine from the traffic equations but obtaining $\mu_k(n)$ is normally a harder problem. The conditional throughput can be determined exactly by solving the entire network, but this is the original problem. Approximate methods are required to find the conditional throughput by just using information about sub-network k. So solving the big queueing network problem is reduced to solving many smaller problems. The FES method is just one way of finding the conditional throughput. In the next section, we will see another similar method (Marie's method) to find the same unknown parameters.

Suppose the equivalent network has M nodes (one for each sub-network) and population K. Then the queue length state vector has steady state distribution given by

$$p(n_1, \ldots, n_M) = \frac{1}{G(M, K)} \prod_{i=1}^{M} x_i(n_i)$$

where

$$x_i(n_i) = \left(\frac{(e_i)^{n_i}}{\prod_{j=1}^{n_i} \mu_i(j)} \right) \qquad \sum_{i=1}^{M} n_i = K$$

and $G(M, K)$ is the normalization constant.

Note that there are two levels of approximation here. The first approximation is in finding the conditional throughput (e.g. by using the FES method or Marie's method). However, even if we had exact values for the conditional throughput, the overall model is still approximate because of the assumption of product form. If the assumptions for decomposing the original network are satisfied then the second approximation is believed to be good. But there are no guarantees!

8.1.4 Matrix geometric methods

When a Markov process has a repetitive structure, we can sometimes readily derive the stationary probabilities by using matrix geometric methods. The foundations of this approach were discovered by Neuts (1981). These methods can be applied when the generator matrix of the Markov process has identical repeating submatrices.

Scalar process

Consider a birth–death process with state representing the number of customers in a queue (i.e. $0, 1, 2, \ldots$). For any state $j > 0$, let λ be the birth rate and μ be the death rate. When $j = 0$, the birth rate is λ'. The

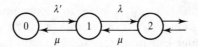

Figure 8.6   Simple birth–death process.

state transition diagram has the simple form shown in Figure 8.6. The generator matrix Q for this birth–death process has the following structure:

$$Q = \begin{bmatrix} -\lambda' & \lambda' & 0 & 0 & \cdots \\ \mu & -(\lambda + \mu) & \lambda & 0 & \cdots \\ 0 & \mu & -(\lambda + \mu) & \lambda & \cdots \\ 0 & 0 & \mu & -(\lambda + \mu) & \lambda \\ \vdots & \vdots & \vdots & \mu & -(\lambda + \mu) \end{bmatrix}$$

The **boundary states** of the process are $j = 0$ and $j = 1$ since the state transitions into these states are not similar to other state transitions. The **repeating states** are $j \geq 2$ because their state transitions are similar.

For each repeating state $j \geq 2$, the balance equation is

$$\pi_{j-1}\lambda - \pi_j(\lambda + \mu) + \pi_{j+1}\mu = 0 \qquad (8.14)$$

where π_j is the stationary probability that the process is in state j. If we are given π_{j+1}, $j \geq 2$, then π_j depends only on transitions between state $j-1$ and state j. Since the transition rates are constant, there exists a constant ρ such that

$$\pi_j = \rho\pi_{j-1} \qquad j \geq 2$$

This is just a hypothesis which will be justified if a solution is found (by the steady state theorem). Our hypothesis implies

$$\pi_j = \rho^{j-1}\pi_1 \qquad j \geq 2 \qquad (8.15)$$

Suppose we substitute our guess (Equation 8.15) into the balance Equation (8.14) for state $j \geq 2$:

$$\rho^{j-2}\pi_1\lambda - \rho^{j-1}\pi_1(\lambda + \mu) + \rho^j\pi_1\mu = 0$$

Dividing by $\rho^{j-2}\pi_1$ gives us a quadratic equation in ρ:

$$\lambda - \rho(\lambda + \mu) + \rho^2\mu = 0 \qquad (8.16)$$

This has solution $\rho = 1$ or $\rho = \lambda/\mu$. We take the minimal solution $\rho = \lambda/\mu$ since $\rho = 1$ does not satisfy the normalization condition.

The boundary states have the following balance equations:

$$\pi_0 \lambda' - \pi_1 \mu = 0 \tag{8.17}$$

$$\pi_0 \lambda' - \pi_1(\lambda + \mu) + \pi_2 \mu = 0 \tag{8.18}$$

Since $\pi_2 = \rho \pi_1$, the matrix form of these equations is

$$(\pi_0, \pi_1) \begin{bmatrix} -\lambda' & \lambda' \\ \mu & -\mu \end{bmatrix} = 0$$

This does not have a unique solution (since there are two unknowns and the rank of the matrix is one). Summing the stationary probabilities and normalizing gives

$$\pi_0 + \pi_1 \sum_{j=1}^{\infty} \rho^{j-1} = \pi_0 + \pi_1/(1 - \rho) = 1$$

From the first balance Equation (8.17), let $\rho' = \lambda'/\mu = \pi_1/\pi_0$, so we have

$$\pi_0 = \frac{1}{[1 + \rho'/(1 - \rho)]} \tag{8.19}$$

$$\pi_1 = \frac{1}{[1/\rho' + 1/(1 - \rho)]} \tag{8.20}$$

Hence the method finds a solution to the whole set of balance equations, which is unique, by the steady state theorem. The stationary performance measures are just linear combinations of π_i. For example, the mean number of queued customers L_Q (i.e. in state $j \geqslant 1$, $j - 1$ are queued) is given by

$$L_Q = \frac{\rho' \rho}{(1 - \rho)(1 - \rho + \rho')}$$

Note that if $\rho' = \rho$, we get $L_Q = \rho^2/(1 - \rho)$, as expected for the M/M/1 queue.

Main approach

As we see from the scalar example above, the matrix geometric method has the following steps:

(1) guessing a geometric solution for the repeating states (with need to calculate the value of an unknown constant)

(2) calculating the value of the constant by substituting the geometric form into the balance equation for the repeating states and finding the root

(3) finding the boundary state probabilities from the repeating states solution and the normalizing condition

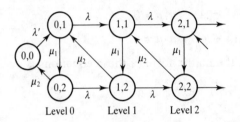

Figure 8.7 State transition diagram for vector state process.

We now use the same approach to analyse a vector state process, as shown in Nelson (1991).

Vector state process

Consider an FCFS queue with arrival rate λ' when no customers are waiting to be served and λ otherwise. Suppose the service time is the sum of two exponential random variables with parameters μ_1 and μ_2 (i.e. a hypoexponential distribution with two stages). The vector state process with two-dimensional state is described by (i, j) where i is the number of customers in the queue excluding any in service and $j = 0, 1, 2$ is the stage of service of the customer in service; $j = 0$ denotes no customer in service, i.e. only occurs in the state $(0, 0)$. Let $\pi(i, j)$ be the stationary probability that the process is in state (i, j). The state transition diagram is shown in Figure 8.7. At level $i \geqslant 0$, the states are $(i, 1)$ and $(i, 2)$. We can order the states by levels to obtain the following sequence: $(0, 0)$, $(0, 1)$, $(0, 2)$, $(1, 1)$, $(1, 2)$, $(2, 1)$ $(2, 2)$, ... Using this ordering, we obtain the following generator matrix:

$$
Q = \begin{bmatrix}
-\lambda' & \lambda' & 0 & 0 & 0 & 0 & 0 & 0 & 0 \\
0 & -a_1 & \mu_1 & \lambda & 0 & 0 & 0 & 0 & 0 \\
\mu_2 & 0 & -a_2 & 0 & \lambda & 0 & 0 & 0 & 0 \\
0 & 0 & 0 & -a_1 & \mu_1 & \lambda & 0 & 0 & 0 \\
0 & \mu_2 & 0 & 0 & -a_2 & 0 & \lambda & 0 & 0 \\
0 & 0 & 0 & 0 & 0 & -a_1 & \mu_1 & \lambda & 0 \\
0 & 0 & 0 & \mu_2 & 0 & 0 & -a_2 & 0 & \lambda \\
\end{bmatrix}
$$

where $a_i = \lambda + \mu_i$, $i = 1, 2$. We can group the states by the number of customers by defining the following:

$$\pi_0 = (\pi(0, 0), \pi(0, 1), \pi(0, 2))$$

$$\pi_i = (\pi(i, 1), \pi(i, 2)), \qquad i \geqslant 1$$

We also define

$$\pi = (\pi_0, \pi_1, \pi_2, \ldots)$$

The generator matrix has the following form:

$$Q = \begin{bmatrix} B_{00} & B_{01} & 0 & 0 & 0 & \ldots \\ B_{10} & A_1 & A_0 & 0 & 0 & \ldots \\ 0 & A_2 & A_1 & A_0 & 0 & \ldots \\ 0 & 0 & A_2 & A_1 & A_0 & \ldots \\ 0 & 0 & 0 & A_2 & A_1 & \ldots \end{bmatrix}$$

where B_{00}, B_{01}, B_{10} are rectangular matrices associated with the boundary states and A_0, A_1, A_2 are 2×2 matrices associated with the repeating states.

The balance equation for the repeating states is given by

$$\pi_{j-1}A_0 + \pi_j A_1 + \pi_{j+1}A_2 = 0 \qquad j \geq 2 \tag{8.21}$$

Given π_{j+1} $(j \geq 2)$, π_j only depends on the state transitions between level $j - 1$ and level j. So our hypothesis is that there is a constant matrix R such that

$$\pi_j = \pi_{j-1}R \qquad j \geq 2$$

Thus the π_j $(j \geq 2)$ are matrix geometric and have the following solution:

$$\pi_j = \pi_1 R^{j-1} \qquad j \geq 2 \tag{8.22}$$

As before, we substitute this guess into the balance Equation (8.21):

$$\pi_1 R^{j-2}A_0 + \pi_1 R^{j-1}A_1 + \pi_1 R^j A_2 = 0 \qquad j \geq 2$$

i.e.

$$A_0 + RA_1 + R^2 A_2 = 0 \tag{8.23}$$

We pick a minimal solution R to this quadratic (minimal in that the spectral radius of R is less than one).

The balance equations for the boundary states are given by

$$\pi_0 B_{00} + \pi_1 B_{10} = 0 \tag{8.24}$$

$$\pi_0 B_{01} + \pi_1 A_1 + \pi_2 A_2 = 0 \tag{8.25}$$

where $\pi_2 = \pi_1 R$. In matrix form, these balance equations become

$$(\pi_0, \pi_1)\begin{bmatrix} B_{00} & B_{01} \\ B_{10} & A_1 + RA_2 \end{bmatrix} = 0$$

This does not have a unique solution. Using the normalizing condition, we obtain

$$\pi_0 e + \pi_1 \sum_{j=1}^{\infty} R^{j-1} e = \pi_0 e + \pi_1 (I - R)^{-1} e = 1$$

where e is the column vector $(1, 1)$. This gives a unique solution for (π_0, π_1) and so for all the π_j $(j \geqslant 0)$.

The various performance measures can be expressed in terms of R. For example, the mean number of customers, L_Q, in the queue but not receiving service is given by assigning a value j to states $(j, 1)$ and $(j, 2)$, where $j > 0$.

$$L_Q = \sum_{j=1}^{\infty} j \pi_j e = \pi_1 \sum_{j=1}^{\infty} j R^{j-1} e$$
$$= \pi_1 (I - R)^{-2} e$$

So we find that the vector state process can be analysed as an extension of the scalar process using the matrix geometric method.

8.2 Fixed point methods

In this section we consider iterative methods for solving queueing networks. The main approach is based on applying the MVA algorithm to queueing networks in general. The main part of the MVA algorithm is the arrival theorem, which is assumed to hold approximately in all the networks that we consider.

8.2.1 Approximate MVA algorithm

Recall the standard MVA recurrence relations for service centre $i = 1$, $2, \ldots, M$ in a closed single class network with population K:

$$Q_i(K) = D_i[Y_i(K) + 1]$$
$$T(K) = \frac{K}{\sum_{i=1}^{M} Q_i(K)}$$
$$L_i(K) = T(K)Q_i(K)$$

where $Q_i(K)$ is the mean total waiting time at service centre i, D_i is the service demand for service centre i, $T(K)$ is the throughput of the closed network, $L_i(K)$ is the mean queue length at service centre i and $Y_i(K)$ is the mean queue length seen by an arrival at service centre i.

The arrival theorem (here the job observer property) gives the relation $Y_i(K) = L_i(K - 1)$, which is exact in product form networks.

For the MVA algorithm given above, we need to evaluate $2M + 1$ quantities (i.e. $Q_i(K)$, $T(K)$, $L_i(K)$) for each population between 1 and K. When the desired population level is K, the only reason for solving the network with smaller population levels is for the response time equation's use of the job observer property. This is because in order to find $Y_i(K)$, we need to find $L_i(K - 1)$, which has one less customer and so we need to solve the same network equations again at the lower population. Hence we can avoid this iteration if we can relate $Y_i(K)$ to $L_i(K)$ instead of $L_i(K - 1)$. In more general terms, we wish to find some function f such that

$$Y_i(K) = f(L_i(K), K)$$

This would give us an algorithm in which the time and space requirements are independent of the population. Unfortunately, there is no function f that gives an exact solution at every K and so we describe an approximate solution.

A simple approximate technique, due to Schweitzer (1979), that is reasonably accurate and widely used in practice because it is much faster than the exact MVA algorithm is based on the following assumption. Suppose we assume that the proportion of the total number of customers (K) at a particular queue remains the same if we reduce the network population by one. Then for each centre i, we have:

$$\frac{L_i(K - 1)}{(K - 1)} = \frac{L_i(K)}{K} \quad \text{for } K > 1$$

This is clearly approximate but it leads to the following:

$$Y_i(K) = L_i(K - 1) = \frac{K - 1}{K} L_i(K) \tag{8.26}$$

This result is exact for $K = 1$ and has the correct asymptotic behaviour as $K \to \infty$, so we are guaranteed good results at the extremes. Typically the errors are less than 5% but in certain cases 20% errors have been found.

Let us briefly look at the dependencies between the variables that we have defined, assuming we are given K and D_i for all i. From the approximation (Equation 8.26), knowing $L_i(K)$ we can find $Y_i(K)$ and hence $Q_i(K)$. From $Q_i(K)$ we can find $T(K)$ and from $Q_i(K)$ and $T(K)$ we can find $L_i(K)$ again. This circularity is illustrated by a simplified dependency graph as follows:

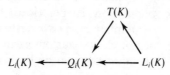

The arrows indicate the relation 'depends on' for unknown variables in the MVA recurrence. This dependency graph is a useful tool for illustrating circularity in the relations and proposing a fixed point equation. The graph here suggests a fixed point equation for $L_i(K)$ but we could also find one for $Q_i(K)$ or $T(K)$. To show this, we now derive a fixed point equation for the throughput $T(K)$.

Using the approximation for $Y_i(K)$ (Equation 8.26) in the MVA recurrences gives the following response time equation:

$$Q_i(K) = D_i\left(\frac{K-1}{K} T(K)Q_i(K) + 1\right)$$

(since $L_i(K) = T(K)Q_i(K)$). Rearranging this gives

$$Q_i(K) = \frac{D_i}{1 - ((K-1)/K)D_iT(K)}$$

and since

$$T(K) = \frac{K}{\sum_{i=1}^{M} Q_i(K)}$$

we obtain the following fixed point equation:

$$T(K) = F(T(K)) \tag{8.27}$$

where

$$F(x) = \frac{K}{\sum_{i=1}^{M} D_i/[1 - ((K-1)/K)D_ix]}$$

To solve this iteration numerically we choose an initial value (e.g. guess a lower bound such as zero) for the throughput $T(K)$ and keep on applying the function F until the difference between successive applications of F is small enough (as desired). Using this or some other numerical method, we can solve the fixed point equation and obtain the fixed point $T(K)$. It has been shown that the fixed point is unique and that the standard methods converge to that fixed point. Once the throughput $T(K)$ is found the other $2M$ unknowns $Q_i(K)$ and $L_i(K)$ can be found directly from the MVA equations. Note that for iterative methods in practice, performance measures such as mean queue length take more iterations to stabilize than throughput or utilizations. So it is better to use performance measures such as mean queue length in the termination conditions.

This approximation extends to multi-class queueing networks also. Suppose the network population is described by $k = (k_1, k_2, \ldots, k_r \ldots k_R)$, where k_r is the number of class r customers. Then we define $L_{ir}(k)$ as the mean number of class r customers in the queue at node i. The recursion in the MVA equations can be broken, analogously to the single class case above, by using the following approximation (Schweitzer 1979), called **Schweitzer's approximation**:

$$L_{is}(k - 1_r) = \begin{cases} L_{is}(k) & s \neq r \\ \dfrac{k_r - 1}{k_r} L_{ir}(k) & s = r \end{cases} \tag{8.28}$$

For multi-class networks, this approximation significantly reduces the amount of computation. Because of its high efficiency, this approximation is often used in practice, even for small networks for which the exact MVA technique is feasible. Schweitzer's approximation has been studied extensively by many researchers and found to be very accurate in practice, especially for throughputs. Mean queue lengths are not as accurate but still acceptable for most purposes.

8.2.2 Marie's method

Marie's method (Marie 1979) is similar to the FES method in that sub-networks are replaced by equivalent exponential servers with state-dependent service rates. The main difference is the way in which this rate is determined. Recall that the FES method analyses a short-circuited closed network. Marie's method, on the other hand, analyses the sub-network in isolation also, but with a state-dependent Poisson arrival process. The isolated network can be analysed by any method provided it gives us a conditional throughput function. Suppose each sub-network is considered as a single node in the original network. Then we can solve the isolated sub-network with a general service time distribution. Let $\lambda(n)$ be the arrival rate when the sub-network population is n. For a closed network with population K, the sub-network in isolation can be analysed as an $M/G/1/K$ queue with arrival rate $\lambda(n)$ when its population is n. This is the same as the closed network shown in Figure 8.8. All sub-networks other than sub-network k are represented collectively by a state-dependent arrival rate to sub-network k.

Let $T_k(n_k)$ be the throughput of sub-network k in the original network when the sub-network population is n_k. This is the rate at which customers flow through this sub-network. We construct an open model to approximate the sub-network in the original network and let $\lambda_k(n_k)$ be the total external arrival rate when the population is n_k, i.e. the state-dependent arrival rate. This arrival rate is supposed to approximate the arrival process to the sub-network in the original network. Normally, this process is neither Poisson nor renewal, but for this approximation we will assume that it is Poisson.

For now let us assume that the arrival rate $\lambda_k(n_k)$ is known. Then the $M/G/1/K$ queue (with arrival rate $\lambda_k(n_k)$ and chosen service time distribution) can be analysed exactly for sub-network k giving marginal

Decomposed network with population K

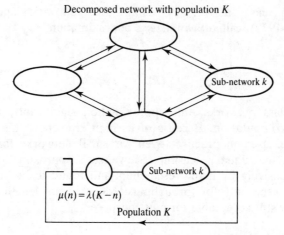

$\mu(n) = \lambda(K-n)$

Population K

Figure 8.8   Decomposition for Marie's method.

probability $p_k^*(n_k)$ for the probability of having n_k customers in the isolated sub-network. The asterisk (*) denotes that the performance measure refers to the M/G/1/K queue, which is used to approximate a sub-network. Let $T_k^*(n_k)$ be the conditional throughput of the M/G/1/K queue (i.e. the throughput when the queue length is n_k). Then for sub-network k, viewed as an M/G/1/K queue, we can show that

$$T_k^*(n_k) = \lambda_k(n_k - 1) \frac{p_k^*(n_k - 1)}{p_k^*(n_k)} \qquad n_k = 1, 2, \ldots, K \qquad (8.29)$$

This is obtained by considering a Coxian service time distribution and analysing the process with state (n, j) where n is the number of customers at the M/G/1/K queue and j is the stage of service of the customer being served. ($j = 0$ when $n = 0$.)

In the equivalent network, the service rate of the corresponding server is set to the conditional throughput:

$$\mu_k(n_k) = T_k^*(n_k) \qquad (8.30)$$

This gives us the required parameter in our equivalent network but we still need to find the arrival rate $\lambda_k(n_k)$. These arrival rates can be determined from the product form solution of the equivalent network, provided the service rates $\mu_k(n_k)$ are known:

$$\lambda_k(n_k) = \mu_k(n_k + 1) \frac{p_k(n_k + 1)}{p_k(n_k)} \qquad n_k = 0, 1, \ldots, K - 1 \qquad (8.31)$$

where $p_k(n_k)$ is the marginal queue length probability in the equivalent network. Thus Equations (8.29), (8.30) and (8.31) imply that the marginal queue length probability of node k in the equivalent network is the same as the state probability of the sub-network in isolation, i.e. $p_k(n_k) = p_k^*(n_k)$. As we saw in Section 6.3.4, the arrival rates can be expressed in terms of normalizing constants from the product form solution:

$$\lambda_k(n_k) = e_k \frac{G(M\backslash k, K - n_k - 1)}{G(M\backslash k, K - n_k)} \qquad n_k = 0, 1, \ldots, K - 1$$

$$(8.32)$$

where e_k is the visitation rate of node k and $G(M\backslash k, K)$ is the normalization constant for the network with node k removed from the M nodes and population K. Note that G is a function of $\mu_k(n_k)$.

Hence we have a fixed point equation because $\mu_k(n_k)$ depends on $\lambda_k(n_k)$, which depends on the node service rates again through the normalizing constant. The dependency graph looks like this for all $k = 1, 2, \ldots, M$ and all $n = 1, 2, \ldots, K$:

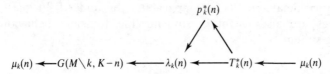

If we define a vector

$$\boldsymbol{\mu} = (\mu_1(1), \mu_1(2), \ldots, \mu_1(K), \ldots, \mu_M(1), \mu_M(2), \ldots, \mu_M(K))$$

then Equations (8.29), (8.30), (8.31) and (8.32) define a function f such that $\mu = f(\mu)$. We can choose some initial value $\mu^{(0)}$ to approximate μ and successively apply the function f until (hopefully) consecutive values of μ are very close. For example, we can choose $\mu^{(0)} = (\mu_1, \mu_1, \ldots, \mu_1, \ldots, \mu_M, \mu_M, \ldots, \mu_M)$, where μ_i is the fixed service rate for all populations.

Marie's algorithm has the following steps (where $n_k = 0, 1, \ldots, K - 1$):

(1)   Let $\mu = \mu^{(0)}$, i.e. some initial value to start the iteration.

(2)   For each sub-network k, calculate $\lambda_k(n_k)$ using $\lambda_k(n_k) = e_k[G(M\backslash k, K - n_k - 1)/G(M\backslash k, K - n_k)]$.

(3)   For the open network approximation to sub-network k, derive the steady state probabilities $p_k^*(n_k)$. Hence find the conditional throughput using $T_k^*(n_k) = \lambda_k(n_k - 1)p_k^*(n_k - 1)/p_k^*(n_k)$.

(4)   Set $\mu_k(n_k) = T_k^*(n_k)$.

(5)   If successive values of $\boldsymbol{\mu}$ are sufficiently close, then determine performance measures from the equivalent product form network; else iterate again from step 2.

Neither the uniqueness of μ nor the convergence of the fixed point procedure has been proved. However, in practical examples, convergence has invariably been demonstrated experimentally.

8.3 Diffusion approximation

So far all the techniques for solving queueing networks that we have covered are discrete in that the population varies in discrete steps as customers arrive or depart. When the population is high (i.e. for heavy loads), each discrete step's increase in population is relatively small when compared to the total population. In such cases, it seems reasonable to approximate the discrete flow of customers by a continuous flow like a fluid. Many such results originate from fluid mechanics, in particular the diffusion equation for an ideal gas. Hence this approximate method is often called the **diffusion approximation**. Some of the approximate results are applicable even under light loads. These techniques are also useful in studying the transient behaviour of a queueing system.

8.3.1 Fluid flow approximation

The fluid flow approximation for queueing networks is useful for studying both transient and steady state behaviour. For example, this method is particularly useful in heavy traffic conditions when the queue is saturated so that equilibrium is never attained or when we want to analyse the transient behaviour before reaching the steady state. The heavy traffic implies that queues are typically much larger than one and so response times are much larger than service times.

Instead of considering the queueing system as a flow of customers with arrivals and departures at discrete time points, we treat it as a continuous flow, rather like fluid entering a piping system. In the queueing system, the number of customers as a function of time is a stochastic process with jumps upward for arrivals and downward for departures. In heavy traffic, when the number of customers is relatively large, these discontinuous jumps are relatively small and we can replace them with a smooth continuous function. This gives us a stochastic fluid flow approximation for the queueing system with continuous sample space as well as continuous parameter space.

Let us now define the arrival and departure processes for an open queueing system. Let $A(t)$ and $D(t)$ be the random variables describing the number of arrivals and the number of departures respectively in

$(0, t)$. Both $A(t)$ and $D(t)$ are monotonically increasing step functions. The number of customers in the system at time t is then given by $N(t) = A(t) - D(t)$, assuming that initially the system is empty. Informally, by the weak law of large numbers, when $A(t)$ gets large it gets close to its mean $\bar{A}(t)$ and similarly as $D(t)$ gets large it also gets close to its mean $\bar{D}(t)$. The fluid flow approximation simply replaces $A(t)$ and $D(t)$ by the continuous deterministic processes $\bar{A}(t)$ and $\bar{D}(t)$. If the queue is non-empty at time t, the process $\{N(t), t \geq 0\}$ can be approximated by the continuous process $\{X(t), t \geq 0\}$ with probability density function defined as $f(x, t) \, dx = P(x \leq X(t) < x + dx)$. Assuming that the system is initially empty ($X(0) = 0$) the approximation gives

$$X(t) = \bar{A}(t) - \bar{D}(t) \tag{8.33}$$

As an example let us consider a water reservoir with water at incoming rate

$$\lambda(t) = d\bar{A}(t)/dt$$

(i.e. the customer arrival rate) and water at outgoing rate

$$\mu(t) = d\bar{D}(t)/dt$$

(i.e. the customer service rate). The amount of water in the reservoir at time t is then approximated by $X(t) = \bar{A}(t) - \bar{D}(t)$.

Since the minimum amount in the reservoir is zero, $X(t) \geq 0$. Suppose now that the service rate is fixed so that $\mu(t) = \mu$ for $X(t) > 0$. As saturation is approached, i.e. $\lambda(t) \to \mu$, we expect a large queue to form, but we find that this model does not capture that aspect. This effect is not modelled because the variability in the arrival and departure processes is not taken into account. In order to obtain a more realistic model of the queue backlog we need to include the variability of $A(t)$ and $D(t)$ as well as the means. This extension makes these processes into diffusion processes, which we now consider.

8.3.2 Diffusion processes

We now consider the case where the number of arrivals $A(t)$ and the number of departures $D(t)$ have variations about their means. Suppose at time $t = 0$, a customer arrives at an empty system and initiates a long busy interval during which many customers arrive and maintain a non-zero queue length. At time $t > 0$, $P(A(t) \geq n) = P(\tau_n \leq t)$ where τ_n is the arrival instant of the nth customer. Thus τ_n is the sum of n inter-arrival times, say $t_1 + t_2 + \ldots + t_n$. Assuming that the times in the set $\{t_i\}$ are independent identically distributed random variables, by the central limit theorem, τ_n has an asymptotically normal distribution as $n \to \infty$. It then follows that $A(t)$ also approaches a normal distribution as $t \to \infty$ under the same independence assumption and a similar argument holds for the departure process $D(t)$ during a long busy period. Assuming that these processes are independent, $N(t) = A(t) - D(t)$ is also asymptotically normally distributed because it is a linear combination of independent normal random variables. The key approximation here is that the queue length process during a finite busy interval can be adequately approximated by the queue length process during an infinite busy interval.

In general, the arrival and departure processes are not independent because they must satisfy the condition $D(t) \leqslant A(t)$. So our independence assumption does not hold all the time. But during a busy interval $[a, b]$, $N(t) > 0$ for all $t \in [a, b]$. Thus the inter-departure times are just service times and so independent of the arrival process. We therefore expect to get good results for heavy loads, but uncertain accuracy for light loads.

We now consider the diffusion approximation of the G/G/1 FCFS queue with independent inter-arrival times and independent service times. We define these two random variables:

$$T = \text{inter-arrival time with } E[T] = 1/\lambda, \text{ Var}[T] = c_a^2/\lambda^2$$

$$S = \text{service time with } E[S] = 1/\mu, \text{ Var}[S] = c_s^2/\mu^2$$

where c_a is the variation coefficient of T and c_s is the variation coefficient of S. We also define the traffic intensity $\rho = \lambda/\mu$. As before, $N(t)$ is the number of customers in the queue at time t and the process $\{N(t), t \geqslant 0\}$ is approximated by the continuous process $\{X(t), t \geqslant 0\}$ with probability density function defined as $f(x, t)\,dx = P(x \leqslant X(t) < x + dx)$. We assume the queue is initially empty $N(0) = 0$. The **drift** or **derivative** of $X(t)$ at time t is defined by

$$\beta(t) = \lim_{h \to 0} \frac{E[X(t + h) - X(t)]}{h}$$

Similarly the **instantaneous variance** of $X(t)$ at time t is defined by

$$\alpha(t) = \lim_{h \to 0} \frac{E[(X(t + h) - X(t))^2]}{h} - \frac{E[X(t + h) - X(t)]^2}{h}$$

In the steady state (as $t \to \infty$) by applying the limit theorem of renewal processes (see Section 4.5) we can show that

$$\beta = \lim_{t \to \infty} \beta(t) = \lambda - \mu \tag{8.34}$$

and

$$\alpha = \lim_{t \to \infty} \alpha(t) = \lambda c_a^2 + \mu c_s^2 \qquad (8.35)$$

We also need to define a **Brownian motion**, which classically represents the movement of particles in an ideal gas. A normalized Brownian motion $b(t)$ has the following properties:

$b(0) = 0$
$b(t) - b(s)$ is independent of $b(s)$, $t > s$
$b(t) - b(s)$ is normally distributed with mean 0 and
              variance $t - s$, $t > s$

Suppose, according to the discussion at the beginning of the section, that for $t > s$, $X(t) - X(s)$ is independent of $X(s)$ and has a normal distribution with mean $(t - s)\beta$ and variance $(t - s)\alpha$. Then we can normalize $X(t)$ using the standard technique of changing the variable, i.e. subtracting the mean from the normal variable and dividing by the standard deviation (only that we want to end up with a variance of t instead of 1):

$$b(t) = \frac{X(t) - \beta t}{\sqrt{\alpha}}$$

Thus we have

$$X(t) = \beta t + \sqrt{\alpha} b(t) \qquad (8.36)$$

where $b(t)$ is a normalized Brownian motion. $X(t)$ has a normal density with mean βt and variance αt:

$$f(x, t) = \frac{1}{(2\pi\alpha t)^{1/2}} \exp\left(-\frac{(x - \beta t)^2}{2\alpha t}\right) \qquad (8.37)$$

This satisfies the **diffusion equation** (also called the Fokker–Planck equation):

$$\frac{\partial}{\partial t} f(x, t) = \frac{\alpha}{2} \frac{\partial^2}{\partial x^2} f(x, t) - \beta \frac{\partial}{\partial x} f(x, t) \qquad (8.38)$$

To solve this partial differential equation, we need initial values $f(x, 0)$ for all values of $x \geq 0$ and boundary conditions for $f(0, t)$ and $\partial f(0, t)/\partial t$.

So we have the probability density function $f(x, t)$ for X(t) that satisfies the diffusion equation and we can use $X(t)$ to approximate $N(t)$, the queue length at time t. In fact, it is a Brownian motion with drift parameter β and variance parameter α. We can now map the queue length problem to a diffusion problem that considers the motion of a particle in an ideal gas. If a steady state exists, we want to find the limiting distribution $f(x) = \lim_{t \to \infty} f(x, t)$ using the diffusion equation. Since the number of customers in the queue cannot be negative, we need to do something to the continuous process when it approaches $X(t) = 0$. Typically, a barrier of some form is introduced at the origin $x = 0$ to keep $X(t)$ non-negative.

The reflecting barrier

With a reflecting barrier the process is reflected back into the positive side at $X(t) = 0$ for all times t. Thus no probability mass accumulates at zero since $X(t) > 0$. We integrate the diffusion equation with respect to x over the interval $(0, \infty)$:

$$\int_0^\infty \frac{\partial}{\partial t} f(x, t)\, dx = \int_0^\infty \left[\frac{\alpha}{2} \frac{\partial^2}{\partial x^2} f(x, t) - \beta \frac{\partial}{\partial x} f(x, t) \right] dx \quad \textbf{(8.39)}$$

Assuming a steady state exists, we can set $(\partial/\partial t)f(x, t) = 0$ (which makes the LHS of Equation 8.39 zero). For the reflecting barrier, the boundary values are $f(0, t) = 0$ and $\partial f(0, t)/\partial t = 0$ for all t, and so Equation (8.38) simplifies to

$$\beta f(x) = \frac{\alpha}{2} f'(x)$$

For the steady state $(\rho < 1)$, the only solution to the diffusion equation (with the normalizing condition for $f(x)$ and given boundary values) is the exponential distribution, namely

$$f(x) = \begin{cases} \gamma e^{-\gamma x} & \text{if } x \geq 0 \\ 0 & \text{otherwise} \end{cases} \quad \textbf{(8.40)}$$

where $\gamma = -2\beta/\alpha$, $\beta = \lambda - \mu$, $\alpha = \lambda c_a^2 + \mu c_s^2$.

Since we have zero probability at $x = 0$, this result is reasonable only when $\rho = \lambda/\mu$ is close to one. We can return to the discrete probability distribution for the queue length by integrating the continuous function $f(x)$. Let $p(n)$ be the equilibrium probability that the queue length is n. Then we approximate $p(n)$ using the following discretization method:

$$p(n) = \int_n^{n+1} f(x)\, dx \quad n = 0, 1, 2, \ldots \quad \textbf{(8.41)}$$

By construction, the probability is automatically normalized. For the exponential case, we get

$$p(n) = \int_n^{n+1} \gamma e^{-\gamma x}\, dx = [-e^{-\gamma x}]_n^{n+1} = (e^{-\gamma})^n (1 - e^{-\gamma})$$

This has a form that closely resembles the M/M/1 queue:

$$p(n) = (1 - \hat{\rho})\hat{\rho}^n \qquad n = 0, 1, 2, \dots \tag{8.42}$$

where $\hat{\rho} = e^{-\gamma}$.

However, since we know that $p(0) = 1 - \rho$ for a single server queue, the distribution is modified to

$$p(0) = 1 - \rho \text{ and } p(n) = \rho(1 - \hat{\rho})\hat{\rho}^{n-1} \qquad n = 1, 2, \dots \tag{8.43}$$

Analogously to the M/M/1 queue, the mean queue length is given by

$$L = \frac{\rho}{1 - \hat{\rho}} \tag{8.44}$$

This approximation becomes more accurate as ρ tends to one and for $\rho < 1$ it has good accuracy when the variation coefficients are close to one. Comparisons can be made with exact results that can be obtained for queues such as the M/G/1.

The absorbing barrier

In this model, the process is not reflected at the $x = 0$ boundary, but is absorbed. After some random time the process is instantaneously returned to the point $x = 1$. The absorbing state corresponds to the empty state and the instantaneous return corresponds to an arrival to an empty queue. A probability mass is assigned to point $x = 0$ to take into account the empty system. For an absorbing barrier, the diffusion equation becomes

$$\frac{\partial}{\partial t} f(x, t) = \frac{\alpha}{2} \frac{\partial^2}{\partial x^2} f(x, t) - \beta \frac{\partial}{\partial x} f(x, t) + \lambda R(t)\delta(x - 1)$$

where $1/\lambda$ is the mean time that the process remains at zero, $R(t)$ is the probability that the process reaches the boundary at time t and $\delta(x - 1)$ is the Dirac function at the point of return (i.e. 1).

In the limit, $\lim_{t \to \infty} R(t) = 1 - \rho$ and $\lim_{t \to \infty} f(x, t) = f(x)$, which has the following solution (after normalization):

$$f(x) = \begin{cases} \rho(1 - e^{-\gamma x}) & \text{if } 0 \leqslant x \leqslant 1 \\ \rho(e^{\gamma} - 1)e^{-\gamma x} & \text{if } x > 1 \end{cases} \tag{8.45}$$

where $\gamma = -2\beta/\alpha$, $\beta = \lambda - \mu$, $\alpha = \lambda c_a^2 + \mu c_s^2$.

The probability of the process being at $x = 0$ is taken to be $1 - \rho$ and it is easy to verify that

$$\int_0^\infty f(x)\, dx = \rho$$

Now we apply the following discretization method which is a slight variation of the previous formula (but equally valid):

$$p(n) = \int_{n-1}^n f(x)\, dx \qquad n = 1, 2, \ldots \tag{8.46}$$

For the continuous function $f(x)$ given in Equation (8.45) for the absorbing barrier, we obtain, using Equation (8.46),

$$p(0) = 1 - \rho$$

$$p(1) = \frac{\rho}{\gamma}(\gamma + e^{-\gamma} - 1) \tag{8.47}$$

$$p(n) = \frac{\rho}{\gamma} e^{-n\gamma}(e^\gamma - 1)^2 \qquad n = 2, 3, \ldots$$

We do not need to normalize this distribution because it sums to one by construction. The mean queue length is then approximated by

$$L = \sum_{n=1}^\infty np(n) = \rho\left(1 + \frac{1}{\gamma}\right) = \rho\left(1 + \frac{\rho c_a^2 + c_s^2}{2(1 - \rho)}\right) \tag{8.48}$$

This is similar to the Pollaczek–Khintchine formula, which is exact for the M/G/1 queue. The only difference is the subexpression $\rho c_a^2 + c_s^2$ in the formula for L. For the M/G/1 queue, arrivals are Poisson ($c_a = 1$) so the subexpression becomes $\rho + c_s^2$ whereas in the exact result, the subexpression is $\rho(1 + c_s^2)$.

Note that we calculated the mean queue length from the discrete queue length distribution $p(n)$. We could also compute the mean queue length from the density $f(x)$, but then we get a different result. By this method, the mean queue length is given by

$$\int_0^\infty xf(x)\, dx = \rho\left(\frac{1}{2} + \frac{1}{\gamma}\right) = \rho\left(\frac{1}{2} + \frac{\rho c_a^2 + c_s^2}{2(1 - \rho)}\right)$$

This differs from the discrete case by $\rho/2$. We will adopt the discrete method since it is consistent with the probability distribution $p(n)$.

If we choose another discretization method we get a different result. The method we use here is simply

$$p(n) = f(n) \qquad n = 1, 2, 3, \ldots \tag{8.49}$$

This simple method gives the following distribution:

$$p(0) = 1 - \rho$$
$$p(n) = \rho(1 - \hat{\rho})\hat{\rho}^{n-1} \qquad n = 1, 2, \ldots \tag{8.50}$$

This is the same as the modified solution given for the reflecting barrier (i.e. Equation 8.43).

Since the Pollaczek–Khintchine formula gives exact results for the M/G/1 queue we want to find an approximate formula for the G/G/1 which degenerates to the exact M/G/1 result when arrivals are Poisson. One additional fact that we have at our disposal is that the variation coefficient for inter-departure times is exactly the same as the variation coefficient of the service time when the server is busy. This happens a proportion ρ of the time so we alter the instantaneous variance of $N(t)$ by introducing a factor ρ. This heuristic allows us to tune the result as follows. The drift is unchanged as $\beta = \lambda - \mu$ but α is changed to

$$\alpha' = \lambda c_a^2 + \mu c_s^2 \rho = \lambda(c_a^2 + c_s^2) \tag{8.51}$$

and we use $\gamma' = -2\beta/\alpha'$. Solving the diffusion equation with these parameters and using

$$p(n) = \int_{n-1}^{n} f(x)\, dx$$

as the discretization method we obtain a queue length distribution which is similar to the one above:

$$p(0) = 1 - \rho$$
$$p(1) = \frac{\rho}{\gamma'} (\gamma' + e^{-\gamma'} - 1) \tag{8.52}$$
$$p(n) = \frac{\rho}{\gamma'} e^{-n\gamma'}(e^{\gamma'} - 1)^2 \qquad n = 2, 3, \ldots$$

As before, we can find the mean queue length from the distribution $p(n)$ to obtain

$$L = \frac{\rho}{\gamma'} (\gamma' + 1) = \rho\left(1 + \frac{\rho(c_a^2 + c_s^2)}{2(1 - \rho)}\right) \tag{8.53}$$

This is identical to the Pollaczek–Khintchine formula when $c_a = 1$ and was first proposed by Kingman. **Kingman's formula** is known to be generally very accurate. The other formulae for the mean queue length (Equations 8.44 and 8.48) can sometimes give more accurate results. Of all the formulae derived for L, none seems to stand out as the best one in general. Numerical results for various solutions based on the diffusion approximation may be found in Gelenbe and Pujolle (1987).

To summarize, we list some options that need to be considered when dealing with diffusion approximations:

(1)   the way in which the diffusion parameters α and β are chosen

(2)   the type of barrier that is used: reflecting or absorbing

(3)   the discretization method employed to obtain the discrete probability distribution from the probability density function

(4)   the modification applied to the discrete probability distributions to make them close to known results

(5)   the method for computing the mean queue length

8.3.3   Diffusion approximation for queueing networks

We can use the diffusion approximation method to analyse queueing networks with FCFS queues and general service times. In order to apply the method we need to make one key assumption: that the arrival process at each service centre is a renewal process. In this way, we can treat the centre as a $G/G/1$ queue and use the diffusion approximation. For some arbitrary node, let us define the random variables T and S as the inter-arrival time and the service time respectively. By solving the traffic equations, we can find the arrival rates and hence $E(T)$. For open networks these equations have a unique solution, but for closed networks we need to fix one variable to a particular value to allow a solution for the visitation rates. The variance of T needs to be estimated somehow in terms of the means and variances of S and T for the other nodes in the network and the routing probabilities. Many methods to find the variance have been proposed (see Kuehn (1979) and Whitt (1983)). Once the mean and variance of S and T are known, we can use the $G/G/1$ diffusion approximation to obtain the queue length distribution.

Remember that the arrival process is neither Poisson nor even renewal in these networks in general. However, the results are more accurate than product form solution results which assume Poisson arrivals and exponential service times. As expected, the errors increase when the variation coefficients of S and T are not close to one. However, when the node utilization is low, the absorbing barrier gives good results because it caters for the empty queue case.

8.4 Maximum entropy methods

A completely different approach to finding probability distributions uses ideas from information theory. The more **information** one obtains on observing the state of a system (a random variable), the greater the **surprise** that observation causes, or equivalently, the more uncertainty there is associated with the state. In information theory, the expected measure of surprise (or information) associated with a random variable X is called the **entropy** of X – conventionally written $H(X)$. Now, one method of assigning probabilities to events – see the discussion in Section 1.1 – is based on Bernoulli's **principle of insufficient reason** which states that all events over a sample space should have the same probability unless there is evidence to the contrary. Now, the entropy of a random variable is minimum, in fact equal to zero, when its value is certain; an observation can yield no information about the random variable. Similarly, the entropy is *maximum* when the random variable is *uniformly distributed*; the outcome of an experiment has maximum uncertainty. Thus, the principle of insufficient reason requires that entropy be maximized, subject to the constraints imposed by any 'additional evidence', specified as equations involving the probability distribution. For example, the 'additional evidence' may relate the mean values or higher moments of the random variables involved. Thus, for a single server queue, given the server's utilization and mean queue length, we may (and will below) obtain the maximum entropy approximation for the queue length *mass function*.

The entropy of a random variable, $H(X)$, is defined in terms of F_X (or p_X if X is discrete, f_X if X is continuous) and we now give a derivation for the discrete case. We have to quantify the notion of surprise, which we have already concluded depends on the probability p associated with the random variable in question. We therefore consider the quantity $S(p)$, and deduce the form of the function S from the properties required of 'surprise'. There are four such properties:

- There is no surprise at $p = 1$, i.e. $S(1) = 0$.

- The more unlikely an event, the greater the surprise its occurrence engenders. Thus S is strictly decreasing, i.e. $p > q \Rightarrow S(p) < S(q)$.

- Small changes in p should result in small changes in $S(p)$. Thus we require S to be continuous.

- Surprise is additive for independent events. Suppose A and B are independent events with probabilities p and q respectively. Then $S(pq)$ is the surprise engendered by the occurrence of both A and B. An equivalent view is that first A is observed with surprise $S(p)$ and then B is observed with surprise $S(q)$ since the observation of A cannot affect this surprise if A and B are independent. The total surprise is therefore $S(p) + S(q)$, by additivity, and it follows that S must have the property that $S(pq) = S(p) + S(q)$ for $0 < p$, $q \leqslant 1$.

These four axioms give us enough information to determine the form of the function S.

Proposition 8.1

$S(p) = -C \log_2 p$ for arbitrary constant $C > 0$.

Proof   By the fourth axiom satisfied by S, for $0 < p \leqslant 1$,

$$S(p^n) = nS(p)$$

for all integers $n \geqslant 0$. Similarly, $S(p) = mS(p^{1/m})$ for any integer $m > 0$. Thus we have

$$S(p^{n/m}) = \frac{n}{m} S(p)$$

and so $S(p^q) = qS(p)$ for any non-negative rational q. Hence, by continuity of S, $S(p^x) = xS(p)$ for all reals $x \geqslant 0$. Now let $x = -\log_2 y$, so that $y = 2^{-x}$, for $0 < y \leqslant 1$. Then we have

$$S(y) = xS(\tfrac{1}{2}) = -C \log_2 y$$

where $C = S(\tfrac{1}{2}) > S(1) = 0$ by the first two properties of S. However, it is easy to check that if a function S_0 satisfies all of the four properties, then so does the function S defined by $S(p) = kS_0(p)$ for any positive constant k.   ∎

Without loss of generality, we may take $C = 1$ whereupon the unit of surprise (or information) is the familiar *bit* (binary digit). For example, the number 16 has four bits of information and can be encoded in four bits (since we do not allow the number 0). However, we take $C = \ln 2$ so that $S(p) = -\ln p$.

Now consider the discrete random variable X with probability mass function given by $\{p_i = P(X = x_i) | i = 1, 2, \ldots\}$. Then the expectation of the surprise of X, i.e. the entropy of X, is

$$H(X) = -\sum_{i=1}^{\infty} p_i \ln p_i$$

Since $H(X)$ is solely a function of $\{p_i\}$, it is often written $H(p)$ whereupon it can be manipulated as a mathematical function without regard to its probabilistic or information theoretic interpretation.

8.4.1 The maximum entropy method

We apply the preceding ideas to assign equilibrium probabilities to the countable number of states of some discrete stochastic process Z. Without loss of generality, assume that Z is stationary and has state space $S = \{0, 1, 2, \ldots\}$, where state i has equilibrium probability p_i. (Of course, we include here the possibility that S is finite, i.e. $S = \{0, 1, \ldots, n\}$ for some $n \geq 0$.) Suppose further that given information about Z imposes constraints on $\{p_i | i \in S\}$ which can be expressed in the form of equations relating the mean values of functions $\{f_j | 0 \leq j \leq m\}$ of the state, where m is less than the number of possible states. In particular, one such constraint must be defined by (for $j = 0$, say) $f_0(i) = 1$ for all $i \in S$, so that the probabilities $\{p_i\}$ can be made to sum to unity.

Based on the principle of insufficient reason, the **principle of maximum entropy** states that, of all the mass functions satisfying the constraints given, the minimally prejudiced – the 'best to choose' – is the one that maximizes the entropy function

$$H(p) = -\sum_{i \in S} p_i \ln p_i \tag{8.54}$$

subject to the constraints

$$\sum_{i \in S} p_i = 1$$

and

$$\sum_{i \in S} f_j(i) p_i = \bar{f}_j \qquad \text{for } 1 \leq j \leq m$$

where $\{\bar{f}_j | 1 \leq j \leq m\}$ are prescribed mean values of the functions $\{f_j\}$. The resulting solution for $\{p_i\}$ is called the **maximum entropy solution** and the technique is most commonly called the **maximum entropy method**, abbreviated to MEM. This maximization problem can be solved by the method of Lagrange multipliers as in the following.

Proposition 8.2

The maximum entropy solution for the probabilities p_i in the above problem is

$$p_i = G^{-1} \prod_{j=1}^{m} x_j^{f_j(i)} \tag{8.55}$$

where

$$G = \sum_{i \in S} \prod_{j=1}^{m} x_j^{f_j(i)}$$

The positive constants $\{x_j | 1 \leq j \leq m\}$ are the solutions to the m constraint equations after substituting each p_i by the above expression.

Proof The solution to the maximization problem is that of the following set of linear equations, together with the $m + 1$ given constraints:

$$\frac{\partial}{\partial p_k}\left(H(p) + \sum_{j=0}^{m}\lambda_j\sum_{i\in S}f_j(i)p_i\right) = 0 \qquad (k \in S)$$

where

$$H(p) = -\sum_{i\in S}p_i \ln p_i$$

The constants $\{\lambda_j | 0 \leq j \leq m\}$ are the Lagrange multipliers of the maximization problem, where λ_j corresponds to the constraint involving f_j. We therefore have a total of $m + 1 + |S|$ equations in the same number of variables, $\lambda_0, \lambda_1, \ldots, \lambda_m, p_0, p_1, \ldots$. Performing the differentiation, we obtain the system of equations

$$\ln p_k + 1 + \sum_{j=0}^{m}\lambda_j f_j(k) = 0 \qquad (k \in S)$$

$$\sum_{i\in S}f_j(i)p_i = \bar{f}_j \qquad (1 \leq j \leq m)$$

$$\sum_{i\in S}p_i = 1$$

The first equation gives (remembering that $f_0(k) = 1$ for all $k \in S$) $p_k = e^{-1}x_0\prod_{j=1}^{m}x_j^{f_j(k)}$ where $x_j = e^{-\lambda_j}$ $(0 \leq j \leq m)$. Substituting into the normalizing equation, we obtain

$$ex_0^{-1} = \sum_{i\in S}\prod_{j=1}^{m}x_j^{f_j(i)}$$

giving the required normalizing constant G with $G^{-1} = e^{-1}x_0$ so that $G \equiv e^{1+\lambda_0}$.

The Lagrange multipliers $\{\lambda_j | 1 \leq j \leq m\}$, or equivalently the positive constants $\{x_j | 1 \leq j \leq m\}$, are now obtained by substituting the expressions for the p_i $(i \in S)$ into the m constraint equations and solving. That the stationary point thus found is a maximum is left as an exercise to the reader; proved, for example, by considering second derivatives. ■

The principle of maximum entropy is often useful for deriving approximate solutions to queueing problems and other stochastic models, since often the expected values of the random variables of interest can be found in terms of the first few moments of given distributions – for example inter-arrival time or service time distributions. Besides this, the main appeal of the method is that it always gives results in *product form* which facilitates further simplification and efficient numerical algorithms of the kind we have seen in this and the previous chapters. We consider next the single server queue and then networks of queues, but the method has been applied to many other systems, for example with multiple servers and classes, blocking and priorities.

First, let us suppose there are no constraints apart from the normalization. Then we have $p_i = G^{-1} \times 1$ where $G \equiv e^{1+\lambda_0} = \sum_{i \in S} 1 = |S|$. Thus we must have a finite state space S for a solution to exist, whereupon all states are assigned the same probability $|S|^{-1}$. This is entirely as expected from the preceding discussion.

8.4.2 Application to the single server queue

For queues, we know from Little's result how to determine utilizations, and for $M/G/1$ queues, mean queue lengths too. We use these quantities as the constraints in the maximum entropy method. For a single server queue with arrival rate λ and service rate μ, both independent of the queue length, we proved in Chapter 5 that the utilization is $\rho \equiv \lambda/\mu$, i.e. that the equilibrium probability that the queue length is 0 is $1-\rho$. This very general result holds for any $G/G/1$ queue, so let us see what the maximum entropy method can do to give us the equilibrium queue length distribution. With this single constraint, we have, in the terminology of Proposition 8.2, $f_1(0) = 1$, $f_1(i) = 0$ for $i > 0$ and $\bar{f}_1 = 1-\rho$. The equilibrium probability p_k that the queue length is k is therefore estimated as $p_0 = G^{-1}x_1$ and $p_k = G^{-1}$ for $k \geqslant 1$. Clearly, therefore, this cannot give a mass function when the state space is infinite, and when it is finite the result is unacceptable, giving the same probability for all queue lengths greater than zero. In fact, substituting into the constraint equation, we have

$$G^{-1}x_1 = 1 - \rho$$

and normalization yields $G = (|S| - 1)/\rho$.

To obtain a more realistic result needs another constraint and so we recall the result for the mean queue length in an $M/G/1$ queue – L say. The new constraint equation has $f_2(i) = i$ for $i \geqslant 0$ and $\bar{f}_2 = L$. This constraint and the utilization equation then give the solution

$$p_0 = G^{-1}x_1$$

$$p_i = G^{-1}x_2^i \qquad (i \geqslant 1)$$

Substituting into the constraint equations we then have

$$G^{-1}x_1 = 1 - \rho$$

$$G^{-1}\sum_{i=1}^{\infty} ix_2^i = L$$

Simplifying and performing the summation gives $G^{-1}x_2 = L(1 - x_2)^2$, and normalizing we obtain $G = x_1 + x_2/(1 - x_2)$, i.e. $G\rho = x_2/(1 - x_2)$. Thus,

$$G^{-1}x_2 = \rho(1 - x_2) = L(1 - x_2)^2$$

and so $x_2 = (L - \rho)/L$, $G = (L - \rho)/\rho^2$ and $x_1 = (1 - \rho)(L - \rho)/\rho^2$. The final solution is therefore

$$p_0 = 1 - \rho$$

$$p_i = \frac{\rho^2}{L}\left(\frac{L - \rho}{L}\right)^{i-1} \qquad (i \geqslant 1) \tag{8.56}$$

For an M/M/1 queue, where $L = \rho/(1 - \rho)$, the result simplifies to $p_i = (1 - \rho)\rho\rho^{i-1}$ and so is exact. This is encouraging, and begs the question 'for what other service time distributions is the result exact?'. The answer is 'not many, but some'. In fact, it can be shown using the Pollaczek–Khintchine formula for the mean queue length L that the maximum entropy solution for $\{p_i | i \geqslant 0\}$ is exact when the service time density function f_S is a generalized exponential (GE) given by

$$f_S(t) = \left(\frac{C_S^2 - 1}{C_S^2 + 1}\right)\delta(t) + \frac{4\mu}{(C_S^2 + 1)^2}\,e^{-2\mu t/(C_S^2 + 1)} \tag{8.57}$$

where C_S is the coefficient of variation of the service time random variable. The property holds for both proper and improper ($C_S < 1$) GE distributions. The proof is given in El-Affendi and Kouvatsos (1983). This lends further support for the use of the GE distribution to approximate general distributions:

- It provides exact queue length distributions given only the first two moments of service time distribution in an M/G/1 queue, and has been seen to give good approximations in other systems such as networks of queues.
- It has a memoryless property, in that residual service time is exponentially distributed. This aids the analysis of flows of customers through a system since the remaining service time, upon

the arrival of a customer at a node, has known (exponential) distribution. Thus, for example, calculation of waiting time distributions is simplified.

- As we saw in Chapter 5, the GE distribution can be used to represent bulk processing with geometrically distributed bulk sizes with mean $(C_S^2 + 1)/2$ and squared coefficient of variation $(C_S^2 - 1)/(C_S^2 + 1)$.

Finally we pose the following question. The constraints used in the MEM are somewhat arbitrary and depend on the application rather than being inherent to the method. We saw that, for the single server queue, utilization alone was inadequate but utilization and mean queue length together provide a reasonable approximation. The question is, how would we have fared using only the mean queue length? The answer is, actually, quite well, the result being

$$p_n = \frac{1}{1 + L}\left(\frac{L}{1 + L}\right)^n \quad (n \geqslant 0) \tag{8.58}$$

where L is the prescribed mean queue length. The proof is a routine application of the MEM and is the subject of Exercise 8.5.

8.4.3   Application to networks of queues

We can now extend the use of the MEM to networks of queues with some confidence; in view of its accuracy when applied to the M/G/1 queue (exactness for M/GE/1) and also because we already know that product form solutions exist for many networks. Remember that *some* product form is guaranteed by the MEM, even though it may provide a poor approximation. Again, the method depends for its success on independent calculation of the mean values of appropriate functions of the state of the network in equilibrium. These mean values provide the constraints of the maximization problem, and, generalizing the analysis for the single server queue, we use the utilization and mean queue length of each server for our constraints. Not surprisingly this gives a result akin to Jackson's theorem (Section 6.6.2), although it applies to *any* network (by the very definition of the method), albeit approximately. The obvious question of when the result is exact will be considered after the following statement and proof.

Proposition 8.3

For an open queueing network with M single server nodes with prescribed utilizations ρ_i and mean queue lengths L_i $(1 \leqslant i \leqslant M)$, the equilibrium state space probability mass function, p, is given by

$$p(n) = \prod_{i=1}^{M} p_i(n_i)$$

where $n = (n_1, \ldots, n_M)$ and p_i is the probability mass function for the queue length at node i given by the MEM in isolation, subject to the constraints that the utilization is ρ_i and the mean queue length is L_i $(1 \le i \le M)$.

Proof There are $2M$ constraints – M utilizations and M mean queue lengths – with corresponding functions and constants which we label f_{1j}, f_{2j} and x_{1j}, x_{2j} $(1 \le j \le M)$, following the method of Proposition 8.2. Then, the maximum entropy solution is

$$p(n) = G^{-1} \prod_{j=1}^{M} x_{1j}^{f_{1j}(n)} \prod_{j=1}^{M} x_{2j}^{f_{2j}(n)}$$

where G is the normalization constant. The utilization constraints are

$$\sum_{n:n_i=0} p(n) = 1 - \rho_i \qquad (1 \le i \le M)$$

and the mean queue length constraints are

$$\sum_{n} p(n) n_i = L_i \qquad (1 \le i \le M)$$

Thus we have $f_{1j}(n) = 1$ if $n_j = 0$ and 0 otherwise and $f_{2j}(n) = n_j$ $(1 \le j \le M)$. Observing that

$$f_{1j}(n) = 1 \Rightarrow f_{2j}(n) = 0$$
$$f_{2j}(n) \ne 0 \Rightarrow f_{1j}(n) = 0$$

we may write $p(n)$ in the simpler form

$$p(n) = G^{-1} \prod_{j=1}^{M} y_j(n_j)$$

where

$$y_j(k) = \begin{cases} x_{1j} & \text{if } k = 0 \\ x_{2j}^{k} & \text{if } k > 0 \end{cases}$$

Substituting into the constraint equations, we obtain

$$1 = G^{-1}\sum_{n}\prod_{j=1}^{M}y_j(n_j) = G^{-1}\prod_{j=1}^{M}\sum_{k=0}^{\infty}y_j(k)$$

$$= G^{-1}\prod_{j=1}^{M}\left(x_{1j} + \sum_{k=1}^{\infty}x_{2j}^k\right)$$

i.e. $G = \prod_{j=1}^{M}\left[x_{1j} + \dfrac{x_{2j}}{1-x_{2j}}\right] = \prod_{j=1}^{M}\dfrac{x_{1j} + x_{2j} - x_{1j}x_{2j}}{1-x_{2j}}$

$$1 - \rho_i = G^{-1}x_{1i}\sum_{n:n_i=0}\prod_{j\neq i}y_j(n_j)$$

$$= G^{-1}x_{1i}\prod_{j\neq i}\sum_{k=0}^{\infty}y_j(k) = \dfrac{x_{1i}(1-x_{2i})}{x_{1i} + x_{2i} - x_{1i}x_{2i}}$$

and

$$L_i = G^{-1}\sum_{n}n_i\prod_{j=1}^{M}y_j(n_j) = G^{-1}\left(\sum_{k=1}^{\infty}kx_{2i}^k\right)\prod_{j\neq i}\sum_{k=0}^{\infty}y_j(k)$$

$$= \dfrac{x_{2i}}{(1-x_{2i})(x_{1i} + x_{2i} - x_{1i}x_{2i})}$$

Thus,

$$G^{-1} = \prod_{j=1}^{M}\dfrac{1-\rho_j}{x_{1j}}, \qquad x_{1i} = \dfrac{(1-\rho_i)x_{2i}}{\rho_i(1-x_{2i})}$$

$$\text{and } L_i = \dfrac{x_{2i}(1-\rho_i)}{x_{1i}(1-x_{2i})^2}$$

We therefore obtain $p(n) = \prod_{j=1}^{M}z_j(n_j)$ where

$$z_j(k) = \begin{cases}1 - \rho_j & \text{if } k = 0 \\ \rho_j(1 - x_{2j})x_{2j}^{k-1} & \text{if } k > 0\end{cases}$$

But

$$L_j = \dfrac{x_{2j}(1-\rho_j)}{x_{1j}(1-x_{2j})^2} = \dfrac{\rho_j}{1-x_{2j}}$$

and so

$$x_{2j} = \dfrac{L_j - \rho_j}{L_j}$$

Hence,

$$z_j(k) = \begin{cases}1 - \rho_j & \text{if } k = 0 \\ \dfrac{\rho_j^2}{L_j}\left(\dfrac{L_j - \rho_j}{L_j}\right)^{k-1} & \text{if } k > 0\end{cases}$$

We observe that $z_j(k)$ is the MEM estimate of the queue length probability mass function for a single server queue with utilization ρ_j and mean queue length L_j and so the proof is complete.   ∎

In particular, if we have a Jackson network of exponential servers, the MEM result is exact. This is a consequence of the fact that the MEM estimate for the marginal probability distribution of the length of each queue is exact, as we proved in the previous section. In fact, we can derive a maximum entropy solution for the equilibrium joint queue length probabilities neglecting the utilizations, i.e. using only mean queue lengths. The analysis is a direct extension of that for the single server queue and is the subject of Exercise 8.5. The result is again exact for networks of exponential servers, but in networks which violate this assumption the inclusion of the utilization constraints gives much greater accuracy; this is to be expected, since the former case just attempts to apply Jackson's theorem in situations where its assumptions do not hold.

In the case of a closed queueing network, an analogous analysis can be applied, giving a similar result. Again, this relies on expressions for the utilization, ρ_i, and mean queue length, L_i, at each node i being given, and gives steady state probability estimate

$$p(\boldsymbol{n}) = G^{-1}\prod_{j=1}^{M}y_{1j}^{f_{1j}(\boldsymbol{n})}\prod_{j=1}^{M}y_{2j}^{f_{2j}(\boldsymbol{n})}$$

for $\boldsymbol{n} \in S = \{(n_1, \ldots, n_M)|\sum_{i=1}^{M} n_i = K,\ n_i \geq 0\}$. However, the expressions for the y_{ij} are not the same as those for the corresponding x_{ij} since the state space S is now finite. Nevertheless, the method is exactly the same.

As we noted above, the MEM depends on the availability of expressions or values for the means of the 'constraint' functions of the state random variable. Approximate expressions can often be derived for the mean queue lengths, even in complex networks, and in the worst case, numerical estimates based on simulation or measurement can be used to parameterize an MEM model. Therein lies the practical value of the maximum entropy approach; combined with its empirically observed accuracy in a range of applications. The method has been applied to priority queues, multi-class networks with blocking and optimal flow control problems. The main objection to the MEM is its lack of an underlying cause and effect relationship, but against this must be set some accurate predictions which can be generated relatively efficiently for a wide range of problems. For a full discussion, the reader is referred to Kouvatsos' forthcoming book (Kouvatsos, in press).

Numerous approximate methods have been proposed in the literature and most of them are *ad hoc*. They are typically guided by intuition and so many assumptions are made and the final result cannot be guaranteed to be accurate. Validation for such a model is initially by comparison with simulations and exact models (where they exist) in simple cases. However, ultimately a model can only be deemed valid when compared with measurements made on the real system being modelled in a controlled experimental environment. Many *ad hoc* techniques lack an exact analysis with respect to the approximating assumptions from which bounds on the performance measures predicted can be obtained.

SUMMARY

- Approximate methods are necessary for most analytical modelling studies in practice. They are often used for solving queueing networks in cases where an exact solution is not known or computationally intractable.

- One commonly used approximate technique is the decomposition method for Markov processes, and this provides a theoretical basis for the flow equivalent server method.

- Matrix geometric methods also exploit the structure of the generator matrix for the Markov process.

- Often, approximate relationships between unknown variables lead to a fixed point equation that can be solved numerically, as in the approximate mean value analysis algorithm.

- Marie's method is an iterative technique for solving queueing networks with FCFS service disciplines and general service time distributions.

- Diffusion methods approximate the discrete flows of customers by continuous flows (like a fluid) and are most accurate under heavy traffic conditions. With appropriate modifications, some of the results also apply under light traffic conditions.

- The maximum entropy method provides a way of obtaining approximate results for fairly complex networks when given certain known results (constraints) that are obtained independently by some other technique.

EXERCISES

8.1   (30 FES method)

Consider a computer system with a very fast instruction processing unit (IPU) and relatively slow memory. (Main memory is normally modelled as a passive resource because the processor stops processing during a memory request.) In this new design, there is a large cache and the context switching overhead is minimal. When there is a cache miss, the process waits for the memory access but the IPU starts processing another task. Consider the simplified diagram below, of M requesters, a single IPU and main memory.

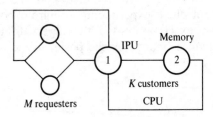

The requesters generate SQL queries on a main memory database, with average think time $1/\gamma$. Under no contention and if all required data records are in cache, the IPU takes D_1 seconds on average to service each query. When there are K queries in the CPU system, the demand for the memory is D_2. Suppose $1/\mu_2$ is the time taken to service a cache fill request, and the cache has c lines. When each task is using x cache lines, the average time between cache fill requests is $h(x)$, an increasing function of x that is determined empirically. Find an expression for D_2 and show how to use the FES method to find the mean response time for a query. Under heavy loads, discuss whether such a design suffers from 'memory thrashing' (which is analogous to page thrashing in more traditional computer systems). Suggest a way of modelling the case where some of the database resides in external storage devices.

8.2   (20 Approximate MVA)
Using Schweitzer's approximation, derive a fixed point equation for the mean queue length vector for a Gordon–Newell network with M nodes, constant service rates and population K. Suggest starting values for an iterative solution.

8.3   (20 Approximate MVA)
For the same type of network as in the previous exercise, derive a fixed point equation for the mean total waiting time vector. Again suggest starting values for an iterative solution.

8.4   (20 Marie's method)
Suppose we apply Marie's method to a single class network that has a product form solution. Verify that the equivalent network has the same parameters as the original network, so the fixed point equation is satisfied after just one iteration.

8.5   (30 Maximum entropy method)
Apply the maximum entropy method to find approximations for

(a)   the equilibrium queue length distribution at a single server queue given that the mean queue length is L

(b)   the joint equilibrium distribution of the queue lengths in an open queueing network of M single server nodes with prescribed mean queue lengths L_i $(1 \leq i \leq M)$

Show that the results are exact for exponential queues with fixed service rates.

Chapter 9
Time Delays

9.1 Time delays in the
single server queue   352
9.2 Time delays in
networks of queues   360

9.3 Inversion of the
Laplace transforms   372
9.4 Approximate methods   377

Most of the performance measures we have considered so far in this book have been *resource-based*, for example mean queue length at a server, throughput of a server or network, utilization of a server etc. However, an equally important aspect of performance is that perceived by the user of a system, characterized by *task-based* measures. The most common of these relate to response time or some other time delay. Of course, if we are only interested in mean time delays, we can just use Little's result together with certain resource-based measures, namely the mean number of customers in a subsystem and the throughput of that subsystem. (We still assume that the system is in equilibrium. To do otherwise would quickly leave the scope of this book, and the current state-of-the-art soon afterwards!) The same might sometimes be said of the variance of a time delay and higher moments if an appropriate extension of Little's result is available.

However, there are many situations in which the mean response time (or other delay) is inadequate. The variability of response time is also important. For example, in multi-access systems, a response time with a mean of a minute or more might be tolerable provided that it does not vary too much, i.e. that its standard deviation is not too large. If response times are consistently close to a minute, users are likely to be patient, but if it often happens that response times exceed five minutes, the system's service will likely be deemed unacceptable. More importantly still, response time *distributions* are required in reliability models. For example, in many real time systems, it is often important that sensors are checked at regular instants, which must never be separated by more than some given time, say 5 seconds. The management will therefore be interested in the probability that consecutive checks take place more than 5 seconds apart. In a sensitive environment, such as a nuclear plant or a military system, this probability must be small, say 0.001%, so moments of the time between checks will be useless.

Recently, there has been a growing interest in the distribution of response times as networks for transaction processing (TP) have become more widespread; for example 'hole in the wall' automated teller machines (ATMs; not to be confused with the term ATM used in Chapter 11). The prediction of quantiles is becoming even more important with the increasing use of diverse parallel computer systems. These can often execute tasks in various different ways with potentially large variations in performance. Consequently, international standards for transaction processing, such as the TPC benchmarks, now include requirements for the 90% and 95% quantiles. For example, it may be specified that a TP system should have a response time of less than 2 seconds at least 95% of the time (the position of the 95% quantile should be to the left of 2 seconds) and less than 1 second at least 90% of the time.

There is therefore a need to derive the probability distribution (or density) of time delay random variables in queueing models. Such analysis is notoriously difficult and exact results have been obtained only in rather special cases. Certainly, when we consider networks of queues, a very much smaller class than we considered in Chapters 6 and 7 can be solved – essentially networks with a 'tree-like' structure in which paths are overtake-free. However, for the single server queue, the distribution of waiting (and other) times can be derived for a variety of queueing disciplines and the results are not restricted to the $M/M/1$ case. We consider these problems in the next section, before going on to look at queueing networks in Section 9.2. Unfortunately, the required densities are often obtained as Laplace transforms, which can be difficult to invert analytically. Although numerical inversion techniques are available, these can be expensive to implement and/or lack precision, especially in the often crucial tail region of the density. We shall see in Section 9.3 that the actual density of response times can be obtained in tree-like networks – as a function of time – by analytical inversion of its Laplace transform. This chapter concludes with a brief discussion of approximate methods, which are essential for non-trivial networks that lack tractable exact solutions.

9.1   Time delays in the single server queue

There are many intervals of time that are of interest in queueing systems, for example the waiting and queueing times of a customer, which we considered for the M/M/1 and M/G/1 queues with FCFS discipline in Section 5.1.2. Another important time interval is the **busy period** (or **busy time**) of the server, i.e. the interval between successive idle periods. In fact, the analysis of busy times will prove a powerful technique and lead, in particular, to the waiting time distribution of an M/G/1 queue with LCFS queueing discipline. PS queueing discipline will also be considered, but only for M/M/1 queues where we can make use of properties of the continuous time Markov chain. In fact, we will see that the method used for PS can also be used for other queueing disciplines in an M/M/1 queue.

9.1.1   Busy periods

To investigate the busy period, we first observe that its distribution is the same for all queueing disciplines that are work-conserving and for which the server is never idle when the queue is non-empty. Suppose that, in equilibrium, whilst an initial customer C_1 is being served, customers $C_2, \ldots, C_{Z+1}$ arrive, where the random variable Z, conditional on service time S for C_1, is Poisson with mean λS. Without loss of generality, we assume an LCFS queueing discipline with no pre-emption so that, if $Z \neq 0$, the second customer to be served is C_{Z+1}. Any other customers that arrive while C_{Z+1} is being served will also be served before C_Z. Now, let N be the random variable for the number of customers served during a busy period and let N_i be the number of customers served between the instants at which C_{i+1} commences service and C_i commences service $(1 \leqslant i \leqslant Z)$. Then $N_1, \ldots, N_Z$ are independent and identically distributed as N. This is because the sets of customers counted by $N_Z, N_{Z-1}, \ldots, N_1$ are disjoint and (excluding $C_{Z+1}, C_Z, \ldots, C_2$ respectively) arrive consecutively after C_{Z+1}. Thus,[1]

$$N \stackrel{\mathcal{D}}{=} \begin{cases} 1 & Z = 0 \\ 1 + N_Z + N_{Z-1} + \ldots + N_1 & Z \geqslant 1 \end{cases}$$

Now, denoting the busy time random variable by T, its distribution function by H and the Laplace–Stieltjes transform of H by H^*, we have

---

[1] $\stackrel{\mathcal{D}}{=}$ means 'equal in distribution'.

$$H^*(\theta) = E[e^{-\theta T}] = E[E[e^{-\theta T}|N]] = E[E[e^{-\theta(S_1+\cdots+S_N)}|N]]$$
$$= E[E[e^{-\theta S}]^N]$$

where $S_1, \ldots, S_N$ are independent service time random variables, distributed as S, say. Thus, $H^*(\theta) = \Phi(B^*(\theta))$ where Φ is the probability generating function of N, which we determine as follows using conditional expectations.

$$\Phi(y) = E[y^N] = E[E[E[y^N|Z, S]|S]]$$
$$= E[E[yE[y^N]^Z|S]]$$
$$= yE[E[\{\Phi(y)\}^Z|S]$$
$$= yE[e^{-\lambda S(1-\Phi(y))}]$$

since Z (conditioned on S) is Poisson with mean λS. This argument was used on several occasions in Chapter 5. The reader who is not confident with the manipulation of conditional expectations should either look at Proposition 3.3 or else follow the corresponding steps using explicit summations and integration. Thus,

$$\Phi(y) = yB^*(\lambda(1 - \Phi(y)))$$

which is an integral equation of $\Phi(y)$ which in general cannot be solved analytically. However, it can be solved for the M/M/1 case, i.e. when $B^*(s) = \mu/(s + \mu)$; this is left as an exercise. Returning to the busy time distribution, we now have

$$H^*(\theta) = \Phi(B^*(\theta)) = B^*(\theta)B^*(\lambda[1 - H^*(\theta)])$$
$$= B^*(\theta + \lambda[1 - H^*(\theta)])$$

Although this equation cannot be solved in general for $H^*(\theta)$, we can obtain the moments of busy time by differentiating at $\theta = 0$. For example, the mean busy period, m say, is given by

$$-m = H^{*\prime}(0) = B^{*\prime}(0)\{1 + \lambda[-H^{*\prime}(0)]\} = -(1 + \lambda m)\mu^{-1}$$

since $H^*(0) = 1$, and so $m = (\mu - \lambda)^{-1}$, the M/M/1 queue result. The above technique, in which a time delay is defined in terms of independent, identically distributed time delays, is often called 'delay cycle analysis' and is due to Takacs (1962).

9.1.2 Waiting times in LCFS queues

Now let us consider waiting times under LCFS disciplines. For the pre-emptive–resume variant, we note that a task's waiting time is independent of the queue length it faces on arrival, since the whole of the queue already there is suspended until after this task completes service. Thus without loss of generality we may assume that the task arrives at an idle server. Waiting time then becomes identical to the busy period. We therefore conclude that the waiting time distribution in an LCFS-PR M/G/1 queue has Laplace–Stieltjes transform $H^*(\theta) = B^*(\theta + \lambda(1 - H^*(\theta)))$.

For LCFS without pre-emption we can modify the busy period analysis. First, if a task arrives at an empty queue, its waiting time is the same as a service time. Otherwise, its *queueing* time Q is the sum of the residual service time R of the customer in service and the service times of all other tasks that arrive before it commences service. This definition is almost the same as that of a busy period given above. The only differences are that the time spent in service by the initial customer C_1' (C_1 above) is not a service time but a residual service time and the random variable N is now the number of customers served during the queueing time Q; call it N'. Proceeding as before, we obtain the Laplace–Stieltjes transform of the distribution function of Q as follows:

$$Q^*(\theta) = E[E[e^{-\theta(R+S_1+\ldots+S_{N'-1})}|N']] = E[e^{-\theta R}]E[E[e^{-\theta S}]^{N'-1}]$$

since R is independent of the S_i ($1 \leqslant i \leqslant N' - 1$). Thus, $Q^*(\theta) = R^*(\theta)\Psi(B^*(\theta))/B^*(\theta)$ where Ψ is the probability generating function of N' defined by $\Psi(y) = E[y^{N'}]$. Now, N' satisfies a similar recurrence formula in terms of Z', the number of customers that arrive whilst C_1' is in (residual) service, to that given for N above in terms of Z:

$$N' \stackrel{\mathcal{D}}{=} \begin{cases} 1 & Z' = 0 \\ 1 + N_{Z'} + N_{Z'-1} + \ldots + N_1 & Z' \geqslant 1 \end{cases}$$

The '1' represents the service completion of C_1' and N_i represents the number of arrivals during the (full) residence time of the ith customer to arrive during the residual service time of C_1' ($1 \leqslant i \leqslant Z'$). We now have

$$\begin{aligned} \Psi(y) &= E[E[E[y^{N'}|Z', R]|R]] \\ &= yE[E[E[y^N]^{Z'}|R]] \\ &= yE[E[\Phi(y)^{Z'}|R]] \\ &= yE[e^{-\lambda R[1-\Phi(y)]}] \\ &= yR^*(\lambda[1 - \Phi(y)]) \end{aligned}$$

Now, by the result obtained for forward recurrence times in Section 4.5.2 (note the change in the role of μ), the residual service time has density $f_R(t) = \mu[1 - F_S(t)]$. Thus, the Laplace transform of this density is $R^*(\theta) = \mu[1 - B^*(\theta)]/\theta$ which follows by a simple integration by parts. Hence we have:

$$Q^*(\theta) = R^*(\theta)R^*(\lambda\{1 - \Phi(B^*(\theta))\}) = R^*(\theta + \lambda[1 - H^*(\theta)])$$

$$= \frac{\mu(1 - B^*(\theta + \lambda[1 - H^*(\theta)]))}{\theta + \lambda[1 - H^*(\theta)]}$$

$$= \frac{\mu[1 - H^*(\theta)]}{\theta + \lambda[1 - H^*(\theta)]}$$

Finally, since a customer arrives at an empty queue with probability $1 - \rho$ in equilibrium (as we have seen already), we obtain for the transform of the waiting time distribution

$$W^*(\theta) = (1 - \rho)B^*(\theta) + \rho B^*(\theta)Q^*(\theta)$$

$$= B^*(\theta)\left(1 - \rho + \frac{\lambda(1 - H^*(\theta))}{\theta + \lambda(1 - H^*(\theta))}\right)$$

since waiting time is the sum of queueing time and service time and these two random variables are independent.

The third variant of the LCFS discipline, pre-emptive-restart, cannot be handled in this way since it is not work-conserving and so the analysis that produced the integral equation for H^* does not apply. We will not consider it further.

Example 9.1 _____

Let us compare the response time variability in a computer system, modelled by an $M/G/1$ queue, with FCFS and LCFS scheduling policies. We can do this to a great extent by comparing the first two moments, which are obtained by differentiating the respective formulae for $W^*(\theta)$ at $\theta = 0$. We obtain the same result for the mean waiting time, which is as expected from Little's result since the mean queue lengths are the same under each discipline. This is because, if there is no pre-emption, the same argument we used to find the queue length distribution (e.g. the embedded Markov chain method) holds whichever customer is selected next for service after a service completion. However, it turns out that the second moment of waiting time for FCFS discipline is $(1 - \rho)$ times that for LCFS. Thus, LCFS discipline suffers a much greater variability as ρ approaches 1, i.e. as the queue begins to saturate. The qualitative result is quite obvious, but the preceding analysis enables the load at which the effect becomes serious to be estimated quantitatively.

_____

Notice that LCFS-PR also gives a different *mean* waiting time in general. This is reasonable because we cannot expect the mean queue length (and hence, using Little's result, the mean waiting time) to be the same since the pre-emption invalidates the argument used to derive the queue length distribution. Intuitively, the average amount of work left to do in the queue should be the same, but since the queue will, in general, contain partially served customers, its expected length should be different. In fact, as we saw above, mean waiting time is the same as for the case of an M/M/1 queue. This is a consequence of the memoryless property of the exponential distribution: a partially served customer is stochastically identical to one that has received no service. For more discussion, the reader might wish to consult Chapter 5 where various queueing disciplines are considered. The determination of the second moment of waiting time for LCFS disciplines is left as an exercise.

9.1.3 Waiting times with processor-sharing discipline

A customer's waiting time at a queue with PS discipline was discussed briefly in Section 5.1.2 for the M/M/1 queue and here we derive the result quoted there. We do not consider the M/G/1 queue (or any other) because the method does not generalize, requiring the Markov property at every point in continuous time. Indeed, the problem is still unsolved in the more general case. The problem with PS discipline is that the rate at which a customer receives service during its sojourn at a server varies as the queue length changes due to new arrivals and other departures. Thus, we begin by analysing the waiting time density (or rather its Laplace transform) of a customer with a given service time requirement.

Proposition 9.1

In a PS M/M/1 queue with fixed arrival rate λ and fixed service rate μ, the Laplace transform of the waiting time distribution, conditional on a customer's service time being x, is

$$W^*(s|x) = \frac{(1 - \rho)(1 - \rho r^2)e^{-[\lambda(1-r)+s]x}}{(1 - \rho r)^2 - \rho(1 - r)^2 e^{-(\mu/r - \lambda r)x}}$$

where r is the smaller root of the equation $\lambda r^2 - (\lambda + \mu + s)r + \mu = 0$ and $\rho = \lambda/\mu$.

Proof Suppose a given customer C arrives at time 0, faces a queue length N, requires a service time X and has waiting time T for random variables X, T, N. For $t > 0$, consider the interval $(0, t + h)$ and the initial infinitesimal sub-interval $(0, h)$. If the queue length faced (N) is $n > 0$ and the service time requirement (X) is $x > 0$, in $(0, h)$ there may be either an arrival or a service completion of a customer other than C, to order h. Hence, by the Random Observer Property, we have the following equation:

$$P(T \leqslant t + h \mid X = x, N = n)$$
$$= [1 - \lambda h - \mu_n h] P(T \leqslant t \mid X = x - h/(n + 1), N = n)$$
$$+ \lambda h P(T \leqslant t \mid X = x, N = n + 1)$$
$$+ \mu_n h P(T \leqslant t \mid X = x, N = n - 1) + o(h)$$

where $\mu_n = n\mu/(n + 1)$ is the total service rate received by all customers other than C. All customers have exponential service requirements with unit mean in this Markovian queue. We can use the same random variable T throughout the right-hand side by the Random Observer Property applied to both the Poisson arrival process and combined departure process of the n customers other than C. Consequently, our method would break down for any queue other than M/M/m. In the case $n = 0$, the same equation holds since $\mu_0 = 0$, suppressing the terms representing departures from an empty set of customers. Letting $F_n(t, x) = P(T \leqslant t \mid X = x, N = n)$, we now obtain

$$\frac{F_n(t + h, x) - F_n(t, x)}{h} = -\frac{1}{n + 1} \frac{\partial F_n}{\partial x} - (\lambda + \mu_n) F_n$$
$$+ \lambda F_{n+1} + \mu_n F_{n-1} + o(1)$$

Multiplying throughout by $n + 1$ and taking the limit $h \to 0$ then gives

$$(n + 1) \frac{\partial F_n}{\partial t} = -\frac{\partial F_n}{\partial x} - [(n + 1)\lambda + n\mu] F_n$$
$$+ (n + 1)\lambda F_{n+1} + n\mu F_{n-1}$$

Differentiating with respect to t gives the same equation, with F substituted by f, for the conditional density function $f_n(t, x) = \partial F_n(t, x)/\partial t$. We now take Laplace transforms, noting that the Laplace transform of $\partial f/\partial t$ is, integrating by parts,

$$\int_0^\infty \frac{\partial f}{\partial t} e^{-st}\, dt = -f(0) + s \int_0^\infty f(t) e^{-st}\, dt$$

Thus, if $L_n(s, x)$ is the Laplace transform of $f_n(t, x)$, we have

$$(n + 1)s L_n = -\frac{\partial L_n}{\partial x} - [(n + 1)\lambda + n\mu] L_n$$
$$+ (n + 1)\lambda L_{n+1} + n\mu L_{n-1}$$

since $f(0) = 0$ for $x > 0$. We solve this recurrence relation by introducing the generating function $G(z, s, x) = \sum_{n=0}^{\infty} L_n(s, x) z^n$. Multiplying throughout by z^n and summing from $n = 0$ to ∞ then gives, after some simplification,

$$[\mu z^2 - (\lambda + \mu + s)z + \lambda] \frac{\partial G}{\partial z} - \frac{\partial G}{\partial x} = (\lambda + s - \mu z)G$$

This is a somewhat simple first-order partial differential equation for G and the result we seek for $W^*(s|x)$ is $(1 - \rho)G(\rho, s, x)$. To solve the equation, we solve the auxiliary equations

$$\frac{dz}{\mu z^2 - (\lambda + \mu + s)z + \lambda} = -dx = \frac{dG}{(\lambda + s - \mu z)G}$$

For z and x, we have

$$\frac{dz}{\lambda(1 - r_1 z)(1 - r_2 z)} = \frac{1}{\lambda(r_1 - r_2)} \left(\frac{r_1}{1 - r_1 z} - \frac{r_2}{1 - r_2 z} \right) dz$$

$$= -dx$$

where r_1 and r_2 are the roots of the equation $\lambda r^2 - (\lambda + \mu + s)r + \mu = 0$. Thus,

$$\ln \left(\frac{1 - r_2 z}{1 - r_1 z} \right) = \lambda(r_2 - r_1)x + A$$

where A is an arbitrary constant to be determined by the boundary conditions. For G and z, we have similarly,

$$\frac{dG}{G} = \frac{\lambda + s}{\lambda(r_1 - r_2)} \left(\frac{r_1}{1 - r_1 z} - \frac{r_2}{1 - r_2 z} \right) dz$$

$$- \frac{\mu}{\lambda(r_2 - r_1)} \left(\frac{1}{1 - r_1 z} - \frac{1}{1 - r_2 z} \right) dz$$

so that

$$\ln(G) = \frac{1}{\lambda(r_1 - r_2)} [(\lambda + s - \mu/r_2) \ln(1 - r_2 z)$$

$$- (\lambda + s - \mu/r_1) \ln(1 - r_1 z)] + B$$

where B is a function of A (because there can be only one arbitrary constant for a first-order equation). Using the equation for x to eliminate $\ln(1 - r_2 z)$ we obtain

$$\ln(G) = \frac{1}{\lambda(r_1 - r_2)}\{(\lambda + s - \mu/r_2)\lambda(r_2 - r_1)x$$
$$- [(\lambda + s - \mu/r_1) - (\lambda + s - \mu/r_2)]\ln(1 - r_1 z)\}$$
$$+ \phi(A) \qquad \text{for some function } \phi$$
$$= -(\lambda + s - \lambda r_1)x - \ln(1 - r_1 z) + \phi(A)$$

since $r_1 r_2 = \rho^{-1}$, r_1 and r_2 being the roots of the given quadratic equation. We determine ϕ from the boundary condition at $x = 0$ that $G(z, s, 0) = 1/(1 - z)$ for all s, $0 \leqslant z < 1$, since $F_n(t, 0) = 1$ for all $t \geqslant 0$, $n \geqslant 0$ ($f_n(t, 0) = \delta(t)$) so that $L_n(s, 0) = 1$. At $x = 0$,

$$A = \ln\left(\frac{1 - r_2 z}{1 - r_1 z}\right)$$

so that

$$\phi\left[\ln\left(\frac{1 - r_2 z}{1 - r_1 z}\right)\right] = \ln(1 - r_1 z) - \ln(1 - z)$$

Now, if $u = (1 - r_2 z)/(1 - r_1 z)$, $z = (1 - u)/(r_2 - r_1 u)$ so that

$$\phi(\ln(u)) = \ln\left(1 - r_1\frac{1 - u}{r_2 - r_1 u}\right) - \ln\left(1 - \frac{1 - u}{r_2 - r_1 u}\right)$$

$$= \ln\left(\frac{r_2 - r_1}{(r_2 - 1) - (r_1 - 1)u}\right)$$

Thus, the function ϕ is defined by

$$\phi(y) = \ln\left(\frac{1 - \rho r_1^2}{(1 - \rho r_1) - \rho r_1(r_1 - 1)e^y}\right)$$

using $r_1 r_2 = \rho^{-1}$ again. In general,

$$A = \ln\left(\frac{1 - r_2 z}{1 - r_1 z}\right) - \lambda(r_2 - r_1)x$$

and so

$$\phi(A)$$
$$= \ln\left(\frac{1 - \rho r_1^2}{(1 - \rho r_1) - \rho r_1(r_1 - 1)[(1 - r_2 z)/(1 - r_1 z)]e^{-\lambda(r_2 - r_1)x}}\right)$$
$$= \ln\left(\frac{(1 - \rho r_1^2)(1 - r_1 z)}{(1 - \rho r_1)(1 - r_1 z) - \rho r_1(r_1 - 1)(1 - r_2 z)e^{-\lambda(r_2 - r_1)x}}\right)$$

whereupon,

$$\ln(G) = -(\lambda + s - \lambda r_1)x - \ln(1 - r_1 z)$$

$$+ \ln\left(\frac{(1 - \rho r_1^2)(1 - r_1 z)}{(1 - \rho r_1)(1 - r_1 z) - \rho r_1(r_1 - 1)(1 - r_2 z)e^{-\lambda(r_2 - r_1)x}}\right)$$

so that

$$G = \frac{(1 - \rho r_1^2)e^{-(\lambda + s - \lambda r_1)x}}{(1 - \rho r_1)(1 - r_1 z) - \rho r_1(r_1 - 1)(1 - r_2 z)e^{-\lambda(r_2 - r_1)x}}$$

This defines G uniquely up to the choice of the roots r_1 and r_2. Now, at $s = 0$, the roots are easily seen to be 1 and ρ^{-1} so that 1 is the smaller since $\rho < 1$ for a steady state to exist. But $L_n(0, x) = 1$ for all n, x and so $G(z, 0, x) = 1/(1 - z)$ for all x, $0 \leq z < 1$. This boundary condition holds if and only if $r_1 = 1$ at $s = 0$ so that r_1 is the smaller root. The result now follows by setting $z = \rho$, multiplying by $1 - \rho$ and taking $r_2 = 1/\rho r_1$.   ∎

This result was first derived by Coffman et al. (1970). Near to $s = 0$, the roots of this equation are close to 1 and μ/λ, so that the smaller root is 1 by stationarity. Of course, we can obtain the Laplace transform of the unconditional waiting time density as

$$W^*(s) = \int_0^\infty W^*(s|x)\mu e^{-\mu x}\,dx$$

and attempt a complicated integration. This result follows because the service time of each customer is exponential with parameter μ.

The essential technique used in the proof of Proposition 9.1 splits the waiting time in an M/M/1 queue into an infinitesimal initial interval and the remaining waiting time. In fact the technique is quite general, applying to more disciplines than PS. In particular, it can be used to find the Laplace transform of the waiting time density in an M/M/1 queue with 'random' discipline or FCFS discipline with certain queue length dependent service rates and in M/M/1 queues with 'negative customers' (Gelenbe et al. 1991; Harrison and Pitel 1992).

Observe how complex a problem it is to obtain waiting time densities in single queues with non-FCFS queueing discipline. It is hardly surprising, therefore, that we restrict our attention to FCFS in the next section.

9.2   Time delays in networks of queues

Networks of queues present an entirely different kettle of fish to the case of a single server queue – even a stationary Markovian network. This is because, although we know the distribution of the queue lengths at the time of arrival of a given (tagged) customer at the first queue in

Figure 9.1   A tandem series of queues.

its path (by the Random Observer Property or the Job Observer Property), we cannot assume this stationary distribution exists upon arrival at subsequent queues. The reason is that the arrival times at the subsequent queues are only finitely later than the arrival time at the first queue. Hence, the state existing at the subsequent arrival times must be conditioned on the state that existed at the time of arrival at the first queue. Effectively, a new time origin is set at the first arrival time, with known initial joint queue length probability distribution – actually a stationary distribution. Even in open networks with no feedback, where it is easy to see that all arrival processes are Poisson, this conditioning cannot be overlooked and we cannot assume all queues on a path are independent and in an equilibrium state at the arrival times of the tagged customer. This is in contrast to Jackson's theorem (Chapter 6), because we are not considering the queues at the same time instant. The situation appears even more hopeless in open networks with feedback and closed networks.

However, things are not quite as hopeless as they seem. First, we can prove that the FCFS queues in an **overtake-free** path in a Markovian open network behave *as if* they were independent and in equilibrium when observed at the successive arrival times of a tagged customer. By an overtake-free path, or a path with **no overtaking**, we mean that a customer following this path will depart from its last queue before any other customer that joins any queue in that path *after* the said customer. Moreover, such other customers can have no influence of any kind on the said customer. Surprisingly, a similar result holds for overtake-free paths in closed networks, e.g. all paths in networks with a tree-like structure – see Figure 9.2. In the next two subsections, we consider respectively those open and closed networks for which a solution for the time delay density along a given path can be derived. These are followed by a discussion of the problems that confront us when we attempt to generalize the network structure.

9.2.1 Open networks

The simplest open network we can consider is a pair of queues in series. However, it is almost as easy to analyse a tandem series of any number of queues, as shown in Figure 9.1. In fact, we can be more general than this, as we will see shortly. Now, the distribution of the time delay of a customer passing through a tandem series of queues is the convolution of the stationary waiting time distributions of each queue in the series considered in isolation. This follows from the following stronger result.

Proposition 9.2

In a series of stationary M/M/1 queues with FCFS discipline, the waiting times of a given customer in each queue are independent.

Proof First we claim that the waiting time of a tagged customer, C say, in a stationary M/M/1 queue is independent of the departure process before the departure of C. This is a direct consequence of reversibility since C's waiting time is clearly independent of the arrival process after C's arrival under FCFS discipline at a single server. Applying this property to the stochastically identical reversed process, a corresponding customer C' arrives at the negative time of departure of C and departs at the negative time of arrival of C. It therefore has the same waiting time as C and the claim follows in the original process by the duality established in Section 5.1.3.

To complete the proof, let A_i, T_i denote C's time of arrival and waiting time respectively at queue i in a series of m queues $(1 \leq i \leq m)$. Certainly, by our claim, T_1 is independent of the arrival process at queue 2 before A_2 and so of the queue length faced by C on arrival at queue 2. Thus, T_2 is independent of T_1. Now, we can ignore customers that leave queue 1 after C since they cannot arrive at any queue in the series before C, again because all queues have single servers and FCFS discipline. Thus, T_1 is independent of the arrival process at queue i before A_i and so of T_i for $2 \leq i \leq m$. Similarly, T_j is independent of T_k for $2 \leq j < k \leq m$. ∎

From this proposition it follows that, since the waiting time probability density at the stationary queue i, considered in isolation $(1 \leq i \leq m)$, has Laplace transform $(\mu_i - \lambda)/(s + \mu_i - \lambda)$, the density of the time to pass through the whole series of m queues is the convolution of these densities, with Laplace transform $\prod_{i=1}^{m} (\mu_i - \lambda)/(s + \mu_i - \lambda)$.

There is one obvious generalization of this result: the final queue in the series need not be M/M/1 since we are not concerned with its output. Also, the same result holds, by the same reasoning, when the final queue is M/G/n for $n \geq 1$. Moreover, Proposition 9.2 generalizes to **tree-like networks** which are defined as follows, and illustrated in Figure 9.2. A tree-like network consists of:

- a linear **trunk segment** containing one or more queues in tandem, the first being called the **root** queue

- a number (greater than or equal to zero) of disjoint **subtrees**, i.e. tree-like sub-networks, such that customers can pass to the roots of the subtrees from the last queue in the trunk segment or else leave the network with specified routing probabilities (which sum to 1)

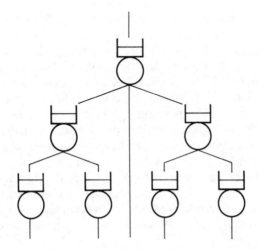

Figure 9.2   An open tree-like network of queues.

The **leaf** queues (or **leaves**) are those from which customers leave the network.

The proof of Proposition 9.2, extended to tree-like networks, carries through unchanged since every path in the network is overtake-free. Hence we can ignore the customers that leave any queue on the path after the tagged customer. Indeed, we can generalize further to overtake-free paths in *any* Markovian open network for the same reason. Conditional on the choice of path of queues numbered, without loss of generality, $1, \ldots, m$, the Laplace transform of the passage time density is the same as for the tandem queue of m servers considered above. Thus, by the Law of Total Probability, the unconditional passage time density has Laplace transform

$$p_{12}p_{23} \cdots p_{m-1,m} \prod_{i=1}^{m} \frac{\mu_i - \lambda}{s + \mu_i - \lambda}$$

where $p_{12}p_{23} \cdots p_{m-1,m}$ is the probability that a customer arriving at queue 1 selects path $1, 2, \ldots, m$.

To generalize the network structure further leads to serious problems and solutions have been obtained only for very special cases. The simplest case of a network with overtaking is the following three-queue network:

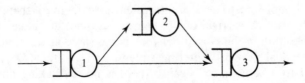

In this network the path of queues numbered $\{1, 3\}$ is overtake-free and so the passage time density can be obtained as described above. However, overtaking is possible on the path $\{1, 2, 3\}$ since when the tagged customer C is at queue 2, any customers departing queue 1 (after C) can reach queue 3 first. The arrival processes to every queue in this network are independent Poisson, by Burke's theorem together with the decomposition and superposition properties of Poisson processes. However, this is not sufficient for the passage time distribution to be the convolution of the stationary sojourn time distributions at each queue on a path with overtaking: the proof of Proposition 9.2 breaks down. This particular problem has been solved, by considering the state of the system at the departure instant of the tagged customer from server 1 and using complex variable methods in an analysis similar to ours for a PS queue (Mitrani 1985). However, more general networks appear intractable.

Even more complex are networks with feedback. Even a network consisting of one queue with feedback is difficult to solve (Takacs 1963). This might suggest that a study of closed networks would be hopeless, but this is not the case provided we consider only overtake-free paths with no feedback. This is the subject of the next section.

9.2.2 Closed networks

As for the case of open networks, we begin with the simplest case, a cyclic network that comprises a tandem network with departures from its last queue fed back into the first queue. There are no external arrivals and hence a constant population. Again, all service disciplines are FCFS and all service rates are constant.

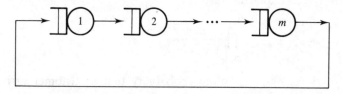

We solve for the Laplace transform of the cycle time density by considering a *dual* network, namely the tandem, open network consisting of the same servers $1, \ldots, m$ with *no external arrivals*. Eventually, therefore, the dual network has no customers, i.e. its state is $e = (0, 0, \ldots, 0)$, the empty state, with probability 1. All other states with one or more customers are transient. Now, given that the state immediately after the arrival of the tagged customer at queue 1 is i, the ensuing cycle time in the closed network is the same as the time interval between the dual network entering states i and e – the (*first*) *passage time* from i to e. This is so because there is no overtaking and service rates are constant. Thus the progress of the tagged customer in its cycle cannot be influenced by any customer behind it. We only need consider customers ahead of the tagged customer and can ignore those recycling after leaving the last queue. Observe that if service rates varied with queue length, we could *not* ignore customers behind the tagged customer, even though they could not overtake, because they would influence the service rate received by the tagged customer.

We therefore seek the density of the passage time from state i to e in the dual network, $f(t|i)$, where i is a state of the form $(i_1, \ldots, i_m)$ with $i_1 > 0$, corresponding to the tagged customer having just arrived at server 1. We know the probability distribution of the state seen by the tagged customer on arrival at the first queue by the Job Observer Property (Chapter 6) and so can calculate the cycle time density by deconditioning f using the Law of Total Probability.

Given a cyclic network of population n, let the state space of the dual network be $S_n = \{(u_1, \ldots, u_m) | 0 \le u_i \le n, 1 \le i \le m; \sum_{i=1}^{m} u_i \le n\}$ and define, for $u \in S_n$,

$$\lambda_u = \sum_{i=1}^{m} \mu_i \varepsilon(u_i)$$

where μ_i is the service rate of server i, $\varepsilon(n) = 1$ if $n > 0$ and $\varepsilon(0) = 0$. Thus λ_u is the total service rate in state u, i.e. the instantaneous transition rate out of state u in the Markov process defining the queueing network. The length of time spent in state u, called the **holding time** in state u, is an exponential random variable with parameter λ_u and so has a density with Laplace transform $\lambda_u/(s + \lambda_u)$. Now, given that the network next enters state v after u, the passage time from u to e is the sum of the holding time in state u and the passage time from v to e. Thus, the density of the passage time from u to e, $f(t|u)$, has Laplace transform $L(s|u)$ given by the equations

$$L(s|u) = \sum_{v \in S} q_{uv} \frac{\lambda_u}{s + \lambda_u} L(s|v) \qquad u \ne e$$

$$L(s|e) = 1$$

where q_{uv} is the one-step transition probability from state u to v. Now let $\mu(u, v)$ denote the rate of the server from which a departure causes the state transition $u \to v$. Then $q_{uv} = \mu(u, v)/\lambda_u$. Thus, defining $q_{uv}^* = \mu(u, v)/(s + \lambda_u)$, we have the matrix equation

$$L = Q^* L + 1_e$$

where $L = (L(s|u) | u \in S_n)$, $Q^* = (q_{uv}^* | u, v \in S_n)$ and 1_e is the vector with component corresponding to state e equal to 1 and the rest 0.

The above equations apply to (first) passage times to a given state e in any Markovian network, and for our cyclic network we may write, for $u \neq e$,

$$L(s|u) = \sum_{i=1}^{m} \varepsilon(u_i) \frac{\mu_i}{s + \lambda_u} L(s|u^i)$$

where $u^i = (u_1, \ldots, u_i - 1, u_{i+1} + 1, \ldots, u_m)$ if $i < m$, $u^m = (u_1, \ldots, u_{m-1}, u_m - 1)$. Multiplying throughout by $(s + \lambda_u)$ and noting that $\lambda_u = \sum_{i=1}^{m} \varepsilon(u_i)\mu_i$ then gives

$$sL(s|u) = \sum_{i=1}^{m} \varepsilon(u_i)\mu_i\{L(s|u^i) - L(s|u)\}$$

Now, let π_u be the equilibrium probability that an arrival at queue 1 in the cyclic network sees state u (including itself) and let $S = \{(u_1, \ldots, u_m) | \sum_{i=1}^{m} u_i = n, u_1 > 0\}$ be the set of all valid initial states u, where n is the population of the cyclic network (the initial population of the dual network). Referring to Chapter 6, in an equilibrium cyclic network, all visitation rates are the same and we take them to be one. Thus, by the Job Observer Property

$$\pi_u = \frac{1}{G(n-1)} \mu_1 \prod_{i=1}^{m} \mu_i^{-u_i}$$

where G is the normalizing constant function for the cyclic network. Now, the unconditional Laplace transform of the cycle time density, a function of the network's population n, is

$$L_n(s) = \sum_{u \in S} \pi_u L(s|u)$$

Thus, multiplying the equation for $L(s|u)$ throughout by $G(n-1)\pi_u$ and summing over $u \in S$ now gives

$$G(n-1)L_n(s)s = \mu_1 \sum_{i=1}^{m} \mu_i \sum_{u \in S} \varepsilon(u_i) \prod_{j=1}^{m} \mu_j^{-u_j}\{L(s|u^i) - L(s|u)\}$$

But for $2 \leq i < m$,

$$\sum_{u \in S} \varepsilon(u_i)f(u^i) = \sum_{v \in S} \varepsilon(v_{i+1})f(v)$$

for any function f, by a simple change of summation variable. Similarly,

$$\sum_{u\in S}\varepsilon(u_1)f(u^1) = \sum_{v\in S}\varepsilon(v_2)f(v) + \sum_{v\in S_1}f(v)$$

where $S_1 = \{(0, u_1, \ldots, u_{m-1})|\sum_{i=1}^{m-1}u_i = n,\ u_1 > 0\}$. Furthermore,

$$\mu_i\prod_{j=1}^{m}\mu_j^{-u_j} = \mu_{i+1}\prod_{j=1}^{m}\mu_j^{-v_j}$$

where $v = u^i$, for $1 \leq i < m$. We therefore obtain

$$G(n-1)L_n(s)s$$

$$= \mu_1\sum_{i=1}^{m-1}\left\{\mu_{i+1}\sum_{u\in S}\varepsilon(u_{i+1})\prod_{j=1}^{m}\mu_j^{-u_j}L(s|u) - \mu_i\sum_{u\in S}\varepsilon(u_i)\prod_{j=1}^{m}\mu_j^{-u_j}L(s|u)\right\}$$

$$+ \mu_1\mu_2\sum_{u\in S_1}\prod_{j=2}^{m}\mu_j^{-u_j}L(s|u)$$

$$+ \mu_1\mu_m\sum_{u\in S}\varepsilon(u_m)\prod_{j=1}^{m}\mu_j^{-u_j}\{L(s|u^m) - L(s|u)\}$$

Cancelling terms, this reduces to

$$G(n-1)L_n(s)s = -\mu_1^2\sum_{u\in S}\varepsilon(u_1)\prod_{j=1}^{m}\mu_j^{-u_j}L(s|u)$$

$$+ \mu_1\mu_2\sum_{u\in S_1}\prod_{j=2}^{m}\mu_j^{-u_j}L(s|u)$$

$$+ \mu_1\mu_m\sum_{u\in S}\varepsilon(u_m)\prod_{j=1}^{m}\mu_j^{-u_j}L(s|u^m)$$

But $\sum_{u\in S}\varepsilon(u_m)f(u^m) = \sum_{v\in S'}f(v)$ for any function f, where $S' = \{(u_1, \ldots, u_m)|\sum_{i=1}^{m}u_i = n-1,\ u_1 > 0\}$, and $\mu_m\prod_{j=1}^{m}\mu_j^{-u_j} = \prod_{j=1}^{m}\mu_j^{-v_j}$ where $v = u^m$. Thus, noting too that $u_1 > 0$ for $u \in S$, we find

$$G(n-1)L_n(s)s = -G(n-1)L_n(s)\mu_1 + G_1(n-1)L_{1,n}(s)\mu_1$$

$$+ G(n-2)L_{n-1}(s)$$

where G_i is the normalizing constant function for the network with server i removed ($1 \leq i \leq m$), and $L_{i,n}(s)$ is the Laplace transform of the cycle time density in this network when its population is n. Writing $H(n) = G(n-1)L_n(s)$ and $H_i(n) = G_i(n-1)L_{i,n}(s)$ similarly for the network with server i removed, we obtain the recurrence relation

$$(s + \mu_1)H(n) = \mu_1 H_1(n) + H(n-1)$$

with the boundary conditions that for $m = 1$, $n \geq 1$,

$$H(n) = \mu_1^{-(n-1)}\left(\frac{\mu_1}{\mu_1 + s}\right)^n = \frac{\mu_1}{(\mu_1 + s)^n}$$

and for $m \geq 1$,

$$H(1) = \prod_{j=1}^{m} \frac{\mu_j}{\mu_j + s}$$

The recurrence can be seen more easily if we renumber the servers in reverse order and define $H(m, n)$ to be $H(n)$ above when the network has m servers. Then we obtain, for $n \geq 2$,

$$(s + \mu_m)H(m, n) = \mu_m H(m - 1, n) + H(m, n - 1)$$

with boundary conditions $H(1, n) = \mu_1/(\mu_1 + s)^n$ and $H(m, 1) = \prod_{j=1}^{m} \mu_j/(\mu_j + s)$ $(m, n \geq 1)$. In this form, the recurrence relation appears very much like the one we derived for normalizing constants in Chapter 6. We can use it to compute the required Laplace transform or else to obtain its expansion as a sum of products. However, this result is a special case of a more powerful theorem which is derived below using a generalization of the above approach.

We consider cycle times in **closed tree-like** queueing networks. Such networks are defined in the same way as open tree-like networks except that customers departing from leaf-queues next visit the root queue. Clearly such networks have the no-overtaking property and if paths are restricted to start at one given server (here the root), they define the most general class for which it holds. We will assume all trunk segments to have just one node – the root – by assigning one subtree to the root if necessary.

Now let Z denote the set of all paths through a closed tree-like network A, i.e. sequences of servers entered in passage through A. For all $z = (z_1, \ldots, z_k) \in Z$, $z_1 = 1$, z_k is a leaf server and the order of Z is the number of leaf servers since there is only one path from the root to a given leaf in a tree. The probability of choosing path z is equal to the product of the routing probabilities between successive component centres in z. The Laplace transform of cycle time distribution is given by Proposition 9.3 below, obtained in different forms independently by various authors, e.g. Daduna (1982), Harrison (1984) and Kelly and Pollett (1983). The last of these references gives the most general result, namely the multidimensional Laplace transform of the *joint* density of the sojourn times spent by the tagged customer at each server on *any* overtake-free path in a network with multiple classes. The proof we give below is simpler, being based on the recursive properties of trees. At the same time the result is almost as general in that any overtake-free path must be tree-like (although several such intersecting paths could exist in the whole network) and the extension to multiple classes and joint sojourn times is straightforward.

Consider then a closed tree-like network A of M servers, with root server numbered 1, and r subtrees. The dual, open tree-like network is denoted by A° (with departures from the leaves), the set of leaf servers by *Leaf* and we will use the following additional notation:

- $\{p_{ij}|1 \leq i, j \leq M\}$ are the routing probabilities of A
- $\{p_{ij}^*|1 \leq i, j \leq M\}$ are the routing probabilities of the corresponding open network, so that $p_{ji}^* = p_{ji}$ if $j \notin Leaf$ and we set $p_{ji}^* = 0$ if $j \in Leaf$ $(1 \leq i \leq M)$

We will also use various sets of states and associated stationary probabilities, defined as follows:

- $S_m(n) = \{(u_1, \ldots, u_m)|\sum_{i=1}^{m} u_i = n, \ u_1 \geq 0\}$ is the state space of the sub-network of servers numbered $1, 2, \ldots, m$ when its population is $n \geq 1$. We abbreviate $S_M(n)$ by $S(n)$ but will need the more general set later in Section 9.3.2.

- $U \equiv U(n) = \{u \in S(n)|u_1 > 0\}$ is the subset of *initial* states in $S(n)$ where the tagged customer has just arrived at server 1. $U(n)$ has stationary probability mass function $P(\bullet, n)$, i.e. $P(u, n)$ is the probability that, in equilibrium, the state seen by the tagged customer on arrival at server 1 is u (including itself).

- $U^{(h)} \equiv U^{(h)}(n) = \{u \in S(n)|u_1 = 0, \ u_h > 0\}$ for each root server numbered h in the r subtrees $(1 \leq h \leq r)$, are the subsets of states in which the tagged customer has just entered the hth subtree. $U^{(h)}$ has stationary probability mass function $P^{(h)}(\bullet, n)$. Thus $P^{(h)}(u, n)$ is the probability that, in equilibrium, the state seen by the tagged customer on arrival at server h is u. Notice that although we may assume a steady state network on arrival of the tagged customer at server 1, the stationary probabilities $P^{(h)}$ will *not* be correct for the state seen on arrival at server h (and similarly for any other subsequent server in the path) by the *same* customer since we will have conditioned on the state existing on its arrival at server 1.

By the Job Observer Property (see Chapter 6) we have

$$P(u, n) = \frac{1}{G(n-1)}\left(\frac{\mu_1}{e_1}\right)\prod_{i=1}^{M}\left(\frac{e_i}{\mu_i}\right)^{u_i} \qquad \text{for } u \in U$$

$$P^{(h)}(u, n) = \frac{1}{G^{(h)}(n-1)}\left(\frac{\mu_h}{e_h}\right)\prod_{i=2}^{M}\left(\frac{e_i}{\mu_i}\right)^{u_i} \qquad \text{for } u \in U^{(h)}$$

where G and $G^{(h)}$ are the corresponding normalizing constant functions, the arguments of which we will drop henceforth when equal to $n - 1$; i.e. $G \equiv G(n-1)$, $G^{(h)} \equiv G^{(h)}(n-1)$. We usually write P_u for $P(u, n)$, $P_u^{(h)}$ for $P^{(h)}(u, n)$ and also denote the stationary probabilities for the initial states in the network with one customer removed by $P'_u \equiv P(u, n-1)$. We can now state and prove the following.

Proposition 9.3

For the closed tree-like network A, the Laplace transform of cycle time distribution, conditional on choice of path $z \in Z$ is

$$L(s|z) = \frac{1}{G(n-1)} \sum_{u \in S(n-1)} \prod_{i=1}^{M} \left(\frac{e_i}{\mu_i}\right)^{u_i} \frac{|z|}{\prod_{j=1}} \left\{\frac{\mu_{z_j}}{s + \mu_{z_j}}\right\}^{u_{z_j}+1}$$

where $|z|$ is the number of servers in path z.

Proof Without loss of generality we may assume that the path $z = (1, 2, \ldots, |z|)$ and that A (and A°) has only one server in its root segment since otherwise the second server could be regarded as the root of a single subtree. In the open network A°, let $L_u(s|z)$ denote the Laplace transform of the passage time from state $u \in U$ to the state immediately following departure of the tagged customer from A°, conditional on choice of path z. (Henceforth in the proof we will drop the argument $(s|z)$.) Now, the Laplace transform of the holding time in state $u \in U$ is $\lambda_u/(s + \lambda_u)$ where $\lambda_u = \sum_{i=1}^{M} \varepsilon(u_i)\mu_i$ is the total service rate in state u. Thus we have:

$$L_u = \sum_{\substack{1 \le i,j \le M \\ i \notin Leaf}} \varepsilon(u_i)p_{ij}^*(z, u) \frac{\mu_i}{s + \lambda_u} L_{u^{ij}} + \sum_{i \in Leaf} \varepsilon(u_i) \frac{\mu_i}{s + \lambda_u} L_{u^i}$$

where $u^{ij} = (u_1, \ldots, u_i - 1, \ldots, u_j + 1, \ldots, u_M)$ $(1 \le i \ne j \le M)$ and $u^i = (u_1, \ldots, u_i - 1, \ldots, u_M)$ $(i \in Leaf)$. $\{p_{ij}^*(z, u)\}$ are routing probabilities in A°, conditional on the tagged customer's path being z. Thus for customers completing service at server i other than the tagged one, $p_{ij}^*(z, u) = p_{ij}^*$ for $1 \le i$, $j \le M$. For the tagged customer, $p_{ij}^*(z, u) = 1$ if $j = i + 1$ $(1 \le i < |z|)$ and 0 otherwise. Now for $u \in U$ with $u_i > 0$, we have

$$P_u = \frac{e_i\mu_j}{e_j\mu_i} P_{u^{ij}} \qquad \begin{array}{l} \text{if } (u^{ij})_1 \ne 0 \text{ so that } u^{ij} \in U \\ \text{(i.e. either } i \ne 1 \text{ or } u_i > 1) \end{array}$$

Similarly, $GP_u = (e_i/\mu_i)G(n-2)P'_{u^i}$ if $i \in Leaf$ and $u_i > 0$. Multiplying throughout by $(s + \lambda_u)GP_u$ and summing over $u \in U$ we then obtain

$$\sum_{u \in U} (s + \lambda_u)GP_uL_u = \sum_{1 \le i,j \le M} \frac{e_i}{e_j} \sum_{u \in U} p_{ij}^*(z, u)\varepsilon(u_i)\mu_jGP_{u^{ij}}L_{u^{ij}}$$

$$+ \sum_{1 \le j \le M} \mu_1 \sum_{\substack{u \in U \\ u_1 = 1}} p_{1j}^*(z, u)GP_uL_{u^{1j}}$$

$$+ \sum_{i \in Leaf} \sum_{u \in U} \varepsilon(u_i)e_iG(n-2)P'_{u^1}L_{u^i}$$

where we define $P_{u^{ij}} = 0$ if $i = 1$ and $u_1 = 1$ so that terms involving $u^{ij} \notin U$ are suppressed in the first sum and considered only in the second. Thus in the first sum, the non-zero contributions cannot represent a service completion of the tagged customer so that $p_{ij}^*(z, u)$ can be replaced by p_{ij}^*. Furthermore, $\sum_{i=1}^{M} e_i p_{ij}^* = \sum_{i=1}^{M} e_i p_{ij} = e_j$ if $j \neq 1$ and $= 0$ if $j = 1$ since for $1 \leq i \leq M$, $p_{ij}^* = p_{ij}$ if $j \neq 1$ and $= 0$ otherwise.

All terms in the second sum represent the departure of the tagged customer from server 1 (the state transitions are all of the form $u \to u^{1j}$ with $u_1 = 1$) so that $p_{1j}^*(z, u) = 1$ if $j = 2$ and $= 0$ otherwise, giving only one term. Furthermore, if $u_1 = 1$ then $GP_u = G^{(h)} P_{u^{1h}}^{(h)}$ for each subtree with root server numbered h. Changing the summation domains on the right-hand side and simplifying now yields

$$\sum_{u \in U} (s + \lambda_u) GP_u L_u = \sum_{v \in U} \left(\sum_{j \neq 1} \varepsilon(v_j) \mu_j \right) GP_v L_v$$

$$+ \mu_1 \sum_{\substack{u \in U \\ u_1 = 1}} G^{(2)} P_{u^{12}}^{(2)} L_{u^{12}}$$

$$+ \sum_{i \in Leaf} e_i \sum_{v \in U(n-1)} G(n-2) P_v' L_v$$

Now, $L = \sum_{u \in U} P_u L_u$ and more generally we write $L_n = \sum_{u \in U(n)} P(u, n) L_u$ (again dropping the argument $(s|z)$), so that $L_{n-1} = \sum_{u \in U(n-1)} P_u' L_u$ for the network A with population $n - 1$. Let A_i denote the network A with servers $1, \dots, i$ removed and let P_i, G_i be the stationary probability and normalizing constant functions for 'initial' states in A_i (i.e. with at least one customer at server $i + 1$) defined by

$$P_i(u, n) = \frac{1}{G_i(n-1)} \left(\frac{\mu_{i+1}}{e_{i+1}} \right) \prod_{j=i+1}^{M} \left(\frac{e_j}{\mu_j} \right)^{u_{j-i}}$$

for $u \in \{(u_1, \dots, u_{M-i}) | u_1 > 0, u_j \geq 0 \ (2 \leq j \leq M - i), \Sigma u_i = n\}$. Notice that because of the non-overtaking property, when the tagged customer arrives at server $i + 1$ $(0 \leq i < |z|)$, the queues at servers $1, \dots, i$ in A° must be empty. Let $L_i(n)$ be the Laplace transform of the distribution of the passage time for *any* customer arriving in the steady state at server $i + 1$ in A_i with population n. Rearranging the previous equation now gives

$$(s + \mu_1) G(n-1) L(n) = \mu_1 G_1(n-1) L_1(n)$$

$$+ e_1 G(n-2) L(n-1)$$

since $\{u^{12}|u \in U\}$ is the set of all states that might exist as the tagged customer enters the subtree with root server 2 and $\sum_{i \in Leaf} e_i = e_1$.

Defining $H_{i,n} = G_i(n-1)L_i(n)$ $(0 \leq i < |z|, \; 1 \leq n \leq N)$ and repeating the above procedure for the remaining servers in the path z, we obtain the recurrence relation

$$(s + \mu_i)H_{i-1,n} = \mu_i H_{i,n} + e_i H_{i-1,n-1}$$
$$\text{for } 1 \leq i \leq |z|, 1 \leq n \leq N$$

Now, for $|z| \leq i \leq M$, we may take $L_i(n) = 1$ or $s = 0$, representing zero contribution to the time delay from servers not in z. We then have $H_{i,n} = G_i(n-1)$ for $|z| \leq i \leq M$ and so obtain

$$X_i H_{i-1,n} = \mu_i H_{i,n} + e_i H_{i-1,n-1}$$
$$\text{for } 1 \leq i \leq M, 1 \leq n \leq N$$

where

$$X_i = \begin{cases} s + \mu_i & \text{for } 1 \leq i \leq |z| \\ \mu_i & \text{for } |z| < i \leq M \end{cases}$$

The boundary conditions are $H_{m-1,n} = \mu_1/(\mu_1 + s)^n$ and $H_{01} = \prod_{j=1}^{|z|} \mu_j/(\mu_j + s)$ $(m, n \geq 1)$. Thus

$$H_{i1} = \begin{cases} 1 & \text{for } |z| \leq i < M \\ \displaystyle\prod_{j=i+1}^{|z|} \frac{\mu_j}{\mu_j + s} & \text{for } 0 \leq i < |z| \end{cases}$$

$$H_{Mn} = 0 \quad \text{for } 1 \leq n \leq N$$

This recurrence for $H_{i,n}$ is now easily solved for H_{0N}, for example by defining the generating functions $F_i(x) = \Sigma H_{in} x^n$. The required result (with N substituted for n) then follows on dividing by $G_0(N-1) \equiv G(N-1)$. ∎

In fact Proposition 9.3 holds for any overtake-free path in a closed Jackson queueing network (recall the preceding discussion) and we will use it in this more general form in the next section.

9.3   Inversion of the Laplace transforms

The majority of results on distributions of time delays in queueing networks and passage times in more general stochastic processes are given as Laplace (or Laplace–Stieltjes) transforms. The preceding is no exception. In general, numerical methods must be used to invert the Laplace transform, which can be expensive to implement and are sometimes unreliable, especially in the tail region of a density which is often the prime objective of a performance study. However, in certain cases, analytical inversion is possible, typically when a stochastic model is based on exponential distributions. The result of Proposition 9.3 is a good example. First, we can simplify the summation giving $L(s|z)$ by partitioning the sum over $S(n-1)$ according to the total number of customers, p, at servers in the overtake-free path $1, 2, \ldots, m$ (without loss of generality). This gives:

$$L(s) = \frac{1}{G(n-1)} \sum_{\substack{p=0 \\ }}^{n-1} \sum_{\substack{\Sigma_{i=m+1}^{M} n_i = n-p-1 \\ n_i \geq 0}}$$

$$\prod_{i=m+1}^{M} \left(\frac{e_i}{\mu_i}\right)^{n_i} \sum_{\substack{\Sigma_{i=1}^{m} n_i = p \\ n_i \geq 0}} \prod_{i=1}^{m} \left(\frac{e_i}{\mu_i}\right)^{n_i} \prod_{j=1}^{m} \left(\frac{\mu_j}{s + \mu_j}\right)^{n_j+1}$$

$$= \frac{1}{G(n-1)} \sum_{p=0}^{n-1} G_m(n-p-1) \sum_{\substack{\Sigma_{i=1}^{m} n_i = p \\ n_i \geq 0}} \prod_{i=1}^{m} \left(\frac{e_i}{\mu_i}\right)^{n_i} \prod_{j=1}^{m} \left(\frac{\mu_i}{s + \mu_j}\right)^{n_j+1}$$

$$(9.1)$$

where $G_m(k)$ is the normalizing constant of the whole network with servers $1, \ldots, m$ removed and population $k \geq 0$, i.e.

$$G_m(k) = \sum_{\substack{\Sigma_{i=m+1}^{M} n_i = k \\ n_i \geq 0}} \prod_{i=m+1}^{M} \left(\frac{e_i}{\mu_i}\right)^{n_i}$$

Now, the Laplace transforms in the inner sum are products of the Laplace transforms of Erlang densities. Moreover, their coefficients are geometric. Such transforms can be inverted analytically. In the simplest case, all the servers on the overtake-free path are identical, i.e. have the same rate, and the inversion can be done by inspection. In the case that the μ_i are all distinct ($1 \leq i \leq m$), the density function is derived in Harrison (1990) and the question of degenerate μ_i is considered in Harrison (1991). These results are considered in the next two sections.

9.3.1 Overtake-free paths with identical servers

When all the rates μ_i in the path $i = 1, 2, \ldots, m$ are the same, equal to μ say, the above Laplace transform (Equation 9.1) is a mixed sum of terms of the form $(\mu/(s + \mu))^{p+m}$ since in the inner summation

$\sum_{i=1}^{m} n_i + 1 = p + m$. Each term can therefore be inverted by inspection to give a corresponding mixture of Erlangians for the passage time density. We therefore have:

Proposition 9.4

If the centres in overtake-free path $(1, 2, \ldots, m)$ in the network of Proposition 9.3 all have service rate μ, the path's time delay density function is

$$\frac{\mu^m e^{-\mu t}}{G(n-1)} \sum_{p=0}^{n-1} G_m(n-p-1) G^m(p) \mu^p \frac{t^{p+m-1}}{(p+m-1)!}$$

where $G^m(k)$ is the normalizing constant for the sub-network comprising servers $1, \ldots, m$ only, with population $k \geqslant 0$, defined by

$$G^m(k) = \sum_{\substack{\Sigma_{i=1}^m n_i = k \\ n_i \geqslant 0}} \prod_{i=1}^{m} \left(\frac{e_i}{\mu_i}\right)^{n_i}$$

Proof Equation (9.1) simplifies to

$$L(s) = \frac{1}{G(n-1)} \sum_{p=0}^{n-1} G_m(n-p-1) \left(\frac{\mu}{s+\mu}\right)^{p+m} \sum_{\substack{\Sigma_{i=1}^m n_i = p \\ n_i \geqslant 0}} \prod_{i=1}^{m} \left(\frac{e_i}{\mu}\right)^{n_i}$$

The result now follows since the Erlang density $\mu^{p+m}[t^{p+m-1}/(p+m-1)!]e^{-\mu t}$ has (uniquely) Laplace transform $[\mu/(s+\mu)]^{p+m}$ and by definition of $G^m(p)$. ∎

From this result we can immediately obtain formulae for moments higher than the mean of a customer's transmission time.

Corollary For a path of equal rate servers, message transmission time has kth moment equal to

$$\frac{1}{\mu^k G(n-1)} \sum_{p=0}^{n-1} G_m(n-p-1) G^m(p)(p+m) \ldots$$

$$(p+m-k+1) ∎$$

9.3.2 Overtake-free paths with distinct servers

The case of paths with equal rate servers is easy, involving only some algebraic manipulation of summations. However, even when the rates are different, the inversion can be done analytically to give a closed form result. The analysis is now rather more difficult, however, and we just state the main result after giving a sketch of its derivation. Two examples then follow for illustration, the second giving a simple result for cyclic networks of arbitrary size and population.

The result was first derived by Harrison (1990) for the case where all the service rates on the overtake-free path are distinct, the opposite extreme to the previous section. The first step is to invert the Laplace transform $L(n, s) = \prod_{i=1}^{m}[\mu_i/(s + \mu_i)]^{n_i}$ where $n = (n_1, \ldots, n_m)$, $n_i \geq 1$ and the μ_is are distinct. This yields the density function

$$f(n, t) = \left(\prod_{i=1}^{m}\mu_i^{n_i}\right)\sum_{j=1}^{m}D_j(n, t)$$

where the $D_j(n, t)$ are given by a recurrence on n. Next, given real numbers $a_1, \ldots, a_M$ for integer $M \geq m$, let

$$H_{jm}(z) = \sum_{n \in S(M+m)} D_j(n, t)\prod_{i=1}^{M}(a_i z_i)^{n_i-1}$$

so that passage time density is obtained from the $H_{jm}(1, \ldots, 1)$ with $a_i = e_i/\mu_i$. The central result is that

$$H_{jm}(z) = \frac{e^{-\mu_j t}}{\displaystyle\prod_{1 \leq i \neq j \leq M} (\mu_i - \mu_j)}$$
$$\times \left[\sum_{i=0}^{m} \frac{(a_j z_j t)^{m-i}}{(m - i)!} \sum_{\substack{n \in S(M+i) \\ n_j=1}} \prod_{\substack{k=1 \\ k \neq j}}^{M}\left(\frac{(a_k z_k - a_j z_j)}{\mu_k - \mu_j}\right)^{n_k-1}\right]$$

We therefore have the following.

Proposition 9.5

If the servers in an overtake-free path $(1, 2, \ldots, m)$ have distinct service rates $\mu_1, \mu_2, \ldots, \mu_m$, the passage time density function, conditional on the choice of path, is

$$\frac{\displaystyle\prod_{i=1}^{m}\mu_i}{G(n - 1)}\sum_{p=0}^{n-1} G_m(n - p - 1)\sum_{j=1}^{m}\frac{e^{-\mu_j t}}{\displaystyle\prod_{1 \leq i \neq j \leq m} (\mu_i - \mu_j)}$$
$$\times \sum_{i=0}^{p} \frac{(e_j t)^{p-i}}{(p - i)!} \sum_{\substack{n \in S_m(m+i) \\ n_j=1}} \prod_{\substack{k=1 \\ k \neq j}}^{m}\left(\frac{(e_k - e_j)}{\mu_k - \mu_j}\right)^{n_k-1}$$

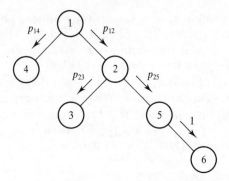

Figure 9.3 A tree-like network and its routing probabilities.

The summations over $S_m(m + 1)$ are just normalizing constants that may be computed efficiently along with the $G_m(n - p - 1)$ and $G(n - 1)$ by Buzen's algorithm; see Chapter 6. However, in simple cases, such as the following example, direct summation is easier and more illustrative. ∎

Example 9.2

We show the computation of the cycle time density for a path in a closed tree-like network with dual open network shown in Figure 9.3. The network of Figure 9.3 has six servers with rates $\mu_1, \ldots, \mu_6$, population 3 and non-zero routing probabilities as shown. Thus the visitation rates $e_1, \ldots, e_6$ for servers 1–6 are respectively proportional to 1, p_{12}, $p_{12}p_{23}$, p_{14}, $p_{12}p_{25}$, $p_{12}p_{25}$. Now let

$$E_{jk} = \frac{(e_j t)^k e^{-\mu_j t}}{k! \prod_{\substack{1 \leq i \neq j \leq m}} (\mu_i - \mu_j)} \quad \text{for } j = 1, 2, 3 \text{ and } k = 0, 1, 2$$

and for $j \in \{1, 2, 3\}$ let j', $j'' \in \{1, 2, 3\}$ be such that $j', j'' \neq j$ and $j' \neq j''$ (i.e. $\{j, j', j''\} = \{1, 2, 3\}$).

Then by Proposition 9.4, the cycle time density for the path $(1, 2, 3)$ is $D_1 + D_2 + D_3$ where, for $j = 1, 2, 3$

$$\frac{G(3)}{\mu_1 \mu_2 \mu_3} D_j = G_3(3) E_{j0} + G_3(2) \left\{ E_{j1} + \left[\left(\frac{e_{j'} - e_j}{\mu_{j'} - \mu_j} \right) + \left(\frac{e_{j''} - e_j}{\mu_{j''} - \mu_j} \right) \right] E_{j0} \right\}$$

$$+ \left\{ E_{j2} + \left[\left(\frac{e_{j'} - e_j}{\mu_{j'} - \mu_j} \right) + \left(\frac{e_{j''} - e_j}{\mu_{j''} - \mu_j} \right) \right] E_{j1} \right.$$

$$+ \left. \left[\left(\frac{e_{j'} - e_j}{\mu_{j'} - \mu_j} \right)^2 + \left(\frac{e_{j'} - e_j}{\mu_{j'} - \mu_j} \right)\left(\frac{e_{j''} - e_j}{\mu_{j''} - \mu_j} \right) + \left(\frac{e_{j''} - e_j}{\mu_{j''} - \mu_j} \right)^2 \right] E_{j0} \right\}$$

Example 9.3 _____

For a *cyclic* network of M exponential servers and population N, cycle time distribution is

$$\frac{\left(\prod\limits_{i=1}^{M}\mu_i\right)t^{N-1}}{G(N)(N-1)!}\sum_{j=1}^{M}\frac{e^{-\mu_j t}}{\prod\limits_{1\leqslant i\neq j\leqslant M}(\mu_i-\mu_j)}$$

This follows by setting $e_1 = \ldots = e_M = 1$ in Proposition 9.4, so that all terms are zero in the rightmost sum except when $n_k = 1$ for all k, i.e. when $i = 0$. Finally, note there is only one partition of the state space, namely the one with all $N - 1$ customers at the servers $1, \ldots, M$. Thus we have $G_M(n) = 1$ if $n = 0$ and $= 0$ if $n > 0$, so that only terms with $p = N - 1$ give a non-zero contribution.

_____

Proposition 9.4 can be generalized to allow arbitrary service rates at the nodes on an overtake-free path: not necessarily all the same nor all distinct. Essentially, we start with the case of distinct rates and successively combine any two servers with equal rates. The combination involves manipulation of the summations and reduces the problem to two similar problems on networks with one less node in the overtake-free path. Thus, in each step, one degenerate server is removed until all the remaining problems are on paths with distinct rate servers. The details may be found in Harrison (1991).

9.4 Approximate methods

We have seen that finding time delay densities is a hard problem, often with complex and computationally expensive solutions (when they can be solved at all). Consequently, in most practical applications, the performance engineer requires approximate methods. There is no single established methodology for such approximation and most of the techniques used are *ad hoc*. In increasing order of sophistication, the following techniques have been used:

• A particular form is prescribed for the required distribution and its parameters are determined by matching moments. Moments may be predicted by an analytical model or estimated by simulation or actual measurement. Typical distributions include Coxian (with a small number of phases), generalized exponential and (mixtures of) Erlang. Although adequate for some purposes, involving probabilities near the median, for example, this approximation lacks a cause and effect relationship and is likely to be poor in the tail region in particular.

- A common simplifying assumption is that the queues in the path of a tagged customer in a queueing network behave as if independent, isolated and in equilibrium at the times of arrival of that customer; the **independence approximation**. The assumption is always true for the first queue in the path by the arrival theorem (with one fewer customer in the case of a closed network) but approximate for all the other queues, except in the case of simple open networks of the type we considered in Section 9.2.1. The approximation is poorest when the ordering of customers in the network is most highly constrained, since then the independence assumption is clearly invalid. For example, in a two-node cyclic network with FCFS queues and population N, it is known with probability one that if there are k customers at queue 1 at any time, then there are $N - k$ at server 2. In particular, suppose server 1 is fast and its queue is empty on arrival of the tagged customer. Then it is very unlikely that queue 2 will be empty on arrival there and very likely that it will contain $N - 1$ or $N - 2$ customers. It does turn out that cyclic networks with FCFS queues give poor results under the independence approximation, but in networks where the ordering of customers has few constraints, for example richly connected networks or networks with PS discipline at many queues, it is usually quite accurate.

- An enhancement of the independence approximation admits limited dependence of the queue lengths faced by the tagged customer at successive servers. It is assumed that the queue length faced at any queue entered after the first in the path (which is independent by the arrival theorem) depends only on that faced at the previous node. This is called the **paired centre approximation** and gives highly accurate results in a variety of queueing networks (Harrison 1986).

- Finally, it might be possible to use maximum entropy methods in continuous time to give the 'least surprising' density function for a time delay subject to the constraints imposed by its moments. In Section 8.4 we considered maximum entropy for discrete random variables and noted that the method gave accurate approximations for the state space distributions in a variety of networks. A continuous time analogue exists and appears well suited to predicting time delay distributions efficiently, given the expected values of certain functions of the state random variable. As before, the most important step would be to identify and estimate the crucial constraints, but this is an open problem.

As with any approximate model, the above methods are subject to validation. The exact results described in the previous sections provide valuable benchmarks for this purpose. An approximation that passes these tests should be subjected to simulation testing and compared with real observations before being accepted as a performance engineering tool.

SUMMARY

- Time delay distributions are, in general, difficult to obtain and exact results are restricted to single server queues and overtake-free paths in simple Jackson networks.

- Delay analysis is a powerful method that exploits the Random Observer Property in an M/G/1 queue to give a fixed point equation. It yields the busy time distribution which in turn gives the waiting time distribution under LCFS queueing discipline.

- Waiting time distribution in an M/M/1 queue under processor sharing queueing discipline can be obtained using an explicit analysis of the transitions that can occur immediately after the arrival of a tagged customer. This leads to a partial differential equation for the Laplace transform of the waiting time density, conditioned on the service requirement of the tagged customer.

- Time delay densities in tandem or tree-like open Jackson networks are easy to obtain using reversibility arguments. The result is the convolution of the exponential waiting time densities of the corresponding M/M/1 queues.

- For both open and closed Jackson networks, time delay densities can be obtained for overtake-free paths. The result in the open case is a simple convolution as above. For closed networks, the Laplace transform takes a product form.

- Time delay densities are typically obtained as Laplace transforms which, in general, have to be inverted numerically. However, analytical inversion is possible for overtake-free paths in Jackson networks.

- Approximate methods are usually necessary in practical performance engineering studies.

EXERCISES

9.1 (20 M/M/1 queueing time delay)
Requests arrive as a Poisson stream with rate λ and queue to use a communication channel. Each request holds the channel for an exponentially distributed time with mean $1/\mu$. We want to find the

rate at which the channel should serve requests so that a proportion p of them have to queue for service for no more than t_0 time units. Derive a fixed point equation for μ, which can be used to compute μ numerically (given values of λ, p and t_0). Suggest a good starting value for the iteration.

9.2   (20 M/M/1 with LCFS)
Derive the mean waiting time in an M/M/1 queue with LCFS queueing discipline, with and without pre-emption, by differentiating the expressions for $H^*(\theta)$ and $W^*(\theta)$ in Section 9.1.2 and setting $\theta = 0$. (Use L'Hôpital's rule often!)

9.3   (40 M/M/1 waiting time distribution)
The essential technique used in the proof of Proposition 9.1 splits the waiting time in an M/M/1 queue into an infinitesimal initial interval and the remaining waiting time. Using this method (i.e. for processor sharing) find the Laplace transform of the waiting time density in an M/M/1 queue

(a)   with a 'random' service discipline (i.e. polling)

(b)   with the FCFS discipline with queue length dependent service rate

9.4   (20 Busy period)
Show that the Laplace transform of the density function of busy period for an M/M/1 queue is given by

$$\Phi(y) = \frac{\lambda + \mu}{2\lambda}\left[1 - \left(1 - \frac{4\lambda\mu s}{(\lambda + \mu)^2}\right)^{1/2}\right]$$

9.5   (30 Queueing time distribution)
Find the queueing time distribution for a G/M/1 queue.

Chapter 10
Blocking in Queueing Networks

10.1 Introduction   382
10.2 Types of blocking   383
10.3 Two finite queues in
    a closed network   388
10.4 Aggregating Markovian
    states   390

10.5 BAS blocking   392
10.6 BBS blocking   405
10.7 Repetitive service
    blocking   409

In the queueing networks discussed so far, we have assumed that the buffers at each node are infinite. Sometimes this assumption is reasonable, especially if the mean queue lengths at the nodes are much smaller than the available buffer size in the real system. However, real systems invariably have finite buffers and often we want our model to represent the blocking effects of a full buffer at one node. Typically, the full node causes other nodes to stall (i.e. stop processing), and this can have a significant performance impact. This is the main motivation for studying queueing networks with finite buffers and therefore blocking.

In queueing networks with blocking, customers can be blocked because the server either stops serving or repeats service. The server waits for some condition to become satisfied or some event to occur before it can resume service. For example, the condition may be that some other node completes serving a customer. This is a very general description of blocking and we will classify different types of blocking in Section 10.2. We then consider an open tandem network with finite buffers and a closed queueing network with finite queues at each node. To get a good understanding of the problem of blocking in closed networks, we will initially consider two-node queueing networks before analysing larger networks. First, let us look at blocking from a more general viewpoint.

10.1   Introduction

In product form queueing networks we have already seen the use of local state dependencies for the service rate at a node (i.e. the service rate of a node depends on the queue length at that node). Now we extend this dependence so that the service rate of a server depends on the state of the entire network (i.e. all the queue lengths) giving global state dependence. This does not satisfy the conditions for a product form solution but, provided the service times are exponential, we can represent the network by a Markov process. One form of blocking is a type of dependency that makes some node's service rate go to zero. This is what happens in queueing networks with finite capacity queues when the destination node is full and cannot accept any more customers.

Blocking often occurs in real systems and is an important feature to model because in practice, incorrect structural assumptions can lead to large errors. In general, blocking effects are more important than assumptions like 'exponential service times only at FCFS nodes' because incorrect distributional assumptions typically lead to smaller errors. Since exact solutions are not practical for blocking networks, many efficient approximate algorithms have been proposed. The remainder of this chapter is devoted to developing good algorithms for solving queueing networks with finite capacity queues. The approximation techniques in Chapter 8 (e.g. decomposition or the maximum entropy methods) can also be adapted to solve blocking networks.

Another feature of a system that is useful to represent in a queueing network is contention for passive resources. An **active resource** is represented by a service node in a queueing network and provides service that advances customers towards their completion. In contrast, a **passive resource** needs to be held by an active resource for it to provide its service. A common example of a passive resource is computer memory, where the active resource is the main processor. This can be viewed as an example of simultaneous resource possession: for example the processor and computer memory both need to be held at the same time. There is memory contention because other components, such as a direct memory access (DMA) i/o channel processor, also need to access memory. We can think of a finite queue as a passive resource because a slot in the queue buffer is a passive resource that needs to be held by a customer so that a server can provide service. Thus a full queue at the destination node can lead to blocking and the customer has to wait in another node's queue.

For the single server queue we have already considered finite queues, so now we extend that to queueing networks. Product form

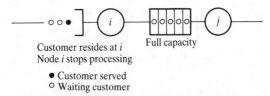

Customer resides at i
Node i stops processing

Full capacity

● Customer served
○ Waiting customer

Figure 10.1 Blocking after service.

queueing networks require infinite capacities at each node, but memory is finite and so we need to model finite capacity queues for a more accurate representation. As we have seen, full nodes downstream cause blocking of nodes upstream. For example, in a data communication network, a full node cannot accept messages from other nodes and so blocks those nodes. This is where some form of flow control is needed. A similar situation arises in telephone networks when a circuit cannot be completed because an intermediate link is in full use (see Chapter 11). There are numerous examples of this type of blocking caused by finite queues. The effect of full nodes depends on the type of blocking, so we give one classification, into three types, in the next section.

We assume the queueing network under consideration has the following characteristics:

M = number of nodes
K = number of customers (for the closed network)
C_i = capacity of node i
p_{ij} = transition probability from node i to node j
μ_i = constant service rate of node i (exponential distribution with mean $1/\mu_i$)

Note that we restrict our analysis to exponential service times, unless otherwise stated. For a Coxian service time distribution, we effectively have a series of exponential servers within each node. The customer in a Coxian service (i.e. in one of the exponential servers at the node) blocks any customers from entering the first stage of service. Thus by replacing the Coxian nodes with a series of exponential servers, we create a large exponential network with blocking that is more complicated but of the same type that we are considering. We assume that the service discipline at all nodes is FCFS with various blocking mechanisms. We now describe a way of classifying these blocking mechanisms.

10.2 Types of blocking

10.2.1 Blocked after service

Probably the most common form of blocking is **blocked after service (BAS) blocking** (or **transfer blocking**). Suppose node j is full and a customer at node i completes its service and chooses to go to node j, as illustrated by Figure 10.1. Then node i becomes blocked and stops

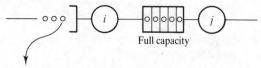

Customer declares that its destination is *i* before it starts
service and starts receiving service only after a departure from *j*

Figure 10.2   Blocking before service.

processing. Node *i* is called the blocked node and node *j* is called the
blocking node.

Other nodes can also get blocked by node *j*, so when a space
becomes available at node *j* there is a choice of which node to unblock.
So we need to impose an ordering on blocked nodes so that the first in
the ordering is unblocked first. We will assume that there is an arrival
time ordering so the first node that is blocked is also the first to be
released. Note that a node can only get blocked by one other node at a
time.

10.2.2   Blocked before service

Another common type of blocking mechanism is **blocked before service
(BBS) blocking** (also called **service blocking**). In this type of blocking a
customer declares its destination node (*j* for example) before starting
service at node *i*. If node *j* is full then node *i* becomes blocked and will
become unblocked when space is available at the destination node. This
type of blocking is illustrated in Figure 10.2. Sometimes, node *j* may
become full only after the customer at node *i* has started its service.
When this happens, the service is interrupted and node *i* becomes
blocked. Service is resumed from the point of interruption when space
becomes available at the destination. The interrupted customer may
restart its service (by taking another value from the same random
variable), but for an exponential service time, the two policies are
equivalent.

Unlike BAS blocking, BBS blocking does not require an ordering
to be imposed on blocked nodes. When a full node *j* blocks more than
one node and then a space becomes available at node *j*, all blocked
customers begin their service in their respective nodes; the first one to
complete will move on to node *j* and possibly block the other nodes
again (if node *j* is full).

When a node is blocked, the blocked customer may or may not
occupy the node's buffer (depending on the application that is being
modelled). We distinguish these types of service blocking by:

BBS-SNO: server is not occupied (i.e. service node does not hold the
blocked customer)

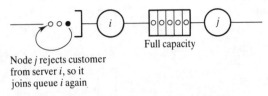

Node j rejects customer
from server i, so it
joins queue i again

Figure 10.3   Repetitive service blocking.

BBS-SO: server is occupied (i.e. service node can hold blocked customer)

In effect, for BBS-SNO blocking, the blocked customer prevents the node from operating but does not use up any of its buffer space. The distinction of these two types becomes important when the blocked node itself becomes full, and by that gaining the potential to block other nodes. When the population is low enough, the SO and SNO types are identical since then only one node can be blocked and the blocked node still has space to accept another customer. The maximum such population K' is obtained by finding the minimum total capacities of two connected nodes:

$$K' = \min\left(C_i + C_j \mid i, j = 1, 2, \ldots, M \text{ and } p_{ij} > 0\right)$$

As an example, consider a communication channel where a message needs to be transferred from some source to a destination node via a channel. When the destination node is full, the channel cannot transmit its message, but it also cannot store the message. Since the customer cannot occupy the channel (we can think that the message is not created but pending) we have BBS-SNO blocking for the channel resource. The other type of blocking, BBS-SO, is common in open networks for manufacturing systems as well as computer systems. Consider a backup system that transfers data on disk to tape via main memory buffers and the CPU. When memory buffers become full, the transfer cannot continue and we have BBS-SO blocking because the disk can only start transferring data when memory is available. Note that in all these examples for BBS blocking, the servers do no real work except move customers between nodes.

10.2.3   Repetitive service blocking

The third type of blocking we consider is **repetitive service (RS) blocking** or **rejection blocking**. For this type, when a customer completes its service at node i only to find its destination node j full, it repeats its service at node i, as illustrated in Figure 10.3. RS blocking is different from BAS and BBS blocking in that nodes that are blocked do not completely stop processing customers.

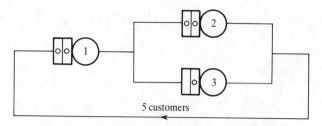

Figure 10.4   A three-node queueing network with finite queues.

Again there are two options: RS-FD (fixed destination) and RS-RD (random destination). In RS-FD blocking, the destination is unchanged for each repeated attempt whereas in RS-RD blocking, the destination is randomly chosen on each attempt.

RS blocking has applications in telecommunication systems and arises in reversible queueing networks. For example, RS-FD blocking can be used in a packet-switched network with fixed routing in which each node sends a packet and waits for a reply. If no acknowledgement arrives, the packet is sent again. In loss networks, a customer that arrives to find a full queue is simply lost. We will learn more about this in Chapter 11 on switching networks. RS-FD and RS-RD blocking also arise in flexible manufacturing systems where, for example, a work-piece cannot be processed at a particular station (because it is full) and has to join a queue of work-pieces for another attempt.

10.2.4   Deadlock in blocking networks

The finite buffers in blocking networks introduce the possibility of deadlock. Here, we state some conditions of deadlock avoidance for the different types of blocking. In the remainder of the chapter, we will assume that the network is deadlock-free. For a more detailed analysis of the conditions for deadlock in finite buffer queueing networks, the reader is referred to Akyildiz and Liebeherr (1991).

Example 10.1 _____

Let us consider the three-node network in Figure 10.4 with population 5, all queues with capacity for two customers and BAS blocking. Now consider the state $(2, 2, 1)$ representing the queue lengths at nodes $1, 2$ and 3. All nodes are busy in this state. Suppose customers at nodes 2 and 3 complete before the customer at node 1. Then both nodes 2 and 3 are blocked by node 1 so we need an ordering to determine which node gets unblocked when node 1 completes a service. Now suppose that node 1 completes serving a customer and this customer then selects destination node 2. Since node 2 is also full, node 1 cannot continue and becomes blocked. But node 2 is also blocked by node 1 and so they are **deadlocked**. These deadlocks can be detected easily and resolved by simultaneously moving blocked customers on. For example, the deadlock in the example can be removed if the customer at node 1 moves to node 2 and the one at node 2 moves to node 1. Note that this resolution still leaves node 3 blocked by node 1 even if it was blocked before node 2.

We define a **cycle** as a directed path starting from one node, passing through some intermediate nodes and returning back to the same node. So a cycle c is an ordered set with elements from $\{1, 2, \ldots, M\}$. We use cycles to identify possible deadlock situations. For example, if nodes were blocked in the cycle $i \to j \to i$, where $a \to b$ denotes 'a is blocked by b', then both nodes i and j are blocked by each other and so cannot be released. The example above has two cycles: $1 \to 2 \to 1$ and $1 \to 3 \to 1$, which show possible deadlocks.

When the number of customers K is small enough there is no possibility of deadlock. For BAS blocking, it can be shown that if for all cycles c:

$$K < \sum_{j \in c} C_j$$

then the network is **deadlock-free**.

It is also possible to construct networks with BBS blocking that are deadlock-free if the population is low enough. The conditions for deadlock-free queueing networks with BBS blocking and RS blocking are given below.

BBS-SNO: for each cycle c, $K < \sum_{j \in c}(C_j - 1)$

BBS-SO: for each cycle c, $K < \sum_{j \in c} C_j$

RS-FD: for each cycle c, $K < \sum_{j \in c} C_j$

RS-RD: $K < \sum_{i=1}^{M} C_i$

Note that BAS, BBS-SO and RS-FD have the same deadlock-free condition, namely that the number of customers is less than the sum of the capacities in any cycle. For RS-RD, we just require a single empty slot to avoid deadlock because then the slot can always be filled, causing a node to be unblocked.

10.2.5 Equivalent blocking mechanisms

As the deadlock-free conditions may suggest, some blocking mechanisms are equivalent in that they generate the same state transition rate matrix. The proof of these equivalences, and many more, can be found in Onvural (1987). Here, we just list some of the more useful equivalences. In closed networks with arbitrary topologies, both BBS-SO and RS-RD are equivalent and for cyclic networks, RS-RD and RS-FD are equivalent. So the BBS-SO results also apply to repetitive service blocking mechanisms.

10.3   Two finite queues in a closed network

We first consider closed queueing networks with just two exponential servers and population $K < C_1 + C_2$, as shown in Figure 10.5. This simple network captures some features of the different blocking mechanisms and has many interesting properties. Moreover, the network can be represented by a simple Markov process that is easy to solve exactly. We also find that some blocking mechanisms are equivalent for two-node networks in that their generator matrices are identical. We will discuss these equivalences and the conditions under which they extend to larger networks.

10.3.1 Blocked after service

We begin by analysing the two-node network with BAS blocking. We first derive the steady state queue length distribution of this network exactly. Let the state of the network be described by n, the queue length at node 1, with stationary distribution $p(n)$. Let $k_{\min} = \max(0, K - C_2)$ be the minimum occupancy of node 1 and $k_{\max} = \min(K, C_1)$ be the maximum occupancy of node 1. There are then two blocked states which we denote by $k_{\min} - 1$ (which represents node 1 blocked by node 2) and $k_{\max} + 1$ (which represents node 2 blocked by node 1).

First suppose $K \le C_2$ and $K > C_1$, so that there is always a space

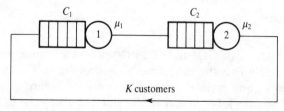

Figure 10.5 Two finite queues in a closed network.

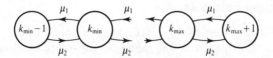

Figure 10.6   State diagram for BAS blocking.

available at node 2 (i.e. node 1 cannot get blocked but node 2 can get blocked). In this case, node 1 is an $M/M/1/C_1 + 1$ queue with arrival rate μ_2 and service rate μ_1. The additional space in node 1 is for the blocked customer (in node 2) that has completed service at node 2 but cannot transfer to the full queue. So in effect, the node 2 service area is used as a holding place just as if it were part of the queue at node 1.

Now suppose $K > \max(C_1, C_2)$, so that both nodes can get blocked and $k_{\min} = K - C_2$ and $k_{\max} = C_1$. The state transition diagram is shown in Figure 10.6 with the two end states representing the blocking situation. The number of states is $(k_{\max} + 1) - (k_{\min} - 1) + 1 = C_1 + C_2 + 3 - K$. The balance equations are easy to write down, as follows. For $i = 0, 1, \ldots, k_{\max} - k_{\min} + 1$,

$$\mu_2 p(k_{\min} + i - 1) = \mu_1 p(k_{\min} + i)$$

So we have

$$p(k_{\min} + i) = \left(\frac{\mu_2}{\mu_1}\right)^{i+1} p(k_{\min} - 1) \tag{10.1}$$

where $p(k_{\min} - 1)$ can be found from normalizing the probabilities

$$p(k_{\min} - 1)^{-1} = \sum_{i=0}^{k_{\max} - k_{\min} + 2} \left(\frac{\mu_2}{\mu_1}\right)^i \tag{10.2}$$

For the two-node BAS blocking network, there is an equivalent non-blocking network that can be used to give exact results. If the blocking network has population K, then the equivalent non-blocking network has population given by

$$K' = \min(K, C_1 + 1) + \min(K, C_2 + 1) - K \tag{10.3}$$

The probability $p(n)$ is represented by the queue length probability $p'(n')$ in the non-blocking network where $n' = 0$ represents that node 1 is blocked by node 2 and $n' = K'$ represents that node 2 is blocked by node 1. This assignment gives the two networks the same number of states and $n' = n - k_{\min} + 1$ transforms the states appropriately. The equivalence is easy to verify using the balance equations since the state transition rates are the same: for $j = 1, 2, \ldots, K'$,

$$\mu_2 p'(j - 1) = \mu_1 p'(j)$$

which gives $p'(j) = p(j + k_{\min} - 1)$.

10.3.2 Blocked before service

For BBS-SNO blocking in any cyclic network with node capacities C_i, the transition rate matrix is the same as for BAS blocking with node capacities $C_i - 1$. Intuitively for cyclic networks, we can view BAS blocking as mimicking BBS-SNO blocking as follows. A customer being blocked under BBS-SNO blocking (because its next node i is full with C_i customers) is represented by some customer blocked under BAS blocking (because its next node is full with $C_i - 1$ customers). Effectively, the first slot at a source node $i - 1$, say, is used as a slot for the next node i. This causes blocking after service for the first customer (because node i has $C_i - 1$ customers) but effectively blocking before service for the next customer, i.e. the second in queue $i - 1$, (which sees C_i customers in front of it). Since the two-node network is cyclic, we can use the BAS results by reducing the node capacities by one to obtain the BBS-SNO results.

Now let us consider BBS-SO blocking with no deadlock (i.e. $K < C_1 + C_2$). As before, if $K \geq C_1$ but $K \leq C_2$ then node 1 is $M/M/1/C_1$ with arrival rate μ_2 and service rate μ_1. Suppose $K \geq \max(C_1, C_2)$ and the state of the network can be represented by the number of customers at node 1. The blocked states are $k_{\min}$ and $k_{\max}$, which represent node 1 blocked and node 2 blocked, respectively. We can write down the following balance equations. For $i = 1, 2, \ldots,$ $k_{\max} - k_{\min}$,

$$\mu_2 p(k_{\min} + i - 1) = \mu_1 p(k_{\min} + i)$$

So we have

$$p(k_{\min} + i) = \left(\frac{\mu_2}{\mu_1}\right)^i p(k_{\min}) \tag{10.4}$$

where $p(k_{\min})$ can be found from normalizing the probabilities.

By looking at the state transition diagram for the two-node network with BBS-SO blocking, we can show that it is equivalent to the non-blocking network with population given by:

$$K' = \min(K, C_1) + \min(K, C_2) - K \tag{10.5}$$

10.4 Aggregating Markovian states

In this section, we describe a general method that aggregates states in a Markov model of a blocking network. As before, we assume the service times at all nodes are exponentially distributed and that all queues are

FCFS. Hence the exact solution for the steady state queue length distribution is possible since the underlying stochastic process is Markovian. In simple cases, we can solve the global balance equations directly, but in general the state space is typically too large to solve exactly and we need some simplifying assumptions. We consider closed queueing networks with K customers and M nodes. The capacity of node i is C_i and the service time is exponentially distributed with mean $1/\mu_i$. For simplicity, the network is assumed to be deadlock-free.

In small blocking networks, we can sometimes simplify the state space by considering the structure of the state diagram and identifying symmetrical states. This approach can reduce the state space M-fold (for M nodes) and so allow an efficient solution that can be used for validation of the approximate methods. For example, consider a cyclic queueing network with identical nodes under some form of blocking (BAS, BBS or RS). All buffers are of size B and all service rates are μ. By looking at the state transition diagram, we can identify a repeating pattern because all nodes have identical characteristics (cf. the matrix geometric methods in Chapter 8). This repetition occurs because in a cyclic network, each node 'sees' another identical node in front. Suppose the state is represented by $n = (n_1, n_2, \ldots, n_M)$ for an M-node cyclic network, then we can rotate the vector by one and still have an equivalent network (by symmetry). If the joint queue length distribution is represented by $\pi(n)$ then we have:

$$\pi(n_1, n_2, \ldots, n_M) = \pi(n_M, n_1, \ldots, n_{M-1})$$

In this way, we can determine transition rates between M equivalence (symmetry) classes S_i and set up a much smaller transition rate matrix. We can then solve the balance equations for $\pi(S_i)$. Dividing this by the number of states in the equivalence class S_i, we obtain the corresponding state probability $\pi(n)$.

Although this type of aggregation is possible in more general topologies, it is not always trivial to identify the equivalent states. Nevertheless, it is widely used in solving specific models that otherwise would be computationally intractable.

In the next few sections, we consider open and closed queueing networks with more than two nodes and under the various blocking mechanisms. Many of the approaches are based on empirical observations but give good approximations in most cases. For certain topologies, we can derive exact results, but normally we have to resort to approximate solutions. When we have infinite queues, the steady state queue length distribution has a product form which, as we have seen, considerably simplifies the derivation of performance measures. One approach to solving a blocking network is to find an equivalent non-blocking network so that the product form solution can be used.

10.5 BAS blocking

BAS blocking was originally motivated by applications in production systems. Thus open networks were best suited for this and the approximations analysed individual queues to obtain marginal queue length distributions. Interest in closed networks with BAS blocking has developed more recently mainly from computer and communication systems. We will analyse both open and closed queueing networks with blocking in this section. Although we restrict ourselves to BAS blocking in this section, some of the techniques also apply to other blocking mechanisms.

We begin by considering a closed queueing network with K customers and M nodes. The capacity of node i is C_i and the service time is exponentially distributed with mean $1/\mu_i$. As before, the network is assumed to be deadlock-free.

When the population of the network is low enough, a product form solution is possible even in a closed blocking network. For example, when $1 \leqslant K \leqslant \min\{C_i\}$, there is no blocking because the entire population can reside in any node. Hence in this case the network has a product form solution. Perhaps surprisingly, when $K = \min\{C_i\} + 1$, the network still has a product form solution. The reason is that for this special case, there can be at most one node blocked at any one time and the blocked node has only one customer (namely the blocked customer). Hence the blocked customer can be thought of as being in the destination node's queue (at which it just waits because the queue is FCFS) and the blocked node is just like an empty node (i.e. not serving any customers). Effectively, the slot for the blocked customer is used as an extra slot for the destination node. Also, the blocked customer cannot affect any other customers at its node (because if one arrives, the blocked customer will immediately become unblocked and continue to its next node). In this way, we see that under BAS blocking and $K = \min C_i + 1$ customers, the network has a product form solution.

When $K > \min C_i + 1$, blocking is possible such that a customer can be denied service because the customer in front of it is blocked. At this population level, a product form solution is not possible in general and this is the case in which we are most interested and now investigate.

10.5.1 FES approach

A popular method used to solve closed networks with BAS blocking decomposes a network into blocking and non-blocking sub-networks and uses the flow equivalent server (FES) approach. We can short-circuit the blocking network, solve the non-blocking network (which now has a

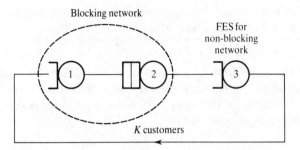

Figure 10.7   Example of FES representation to isolate the blocking network.

product form) for various populations and obtain an FES node. Then the FES node can replace the non-blocking network in the closed network and we can numerically solve the reduced network. Alternatively, we can short-circuit the non-blocking network and numerically solve the blocking network first to obtain an FES node. In this case, the reduced network has a product form solution. Both of these approaches are equally valid and the one chosen depends on the characteristics of the system being modelled.

Suppose we choose the first approach, that is, creating an FES for the non-blocking network by short-circuiting the blocking network. In isolation, the non-blocking network in equilibrium has a product form solution for its joint queue length distribution $p(m|n)$, say, where m is a vector of queue lengths that sum to n. This product form solution allows us to compute the throughput $T(n)$ when the non-blocking network has n customers. The throughput we require here is for the arc that is short-circuiting the blocking network and the FES node is assigned the service rate function $T(n)$. We substitute the FES node back into the original network to obtain the reduced network, which we solve numerically.

Example 10.2

As an example, consider the reduced network in Figure 10.7 where the non-blocking network is represented by the FES node (labelled 3). The blocking sub-network has just two nodes: an infinite buffer node (labelled 1) at which BAS blocking occurs because the other node (labelled 2) has a finite queue. In the original network, all arcs entering the blocking network from the non-blocking network go to node 1 and these arcs are collectively represented by the arc from node 3 to node 1 in Figure 10.7. For this simple example, the steady state queue length distribution can be computed directly by solving the balance equations. In this way, the numerical solution of the reduced network gives the marginal queue length distribution at the FES node, $p_3(n)$ say, from which we can determine the individual queue length distributions in the non-blocking network by using $p(\boldsymbol{m}) = p(\boldsymbol{m}|n) \, p_3(n)$.

The decomposition of the original network into two sub-networks is not exact when the network does not have a product form. This is the main approximation of this approach, but the accuracy is typically better than 1% in practical applications.

10.5.2   Equivalence by size of state space

This approach computes the number of states in the blocking network with population K and finds a non-blocking network with the same set of nodes and routing probabilities (or visitation rates) and population K' such that the number of states in both networks is very close. The number of states in a non-blocking network with M nodes and population K' is the same as the number of arrangements of K' items in M urns. As we have already seen, the size of this state space is given by

$$\binom{M + K' - 1}{M - 1}$$

The number of states in a similar network with finite queues is less than this because a queue length higher than a node capacity is not possible. To obtain the number of states with bounded queues, let us first define the vector y^i to represent node i as follows:

$$y^i = (y^i_0, y^i_1, \ldots, y^i_K)$$

where

$$y^i_j = \begin{cases} 1 & j = 0, 1, \ldots, C_i + 1 \\ 0 & \text{otherwise} \end{cases}$$

We increase the node capacity by one to cater for the state in which an arriving customer is blocked by a full queue. The blocked customer remains in the source node but we need the fictitious space to distinguish the blocked state from the non-blocked state. All the vectors are indexed from zero since a node has zero customers or more.

We first define the **convolution operator** $(*)$ on vectors. If $\boldsymbol{a} = (a_0, a_1, a_2, \ldots, a_K)$ and $\boldsymbol{b} = (b_0, b_1, b_2, \ldots, b_K)$ are vectors then their convolution is defined by $\boldsymbol{a}*\boldsymbol{b} = \boldsymbol{c}$, where $\boldsymbol{c} = (c_0, c_1, c_2, \ldots, c_K)$ and $c_k = \sum_{i=0}^{k} a_i b_{k-i}$ for $k = 0, 1, 2, \ldots, K$. Note that the convolution operator is associative.

The number of states in the blocking network is represented by the vector

$$z = y^1 * y^2 * \ldots * y^M$$

So the $(K + 1)$th element of z, z_k is the number of states in the blocking network.

Example 10.3

As an example, consider a closed network with just two nodes that have capacities 3 and 2. Node 1 can have 0, 1, 2 or 3 customers or can be a blocking node with 3 customers. Similarly, node 2 can have 0, 1 or 2 customers or be a blocking node with 2 customers. Then we have:

$$y^1 = (1, 1, 1, 1, 1, 0)$$
$$y^2 = (1, 1, 1, 1, 0, 0)$$
$$z = y^1 * y^2 = (1, 2, 3, 4, 4, 3)$$

When there are 5 customers, we have $z_6 = 3$ states: one non-blocked state $(3, 2)$ and two blocked states $(3', 2)$ and $(3, 2')$ where n' indicates a blocked queue of length n.

The algorithm merely finds the number of states in the blocking network and finds a non-blocking network with the same number of nodes but with population K' for which the difference in the state space size is minimum. In other words, it finds a K' that minimizes:

$$\binom{M + K' - 1}{M - 1} - z_{K+1}$$

The throughput of the non-blocking network is computed (using the original visitation rates) and used as an approximation for the blocking network throughput. This approximation can be surprisingly accurate, but sometimes leads to large errors (over 25%) because it is insensitive to the node topology and service rates.

This algorithm has been extended to include Coxian service time distributions. Since a product form does not then exist for FCFS networks, Marie's method (see Chapter 8) is used to approximate the throughput. However, this extra approximation leads to more errors.

10.5.3 Curve fitting approach

As we increase the population of a closed network with finite queues, the throughput initially increases. However, after a certain population K^* the throughput begins to drop because there is greater contention for empty spaces by customers and blocking becomes more likely. From this point the throughput steadily declines as more customers are added. (This is similar to the page thrashing that we saw in Chapter 8.) Many points on the throughput curve are easy to determine because product form solutions are available for $K = 1, 2, \ldots, \min C_i + 1$. At the maximum population $K = \sum_{i=1}^{M} C_i$, we can solve the network to obtain the throughput; see below. If the population that gives maximum throughput can be determined (even approximately) and the throughput when the population is maximum is known, we can fit a suitable curve through those points to estimate throughput for all values of K. The crucial step in this approach is to find the population that gives the highest throughput.

For cyclic networks with maximum population (i.e. $K = \sum_i C_i$), all customers in service move on to the next queue at the same time (when every service is completed). Hence the bottleneck is the slowest server and so the throughput is $1/E[\max(X_1, X_2, \ldots, X_M)]$ where the random variable X_i is the service time at node i. If X_i has the exponential distribution with rate μ_i then

$$E[\max(X_1, X_2, \ldots, X_M)] = \int_0^\infty \left(1 - \prod_{i=1}^{M}(1 - e^{-\mu_i t})\right) dt \qquad (10.6)$$

The integrand is the complement of the cumulative distribution function of the node service times (see Exercise 10.1). In cyclic networks, the approximation $K^* = (M + \sum_i C_i)/2$ for various capacities has been shown to be accurate (Onvural and Perros 1989).

For other topologies, K^* is obtained as follows. Suppose node 1 has the largest buffer in a closed network with BAS blocking and let $C' = \sum_{i=2}^{M} C_i$ (i.e. the total capacities of the remaining nodes). If $C_1 > C'$ then for all populations $K \geq C' + 1$, node 1 is always occupied and the network throughput is the same (approximately). This is exact when effectively node 1 has infinite capacity, $C_1 \geq K$. (Adding more customers to the network with population $C' + 1$ just increases the minimum queue length at node 1.) For the curve fitting approach, we can use $K^* = C' + 1$ as the population that gives maximum throughput.

10.5.4 Open tandem networks

We now consider open tandem networks with BAS blocking by analysing individual queues in isolation. This approach takes blocking into account by modifying both the service rates and the arrival rates. It can be used for both open and closed networks, and we consider the open network case as described by Jun and Perros (1990).

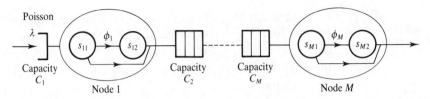

Figure 10.8   Tandem network with blocking.

We consider an open network of M nodes in tandem where node i has capacity C_i as shown in Figure 10.8. The service time at node i has a Coxian-2 distribution described by $s_i = (s_{i1}, s_{i2}, \phi_i)$ where s_{ij} is the service rate in phase j and ϕ_i is the probability that a customer goes through the second phase of service. The queueing discipline at all nodes is FCFS and the finite buffers cause BAS blocking at nodes $1, 2, \ldots, M - 1$.

Here, we assume that the capacity at node 1 is infinite ($C_1 = \infty$), but this restriction can be relaxed (see Jun and Perros 1990). The overall approach is to isolate each node and analyse individual nodes by approximating the arrival and departure processes. Although the arrival process at node 1 is Poisson with rate λ, it is unknown at nodes $2, 3, \ldots, M$. As a first approximation, we assume that all arrival processes are Poisson. For the second approximation, we will approximate both the arrival and departure processes by renewal processes with renewal periods having two-phase Coxian distributions. When blocking occurs, the blocked customer actually resides in the blocked node, but we can also imagine that there is a fictitious slot in the next node, which the blocked customer can occupy (still blocking the original node). So for an isolated node (one of nodes $2, 3, \ldots, M$), we increase the capacity by one to allow for this.

We define the following probabilities for the system, assumed to be in a steady state:

ω_i = the equilibrium probability that on service completion at node i, the next queue (at node $i + 1$) is full ($i = 1, 2, \ldots, M - 1$)

w_{ij} = the equilibrium probability that server i is in phase j when a customer arrives to find queue i full ($i = 2, 3, \ldots, M$ and $j = 1, 2$)

$p_i(n, j)$ = the equilibrium probability that node i has n customers and the customer in service is in phase j ($n = 1, 2, \ldots, C_i + 1$ and $j = 1, 2$)

$p_i(n)$ = the equilibrium probability that node i has n customers ($n = 0, 1, \ldots, C_i + 1$), so for $n > 0$ $p_i(n) = p_i(n, 1) + p_i(n, 2)$

$q_i(n, j)$ = the probability that an arrival to node i finds n customers in queue i and the customer in service is in phase j ($n = 1, 2, \ldots, C_i + 1$ and $j = 1, 2$)

$q_i(n)$ = the probability that an arrival to node i finds n customers in queue i

The overall arrival rate to node i is λ_i, which is slightly higher than the throughput λ of the open network because arrivals after a queue becomes full are rejected (when analysing the node in isolation). We have to thin the overall arrival rate (according to the probability of rejection) to obtain the correct throughput λ.

Model with Poisson arrival processes

For the first approximate model, the algorithm begins at node M and iterates backwards towards node one. Since node M is never blocked, it can be analysed as an M/Cox-2/1/$C_M + 1$ queue in isolation with arrival rate λ. Thus using Neuts' matrix geometric method (Neuts 1981), we can obtain the equilibrium probability, $p_M(n, j)$, and hence $p_M(n)$.

Now let us consider the server at node $M - 1$. On service completion at server $M - 1$, the completing customer either joins queue M without blocking (with probability $1 - \omega_{M-1}$) or gets blocked (with probability ω_{M-1}). When server $M - 1$ is blocked, server M is either in phase 1 (with probability $w_{M,1}$) or phase 2 (with probability $w_{M,2}$). If server M is in phase 1, the residual service time is a Coxian-2 distribution with parameter $s_M = (s_{M1}, s_{M2}, \phi_M)$ by the Random Observer Property. Similarly, if it is in phase 2, the residual service time is exponential with mean service time $1/s_{M2}$. So the effective service time at node $M - 1$ has two parts:

(1)   the actual service time

(2)   the residual service time at node M at the time of blocking

For node i, let $S_i^*(s)$ be the Laplace transform of the density function of the original service time. Thus we have for $i = 1, 2, \ldots, M$:

$$S_i^*(s) = (1 - \phi_i)\frac{s_{i1}}{s + s_{i1}} + \phi_i\frac{s_{i1}}{s + s_{i1}}\frac{s_{i2}}{s + s_{i2}} \tag{10.7}$$

Now let $B_i^*(s)$ be the Laplace transform of the density function of the *effective* service time at node i (which includes time spent waiting to become unblocked). For node $M - 1$, we have

$$B^*_{M-1}(s) = (1 - \omega_{M-1})S^*_{M-1}(s)$$

$$+ \omega_{M-1}S^*_{M-1}(s)\left[w_{M,1}B^*_M(s) + w_{M,2}\frac{s_{M2}}{s + s_{M2}}\right] \quad \textbf{(10.8)}$$

where $B^*_M(s) = S^*_M(s)$ since server M is never blocked.

We approximate $B^*_{M-1}(s)$ by a Coxian-2 distribution by finding the first three moments. Let $b_i = (b_{i1}, b_{i2}, \beta_i)$ be the parameters for the Coxian-2 distribution that approximates the effective service time at node i. Then for node $M - 1$, we have

$$B^*_{M-1}(s) \approx (1 - \beta_{M-1})\frac{b_{M-1,1}}{s + b_{M-1,1}}$$

$$+ \beta_{M-1}\frac{b_{M-1,1}}{s + b_{M-1,1}}\frac{b_{M-1,2}}{s + b_{M-1,2}} \quad \textbf{(10.9)}$$

The unknown parameters in Equation (10.9), $b_{M-1} = (b_{M-1,1}, b_{M-1,2}, \beta_{M-1})$, can be expressed in terms of $\omega_{M-1}, w_{M,1}, w_{M,2}$, which we now consider. The probability that a blocked customer finds server M in phase j is given by

$$w_{M,j} = \frac{q_M(C_M, j)}{q_M(C_M)} \quad \textbf{(10.10)}$$

Since arrivals are assumed to be Poisson, they see the queue in the steady state and so $q_M(C_M, j) = p_M(C_M, j)$ and $q_M(C_M) = p_M(C_M)$.

Applying Little's result to the fictitious position in queue M (slot $C_M + 1$), which has a mean number of customers $p_M(C_M + 1)$, we obtain

$$p_M(C_M + 1) = \lambda\omega_{M-1}\left[w_{M,1}\left(\frac{1}{s_{M1}} + \frac{\phi_M}{s_{M2}}\right) + w_{M,2}\frac{1}{s_{M2}}\right] \quad \textbf{(10.11)}$$

from which we can determine ω_{M-1}.

Now node $M - 1$ can be analysed as an M/Cox-2/1/$C_{M-1} + 1$ queue using Neuts' matrix geometric method (Neuts 1981). We need the *overall* arrival rate (λ_{M-1}) to node $M - 1$, which guarantees that the throughput is λ. We can obtain this from the following fixed point equation (since λ_{M-1} is needed to compute the denominator:

$$\lambda_{M-1} = \frac{\lambda}{1 - p_{M-1}(C_{M-1} + 1)} \quad \textbf{(10.12)}$$

We can now analyse node $M - 2$ in the same way as node $M - 1$, namely by deriving the effective service time as a Cox-2 distribution and analysing the M/Cox-2/1/$C_{M-2} + 1$ queue. In this way, we iterate back to the first queue, which is M/Cox-2/1 because it has infinite capacity.

Model with Coxian arrival processes

For the second approximate model, the algorithm iterates from node one to node M. Instead of a Poisson arrival stream at nodes $2, 3, \ldots, M$, we now use a Coxian-2 distribution to represent the arrival process. We define the following additional terms:

$d_i(t) =$ the density function of the inter-departure time of node i

$D_i^*(s) =$ the Laplace transform of $d_i(t)$

$r_i(t) =$ the density function of the overall inter-arrival time of node i

$R_i^*(s) =$ Laplace transform of $r_i(t)$

Let us consider the departure times of node 1. We obtain the Laplace transform $D_1^*(s)$ by assuming that successive effective services are independent and using the argument of Chapter 5. If on a departure the queue is non-empty, the next customer comes into service and the next departure occurs at the end of its service. If the departure leaves behind an empty queue (with probability $p_1(0)$), then the next departure occurs after an arrival and its service time. Thus we have

$$D_1^*(s) = (1 - p_1(0))B_1^*(s) + p_1(0)\frac{\lambda}{\lambda + s}B_1^*(s) \tag{10.13}$$

The departure process at node 1 is identical to what we call the *effective* arrival process at node 2. In order to study node 2 in isolation, we need to find the overall arrival process, which when thinned gives the same effective arrival process (as the one described by $D_1^*(s)$). Suppose f_2 is the probability that an arrival at node 2 finds queue 2 full and is lost; f_2 will be defined by a fixed point equation later. By decomposing the renewal process representing the overall arrival process at node 2 (see Kuehn 1979) with thinning probability f_2, we obtain the relationship:

$$D_1^*(s) = \frac{(1 - f_2)R_2^*(s)}{1 - f_2 R_2^*(s)} \tag{10.14}$$

Rearranging Equation (10.14) gives us the Laplace transform $R_2^*(s)$ of the overall inter-arrival time density that we need for analysing node 2 in isolation, provided f_2 is known:

$$R_2^*(s) = \frac{D_1^*(s)}{1 - f_2 + f_2 D_1^*(s)} \tag{10.15}$$

So the first three moments of $r_2(t)$ can be expressed in terms of f_2 and the first three moments of $d_1(t)$. The overall arrival rate to node 2, λ_2 is equal to the reciprocal of the first moment of $r_2(t)$. The value of f_2 (the thinning probability) can be found by solving the following fixed point problem:

$$\lambda_2 = \frac{\lambda}{(1 - f_2)} \tag{10.16}$$

This ensures that the throughput at node 2 is λ. The first three moments of $r_2(t)$ allow us to construct a Cox-2 representation of the arrival process at node 2 (i.e. with parameters $a_2 = (a_{21}, a_{22}, \alpha_2)$). So now we can analyse node 2 as a Cox-2/Cox-2/1/$C_2 + 1$ queue.

For the analysis of node $i + 1$ ($i = 2, 3, \ldots, M - 1$), we need to determine the departure process of node i. Let δ_{ij} be the probability that a departing customer leaves the node empty and the next arrival to node i is in phase j of the arrival process. This can be found from the mass function p_i and gives the following Laplace transform:

$$D_2^*(s) = (1 - \delta_{21} - \delta_{22})B_2^*(s) + \delta_{21}R_2(s)B_2^*(s) + \delta_{22}\frac{a_{22}}{a_{22} + s}B_2^*(s) \tag{10.17}$$

In this way, we can analyse nodes $3, 4, \ldots, M$ numerically.

For the third approximate model, we iterate again backward from node $M - 1$ to node 1 as in the first approximate model. However, now we use Coxian-2 arrival processes and recompute the effective service time distributions. The mass functions q_i are determined using the corresponding p_i already calculated.

This analysis of individual Cox-2/Cox-2/1/$C_i + 1$ queues yields the desired queue length distribution at each node. Jun and Perros found that this algorithm gives very accurate results when compared to simulation. With somewhat more notation, Coxian distributions with more phases can be used. The approach can also be extended to allow a finite capacity at the first node. All we need in addition for this case is the throughput of the tandem network, which can be obtained by solving a fixed point problem.

10.5.5 Variable buffer approach for cyclic networks

We now consider closed cyclic networks with BAS blocking and M exponential nodes. Node i has capacity C_i and service rate μ_i as shown in Figure 10.9. The network population is denoted by $K = 1, 2, \ldots, K_{\max}$. One of the nodes, node 1 say, has effectively infinite capacity in that $C_1 \geqslant K_{\max}$.

This approach uses a two-node closed network as a building block for cyclic networks with finite buffers. We first analyse nodes

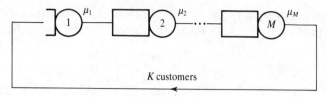

Figure 10.9 The cyclic network.

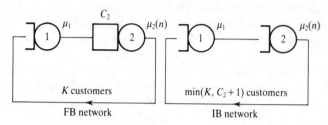

Figure 10.10 The two-node cyclic networks.

$\{M - 1, M\}$ to create a composite node $(M - 1)'$ say. We then analyse nodes $\{M - 2, (M - 1)'\}$ to create node $(M - 2)'$ and continue to iterate to nodes $\{1, 2'\}$. The main idea in this approach is to view the rest of the network seen at a node as a single composite server. Blocking by that composite server depends on the distribution of customers in the original nodes and so we need a variable buffer size (which we describe in more detail later).

The composite server is in effect a flow equivalent server and so the approach can be extended to model topologies other than cyclic. Initially, we short-circuit nodes $1, 2, \ldots, M - 2$ and analyse nodes $M - 1$ and M in a closed network. The throughput of this sub-network is the service rate of FES_{M-1} where FES_i is the flow equivalent server node for nodes $i, i + 1, \ldots, M$ in the original network. At the next step, we analyse the sub-network with node $M - 2$ and FES_{M-1} in a closed network to obtain FES_{M-2}, and so on. Eventually, FES_1 gives the throughput of the cyclic network.

First let us consider the two-node networks that we will be using (shown in Figure 10.10). The finite buffer (FB) sub-network with K customers has one infinite node (with rate μ_1) and one finite node (with rate $\mu_2(n)$ when its queue length is n). The infinite buffer (IB) sub-network has two infinite nodes with the same rates but with population $\min(K, C_2 + 1)$. Clearly when $K \leq C_2 + 1$, both networks are equivalent with the same population. When $K > C_2 + 1$ in the FB network, node 1 is always occupied by at least $K - C_2$ customers. The additional customers (above $C_2 + 1$) are effectively dummy customers occupying space at node 1 and so the throughput-equivalent IB network only has population $C_2 + 1$.

The performance measures we are interested in include the throughput and the queue length distribution. We define the following for these networks in equilibrium:

$X^{FB}(K|C_2)$ = the throughput of the FB network with K customers

$P^{FB}(n_1, n_2|C_2)$ = the probability that the queue lengths in the FB network are n_1 and n_2

$X^{IB}(K)$ = the throughput of the IB network with K customers

$P^{IB}(n_1, n_2)$ = the probability that the queue lengths in the IB network are n_1 and n_2

By looking at the state transition diagram for these networks, it is easy to see that they are isomorphic so that the performance measures for the FB network can be determined from the IB network for $K \geq C_2 + 1$ as follows:

$$X^{FB}(K|C_2) = X^{IB}(C_2 + 1) \tag{10.18}$$

$$P^{FB}(K - j, j|C_2)$$
$$= \begin{cases} P^{IB}(C_2 + 1 - j, j) & j = 0, 1, \ldots, C_2 - 1 \\ P^{IB}(1, C_2) + P^{IB}(0, C_2 + 1) & j = C_2 \end{cases} \tag{10.19}$$

Since the IB network has a product form solution for the queue length distribution, these performance measures can be computed efficiently.

The variable buffer (VB) network behaves like the FB network, but the capacity C_2 varies over time. We introduce non-negative weights $p(1|K)$, $p(2|K)$, $\ldots$, $p(K|K)$ that sum to unity. The term $p(k|K)$ can be thought of as the proportion of time that the buffer has capacity k when K customers are in the network. So $p(K|K)$ indicates the proportion of time that the buffer is effectively infinite.

We can now define the following performance measures for the VB network in terms of the FB network and buffer size weights:

$$X^{VB}(K) = \sum_{k=1}^{K} X^{FB}(K|k)p(k|K) \tag{10.20}$$

$$P^{VB}(K - j, j)$$
$$= \sum_{k=1}^{K} P^{FB}(K - j, j|k)p(k|K) \quad j = 0, 1, \ldots, K \tag{10.21}$$

The VB network is the basic building block used to solve the cyclic network. Node i sees all downstream nodes $(i + 1, \ldots, M)$ as a single composite server with queue length dependent service rate and

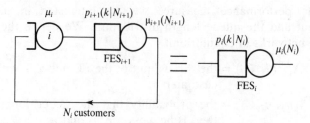

N_i customers

Figure 10.11 The variable buffer model.

capacity C. If we make $C = \sum_{j=i+1}^{M} C_j$ then node i blocking is underestimated because node i can be blocked with fewer than C customers in the FES node (since it represents several finite capacity queues, only the first of which need be full). However, if we make $C = C_{i+1}$ then node i blocking is overestimated because the FES node can accept C_{i+1} or more customers without blocking the previous node. This is why we need to view the FES node buffer with variable size.

Let N_i $(i = 1, 2, \ldots, M)$ denote the number of customers in nodes $i, i + 1, \ldots, M$ so $N_i = 1, 2, \ldots, \min(K, \sum_{j=i}^{M} C_j)$. Let $p_{i+1}(k|N_{i+1})$ be the proportion of time that node i sees a buffer of size k when N_{i+1} customers are downstream (i.e. in nodes $i + 1, i + 2, \ldots, M$) where $k = C_{i+1}, C_{i+1} + 1, \ldots, N_{i+1}$. Let $\mu_i(N_i)$ be the service rate of the FES node representing nodes i to M. We now want to analyse the network shown in Figure 10.11. For the base case, (just nodes $M - 1$ and M) we have:

$$p_M(k|N_M) = \begin{cases} 1 & \text{if } k = C_M \\ 0 & \text{otherwise} \end{cases} \tag{10.22}$$

$$\mu_M(N_M) = \mu_M \tag{10.23}$$

For other cases, we want to obtain $p_i(k|N_i)$ and $\mu_i(N_i)$ from $p_{i+1}(k|N_{i+1})$ and $\mu_{i+1}(N_{i+1})$ where $i = M - 1, M - 2, \ldots, 1$.

So at the step for node i, nodes $1, 2, \ldots, i - 1$ are short-circuited and node i remains with nodes $i + 1, i + 2, \ldots, M$ forming an FES with a variable buffer. We can solve this two-node network by using the VB network model and thereby obtain the throughput function $\mu_i(N_i)$. The values of $p_i(k|N_i)$ are derived as follows for the view seen by node $i - 1$. A buffer of capacity k means that when there are k customers in nodes $i, i + 1, \ldots, M$ blocking occurs at node $i - 1$ where $k = C_i$, $C_i + 1, \ldots, \sum_{j=i}^{M} C_j$. In the original cyclic network, blocking occurs at node $i - 1$ when C_i customers are at node i and so $k - C_i$ customers are downstream at nodes $i + 1, i + 2, \ldots, M$. Thus we estimate the proportion of time that node $i - 1$ sees a buffer of size k by

$$p_i(k|N_i) = P_i^{\text{VB}}(N_i - (k - C_i), k - C_i) \tag{10.24}$$

$$k = C_i, C_i + 1, \ldots, N_i - 1$$

where $P_i^{VB}(\bullet)$ is $P^{VB}(\bullet)$ defined above for a two-node cycle with rates μ_i and $\mu_{i+1}(\bullet)$. When $k = N_i$, $N_i - C_i$ customers are downstream and blocking is not possible. Likewise, we need to consider the cases when up to N_i customers are downstream. The buffer is effectively infinite when $k = N_i, N_i + 1, \ldots, N_i + C_i$. So collecting all the terms gives

$$p_i(N_i|N_i) = \sum_{j=0}^{C_i} P^{VB}(C_i - j, N_i - C_i + j) \tag{10.25}$$

In this way, we can iterate over all the nodes to obtain the network throughput $\mu_1(K)$. The approach is very accurate (typically less than 1% error) when compared to the exact Markov models and is more efficient. Since it is based on a product form solution, it can make use of existing queueing network software. Certain more general topologies can also be solved using this approach if all the finite buffers form a tandem sub-network and so can be replaced by an FES node. Further details can be found in Suri and Diehl (1986).

10.6 BBS blocking

The distinction between BBS blocking and BAS blocking has been demonstrated by the different performance impact on modelled systems. However, for certain network topologies, such as the cyclic network, the two types of blocking are equivalent. For example, a cyclic network with BBS-SNO blocking and C_i spaces at node i is equivalent to the same network with BAS blocking but with $C_i - 1$ spaces at node i. For general topologies, we find that the modelling technique used for one type of blocking can also be applied to the other type. In this section we will consider BBS-SO blocking in cyclic networks.

10.6.1 Concept of holes

When a finite buffer node with C_i spaces has n_i customers we call the $C_i - n_i$ unoccupied spaces **holes** and treat them as active entities. Just as customers flow through the network the holes flow through the network in a similar way. Each state transition caused by a customer changing nodes corresponds to a hole moving in the reverse direction. Let us describe a cyclic network with K customers by a vector of capacities and service rates, such as

$$\{(C_1, \mu_i), (C_2, \mu_2), \ldots, (C_M, \mu_M)\}$$

The dual network with $\Sigma C_i - K$ customers (holes) can then be described by

$$\{(C_1, \mu_M), (C_M, \mu_{M-1}), \ldots, (C_2, \mu_1)\}$$

Thus the steady state distributions for the joint queue lengths in the cyclic network and its dual network are related as follows:

$$\pi(n_1, n_2, \ldots, n_M) = \pi^P(C_1 - n_1, C_M - n_M, \ldots, C_2 - n_2)$$

If the population is such that no node is ever empty, then in the dual queueing network, holes always have enough 'space' in the destination node. In this case, the dual network is non-blocking and has a product form solution. In a cyclic network with BBS-SO blocking this condition is

$$K \geq \sum_{i=1}^{M} C_i - \min_{j} (C_j)$$

So for populations that satisfy this condition, we can easily write down the product form solution $\pi^P(C_1 - n_1, C_M - n_M, \ldots, C_2 - n_2)$ of the dual network and thereby obtain $\pi(n_1, n_2, \ldots, n_M)$.

10.6.2 Properties of cyclic networks

We now state some properties of cyclic networks that are useful for developing techniques. Let us consider a cyclic network with BBS-SO blocking and state-dependent service rates. We define the following terms:

$\boldsymbol{\mu} = (\mu_1(n_1), \mu_2(n_2), \ldots, \mu_M(n_M))$ (the vector of service rates at population vector $(n_1, n_2, \ldots, n_M)$)

$\boldsymbol{C} = (C_1, C_2, \ldots, C_M)$ (the vector of node capacities)

$T(\boldsymbol{\mu}, \boldsymbol{C}, K) =$ the throughput function for the cyclic network for service rates $\boldsymbol{\mu}$, node capacities C and population K

Suppose we have two service rate vectors $\boldsymbol{\mu}$ and $\boldsymbol{\mu}'$ such that for all nodes i, $\mu_i'(k) > \mu_i(n)$ for $k \geq n$. Then for cyclic networks we have the property $T(\boldsymbol{\mu}', \boldsymbol{C}, K) > T(\boldsymbol{\mu}, \boldsymbol{C}, K)$. Likewise, if we increase the node capacities to $\boldsymbol{C}'$ and the service rate functions are monotonically increasing with queue length, we have $T(\boldsymbol{\mu}, \boldsymbol{C}', K) > T(\boldsymbol{\mu}, \boldsymbol{C}, K)$. Supposing $C^* = \max C_i$ then for $K = 1, 2, \ldots, C^* - 1$, $T(\boldsymbol{\mu}, \boldsymbol{C}, K + 1) > T(\boldsymbol{\mu}, \boldsymbol{C}, K)$. Most of these properties are intuitively correct and have been shown by Shanthikumar and Yao (1989).

These properties are useful in formulating new algorithms to solve cyclic networks. For example, the maximum throughput occurs at population $K^* = \Sigma_i C_i/2$ and we use this in the curve fitting algorithm. This gives more accurate results than BAS blocking because K^* is known exactly.

10.6.3 Closed cyclic networks

Now let us consider a closed queueing network with K customers and M nodes in tandem labelled $i = 1, 2, \ldots, M$. The capacity of node i is C_i and the service time is exponentially distributed with mean $1/\mu_i$. For now let us assume that C_1 is infinite and $C_2, C_3, \ldots, C_M$ are finite and cause BBS-SO blocking. It is easy to extend this to all finite buffers with more notation. This approach is considered by Frein and Dallery (1989).

As for the open tandem network (Section 10.5.4), the approach we describe here decomposes the network into M individual nodes. We need to determine arrival rates and effective service times at each of the nodes in isolation. For the isolated node labelled i ($i = 1, 2, \ldots, M$), we first derive the following:

$C_i' = \min(K, C_i)$

$\lambda_i' = $ the arrival rate at node i

$\mu_i'(n) = $ the effective service rate when node i has n customers

Given these parameters, we model the isolated node by an $M/M/1/C_i'$ queue with losses. Thus using standard formulae, we can obtain the following performance measures.

$p_i'(n) = $ the probability that the queue length at node i is n

$L_i' = $ the mean queue length at node i

$X_i' = $ the throughput of node i

So we simply need to find λ_i' and $\mu_i'(n)$ for each node i. For now, suppose we know the arrival rate λ_i' and attempt to find $\mu_i'(n)$ for each node i. We consider nodes starting from node M and proceeding backwards. The server at node M is never blocked since the capacity at node 1 is infinite, so $\mu_M'(n) = \mu_M$. Now consider node $M - 1$. If it is not blocked, its mean service time is $1/\mu_{M-1}$. But if it is blocked (i.e. queue M is full), it has to wait for server M to complete serving its current customer before the customer at node $M - 1$ can begin service. In this case, the mean service time at node $M - 1$ is $1/\mu_M + 1/\mu_{M-1}$. Similarly, node $M - 2$ can be blocked by node $M - 1$ (if queue $M - 1$ is full but queue M is not full) or it can be blocked by node M (if both queues $M - 1$ and M are full). So let us define $b_{ij}(n)$ ($1 \leq i, j \leq M$) as the probability that node j is causing the blocking of server i when queue i

has n customers, i.e. for $j \leq M$, the probability that queues $i+1, i+2$, ..., j are full and queue $j+1$ is not full. Thus for $i = 1, 2, \ldots, M-1$ we have

$$\frac{1}{\mu_i'(n)} = \frac{1}{\mu_i} + \sum_{j=i+1}^{M} b_{ij}(n) \sum_{k=i+1}^{j} \frac{1}{\mu_k} \qquad (10.26)$$

since there is BBS-SO blocking.

Let C_{ij} be the total capacity of nodes $i+1, i+2, \ldots, j$ so that

$$C_{ij} = \sum_{k=i+1}^{j} C_k$$

We identify three cases to estimate $b_{ij}(n)$:

(1)   If n is large enough, queues $i+1, i+2, \ldots, j$ cannot be simultaneously full, i.e. the surplus customers $K - n < C_{ij}$:

$$b_{ij}(n) = 0 \qquad \text{for } n > K - C_{ij} \qquad (10.27)$$

(2)   If n is such that queues $i+1, i+2, \ldots, j$ can be simultaneously full but queue $j+1$ cannot be full, i.e. the surplus customers $K - n \geq C_{ij}$ and $K - n < C_{i,j+1}$:

$$b_{ij}(n) = \prod_{k=i+1}^{j} p_k'(C_k') \qquad \text{for } K - C_{i,j+1} < n \leq K - C_{ij}$$

$$(10.28)$$

(3)   If n is such that queues $i+1, i+2, \ldots, j+1$ can be simultaneously full, i.e. the surplus customers $K - n \geq C_{i,j+1}$:

$$b_{ij}(n) = (1 - p_{j+1}'(C_{j+1}')) \prod_{k=i+1}^{j} p_k'(C_k') \qquad \text{for } n \leq K - C_{i,j+1}$$

$$(10.29)$$

We also need the arrival rates to each isolated node and we obtain these by two conservation principles. The conservation of flow yields (say)

$$X_1' = X_2' = \ldots = X_M' = X$$

For a given throughput X, we can find λ_i' by solving the following fixed point equation:

$$\lambda_i' = \frac{X}{(1 - p_i'(C_i'))}$$

The conservation of population yields

$$\sum_{i=1}^{M} L_i' = K$$

where each L_i' is obtained as a function of λ_i' and $\mu_i'(n)$. This is used as the stopping condition of the iteration.

These equations allow us to solve for the unknowns iteratively for a given network population. We bound the throughput by $X_{\min} = 0$ and $X_{\max} = \min \mu_i$ and estimate the throughput by $X = (X_{\min} + X_{\max})/2$. The algorithm finds better bounds $(X_{\min}, X_{\max})$ on each outer iteration. For the inner iteration, we initially let $p_i'(C_i') = 0$ for all i and for a given throughput X (which influences the $p_i'(C_i')$) we find the service rates $\mu_i(n)$. Now we use the $M/M/1/C_i'$ approximation to calculate the new $p_i'(C_i')$, mean queue lengths L_i' and total population $L = \sum_{i=1}^{M} L_i'$. If L is close to K then the iteration stops, but if $L > K$ then $X_{\max} = X$ and if $L < K$ then $X_{\min} = X$.

The algorithm is reasonably accurate (typically 4% accuracy) for both mean queue length and throughput. This approach can be extended easily to the case where all queues in the cyclic network are finite. In this case, node M can be blocked by node 1 (which now has finite capacity) and so $\mu_M'(n) = \mu_M$ no longer holds and Equation (10.26) has to be extended for node M. The other equations remain mostly unchanged, only now a cycle of blocked nodes can include node M. Furthermore, since the BBS-SO blocking mechanism is equivalent to RS-FD blocking, this approach can be used for that case also.

10.7   Repetitive service blocking

Repetitive service blocking or rejection blocking has numerous applications, mainly in communication networks in which data transmission has to be repeated until the destination can accept the message. This is similar to the loss networks used to model telephone networks in which blocked customers are lost. The lost customers are taken into account by increasing the arrival rate to the network. In effect, this causes some customers to repeat service at some nodes because the amount of additional traffic depends on the rate of lost customers.

For exponential servers, it can be shown that RS-FD (i.e. repetitive service blocking with fixed destination) is equivalent to BBS-SO blocking because we can view the repeat service as a wasted service (see Section 10.2.5). Since we have just considered BBS-SO blocking, in this section we will only consider RS-RD blocking (i.e. repetitive service blocking with random destination).

10.7.1 RS-RD blocking with reversible routing

We now consider closed networks with RS-RD blocking and a special property called **reversible routing**. The routing probabilities p_{ij} are reversible if there exist $\lambda_i > 0$ such that

$$p_{ij}\lambda_i = p_{ji}\lambda_j \qquad \text{for } i, j = 1, 2, \ldots, M \tag{10.31}$$

We also define the following parameters:

$1/\mu_i$ = mean service time at node i

C_i = capacity of node i

$f_i(n_i)$ = rate at which node i works when n_i customers are in the queue so that $f_i(0) = 0$ and $f_i(n_i) > 0$ if $n_i > 0$

$b_i(n_i)$ = probability that a customer is admitted to node i when it has n_i customers

For RS-RD blocking nodes we have $b_i(C_i) = 0$ and $b_i(n_i) = 1$ for $n_i = 0, 1, \ldots, C_i - 1$.

Suppose $\pi(n)$ is the steady state probability that the network is in state $n = (n_1, n_2, \ldots, n_M)$ where n_i is the queue length at node i. For all feasible states we have $K = \Sigma_i n_i$ and $n_i \leq C_i$.

The stochastic process that describes a closed network with RS-RD blocking and has reversible routing is a truncated process of the process that describes the corresponding infinite buffer network (i.e. with the same routing probabilities and service rates but with no blocking). So if the infinite buffer network has a product form solution then so does the finite buffer network (see Kelly (1979) for the proof). Note that a truncated process has the same queue length distribution as the process, but is normalized over a smaller state space. In our case, the smaller state space excludes all states that cause buffer overflow at any node. Since the blocking network has reversible routing, it is quasi-reversible (see Chapter 7) and has the following product form solution:

$$\pi(n) = \frac{1}{G}\prod_{i=1}^{M}\lambda_i\prod_{k=1}^{n_i}\frac{b_i(k-1)}{\mu_i f_i(k)}$$

If the network has fixed blocking ($b_i(n_i) = b_i$) or constant service rates ($f_i(n_i) = f_i$) then it is quasi-reversible and has a product form regardless of whether the routing probabilities are reversible.

For constant service rates, the equilibrium queue length distribution becomes

$$\pi(n) = \frac{1}{G(M, K)}\prod_{i=1}^{M}x_i^{n_i}$$

where $x_i = e_i/\mu_i$, e_i is the visitation rate of node i and $G(M, K)$ is the normalizing constant. The product form solution is the same as for the infinite buffer case, but the state space is restricted by the finite capacities and so the normalizing constant is different. $G(M, K)$ is defined as follows:

$$G(M, K) = \sum_{n \in S(M,K)} \prod_{i=1}^{M} x_i^{n_i} \tag{10.32}$$

where $S(M, K) = \{(n_1, \ldots, n_M)|0 \le n_i \le C_i, \sum_{i=1}^{M} n_i = K\}$.

The performance measures are easy to determine from the normalizing constant, just as we found for the infinite buffer queueing networks with product form solutions. The marginal queue length distribution is then given by

$$\pi_i(n) = x_i^n \frac{G(M\backslash i, K - n)}{G(M; K)}$$

where $G(M\backslash i, k)$ is the normalization constant for the network with node i removed and population k.

The total utilization of node i is $U_i^T = 1 - \pi_i(0)$. But if the node is blocked, it cannot serve any of the customers waiting in its queue. So the effective utilization $U_i^E = \lambda_i/\mu_i$ where λ_i is the throughput of node i. Because of the blocking, the node throughput is harder to determine but can be expressed using convolution operators, and is proportional to the visitation rate as in the non-blocking case (see Akyildiz (1989) for a derivation). Once the throughput and mean queue length are known the mean waiting time follows from Little's result.

The reversible routing in these networks can be extended to include state-dependent routing and Coxian service time distributions (see Kelly 1979). Again the product form solution for the joint queue length distribution allows efficient computation of the performance measures.

10.7.2 Maximum entropy method

The maximum entropy method can be applied to queueing networks with RS-RD blocking. In this approach we decompose the network into single nodes and analyse each node in isolation. Each node is a $GE/GE/1/C$ server where GE is the generalized exponential distribution and C is the capacity.

Suppose $p(n)$ is the equilibrium probability that there are n customers in a $GE/GE/1/C$ queue. Then we define:

$$p(n) = p(0)g^{h(n)}x^n y^{f(n)}$$

where $h(n) = I_{(n>0)}$, $f(n) = I_{(n=C)}$, $g = e^{-\beta_1}$, $x = e^{-\beta_2}$, $y = e^{-\beta_3}$ and $I_B = 1$ if B is true and 0 otherwise.

The β_i are the Lagrange multipliers in the following optimization problem (see Chapter 8):

$$\max \sum_{n=0}^{C} p(n) \log p(n) \tag{10.33}$$

under the constraints:

(1) normalization:

$$\sum_{n=0}^{C} p(n) = 1$$

(2) utilization:

$$\sum_{n=1}^{C} p(n) = \rho = \sum_{n=0}^{C} h(n)p(n)$$

(3) mean number of customers:

$$\sum_{n=0}^{C} np(n) = L$$

(4) probability of a full node:

$$\sum_{n=0}^{C} f(n)p(n) = \phi$$

We assume that ϕ, L and ρ are known (using some other method such as applications of Little's result).

Let us add a suffix i to all these terms to indicate node i in the network so the service time has the generalized exponential distribution with mean $1/\mu_i$ and square of variation coefficient (svc) c_{si}^2. To take blocking into account, we need to revise this service time. The effective service time is a random number of GE service times because of the repeated service that customers go through. Let π_i be the probability that a customer at node i finds the destination node full. We approximate this by

$$\pi_i = \sum_{j=1}^{M} p_{ij}p_j(C_j)$$

where p_{ij} is the routing probability from i to j.

The effective service time at node i is a GE distribution with parameters

$$(\mu_i^{*-1}, c_{si}^{*2}) = \left(\frac{1}{\mu_i(1 - \pi_i)}, \pi_i + c_{si}^2(1 - \pi_i) \right)$$

The effective service rate $\mu_i^* = \mu_i(1 - \pi_i)$, i.e. obtained by thinning the service rate by the probability $(1 - \pi_i)$. Notice that for exponential service times $c_{si}^2 = 1$, so $c_{si}^{*2} = 1$. The arrival process to node i is formed by the superposition of departure processes from nodes j with $p_{ji} > 0$. The departure process has mean $1/\lambda_i$ and svc approximated by

$$c_{di}^2 = \rho_i^*(1 - \rho_i^*) + \rho_i^* c_{si}^{*2} + (1 - \rho_i^*)c_{ai}^2$$

where $\rho_i^* = \lambda_i/\mu_i^*$

$$c_{ai}^2 = -1 + \sum_{j=1}^{M} \frac{\lambda_j p_{ji}}{\lambda_i}(c_{dji}^2 + 1)$$

$$c_{dji}^2 = 1 - p_{ji} + p_{ji}c_{di}^2$$

These approximations have been given by Kouvatsos amd Xenios (1989), which contains further justification for their use.

For open networks, we can initialize the values of c_{di}^2 and c_{ai}^2 for all nodes i. Then we can iterate among the nodes until the convergence criteria for the arrival and service rates are satisfied for each node. For closed networks, we need an additional condition: the **fixed population constraint** $\Sigma_i L_i = K$, which is also called conservation of population. This incurs further approximation, but overall the approach gives good accuracy and is also applicable to other types of blocking.

SUMMARY

- In general, when finite buffers are put into a product form network, the steady state queue length distribution no longer has a product form because nodes can become blocked.

- Blocking after service causes a node to stop serving customers when it completes a service and finds that the destination queue is full.

- In the blocking before service mechanism, a customer declares its destination before starting service and the node stops providing service at any point when the destination queue becomes full. Service resumes only when space becomes available at the destination node.

- Repetitive service blocking is similar to blocking after service, but when the destination queue is full, instead of stalling the server the blocked customer rejoins its original queue for a repeat service.

- Most of the models for blocking networks are approximate, but certain small cases (e.g. with just two nodes) are exact. One approach is to consider all nodes in isolation, and approximate the input and output traffic streams.

- Blocking networks with nodes in series, e.g. tandem networks and cyclic networks, have been studied extensively and have many accurate models.

- Some of the general approximation techniques covered in Chapter 8 are also applicable to blocking networks.

EXERCISES

10.1 (20 BAS blocking)
A cyclic network has two identical nodes each with capacity C and BAS blocking. Assuming that the service time is exponential, find the equilibrium queue length distribution of each node when the total population is $K > C$.

10.2 (20 BBS-SO blocking)
Repeat the previous question for BBS-SO blocking instead of BAS blocking. Hence show that in this case, the equilibrium queue length distribution for the BBS-SO network is not the same as for the BAS network with one fewer buffer slot in each queue.

10.3 (30 BBS-SO blocking in a cyclic network)
A cyclic network with M nodes (where node i has capacity C_i and service rate μ_i) has BBS-SO blocking. Find the equilibrium queue length distribution when there are K customers such that

$$K \geqslant \sum_i C_i - \min_j C_j$$

10.4 (20 Expected maximum of a set of exponentials)
Show that for random variables X_i with exponential distribution with rate μ_i,

$$E[\max(X_1, X_2, \ldots, X_M)] = \int_0^\infty \left[1 - \prod_{i=1}^M (1 - e^{-\mu_i t})\right] dt$$

10.5 (20 Normalizing constant for closed network with finite queues)
Consider an M-node blocking network with RS blocking and where node i ($i = 1, 2, \ldots, M$) has a finite queue of capacity C_i, constant service rate μ_i and visitation rate e_i. The normalizing constant for this network with K customers is given by:

$$G(M, K, C) = \sum_{n \in S(M,K)} \prod_{i=1}^M x_i^{n_i}$$

where $S(M, K, C) = \{(n_1, \ldots, n_M)|0 \le n_i \le C_i, \sum_{i=1}^{M} n_i = K\}$ and $x_i = e_i/\mu_i$. Show that this satisfies the following recurrence for $M > 0$ and $K > 0$:

$$G(M, K, C) = G(M - 1, K, C)$$

$$+ x_M G(M, K - 1, (C_1, C_2, \ldots, C_M - 1))$$

Suggest boundary values for this recurrence.

10.6 (40 Urn model with restricted capacity)
A closed queueing network has M nodes each with finite buffer of size C. Show that the number of states in this network when there are K customers is

$$\sum_{j=0}^{M} (-1)^j \binom{M}{j} \binom{K + M - j(C + 1) - 1}{M - 1}$$

Chapter 11
Switching Network Models

11.1 Telephone networks 417

11.2 Interconnection networks for parallel processing systems 420

11.3 Models of the full crossbar switch 423

11.4 Multi-stage interconnection networks 427

11.5 Models of synchronous MINS 431

11.6 Models of asynchronous MINS 433

11.7 Interconnection networks in a queueing model 440

Switching networks are important components for computer systems and communication networks and models are needed to evaluate the different types. This is especially true for new parallel systems, where they provide the means to access shared memory modules from any processor module. For many system architectures, a switching fabric can be used to switch between high speed fibre channels and so provide fast data movement between various system components. In this chapter, we begin by considering large circuit-switched networks that are used to carry telephone calls. We then consider the use of switching networks in parallel processing systems and describe some models of a crossbar switch. We also look at the characteristics and models of switching networks constructed from multiple stages of crossbars. Finally, we describe a way of representing a switching network in a queueing model of the system that uses the network.

11.1 Telephone networks

The modelling of large circuit-switched networks has long been of interest to telephone engineers, designers of large computer communication networks and, more recently, architects of parallel computers. Here we summarize some of the work presented by Kelly (1986). We start by considering a Markov model for general circuit-switched networks that is exact but computationally impractical for large networks. In limiting cases, however, links behave *as if* they were independent even though they are not independent in general. This property allows us to derive a fixed point equation, **Erlang's fixed point approximation** (Erlang 1948), which is computationally tractable and gives very accurate results.

11.1.1 Markov model of circuit-switched networks

As an example of a simple circuit-switched network, consider the network in Figure 11.1.

In general, the circuit-switched network may have an arbitrary topology. Suppose that there are J links labelled $j = 1, 2, \ldots, J$ with link j comprising C_j circuits. A call on a route r simultaneously holds $A_{jr} \in \{0, 1\}$ circuits from link j. (More generally, a call may use more than one circuit from a link, but here we only consider the simpler case to simplify the notation.) Thus route r can be identified by $\{j | A_{jr} = 1\}$ and the set of routes R is a subset of the power set of $\{1, 2, \ldots, J\}$. Calls requesting route r arrive as an independent Poisson process with rate v_r and are lost if a required link has no free circuits; for this reason, such networks are often called **loss networks**. Successful calls on route r hold all links $j \in r$ for a random period of time with exponential distribution of unit mean. We define the following terms:

n_r = the number of calls in progress on route r

$n = (n_r | r \in R)$ describes the state of the network

$C = (C_j | j = 1, 2, \ldots, J)$ is the set of link capacities

$A = \{(A_{jr} | j = 1, 2, \ldots, J) | r \in R\}$ defines the set of routes through the network

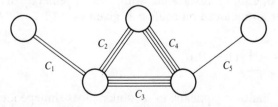

Figure 11.1 An example of a circuit-switched network.

The state space of the network can then be expressed by $S(C) = \{n \in Z^R | An \leqslant C\}$ where Z^R is the set of vectors of length $|R|$ and non-negative integer components. If $\pi(n)$ is the steady state probability of the process being in state n, the detailed balance equations are

$$\pi(n)v_r = \pi(n^{(r)})(n_r + 1) \quad \text{where } n, n^{(r)} \in S(C) \tag{11.1}$$

and $n^{(r)}$ is the vector n with n_r incremented by one.

These Equations (11.1) are satisfied by

$$\pi(n) = \frac{1}{G(C)} \prod_{r \in R} \frac{v_r^{n_r}}{n_r!} \tag{11.2}$$

where

$$G(C) = \sum_{n \in S(C)} \prod_{r \in R} \frac{v_r^{n_r}}{n_r!} \tag{11.3}$$

Since the detailed balance equations can be satisfied, the process is reversible. The steady state probability of acceptance of a call on route r is given by

$$\sum_{n \in S(C - Ae_r)} \pi(n) = \frac{G(C - Ae_r)}{G(C)} \tag{11.4}$$

where $e_r \in S(C)$ is the unit vector describing just one call or route r, i.e. a vector with a 1 in the rth position and zero elsewhere.

These simple equations give the complete solution but the number of routes can grow exponentially with the number of links J (since $|R| \leqslant 2^J$). Because of this, the normalizing constant (Equation 11.3) is effectively only computable for small networks.

11.1.2 Limiting regimes

Suppose the capacities C_j and offered traffic v_r are increased such that the ratios C_j/v_r are kept fixed. Kelly (1986) has shown that in the limit, parameters $B_j \in [0, 1)$ associated with link j emerge such that the probability of losing a call on route r is given by

$$L_r = 1 - \prod_{j \in r}(1 - B_j) \tag{11.5}$$

Thus in the limit, it appears *as if* links block independently, link j blocking with probability B_j.

For star networks, where all calls pass through the central node, it has been shown that in the limit when the number of nodes approaches infinity, the same result holds. These limiting regimes suggest that links behave as if they block independently when link capacities are high and/or when the number of nodes is large.

11.1.3 Erlang's fixed point approximation

Suppose a link of capacity C is offered Poisson traffic with rate λ and is held for some random time with mean one (we can relax the assumption of exponential service times). This forms an M/G/C/C queue and in the steady state the probability that a call is lost is the same as the probability that all circuits are busy since Poisson arrivals 'see' the link in equilibrium (by the Random Observer Property in Chapter 4). This probability is given by Erlang's loss formula (see Chapter 5):

$$E(\lambda, C) = \frac{\lambda^C}{C!} \left(\sum_{n=0}^{C} \frac{\lambda^n}{n!} \right)^{-1} \tag{11.6}$$

The throughput of this link is $\lambda[1 - E(\lambda, C)]$, since the arrival rate is thinned by a factor $[1 - E(\lambda, C)]$, i.e. the probability that the link is not full.

Now let us consider a circuit-switched network with arbitrary topology. We make two assumptions:

(1) Before traffic v_r on route r is offered to link j, it is thinned by a factor $1 - E_i$, for all $i \in r - \{j\}$ (where E_i is the blocking probability for link i)

(2) All thinnings are independent

So if link j is used by route r, then the traffic offered to link j is thinned by using the blocking probabilities at all links in route r except link j. For route r, the offered traffic to link j is given by

$$\lambda_{r,j} = A_{jr} v_r \prod_{i \in r - \{j\}} (1 - E_i) \tag{11.7}$$

Summing Equation (11.7) over all routes r we get the link j arrival rate. Now we can use this arrival rate in Erlang's loss formula:

$$E_j = E\left(\sum_{r \in R} \lambda_{rj}, C_j \right)$$

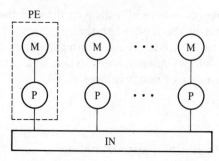

Figure 11.2   IN with a static topology.

Substituting Equation (11.7) then gives

$$E_j = E\left(\sum_{r \in R} A_{jr} v_r \prod_{i \in r - \{j\}} (1 - E_i), C_j\right) \quad \text{where } E_j \in (0, 1) \quad \textbf{(11.8)}$$

Equation (11.8) is **Erlang's fixed point equation** and Kelly (1986) shows that for fixed routing, the fixed point exists and is unique. For dynamic routing, in which alternative routes are attempted when the first route is unavailable, there may be more than one fixed point. Erlang's fixed point approximation is believed to give more accurate results as network complexity increases.

11.2   Interconnection networks for parallel processing systems

At the heart of any parallel processing system lies some form of interconnection network (IN) that provides interprocessor communication. We describe various types of INs associated with parallel systems. The class of homogeneous parallel computer architectures with a large number of processing elements (PEs) and a static topology is shown in Figure 11.2, where processors are labelled P and memories are labelled M. These parallel architectures are sometimes also called **multicomputers**. The topology is static in that the interconnections between processors are fixed (at least for the duration of one program). A multicomputer in which the set of transmission links actually used by a program is fixed is sometimes called a **process network**.

In contrast, the class of homogeneous parallel computer architectures with a large number of PEs and memory modules (MM) and a dynamic IN topology is shown in Figure 11.3. The dynamic IN can make connections from any PE to any MM and, in principle, no MM is favoured by any PE. An example of this type of multiple instruction stream, multiple data stream (MIMD) computer is the NYU Ultracomputer (Gottlieb *et al*. 1983).

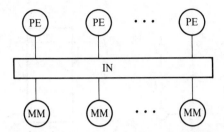

Figure 11.3   IN with a dynamic topology.

Generally in multiprocessing systems, the processors can communicate and cooperate at different levels in solving a given problem, i.e. by sending messages or by sharing memory. It is generally agreed that for interprocessor communication, message passing is slower than sharing memory. If there is relatively little processor interaction via shared memory the parallel system is said to be *loosely coupled*. Thus in loosely coupled multiprocessors, the processors have large local memories from which most of their instructions and data are obtained. Communication between processors is achieved by sending messages across an IN. In this case, full connectivity is not essential as the processors spend little time communicating with each other and an IN with a static topology is suitable.

The principal aim of these parallel processing projects is to achieve massive parallelism on a computer that has a large number of relatively low performance processors. We can also have parallelism by using a small number of high performance processors (e.g. the Cray Y-MP). It remains to be seen if there is enough parallelism in typical problems to make use of many processors. For massive parallelism, we need a large interconnection network for processor communication and this will limit the overall performance. It is these interconnection networks that we now consider.

Both static and dynamic IN topologies can be used for interprocessor communication in multiprocessors. Here we present some dynamic INs specifically for shared-memory multiprocessors. In these architectures the sharing of main memory naturally causes contention and so the IN design must be efficient, otherwise the processors spend most of their time communicating and doing little real work. We assess the relative merits of each type of IN and conclude that the multi-stage IN appears to provide the most cost-effective means of implementing interprocessor communication for large-scale shared-memory multiprocessors.

Shared-memory multiprocessor systems require some kind of switch to connect their processing elements and memory modules, and being a unique shared resource in the parallel machine, the switch is a potential source of high contention. The simplest type of switch for this

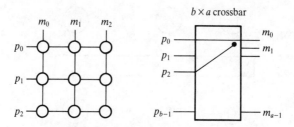

Figure 11.4   Equivalent crossbar switches.

purpose is the common bus which connects to every element. However, the bus derives its simplicity at the expense of increased complexity in each component that it connects. For example, bus request and receive pins are needed by each element, together with several others for control and synchronization, and non-trivial logic is necessary to implement the bus protocol. This increases the overall cost of a large-scale multiprocessor and, moreover, each additional processor that is added to the bus is faced with more contention (along with the others) and so delivers a diminishing increment in performance.

In order to accommodate more processors without increasing contention, the common bus can be extended by using multiple common buses. Multiple bus INs are simple yet fault tolerant and suitable for all algorithms. If there are N processors and M memories a B-bus IN has cost that varies as $O(B(N + M))$. Despite the inherent disadvantages of the common bus, multiple bus INs are good for medium-scale parallel systems because the number of buses can be increased until reasonable performance is attained. Towsley (1986) describes an approximate model of a multiple bus IN for a multiprocessor system with Poisson arrivals and general service times.

At the other end of the spectrum, the switch might be a full crossbar which provides parallel communication between any number of distinct pairs of processors connected through it. For example, a crossbar may have two types of links – one for processors and the other for memory modules – and a way of dynamically connecting any pair of the two types. This allows parallel access to the shared memory provided that there are no *memory conflicts* (i.e. two or more processors attempting to access the same memory module). Figure 11.4 shows a simple crossbar switch connecting processors to memory modules using a grid of small switches (circles in the diagram). This structure is normally drawn differently to indicate the blocking of certain paths by other active paths.

A $b \times a$ crossbar can switch any of its b input pins to any of its a output pins on the appropriate clock cycle. The only possible contention is for the destination processors (i.e. contention is internal in the switch for the output pins).

Each additional input processor that is added to the crossbar requires a new parallel link to each output pin (and similarly interchanging input and output). Thus for an $N \times N$ or N-way crossbar the complexity and cost grow as $O(N^2)$ and the very large crossbars required for large-scale multiprocessors would become hopelessly complex and expensive. However, crossbars have good characteristics for medium-scale multiprocessing and can be combined to obtain higher connectivity. We now consider models of such crossbars.

11.3   Models of the full crossbar switch

Before looking at various models of crossbars, we need to consider the types of workload passing through them. The simplest type of workload has a uniform traffic pattern, i.e. requests originating from any of the input pins select each output pin with equal probability. Many of these models can be extended to include non-uniform traffic in which the output pin selection probabilities are not all the same. Still further we can model favourite routing in which each input pin has its own set of selection probabilities for the output pins. All the crossbar models can be divided into two classes: synchronous and asynchronous. For the synchronous case, requests arrive at the beginning of a clock cycle with a certain probability and complete at the end of the cycle. This probability effectively defines the rate at which requests arrive. For the asynchronous case, requests arrive at the inputs at random time points according to some inter-arrival time distribution.

11.3.1   Synchronous crossbar models

We start by considering a model of an $n \times b$ crossbar operating in synchronous mode. Bhandarkar (1975) presents a discrete Markov chain model in which the state $(k_1, k_2, \ldots, k_b)$ (with $\sum_i k_i = n$) represents the number of requests at each output pin. At the beginning of a cycle all free inputs request any output with equal probability. Of course, some inputs will request the same output and form a queue. The request that is at the front of the queue completes at the end of the cycle. Therefore, if there are k non-empty queues just before the end of the cycle, then k requests will complete at the end of this cycle and the other $n - k$ requests will remain in the output queues. These k requests need reassigning to the output queues because they effectively recycle, again to join one of the output queues with equal probability. By adding the recycled requests one by one to the queues, all the possible terminal states can be determined and hence the transition probability matrix and steady state probabilities can be calculated. However, this is computationally complex and difficult to extend to arbitrary memory selection probabilities.

The complexity of the above Markov model can be reduced by assuming that all blocked requests in a given cycle retry independently on the next cycle. Essentially, this is a loss model which has no output buffers. The assumption has come to be known as **Strecker's approximation** (Strecker 1970). Let p be the probability that the processor attached to an input pin generates a request in a particular cycle (which is the same for all free inputs). We can also think of p as a rate since the mean number of requests per cycle is p. Then the probability that the uppermost output is connected to the uppermost input is p/b (since p is the probability that the top input sends a request and $1/b$ is the probability that it selects the top output). From the independence assumption, the probability that the top output is *not* connected via any of the n inputs is given by

$$\left(1 - \frac{p}{b}\right)^n$$

Since all outputs are identical, the bandwidth (B) or the expected number of busy output ports is given by

$$B = b\left[1 - \left(1 - \frac{p}{b}\right)^n\right] \tag{11.9}$$

Then the probability of acceptance (P_A) is (by conditioning on the number of other requests m selecting the chosen output so that the conditional probability of acceptance is $1/(m + 1)$)

$$P_A = \frac{B}{np} \tag{11.10}$$

The error is about 6–8% for $b/n > 0.75$ when $p = 1$. The closed form solution is widely used despite its underestimation of bandwidth at low request rates (p) and overestimation for higher p.

In Yen *et al.* (1982) the rate p is increased to take account of the rejected requests that are resubmitted. The new rate p' is given by

$$p' = \frac{1}{1 - P_A(1 - 1/p)} \tag{11.11}$$

This overestimates the bandwidth because it assumes that the *queued* requests are distributed uniformly over the outputs. By restricting the uniformity of the distribution, the model is refined to give very accurate results.

A queueing system approach assuming binomially distributed arrivals to the crossbar is investigated in Baskett and Smith (1976). This approach is asymptotically exact as n and/or b tend to infinity and gives accurate results for small values of n and b.

11.3.2 Asynchronous crossbar models

We now consider a crossbar at which customers arrive asynchronously at input pin i with rate λ_i. Each customer holds an input pin and competes for an output pin. Here we solve for the uniform crossbar in the steady state using Little's result. We want to find the probability that a given output pin is active and use this to find the bandwidth B (the expected number of active output pins). The approach is similar to that found in Harrison and Patel (1990) and Patel (1989). First we require the following definitions when the crossbar is in the steady state:

π_i = utilization of input pin i

p = utilization of an output pin (all output pins have the same utilization)

m = mean holding time (MHT) for output pins (i.e. mean time interval for which an output pin is held)

β_i = probability that an arrival at input pin i is blocked

d = mean residual holding time (MRHT) for output pins (i.e. mean time taken for an active output pin to be released after a new customer arrives requesting the same pin)

We can apply Little's result ($L = \lambda W$) to the $b \times a$ crossbar shown in Figure 11.5 assuming only that a steady state exists. Indeed, we apply Little's result to individual pins, which means that the queue length is either zero or one. For an output pin, the queue length is one with probability p and zero with probability $1 - p$. Thus the mean queue length at a pin is the same as the pin utilization since $L = 1 \times p + 0 \times (1 - p) = p$. Note that here we are not considering multiple requests to the same output pin.

For an output pin, the throughput is a fraction $1/a$ of the total throughput since all outputs are equally utilized. Since the mean holding time is m we have

$$p = \left[\frac{\lambda_0 + \lambda_1 + \ldots + \lambda_{b-1}}{a} \right] m \qquad (11.12)$$

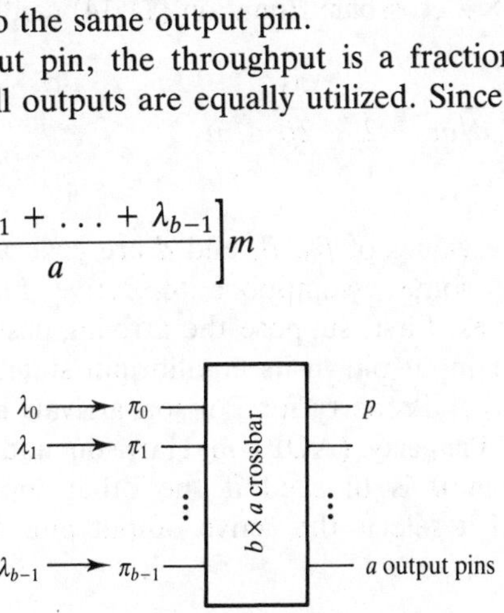

Figure 11.5 Uniform crossbar.

For input pin i, the mean waiting time W is the sum of the delay in acquiring the output (which is non-zero with probability β_i) and the mean pin holding time. This gives

$$\pi_i = \lambda_i[m + \beta_i(d + c_im)] \tag{11.13}$$

where c_i is the expected number of other requests that will be allocated to the output pin i before the request on input pin.

Eliminating the λ_i $(i = 0, 1, \ldots, b - 1)$ in Equations (11.12) and (11.13) gives

$$p = \frac{m}{a} \sum_{i=0}^{b-1} \frac{\pi_i}{m + \beta_i(d + c_im)} \tag{11.14}$$

The value of c_i depends on the arbitration mechanism used in the crossbar (e.g. polling, FCFS etc.). For $b = 2$, there is only one other input pin, which must be connected if the new arrival gets blocked, giving $c_i = 0$. So for our analysis of 2×2 crossbars, we do not need to investigate any further. For larger crossbars, we do need to determine c_i somehow.

Using Equation (11.14), the bandwidth $B = ap$ is given by

$$B = \sum_{i=0}^{b-1} \frac{\pi_i}{1 + \beta_i(d/m + c_i)} \tag{11.15}$$

Uniform 2×2 crossbar

For the uniform 2×2 crossbar, Equation (11.14) can be expressed as

$$p = \frac{\pi_0}{2 + 2\beta_0 d/m} + \frac{\pi_1}{2 + 2\beta_1 d/m} \tag{11.16}$$

and $B = 2p$.

However, the values of β_0, β_1 and d are generally not known and we need to make some assumptions to derive further relationships between the variables. First, suppose the arriving customer at one input pin 'sees' the other input pin in its equilibrium state. This is similar to the Random Observer Property for Poisson arrivals and it is called the **Arriving Observer Property** (AOP) in Harrison and Patel (1990). An arrival on input pin 0 is blocked if the other input is active (with probability π_1) and it selects the active output pin. Thus we have, for $b = 2$:

$$\beta_0 = \pi_1/2 \quad \text{and} \quad \beta_1 = \pi_0/2 \tag{11.17}$$

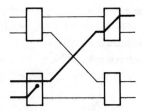

Figure 11.6 Path conflict in the simplest MIN.

Secondly, suppose we have MRHT = MHT, i.e. $d = m$. This is certainly the case if the holding times are exponentially distributed because of the memoryless property. These two assumptions simplify Equation (11.16) to give:

$$p = \frac{\pi_0}{2 + \pi_1} + \frac{\pi_1}{2 + \pi_0} \tag{11.18}$$

If the inputs are identical, i.e. $\pi_0 = \pi_1 = \pi$, we obtain

$$p = \frac{2\pi}{2 + \pi} \tag{11.19}$$

Further, if the crossbar is saturated, i.e. $\pi = 1$, we have $p = \frac{2}{3}$ and $B = \frac{4}{3}$.

11.4   Multi-stage interconnection networks

By interconnecting a matrix of small crossbars, we can form a **multi-stage interconnection network** (MIN). A MIN has a number of levels (or stages) such that the output pins of crossbars in one stage are connected to the input pins of crossbars in the next stage (as shown for the simplest MIN in Figure 11.6). This arrangement provides the same connectivity as a full crossbar (any input pin can be dynamically connected to any output pin if there is a free path), but introduces contention for internal links (*path conflicts*) on top of the memory conflicts. A path conflict occurs when a request across the network cannot establish a complete path because an internal link that it requires is occupied. For example, in Figure 11.6, two paths to different output pins are in conflict because of a shared internal link (shown in bold).

There are several types of MIN, many with similar structure and properties, but here we will consider **banyan networks**, which are also called blocking networks because of their path conflicts. However, there are also MINs like the **Benes network** (Benes 1965) in which all permutations of input and output requests can be realized by rearranging some existing connections. The **Clos network** (Clos 1953) is non-blocking without requiring any rearranging of connections. Both the

Benes and Clos networks require more complex control than banyans and are therefore unsuitable for large-scale multiprocessors. Many types of MIN have been proposed and we consider a sub-class of the banyan network, called a **delta network**, which we define in Section 11.4.2. More recently, banyan networks have been extended in various ways to improve fault tolerance.

MINs provide a cost-effective means of implementing a full connection from processors to memory with higher performance than the common bus and lower cost than the equivalent full crossbar. The main advantage of a MIN is that its cost grows almost linearly, $O(N \log N)$ for $N \times N$ connectivity, compared with $O(N^2)$ for the equivalent crossbar. For example, consider constructing a J-stage MIN from 2×2 crossbars. To provide $N \times N$ connectivity, we need $N/2$ crossbars per stage and at least $J = \log_2 N$ stages (since this is the depth of a binary tree with N leaf nodes). Thus the number of crossbars needed (and so the main cost factor) is $\frac{1}{2} N \log_2 N$. Under light loads, both MINs and crossbars give similar throughput, as we will see.

11.4.1 Banyan networks

A banyan network, named after a type of Indian fig tree with a similar structure, is a MIN with a unique path from each input pin to each output pin. This criterion implies that the network has a tree-like fan-in and fan-out structure; a formal definition of banyan networks in terms of graph theory is given by Goke and Lipovski (1973).

A banyan network is said to be *layered* if its switches can be arranged as a number of distinct stages. A layered banyan comprising J stages of crossbars in which the outputs of one stage connect directly to the inputs of the next stage, is called a *J-level banyan*. There are two main types of J-level banyans: *regular banyans* and *irregular banyans*. Irregular banyans connect any N inputs to M outputs through J stages of crossbars where the ith stage employs c_i $n_i \times m_i$ crossbars. Since no crossbar pin is left unconnected, the number of outputs from one stage has to be the same as the number of inputs to the next stage. In symbols we have:

$$c_i m_i = c_{i+1} n_{i+1} \qquad i = 1, 2, \ldots, J - 1$$

This equation is satisfied by

$$c_i = \prod_{j=1}^{i-1} m_j \prod_{k=i+1}^{J} n_k \qquad i = 1, 2, \ldots, J$$

Thus the number of inputs is $N = n_1 \times c_1 = n_1 \times n_2 \times \ldots \times n_J$ and the number of outputs is $M = c_J \times m_J = m_1 \times m_2 \times \ldots \times m_J$.

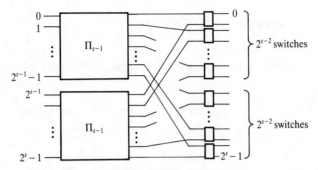

Figure 11.7   The SW banyan structure.

Regular banyans are constructed from a single type of basic crossbar switch (i.e. for $i = 2, 3, \ldots, J$: $n_i = n_1$ and $m_i = m_1$, so $c_i = c_1$). Examples of specific structures, defined in Goke and Lipovski (1973), include CC banyans and SW banyans.

SW banyans can be defined recursively as follows for networks with 2×2 crossbars (the definition can be generalized easily to networks constructed from $b \times a$ crossbars with $b, a \geqslant 2$):

(1)   A one-stage network, Π_1, is the single 2×2 crossbar.

(2)   An s-stage network, Π_s, $(s > 0)$ has 2^s inputs and outputs, so there are 2^{s-1} switches in each stage. It is constructed by connecting a *head stage* (numbered s) of 2^{s-1} switches to the right of 2 *tail networks* of $(s - 1)$ stages according to the partial shuffle topology shown in Figure 11.7. The ith switch in stage s takes its top and bottom input from the ith output pin of the upper sub-network and the ith output pin of the lower sub-network, respectively. This property of the topology is particularly useful in obtaining recurrence formulae for throughput (see Section 11.7.2).

11.4.2 Delta networks

A well-known example of a regular banyan network is the delta network defined by Patel (1981). The definition of delta networks includes the additional property that routing in the network is *digit-controlled*. This means that the choice of which output pin to select at a particular crossbar in the network can be determined by a single digit in the destination address of a packet. A rectangular delta network is constructed from b-way crossbars with the same number of input pins as output pins and is often called a **delta-b network**. There are many different ways of connecting the outputs of one stage of crossbars to the inputs of the next to obtain the desired connectivity. Corresponding

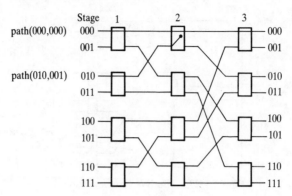

Figure 11.8   Paths through a delta network.

permutation functions define a network's topology, all of which have been shown to be equivalent by Wu and Feng (1980). Each topology can be obtained from any other by permuting the switches in each stage of the network and so all have the same performance characteristics, such as equilibrium throughput. We will be primarily concerned with the partial shuffle topology shown in Figure 11.8 and defined in the previous section.

11.4.3 Operational characteristics of switching networks

MINs are distinguished by three main operational characteristics: *control, timing* and *switching protocol*. Typically, MINs have decentralized control with implicit digit-controlled routing as in delta networks. However, timing characteristics depend on the type of parallel machine that uses the MIN. For SIMD machines, the MIN is normally used in synchronous mode whereas in MIMD machines the MIN is used in asynchronous mode. There are two main types of switching protocols – circuit switching and packet switching – as well as hybrid protocols. In circuit switching, a complete path has to be established across the network before data can be transferred from the input buffer to the destination buffer. In the process of setting up this path there may be a required link already in use, which causes the path to be blocked. The partial path already established may then be held until the link becomes free or may be released, whereupon the source processor may have to retry after some appropriately chosen time. In a packet-switched MIN, there are buffers at each crossbar switch and packets of data are transferred from one buffer to the next in a single hop fashion. This protocol incurs higher transfer delays than circuit switching but introduces greater potential for parallelism and higher throughput. Hybrid protocols can also be used in buffered MINs in which packets can bypass many buffers by forming circuits across any number of stages when possible.

11.5 Models of synchronous MINs

Models of MINs with various operational characteristics have been presented in the literature. Here we briefly describe a selection of these models classified by the timing philosophy: synchronous or asynchronous mode of operation. We further classify these categories by the switching mode: packet switching or circuit switching. We also discuss why asynchronous, circuit-switched MINs are harder to model than MINs with other operational characteristics. Each of the modelling techniques we consider has to overcome the problem of blocking in MINs, i.e. requests being blocked because of unavailable shared resources (links). We find that different types of blocking are involved in MINs with different operational characteristics and different modelling techniques are, in general, required for each type.

As we have seen in Chapter 10, three types of blocking have been identified for general queueing networks: *blocked after service* (BAS), *blocked before service* (BBS) and *repetitive service blocking* (RS). One type of blocking is present in each type of operation mode for a given MIN. A form of RS blocking where rejected tasks receive no service is present in many models of synchronous MINs. In asynchronous, packet-switched MINs with finite capacity buffers there is BAS blocking. Similar approximations as in Akyildiz (1987) can be applied here because the MIN is basically a queueing network with blocking. BBS blocking occurs in the DMA (direct memory access) servers attached to the inputs of the asynchronous, circuit-switched MIN because the data transfer (i.e. DMA service) cannot take place until a complete path across the MIN is established. Furthermore, all links in the path across the MIN need to be held at the same time. Since the links are shared resources, we also have the problem of *simultaneous resource possession* (Whitt 1985) when we view the MIN at the link level.

Numerous synchronous MIN models have been proposed primarily as a result of interest in SIMD computers (i.e. computers with a single instruction stream and multiple data streams where a single control unit acts on many data items synchronously). Much of this work involves the *permutation capability* of MINs (i.e. the number of total, 1–1 functions mapping input ports to output ports that can be realized by the MIN without path conflicts). Other work in this area has concentrated on determining the effective bandwidth of the MIN when requests arrive at an input with a given probability at the beginning of the clock cycle. Here we present an overview of Patel (1981) (for a synchronous circuit-switched network model) and the results of Jenq (1983) (for a synchronous packet-switched network model).

11.5.1 Synchronous, circuit-switched MINs

Consider a J-stage delta network constructed from $a \times b$ crossbars. The following analysis of synchronous circuit-switched delta networks can be found in Patel (1981). In a delta network with uniform request patterns, the transmission rate of requests from each output in a given stage is the same. Thus we only need to consider one switch of each stage where the rate of requests at a switch output is a function of the rate of requests at any switch input (all of which are the same, similarly). Let p_j $(0 < j \leq J)$ be the rate of requests at an output pin of a crossbar in stage j and p_0 be the rate of requests at each input port of the network (stage 1). Applying Strecker's approximation (Equation 11.9) to a crossbar in stage j we have

$$p_j = \left[1 - \left(1 - \frac{p_{j-1}}{b} \right)^a \right] \qquad j = 1, 2, \ldots, J \tag{11.20}$$

Since there are b^J output pins, the bandwidth is given by

$$B = b^J p_J \tag{11.21}$$

where p_J is computed by repeated application of Equation (11.20).

In Kruskal and Snir (1983), an asymptotic expression for p_J (with $a = b$) is derived which approximates to

$$p_J = \frac{2b}{(b - 1)J + 2b/p_0} \tag{11.22}$$

The analysis of Patel (1981) is extended to include favourite memory references in Bhuyan (1985).

11.5.2 Synchronous, packet-switched MINs

The model in Patel (1981) also applies to synchronous packet-switched delta networks provided that switches are unbuffered and packets are generated at the beginning of each cycle. The other models presented here can be classified by the size of the buffers used at each node: single, finite or infinite buffers.

The first paper on modelling buffered packet-switched MINs was by Dias and Jump (1981), which considers single buffers at each input pin. The switch is modelled using petri-nets and results in fairly complicated expressions. Jenq (1983) has a similar analysis but without using petri-nets. Kruskal and Snir (1983) present a model for a uniform MIN with infinite-sized buffers, so that there is no blocking and the request rate p is the same at all stages in the steady state. Finite buffered MINs have been studied by Harper and Jump (1987) and the analysis has been extended to include non-uniform routing in Kim and Garcia (1988).

11.6   Models of asynchronous MINs

Models of asynchronous MINs have been sparse in the literature. However, in recent years there has been considerable interest in developing such models, mainly because of developments in two distinct areas: parallel computer architectures and telecommunication networks. The need to design novel parallel architectures has encouraged the development of new modelling techniques and new applications for more established ones. The other impetus for modelling asynchronous MINs has come from the new integrated services digital communications networks (ISDNs) in which MINs provide a switching function for packets of information which may be data, voice, video or control signals.

11.6.1   Asynchronous, packet-switched MINs

Here, we briefly describe the analysis reported by Mitra and Cieslak (1987), which assumes that buffers at links have infinite capacity. With this assumption, the problem of blocking does not arise and effectively the MIN is a queueing network. Much of its complexity can be reduced because there is no feedback (i.e. no task can ever return after leaving a node) and each node in a particular stage has statistically identical behaviour in uniform traffic. Thus, the analysis considers only one crossbar in each stage and approximates the superposition of arrival processes and the splitting of the departure processes by stationary renewal processes defined by the traffic descriptors: the traffic intensity and the coefficient of variation of waiting time at the node. Assuming that the sources at the first stage are Poisson, the link queues are $M/G/1$ and so the Pollaczek–Khintchine formula gives the mean delay and other results give the coefficient of variation of the inter-departure times. In other stages, the arrival processes are obtained from the departure processes of the previous stage and are used to derive the new departure processes similarly. However, the queues are $GI/GI/1$ and so

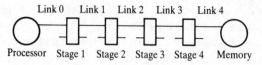

Figure 11.9   Link labelling in a MIN.

further approximations need to be made. Finally, an iterative expression for the mean transmission time from source to destination is derived.

The problem of blocking in asynchronous MINs with finite buffer capacity has been difficult to solve. An MVA algorithm for blocking in general queueing networks is reported in Akyildiz (1988) and this can be applied to MINs. The blocking problem is also addressed by Harrison and Pinto (1991), which generalizes the method of Jun and Perros (1990) to non-tandem, feed-forward networks (see Chapter 10).

11.6.2   Circuit-switched MIN with a drop protocol

In this section we consider an open delta network with a circuit switching protocol, cf. Gelenbe (1989). Here we consider the case where partially established paths are dropped if they are blocked. In the next section we use a similar approach to analyse the case where partially established paths are held. These MINs form the path by which a number of DMA processors at the input pins access memory modules at the output pins. For example, Figure 11.9 shows a path between a processor-memory pair in a 4-stage MIN. Link 0 is always available to a new request from a processor as it is not shared with other processors. All the other links are shared and so may be in use when the processor attempts to form a circuit across the network. The processor generates requests at a rate λ when it is not using the MIN. The main performance measure we want to derive is the total number of memory accesses per second for a given λ.

For a J-stage MIN, a processor can be in one of many states as it attempts to build a circuit across the network. When the processor is not attempting to access memory, it is in state 0 and when it is accessing memory, it is in state $J + 1$. The processor is in state $j = 1, 2, \ldots, J$ if it is attempting to obtain link j in its path having obtained all links up to link $j - 1$. If it fails to obtain a link, it enters a blocked state -1 to retry after some random delay.

We first define the following terms:

λ = the rate at which the processor generates requests from state 0

$1/\mu$ = mean time taken to access memory (after the path is established)

$1/\gamma$ = mean time spent in state -1

α_j = instantaneous transition rate from state j to state $j+1$, $j = 1, 2, \ldots, J$

β_j = instantaneous transition rate from state j to state -1, $j = 1, 2, \ldots, J$

The state transitions for this process are described by Figure 11.10. After the processor enters state j $(j = 1, 2, \ldots, J)$, it takes a short time h_j (on average) to discover whether the next link will be available. At that point the processor either obtains the next link or gets blocked. The probability that a processor gets blocked while attempting to obtain link j is b_j. So we have for $j = 1, 2, \ldots, J$:

$$\alpha_j = (1 - b_j)/h_j \tag{11.23}$$

$$\beta_j = b_j/h_j \tag{11.24}$$

Normally, all the state holding times h_j are constant and small relative to the time spent in states, 0, -1 and $J+1$. So we let $h = h_j$ for $j = 1, 2, \ldots, J$ and let b_j capture the effects of the shared links.

Let π_j denote the steady state probability that the process is in state j $(j = -1, 0, 1, \ldots, J+1)$. Under the approximating assumption that all state holding times are exponentially distributed, we can write down the following balance equations:

$$\gamma\pi_{-1} = \sum_{j=1}^{J} \beta_j\pi_j$$

$$\lambda\pi_0 = \mu\pi_{J+1} + \gamma\pi_{-1}$$

$$(1/h)\pi_1 = \lambda\pi_0$$

$$(1/h)\pi_j = \alpha_{j-1}\pi_{j-1} \qquad j = 2, 3, \ldots, J$$

$$\mu\pi_{J+1} = \alpha_J\pi_J \tag{11.25}$$

This models the processor's access to the MIN. We now need to consider the effect of the state of the network.

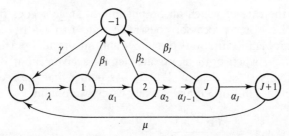

Figure 11.10 State transition diagram for the drop protocol.

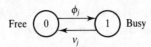

Figure 11.11 State transition diagram for switch in stage j.

To represent the network state, we solve the following model of a switch at stage j of the MIN. The switch output pin (link j) can be in one of two states: $X_j = 0$ (indicating that it is free) and $X_j = 1$ (indicating that it is busy). This gives the state transition diagram shown in Figure 11.11, where $1/v_j$ is the average time that link j spends in state 1 and $1/\phi_j$ is the average time link j spends in state 0.

Again by assuming exponential state holding times, we can write down the balance equation for this 0–1 Markov process:

$$\phi_j P(X_j = 0) = v_j P(X_j = 1) \tag{11.26}$$

where $P(X_j = k)$ is the steady state probability that the link is in state k. Since $P(X_j = 0) + P(X_j = 1) = 1$, we have:

$$P(X_j = 0) = \frac{v_j}{\phi_j + v_j} \tag{11.27}$$

$$P(X_j = 1) = \frac{\phi_j}{\phi_j + v_j} \tag{11.28}$$

We now relate the switch model to the model for the processor access to the network. First, assuming that new arrivals to a switch see the outputs as a random observer, we have:

$$P(X_j = 1) = b_j \tag{11.29}$$

By Equations (11.24), (11.28) and (11.29) we obtain

$$\beta_j = \frac{1}{h} \frac{\phi_j}{\phi_j + v_j} \tag{11.30}$$

Now ϕ_j is the rate at which an output link at stage j goes from state 0 to state 1, i.e. some processor goes from state j to $j + 1$. In the steady state, the probability flux out of state j and into state $j + 1$ is $\alpha_j \pi_j$. For a 2×2 switch, when both inputs are active, a given input is connected with probability $\frac{2}{3}$ (cf. Section 11.3.2). Assuming that the second arrival is successful in 2 out of 3 equally likely cases, we obtain

$$\phi_j = \tfrac{2}{3}\alpha_j \pi_j = \tfrac{2}{3}\frac{(1 - b_j)}{h}\pi_j \tag{11.31}$$

On the other hand, v_j is the rate at which a busy link becomes free. This happens when:

(1)   blocking is encountered downstream and the link is released
(2)   the processor releases the complete path at the end of a memory access

Thus we have

$$v_j = \sum_{i=j+1}^{J} \beta_i \pi_{ji} + \mu \pi_{j,J+1} \tag{11.32}$$

where π_{jk} is the probability that a processor is in state k given that it is in some state $k' \in \{j+1, j+2, \ldots, J+1\}$. This simple conditional probability is given by

$$\pi_{jk} = \frac{\pi_k}{\sum_{i=j+1}^{J+1} \pi_i}$$

Now we can substitute Equation (11.31) for ϕ_j and Equation (11.32) for v_j into Equation (11.30) to obtain β_j.

The performance measure of greatest interest here is the bandwidth, given by

$$B = 2^J \pi_{J+1} \mu \tag{11.33}$$

We also have the normalizing equation

$$\sum_{j=-1}^{J+1} \pi_j = 1$$

We therefore want to find π_{J+1} (from Equations 11.25 to 11.32) and hence the bandwidth from Equation (11.33). The unknowns are β_j and π_j and these can be found numerically (see Gelenbe (1989) for the details).

11.6.3 Circuit-switched MIN with a hold protocol

In this section we model a circuit-switched MIN with the hold protocol, i.e. in which partially established paths are held instead of dropped. All the links obtained in the partial path are maintained and the processor waits until the blocking link becomes available. This of course means that the links are held without being used and are possibly blocking other processors' requests. However, the processor has to obtain each link in the path only once, so there is a trade-off between these two

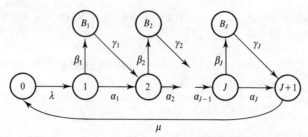

Figure 11.12   State transition diagram for the hold protocol.

protocols. Details of a combined release–hold protocol may be found in Patel (1991). Other practical advantages of the hold protocol are that it is fairer and cheaper to implement.

The states of a processor are similar to the drop protocol, but now the blocked state (previously state -1) becomes a number of states B_j where $j = 1, 2, \ldots, J$ indicates the link that it is blocked on. State 0 is still the non-requesting state of the processor and state $J + 1$ is the state when the memory module is being accessed. State j ($j = 1, 2, \ldots, J$) indicates that the processor is attempting to obtain link j. So the states are described by the set

$$S = \{0, 1, 2, \ldots, J, J + 1, B_1, B_2, \ldots, B_J\}$$

As before we define the following terms:

λ = the rate at which the processor generates requests from state 0

$1/\mu$ = mean time taken to access memory (after the complete path is established)

α_j = instantaneous transition rate from state j to state $j + 1, j = 1, 2, \ldots, J$

β_j = instantaneous transition rate from state j to state $B_j, j = 1, 2, \ldots, J$

$1/\gamma_j$ = mean time spent in state B_j, i.e. before transition to state $j + 1$

The state transition diagram is shown in Figure 11.12. Let π_j be the steady state probability that the processor is in state $j \in S$. As before we let $1/h = \alpha_j + \beta_j$ for $j = 1, 2, \ldots, J$ so that h is the mean time that a processor spends in attempting to obtain link j, after which it gets the link or gets blocked on that link. Assuming that all the state holding times are exponentially distributed we can write down the following balance equations.

$$\lambda \pi_0 = \mu \pi_{J+1}$$

$$\frac{1}{h}\pi_1 = \lambda \pi_0$$

$$\frac{1}{h}\pi_j = \alpha_{j-1}\pi_{j-1} + \gamma_{j-1}\pi_{B_{j-1}} \qquad j = 2, 3, \ldots, J$$

$$\mu \pi_{J+1} = \alpha_J \pi_J + \gamma_J \pi_{B_J}$$

$$\gamma_j \pi_{B_j} = \beta_j \pi_j \qquad\qquad j = 1, 2, \ldots, J \quad (11.34)$$

Since $(1/h)\pi_j = \alpha_{j-1}\pi_{j-1} + \gamma_{j-1}\pi_{B_{j-1}}$ and $\gamma_{j-1}\pi_{B_{j-1}} = \beta_{j-1}\pi_{j-1}$ for $j = 2, 3, \ldots, J$ we have

$$(1/h)\pi_j = \alpha_{j-1}\pi_{j-1} + \beta_{j-1}\pi_{j-1} = (1/h)\pi_{j-1}$$

Thus we have

$$\pi_j = \pi_1 \qquad j = 1, 2, 3, \ldots, J \qquad\qquad (11.35)$$

Similarly we obtain

$$\pi_{J+1} = \frac{1}{h\mu}\pi_J = \frac{1}{h\mu}\pi_1$$

$$\pi_0 = \frac{\mu}{\lambda}\pi_{J+1} = \frac{1}{h\lambda}\pi_J = \frac{1}{h\lambda}\pi_1$$

This gives all the non-blocking probabilities π_j $(j = 0, 1, 2, \ldots, J + 1)$ in terms of π_1. From the last balance Equation (11.34), we have $\pi_{B_j} = \beta_j \pi_1 / \gamma_j$. Substituting these into the normalizing condition we obtain

$$\sum_{j=0}^{J+1} \pi_j + \sum_{j=1}^{J} \pi_{B_j} = 1$$

$$1 = J\pi_1 + \left(\frac{1}{h\lambda} + \frac{1}{h\mu}\right)\pi_1 + \pi_1 \sum_{j=1}^{J} \frac{\beta_j}{\gamma_j} \qquad (11.36)$$

$$\pi_1^{-1} = J + \frac{1}{h\lambda} + \frac{1}{h\mu} + \sum_{j=1}^{J} \frac{\beta_j}{\gamma_j}$$

Now we need to find β_j and γ_j by relating these terms to the crossbar switches at stage j. The switch model is the same as the one considered for the drop protocol where $X_j = 0$ if link j is free and $X_j = 1$ if it is occupied. Again we have

$$\beta_j = \frac{1}{h}P(X_j = 1) = \frac{1}{h}\left(\frac{\phi_j}{\phi_j + \nu_j}\right) \qquad (11.37)$$

where ϕ_j is the rate out of the free state and v_j is the rate out of the occupied state.

The rate at which link j is released depends on the rate that some processor in state $J + 1$ completes its memory access. Upon completion, the processor releases all the acquired links (including link j) and thereby unblocks other processors. Conditioning on the event that the blocking processor must have obtained links $i = j + 1, j + 2, \ldots, J$ (or have been blocked at link i) we obtain

$$v_j = \frac{\mu \pi_{J+1}}{\sum_{i=j+1}^{J+1} \pi_i + \sum_{i=j+1}^{J} \pi_{B_i}} \tag{11.38}$$

Supposing that a processor has obtained all links up to link $j - 1$ and fails to get link j, then the rate (γ_j) at which link j becomes available to it is related to the rate (v_j) at which link j unconditionally becomes available as follows:

$$\gamma_j = v_j \frac{\pi_{B_j}}{\pi_j + \pi_{B_j}} = v_j \frac{\beta_j}{\gamma_j + \beta_j} \tag{11.39}$$

Also the total request rate for link j when it is free is $\phi_j = (1/h)\pi_j$, so Equation (11.37) becomes

$$\beta_j = \frac{1}{h} \left(\frac{\pi_j}{\pi_j + h v_j} \right) \tag{11.40}$$

For a given π_1, we can calculate β_j / γ_j and hence iteratively calculate π_1. As before we are mainly interested in the network bandwidth and so want to find π_{J+1}. The accuracy of this model with respect to simulation is good. Further details can be found in Gelenbe (1989).

11.7 Interconnection networks in a queueing model

In this section we analyse a closed system with a circuit-switched interconnection network in which partial paths are held. The IN is an integral part of the shared-memory multiprocessor and needs to be represented in a queueing model of the whole system. We isolate the IN and its associated DMA processors by short-circuiting the other components of the queueing network. The IN can then be analysed by applying the FES method (see Chapter 8) as in Figure 11.13. Thus the quantity of interest is the throughput of the IN as a function of the population of the closed system. Since each customer represents a network transfer request, the throughput is the number of requests

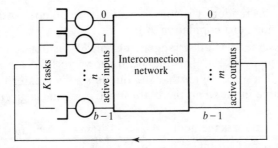

Figure 11.13   Closed system of DMA servers and the IN.

served per unit time. We assume that path set-up and release times are negligible and that transfer times are exponentially distributed with unit mean. The request buffers are on the inputs rather than the outputs because the IN imposes constraints on the input processors (a kind of BBS blocking).

Suppose that the IN has b inputs, b outputs and J stages and that we replace it by an FES with service rate function $T(K)$. Assuming that the memory references are uniform, the state space can be described by:

$$S = \{(n, m) | \Sigma n_i = K, m = 1, 2, \ldots, n\}$$

where $n = (n_0, n_1, \ldots, n_{b-1})$ represents the queue lengths at the inputs (n of which are non-empty) and m represents the number of active output pins. Under the assumption of exponential transfer times, the process $X_t = (N_t, M_t)$ $t > 0$ with state space S is a Markov process. State transitions occur when a path from some input pin is released (freeing an output pin) and this causes a new arrival at some input pin. During a state transition, many free output pins can become active. These pins can be acquired by

(1)   customers blocked by the released path from i (up to J customers unblocked in a J-stage MIN)

(2)   the next customer in queue i (1 customer)

(3)   the recycled customer (1 customer)

Thus transitions are of the form $(n, m) \to (n', m')$ where $m' = m - 1$, m, $m + 1, \ldots, m + J + 1$. When the number of stages J is large, the number of possible state transitions is very large.

We therefore consider the simpler Markov process representing the number of active inputs only:

$$Z(t) = \{N_t | t \geq 0\} \text{ with state space } \Omega_Z = \{n | 1 \leq n \leq \min(b, K)\}$$

where N_t is the random variable indicating the number of active inputs ($N_t \geq 1$, for non-zero population K).

We assume that all arrangements of K customers over n active inputs are equally likely. This has been shown to hold for a crossbar in equilibrium. The probability that the queue size is greater than one at a particular active input when there are n active inputs is given by

$$\frac{\text{Number of arrangements of } K - 1 \text{ items in } n \text{ non-empty queues}}{\text{Number of arrangements of } K \text{ items in } n \text{ non-empty queues}}$$

$$= \binom{K-2}{n-1} \bigg/ \binom{K-1}{n-1} = \frac{K-n}{K-1}$$

Using this result it is easy to write down the state transition probabilities. Let p_{ij} be the state transition probability from state i to state j. The state can only increase by one, decrease by one or stay the same. When the state increases by one the departing customer must leave behind a non-empty queue and must join one of the $b - n$ empty queues:

$$p_{n,n+1} = \left(\frac{K-n}{K-1}\right)\left(\frac{b-n}{b}\right) \tag{11.41}$$

Conversely, when the state decreases by one the departing customer must leave an empty queue and join one of the n active queues:

$$p_{n+1,n} = \left(\frac{n}{K-1}\right)\left(\frac{n}{b}\right) \tag{11.42}$$

Let π_n be the steady state probability that the process is in state n and let μ_n be the throughput when n inputs are active (i.e. this is the conditional throughput function). Then for $n = 1, 2, \ldots, b - 1$ the balance equations are

$$\mu_n \pi_n p_{n,n+1} = \mu_{n+1} \pi_{n+1} p_{n+1,n} \tag{11.43}$$

Substituting Equations (11.41) and (11.42) gives

$$\mu_n \pi_n (b - n)(K - n) = \mu_{n+1} \pi_{n+1} n^2 \tag{11.44}$$

Solving Equation (11.44) yields the following unnormalized solution:

$$\pi_n = \frac{p_1 \mu_1 \prod_{j=1}^{n-1}[(b - j)(K - j)]}{\mu_n (n - 1)!^2} \qquad n = 1, 2, \ldots, b \tag{11.45}$$

11.7.1 The FES service rate function

Assuming that μ_n is known it is easy to write down the throughput when the FES network population is K:

$$T(K) = \sum_{n=1}^{b} \mu_n \pi_n$$

In order to find a closed form solution, let $t_n = \mu_n \pi_n$ and rewrite the balance Equations (11.44) as

$$(b - n)(K - n)t_n = n^2 t_{n+1} \qquad n = 1, 2, \ldots, b - 1 \qquad \textbf{(11.46)}$$

The boundary condition for this recurrence is:

$$\sum_{n=1}^{b} t_n/\mu_n = 1 \qquad \textbf{(11.47)}$$

corresponding to the normalization of the probabilities π_n.

We now define the following generating functions, where $t_n = 0$ for $n > b$:

$$G(z) = \sum_{n=1}^{\infty} t_n z^n$$

$$H(z) = \sum_{n=1}^{\infty} \frac{t_n z^n}{n}$$

We now have $T(K) = G(1)$ and we can rewrite the recurrence Equation (11.46) as

$$Kb(t_n/n) - (K + b)t_n + nt_n + t_{n+1} - (n + 1)t_{n+1} = 0$$

Multiplying this equation by z^n and summing over all n yields

$$KbH(z) - (K + b)G(z) + zG'(z) + z^{-1}(G(z) - t_1 z)$$
$$- G'(z) + t_1 = 0$$

which simplifies to

$$(1 - z)G'(z) + (K + b - z^{-1})G(z) - KbH(z) = 0$$

Thus, setting $z = 1$, we obtain the required expression for the throughput $T(K)$:

$$T(K) = G(1) = \frac{bK}{b + K - 1}H(1) \qquad \textbf{(11.48)}$$

The value of $H(1)$ can be found from the boundary condition. Let us consider some simple cases.

Multiple server (i.e. no switching network)

Suppose each server has rate μ and there is no network contention (so that $\mu_n = n\mu$). The boundary condition (Equation 11.47) gives $H(1) = \mu$, so substituting this in Equation 11.48 gives

$$T(K) = \frac{bK}{b + K - 1}\mu \tag{11.49}$$

This is the result derived in Section 6.6 for multiple server sub-networks.

Full b-way crossbar

For the b-way crossbar ($J = 1$), the state transitions for the process X_t are simpler but the balance equations still remain large. However, if we artificially force the number of active inputs to be fixed (i.e. ignore all transitions that change the value of n) then the balance equations are satisfied by

$$P(m|n) = \binom{n-1}{m-1}\binom{b}{m}\bigg/\binom{b+n-1}{n} \qquad m = 1, 2, \ldots, n \tag{11.50}$$

where $P(m|n)$ is the steady state probability for any state with m active outputs and n active inputs. For a proof of this, see Patel (1989). Note that this expression is independent of the network population K (as we would expect, since the process is constrained to keep the number of active inputs constant and $K \geq n$). This is, in fact, an asymptotically exact result as $K \to \infty$ since then all input pins are always active with probability one, i.e. $n = b$. For each value of n we define the conditional throughput as

$$\mu_n = \mu \sum_{m=1}^{n} mP(m|n) \tag{11.51}$$

Thus μ_n is the throughput given that n inputs are active. This is approximate since the actual throughput conditioned on the number of active inputs depends on the overall population K. Nevertheless, this approach provides a good approximation, which is exact when $n = b$.

Standard results for sums of binomial coefficients yield a simple expression for the conditional throughput of a b-way crossbar:

$$\mu_n = \frac{bn}{b + n - 1}\mu \qquad n = 1, 2, \ldots, b \tag{11.52}$$

From the boundary condition, we obtain a relationship between $G(1)$ and $H(1)$, which yields

$$T(K) = \frac{b^2 K}{(2b - 1)K + (b - 1)^2}\mu \tag{11.53}$$

Details may be found in Harrison and Patel (1990).

Delta network

For a delta network, μ_n is not a simple expression, and a closed form solution for the FES rate is not possible. In such cases we numerically compute $\mu_1, \mu_2, \ldots, \mu_b$ and evaluate $\pi_1, \pi_2, \ldots, \pi_b$ from Equation (11.45). Then summing all the *little* throughputs t_i gives the required FES rate:

$$t_1 + t_2 + \ldots + t_b = T(K)$$

We will now briefly consider the simplest case of the delta-2 network.

11.7.2 Saturated delta-2 networks

The analysis of a simple crossbar relates the input utilization to the output utilization. The successive application of the same result to each stage of a delta network can yield a corresponding expression that relates the network input utilization to its output utilization. Suppose we define u_s as the utilization of an output pin in stage s ($s = 1, 2, \ldots, J$) and u_0 as the utilization of an input pin ($u_0 = 1$ in the saturated case). Thus a crossbar in stage s has inputs with utilization u_{s-1} and outputs with utilization u_s and under uniform routing we have, from Equation (11.19),

$$u_s = \frac{2u_{s-1}}{2 + u_{s-1}} \tag{11.54}$$

If we let $v_s = 1/u_s$ then Equation (11.54) becomes

$$v_s = v_{s-1} + \tfrac{1}{2}$$

Expanding this recurrence (with boundary value $v_0 = 1$ since the network is saturated) gives

$$v_s = v_{s-2} + \tfrac{1}{2} + \tfrac{1}{2} = v_0 + s/2 = \frac{s + 2}{2}$$

Therefore, in a saturated network, the output pin utilization at stage s is:

$$u_s = \frac{2}{s + 2} \tag{11.55}$$

For a J-stage network with unit mean transmission times ($\mu = 1$), the throughput or bandwidth is given by

$$B = 2^J u_J = \frac{2^{J+1}}{J + 2} \tag{11.56}$$

As an example, consider a saturated 10-stage delta-2 network. Using Equation (11.56) we find that, out of the 1024 requests in the saturated network, only 170.7 requests will have complete paths on average. Thus by applying Little's result to the requests in the network we find that the mean waiting time is $(J + 2)/2 = 6.0$. Let us compare this with the equivalent single 1024×1024 crossbar. Using Equation (11.52), we find that in saturation 512.25 requests will be connected on average and the mean waiting time for customers at the head of the queue is just 2.0. Clearly, a large number of stages in the MIN is not suitable for heavy traffic.

This approach has been extended to allow non-uniform routing to the output pins of the MIN (Harrison and Patel 1990). The more detailed analysis yields some very accurate results with respect to simulation: less than 1% error in the saturated uniform case and about 3% in other cases.

11.7.3 Recent research and open problems

Packet-switched MINs with finite buffers pose extra complications because the shared buffers cause blocking. This is similar to the blocking encountered in queueing networks and approximation methods are needed. The MIN model in Harrison and Pinto (1991) provides an accurate method for evaluating these types of MINs. Other open problems include finding time delay distributions (see Chapter 9 for further discussion) for message latency across a MIN. Since the delta network is overtake-free, this generally hard problem has been tackled in the special case of exponential servers and infinite buffers (Harrison 1990). Fault tolerant MINs also need to be modelled. They usually have multiple paths for any input–output pair and are constructed in novel ways. These redundant paths were considered in Mitra and Cieslak (1987), which could be extended to handle general link transmission times. Other features of switching networks that could be modelled include more general workloads, e.g. dependent arrival processes of inputs of synchronous MINs.

SUMMARY

- Circuit-switched networks, such as telephone networks, can be modelled by an exact Markov model. However, this is not computationally tractable and Erlang's fixed point approximation, which is exact in limiting cases, provides very accurate results.

- In parallel processing systems, much smaller switching networks are required. The simplest case is the full crossbar switch, which allows a number of inputs (from processors) to connect to any one of the outputs (to the memory modules).

- Models of the full crossbar represent either synchronous or asynchronous modes of operation. For the synchronous case, Strecker's approximation provides throughput measures. Little's result provides many useful relationships between variables in the asynchronous case.

- A matrix of crossbars can be interconnected to form a multi-stage interconnection network, which is a more cost-effective way of providing high connectivity.

- The packet-switched network provides buffers at each stage and allows transfer of packets point-to-point across stages according to buffer availability. So the network can be modelled as a queueing network with finite buffers.

- The circuit-switched network first establishes a path across all stages before sending the data. A Markov model can provide some of the desired performance measures.

- Multi-stage interconnection networks can be represented in models of parallel computers by extending the flow equivalent server method.

EXERCISES

11.1 (20 Synchronous switch)

For the synchronous switch model of Bhandarkar (1975), analyse the 2×2 crossbar where a new request is generated at each free input on every cycle. Find the steady state probability for each of the three states of the output queues. Find the bandwidth of the switch and compare with Strecker's approximation.

11.2 (20 Asynchronous switch)

In a saturated, symmetrical 2×2 crossbar switch, both inputs are always busy and each output is selected with probability $\frac{1}{2}$ by all tasks. Each output is connected to a server with fixed rate μ and the system is in equilibrium.

(a) What is the probability that a new arrival on either input is blocked by the task holding the other input?

(b) Given that the steady state arrival rate on each input is λ, show that the switch has throughput $4\mu/3$.

(c) Show that for a *non-saturated* crossbar connected to the same servers, the conditional probability that the upper output is active, given that both inputs are busy, is $\frac{2}{3}$ under the additional approximating assumption that Little's result may be applied just over periods when such a state exists.

11.3 (20 Full crossbar)
Consider the FES for an $a \times b$ crossbar in a closed network with $K > 0$ customers. Assuming that the conditional throughput is $\mu_n = [bn/(b + n - 1)]\mu$ when there are n active inputs ($n = 1, 2, \ldots, b$), derive an expression for the FES service rate $T(K)$. Hence show that the throughput of an $a \times b$ crossbar is the same as that of a $b \times a$ crossbar.

11.4 (20 Packet-switched delta-2 network)
A packet-switched 4×4 delta-2 network is embedded in a computer architecture which is modelled by a closed Markovian queueing network with population N. All 4 inputs and all 4 outputs are selected with equal probability by any packet. Buffers of size greater than N are located at each of the 8 crossbar output pins, numbered 1 to 8. Packets are queued FCFS, there is no blocking and all transfer times between buffers are exponentially distributed with mean one. Apply the FES decomposition method to the delta network, and:

(a) show that all visitation rates in the short-circuited network are equal and hence that all its states have the same equilibrium probability

(b) show that in the steady state, any buffer is empty with probability S_7/S_8 where S_m is the number of states in a closed network of m nodes and population N

(c) given that

$$S_m = \frac{(N + m - 1)!}{N!(m - 1)!}$$

show that the FES rate is $4N/(N + 7)$.

Appendix: Outline Solutions

1.1 $\frac{1}{36}, \frac{1}{216}$

1.2   This can be proved using mathematical induction. For the base case, we can take $n = 2$ and use Proposition 1.2. The inductive case also uses the same proposition. Notice that the domain of the rth sum on the right-hand side has $\binom{n}{r}$ elements corresponding to each of the (ordered) subsets of $\{1, 2, \ldots, n\}$ of size r.

1.3   Consider $N + M - 1$ items arranged in a straight line. Suppose we choose $M - 1$ items and make them into lines perpendicular to the line of items. This divides the items into M partitions (urns). The remaining N items become balls. So the number of ways of arranging N balls in M urns is given by

$$\binom{N + M - 1}{M - 1}$$

Notice that if the urn capacity is restricted, the problem becomes somewhat more complicated.

1.4   Consider a person x in the group and let $P(D) = p$ be the probability that he or she has the disease, $P(V|D) = v$ be the probability that he or she tests positive given that he or she has the disease, and $P(\bar{V}|\bar{D}) = c$ be the probability that he or she tests negative given that he or she does not have the disease. Using Bayes' formula, the required probability is given by:

$$P(D|V) = \frac{P(D)P(V|D)}{P(D)P(V|D) + P(\bar{D})P(V|\bar{D})}$$

$$= \frac{pv}{pv + (1 - p)(1 - c)}$$

1.5   The solution is counter-intuitive to many people, and depends on how they view the problem. It is important to consider the extra information provided by each event and the order in which events occur. On the first selection, the grand prize is selected with probability $\frac{1}{3}$, a bogus prize is selected with probability $\frac{2}{3}$. However, when the host opens one of the doors to reveal one of the bogus prizes, he or she only has a choice in 1 of 3 cases (if the contestant had first selected the 'correct' door). Hence in 2 out of 3 cases, the host is forced to open a particular door because he or she cannot open the door which hides the grand prize. So the probability of winning the grand prize is $\frac{2}{3}$ if the contestant changes his selection and $\frac{1}{3}$ otherwise.

2.1 P(nobody (in n people) has the same birthday)

$$= \underbrace{\left(\frac{364}{365}\right)\left(\frac{363}{365}\right)\cdots\left(\frac{365-(n-1)}{365}\right)}_{(n-1)\ \text{terms}}$$

P(at least 2 people (from n) have the same birthday)

$$= 1 - \frac{\prod_{i=1}^{n-1}(365-i)}{365^{n-1}}$$

For $n = 22$, this probability is 0.4757, and for $n = 23$, it is 0.5073.

2.2 Let

$$P_t(X = r) = \frac{(\lambda t)^r}{r!}\,e^{-\lambda t}$$

be the probability of r crashes in t months. The required probability is

P(1 occurrence on 31 Jan.|exactly one occurrence in Jan.)

$$= \frac{P(1\ \text{occurrence on 31 Jan.}\ \textit{and}\ \text{exactly one occurrence in Jan.})}{P(\text{exactly one occurrence in Jan.})}$$

$$= \frac{P_{30/31}(X=0)P_{1/31}(X=1)}{P_1(X=1)} = \frac{1}{31}$$

2.3 Let X_1 be the time for T_1 and X_2 be the time for T_2, so that $F_1(x) = 1 - e^{-\lambda x}$, $f_1(x) = \lambda e^{-\lambda x}$, $F_2(x) = 1 - e^{-\mu x}$, $f_2(x) = \mu e^{-\mu x}$.

$$P(X_1 > X_2) \approx \sum_i P(X_2 < x_i)P(X_1 \in (x_i, x_i + h))$$

$$\approx \sum_i P(X_2 < x_i)\frac{P(X_1 < x_i + h) - P(X_1 < x_i)}{h}\,h$$

$$= \int_0^\infty F_2(x)f_1(x)\,\mathrm{d}x = \frac{\mu}{\lambda + \mu}$$

Alternatively, consider two Poisson streams: one of type 1 transactions and the other of type 2 transactions. The superposition of the two Poisson streams is also a Poisson stream with rate $\lambda + \mu$. The proportion of type 2 transactions is $\mu/(\lambda + \mu)$, which is the same as the probability that the next transaction to complete is of type 2.

2.4 Let $T = \max(X_1, X_2)$ where X_1 and X_2 are exponentially distributed with rate μ. Then $P(T \leq t) = P(X_1 \leq t)P(X_2 \leq t) = (1 - e^{-\mu t})(1 - e^{-\mu t}) = 1 + e^{-2\mu t} - 2e^{-\mu t}$. Differentiating w.r.t. t gives the density function: $2\mu e^{-2\mu t}(e^{\mu t} - 1)$.

2.5 Suppose λ is the arrival rate and $F(t) = P(T \leq t)$ is the probability that the next arrival occurs before time t. The probability of an arrival in a small interval $(t, t + h)$ is $\lambda h + o(h^2)$ and so we have for small h: $P(T \leq t + h) = P(T \leq t) + P(T > t)\lambda h$.

Rearranging and letting $h \to 0$, we obtain $F'(t) = \lambda[1 - F(t)]$ with boundary values $F(0) = 0$ and $F(\infty) = 1$, so $F(t) = 1 - e^{-\lambda t}$.

2.6   Let $Y = \min(X_1, X_2, \ldots, X_n)$, so $P(Y > t) = P(X_1 > t)P(X_2 > t)$ $\ldots P(X_n > t)$, i.e. $F_Y(t) = 1 - (1 - F_{X_1}(t)) \ldots (1 - F_{X_n}(t))$.

For the exponential distribution, where $F_{X_2}(t) = P(X_i \leq t) = 1 - \exp(-\mu_i t)$, $F_Y(t) = 1 - \exp - (\mu_1 + \mu_2 + \ldots + \mu_n)t$. Hence the distribution of the minimum of a set of exponentials is also exponential.

2.7   Let $Z = \max(X_1, X_2, \ldots, X_n)$, so $P(Z \leq t) = P(X_1 < t)P(X_2 < t) \ldots P(X_n \leq t)$, i.e. $F_Z(t) = F_{X_1}(t) \ldots F_{X_n}(t)$.

For the exponential distribution, where $F_{X_i}(t) = P(X_i \leq t) = 1 - \exp(-\mu_i t)$, $F_Z(t) = [1 - \exp(-\mu_1 t)] \ldots [1 - \exp(-\mu_n t)]$.

2.8   This is the Erlang-n distribution function. Let X be the number of arrivals in the interval $(0, t)$, i.e. a Poisson variable. So

$$P[X < n] = \sum_{k=0}^{n-1} \frac{(\lambda t)^k}{k!} e^{-\lambda t}$$

The result follows since $P[T_n \leq t] = P[X \geq n] = 1 - P[X < n]$.

2.9   Generalizing from small cases, guess that

$$f_n(t) = \lambda \frac{(\lambda t)^{n-1}}{(n - 1)!} e^{-\lambda t}$$

and prove by induction on n. Alternatively, find the distribution function $F_n(t)$ by considering the probability that the nth arrival of a Poisson process occurs before time t and differentiate with respect to t.

2.10   Let X_1, X_2 be the random variables for inter-arrival times for process 1 and 2.

$$P(X_2 > X_1) = \int_0^{2/\lambda} (1 - e^{-\lambda x})\lambda/2 \, dx = \tfrac{1}{2}(1 + e^{-2})$$

3.1   Expected loss of 0.50

3.2 $E[X] = 20/3$

3.3 $E[X] = 2$

3.4   The probabilities $\tfrac{1}{2}, \tfrac{1}{4}, \tfrac{1}{8}, \ldots$ form a geometric series with ratio $\tfrac{1}{2}$ and sum to one. However, the expectation is $1 + 1 + 1 + \ldots$ and so not finite.

3.5   (a) $E[X] = p$ and $E[X^2] = p$ so $\text{Var}[X] = p - p^2 = p(1 - p)$. For n independent Bernoulli trials, we just multiply these expectations by n.

(b)   Suppose we split the interval $(0, t)$ into n divisions each of length $h = t/n$. Then the probability of success in one division is $p = \lambda t/n$. Taking the limit as $n \to \infty$, we have $S_n \to K_t$ and the result follows.

3.6 $\phi(t) = \dfrac{1}{\sqrt{2\pi}} \displaystyle\int_{-\infty}^{\infty} e^{tx} e^{-x^2/2}\, dx = \dfrac{e^{t^2/2}}{\sqrt{2\pi}} \displaystyle\int_{-\infty}^{\infty} e^{-(x-t)^2/2}\, dx = e^{t^2/2}$

3.7 Assuming failures occur independently, then the number of cycles to the first failure has a geometric distribution. Hence the mean time to failure of a single component is $1/p$ cycles. For n independent components, the probability that at least one fails is $1 - (1 - p)^n$ which is np for small p. Similarly, the mean time to failure is $1/(np)$.

3.8 Assume failures occur independently with probability $p = 1/m$ in any cycle. Then the probability that both disks fail in a given cycle is p^2. Hence the mean time before failure is m^2.

4.1 Take limits as $k \to \infty$:
$$\lim_{k \to \infty} P(K_j = k) = (1 - v_{jj}) \lim_{k \to \infty} v_{jj}^{k-1} = 0 \text{ since } v_{jj} < 1.$$

4.2 The result follows from the balance equations: $(1 - \alpha)p_{j-1} = \alpha p_j$ for $j = 1, 2, \ldots$.

4.3 Let states 1 and 2 denote that the particle is at an odd number and even number respectively. Then the 2-step matrix is
$$Q = \begin{bmatrix} 0 & 1 \\ 1 - \omega & \omega \end{bmatrix}$$

(a) $Q^4 =$
$$\begin{bmatrix} (1 - \omega)(1 - \omega + \omega^2) & \omega(2 - 2\omega + \omega^2) \\ \omega(1 - \omega)(2 - 2\omega + \omega^2) & (1 - \omega)(1 - \omega + 3\omega^2) + \omega^4 \end{bmatrix}$$

(b) (i) aperiodic if $\omega > 0$; (ii) recurrent if $\omega < 1$

(c) Balance equations are $p_1 = p_2(1 - \omega)$, so $p_2 = 1/(2 - \omega)$

4.4 Let p_j be the probability that there are j messages in the buffer. The balance equation is $\alpha(1 - \beta)p_{j-1} = \beta p_j$ for $j = 1, 2, \ldots, M$. The normalized probability distribution is $p_j = \gamma^j(1 - \gamma)/(1 - \gamma^{M+1})$ where $\gamma = \alpha(1 - \beta)/\beta$ from which the buffer full probability is $\gamma^M(1 - \gamma)/(1 - \gamma^{M+1})$.

4.5 If p_j is the equilibrium probability that the executing job is in phase j, then the balance equations are: $\mu_j p_j = \alpha_{j-1}\mu_{j-1}p_{j-1}$ for $j = 2, 3, \ldots, M$. Thus we have
$$p_j = p_1 \frac{\mu_1}{\mu_j} \prod_{k=1}^{j} \alpha_k$$

where p_1 can be found by normalizing. Then the mean number of jobs that complete normally per unit time is $\mu_M p_M$ and the mean number that abort per unit time is $\mu_1 p_1 - \mu_M p_M$.

4.6 (a) The state at the next clock pulse depends only on the state at the current pulse so we have a Markov chain with transition probability matrix
$$P = \begin{bmatrix} 1 - \alpha & \alpha \\ \beta & 1 - \beta \end{bmatrix}$$

(b)   Prove by induction on n

(c)   Post-multiply result of (b) by M^{-1}, to obtain P^n.

(d)   As $n \to \infty$, $\omega^n \to 0$ if $-1 < \omega < 1$, and so

$$P^\infty = \frac{1}{\alpha + \beta} \begin{bmatrix} \beta & \alpha \\ \beta & \alpha \end{bmatrix}$$

P^n does not converge if $\omega = -1$ (i.e. $\alpha = \beta = 1$) because the chain is periodic. If $\omega = 1$ (i.e. $\alpha = \beta = 0$), $P = I$ and so the chain remains in the initial state.

4.7   By the superposition property of the Poisson streams, the overall arrival process is Poisson with rate $m\lambda$. This forms a very simple Markov chain since the number of packets at a clearance instant is independent of any previous clearances. The buffer is empty if no packets arrive in time t_0. This occurs with probability $\exp(-m\lambda t_0)$.

4.11 The number of records in the buffer is a Markov process with state space $\{0, 1, 2\}$. Let p_i denote the equilibrium probability that i records are in the buffer. The balance equations are: $\mu p_2 = \lambda p_1$, $(\lambda + \mu)p_1 = \lambda p_0$ and $\lambda p_0 = \mu p_1 + \mu p_2$. With the normalizing condition, we obtain $p_2 = [\lambda/(\lambda + \mu)]^2$, as required.

4.12 Using $|p_{jk}(h)/h - q_{jk}| \leq \Sigma_l q_{jl} q_{lk} h_1 h_2 \leq \Sigma qq h^2 \leq q_j q_l h^2 \leq M^2 h^2 \to 0$ uniformly. Also, even if q_i is not bounded, if $p_{ij}(t) \to 0$ as $j \to \infty$ 'faster than j^{-2}', we can still get uniformity. Using $P(t) = P(t/n)^n$, we get $p_{ij}(t) \leq (t/n)^n \Sigma \Pi q_{ki,ki+1} \leq (t/n)^n A^n \Pi M_i$ where A is the maximum number of states that can be transited to (if it exists) M_i, which is bound on q_{ki} after i transitions, e.g. i. Then Stirling's formula gives $\leq (Xt)^n \sqrt{n} e^{-n} \to 0$ faster than n^{-k} for any k. Choose $n = j$.

4.14 $R(t) = \lambda t$ and $r(t) = \lambda$.

4.15 $P(\text{renewal in } (t, t + h] | \text{renewal at } 0) = P(\text{1st renewal in } (t, t + h] | \text{renewal at } 0) + \int_0^t P(\text{1st renewal in } (s, s + ds] \text{ and renewal in } (s + (t - s), s + (t - s) + h] | \text{renewal at } 0) = f(t)h + \int_0^t f(s)\lambda_{t-s} h \, ds + o(h)$.

4.17 (a)   The probability that an observed inter-arrival time is of length s is proportional to both s (since the observation point is more likely to fall in a large interval than a small one) and the frequency at which intervals of length s occur. Integrating shows that the constant of proportionality is $1/m$, since the area under the density function is one.

(b)   If the observed period is of length s, then the observation point is uniformly distributed over the interval $(0, s)$, i.e. the residual life density is $(1/s)$.

$P(\text{residual life} = u | \text{observed period} = s) = (1/s) \, du$
$P(\text{observed period} = s) = f_0(s) \, ds$
$P(\text{residual life} = u \text{ and observed period} = s)$
$\qquad\qquad\qquad\qquad\qquad = (1/s) \, du (1/m) s f(s) \, ds$

Integrating over all observed periods from s to infinity gives the probability that the residual life $= u$ (from the total probability formula)

$$f_R(u) = \int_u^\infty \frac{1}{m} f(s)\,ds = \frac{1}{m}(1 - F(u))$$

(c)   Finding the mean of this density by integrating by parts gives

$$\text{mean residual life} = \int_0^\infty \frac{1}{m} u(1 - F(u))\,du$$

$$= \frac{1}{2m}\int_0^\infty u^2 f(u)\,du$$

4.18 $r(t - \tau - h)h + o(h)$

5.1   The balance equations are $\mu p_j = p_{j-1}\lambda/j$ for $j = 1, 2, \ldots$ and have solution $p_j = (\rho^j/j!)e^{-\rho}$ for $j = 0, 1, 2, \ldots$, i.e. Poisson with parameter $\rho = \lambda/\mu$. So we have utilization $= (1 - e^{-\rho})$; throughput $= \mu(1 - e^{-\rho})$; mean queue length $= \rho$; mean response time $= \rho/\mu(1 - e^{-\rho})$.

5.2   The balance equations are $\mu(j)p_j = \lambda(j - 1)p_{j-1}$ for $j = 1, 2, \ldots$ and have solution $p_j = (\rho^j/(j!)^{b+c})p_0$ for $j = 0, 1, 2, \ldots$, where $\rho = \lambda/\mu$, which becomes the Poisson distribution with parameter ρ when $b + c = 1$.

5.3   Let X and Y be the inter-arrival time and the service time random variables with densities $f_X(x)$ and $f_Y(x)$. Find the convolution $X + Y$, i.e. the density. $f_{X+Y}(x) = \lambda\mu(e^{-\lambda x} - e^{-\mu x})/(\mu - \lambda)$ which occurs with probability $(1 - U)$ where $U = \rho = \lambda/\mu$. Then $f_D(x) = (1 - \rho)f_{X+Y}(x) + \rho f_Y(x) = \lambda e^{-\lambda x}$.

5.4 $P(\text{state } j + 1 \text{ at time } t - h | \text{ state } j \text{ at time } t)$

$$= P(\text{state } j \text{ at time } t | \text{state } j + 1 \text{ at time } t - h)\,\frac{P(\text{state } j + 1 \text{ at time } t - h)}{P(\text{state } j \text{ at time } t)}$$

$$= (I_{(j<n)}[(j + 1)\mu h] + I_{(j\geq n)}[n\mu h] + o(h))\pi_{j+1}/\pi j$$

where π_j is the stationary probability that there are j customers in the queue. From the balance equations, we have $\pi_{j+1}/\pi_j = \{I_{(j<n)}[\lambda/(j + 1)\mu] + I_{(j\geq n)}(\lambda/n\mu)\}$. And so $P(\text{state } j + 1 \text{ at time } t - h | \text{state } j \text{ at time } t) = \lambda h + o(h)$ $j = 0, 1, 2, \ldots$.
    Similarly, we can show that

$$P(\text{state } j \text{ at time } t - h | \text{state } j + 1 \text{ at time } t)$$

$$= I_{(j<n)}[(j + 1)\mu h] + I_{(j\geq n)}[n\mu h] + o(h) \qquad j = 0, 1, 2, \ldots$$

5.6   The number of non-empty queues encountered on the token's cycle is binomially distributed. This gives the distribution of the number of delays (each of length d) that the token encounters (on top of the transmission delay of Mx). Thus we can find the mean and second moment of the service time and use the Pollaczek–Khintchine formula to determine the mean waiting time for the M/G/1 queue.

5.7   Let L_Q and W_Q be the mean queue length excluding any in service and the mean queueing time respectively. Little's result gives $L_Q = \lambda W_Q$ and $L = \lambda(W_Q + (1/\mu))$. Poisson arrivals find the server busy with probability $\rho = \lambda/\mu$. So an arrival has to wait for the customer in service and all the customers waiting to be served. Since the arrival process is Poisson, by the Random Observer Property: $W_Q = \rho r + (1/\mu)L_Q$. Thus $W_Q = \rho r/(1 - \rho)$ and the result follows.

6.1 Mean waiting time

$$W = \frac{1}{\mu_1 - \gamma} + \frac{p}{\mu_2 - p\gamma} + \frac{q}{\mu_3 - q\gamma}$$

which is minimum when $p = \frac{1}{2}$.

6.2 All strings start with the character 0 and every choice of $m - 1$ zeros among the remaining $n + m - 1$ characters corresponds to a different state. The number of arrangements of n customers on m non-empty queues is the same as the number of arrangements of $n - m$ customers on m queues (we remove m customers and place them in each of the queues, which leaves $n - m$ customers on m queues).

6.3 Let $x_i = e_i/\mu_i$, so

$$P(N_j \geqslant h) = x_j^h \frac{G(K - h)}{G(K)} \quad \text{and}$$

$$P(N_i = k \text{ and } N_j \geqslant h) = x_i^k x_j^h \frac{G_i(K - k - h)}{G(K)}$$

Dividing these results gives the required conditional probability (a). Part (b) follows from

$$P(N_j = h) = x_j^h \frac{G_j(K - h)}{G(K)} \quad \text{and}$$

$$P(N_i = k \text{ and } N_j = h) = x_i^k x_j^h \frac{G_{ij}(K - k - h)}{G(K)}$$

6.4 Removing the subscripts, we have $L(n) = U(n)(1 + L(n - 1))$.

(a) We first show that the sequence $(L(k), k = 0, 1, 2, \ldots)$ is increasing (by induction on k). Basis: $L(1) = U(1)(1 + L(0)) = U(1) > 0 = L(0)$. Assume $L(k) > L(k - 1)$ for $k > 1$, then $L(k + 1) = U(k + 1)(1 + L(k)) > U(k + 1)(1 + L(k - 1))$ by the inductive hypothesis. Since $(U(k))$ is increasing, $L(k + 1) > U(k)(1 + L(k - 1)) = L(k)$.

(b) Case $u < 1$. Since $U(k)$ is increasing and has a limit, $L(k) \leqslant u(1 + L(k - 1))$, and by induction we can show $L(k) \leqslant u/(1 - u)$. Thus $(L(k))$ is increasing (by (a)) and is bounded and so must have a limit (L, say). Since $L = u(1 + L)$, $L = u/(1 - u)$ as required.

(c) Case $u = 1$. As $k \to \infty$, we must have $L(k)/(1 + L(k)) \to 1$. If $(L(k))$ has a limit L, then we require $L/(1 + L) = 1$, which is a contradiction. So $L(k) \to \infty$, as $k \to \infty$.

6.5 (a) From the product form solution, we can obtain the probability distribution of the number of customers in the first m nodes:

$$p_{1m}(k) = \frac{G_{m+1,M}(k)G_{1m}(N - k)}{G(N)}$$

The result follows by finding the mean of this distribution.

(b)   The queue length distribution at node i is

$$p_i(k) = \frac{x_i^k G_{i,i}(N-k)}{G(N)}$$

Finding the mean and summing over $i = 1, 2, \ldots, m$ gives the mean number in the first m nodes. Equating with the result from (a) gives the desired result.

6.6   (a)   Assume each processor has an exponential service time with unit mean. Collection A can be modelled as a single queue with multiple servers, so the service rate is

$$\mu_A(n) = \begin{cases} n & n \leqslant m_1 \\ m_1 & n \geqslant m_1 \end{cases}$$

Collection B consists of multiple parallel servers and so we can create an FES node with rate

$$\mu_B(n) = \frac{m_2 n}{m_2 + n - 1}$$

(b)   The 2-node network has a product form solution: $p(n, N - n) = p(n)q(N - n)/G$. Since visitation rates are one: $p(i)^{-1} = \mu_A(1)\mu_A(2) \ldots \mu_A(i)$ and $q(i)^{-1} = \mu_B(1)\mu_\beta(2) \ldots \mu_B(i)$.

6.7   Define $G_n(z) = \sum_{b=0}^{\infty} v_{b|n} z^b$ so that $G_n'(1) = A(n)$ and $G_n(1) = 1$. By multiplying the recurrence by z^b and summing over all b, we can introduce the generating function to get

$$(m + n - 1)G_n(z) = mzG_{n-1}(z) + (n - 1)G_{n-1}(z)$$
$$+ (1 - z)zG_{n-1}'(z)$$

Differentiating this w.r.t. z and setting $z = 1$, we obtain

$$(m + n - 1)A(n) = (m + n - 2)A(n - 1) + m$$

which has solution $A(n) = mn/(m + n - 1)$.

7.1   Consider the dot product of two vectors $Z = X \cdot Y$ where $X = (X_1, X_2, \ldots, X_R)$ and $Y = (Y_1, Y_2, \ldots, Y_R)$ (which is a unit vector with a one in position r with probability p_r and zero elsewhere). Then we have the following properties: for all n $E[Y_r^n] = p_r$ and $E[Y_r Y_s] = 0$ if $r \neq s$. (Note that Z has a hyperexponential distribution.)

(a) $E[Z^n] = E[(X \cdot Y)^n] = \sum_{r=1}^{R} E[Y_r^n]E[X_r^n]$

(b) $\text{Var}[Z] = E[Z^2] - E[Z]^2$, and the result follows by substitution and rearranging. (Note that this result is similar to the parallel axis theorem for moment of inertia in applied mechanics.)

7.2   (a)   Integrating $\Gamma(k)$ by parts, we have $\Gamma(k + 1) = k\Gamma(k)$ and $\Gamma(1) = 1$, so $\Gamma(k) = (k - 1)!$ for $k = 1, 2, \ldots$. The Erlang-k random variable with k exponential stages each with service rate μ is the gamma variable with parameters $\beta = k$ and $\alpha = \mu$.

(b)   From the Laplace transform, we show that for a gamma variable X, $E[X] = \beta/\alpha$ and $\text{svc}(X) = 1/\beta$. So we set $\beta = 1/c_Y^2$ and $\alpha = 1/(c_Y^2 m_Y)$.

(c)   Choose $k = \text{Floor}(1/c_Y^2)$ and $\mu = k/m_Y$. This gives the same mean but slightly different variance.

7.3 $E[X] = \mu_1 + b_1\mu_2 = 1/\mu$. Let X_i be the random variable for the exponential delay in stage $i = 1, 2$, so that $E[X_i^2] = 2/\mu_i^2$. $E[X^2] = E[X_1^2] + b_1 E[(X_1 + X_2)^2] = (1 + c^2)/\mu^2$.

8.1   This exercise is analogous to the interactive paging example, and

$$D_2 = \frac{D_1}{\mu_2 h(c/K)}$$

If $h(0)$ is close to 0, then this model also predicts memory thrashing as K gets large. Using hierarchical modelling, the FES for IPU and the memory can be used as the CPU node in the higher level model of interactive paging.

8.2   Using notation given in the text, $L_i(K) = T(K)Q_i(K)$

$$L_i(K) = \frac{KD_i\{1 + [(K - 1)/K]L_i(K)\}}{\sum_{j=1}^M D_j\{1 + [(K - 1)/K]L_j(K)\}}$$

Starting values could be $L_i(K) = K/M$

8.3 $Q_i(K) = D_i\left(1 + \frac{K - 1}{K} L_i(K)\right)$

$$= D_i\left(1 + \frac{(K - 1)Q_i(K)}{\sum_{j=1}^M Q_j(K)}\right)$$

Starting values could be $Q_i(K) = D_i$

8.4   For an M/M/1 queue with state-dependent arrival and service rates, we have from the balance equations

$$\frac{p_k^*(n_k - 1)}{p_k^*(n_k)} = \frac{\mu_k(n_k)}{\lambda_k(n_k - 1)}$$

so that $T_k^*(n_k) = \mu_k(n_k)$

8.5   (a)   There is one constraint, so Proposition 8.2 gives

$$p(n) = G^{-1}x^n$$

Substituting into the mean queue length constraint equation, we obtain

$$L = G^{-1}\frac{x}{(1 - x)^2}$$

and normalization yields $G^{-1} = 1 - x$. Thus, $L = x/(1 - x)$ and so $x = L/(1 + L)$. Thus,

$$p_n = \frac{1}{1 + L}\left(\frac{L}{1 + L}\right)^n \quad (n \geqslant 0)$$

(b)   We now have M constraints so

$$p(\boldsymbol{n}) = G^{-1} \prod_{j=1}^M x_j^{n_j}$$

Normalization gives (after interchanging sum and product)

$$1 = G^{-1} \prod_{j=1}^{M} \sum_{k=0}^{\infty} x_j^k$$

so that $G^{-1} = \prod_{j=1}^{m}(1 - x_j)$. The queue length constraint equations are

$$L_i = G^{-1} \sum_n n_i \prod_{j=1}^{M} x_j^{n_j} = G^{-1} \left(\sum_{k=1}^{\infty} k x_i^k \right) \prod_{j \neq i} \sum_{k=0}^{\infty} x_j^k$$

$$= G^{-1} \frac{x_i}{(1 - x_i)^2} G(1 - x_i) = \frac{x_i}{1 - x_i}$$

Thus, $x_i = L_i/(1 + L_i)$, $1 - x_i = 1/(1 + L_i)$ and so

$$p(n) = \prod_{j=1}^{M} \frac{1}{1 + L_j} \left(\frac{L_j}{1 + L_j} \right)^{n_j}$$

For an M/M/1 queue, $L = \rho/(1 - \rho)$ where ρ is the utilization. Thus, $1 + L = 1/(1 - \rho)$ and so the result of (a) becomes $p_n = (1 - \rho)\rho^n$ for $n \geq 0$, which is exact.

9.1 The queueing time distribution for this M/M/1 queue is $F_Q(t) = 1 - \rho e^{-(\mu-\lambda)t}$ where $\rho = \lambda/\mu$, so $p = 1 - \rho \exp[-(\mu - \lambda)t_0]$. Rearranging this gives $\mu = \lambda - (1/t_0) \ln[(1 - p)\mu/\lambda]$. We can iteratively compute μ, starting with $\mu = \lambda$.

10.1 Let $k_{min} = K - C$ and $k_{max} = C$. The states $k_{min} - 1$ and $k_{max} + 1$ represent the blocking situation with node 1 and node 2 blocked respectively. The process with state space $\{k_{min} - 1, \ldots, k_{max} + 1\}$ is a simple birth-death process with identical transition rates, so that all states are equally likely. The number of states is $2C - K + 3$, so the probability that one node has n customers is

$$p(n) = \begin{cases} 2/(2C - K + 3) & \text{if } n = K - C \text{ or } n = C \\ 1/(2C - K + 3) & \text{if } n = K - C + 1, \ldots, C - 1 \end{cases}$$

10.2 Let the buffer size be B. Now states $k_{min} = K - B$ and $k_{max} = B$ represent the blocking situation with node 1 and node 2 blocked respectively. The number of states is $2B - K + 1$ and for $n = K - B, \ldots, B$: $p(n) = 1/(2B - K + 1)$. With $C = B - 1$, this distribution is different from the previous question, even though the corresponding birth–death processes are identical.

10.3 The dual network of holes (instead of customers) is such that there is always a slot for a hole, which means that it is non-blocking. Hence the dual network has a product form solution and the joint queue length distribution is given by

$$\pi(n_1, n_2, \ldots, n_M) = \frac{1}{G} \frac{1}{\mu_M^{(C_1-n_1)}} \prod_{i=2}^{M} \frac{1}{\mu_{i-1}^{(C_i-n_i)}}$$

where G is the normalizing constant.

10.4 Let $T = \max(X_1, X_2, \ldots, X_M)$, $P(T > t) = 1 - P(X_1 \leq t)P(X_2 \leq t) \cdots P(X_M \leq t)$.

10.5 $G(M, K, C) = 0$ if $M = 0$ or any component of C is negative. $G(M, 0, C) = 1$.

11.1   Define the following equilibrium probabilities $p_1 = P(\text{state} = (2, 0))$, $p_2 = P(\text{state} = (0, 2))$, $p_3 = P(\text{state} = (1, 1))$. So the balance equations are: $p_1 = \frac{1}{2}p_1 + \frac{1}{4}p_3$; $p_2 = \frac{1}{2}p_2 + \frac{1}{4}p_3$; $p_3 = \frac{1}{2}p_1 + \frac{1}{2}p_2 + \frac{1}{2}p_3$. By symmetry, $p_1 = p_2$ and from the normalizing condition we obtain $p_1 = \frac{1}{4}$, $p_2 = \frac{1}{4}$ and $p_3 = \frac{1}{2}$. The bandwidth $B = \frac{1}{4} + \frac{1}{4} + 2 \times \frac{1}{2} = 1.5$ which is the same value given by Strecker's approximation.

11.2   (a) $\frac{1}{2}$

(b)   Applying Little's result to an output pin gives its utilization $U = \lambda(1/\mu)$. The mean waiting time for a new arrival is

$$\frac{1}{2}\frac{1}{\mu} + \frac{1}{2}\frac{2}{\mu} = \frac{3}{2\mu}$$

so applying Little's result to one input gives $1 = \lambda(3/2\mu)$. So $U = \frac{2}{3}$ and the throughput is $2U\mu = 4\mu/3$

(c) $P(\text{upper output is active}|\text{both inputs are active}) = U = \frac{2}{3}$ assuming we can apply Little's result only at times when both inputs are active.

11.3   By a similar analysis to that given in the text:

$$T(K) = \frac{abK}{(a + b - 1)K + (a - 1)(b - 1)}\mu$$

where a and b can be interchanged without affecting $T(K)$.

11.4   (a)   Since all outputs are selected with equal probability, the visitation rates of all buffers in stage 2 are the same (and similarly for stage 1). The visitation rate of stage 1 is the same as that of stage 2, so the visitation rates of all buffers are the same. Since all the service rates are constant, the equilibrium queue length distribution is $p(n) = 1/S_8$, from the product form solution.

(b)   Of the S_8 states, S_7 have no customers at any given node, so any given buffer is empty with probability S_7/S_8.

(c)   For m nodes, the probability that a buffer is non-empty is $1 - S_{m-1}/S_m = N/(N + m - 1)$. Since there are 4 buffers per stage the throughput is 4 times this probability.

References

Akyildiz, I. F. (1987). General closed queueing networks with blocking. In *Proc of the 12th Annual International Symposium on Computer Performance Modelling*, Brussels, Belgium. Elsevier/North-Holland, Amsterdam.

Akyildiz, I. F. (1988). Mean value analysis for blocking queueing networks. *IEEE Trans. Software Eng.* **SE-14** (1), 418–29.

Akyildiz, I. F. (1989). Analysis of queueing networks with rejection blocking. In *Workshop on Queueing Networks with Blocking* (eds H. G. Perros and T. Atiok). North-Holland, Amsterdam.

Akyildiz, I. F. and Liebeherr, J. (1991). Optimal deadlock free buffer allocation in multiple chain blocking networks of queues. In *Proc. Conf. on the performance of Distributed Systems and Integrated Communication Networks*, Kyoto (Sept 10–12, 1991).

Barbour, A. D. (1976). Networks of queues and the method of stages. *Adv. Appl. Prob.* **8**, 584–91.

Bard, Y. (1974). Some extensions to multiclass queueing analysis. In *Performance of Computer Systems* (ed. M. Arato, A. Butrimenko and E. Gelenbe) North-Holland, Amsterdam.

Baskett, F. and Smith, A. J. (1976). Interference in multiprocessor computer systems with interleaved memory. *Comm. ACM* **19** (6), 323–34.

Baskett, F., Chandy, K. M., Muntz, R. R. and Palacios, F. G. (1975). Open, closed and mixed networks of queues with different classes of customers. *J. ACM* **22** (2), 248–60.

Benes, V. (1965). *Mathematical theory of connecting networks*. Academic Press, New York.

Bhandarkar, D. (1975). Analysis of memory interference in multiprocessors. *IEEE Trans. Comp.* **C-24** (9), 897–908.

Bhuyan, L. N. (1985). An analysis of processor–memory interconnection networks. *IEEE Trans. Comp.* **C-34** (3), 279–83.

Billingsley, P. (1968). *Convergence of probability measures*. John Wiley, New York.

Buzen, J. P. (1973). A computational algorithm for closed queueing networks with exponential servers. *Comm. ACM* **14** (9), 527–31.

Chandy, K. M. and Neuse, D. (1982). Linearizer: a heuristic algorithm for queueing networks models of computing systems. *Comm. ACM* **25** (2), 126–34.

Chandy, K. M., Herzog, U. and Wu, L. (1975). Parametric analysis of queueing networks. *IBM J. Res. Develop.* **19** (1), 36–42.

Cinlar, E. (1975). *Introduction to stochastic processes*. Prentice-Hall, Englewood Cliffs NJ.

Clos, C. (1953). A study of nonblocking switching networks. *Bell System Tech. J.* **32**, 406–24.

Cobham, A. (1954). Priority assignment in waiting line problems. *Op. Research* **2**, 70–6.

Coffman, E. G. Jr, Muntz, R. R. and Trotter, H. (1970). Waiting time distribution for processor-sharing systems. *J. ACM* **17**, 123–30.

Cohen, J. W. (1982). *The single server queue*, rev. edn. North-Holland, Amsterdam.

Cohen, J. W. and Boxma, O. J. (1983). *Boundary value problems in queueing system analysis* (Mathematical Studies 79). North-Holland, Amsterdam.

Cox, D. P. (1955). A use of complex probabilities in the theory of stochastic processes. *Proc. Cambridge Phil. Soc.* **51**, 313–19.

Courtois, P. J. (1977). *Decomposability: queueing and computer system applications*, Academic Press, New York.

Conway, A. E., de Souza e Silva, E. and Lavenburg, S. S. (1989). Mean value analysis by chain of product form queueing networks. *IEEE Trans. Comput.* **38** (3), 432–41.

Daduna, H. (1982). Passage times for overtake-free paths in Gordon-Newell networks. *Adv. Appl. Prob.* **14**, 672–86.

Dallery, Y. and Cao, X. R. (1992). Operational analysis of stochastic closed queueing networks. *Performance evaluation* **14**, 43–61.

Denning, P. J. and Buzen, J. P. (1978). The operational analysis of queueing network models. *Comp. Surv.* **10** (3), 225–61.

Dias, D. M. and Jump, J. R. (1981). Analysis and simulation of buffered delta networks. *IEEE Trans. Comp.* **C-30** (4), 273–82.

Disney, R. L. and Konig, D. (1985). Queueing networks: a survey of their random processes. *SIAM Rev.* **27** (3), 335–403.

El-Affendi, M. A. and Kouvatsos, D. D. (1983). A maximum entropy analysis of the M/G/1 and G/M/1 queueing systems at equilibrium. *Acta Informatica* **19**, 339–55.

Erlang, A. K. (1948). On the rational determination of the number of circuits. In *The life and works of A. K. Erlang* (E. Brockmeyer, H. L. Halstrom and Arne Jensen). *Trans. Danish Academy of Tech. Sci.* 216–21.

Fagin, R. and Halpern, J. Y. (1988a). Reasoning about knowledge and probability, preliminary report. In *Proceedings of the 2nd Conference on Theoretical Aspects of Reasoning about Knowledge* (ed M. Y. Vardi), pp. 277–93. Morgan Kaufmann, San Mateo CA.

Fagin, R. and Halpern, J. Y. (1988b). Belief, awareness and limited reasoning. *Artif. Intel.* **34**, 39–76.

Feller, W. (1968). *An introduction to probability theory and its applications*, Vol. I, 3rd edn. John Wiley, New York.

Feller, W. (1971). *An introduction to probability theory and its applications*, Vol. II, 2nd edn. John Wiley, New York.

Frein, Y. and Dallery, Y. (1989). Analysis of cyclic queueing networks with finite buffers and blocking before service. *Perf. Eval.* **10**, 197–210.

Gelenbe, E. (1989). *Multiprocessor performance*. John Wiley, New York.

Gelenbe, E. and Mitrani, I. (1980). *Analysis and synthesis of computer systems*. Academic Press, London.

Gelenbe, E. and Pujolle, G. (1987). *Introduction to queueing networks*. John Wiley, New York.

Gelenbe, E., Glynn, P. and Sigman, K. (1991). Queues with negative arrivals. *J. Appl. Prob.* **14**, 245–50.

Gottlieb, A., Grishman, R., Kruskal, C. P., McAuliffe, K. P., Rudolph, L. and Snir, M. (1983). The NYU ultracomputer – designing an MIMD shared memory parallel computer. *IEEE Trans. Comp.* **C-32** (2), 173–89.

Goke, L. R. and Lipovski, G. L. (1973). Banyan networks for partitioning multiprocessor systems. In *Proc. of the First Annual Symposium on Computer Architecture*. IEEE/ACM, New York.

Gordon, W. J. and Newell, G. F. (1967). Closed queueing systems with exponential servers. *Operations Research* **15** (2), 254–65.

Harper, D. T. III and Jump, J. R. (1987). Performance evaluation of reduced bandwidth multi-stage interconnection networks. In *Proc. International Symposium in Computer Architecture*. IEEE/ACM, New York.

Harrison, J. M. (1985). *Brownian motion and stochastic flow systems*. John Wiley, Chichester.

Harrison, P. G. (1984). The distribution of cycle times in tree-like networks of queues. *Computer J.* **27** (1), 27–36.

Harrison, P. G. (1986). An enhanced approximation by pair-wise analysis of servers for time delay distributions in queueing networks. *IEEE Trans. Comp.* **C-35** (1), 54–61.

Harrison, P. G. (1990) Laplace transform inversion and passage time distributions in Markov processes. *J. Appl. Prob.* **27**, 74–87.

Harrison, P. G. (1991). On non-uniform packet-switched networks and the hot-spot effect. *IEE Proceedings*, 123–30.

Harrison, P. G. and Patel, N. M. (1990). The representation of multi-stage interconnection networks in queueing models of parallel systems. *J. ACM* **37** (4), 863–98.

Harrison, P. G. and Pitel, E. (1992). Sojourn times in single server queues with negative customers. *Research Report No. DoC92/10*. Department of Computing, Imperial College, University of London.

Hartman, P. and Wintner, A. (1941). On the law of the iterated logarithm. *Am. J. Math.* **63**, 169–76.

Heidelberger, P. (1988). Discrete event simulations and parallel processing: statistical properties. *SIAM J. Stat. Comput.* **9** (6), 1114–32.

Hordijk, A. and van Dijk, N. M. (1983). Network of queues. In *Lecture notes in control and information sciences* **60**, 158–205.

Jackson, J. R. (1957). Networks of waiting lines, *Operations Research* **5** (4), 518–21.

Jackson, J. R. (1963). Jobshop-like queueing systems. *Management Science* **10** (1), 131–42.

Jenq, T. (1983). Performance of a packet switch based on single buffered banyan networks. *IEEE J. Selected Areas Comm.* **SAC-1** (6), 1014–21.

Jun, K. P. and Perros, H. G. (1990). An approximate analysis of open tandem queueing networks with blocking and general service times. *Eur. J. Op. Res.* **46**, 123–35.

Karlin, S. and Taylor, M. (1975). *A first course in stochastic processes*, 2nd edn. Academic, London.

Kelly, F. P. (1975). Networks of queues with customers of different types. *J. Appl. Prob.* **12**, 542–54.

Kelly, F. P. (1979). *Reversibility and stochastic networks*. John Wiley, Chichester.

Kelly, F. P. (1986). Blocking probabilities in large circuit-switched networks. *Adv. Appl. Prob.* **18**, 473–505.

Kelly, F. P. and Pollett, P. K. (1983). Sojourn times in closed queueing networks. *Adv. Appl. Prob.* **15**, 638–56.

Kim, H. S. and Garcia, A. L. (1988). Performance of buffered banyan networks under non-uniform traffic patterns. *Proc. IEEE INFOCOM* 344–53.

King, P. J. B. (1990). *Computer and communication systems performance modelling*. Prentice Hall, Hemel Hempstead.

Kingman, J. F. C. and Taylor, S. J. (1966). *Introduction to measure and probability*. Cambridge University Press, Cambridge.

Kleinrock, L. (1975). *Queueing systems I: Theory*. John Wiley, Chichester.

Kleinrock, L. (1976). *Queueing systems II: Computer Applications*. John Wiley, Chichester.

Kouvatsos, D. D. (in press). *Maximum entropy*. Blackwell Scientific, Oxford.

Kouvatsos, D. D. and Xenios, N. P. (1989). Maximum entropy analysis of general queueing networks with blocking. In *Workshop on queueing networks with blocking* (eds H. G. Perros and T. Atiok). North-Holland, Amsterdam.

Kruskal, C. P. and Snir, M. (1983). The performance of multi-stage interconnection networks for multiprocessors. *IEEE Trans. Comp.* **C-32** (12), 1091–8.

Kuehn, P. J. (1979). Approximate analysis of general queueing networks by decomposition. *IEEE Trans Comm.* COM-27 (1), 113–26.

Liu, Z. and Nain, P. (1991). Sensitivity results in open, closed and mixed product form queueing networks. *Performance Evaluation* **13**, 237–51.

Lazowska, E., Zahorjan, J., Graham, G. S. and Sevcik, K. C. (1984). *Quantitative system performance*. Prentice-Hall, Englewood Cliffs NJ.

Marie, R. A. (1979). An approximate analytical method for general queueing networks. *IEEE Trans. Soft. Eng.* SE-5 (5), 530–8.

Mitra, D. and Cieslak, R. (1987). Randomized parallel communications on an extension of the omega network. *J. ACM* **34** (4), 802–24.

Mitrani, I. (1985). Response time problems in communication networks. *J. Roy. Stat. Soc.* **B-47** (3), 396–406.

Mitrani, I. (1987). *Modelling of computer and communication systems*. Cambridge University Press, Cambridge.

Neuts, M. F. (1981). *Matrix geometric solutions in stochastic models*. Johns Hopkins University Press, Baltimore.

Nelson, R. (1991). Matrix geometric techniques. In *ACM SIGMetrics conference, Tutorial Proceedings*. ACM, New York.

Onvural, R. O. (1987). Closed queueing networks with finite buffers. *PhD dissertation*, CSE/OR. North Carolina State University.

Onvural, R. O. and Perros, H. G. (1989). Throughput analysis in cyclic queueing networks with blocking. *IEEE Trans. Soft. Eng.* SE-15 (6), 800–8.

Patel, J. H. (1981). Performance of processor–memory interconnections for multiprocessors. *IEEE Trans. Comp.* **C-30** (10), 771–80.

Patel, N. M. (1989). Models of circuit-switched interconnection networks. *PhD thesis*, Dept. of Computing, Imperial College, University of London.

Patel, N. M. (1991). New protocol for multistage interconnection networks, *IEE Proceedings-E* **138** (4), 269–75.

Priestley, H. A. (1985). *Introduction to complex analysis*. Oxford University Press, Oxford.

Reiser, M. and Lavenburg, S. S. (1980). Mean-value analysis of closed multi-chain queueing networks. *J. ACM* **27** (2), 313–22.

Ross, S. M. (1988). *A first course in probability*, 3rd edn. Macmillan, New York.

Schweitzer, P. (1979). Approximate analysis of multiclass closed networks of queues. In *Int. Conf. on Stochastic Control and Optimization*, Amsterdam.

Sevcik, K. C. and Mitrani, I. (1981). The distribution of queueing network states at input and output instants. *J. ACM* **28** (2), 358–71.

Shafer, G. (1976). *A mathematical theory of evidence*. Princeton University Press, Princeton.

Shanthikumar, G. J. and Yao, D. D. (1989). Monotonic properties in cyclic queueing networks with finite buffers. In *Workshop on queueing networks with blocking* (eds H. G. Perros and T. Atiok). North-Holland, Amsterdam.

Strecker, W. D. (1970). Analysis of the instruction execution rate in certain computer structures. *PhD dissertation*, Carnegie-Mellon University.

Suri, R. and Diehl, G. W. (1986). A variable buffer size model and its use in analyzing closed queueing networks with blocking. *Management Science* **32** (2), 206–24.

Takacs, L. (1962). *Introduction to the theory of queues*. Oxford University Press, Oxford.

Takacs, L. (1963). A single server queue with feedback. *Bell Systems Tech. J.* **42**, 505–19.

Towsley, D. (1980). Queueing network models with state-dependent routing. *J. ACM* **27** (2), 323–37.

Towsley, D. (1986). Approximate models of multiple bus multiprocessor systems. *IEEE Trans. Comp.* **35**, 220–8.

Whitt, W. (1983). The queueing network analyzer. *Bell System Tech. J.* **62** (9), 2779–813.

Whitt, W. (1985). Blocking when service is required from several facilities simultaneously. *AT&T Tech. J.* **64** (8), 1807–56.

Whittle, P. (1970). *Probability*. Penguin, London.

Wu, C. and Feng, T. (1980). On a class of multistage interconnection networks. *IEEE Trans. Comp.* **29** (8), 694–702.

Yen, D., Patel, J. H. and Davidson, E. (1982). Memory interference in synchronous multiprocessor systems. *IEEE Trans. Comp.* **C-31** (11), 1116–21.

Index

absolutely integrable 146
absorbing barrier 85, 333
absorbing state 85, 123
abstraction 2
active resource 299, 382
adaptive routing 219
aggregation
  of Markov states 390–1
alternating renewal process 155
aperiodic 96
arithmetic 146
arrival rate lemma 145
arrival theorem 240–2, 294, 323
arrivals
  in bulk 176–9
arriving observer property 426

backward Kolmogorov equation 124
backward recurrence time 149
balance equations
  aggregated 127
  definition 127
  detailed 132
  global 127
  local 223
  multi-class networks 274
  for single class
    closed networks 233
    open networks 222
banyan networks 428–9
barrier
  absorbing 333
  reflecting 332
BAS see blocking after service

basic renewal theorem 146
batch arrivals see bulk arrivals
Bayes' formula 12
BBS see blocking before service
BCMP network
  computational algorithms 276–81
  extensions 275
BCMP theorem 271–5
Benes network 427
Bernoulli see distribution
Bernoulli trials 24, 52
binomial see distribution
birth and death process 128
birthday problem 48
Blackwell's theorem 147
block diagonal matrix 303–5
blocking 382
  curve fitting approach 395–6
  and deadlock 386–7
  equivalent mechanisms 388
  FES approach 392–4
  finding equivalent state
    space 394–5
  types of 383–8
blocking after service
  definition 383
  in queueing networks 392–405
  simple closed network 388–9
blocking before service
  definition 384–5
  in queueing networks 405–9
  simple closed network 390
blocking networks
  for switching 427

bottleneck node   243
boundary states   318
Brownian motion   331
bulk arrivals   176–9
   M/G/1 queue   202–3
Burke's theorem   184, 214, 221
busy period   352, 353
   of M/M/1 queue   380

c.d.f. *see* cumulative distribution
      function
central limit theorem   73
   for diffusion processes   329
centre of mass   52
Chapman–Kolmogorov equation   91
characteristic function   70
Chebyshev's inequality   76
circuit-switched *see* switching networks
Clos network   427
closed networks   217
   cyclic
      with BAS blocking   401–5
      with BBS blocking   407–9
      properties of 406
   of quasi-reversible nodes   294–5
   single class *see* Gordon–Newell
      networks
   time delay distribution   364–72
Cobham's formula   285
coefficient of variation   259
communicating states   95
complete probability formula *see* law
      of total probability
conditional expectation   59–63
conditional probability   9–13
   definition   10
   distribution   39–43
conditional throughput
   for FES approach   313
   in Marie's method   325
conditional variance   61
conservative queueing discipline   166
contention for passive resources   382
convolution
   definition of   46
   operator (∗) on vectors   394
convolution algorithm
   multi-class network   277
   single class network   245–8

covariance   62
Coxian *see* distribution
Coxian model   261
crossbar switches   423–7
   asynchronous models   425–7
   synchronous models   423–4
cumulative distribution function   21
curve fitting approach   395–6
cycles
   in blocking networks   387
cyclic networks *see* closed networks

deadlock
   in blocking networks   386–7
decomposition   300–22
   error analysis   307–10
   of a Markov process   301–15
   of queueing networks   316–17
decomposition property *see* Poisson
      process
delay cycle analysis   353
delay server *see* infinite server
delayed renewal process   154
delta networks   429–30
delta-*b* network   429
density function   28
departure process *see* quasi-reversible
   of M/M/1 queue   183
derivative
   in diffusion process   330
detailed balance equations   132
diffusion approximation   328–36
   queueing networks   336
diffusion equation   331
diffusion process   329–36
Dirac delta function   29
discretization method   332
distribution
   Bernoulli   24
      mean   52
   binomial   24
      mean   53
   Coxian   261–2
      example   296
   Erlang   33, 259
      c.d.f.   49
   exponential   31
      mean   54

gamma 32
  example 296
generalized exponential 177–8, 262
geometric 24
  mean 68
hyperexponential 260
hypoexponential 260
negative binomial 25
normal 34
  mean 54
Poisson 26
  mean 53
uniform
  continuous 30
  discrete 26
distribution function 2, 20–3
  definition 21
drift 330

elementary renewal theorem 145
embedded Markov chain 124–6
EMC *see* embedded Markov chain
entropy 337
equilibrium 105
equivalent open network 239–42
ergodic 106
ergodic theorems 105
Erlang *see* distribution
Erlang's fixed point
  approximation 419–20
Erlang's fixed point equation 420
Erlang's loss formula 173–4
  for switching networks 419
event space 4
events in probability 3
exceptional first service times 199
expectation 51–63
expectation function 55

factorial moment 67
FCFS *see* first come first served
FCFS node 264
feedforward networks 219
FES *see* flow equivalent server method
finite queues 382
first come first served 165
first moment 57
first passage time 97
first return time 96

fixed point equation 324
fixed point methods 322–8
fixed population constraint 413
flow equivalent server 249–53
fluid flow approximation 328–9
Fokker–Planck equation 331
fork node 316
forward Kolmogorov equation 124
forward recurrence time 118, 149

G/M/1 queue 207, 212
G/M/1 queue 207
gambler's ruin 85
gamma *see* distribution
gamma function 32
Gaussian distribution *see* normal
  distribution
GE/M/1 queue 178
generalized exponential *see*
  distribution
generating function 63–72
generators
  of a Markov process 122
geometric *see* distribution
Gordon–Newell networks 231–8
Gordon–Newell theorem 233

hazard function 204
head of line *see* non-pre-emptive
hierarchical decomposition 315
holding time 365
holes 405–7
hyperexponential *see* distribution
hypoexponential *see* distribution

i.i.d. *see* independent, identically
  distributed random variables
IN *see* interconnection network,
  switching networks
independence 13–16, 44–8
independence approximation 378
independent
  events 2
  increments 82
    for Poisson process 113
  random variables 44
independent, identically distributed
  random variables 87
indicator random variable 55

infinite server 166, 218
instantaneous transition rate 122
instantaneous variance 330
integrated services digital
    communications networks 433
interactive computer system 310
interchangeable relation 270
interconnection networks
    for parallel processing 420–3
irreducible 95
IS *see* infinite server
IS node 266–7
ISDN *see* integrated services
iterative methods *see* fixed point
    methods

Jackson networks 218–31
    balance equations 222
    definition 219
    performance measures 225–6
    traffic equations 220–1
Jackson's theorem 221–5
job observer property 240
    for tandem queues 365
join node 316
joint distribution function 35
joint random variables 35–9

Kendall's notation 165–7
key renewal theorem 146
Kingman's formula 335
Kolmogorov's criteria for
    reversibility 134
Kolmogorov's theorem 105
Kronecker delta function 87

Laplace transform 69–71
    inversion of 372–7
last come first served 165, 218
law of
    the iterated logarithm 75
    large numbers 75
    total probability 12
        for continuous random
            variables 41
        for discrete random variables 39
LCFS *see* last come first served
LCFS-PR node 267–70
lifetime function 311

Lindley's integral equation 209
Little's result 167–71
    extension to higher moments 169
load of a single server queue 209
local balance equations 223
    for BCMP network 275
    of quasi-reversible queues 290
loss networks 417
lumpable matrix 305–6
    definition 305

M/G/1 queue 188–207
    outstanding service demand 215
    with vacations 199–210
    variants 198–203
M/M/1 queue 171–3
M/M/m queue 173
M/M/m/m queue 173, 174
M/M/m/N queue 174–6
$M \Rightarrow M$ property 275
marginal distribution 36
Marie's method 325–8
Markov chain 89–112
    classification 94–105
    embedded 125
Markov process 83, 112–31
    quasi-reversible 288
    reversible 132
    stationary 132
Markov property 83, 112
Markov renewal process *see*
    semi-Markov process
Markov's inequality 75
mass function 2, 23
massive parallelism 421
matrix geometric methods 317–22
maximum
    of a set of random variables 396
maximum entropy method 339–46
    application to queueing
        networks 343–6
    application to RS blocking 411–3
    application to simple queue 341–3
    example 349
maximum entropy solution 339
mean *see* expectation
mean value analysis 238–44
    approximate 322–5
    multi-class networks 278–81

recurrence equations   280
  state dependent case   248–9
MEM *see* maximum entropy method
memory conflicts   422
memoryless *see* Poisson process
method of stages *see* Coxian model
MIN *see* multi-stage interconnection
    networks, switching networks
mirrored disk example 80
mixed network
  definition   217
  fixed rate servers   272
  state dependent servers   273
moment generating function   64–6
moments of a random variable   57
multi-access system   174
multicomputers   420
multinomial theorem   263–4
multiple parallel servers   252–3
multiprogramming computer
    system   243–4
multi-server   173
multi-stage interconnection networks
    types   427–31
mutually exclusive events   5
MVA *see* mean value analysis

NCD *see* nearly completely
    decomposable
nearly completely decomposable   301
  definition   302
negative binomial *see* distribution
negative customers   360
negative exponential *see* distribution
non-pre-emptive discipline   282,
    283–6
normal *see* distribution
normalizing condition   28
normalizing constant   233
Norton's theorem   250–2
null-recurrence   99
null-recurrent state   96

observables   3
open networks   217
  fixed rate servers   272
  of quasi-reversible nodes   291–4
  single class *see* Jackson networks
  in tandem   396–401

time delay distribution   361–4
operational analysis   253
optimal allocation
  in Jackson networks   230
orderly   113
overtake-free path   361

paired centre approximation   378
parallel processing *see* interconnection
    networks
partial balance equations *see* local
    balance
partition   5
passive resource   299, 382
path conflicts   427
p.d.f. *see* probability density function
periodicity   99
petri-nets   433
Poisson *see* distribution
Poisson process   112–20
  definition   113
  property
    decomposition   119
    memoryless   117
    random observer   117
    recurrence time   153
    superposition/union   118
Pollaczek–Khintchine formula   189
Pollaczek–Khintchine transform
    equation   197
positive-recurrence   99
positive-recurrent state   96
pre-emptive discipline   282
pre-emptive repeat discipline   282
pre-emptive resume discipline   287–8
principle of insufficient reason   337
principle of maximum entropy   339
priority discipline   281–8
probability   3–9
  axioms of   5
probability density function   28
probability flux   127
probability generating function   66–9
  definition   66
process network   420
processor sharing   166, 218
product form   233
PS *see* processor sharing
PS node   264–6

QLD *see* queue length dependent
  node
quasi-reversibility 288–95
quasi-reversible queues
  in blocking networks 410
  local balance 290
  properties of 289–91
queue length 165
queue length dependent node 218
queue length distribution
  M/G/1 192
  multi-class FCFS node 264
  multi-class IS node 266
  multi-class LCFS-PR node 268
  multi-class PS node 265
  symmetric queues 269
queueing discipline *see* service
  discipline
queueing time 179

random observer property 228–30, 284
  see also Poisson process,
random variables 19
  continuous 28–35
  discrete 23–8
  sums of *see* convolution
random walk 83–89
  with barriers 85–9
  unrestricted 84
recurrence relation 71
recurrence time 149–54
  for Poisson process 153
reflecting barrier 332
regenerative process 208
rejection *see* repetitive service
  blocking
relative visitation rate 232
renewal density 144
renewal equation 97, 142–4
renewal function 143
renewal process 141
  alternating 155
  delayed 154
  Markov *see* semi-Markov process
  superposition of 157
renewal theory 140–58
repeating states 318
repetitive service blocking
  definition 385

maximum entropy method 411–13
  in networks with reversible
    routing 410–11
  in queueing networks 409–13
residual life *see* forward recurrence
  time
reversed process 136
reversibility 131–40
reversible process 132
reversible routing 410
reversible systems 288
routing chain 270
routing probability 219
RS *see* repetitive service blocking

sample path 82
sample space 3
Schweitzer's approximation 325
semi-Markov process 141, 156
separable queueing networks 316
service blocking *see* blocking before
  service
service discipline
  in BCMP nodes 264
  FCFS 165
  for single class nodes 218
service node
  multi-class 262–70
service time distribution 259–62
shortest processing time first 286
simultaneous resource
  possession 299, 382
single class queueing network 216
single server fixed rate node 218
sojourn time 43, 226
square of the variation
  coefficient 259
SSFR *see* single server fixed rate node
standard deviation 58
standard normal 34
star networks 419
state
  absorbing 85, 123
  class property 95
  communicating 95
  essential 96
  inessential 96
  instantaneous 123
  periodic 96

recurrent   96
 stable   123
 steady   105
state holding time   122
state space of a stochastic process   81
state transition graph   102
stationary   82
stationary process   132
stationary probability   105
steady state   105
steady state equation   106
steady state solutions *see* ergodic
   theorems
steady state theorem   125–6
Stieltjes integral
   definition   41
stochastic matrix   90
stochastic process   81
Strecker's approximation   424
strong law of large numbers   77
superposition of renewal
   processes   157
superposition property *see* Poisson
   process
supplementary variables   204, 207
svc *see* square of the variation
   coefficient
switching networks
   asynchronous   433–40
      circuit-switched with
         dropping   434–7
      circuit-switched with
         holding   437–40
      packet-switched   433–4
   circuit-switched   417–20
   operational characteristics   430
   representation in queueing
      models   440–6
   synchronous   431–3
symmetric queueing
   disciplines   269–70

tandem networks *see* open networks
tandem queues   138
task-based measure   350
tau-equivalent   302
Tauberian theorem   149
telephone networks   417–20
terminal system   310

think time   175
thrashing   312
time delays
   approximate methods   377–9
   overtake-free paths   373–7
   queueing networks   360–72
   single server queue   352–360
time dependent solution
   for M/M/1 queue   187
time-homogeneous   113, 120
token ring   191
traffic equations
   Gordon–Newell network   232
   Jackson network   220
   multi-class   271
traffic intensity   209
transfer blocking *see* blocking after
   service
transforms   63–72
transience   99
transient state
   definition   96
transition maxtrix   90
transition probability   89
tree-like networks
   closed   368
   general   219
   open   362
trials   16
trunk segment   362

uniform
   continuous *see* distribution
   discrete *see* distribution
union property *see* Poisson process
urn model
   with restricted capacity   415
   unrestricted   17
utilization
   effective   411
   total   411

variable buffer approach   401–5
variance   58
   conditional   61
variation coefficient   259
visit ratio   227

waiting time   179
waiting time distribution   179–83
  for LCFS queue   353–6
  M/M/1   179–80
  M/M/m   180–2
  PS discipline   182–3

  for PS queue   356–60
Wald's identity   87
weak law of large numbers   77, 329

z-transform *see* probability generating
  function